DELETED

Bloom's Classic Critical Views

WILLIAM SHAKESPEARE

Bloom's Classic Critical Views

Alfred, Lord Tennyson
Benjamin Franklin
The Brontës
Charles Dickens
Edgar Allan Poe
Geoffrey Chaucer
George Eliot
George Gordon, Lord Byron
Henry David Thoreau
Herman Melville
Jane Austen
John Donne and the Metaphysical Poets
John Milton
Jonathan Swift
Mark Twain
Mary Shelley
Nathaniel Hawthorne
Oscar Wilde
Percy Shelley
Ralph Waldo Emerson
Robert Browning
Samuel Taylor Coleridge
Stephen Crane
Walt Whitman
William Blake
William Shakespeare
William Wordsworth

Bloom's Classic Critical Views

WILLIAM SHAKESPEARE

Edited and with an Introduction by
Harold Bloom
Sterling Professor of the Humanities
Yale University

**BLOOM'S
LITERARY CRITICISM**
An imprint of Infobase Publishing

Bloom's Classic Critical Views: William Shakespeare

Copyright © 2010 Infobase Publishing

Introduction © 2010 by Harold Bloom

Bloom's Literary Criticism

An imprint of Infobase Publishing

132 West 31st Street

New York NY 10001

Library of Congress Cataloging-in-Publication Data

William Shakespeare / edited and with an introduction by Harold Bloom : Neil Heims, volume editor.

    p. cm. — (Bloom's classic critical views)

  Includes bibliographical references and index.

  ISBN 978-1-60413-723-1 (acid-free paper)

  1. Shakespeare, William, 1564–1616—Criticism and interpretation.   I. Bloom, Harold.
II. Heims, Neil.

  PR2976.W5352 2010

  822.3'3—dc22

                       2010010067

You can find Bloom's Literary Criticism on the World Wide Web at http://www.chelseahouse.com

Volume editor: Neil Helms

Series design by Erika K. Arroyo

Cover designed by Takeshi Takahashi

Composition by IBT Global, Inc.

Cover printed by IBT Global, Inc., Troy NY

Book printed and bound by IBT Global, Inc., Troy NY

Date printed: August 2010

Printed in the United States of America

10 9 8 7 6 5 4 3 2 1

Contents

Series Introduction

Bloom's Classic Critical Views is a new series presenting a selection of the most important older literary criticism on the greatest authors commonly read in high school and college classes today. Unlike the Bloom's Modern Critical Views series, which for more than 20 years has provided the best contemporary criticism on great authors, Bloom's Classic Critical Views attempts to present the authors in the context of their time and to provide criticism that has proved over the years to be the most valuable to readers and writers. Selections range from contemporary reviews in popular magazines, which demonstrate how a work was received in its own era, to profound essays by some of the strongest critics in the British and American tradition, including Henry James, G.K. Chesterton, Matthew Arnold, and many more.

Some of the critical essays and extracts presented here have appeared previously in other titles edited by Harold Bloom, such as the New Moulton's Library of Literary Criticism. Other selections appear here for the first time in any book by this publisher. All were selected under Harold Bloom's guidance.

In addition, each volume in this series contains a series of essays by a contemporary expert, who comments on the most important critical selections, putting them in context and suggesting how they might be used by a student writer to influence his or her own writing. This series is intended above all for students, to help them think more deeply and write more powerfully about great writers and their works.

Introduction by Harold Bloom

> I greet you at the beginning of a great career, which yet must have
> had a long foreground somewhere, for such a start.
>
> —Emerson to Whitman, 1855

The "foreground" Emerson sees in Whitman's career is not, as he makes clear by his strange and original use of the word, a background. That latter term has been employed by literary historians during the twentieth century to mean a context, whether of intellectual, social, or political history, within which works of literature are framed. But Emerson means a temporal foreground of another sort, a precursory field of poetic, not institutional, history; perhaps one might say that its historiography is written in the poetry itself. *Foregrounding*, the verb, means to make prominent, or draw attention to, particular features in a literary work.

What is the long foreground of Sir John Falstaff, or of Prince Hamlet, or of Edmund the Bastard? A formalist or textualist critic might say there is none, because these are men made out of words. A contextualist or historicist critic might say, There is background but no foreground. I have argued throughout *Shakespeare: The Invention of the Human* that Shakespeare invents (or perfects, Chaucer being there before him) a mode of representation that depends on his foregrounding of his characters. Shakespeare calls upon the audience to surmise just how Falstaff and Hamlet and Edmund got to be the way they are, by which I mean: their gifts, their obsessions, their concerns. I am not going to ask what made Falstaff so witty, Hamlet so skeptical, Edmund so icy. The mysteries or enigmas of personality are a little to one side of Shakespearean foregrounding.

Shakespeare's literary art, the highest we ever will know, is as much an art of omission as it is of surpassing richness. The plays are greatest where they are most elliptical. Othello loves Desdemona yet seems not to desire her sexually, since evidently he has no knowledge of her palpable virginity and never makes love to her. What are Antony and Cleopatra like when they are alone together? Why are Macbeth and his fierce lady childless? What is it that so afflicts Prospero and causes him to abandon his magical powers and to say that, in his recovered realm, every third thought shall be of his grave? Why does no one behave other than zanily in *Twelfth Night* or other than madly in *Measure for Measure*? Why must Shylock be compelled to accept Christian conversion or Malvolio be so outrageously tormented? Foregrounding is necessary to answer these questions. I will begin with *Hamlet*, partly because I will argue that Shakespeare all but began with him, since there is no *Ur-Hamlet* by Thomas Kyd, and probably there was a *Hamlet* by Shakespeare as early as 1588. Another reason for starting with *Hamlet* is that the play, contra T. S. Eliot, indeed is Shakespeare's masterpiece, cognitively and aesthetically the furthest reach of his art.

In the final *Hamlet*, the prince we first encounter is a student home from Wittenberg, where his companions included Rosencrantz, Guildenstern, and Horatio. It is less than two months since the sudden death of his father and only a month since his mother's marriage to his uncle, who has assumed the crown. Critics have been too ready to believe that Hamlet's melancholia results from these traumas and from the Ghost's subsequent revelation that Claudius bears the mark of Cain. Yet the long foreground of Hamlet in Shakespeare's life and career, and of Hamlet in the play, suggests quite otherwise. This most extraordinary of all the Shakespearean characters (Falstaff, Iago, Lear, Cleopatra included) is, amidst much else, a despairing philosopher whose particular subject is the vexed relationship between purpose and memory. And his chosen mode for pursuing that relationship is the theater, of which he will display a professional's knowledge and an active playwright's strong opinions. His Wittenberg is pragmatically London, and his university must certainly be the London stage. We are allowed to see his art in action and in the service of his philosophy, which transcends the skepticism of Montaigne and, by doing so, invents Western nihilism.

Hamlet's aptest disciple is Iago. As I have already noted, Harold Goddard, a now greatly neglected Shakespearean critic who possessed true insight, remarked that Hamlet was his own Falstaff. I would add that Hamlet also was his own Iago. A. C. Bradley suggested that Hamlet was the only Shakespearean character who could have written the play in which he appears. Again, I would add that Hamlet was capable of composing *Othello, Macbeth*, and *King Lear*. There is pragmatically something very close to a fusion of Hamlet and Shakespeare the tragedian, by which I do not mean that Hamlet was any more a representation of William Shakespeare than Ophelia was, or whom you will, but rather that Hamlet, in taking on Shakespeare's function as playwright-actor, assumes also the power of making Shakespeare his mouthpiece, his Player King who takes instruction. This is very different from Hamlet's serving as Shakespeare's mouthpiece. Rather, the creature usurps the creator, and Hamlet exploits Shakespeare's memory for purposes that belong more to the Prince of Denmark than to Shakespeare the man. Paradoxical as this must sound, Hamlet "lets be" Shakespeare's empirical self, while taking over the dramatist's ontological self. I do not think that this was Shakespeare's design or his overt intention, but I suspect that Shakespeare, apprehending the process, let it be. Foregrounding Hamlet, as I will show, depends entirely on conclusions and inferences drawn only from the play itself; the life of the man Shakespeare gives us very few interpretative clues to help us apprehend Hamlet. But Hamlet, fully foregrounded, and Falstaff are clues to what, in a Shakespearean term, we could call the "selfsame" in Shakespeare. That sense of "selfsame" is most severely tested by the character of Hamlet, the most fluid and mobile of all representations ever.

Presumably, Shakespeare had read Montaigne in Florio's manuscript version. Nothing seems more Shakespearean than the great, culminating essay, "Of Experience," composed by Montaigne in 1588, when I suspect that Shakespeare was finishing his first Hamlet. Montaigne says that we are all wind, but the wind is wiser than we are, since it loves to make a noise and move about and does not long for solidity and stability, qualities alien to it. As wise as the wind, Montaigne takes a positive view of our mobile selves, metamorphic yet surprisingly free. Montaigne, like Shakespeare's greatest characters, changes because he overhears what he himself has said. It is in reading his own text that Montaigne becomes Hamlet's precursor at representing reality in and by himself. He becomes also Nietzsche's forerunner or perhaps melds with Hamlet as a composite precursor whose mark is always on the aphorist of *Beyond Good and Evil* and *The Twilight of the Idols*. Montaigne's experiential man avoids Dionysiac transports, as well as the sickening descents from such ecstasies. Nietzsche unforgettably caught this aspect of Hamlet in his early *The Birth of Tragedy*, where Coleridge's view that Hamlet (like Coleridge) thinks too much is soundly repudiated in favor of the truth, which is that Hamlet thinks too well. I quote this again because of its perpetual insight:

For the rapture of the Dionysian state with its annihilation of the ordinary bounds and limits of existence contains, while it lasts, a *lethargic* element in which all personal experiences of the past become immersed. This chasm of oblivion separates the worlds of everyday reality and of Dionysian reality. But as soon as this everyday reality re-enters consciousness, it is experienced as such, with nausea: an ascetic, will-negating mood is the fruit of these states.

In this sense the Dionysian man resembles Hamlet: both have once looked truly into the essence of things, they have gained *knowledge*, and nausea inhibits action; for their action could not change anything in the eternal nature of things; they feel it to be ridiculous or humiliating that they should be asked to set right a world that is out of joint. Knowledge kills action; action requires the veils of illusion: that is the doctrine of Hamlet, not that cheap wisdom of Jack the Dreamer who reflects too much and, as it were, from an excess of possibilities does not get around to action. Not reflection, no—true knowledge, an insight into the horrible truth, outweighs any motive for action, both in Hamlet and in the Dionysian man.

To see that for Hamlet knowledge kills action is to repeat the nihilist arguments that Hamlet composes for the Player King (quite possibly spoken by Shakespeare himself, onstage at the Globe, doubling the role with the Ghost's). In his later *The Twilight of the Idols*, Nietzsche returned to the Dionysiac Hamlet, though without mentioning him. Recalling the "O what a rogue and peasant slave am I!" soliloquy, where Hamlet denounces himself as one who "Must like a whore unpack my heart with words," Nietzsche arrives at a formulation that is the essence of Hamlet: "That for which we find words is something already dead in our hearts. There is always a kind of contempt in the act of speaking." With faith neither in language nor in himself, Hamlet nevertheless becomes a dramatist of the self who surpasses St. Augustine, Dante, and even Montaigne, for that is Shakespeare's greatest invention, the inner self that is not only ever-changing but also ever-augmenting.

J. H. Van den Berg, a Dutch psychiatrist from whom I've learned much, disputes Shakespeare's priority as the inventor of the human by assigning "the birth date of the inner self" to 1520, two generations before *Hamlet*. For Van den Berg, that undiscovered country was found by Martin Luther, in his discourse on "Christian Freedom," which distinguishes the "inner" man from the physical one. It is the inner man who has faith and who needs only the

Word of God. Yet that Word does not dwell within man, as it did for Meister Eckhart and Jakob Böhme, mystics extraordinary, and must come from above. Only the Ghost's word comes to Hamlet from above, and for Hamlet it both does and does not have authority. If you scorn to unpack your heart with words, then why have faith in the Ghosts act of speaking? The deadness in Hamlet's heart long precedes the Ghost's advent, and the play will show us that it has been with Hamlet since early childhood. Foregrounding Hamlet is crucial (and anguishing), because it involves the prehistory of the first absolutely inner self, which belonged not to Martin Luther but to William Shakespeare. Shakespeare allowed something very close to a fusion between Hamlet and himself in the second quarter of the tragedy, which begins with the advent of the players in act 2, scene 2 and continues through Hamlet's antic glee when Claudius flees *The Mousetrap* in act 3, scene 3.

We are overfamiliar with *Hamlet,* and we therefore neglect its wonderful outrageousness. The Prince of Denmark evidently is a frequent truant from Wittenberg and haunts the London playhouses; he is eager to hear all the latest gossip and fireworks of Shakespeare's theatrical world and happily is brought up to date by the Player King. Clearly referring to Shakespeare and his company, Hamlet asks, "Do they hold the same estimation they did when I was in the city? Are they so followed?" and the Globe audience is free to roar when Rosencrantz answers, "No, indeed, are they not." The war of the theaters is discussed with great gusto in Elsinore, just down the street from the Globe. A greater outrageousness comes just a touch later when Hamlet becomes Shakespeare, admonishing the players to act what he has written. Not Claudius but the clown Will Kemp becomes the drama's true villain, and revenge tragedy becomes Shakespeare's revenge against poor players. Ophelia, in her lament for Hamlet, elegizes her lover as courtier, soldier, and scholar; as I have already mentioned, she might have added playwright, actor, and theater manager, as well as metaphysician, psychologist, and lay theologian. This most various of heroes (or hero-villains, as a few would hold) is more interested in the stage than all Shakespeare's other personages taken together. Playing a role is for Hamlet anything but a metaphor; it is hardly *second* nature but indeed is Hamlet's original endowment. Fortinbras, crying out for military honors because Hamlet, had he ascended the throne, would have merited them, has gotten it all wrong. Had he lived, on or off a throne, Hamlet would have written *Hamlet* and then gone on to *Othello, King Lear,* and *Macbeth.* Prospero, Shakespeare's redeemed Faustus, would have been Hamlet's final epiphany.

Shakespeare might have been everyone and no one, as Borges suggested, but from act 2, scene 2, through act 3, scene 3, Shakespeare can be distinguished from Hamlet only if you are resolved to keep the Prince and the actor-dramatist apart. Hamlet's relationship to Shakespeare precisely parallels the playwright's stance toward his own *Ur-Hamlet;* one can say that the Prince revises Shakespeare's career even as the poet revises the earlier protagonist into the Prince. It cannot be accidental that nowhere else in his work can we find Shakespeare risking so deliberate a conflation of life and art. The sonnets dramatize their speaker's ejection, akin to the pathos of Falstaff's ruin, while no intrusion from the life of the theater is allowed in *Henry IV, Part 2.* It would make no sense to speak of "intrusions" in the "poem unlimited," *Hamlet,* where all is intrusion, and nothing is. The play as readily could have been expanded into a two-part work, because it could absorb even more of Shakespeare's professional concerns. When Hamlet admonishes and instructs the players, neither he nor the play is the least out of character: *The Mousetrap* is as natural to the world of *Hamlet* as is the crooked duel arranged by Claudius between Hamlet and Laertes.

But what does that tell us about Hamlet in his existence before the play begins? We cannot avoid the information that this was always a man of the theater, as much a critic as an observer, and very possibly more of an actual than a potential playwright himself. Foregrounding Hamlet will teach us his greatest paradox: that long before his father's murder and mother's seduction by Claudius, Hamlet was already a self-dramatizing genius of the theater, driven to it out of his contempt for the act of speaking what was already dead in his heart. The apocalyptic self-consciousness of this charismatic personality could have led to dangerous action, a murderousness prophetic of Macbeth's, had it not been for the outlet of this theatrical vocation. Hamlet is only secondarily a courtier, soldier, and scholar; primarily he is that anomaly (and knows it): a royal playwright, "The play's the thing" in every possible sense. Of all Shakespeare's works, this is the play of plays because it is the play of the play. No theory of the drama takes us further than the sequence from act 2, scene 2, through act 3, scene 3, if we realize that, compared with it, everything that comes before and after in *Hamlet* is interruption. The mystery of Hamlet and the enigma of Shakespeare are centered here.

Backgrounding Shakespeare is a weariness, because it does nothing to explain Shakespeare's oceanic superiority to even the best of his contemporaries, Marlowe and Ben Jonson. Marlowe's Faustus is a cartoon; Shakespeare's Faustus is Prospero. Dr. Faustus in Marlowe acquires Mephistopheles, another cartoon, as familiar spirit. Ariel, Prospero's "sprite," though necessarily other than human, has a personality nearly as distinct as that of the great magus. What Shakespeare shared with his era can explain everything about Shakespeare, except what made him so different in degree

from his fellows that at last it renders him different in kind. Foregrounding
Shakespeare's characters begins by noting what Shakespeare himself implied
about them; it cannot conclude by compiling what they imply about
Shakespeare. We can make surmises, particularly in regard to Hamlet and
Falstaff, who seem in many ways to live at the limits of Shakespeare's own
consciousness. With just a handful of Shakespearean roles—Hamlet, Falstaff,
Rosalind, Iago, Macbeth, Lear, Cleopatra—we sense infinite potential, and
yet we cannot surpass Shakespeare's employment of them. With Lear—as to
a lesser degree with Othello and Antony—we feel that Shakespeare allows
us to know their limits as what Chesterton called "great spirits in chains."
Perhaps the Falstaffian Chesterton thought of Hamlet as another such figure,
since from a Catholic perspective Hamlet (and Prospero) are purgatorial
souls at best. Dante foregrounds only Dante the Pilgrim; all others in him
no longer can change, since those souls sustaining Purgatory only can be
refined, not fundamentally altered. It is because of his art of foregrounding
that Shakespeare's men and women are capable of surprising changes, even at
the final moment, as Edmund changes at the close of *King Lear*. Unless you
are adequately foregrounded, you can never quite overhear yourself.

Shakespeare is a great master of beginnings, but how far back does a
Shakespearean play begin? Prospero foregrounds *The Tempest* in his early
conversation with Miranda, but does the drama truly commence with his
expulsion from Milan? Most would say it starts with the storm that rather
oddly gives the play its title, a tempest that ends after the first scene. Since
there is almost no plot—any summary is maddening—we are not surprised
that scholars tell us there is no source for the plot. But the foreground begins
with Shakespeare's subtle choice of a name for his protagonist, Prospero,
which is the Italian translation of the Latin Faustus, "the favored one."
Presumably Shakespeare, like Marlowe, knew that the name Faustus began
as the cognomen that Simon Magus of Samaria took when he went to Rome,
there to perish in an unlikely flying contest with St. Peter. *The Tempest*, most
peculiarly, is Shakespeare's *Dr. Faustus*, all unlike Marlowe's last play. Think
how distracting it would be had Shakespeare named his Mage Faustus, not
Prospero. There is no devil in *The Tempest*, unless you argue with Prospero that
poor Caliban is one, or at least a sea devil's child. The ultimate foregrounding
of *The Tempest* is its magician's name, since its substitution for Faust means
that Christianity is not directly relevant to the play. A distinction between
"white" and "black" magic is not crucial; an art, Prospero's, is opposed to the
sale and fall of a soul, Faustus's.

Hamlet, Prospero, Falstaff, Iago, Edmund: All have evolved through
a foretime that itself is the implicit creation of Shakespeare's imaginings.

While Hamlet and Prospero intimate dark sensibilities that preceded their catastrophes, Falstaff suggests an early turning to wit, even as Hamlet turned to theater and Prospero to hermetic magic. The despair of having thought too well too soon seems shared by Hamlet and by Prospero, while Falstaff, a professional soldier who long ago saw through chivalry and its glories, resolutely resolves to be merry and will not despair. He dies of brokenheartedness, according to his fellow scamps, and so Hal's rejection does seem the Falstaffian equivalent of Hamlet's rejection of, and by, life itself.

It seems appropriate that I conclude this introduction with Falstaff and with Hamlet, as they are the fullest representations of human possibility in Shakespeare. Whether we are male or female, old or young, Falstaff and Hamlet speak most urgently for us and to us. Hamlet can be transcendent or ironic; in either mode his inventiveness is absolute. Falstaff, at his funniest or at his most reflective, retains a vitalism that renders him alive beyond belief. When we are wholly human and know ourselves, we become most like either Hamlet or Falstaff.

BIOGRAPHY

William Shakespeare was born in Stratford-on-Avon in April 1564 into a family of some prominence. His father, John Shakespeare, was a glover and merchant of leather goods, who earned enough to marry the daughter of his father's landlord, Mary Arden, in 1557. John Shakespeare was a prominent citizen in Stratford, and at one point, he served as an alderman and bailiff.

Shakespeare presumably attended the Stratford grammar school, where he would have received an education in Latin, but he did not go on to either Oxford or Cambridge universities. Little is recorded about Shakespeare's early life; indeed, the first record of his life after his christening is of his marriage to Anne Hathaway in 1582 in the church at Temple Grafton, near Stratford. He would have been required to obtain a special license from the bishop as security that there was no impediment to the marriage. Peter Alexander states in his book *Shakespeare's Life and Art* that marriage at this time in England required neither a church nor a priest or, for that matter, even a document—only a declaration of the contracting parties in the presence of witnesses. Thus, it was customary, though not mandatory, to follow the marriage with a church ceremony.

Little is known about William and Anne Shakespeare's marriage. Their first child, Susanna, was born in May 1583, and twins, Hamnet and Judith, in 1585. Later on, Susanna married Dr. John Hall, but the younger daughter, Judith, remained unmarried. When Hamnet died in Stratford in 1596, the boy was only eleven years old.

We have no record of Shakespeare's activities for the seven years after the birth of his twins, but by 1592 he was in London working as an actor. He was also apparently well-known as a playwright, for reference is made of him by his contemporary, Robert Greene, in *A Groatsworth of Wit*, as "an upstart crow."

Several companies of actors were in London at this time. Shakespeare may have had connection with one or more of them before 1592, but we have no record that tells us definitely. However, we do know of his long association with the most famous and successful troupe, the Lord Chamberlain's Men. (When James I came to the throne in 1603, after Elizabeth's death, the troupe's name changed to the King's Men.) In 1599, the Lord Chamberlain's Men provided the financial backing for the construction of their own theater, the Globe.

The Globe was begun by a carpenter named James Burbage and finished by his two sons, Cuthbert and Robert. To escape the jurisdiction of the Corporation of London, which was composed of conservative Puritans who opposed the theater's "licentiousness," James Burbage built the Globe just outside London, in the Liberty of Holywell, beside Finsbury Fields. This also meant that the Globe was safer from the threats that lurked in London's crowded streets, like plague and other diseases, as well as rioting mobs. When James Burbage died in 1597, his sons completed the Globe's construction. Shakespeare played a vital role, financially and otherwise, in the construction of the theater, which was finally occupied some time before May 16, 1599.

Shakespeare not only acted with the Globe's company of actors; he was also a shareholder and eventually became the troupe's most important playwright. The company included London's most famous actors, who inspired the creation of some of Shakespeare's best-known characters, such as Hamlet and Lear, as well as his clowns and fools.

In his early years, however, Shakespeare did not confine himself to the theater. He also composed some mythological-erotic poetry, such as *Venus and Adonis* and *The Rape of Lucrece*, both of which were dedicated to the earl of Southampton. Shakespeare was successful enough that in 1597 he was able to purchase his own home in Stratford, which he called New Place. He could even call himself a gentleman, for his father had been granted a coat of arms.

By 1598 Shakespeare had written some of his most famous works: *Romeo and Juliet*, *The Comedy of Errors*, *A Midsummer Night's Dream*, *The Merchant of Venice*, *Two Gentlemen of Verona*, and *Love's Labour's Lost*, as well as his historical plays *Richard II*, *Richard III*, *Henry IV*, and *King John*. Around the turn of the century, Shakespeare wrote his romantic comedies: *As You Like It*, *Twelfth Night*, and *Much Ado about Nothing*, as well as *Henry V*, the last of his history plays in the Prince Hal series. During the next ten years he wrote his great tragedies, *Hamlet, Macbeth, Othello, King Lear,* and *Antony and Cleopatra.*

At this time, the theater was burgeoning in London; the public took an avid interest in drama, the audiences were large, the plays demonstrated an enormous range of subjects, and playwrights competed for approval. By 1613, however, the rising tide of Puritanism had changed the theater. With the desertion of the theaters by the middle classes, the acting companies were compelled to depend more on the aristocracy, which also meant that they now had to cater to a more sophisticated audience.

Perhaps this change in London's artistic atmosphere contributed to Shakespeare's reasons for leaving London after 1612. His retirement from the theater is sometimes thought to be evidence that his artistic skills were waning. During this time, however, he wrote *The Tempest* and *Henry VIII.* He also wrote the "tragicomedies": *Pericles, Cymbeline,* and *The Winter's Tale.* These were thought to be inspired by Shakespeare's personal problems, and have sometimes been considered proof of his greatly diminished abilities.

However, so far as biographical facts indicate, the circumstances of his life at this time do not imply any personal problems. He was in good health, was financially secure, and enjoyed an excellent reputation. Indeed, although he was settled in Stratford at this time, he made frequent visits to London, enjoying and participating in events at the royal court, directing rehearsals, and attending to other business matters.

In addition to his brilliant and enormous contributions to the theater, Shakespeare remained a poetic genius throughout the years, publishing a renowned and critically acclaimed sonnet cycle in 1609 (most of the sonnets were written many years earlier). Shakespeare's contribution to this popular poetic genre are all the more amazing in his break with contemporary notions of subject matter. Shakespeare idealized the beauty of man as an object of praise and devotion (rather than the Petrarchan tradition of the idealized, unattainable woman). In the same spirit of breaking with tradition, Shakespeare also treated themes that hitherto had been considered off limits—the dark, sexual side of a woman as opposed to the Petrarchan ideal of a chaste and remote love object. He also expanded the sonnet's emotional range, including such emotions as delight, pride, shame, disgust, sadness, and fear.

When Shakespeare died in 1616, no collected edition of his works had ever been published, although some of his plays had been printed in separate unauthorized editions. (Some of these were taken from his manuscripts and from the actors' prompt books, and others were reconstructed from memory by actors or spectators.) In 1623, two members of the King's Men, John

Heminge and Henry Condell, published a collection of all the plays they considered to be authentic, the First Folio.

Included in the First Folio is a poem by Shakespeare's contemporary Ben Jonson, an outstanding playwright and critic in his own right. Jonson paid tribute to Shakespeare's genius, proclaiming his superiority to what previously had been held as the models for literary excellence—the Greek and Latin writers. "Triumph, my Britain, thou hast one to show / To whom all scenes of Europe homage owe. / He was not of an age, but for all time!"

Jonson was the first to state what has been said so many times since. Having captured what is permanent and universal to all human beings at all times, Shakespeare's genius continues to inspire us—and the critical debate about his works never ceases.

PERSONAL

Robert Greene (1592)

Shakespeare emerged as an actor and a playwright in a London teeming with popular theatrical and literary activity at a time when the English could celebrate their position in the world—the English navy had defeated the Spanish Armada in 1588—and when the social climate was bracing. Returning veterans, unmoored by the war, added a degree of instability and excitement to a society that was being redefined by the reemergence of classical knowledge, the birth of modern science, and a humanist vision of the creative capacities of mankind.

Robert Greene's (1558–92) life and career were representative of the time's spirit and embodied its contradictions. Cambridge-educated, while in London, Greene led the bohemian life of an artist, carousing and gaming, yet also producing a respectable body of work, including *Pandosto*, a 1588 novel that became a source for Shakespeare's own late romance, *The Winter's Tale*.

The following excerpt is regarded as the first allusion to Shakespeare and, as such, the first documentation of his existence, work, and whereabouts. In it, Greene criticizes Shakespeare as an "upstart," as an up-and-coming theater man whose entrance into the London literary and theater scene threatens to eclipse those, like Greene, who had already made a name for themselves. Greene vilifies the public that had once applauded him but has abandoned him for a newer author. Indeed, *Pandosto* is read now primarily for the study of Shakespeare's source material, and Greene is remembered primarily for the following passage. The reader will recognize Greene's sly allusions to Shakespeare as he makes a pun of his name. The phrase *"Tygers heart wrapt in a Players hide"* suggests the line from Shakespeare's *3 Henry VI*, I.iv.137, "O tiger's heart wrapp'd in a woman's hide!" Greene's dismissal of Shakespeare and of his talents, as in his scorn for Shakespeare's skill in writing blank verse, ironically constitutes an early acknowledgment.

Blank verse consists of unrhymed lines of iambic pentameter. Each line has five iambic feet, thus constituting ten beats to a line. An iambic foot is a foot of two beats in which the first is unstressed and the second is stressed. "Shall **I**/ com**pare**/ thee **to**/ a **sum**/mer's **day**," the first line of Shakespeare's eighteenth sonnet, offers a good example of an iambic line. However, a traditional sonnet, since it is rhymed, is not an example of blank verse. Hamlet's well-known soliloquy, starting "To be or not to be, that is the question," since it is composed of unrhymed iambic pentameter lines, is.

Is it not strange that I, to whom they al haue beene beholding: is it not like that you, to whome they all haue beene beholding, shall (were ye in that case that I am now) be both at once of them forsaken? Yes, trust them not: for there is an vpstart Crow, beautified with our feathers, that with his *Tygers heart wrapt in a Players hide*, supposes he is as well able to bumbast out a blanke verse as the best of you: and being an absolute *Iohannes fac totum* [Jack of all trades], is in his owne conceit the onely Shake-scene in a countrie.

—Robert Greene, *A Groatsworth of Wit*, 1592

JOHN DAVIES (CA. 1611)

John Davies (1565–1618) was a poet and a teacher of penmanship whose students included King James's son, Prince Henry. His verses dedicated to Shakespeare, inconsequential as poetry, show the kind of regard that was attached to Shakespeare even in his lifetime. Davies praises Shakespeare not only for his prowess as a playwright but as a generous and gentle man.

Terence was a Roman playwright of comedies. The spirit of his work is well characterized by a line from one of them, certainly fitting for Shakespeare's works: "*Homo sum, humani nil a me alienum puto*," I am a man and I don't think anything regarding mankind is alien to me.

To our English Terence, Mr. Will. Shakespeare.

Some say (good *Will*) which I, in sport, do sing,
Had'st thou not plaid some Kingly parts in sport,
Thou hadst bin a companion for a *King*;

And, beene a King among the meaner sort.
Some others raile; but, raile as they thinke fit,
Thou hast no rayling, but, a raigning Wit:
And honesty *thou sow'st, which they do reape,*
So, to increase their Stocke *which they do keepe.*

—John Davies, *The Scourge of Folly,* ca. 1611

INSCRIPTION (1616)

The epitaph that Shakespeare composed for himself shows a certain awareness, perhaps, of the interest he would generate in posterity and his desire not to be exhumed for purposes of research. Mark Twain would have much sport with these lines in his essay concerning whether Shakespeare was actually the author of the body of work attributed to him.

Good frend for Iesvs sake forbeare,
To digg the dvst encloased heare:
Bleste be ye man y^t spares thes stones,
And cvrst be he y^t moves my bones.

—Inscription on the tablet above
Shakespeare's grave, April 25, 1616

WILLIAM BASSE "ON MR. WM. SHAKESPEARE" (1622)

A minor poet and an admirer of Shakespeare's great precursor Edmund Spenser, William Basse (1583–1653) in this tribute addresses the corpses of Spenser, Geoffrey Chaucer, and Shakespeare's popular contemporary, the playwright Francis Beaumont, asking them to move a little nearer to one another, as if they were buried in the same grave, so that Shakespeare, in his greatness, can take his place beside them in the tomb as he has in the literary canon.

Renowned Spencer lye a thought more nye
To learned Chaucer, and rare Beaumont lye
A little neerer Spenser, to make roome
For Shakespeare in your threefold, fowerfold Tombe.
To lodge all fowre in one bed make a shift

Vntill Doomesdaye, for hardly will a fift
Betwixt *this* day and *that* by Fate be slayne,
For whom your Curtaines may be drawn againe.
If your precedency in death doth barre
A fourth place in your sacred sepulcher,
Vnder this carued marble of thine owne,
Sleepe, rare Tragoedian, Shakespeare, sleep alone;
Thy vnmolested peace, vnshared Caue,
Possesse as Lord, not Tenant, of thy Graue,
  That vnto us & others it may be
  Honor hereafter to be layde by thee.

—William Basse, "On Mr. Wm.
Shakespeare," 1622

Ben Jonson "To the Reader" (1623)

In 1623, seven years after Shakespeare's death, John Heminge and Henry Condell, two of the partners in the King's Men, the acting company to which Shakespeare had belonged, gathered thirty-six of his plays together in one volume, called the First Folio. *Pericles* and *The Two Noble Kinsmen*, both now thought to be at least in large part by Shakespeare, were omitted. (A folio is a volume whose sheets are folded in half, giving each sheet four sides.) Eighteen of the plays had never been published before. The text of the plays was preceded by several dedicatory pieces by Shakespeare's contemporaries and admirers and by an engraving of Shakespeare by Martin Droeshout. Ben Jonson (1572–1637) was a playwright, poet, and actor. These lines celebrate the closeness of Droeshout's portrait to the man himself but recommend that the reader seek the essence of the man Shakespeare not in his portrait but in his work.

This Figure, that thou here seest put,
It was for gentle Shakespeare cut;
Wherein the Grauer had a strife
With Nature, to out-doo the life:
O, could he but haue drawne his wit
As well in brasse, as he hath hit
His face; the Print would then surpasse
All, that was euer writ in brasse.

But, since he cannot, Reader, looke
Not on his Picture, but his Booke.

—Ben Jonson, "To the Reader,"
Mr. William Shakespeares Comedies,
Histories, & Tragedies, 1623

I. M. "TO THE MEMORIE OF M. W. SHAKESPEARE" (1623)

This verse attributed to the unidentified I. M. has a similar theme, arguing that Shakespeare's death can be seen as an actor's exit. Like an actor, this poem suggests, Shakespeare made his exit as a mortal man. The Folio heralds his reentrance, in the costume of a book, as one worthy of eternal applause.

Wee wondred *(Shake-speare)* that thou went'st so soone
From the Worlds-Stage, to the Graues-Tyring-roome.
Wee thought thee dead, but this thy printed worth,
Tels thy Spectators, that thou went'st but forth
To enter with applause. An Actors Art,
Can dye, and hue, to acte a second part.
That's but an *Exit* of Mortalitie;
This, a Re-entrance to a Plaudite.

—I. M., "To the Memorie of M. W. Shakespeare,"
Mr. William Shakespeares Comedies,
Histories, & Tragedies, 1623

JOHN WARD (1648–79)

A vicar in Stratford, Shakespeare's birthplace, John Ward was an acquaintance of Shakespeare's daughter Judith and a diarist. The following excerpt from his diary suggests that he was less than reliable for accuracy but useful for readers interested in learning the sorts of legends and gossip that grew up around Shakespeare. A reader may gather from Ward's last consideration that, although regarded highly by some, Shakespeare was not viewed by all with the regard he was to attain.

Shakespear had but 2 daughters, one whereof M. Hall, ye physitian, married, and by her had one daughter, to wit, ye Lady Bernard of Abbingdon.

I have heard y^t M^r. Shakespeare was a natural wit, without any art at all; hee frequented ye plays all his younger time, but in his elder days lived at Stratford: and supplied ye stage with 2 plays every year, and for y^t had an allowance so large, y^t hee spent art ye Rate of a 1,000/. a year, as I have heard.

Shakespear, Drayton, and Ben Jhonson, had a merry meeting, and itt seems drank too hard, for Shakespear died of a feavour there contracted.

Whether Dr. Heylin does well, in reckoning up the dramatick poets which have been famous in England, to omit Shakespeare.

—John Ward, *Diary*, 1648–79

THOMAS FULLER (1662)

Thomas Fuller (1608–61) was a churchman, a poet, and a historian. His comments about Shakespeare reinforce the idea of Shakespeare as an untutored genius and advance the image of him as a hearty and sociable man.

Heraclitus was an ancient Greek philosopher known for his idea that everything is in flux. Only fragments of his work are extant. Democritus, also an ancient Greek philosopher, hypothesized the existence of atoms as the fundamental particles of matter.

William Shakespeare was born at Stratford on Avon in this county (Warwickshire); . . . [T]hough his genius generally was jocular, and inclining him to festivity, yet he could (when so disposed) be solemn and serious, as appears by his tragedies; so that Heraclitus himself (I mean if secret and unseen) might afford to smile at his comedies, they were so merry; and Democritus scarce forbear to sigh at his tragedies, they were so mournful.

He was an eminent instance of the truth of that rule, "Poeta non fit sed nascitur," [Poets are not made but born.] Indeed his learning was very little; so that, as Cornish diamonds are not polished by any lapidary, but are pointed and smoothed even as they are taken out of the earth, so Nature itself was all the art which was used upon him.

Many were the wet-combats betwixt him and Ben Jonson; which two I behold like a Spanish great galleon and an English man-of-war: master Jonson (like the former) was built far higher in learning; solid, but slow, in his performances. Shakespeare, with the English man-of-war, lesser in bulk, but lighter in sailing, could turn with all tides, tack about, and take advantage of all winds, by the quickness of his wit and invention. He died anno Domini 1616, and was buried at Stratford-upon-Avon, the town of his nativity.

—Thomas Fuller, *The History of the Worthies of England*, 1662

John Aubrey (1669–96)

John Aubrey (1626–97) was an antiquary and a writer of biographies. His reporting is anecdotal. Derived from hearsay, it suggests the kind of legend that surrounded Shakespeare rather than the actual facts of his life.

Mr. William Shakespeare was born at Stratford upon Avon in the County of Warwick. His father was a Butcher, and I have been told heretofore by some of the neighbours, that when he was a boy he exercised his father's Trade, but when he kill'd a Calfe he would doe it in a high style, and make a Speech. There was at this time another Butcher's son in this Towne that was held not at all inferior to him for a naturall witt, his acquaintance and coetanean, [contemporary] byt dyed young.

This William, being inclined naturally to Poetry and acting, came to London, I guesse about 18: and was an Actor at one of the Play-houses, and did acte exceedingly well: now B[en]. Johnson was never a good Actor, but an excellent Instructor.

He [Shakespeare] began early to make essayes at Dramatique Poetry, which at that time was very lowe; and his Playes tooke well.

He was a handsome, well-shap't man: very good company, and of a very readie and pleasant smoothe Witt.

The Humour of the Constable in *Midsomernight's Dreame*, he happened to take at Grendon, in Bucks (I thinke it was Midsomer night that he happened to lye there) which is the roade from London to Stratford, and there was living that Constable about 1642, when I first came to Oxon. Ben Johnson and he did gather Humours of men dayly where ever they came. . . .

He was wont to goe to his native Countrey once a yeare. I thinke I have been told that he left 2 or 300 pounds per annum there and thereabout to a sister.

I have heard Sir William Davenant and Mr. Thomas Shadwell (who is counted the best Comoedian we have now) say that he had a most prodigious Witt, and did admire his naturall parts beyond all other Dramaticall writers.

His Comoedies will remaine witt as long as the English tongue is understood, for that he handles *mores hominum*. Now our present writers reflect so much on particular persons and coxcombeities that twenty yeares hence they will not be understood.

Though, as Ben Johnson sayes of him, that he had little Latine and lesse Greek, He understood Latine pretty well: for he had been in his younger yeares a schoolmaster in the countrey.

He was wont to say that he never blotted out a line in his life. Sayd Ben: Johnson, I wish he had blotted-out a thousand.

—John Aubrey, *Brief Lives,* 1669–96

NICHOLAS ROWE "SOME ACCOUNT OF THE LIFE, &C. OF MR. WILLIAM SHAKESPEAR" (1709)

Nicholas Rowe (1674–1718) was the first editor of Shakespeare's plays and his first biographer. It was Rowe who inserted act and scene divisions into the plays.

Rowe was a dramatist and a poet. He was appointed England's poet laureate in 1715. Rowe's anecdotal account of Shakespeare's life precedes his edition of Shakespeare's plays.

Inaccurate as it is in many respects, and guided much by hearsay, Rowe's life of Shakespeare became the standard biography of the eighteenth century, establishing the eighteenth century's popular sense of Shakespeare as a man and an author. Rowe's characterization of Shakespeare as a rambunctious youth and as an affable tavern companion in his maturity, and his definition of the nature of Shakespeare's genius have become commonplace, even if doubtful. Rowe's contention that "Art had so little, and Nature so large a Share in what he did," seems more a bias than an insight and suggests a rule-bound conception of art.

Rowe's account of Shakespeare's father's occupation, that he was in the wool trade, differs from John Aubrey's assertion that he was a butcher and supplanted it. It is now believed that Shakespeare's father apprenticed thirteen-year-old William to a butcher. Rowe's argument that Shakespeare was unfamiliar with classical literature is shaky, as he himself concedes in his recognition that *The Comedy of Errors* owes much to *The Menachmi,* by the Roman playwright Plautus. A reader may also think of *Troilus and Cressida* and of the allusions to Ovid in *The Tempest.* Rowe's account of Shakespeare's misadventures in regard to Sir Thomas Lucy, as well as his reference to the ballad Shakespeare allegedly composed against Lucy, come from an account written around 1616 by a Gloucestershire clergyman named Richard Davies. He wrote that "Shakespeare was much given to all unluckiness in stealing venison and rabbits, particularly from Sir — Lucy who oft had him whipped and sometimes imprisoned and at last mad[e] him fly his native country to his great advancement."

The Mr. Rhymer Rowe mentioned is Thomas Rhymer, a historiographer and a critic. He is noted among Shakespeare scholars for *A Short View of Tragedy* (1692), in which he dismisses Shakespeare's *Othello* as a "bloody farce" and suggests that the moral of the play (referring to Desdemona's dropped handkerchief) is that women ought to be careful when it comes to their linen.

He was the Son of Mr. *John Shakespear,* and was Born at *Stratford* upon Avon, in *Warwickshire,* in *April* 1564. His Family, as appears by the Register and Publick Writings relating to that Town, were of good Figure and Fashion there, and are mention'd as Gentlemen. His Father, who was a considerable Dealer in Wool, had so large a Family, ten Children in all, that tho' he was his eldest Son, he could give him no better Education than his own Employment. He had bred him, 'tis true, for some time at a Free-School, where 'tis probable he acquir'd that little *Latin* he was Master of: But the narrowness of his Circumstances, and the want of his assistance at Home, forc'd his Father to withdraw him from thence, and unhappily prevented his further Proficiency in that Language. It is without Controversie, that he had no knowledge of the Writings of the Antient Poets, not only from this Reason, but from his Works themselves, where we find no traces of any thing that looks like an Imitation of 'em; the Delicacy of his Taste, and the natural Bent of his own Great *Genius,* equal, if not superior to some of the best of theirs, would certainly have led him to Read and Study 'em with so much Pleasure, that some of their fine Images would naturally have insinuated themselves into, and been mix'd with his own Writings; so that his not copying at least something from them, may be an Argument of his never having read 'em. Whether his Ignorance of the Antients were a disadvantage to him or no, may admit of a Dispute: For tho' the knowledge of 'em might have made him more Correct, yet it is not improbable but that the Regularity and Deference for them, which would have attended that Correctness, might have restrain'd some of that Fire, Impetuosity, and even beautiful Extravagance which we admire in *Shakespear:* And I believe we are better pleas'd with those Thoughts, altogether New and Uncommon, which his own Imagination supply'd him so abundantly with, than if he had given us the most beautiful Passages out of the *Greek* and *Latin* Poets, and that in the most agreeable manner that it was possible for a Master of the *English* Language to deliver 'em. Some *Latin* without question he did know, and one may see up and down in his Plays how far his Reading that way went: In *Love's Labour Lost,* the Pedant comes out with a Verse of *Mantuan* [Baptista Spagnuoli Mantuanus, 1447–1516]; and in *Titus Andronicus,* one of the *Gothick* Princes, upon reading

Integer vitae scelerisque purus
Non eget Mauri jaculis nee arcu
[He who is upright in his way of life and unstained by guilt,
Needs not Moorish darts nor bow nor quiver loaded with poisoned arrows.
Horace, Ode 22, line 55]

says, "'tis *a Verse in* Horace, *but he remembers it out of his* Grammar: Which, I suppose, was the Author's Case. Whatever *Latin* he had, 'tis certain he understood *French,* as may be observ'd from many Words and Sentences scatter'd up and down his Plays in that Language; and especially from one Scene in *Henry* the Fifth written wholly in it. Upon his leaving School, he seems to have given intirely into that way of Living which his Father propos'd to him; and in order to settle in the World after a Family manner, he thought fit to marry while he was yet very Young. His Wife was the Daughter of one *Hathaway,* said to have been a substantial Yeoman in the Neighbourhood of *Stratford.* In this kind of Settlement he continu'd for some time, 'till an Extravagance that he was guilty of, forc'd him both out of his Country and that way of Living which he had taken up; and tho' it seem'd at first to be a Blemish upon his good Manners, and a Misfortune to him, yet it afterwards happily prov'd the occasion of exerting one of the greatest Genius's that ever was known in Dramatick Poetry. He had, by a Misfortune common enough to young Fellows, fallen into ill Company; and amongst them, some that made a frequent practice of Deer-stealing, engag'd him with them more than once in robbing a Park that belong'd to Sir *Thomas Lucy* of *Cherlecot,* near *Stratford.* For this he was prosecuted by that Gentleman, as he thought, somewhat too severely; and in order to revenge that ill Usage, he made a Ballad upon him. And tho' this, probably the first Essay of his Poetry, be lost, yet it is said to have been so very bitter, that it redoubled the Prosecution against him to that degree, that he was oblig'd to leave his Business and Family in *Warwickshire,* for some time, and shelter himself in *London.*

It is at this Time, and upon this Accident, that he is said to have made his first Acquaintance in the Play-house. He was receiv'd into the Company then in being, at first in a very mean Rank; But his admirable Wit, and the natural Turn of it to the Stage, soon distinguish'd him, if not as an extraordinary Actor, yet as an excellent Writer. His Name is Printed, as the Custom was in those Times, amongst those of the other Players, before some old Plays, but without any particular Account of what sort of Parts he us'd to play; and tho' I have inquir'd, I could never meet with any further Account of him this way, than that the top of his Performance was the Ghost in his own *Hamlet*. I should have been much more pleas'd, to have learn'd from some certain Authority, which was the first Play he wrote; it would be without doubt a pleasure to any Man, curious in Things of this Kind, to see and know what was the first Essay of a Fancy like *Shakespear's*. Perhaps we are not to look for his Beginnings, like those of other Authors, among their least perfect Writings; Art had so little, and Nature so large a Share in what he did, that, for ought I know, the Performances of his Youth, as they were the most vigorous, and had the most fire and strength of Imagination in 'em, were the best. I would not be thought by this to mean, that his Fancy was so loose and extravagant, as to be Independent on the Rule and Government of Judgment; but that what he thought, was commonly so Great, so justly and rightly Conceiv'd in it self, that it wanted little or no Correction, and was immediately approv'd by an impartial Judgment at the first sight. Mr. *Dryden* seems to think that *Pericles* is one of his first Plays; but there is no judgment to be form'd on that, since there is good Reason to believe that the greatest part of that Play was not written by him; tho' it is own'd, some part of it certainly was, particularly the last Act. But tho' the order of Time in which the several Pieces were written be generally uncertain, yet there are Passages in some few of them which seem to fix their Dates. So the *Chorus* in the beginning of the fifth Act of *Henry* V. by a Compliment very handsomly turn'd to the Earl of *Essex*, shews the Play to have been written when that Lord was General for the Queen in *Ireland*: And his Elogy upon Q. *Elizabeth*, and her Successor K. *James*, in the latter end of his *Henry* VIII, is a Proof of that Play's being written after the Accession of the latter of those two Princes to the Crown *of England*. Whatever the particular Times of his Writing were, the People of his Age, who began to grow wonderfully fond of Diversions of this kind, could not but be highly pleas'd to see a *Genius* arise amongst 'em of so pleasurable, so rich a Vein, and so plentifully capable of furnishing their favourite Entertainments. Besides the advantages of his Wit, he was in himself a good-natur'd Man, of great sweetness in his Manners, and a most agreeable Companion; so that it is no wonder if with so many good Qualities he made himself acquainted with the best Conversations of those Times. Queen *Elizabeth* had several of his Plays Acted before her, and without doubt gave him many gracious Marks of her Favour: It is that Maiden Princess plainly, whom he intends by

> A fair Vestal, Throned by the West.
>> *(Midsummer Night's Dream)*

And that whole Passage is a Compliment very properly brought in, and very handsomly apply'd to her. She was so well pleas'd with that admirable Character of *Falstaff,* in the two Parts of *Henry* the Fourth, that she commanded him to continue it for one Play more, and to shew him in Love. This is said to be the Occasion of his Writing *The Merry Wives of* Windsor. How well she was obey'd, the Play it self is an admirable Proof. Upon this Occasion it may not be improper to observe, that this Part *of Falstaff is* said to have been written originally under the Name of *Oldcastle;* some of that Family being then remaining, the Queen was pleas'd to command him to alter it; upon which he made use of *Falstaff.* The present Offence was indeed avoided; but I don't know whether the Author may not have been somewhat to blame in his second Choice, since it is certain that Sir *John Falstaff,* who was a Knight of the Garter, and a Lieutenant-General, was a Name of distinguish'd Merit in the Wars in *France* in *Henry* the Fifth's and *Henry* the Sixth's Times. What Grace soever the Queen confer'd upon him, it was not to her only he ow'd the Fortune which the Reputation of his Wit made. He had the Honour to meet with many great and uncommon Marks of Favour and Friendship from the Earl of *Southampton,* famous in the Histories of that Time for his Friendship to the unfortunate Earl of Essex. It was to that Noble Lord that he Dedicated his *Venus* and *Adonis,* the only Piece of his Poetry which he ever publish'd himself, tho' many of his Plays were surrepticiously and lamely Printed in his Lifetime. There is one Instance so singular in the Magnificence of this Patron of *Shakespear's,* that if I had not been assur'd that the Story was handed down by Sir *William D'Avenant,* who was probably very well acquainted with his Affairs, I should not have ventur'd to have inserted, that my Lord *Southampton,* at one time, gave him a thousand Pounds, to enable him to go through with a Purchase which he heard he had a mind to. A Bounty very great, and very rare at any time, and almost equal to that profuse Generosity the present Age has shewn to *French* Dancers and *Italian* Eunuchs.

What particular Habitude or Friendships he contracted with private Men, I have not been able to learn, more than that every one who had a true Taste of Merit, and could distinguish Men, had generally a just Value and Esteem for him. His exceeding Candor and good Nature must certainly have inclin'd all the gentler Part of the World to love him, as the power of his Wit oblig'd the Men of the most delicate Knowledge and polite Learning to admire him. Amongst these was the incomparable Mr. *Edmond Spencer,* who speaks of him in his *Tears of the Muses,* not only with the Praises due to a good Poet, but even lamenting his Absence with the tenderness of a Friend. The Passage is in *Thalia's* Complaint for the Decay of Dramatick Poetry, and the Contempt the Stage then lay under, amongst his Miscellaneous Works.

> And he the Man, whom Nature's self had made
> To mock her self, and Truth to imitate
> With kindly Counter under mimick Shade,
> Our pleasant *Willy,* ah! is dead of late:
> With whom all Joy and jolly Merriment
> Is also deaded, and in Dolour drent.
>   Instead thereof, scoffing Scurrility
> And scorning Folly with Contempt is crept,
> Rolling in Rhimes of shameless Ribaudry,
> Without Regard or due *Decorum* kept;
> Each idle Wit at will presumes to make,
> And doth the Learned's Task upon him take.
>   But that same gentle Spirit, from whose Pen
> Large Streams of Honey and sweet *Nectar* flow,
> Scorning the Boldness of such base born Men,
> Which dare their Follies forth so rashly throw;
> Doth rather choose to sit in idle Cell,
> Than so himself to Mockery to sell.

I know some People have been of Opinion, that *Shake-spear* is not meant by *Willy* in the first *Stanza* of these Verses, because *Spencer's* Death happen'd twenty Years before *Shake-spear's.* But, besides that the Character is not applicable to any Man of that time but himself, it is plain by the last *Stanza* that Mr. *Spencer* does not mean that he was then really Dead, but only that he had with-drawn himself from the Publick, or at least with-held his Hand from Writing, out of a disgust he had taken at the then ill taste of the Town, and the mean Condition of the. Stage. Mr. *Dryden* was always of Opinion these Verses were meant of *Shakespear;* and 'tis highly probable they were so, since he was three and thirty Years old at *Spencer's* Death; and his Reputation in Poetry must have been great enough before that Time to have deserv'd what is here said of him. His Acquaintance with *Ben Johnson* began with a remarkable piece of Humanity and good Nature; Mr. *Johnson,* who was at that Time altogether unknown to the World, had offer'd one of his Plays to the Players, in order to have it Acted; and the Persons into whose Hands it was put, after having turn'd it carelessly and superciliously over, were just upon returning it to him with an ill-natur'd Answer, that it would be of no service to their Company, when

Shakespear luckily cast his Eye upon it, and found something so well in it as to engage him first to read it through, and afterwards to recommend Mr. *Johnson* and his Writings to the Publick. After this they were profess'd Friends; tho' I don't know whether the other ever made him an equal return of Gentleness and Sincerity. *Ben* was naturally Proud and Insolent, and in the Days of his Reputation did so far take upon him the Supremacy in Wit, that he could not but look with an evil Eye upon any one that seem'd to stand in Competition with him. And if at times he has affected to commend him, it has always been with some Reserve, insinuating his Uncorrectness, a careless manner of Writing, and want of Judgment; the Praise of seldom altering or blotting out what he writ, which was given him by the Players who were the first Publishers of his Works after his Death, was what *Johnson* could not bear; he thought it impossible, perhaps, for another Man to strike out the greatest Thoughts in the finest Expression, and to reach those Excellencies of Poetry with the Ease of a first Imagination, which himself with infinite Labour and Study could but hardly attain to. *Johnson* was certainly a very good Scholar, and in that had the advantage of *Shakespear*, tho' at the same time I believe it must be allow'd, that what Nature gave the latter, was more than a Ballance for what Books had given the former; and the Judgment of a great Man upon this occasion was, I think, very just and proper. In a Conversation betwee Sir *John Suckling*, Sir *William D'Avenant, Endymion Porter,* Mr. *Hales* of *Eaton* and *Ben Johnson;* Sir *John Suckling*, who was a profess'd Admirer *of Shakespear*, had undertaken his Defence against *Ben Johnson* with some warmth; Mr. *Hales*, who had sat still for some time, hearing *Ben* frequently reproaching him with the want of Learning, and Ignorance of the Antients, told him at last, *That if Mr.* Shakespear *had not read the Antients, he had likewise not stollen any thing from 'em;* (a Fault the other made no Conscience of) *and that if he would produce any one Topick finely treated by any of them, he would undertake to shew something upon the same Subject at least as well written by* Shakespear. *Johnson* did indeed take a large liberty, even to the transcribing and translating of whole Scenes together; and sometimes, with all Deference to so great a Name as his, not altogether for the advantage of the Authors of whom he borrow'd. And if *Augustus* and *Virgil* were really what he has made 'em in a Scene of his *Poetaster*, they are as odd an Emperor and a Poet as ever met. *Shakespear*, on the other Hand, was beholding to no body farther than the Foundation of the Tale, the Incidents were often his own, and the Writing intirely so. There is one Play of his, indeed, *The Comedy of Errors*, in a great measure taken from the *Menaichmi* of *Plautus*. How that happen'd, I cannot easily Divine, since, as I hinted before, I do not take him to have been Master of *Latin* enough to read it in the Original, and I know of no Translation of *Plautus* so Old as his Time.

As I have not propos'd to my self to enter into a Large and Compleat Criticism upon Mr. *Shakespear's* Works, so I suppose it will neither be expected that I should take notice of the severe Remarks that have been formerly made upon him by Mr. *Rhymer*. I must confess, I can't very well see what could be the Reason of his animadverting with so much Sharpness, upon the Faults of a Man Excellent on most Occasions, and whom all the World ever was and will be inclin'd to have an Esteem and Veneration for. If it was to shew his own Knowledge in the Art of Poetry, besides that there is a Vanity in making that only his Design, I question if there be not many Imperfections as well in those Schemes and Precepts he has given for the Direction of others, as well as in that Sample of Tragedy which he has written to shew the Excellency of his own *Genius*. If he had a Pique against the Man, and wrote on purpose to ruin a Reputation so well establish'd, he has had the Mortification to fail altogether in his Attempt, and to see the World at least as fond of *Shakespear* as of his Critique. But I won't believe a Gentleman, and a good-natur'd Man, capable of the last Intention. Whatever may have been his Meaning, finding fault is certainly the easiest Task of Knowledge, and commonly those Men of good Judgment, who are likewise of good and gentle Dispositions, abandon this ungrateful Province to the Tyranny of Pedants.

The latter Part of his Life was spent, as all Men of good Sense will wish theirs may be, in Ease, Retirement, and the Conversation of his Friends. He had the good Fortune to gather an Estate equal to his Occasion, and, in that, to his Wish; and is said to have spent some Years before his Death at his native *Stratford*. His pleasurable Wit, and good Nature, engag'd him in the Acquaintance, and entitled him to the Friendship of the Gentlemen of the Neighbourhood. Amongst them, it is a Story almost still remember'd in that Country, that he had a particular Intimacy with Mr. *Combe*, an old Gentleman noted thereabouts for his Wealth and Usury: It happen'd, that in a pleasant Conversation amongst their common Friends, Mr. *Combe* told *Shakespear* in a laughing manner, that he fancy'd, he intended to write his Epitaph, if he happen'd to out-live him; and since he could not know what might be said of him when he was dead, he desir'd it might be done immediately: Upon which *Shakespear* gave him these four Verses.

Ten in the Hundred lies here ingrav'd,
Tis a Hundred to Ten, his Soul is not sav'd:
If any Man ask, Who lies in this Tomb?
Oh! ho! quoth the Devil, 'tis my *John-a-Combe*.

But the Sharpness of the Satyr is said to have stung the Man so severely, that he never forgave it.

He Dy'd in the 53d Year of his Age, and was bury'd on the North side of the Chancel, in the Great Church at *Stratford*, where a Monument, as engrav'd in the Plate, is plac'd in the Wall. On his Grave-Stone underneath is,

Good Friend, for Jesus sake, forbear
To dig the Dust inclosed here.
Blest be the Man that spares these Stones,
And Curst be he that moves my Bones.

He had three Daughters, of which two liv'd to be marry'd; *Judith*, the Elder, to one Mr. *Thomas Quiney*, by whom she had three Sons, who all dy'd without Children; and *Susannah*, who was his Favourite, to Dr. *John Hall*, a Physician of good Reputation in that Country. She left one Child only, a Daughter, who was marry'd first to *Thomas Nash*, Esq; and afterwards to Sir *John Bernard* of *Abbington*, but dy'd likewise without Issue.

—Nicholas Rowe, From "Some Account of
the Life, &c. of Mr. William Shakespear,"
The Works of Mr. William Shakespear,
1709, volume 1, pp. i–xxxvii

WASHINGTON IRVING
"STRATFORD-ON-AVON" (1819–20)

American writer, biographer, and historian Washington Irving (1783–1859), renowned for his tale of Rip Van Winkle and *The Legend of Sleepy Hollow*, recounts his visit to Shakespeare's birthplace and the reveries it induced in him. The Shakespeare that Irving limns here is a figure derived from Irving's own romantic imagination, drawn from anecdotes of Shakespeare's life, rather than a true rendering of the actual man.

Justice Shallow appears in *2 Henry IV* and in *The Merry Wives of Windsor*. It is his second incarnation that is regarded as being an unflattering portrait of the nemesis of Shakespeare's youth, Sir Thomas Lucy.

I had a desire to see the old family seat of the Lucys at Charlecot, and to ramble through the park where Shakespeare, in company with some of the roysters of Stratford, committed his youthful offence of deer stealing. In this harebrained exploit we are told that he was taken prisoner, and carried to the keeper's lodge, where he remained all night in doleful captivity. When brought into the presence of Sir Thomas Lucy, his treatment must have been galling and humiliating; for it so wrought upon his spirit as to produce a rough pasquinade, which was affixed to the park gate at Charlecot.[1]

This flagitious attack upon the dignity of the Knight so incensed him, that he applied to a lawyer at Warwick to put the severity of the laws in force against the rhyming deer stalker. Shakespeare did not wait to brave the united puissance of a Knight of the Shire and a country attorney. He forthwith abandoned the pleasant banks of the Avon and his paternal trade; wandered away to London; became a hanger on to the theatres; then an actor; and, finally, wrote for the stage; and thus, through the persecution of Sir Thomas Lucy, Stratford lost an indifferent wool comber and the world gained an immortal poet. He retained, however, for a long time, a sense of the harsh treatment of the Lord of Charlecot, and revenged himself in his writings; but in the sportive way of a good natured mind. Sir Thomas is said to be the original of Justice Shallow, and the satire is slyly fixed upon him by the Justice's armorial bearings, which, like those of the Knight, had white luces[2] in the quarterings.

Various attempts have been made by his biographers to soften and explain away this early transgression of the poet; but I look upon it as one of those thoughtless exploits natural to his situation and turn of mind. Shakespeare, when young, had doubtless all the wildness and irregularity of an ardent, undisciplined, and undirected genius. The poetic temperament has naturally something in it of the vagabond. When left to itself it runs loosely and wildly, and delights in every thing eccentric and licentious. It is often a turn up of a die, in the gambling freaks of fate, whether a natural genius shall turn out a great rogue or a great poet; and had not Shakespeare's mind fortunately taken a literary bias, he might have as daringly transcended all civil, as he has all dramatic laws.

I have little doubt that, in early life, when running, like an unbroken colt, about the neighbourhood of Stratford, he was to be found in the company of all kinds of odd anomalous characters; that he associated with all the mad caps of the place, and was one of those unlucky urchins, at mention of whom old men shake their heads, and predict that they will one day come to the gallows. To him the poaching in Sir Thomas Lucy's park was doubtless like a foray to a Scottish Knight, and struck his eager, and as yet untamed, imagination, as something delightfully adventurous.[3]

The old mansion of Charlecot and its surrounding park still remain in the possession of the Lucy family, and are peculiarly interesting from being connected with this whimsical but eventful circumstance in the scanty history of the bard. As the house stood at little more than three miles distance from Stratford, I resolved to pay it a pedestrian visit, that I might stroll leisurely through some of those scenes from which Shakespeare must have derived his earliest ideas of rural imagery. . . .

[T]he lark, springing up from the reeking bosom of the meadow, towered away into the bright fleecy cloud, pouring forth torrents of melody. As I watched the little songster, mounting up higher and higher, until his body was a mere speck on the white bosom of the cloud, while the ear was still filled with his music, it called to mind Shakespeare's exquisite little song in *Cymbeline:*

> Hark! hark! the lark at heav'n's gate sings,
>   And Phoebus 'gins arise,
> His steeds to water at those springs,
>   On chaliced flowers that lies.
> And winking mary-buds begin,
>   To ope their golden eyes;
> With every thing that pretty bin,
>   My lady sweet arise!

Indeed the whole country about here is poetic ground: every thing is associated with the idea of Shakespeare. Every old cottage that I saw, I fancied into some resort of his boyhood, where he had acquired his intimate knowledge of rustic life and manners, and heard those legendary tales and wild superstitions which he has woven like witchcraft into his dramas.

Notes

1.   The following is the only stanza extant of this lampoon:—
    A parliament member, a justice of peace,
    At home a poor scarecrow, at London an asse,
    If lowsie is Lucy, as some volke miscalle it,
    Then Lucy is lowsie, whatever befall it.
    He thinks himself great;
    Yet an asse in his state,
    We allow, by his ears, but with asses to mate.
    If Lucy is lowsie, as some volke miscall it,
    Then sing lowsie Lucy whatever befall it.
2.   The luce is a pike, or jack, and abounds in the Avon about Charlecot.
3.   A proof of Shakespeare's random habits and associates in his youthful days, may be found in a traditionary anecdote, picked up at Stratford by the elder Ireland and mentioned in *Picturesque Views on the Avon.*

About seven miles from Stratford lies the thirsty little market town of Bedford, famous for its ale. Two societies of the village yeomanry used to meet, under the appellation of the Bedford topers, and to challenge the lovers of good ale of the neighbouring villages, to a contest of drinking. Among others, the people of Stratford were called out to prove the strength of their heads; and in the number of the champions was Shakespeare, who, in spite of the proverb, that "they who drink beer will think beer," was as true to his ale as Falstaff to his sack. The chivalry of Stratford was staggered at the first onset, and sounded a retreat while they had yet legs to carry them off the field. They had scarcely marched a mile, when, their legs failing them, they were forced to lie down under a crab tree, where they passed the night. It is still standing, and goes by the name of Shakespeare's tree.

In the morning his companions awakened the bard, and proposed returning to Bedford, but he declined, saying he had had enough, having drank with

Piping Pebworth, Dancing Marston,
Haunted Hillbro', Hungry Grafton,
Dudging Exhall, Papist Wicksford,
Beggarly Broom, and Drunken Bedford.

"The villages here alluded to," says Ireland, "still bear the epithets thus given them: the people of Pebworth are still famed for their skill on the pipe and tabor: Hillborough is now called Haunted Hillborough: and Grafton in famous for the poverty of its soil."

—Washington Irving, from "Stratford-on-Avon," *The Sketch Book of Geoffrey Crayon, Gent.*, 1819–20

WALTER BAGEHOT "SHAKESPEARE—THE INDIVIDUAL" (1853)

Walter Bagehot (1826–77) was an English businessman involved in shipping and banking and a writer who wrote about literature, economics, and political philosophy. Bagehot's aim in the following excerpt is to compose a written portrait of Shakespeare by the revelation of the man he believes he can derive from analyzing the substance of his work, the attitudes he believes it professes, and the dispositions of his characters rather than by relying on the biographical anecdotes that had come to be taken to be accurate representations of Shakespeare's life.

Despite his dismissal of the authenticity of the anecdotal accounts of Shakespeare's life that began to be traded soon after Shakespeare's death, Bagehot's conclusions about Shakespeare, drawn from the plays, tend to echo them.

Of interest for the student of the plays is that in attempting to derive Shakespeare's personality from their study, Bagehot often engages in critical analyses of the plays, their language, and their characters.

The greatest of English poets, it is often said, is but a name. 'No letter of his writing, no record of his conversation, no character of him drawn with any fulness by a contemporary,' have been extracted by antiquaries from the piles of rubbish which they have sifted. Yet of no person is there a clearer picture in the popular fancy. You seem to have known Shakespeare—to have seen Shakespeare—to have been friends with Shakespeare. We would attempt a slight delineation of the popular idea which has been formed, not from loose tradition or remote research; not from what some one says some one else said that the poet said, but from data, which are at least undoubted, from the sure testimony of his certain works. . . .

First of all, it may be said, that Shakespeare's works could only be produced by a first-rate imagination working on a first-rate experience. It is often difficult to make out whether the author of a poetic creation is drawing from fancy, or drawing from experience; but for art on a certain scale, the two must concur. Out of nothing, nothing can be created. Some plastic power is required, however great may be the material. And when such a work as *Hamlet* or *Othello*, still more, when both of them and others not unequal have been created by a single mind, it may be fairly said, that not only a great imagination, but a full conversancy with the world was necessary to their production. The whole powers of man under the most favourable circumstances, are not too great for such an effort. We may assume that Shakespeare had a great experience.

In spiritedness, the style of Shakespeare is very like to that of [Sir Walter] Scott. The description of a charge of cavalry in Scott reads . . . as if it was written on horseback. A play by Shakespeare reads as if it were written in a playhouse. The great critics assure you, that a theatrical audience must be kept awake, but Shakespeare knew this of his own knowledge. When you read him you feel a sensation of motion, a conviction that there is something 'up,' a notion that not only is something being talked about, but also that something is being done. We do not imagine that Shakespeare owed this quality to his being a player, but rather that he became a player because he possessed this quality of mind. For after, and not withstanding everything which has, or may be said against the theatrical profession, it certainly does require from those who pursue it a certain quickness and liveliness of mind. Mimics are commonly an elastic sort of persons, and it takes a little levity of disposition to enact even the 'heavy fathers.' If a boy joins a company of strolling players, you may be sure that he is not a 'good boy;' he may be a trifle foolish, or a thought romantic, but certainly he is not slow. And this was in truth the case with Shakespeare. They say, too, that in the beginning he was a first-rate link-boy [a boy who guided people through the streets at night by the light of the torch he carried]; and the tradition is affecting, though we fear it is not quite certain. Anyhow you feel about Shakespeare that he could have been a link-boy. In the same way you feel he may have been a player. You are sure at once that he could not have followed any sedentary kind of life. But wheresoever there was anything *acted* in earnest or in jest, by way of mock representation or by way of serious reality, there he found matter for his mind. If anybody could have any doubt about the liveliness of Shakespeare, let them consider the character of Falstaff. When a man has created *that* without a capacity for laughter, then a blind man may succeed in describing colours. Intense animal spirits are the single sentiment (if they be a sentiment) of the entire character. If most men were to save up all the gaiety of their whole lives, it would come about to the gaiety of one speech in Falstaff. A morose man might have amassed many jokes, might have observed many details of jovial society, might have conceived a Sir John, marked by rotundity of body, but could hardly have imagined what we call his rotundity of mind. We mean that the animal spirits of Falstaff give him an easy, vague, diffusive sagacity which is peculiar to him. A morose man, Iago, for example, may know anything, and is apt to know a good deal, but what he knows is generally all in corners. He knows number 1, number 2, number 3, and so on, but there is not anything continuous or smooth, or fluent in his knowledge. Persons conversant with the works of Hazlitt will know in a minute what we mean. Everything which he observed he seemed to observe from a certain soreness of mind; he looked at people because they offended him; he had the same vivid notion of them that a man has of objects which grate on a wound in his body. But there is nothing at all of this in Falstaff; on the contrary, everything pleases him, and everything is food for a joke. Cheerfulness and prosperity give an easy abounding sagacity of mind which nothing else does give. . . . [T]he happy have a vague and rounded view of the round world, and such was the knowledge of Falstaff.

It is to be observed that these high spirits are not a mere excrescence or superficial point in an experiencing nature; on the contrary, they seem to be essential, if not to its idea or existence, at least to its exercise and employment. How are you to know people without talking to them, but how are you to talk to them without tiring yourself? A common man is exhausted in half an hour; Scott or Shakespeare could have gone on for a whole day . . . all great English writers describe English people, and in describing them, they give, as they must give, a large comic element; and, speaking generally, this is scarcely possible, except in the case of cheerful and easy-living men. There is, no doubt, a biting satire, like that of Swift, which has for its essence misanthropy. There is the mockery of Voltaire, which is based on intellectual contempt; but this is not our English humour,—it is not that of Shakespeare and Falstaff; ours is the humour of a man who laughs when he speaks, of flowing enjoyment, of an experiencing nature.

Yet it would be a great error if we gave anything like an exclusive prominence to this aspect of Shakespeare. Thus he appeared to those around him,—in some degree they knew that he was a cheerful, and humorous, and happy man; but of his higher gift they knew less than we. A great painter of men must (as has been said) have a faculty of conversing, but he must also have a capacity for solitude. There is much of mankind that a man can only learn from himself. Behind every man's external life, which he leads in company, there is another which he leads alone, and which he carries with him apart. . . .

In another point also Shakespeare, as he was, must be carefully contrasted with the estimate that would be formed of him from such delineations as that of Falstaff, and that was doubtless frequently made by casual though only by casual frequenters of the Mermaid. It has been said that the mind of Shakespeare contained within it the mind of Scott; it remains to be observed that it contained also the mind of Keats. For, beside the delineation of human life, and beside also the delineation of nature, there remains also for the poet a third subject—the delineation of *fancies*. Of course, these, be they what they may, are like to, and were originally borrowed either from man or from nature—from one or from both together. We know but two things in the simple way of direct experience, and whatever else we know, must be in some mode or manner compacted out of them. Yet 'books are a substantial world, both pure and good,' and so are fancies too. In all countries men have devised to themselves a whole series of half-divine creations—mythologies Greek and Roman, fairies, angels; beings who may be, for aught we know, but with whom, in the meantime, we can attain to no conversation. The most known of these mythologies are the Greek, and what is, we suppose, the second epoch of the Gothic, the fairies; and it so happens that Shakespeare has dealt with them both and in a remarkable manner. We are not, indeed, of those critics who profess simple and unqualified admiration for the poem of *Venus and Adonis*. It seems intrinsically, as we know it from external testimony to have been, a juvenile production, written when Shakespeare's nature might be well expected to be crude and unripened. Power is shown, and power of a remarkable kind; but it is not displayed in a manner that will please or does please the mass of men. In spite of the name of its author, the poem has never been popular—and surely this is sufficient. Nevertheless it is remarkable as a literary exercise, and as a treatment of a singular though unpleasant subject. The fanciful class of poems differ from others in being laid, so far as their scene goes, in a perfectly unseen world. The type of such productions is Keats's *Endymion*. We mean that it is the type, not as giving the abstract perfection of this sort of art, but because it shows and embodies both its excellencies and defects in a very marked and prominent manner. In that poem there are no passions and no actions, there is no art and no life, but there is beauty, and that is meant to be enough, and to a reader of one-and-twenty it is enough and more. What are exploits or speeches? What is Caesar or Coriolanus? What is a tragedy like *Lear*, or a real view of human life in any kind whatever, to people who do not know and do not care what human life is? In early youth it is, perhaps, not true that the passions, taken generally, are particularly violent, or that the imagination is in any remarkable degree powerful; but it is certain that the fancy (which though it be, in the last resort, but a weak stroke of that same faculty, which, when it strikes hard, we call imagination, may yet for this purpose be looked on as distinct) is particularly wakeful, and that the gentler species of passions are more absurd than they are afterwards. And the literature of this period of human life runs naturally away from the real world; away from the less ideal portion of it, from stocks and stones, and aunts and uncles, and rests on mere half-embodied sentiments, which in the hands of great poets assume a kind of semipersonality, and are, to the distinction between things and persons, 'as moonlight unto sunlight, and as water unto wine.' The 'sonnets' of Shakespeare belong exactly to the same school of poetry. They are not the sort of verses to take any particular hold upon the mind permanently and for ever, but at a certain period they take too much. For a young man to read in the spring of the year among green fields and in gentle air, they are the ideal. . . .

Can it be made out what were Shakespeare's political views? We think it certainly can, and that without difficulty. From the English historical plays, it distinctly appears that he accepted, like everybody then, the Constitution of his country. His lot was not cast in an age of political controversy, nor of reform. What was, was from of old. The Wars of the Roses had made it very evident how much room there was for the evils incident to an hereditary monarchy, for instance, those of a controverted succession, and the evils incident to an aristocracy, as want of public spirit and audacious selfishness, to arise and continue within the realm of England. Yet they had not repelled, and had barely disconcerted our conservative ancestors. They had not become Jacobins; they did not concur—and history, except in Shakespeare, hardly does justice to them—in Jack Cade's notion that the laws should come out of his mouth, or that the commonwealth was to be reformed by interlocutors in this scene.

> *George:* I tell thee, Jack Cade, the clothier means to dress the Commonwealth, and turn it, and set a new nap upon it.
>
> *John:* So he had need, for 'tis threadbare. Well, I say it was never merry world in England since gentlemen came up.
>
> *Geo.:* O miserable age! Virtue is not regarded in handycraftsmen.
>
> *John:* The nobility think scorn to go in leathern aprons.
>
> *Geo.:* Nay more: the king's council are no good workmen.
>
> *John:* True; and yet it is said, labour in thy vocation; which is as much as to say, as let the magistrates be labouring men, and therefore should we be magistrates.
>
> *Geo.:* Thou has hit it, for there is no better sign of a brave mind than a hard hand.
>
> *John:* I see them! I see them!

The English people did see them, and know them, and therefore have rejected them. An audience which, *bona fide,* entered into the merit of this scene, would never believe in everybody's suffrage. They would know that there is such a thing as nonsense, and when a man has once attained to that deep conception, you may be sure of him ever after. And though it would be absurd to say that Shakespeare originated this idea, or that the disbelief in simple democracy is owing to his teaching or suggestions, yet it may, nevertheless, be truly said, that he shared in the peculiar knowledge of men,— and also possessed the peculiar constitution of mind—which engender this effect. The author of *Coriolanus* never believed in a mob, and did something towards preventing anybody else from doing so. But this political idea was not exactly the strongest in Shakespeare's mind. We think he had two others stronger, or as strong. First, the feeling of loyalty to the ancient polity of this country—not because it was good, but because it existed. In his time, people no more thought of the origin of the monarchy than they did of the origin of the Mendip Hills. The one had always been there, and so had the other. God (such was the common notion) had made both, and one as much as the other. Everywhere, in that age, the common modes of political speech assumed the existence of certain utterly national institutions, and would have been worthless and nonsensical except on that assumption. This national habit appears as it ought to appear in our national dramatist. . . . It is to most of us, and to the happiest of us, a thing immutable, and such, no doubt, it was to Shakespeare, which, if any one would have proved, let him refer at random to any page of the historical English plays.

The second peculiar tenet which we ascribe to his [Shakespeare's] political creed is a disbelief in the middle classes. We fear he had no opinion of traders. In this age, we know, it is held that the keeping of a shop is equivalent to a political education. Occasionally, in country villages, where the trader sells everything, he is thought to know nothing, and has no vote; but in a town where he is a householder (as, indeed, he is in the country), and sells only one thing—there we assume that he knows everything. And this assumption is in the opinion of some observers confirmed by the fact. Sir Walter Scott used to relate, that when, after a trip to London, he returned to Tweedside, he always found the people in that district knew more of politics than the Cabinet. And so it is with the mercantile community in modern times. If you are a Chancellor of the Exchequer, it is possible that you may be acquainted with finance; but if you sell Figs it is certain that you will. Now we nowhere find this laid down in Shakespeare. On the contrary, you will generally find that when a 'citizen' is mentioned, he generally does or says something absurd. Shakespeare had a clear perception that it is possible to bribe a class as well as an individual, and that personal obscurity is but an insecure guarantee for political disinterestedness.

> Moreover, he hath left you all his walks,
> His private arbours and new-planted orchards
> On this side Tyber; he hath left them you,
> And to your heirs for ever: common pleasures,
> To walk abroad and recreate yourselves.
> Here was a Caesar! when comes such another?
> [*Julius Caesar*, III.ii.249–54]

He everywhere speaks in praise of a tempered and ordered and qualified polity, in which the pecuniary classes have a certain influence, but no more, and shows in every page a keen sensibility to the large views, and high-souled energies, the gentle refinements and disinterested desires in which those classes are likely to be especially deficient. He is particularly the poet of personal nobility, though, throughout his writings, there is a sense of freedom, just as Milton is the poet of freedom, though with an underlying reference to personal nobility; indeed, we might well expect our two poets to combine the appreciation of a rude and generous liberty, with that of a delicate and refined nobleness, since it is the union of these two elements that characterises our society and their experience.

There are two things—good-tempered sense and ill-tempered sense. In our remarks on the character of Falstaff, we hope we have made it very clear, that Shakespeare had the former; we think it nearly as certain that he possessed the latter also. An instance of this might be taken from that contempt for the perspicacity of the *bourgeoisie* which we have just been mentioning. It is within the limits of what may be called malevolent sense, to take extreme and habitual pleasure in remarking the foolish opinions, the narrow notions, and fallacious deductions which seem to cling to the pompous and prosperous man of business. . . . [An] instance of (what has an odd sound), the malevolence of Shakespeare is to be found in the play of *Measure for Measure.* We agree with Hazlitt, that this play seems to be written, perhaps more than any other, *con amore,* and with a relish, and this seems to be the reason why, notwithstanding the unpleasant nature of its plot, and the absence of any very attractive character, it is yet one of the plays which take hold on the mind most easily and most powerfully. Now the entire character of Angelo, which is the expressive feature of the piece, is nothing but a successful embodiment of the pleasure, the malevolent pleasure, which a warm-blooded and expansive man takes in watching the rare, the dangerous and inanimate excesses of the constrained and cold-blooded. One seems to see Shakespeare, with his bright eyes and his large lips and buoyant face, watching with a pleasant excitement the excesses of his thin-lipped and calculating creation, as though they were the excesses of a real person. It is the complete picture of a natural hypocrite, who does not consciously disguise strong impulses, but whose very passions seem of their own accord to have disguised themselves and retreated into the recesses of the character, yet only to recur even more dangerously when their proper period is expired, when the will is cheated into security by their absence, and the world (and, it may be, the 'judicious person' himself) is impressed with a sure reliance in his chilling and remarkable rectitude.

It has, we believe, been doubted whether Shakespeare was a man much conversant with the intimate society of women. Of course no one denies that he possessed a great knowledge of them—a capital acquaintance with their excellencies, faults, and foibles; but it has been thought that this was the result rather of imagination than of society, of creative fancy rather than of perceptive experience. Now that Shakespeare possessed, among other singular qualities, a remarkable imaginative knowledge of women, is quite certain, for he was acquainted with the soliloquies of women. A woman we suppose, like a man, must be alone, in order to speak a soliloquy. After the greatest possible intimacy and experience, it must still be imagination, or fancy at least, which tells any man what a woman thinks of herself and to herself. There will still— get as near the limits of confidence or observation as you can—be a space which must be filled up from other means. Men can only divine the truth— reserve, indeed, is a part of its charm. Seeing, therefore, that Shakespeare had done what necessarily and certainly must be done without experience, we were in some doubt whether he might not have dispensed with it altogether. A grave reviewer cannot know these things. We thought indeed of reasoning that since the delineations of women in Shakespeare were admitted to be first-rate, it should follow,—at least there was a fair presumption,—that no means or aid had been wanting to their production, and that consequently we ought, in the absence of distinct evidence, to assume that personal intimacy as well as solitary imagination had been concerned in their production. And we meant to cite the 'questions about Octavia,' which Lord Byron, who thought he had the means of knowing, declared to be 'woman all over.'

But all doubt was removed and all conjecture set to rest by the coming in of an ably-dressed friend from the external world, who mentioned that the language of Shakespeare's women was essentially female language; that there were certain points and peculiarities in the English of cultivated English women, which made it a language of itself, which must be heard familiarly in order to be known. And he added, 'except a greater use of words of Latin derivation, as was natural in an age when ladies received a learned education, a few words not now proper, a few conceits that were the fashion of the time, and there is the very same English in the women's speeches in Shakespeare.' He quoted—

Think not I love him, though I ask for him;
'Tis but a peevish boy:—yet he talks well;—
But what care I for words? yet words do well,
When he that speaks them pleases those that hear.
It is a pretty youth:—not very pretty:—
But, sure, he's proud; and yet his pride becomes him;
He'll make a proper man: The best thing in him
Is his complexion; and faster than his tongue

Did make offence, his eye did heal it up.
He is not very tall; yet for his years he's tall:
His leg is but so so: and yet 'tis well.
There was a pretty redness in his lip;
A little riper and more lusty red
Than that mix'd in his cheek; 'twas just the difference
Betwixt the constant red, and mingled damask.
There be some women, Silvius, had they mark'd him
In parcels as I did, would have gone near
To fall in love with him: but, for my part,
I love him not, nor hate him not; and yet
I have more cause to hate him than to love him:
For what had he to do to chide at me?
He said, my eyes were black, and my hair black,
And, now I am remember'd, scorn'd at me:
I marvel, why I answer'd not again:
But that's all one;

[*As You Like It*, III.v.109–33]

and the passage of Perdita's . . . about the daffodils that—

take
The winds of March with beauty; violets dim,
But sweeter than the lids of Juno's eyes,
Or Cytherea's breath;

[*The Winter's Tale*, IV.iv.119–22]

and said that these were conclusive. But we have not, ourselves, heard young ladies converse in that manner. . . .

On few subjects has more nonsense been written than on the learning of Shakespeare. In former times, the established tenet was, that he was acquainted with the entire range of the Greek and Latin classics, and familiarly resorted to Sophocles and Aeschylus as guides and models. This creed reposed not so much on any painful or elaborate criticism of Shakespeare's plays, as on one of the *a priori* assumptions permitted to the indolence of the wise old world. It was then considered clear, by all critics, that no one could write good English, who could not also write bad Latin. Questioning scepticism has rejected this axiom, and refuted with contemptuous facility the slight attempt which had been made to verify this case of it from the evidence of the plays themselves. But the new school, not content with showing that Shakespeare was no formed or elaborate scholar, propounded the idea that he was quite ignorant.... The answer is that Shakespeare wrote his plays, and that those plays show not only a very powerful, but also a very cultivated mind. A hard student Shakespeare was not, yet he was a happy and pleased reader of interesting books. He was a natural reader; when a book was dull, he put it down, when it looked fascinating, he took it up and the consequence is, that he remembered and mastered what he read. Lively books, read with lively interest, leave strong and living recollections.... It is certain that Shakespeare read the novels of his time, for he has founded on them the stories of his plays; he read Plutarch, for his words still live in the dialogue of the 'proud Roman' plays; and it is remarkable that Montaigne is the only philosopher that Shakespeare can be proved to have read, because, he deals more than any other philosopher with the first impressions of things which exist. On the other hand, it may be doubted if Shakespeare would have perused his commentators.... [W]hat would he have thought of the following speculations of an anonymous individual, whose notes have been recently published ... and, according to the periodical essayists, 'contribute valuable suggestions to the illustration of the immortal bard'?

The Two Gentlemen of Verona
Act I. Scene I.
P. 92. The reading of the subsequent line has hitherto been
'Tis true; for you are over boots in love;'
but the manuscript corrector of the Folio, 1632, has changed it to
'Tis true; *but* you are over boots in love;'
which seems more consistent with the course of the dialogue; for
Proteus, remarking that Leander had been 'more than over shoes
in love' with Hero, Valentine answers, that Proteus was even more
deeply in love than Leander. Proteus observes of the fable of Hero and
Leander—
'That's a deep story of a deeper love,
For he was more than over shoes in love.'
Valentine retorts—
'Tis true; *but* you are over boots in love.'
For instead of *but* was perhaps caught by the compositor from the
preceding line.

It is difficult to fancy Shakespeare perusing a volume of such annotations, though we allow that we admire them ourselves. As to the controversy on his school learning, we have only to say, that though the alleged imitations of the Greek tragedians are mere nonsense, yet there is clear evidence that

Shakespeare received the ordinary grammar school education of his time, and that he had derived from the pain and suffering of several years, not exactly an acquaintance with Greek or Latin, but like Eton boys a firm conviction that there are such languages.

Another controversy has been raised as to whether Shakespeare was religious. In the old editions it is commonly enough laid down, that, when writing his plays, he had no desire to fill the Globe Theatre, but that his intentions were of the following description. 'In this play,' Cymbeline, 'Shakespeare has strongly depicted the frailties of our nature, and the effect of vicious passions on the human mind. In the fate of the Queen we behold the worst of perfidy justly sacrificed by the arts she had, with unnatural ambition, prepared for others; and in reviewing her death and that of Cloten, we may easily call to mind the words of Scripture, &c.' And of *King Lear* it is observed, with great confidence, that Shakespeare, '*no doubt,* intended to mark particularly the afflicting character of children's ingratitude to their parents, and the conduct of Goneril and Regan to each other, *especially* in the former's poisoning the latter, and laying hands on *herself,* we are taught that those who want gratitude towards their parents (who gave them their being, fed them, nurtured them to *man's* estate) will not scruple to commit more barbarous crimes, and easily to forget that, by destroying their body, they destroy their soul also.' And Ulrici, a very learned and illegible writer, has discovered that in every one of his plays Shakespeare had in view the inculcation of the peculiar sentiments and doctrines of the Christian religion, and considers the *Midsummer Night's Dream* to be a specimen of the lay or amateur sermon. This is what Dr. Ulrici thinks of Shakespeare; but what would Shakespeare have thought of Dr. Ulrici? We believe that '*Via* goodman dull,' is nearly the remark which the learned professor would have received from the poet to whom his very careful treatise is devoted. . . . had, we suspect, an objection to grim people, and we fear would have liked the society of Mercutio better than that of a dreary divine, and preferred Ophelia or '*that* Juliet' to a female philanthropist of sinewy aspect. And, seriously, if this world is not all evil, he who has understood and painted it best must probably have some good. If the underlying arid almighty essence of this world be good, then it is likely that the writer who most deeply approached to that essence, will be himself good. There is a religion of week-days as well as of Sundays, of 'cakes and ale,' as well as of pews and altar cloths. This England lay before Shakespeare as it lies before us all, with its green fields, and its long hedgerows, and its many trees, and its great towns, and its endless hamlets, and its motley society, and its long history, and its bold exploits, and its gathering power; and he saw that they were good. To him, perhaps, more than to any one else, has it been given to see, that they were a great unity, a great religious object; that if you could only descend to the inner life, to the deep things, to the secret principles of its noble vigour, to the essence of character, to what we know of Hamlet, and seem to fancy of Ophelia, we might, so far as we are capable of so doing, understand the nature which God has made. Let us, then, think of him, not as a teacher of dry dogmas, or a sayer of hard sayings, but as

> A priest to us all,
> Of the wonder and bloom of the world—
> [Matthew Arnold, "Empedocles upon Etna," stanza 5]

a teacher of the hearts of men and women; one from whom may be learned something of that inmost principle that ever modulates

> with murmurs of the air,
> And motions of the forest and the sea,
> And voice of living beings, and woven hymns
> Of night and day and the deep heart of man.
> [Percy Bysshe Shelley, "Alastor"]

. . . Yet it must be allowed that Shakespeare was worldly, and the proof of it is, that he succeeded in the world. Possibly this is the point on which we are most richly indebted to tradition. We see generally indeed in Shakespeare's works the popular author, the successful dramatist; there is a life and play in his writings rarely to be found, except in those who have had habitual good luck, and who, by the tact of experience, feel the minds of their readers at every word, like a good rider feels the mouth of his horse. But it would have been difficult quite to make out whether the profits so accruing had been profitably invested—whether the genius to create such illusions was accompanied with the care and judgment necessary to put out their proceeds properly in actual life. We could only have said, that there was a general impression of entire calmness and equability in his principal works, rarely to be found where there is much pain, which usually makes gaps in the work and dislocates the balance of the mind. But happily here, and here almost alone, we are on sure historical ground. The reverential nature of Englishmen has carefully preserved what they thought the great excellence of their poet—that he made a fortune. It is certain that Shakespeare was proprietor of the Globe Theatre—that he made money there, and invested the same in land at Stratford-on-the-Avon, and probably no circumstance in his life ever gave him so much pleasure. It was a great thing that he, the son of the wool-comber, the poacher, the good-for-nothing, the vagabond (for so we fear the phrase went in Shakespeare's youth), should return upon the old scene a substantial man, a person of capital, a freeholder, a gentleman to be respected, and over whom even a burgess could not affect the least superiority. . . . [W]ith Shakespeare: it pleased him to be respected by those whom he had respected with boyish reverence, but who had rejected the imaginative man—on their own ground and in their own subject, by the only title which they would regard—in a word, as a monied man. We seem to see him eyeing the burgesses with good-humored fellowship and genial (though suppressed and half unconscious) contempt, drawing out their old stories, and acquiescing in their foolish notions, with everything in his head and easy sayings upon his tongue,—a full mind and a deep dark eye, that played upon an easy scene—now in fanciful solitude, now, in cheerful society; now occupied with deep thoughts, now and equally so, with trivial recreations, forgetting the dramatist in the man of substance, and the poet in the happy companion; beloved and even respected, with a hope for every one, and a smile for all.

—Walter Bagehot, from "Shakespeare—the
Individual," 1853, *Collected Works*, ed. Norman
St. John-Stevas, 1965, volume 1, pp. 173–214

NATHANIEL HAWTHORNE
"RECOLLECTIONS OF A GIFTED WOMAN" (1863)

Nathaniel Hawthorne (1804–64), American novelist, essayist, and short story writer is best known for his novel of Puritan New England, *The Scarlet Letter*. After Franklin Pierce was elected the fourteenth president of the United States in 1852, Hawthorne, who wrote Pierce's official campaign biography, was rewarded with the position of U.S. consul in Liverpool. During his stay in England, Hawthorne visited Shakespeare's home and burial place in Stratford. In the following passage, Hawthorne describes the places he saw and the sense of Shakespeare he derived from his visit. His foremost impression is of the distance between the ordinary circumstances of Shakespeare's life, as they appear from his daily surroundings, and the extraordinary quality of his work. Hawthorne concludes with a meditation on the power of Shakespeare's genius to eclipse the power of all other practitioners of art, and the reader senses he is indirectly feeling his own lesser status as a writer in Shakespeare's presence.

William Davenant was a poet and playwright and, in 1638, was appointed poet laureate of England. Shakespeare was his godfather, and the unsubstantiated rumor grew around him that Shakespeare was also his biological father, thus Hawthorne's oblique reference to Davenant's mother.

The spire of Shakespeare's church—the Church of the Holy Trinity—begins to show itself among the trees at a little distance from Stratford. Next we see the shabby old dwellings, intermixed with mean-looking houses of modern date; and the streets being quite level, you are struck and surprised by nothing so much as the tameness of the general scene, as if Shakespeare's genius were vivid enough to have wrought pictorial splendors in the town where he was born. . . .

After wandering through two or three streets, I found my way to Shakespeare's birthplace, which is almost a smaller and humbler house than any description can prepare the visitor to expect; so inevitably does an august inhabitant make his abode palatial to our imaginations, receiving his guests, indeed, in a castle in the air, until we unwisely insist on meeting him among the sordid lanes and alleys of lower earth. The portion of the edifice with which Shakespeare had anything to do is hardly large enough, in the basement, to contain the butcher's stall that one of his descendants kept, and that still remains there, windowless, with the cleaver-cuts in its hacked counter, which projects into the street under a little penthouse-roof, as if waiting for a new occupant.

The upper half of the door was open, and, on my rapping at it, a young person in black made her appearance and admitted me; she was not a menial, but remarkably genteel (an American characteristic) for an English girl, and was probably the daughter of the old gentlewoman who takes care of the house. This lower room has a pavement of gray slabs of stone, which may have been rudely squared when the house was new, but are now all cracked, broken, and disarranged in a most unaccountable way. One does not see how any ordinary usage, for whatever length of time, should have so smashed these heavy stones; it is as if an earthquake had burst up through the floor, which afterwards had been imperfectly trodden down again. The room is whitewashed and very clean, but woefully shabby and dingy, coarsely built, and such as the most poetical imagination would find it difficult to idealize. In the rear of this apartment is the kitchen, a still smaller room, of a similar rude aspect: it has a great, rough fireplace, with space for a large family under the blackened opening of the chimney, and an immense passageway for the smoke, through which Shakespeare may have seen the blue sky by day and the stars glimmering down at him by night. It is now a dreary spot where the long-extinguished embers used to be. A glowing fire, even if it covered only a quarter part of the hearth, might still do much towards making the old kitchen cheerful. But we get a depressing idea of the stifled, poor, sombre kind of life that could have been lived in such a dwelling, where this room seems to have been the gathering-place of the family, with no breadth or scope, no good retirement, but old and young huddling together cheek by jowl. What a hardy plant was Shakespeare's genius, how fatal its development, since it could not be blighted in such an atmosphere! It only brought human nature the closer to him, and put more unctuous earth about his roots.

Thence I was ushered up stairs to the room in which Shakespeare is supposed to have been born: though, if you peep too curiously into the matter, you may find the shadow of an ugly doubt on this, as well as most other points of his mysterious life. It is the chamber over the butcher's shop, and is lighted by one broad window containing a great many small, irregular panes of glass. The floor is made of planks, very rudely hewn, and fitting together with little neatness; the naked beams and rafters, at the sides of the room and overhead, bear the original marks of the builder's broad-axe, with no evidence of an attempt to smooth off the job. Again we have to reconcile ourselves to the smallness of the space enclosed by these illustrious walls,—a circumstance more difficult to accept, as regards places that we have heard, read, thought, and dreamed much about, than any other disenchanting particular of a mistaken ideal. A few paces—perhaps seven or eight—take us from end to end of it. So low it is, that I could easily touch the ceiling, and might have done so without a tiptoe-stretch, had it been a good deal higher; and this humility of the chamber has tempted a vast multitude of people to write their names overhead in pencil. Every inch of the side-walls, even into the obscurest nooks and corners, is covered with a similar record; all the windowpanes, moreover, are scrawled with diamond signatures among which is said to be that of Walter Scott; but so many persons have sought to immortalize themselves in close vicinity to his name, that I really could not trace him out. Methinks it is strange that people do not strive to forget their forlorn little identities, in such situations, instead of thrusting them forward into the dazzle of a great renown, where, if noticed, they cannot but be deemed impertinent.

This room, and the entire house, so far as I saw it, are whitewashed and exceedingly clean; nor is there the aged, musty smell with which old Chester first made me acquainted, and which goes far to cure an American of his excessive predilection for antique residences. An old lady, who took charge of me up stairs, had the manners and aspect of a gentlewoman, and talked with somewhat formidable knowledge and appreciative intelligence about

Shakespeare. Arranged on a table and in chairs were various prints, views of houses and scenes connected with Shakespeare's memory, together with editions of his works and local publications about his home and haunts, from the sale of which this respectable lady perhaps realizes a handsome profit. At any rate, I bought a good many of them, conceiving that it might be the civillest way of requiting her for her instructive conversation and the trouble she took in showing me the house. It cost me a pang (not a curmudgeonly, but a gentlemanly one) to offer a downright fee to the lady-like girl who had admitted me: but I swallowed my delicate scruples with some little difficulty, and she digested hers, so far as I could observe, with no difficulty at all. In fact, nobody need fear to hold out half a crown to any person with whom he has occasion to speak a word in England.

I should consider it unfair to quit Shakespeare's house without the frank acknowledgment that I was conscious of not the slightest emotion while viewing it, nor any quickening of the imagination. This has often happened to me in my visits to memorable places. Whatever pretty and apposite reflections I may have made upon the subject had either occurred to me before I ever saw Stratford, or have been elaborated since. It is pleasant, nevertheless, to think that I have seen the place; and I believe that I can form a more sensible and vivid idea of Shakespeare as a flesh-and-blood individual now that I have stood on the kitchen-hearth and in the birth-chamber; but I am not quite certain that this power of realization is altogether desirable in reference to a great poet. The Shakespeare whom I met there took various guises, but had not his laurel on. He was successively the roguish boy,—the youthful deer-stealer,—the comrade of players,—the too familiar friend of [Sir William] Davenant's mother,—the careful, thrifty, thriven man of property who came back from London to lend money on bond, and occupy the best house in Stratford,—the mellow, red-nosed, autumnal boon-companion of John a' Combe,—and finally (or else the Stratford gossips belied him), the victim of convivial habits, who met his death by tumbling into a ditch on his way home from a drinking-bout, and left his second-best bed to his poor wife.

I feel, as sensibly as the reader can, what horrible impiety it is to remember these things, be they true or false. In either case, they ought to vanish out of sight on the distant ocean-line of the past, leaving a pure, white memory, even as a sail, though perhaps darkened with many stains, looks snowy white on the far horizon. . . . When Shakespeare invoked a curse on the man who should stir his bones, he perhaps meant the larger share of it for him or them who should pry into his perishing earthliness, the defects or even the merits of the character that he wore in Stratford, when he had left mankind so much to muse upon that was imperishable and divine. Heaven keep me from incurring any part of the anathema in requital for the irreverent sentences above written!

From Shakespeare's house, the next step, of course, is to visit his burial-place. The appearance of the church is most venerable and beautiful, standing amid a great green shadow of lime-trees, above which rises the spire, while the Gothic battlements and buttresses and vast arched windows are obscurely seen through the boughs. The Avon loiters past the churchyard, an exceedingly sluggish river, which might seem to have been considering which way it should flow ever since Shakespeare left off paddling in it and gathering the large forget-me-nots that grow among its flags and water-weeds. . . .

The poet and his family are in possession of what may be considered the very best burial-places that the church affords. They lie in a row, right across the breadth of the chancel, the foot of each gravestone being close to the elevated floor on which the altar stands. Nearest to the side-wall, beneath Shakespeare's bust, is a slab bearing a Latin inscription addressed to his wife, and covering her remains; then his own slab, with the old anathematizing stanza upon it; then that of Thomas Nash, who married his granddaughter; then that of Dr. Hall, the husband of his daughter Susannah; and, lastly, Susannah's own. Shakespeare's is the commonest-looking slab of all, being just such a flag-stone as Essex Street in Salem used to be paved with, when I was a boy. Moreover, unless my eyes or recollection deceive me, there is a crack across it, as if it had already undergone some such violence as the inscription deprecates. Unlike the other monuments of the family, it bears no name, nor am I acquainted with the grounds or authority on which it is absolutely determined to be Shakespeare's; although, being in a range with those of his wife and children, it might naturally be attributed to him. But, then, why does his wife, who died afterwards, take precedence of him and occupy the place next his bust? And where are the graves of another daughter and a son, who have a better right in the family row than Thomas Nash, his grandson-in-law? Might not one or both of them have been laid under the nameless stone? But it is dangerous trifling with Shakespeare's dust; so I forbear to meddle further with the grave (though the prohibition makes it tempting), and shall let whatever bones be in it rest in peace. Yet I must needs add that the inscription on the bust seems to imply that Shakespeare's grave was directly underneath it.

The poet's bust is affixed to the northern wall of the church, the base of it being about a man's height, or rather more, above the floor of the chancel. The features of this piece of sculpture are entirely unlike any portrait of Shakespeare that I have ever seen, and compel me to take down the beautiful, lofty-browed, and noble picture of him which has hitherto hung in my mental portrait-gallery. The bust cannot be said to represent a beautiful face or an eminently noble head; but it clutches firmly hold of one's sense of reality and insists upon your accepting it, if not as Shakespeare the poet, yet as the wealthy burgher of Stratford, the friend of John a' Combe, who lies yonder in the corner. I know not what the phrenologists say to the bust. The forehead is but moderately developed, and retreats somewhat, the upper part of the skull rising pyramidally; the eyes are prominent almost beyond the penthouse of the brow; the upper lip is so long that it must have been almost a deformity, unless the sculptor artistically exaggerated its length, in consideration, that, on the pedestal, it must be foreshortened by being looked at from below. On the whole, Shakespeare must have had a singular rather than a prepossessing face; and it is wonderful how, with this bust before its eyes, the world has persisted in maintaining an erroneous notion of his appearance, allowing painters and sculptors to foist their idealized nonsense on us all, instead of the genuine man. For my part, the Shakespeare of my mind's eye is henceforth to be a personage of a ruddy English complexion, with a reasonably capacious brow, intelligent and quickly observant eyes, a nose curved slightly outward, a long, queer upper lip, with the mouth a little unclosed beneath it, and cheeks considerably developed in the lower part and beneath the chin. But when Shakespeare was himself (for nine tenths of the time, according to all appearances, he was but the burgher of Stratford), he doubtless shone through this dull mask and transfigured it into the face of an angel.

Fifteen or twenty feet behind the row of Shakespeare gravestones is the great east-window of the church, now brilliant with stained glass of recent manufacture. On one side of this window, under a sculptured arch of marble, lies a full-length marble figure of John a' Combe, clad in what I take to be a robe of municipal dignity, and holding its hands devoutly clasped. It is a sturdy English figure, with coarse features, a type of ordinary man whom we smile to see immortalized in the sculpturesque material of poets and heroes; but the prayerful attitude encourages us to believe that the old usurer may not, after all, have had that grim reception in the other world which Shakespeare's squib foreboded for him. By the by, till I grew somewhat familiar with Warwickshire pronunciation, I never understood that the point of those ill-natured lines was a pun. "'Oho!' quoth the Devil, 't is my John a' Combe!'"—that is, "My John has come!"

Close to the poet's bust is a nameless, oblong, cubic tomb, supposed to be that of a clerical dignitary of the fourteenth century. The church has other mural monuments and altar-tombs, one or two of the latter upholding the recumbent figures of knights in armor and their dames, very eminent and worshipful personages in their day, no doubt, but doomed to appear forever intrusive and impertinent within the precincts which Shakespeare has made his own. His renown is tyrannous, and suffers nothing else to be recognized within the scope of its material presence, unless illuminated by some side-ray from himself. The clerk informed me that interments no longer take place in any part of the church. And it is better so; for methinks a person of delicate individuality, curious about his burial-place, and desirous of six feet of earth for himself alone, could never endure to lie buried near Shakespeare, but would rise up at midnight and grope his way out of the church-door, rather than sleep in the shadow of so stupendous a memory.

—Nathaniel Hawthorne, from "Recollections of a Gifted Woman," *Our Ol' Home*, 1863

John Richard Green "The England of Shakspere" (1874)

John Richard Green (1837–83) was an English historian and clergyman. In the following entry, Green draws from English history the few anecdotes that attached to Shakespeare and the mood of his works to construct Shakespeare's biography.

A few daring jests, a brawl, and a fatal stab, make up the life of Marlowe; but even details such as these are wanting to the life of William Shakspere. Of hardly any great poet indeed do we know so little. For the story of his youth we have only one or two trifling legends, and these almost certainly false. Not a single letter or characteristic saying, not one of the jests "spoken at the Mermaid," hardly a single anecdote, remain to illustrate his busy life in London. His look and figure in later age have been preserved by the bust over his tomb at Stratford, and a hundred years after his death he was still remembered in his native town; but the minute diligence of the enquirers of the Georgian time was able to glean hardly a single detail, even of the most trivial order, which could throw light upon the years of retirement before his death. It is owing perhaps to the harmony and unity of his temper that no salient peculiarity seems to have left its trace on the memory of his contemporaries; it is the very grandeur of his genius which precludes us from discovering any personal trait in his works. His supposed self-revelation in the *Sonnets* is so obscure that only a few outlines can be traced even by the boldest conjecture. In his dramas he is all his characters, and his characters range over all mankind. There is not one, or the act or word of one that we can identify personally with the poet himself.

He was born in 1564, the sixth year of Elizabeth's reign, twelve years after the birth of Spenser, three years later than the birth of [Francis] Bacon. Marlowe was of the same age with Shakspere: Greene probably a few years older. His father, a glover and small farmer of Stratford-on-Avon, was forced by poverty to lay down his office of alderman as his son reached boyhood; and stress of poverty may have been the cause which drove William Shakspere, who was already married at eighteen to a wife older than himself, to London and the stage. His life in the capital can hardly have begun later than in his twenty-third year, the memorable year which followed Sidney's death, which preceded the coming of the Armada, and which witnessed the production of Marlowe's *Tamburlaine*. If we take the language of the *Sonnets* as a record of his personal feeling, his new profession as an actor stirred in him only the bitterness of self-contempt. He chides with Fortune "that did not better for my life provide than public means that public manners breed;" he writhes at the thought that he has "made himself a motley to the view" of the gaping apprentices in the pit of Blackfriars. "Thence comes it," he adds, "that my name receives a brand, and almost thence my nature is subdued to that it works in." But the application of the words is a more than doubtful one. In spite of petty squabbles with some of his dramatic rivals at the outset of his career, the genial nature of the newcomer seems to have won him a general love among his fellows. In 1592, while still a mere actor and fitter of old plays for the stage, a fellow-playwright, [Henry] Chettle, answered Greene's attack on him in words of honest affection: "Myself have seen his demeanour no less civil than he excellent in the quality he professes: besides, divers of worship have reported his uprightness of dealing, which argues his honesty, and his facetious grace in writing, that proves his art." His partner Burbage spoke of him after death as a "worthy friend and fellow;" and Jonson handed down the general tradition of his time when he described him as "indeed honest, and of an open and free nature."

His profession as an actor was at any rate of essential service to him in the poetic career which he soon undertook. Not only did it give him the sense of theatrical necessities which makes his plays so effective on the boards, but it enabled him to bring his pieces as he wrote them to the test of the stage. If there is any truth in Jonson's statement that Shakspere never blotted a line, there is no justice in the censure which it implies on his carelessness or incorrectness. The conditions of poetic publication were in fact wholly different from those of our own day. A drama remained for years in manuscript as an acting piece, subject to continual revision and amendment; and every rehearsal and representation afforded hints for change which we know the young poet was far from neglecting. The chance which has preserved an earlier edition of his *Hamlet* shows in what an unsparing way Shakspere could recast even the finest products of his genius. Five years after the supposed date of his arrival in London he was already famous as a dramatist. Greene speaks bitterly of him under the name of "Shakescene" as an "upstart crow beautified with our feathers," a sneer which points either to his celebrity as an actor or to his preparation for loftier flights by fitting pieces of his predecessors for the stage. He was soon partner in the theatre, actor, and playwright; and another nickname, that of "Johannes Factotum" or Jack-of-all-Trades, shows his readiness to take all honest work which came to hand.

With his publication in 1593 of the poem of *Venus and Adonis*, "the first heir of my invention" as Shakspere calls it, the period of independent creation fairly began. The date of its publication was a very memorable one. The *Faerie Queen* had appeared only three years before, and had placed [Edmund] Spenser without a rival at the head of English poetry. On the other hand the two leading dramatists of the time passed at this moment suddenly away. Greene died in poverty and self-reproach in the house of a poor shoemaker. "Doll," he wrote to the wife he had abandoned, "I charge thee, by the love of our youth and by my soul's rest, that thou wilt see this man paid; for if he and his wife had not succoured me I had died in the streets." "Oh, that a year were granted me to live," cried the young poet from his bed of death, "but I must die, of every man abhorred! Time, loosely spent, will not again be won! My time is loosely spent—and I undone!" A year later the death of Marlowe in a street brawl removed the only rival whose powers might have equaled Shakspere's own. He was now about thirty; and the twenty-three years which elapsed between the appearance of the *Adonis* and his death were filled with a series of masterpieces. Nothing is more characteristic of his genius than its incessant activity. Through the five years which followed the publication of his early poem he seems to have produced on an average two dramas a year. When we attempt however to trace the growth and progress of the poet's mind in the order of his plays we are met in the case of many of them by an absence of certain information as to the dates of their appearance. The facts on which enquiry has to build are extremely few. *Venus and Adonis*, with the *Lucrece*, must have been written before their publication in 1593–4; the *Sonnets*, though not published till 1609, were known in some form among his private friends as early as 1598. His earlier plays are defined by a list given in the *Wit's Treasury* of Francis Meres in 1598, though the omission of a play from a casual catalogue of this kind would hardly warrant us in assuming its necessary non-existence at the time. The works ascribed to him at his death are fixed in the same approximate fashion through the edition published by his fellow-actors. Beyond these meagre facts and our knowledge of the publication of a few of his dramas in his lifetime all is uncertain; and the conclusions which have been drawn from these, and from the dramas themselves, as well as from assumed resemblances with, or references to, other plays of the period can only be accepted as approximations to the truth.

The bulk of his lighter comedies and historical dramas can be assigned with fair probability to a period from about 1593, when Shakspere was known as nothing more than an adapter, to 1598, when they are mentioned in the list of [Francis] Meres. They bear on them indeed the stamp of youth. In *Love's Labour's Lost* the young playwright, fresh from his own Stratford, its "daisies pied and violets blue," with the gay bright music of its country ditties still in his ears, flings himself into the midst of the brilliant England which gathered round Elizabeth, busying himself as yet for the most part with the surface of it, with the humours and quixotisms, the wit and the whim, the unreality, the fantastic extravagance, which veiled its inner nobleness. Country-lad as he is, Shakspere shows himself master of it all; he can patter euphuism and exchange quip and repartee with the best; he is at home in their pedantries and affectations, their brag and their rhetoric, their passion for the fantastic and the marvelous. He can laugh as heartily at the romantic vagaries of the courtly world in which he finds himself as at the narrow dullness, the pompous triflings, of the country world which he has left behind him. But he laughs frankly and without malice; he sees the real grandeur of soul which underlies all this quixotry and word-play; and owns with a smile that when brought face to face with the facts of human life, with the suffering of man or the danger of England, these fops have in them the stuff of heroes. He shares the delight in existence, the pleasure in sheer living, which was so marked a feature of the age; he enjoys the mistakes, the contrasts, the adventures, of the men about him; his fun breaks almost riotously out in the practical jokes of the *Taming of the Shrew* and the endless blunderings of the *Comedy of Errors*. In these earlier efforts his work had been marked by little poetic elevation, or by passion. But the easy grace of the dialogue, the dexterous management of a complicated story, the genial gaiety of his tone, and the music of his verse promised a master of social comedy as soon as Shakspere turned from the superficial aspects of the world about him to find a new delight in the character and actions of men. The interest of human character was still fresh and vivid; the sense of individuality drew a charm from its novelty; and poet and essayist were busy alike in sketching the "humours" of mankind. Shakspere sketched with his fellows. In the *Two Gentlemen of Verona* his painting of manners was suffused by a tenderness and ideal beauty which formed an effective protest against the hard though vigorous character-painting which the first success of Ben Jonson in *Every Man in His Humour* brought at the time into fashion. But quick on these lighter comedies followed two in which his genius started fully into life. His poetic power, held in reserve till now, showed itself with a splendid profusion in the brilliant fancies of the *Midsummer Night's Dream;* and passion swept like a tide of resistless delight through *Romeo and Juliet.*

Side by side however with these passionate dreams, these delicate imaginings and piquant sketches of manners, had been appearing during this short interval of intense activity a series of dramas which mark Shakspere's relation to the new sense of patriotism, the more vivid sense of national existence, national freedom, national greatness, which gives its grandeur to the age of Elizabeth. England itself was now becoming a source of literary interest to poet and prose-writer. Warner in his *Albion's England,* Daniel in his *Civil Wars,* embalmed in verse the record of her past; Drayton in his *Polyolbion* sang the fairness of the land itself, the "tracts, mountains, forests, and other parts of this renowned isle of Britain." The national pride took its highest poetic form in the historical drama. No plays seem to have been more popular from the earliest hours of the new stage than dramatic representations of our history. Marlowe had shown in his *Edward the Second* what tragic grandeur could be reached in this favourite field; and, as we have seen, Shakspere had been led naturally towards it by his earlier occupation as an adapter of stock pieces like *Henry the Sixth* for the new requirements of the stage. He still to some extent followed in plan the older plays on the subjects he selected, but in his treatment of their themes he shook boldly off the yoke of the past. A larger and deeper conception of human character than any of the old dramatists had reached displayed itself in Richard the Third, in Falstaff, or in Hotspur; while in Constance and Richard the Second the pathos of human suffering was painted as even Marlowe had never dared to paint it.

No dramas have done so much for Shakspere's enduring popularity with his countrymen as these historical plays. They have done more than all the works of English historians to nourish in the minds of Englishmen a love of and reverence for their country's past. When Chatham was asked where he had read his English history he answered, "In the plays of Shakspere." Nowhere could he have read it so well, for nowhere is the spirit of our history so nobly rendered. If the poet's work echoes sometimes our national prejudice and unfairness of temper, it is instinct throughout with English humour, with our English love of hard fighting, our English faith in goodness and in the doom that waits upon triumphant evil, our English pity for the fallen. Shakspere is

Elizabethan to the core. He stood at the meeting-point of two great epochs of our history. The age of the Renascence was passing into the age of Puritanism. Rifts which were still little were widening every hour, and threatening ruin to the fabric of Church and State which the Tudors had built up. A new political world was rising into being; a world healthier, more really national, but less picturesque, less wrapt in the mystery and splendour that poets love. Great as were the faults of Puritanism, it may fairly claim to be the first political system which recognized the grandeur of the people as a whole. As great a change was passing over the spiritual sympathies of men. A sterner Protestantism was invigorating and ennobling life by its morality, its seriousness, its intense conviction of God. But it was at the same time hardening and narrowing it. The Bible was superseding Plutarch. The "obstinate questionings" which haunted the finer souls of the Renascence were being stereotyped into the theological formulas of the Puritan. The sense of a divine omnipotence was annihilating man. The daring which turned England into a people of "adventurers," the sense of inexhaustible resources, the buoyant freshness of youth, the intoxicating sense of beauty and joy, which created Sidney and Marlowe and Drake, were passing away before the consciousness of evil and the craving to order man's life aright before God.

From this new world of thought and feeling Shakspere stood aloof. Turn as others might to the speculations of theology, man and man's nature remained with him an inexhaustible subject of interest. Caliban was among his latest creations. It is impossible to discover whether his religious belief was Catholic or Protestant. It is hard indeed to say whether he had any religious belief or no. The religious phrases which are thinly scattered over his works are little more than expressions of a distant and imaginative reverence. But on the deeper grounds of religious faith his silence is significant. He is silent, and the doubt of Hamlet deepens his silence about the afterworld. "To die," it may be, was to him as it was to Claudio [in *Measure for Measure*], "to go we know not whither." Often as his questionings turn to the riddle of life and death he leaves it a riddle to the last without heeding the common theological solutions around him. "We are such stuff as dreams are made on, and our little life is rounded with a sleep."

Nor were the political sympathies of the poet those of the coming time. His roll of dramas is the epic of civil war. The Wars of the Roses fill his mind, as they filled the mind of his contemporaries. It is not till we follow him through the series of plays from *Richard the Second* to *Henry the Eighth* that we realize how profoundly the memory of the struggle between York and Lancaster had moulded the temper of the people, how deep a dread of civil war, of baronial turbulence, of disputes over the succession to the throne, it had left behind it. Men had learned the horrors of the time from their fathers; they had drunk in with their childhood the lesson that such a chaos of weakness and misrule must never be risked again. From such a risk the Crown seemed the one security. With Shakspere as with his fellow-countrymen the Crown is still the centre and safeguard of the national life. His ideal England is an England grouped around a noble king, a king such as his own Henry the Fifth, devout, modest, simple as he is brave, but a lord in battle, a born ruler of men, with a loyal people about him and his enemies at his feet. Socially the poet reflects the aristocratic view of social life which was shared by all the nobler spirits of the Elizabethan time. Coriolanus is the embodiment of a great noble; and the taunts which Shakspere hurls in play after play at the rabble only echo the general temper of the Renascence. But he shows no sympathy with the struggle of feudalism against the Crown. If he paints Hotspur with a fire which proves how thoroughly he could sympathize with the rough, bold temper of the baronage, he suffers him to fall unpitied before Henry the Fourth. Apart however from the strength and justice of its rule, royalty has no charm for him. He knows nothing of the "right divine of kings to govern wrong" which became the doctrine of prelates and courtiers in the age of the Stuarts. He shows in his *Richard the Second* the doom that waits on a lawless despotism, as he denounces in his *Richard the Third* the selfish and merciless ambition that severs a ruler from his people. But the dread of misrule was a dim and distant one. Shakspere had grown up under the reign of Elizabeth; he had known no ruler save one who had cast a spell over the hearts of Englishmen. His thoughts were absorbed, as those of the country were absorbed, in the struggle for national existence which centred round the Queen. *King John* is a trumpet-call to rally round Elizabeth in her fight for England. Again a Pope was asserting his right to depose an English sovereign and to loose Englishmen from their bond of allegiance. Again political ambitions and civil discord woke at the call of religious war. Again a foreign power was threatening England at the summons of Rome, and hoping to master her with the aid of revolted Englishmen. The heat of such a struggle as this left no time for the thought of civil liberties. Shakspere casts aside the thought of the Charter to fix himself on the strife of the stranger for England itself. What he sang was the duty of patriotism, the grandeur of loyalty, the freedom of England from Pope or Spaniard, its safety within its "water-walled bulwark," if only its national union was secure. And now that the nation was at one, now that he had seen in his first years of London life Catholics as well as Protestants trooping to the muster at Tilbury and hasting down Thames to the fight in the Channel, he could thrill his hearers with the proud words that sum up the work of Elizabeth:—

This England never did, nor never shall,
Lie at the proud foot of a conqueror,
But when it first did help to wound itself.
Now that her princes are come home again,
Come the three corners of the world in arms,
And we shall shock them! Nought shall make us rue
If England to itself do rest but true.

[*King John,* V.vii.112–18]

With this great series of historical and social dramas Shakspere had passed far beyond his fellows whether as a tragedian or as a writer of comedy. "The Muses," said Meres in 1598, "would speak with Shakspere's fine-filed phraze, if they would speak English." His personal popularity was now at its height. His pleasant temper and the vivacity of his wit had drawn him early into contact with the young Earl of Southampton, to whom his *Adonis* and *Lucrece* are dedicated; and the different tone of the two dedications shows how rapidly acquaintance ripened into an ardent friendship. Shakspere's wealth and influence too were growing fast. He had property both in Stratford and London, and his fellow townsmen made him their suitor to Lord Burleigh for favours to be bestowed on Stratford. He was rich enough to aid his father, and to buy the house at Stratford which afterwards became his home. The tradition that Elizabeth was so pleased with Falstaff in *Henry the Fourth* that she ordered the poet to show her Falstaff in love—an order which produced the *Merry Wives of Windsor*—whether true or false, proves his repute as a playwright. As the group of earlier poets passed away, they found successors in Marston, Dekker, Middleton, Heywood, and Chapman, and above all in Ben Jonson. But none of these could dispute the supremacy of Shakspere. The verdict of Meres that "Shakspere among the English is the most excellent in both kinds for the stage," represented the general feeling of his contemporaries. He was at last fully master of the resources of his art. The *Merchant of Venice* marks the perfection of his development as a dramatist in the completeness of its stage effect, the ingenuity of its incidents, the ease of its movement, the beauty of its higher passages, the reserve and self-control with which its poetry is used, the conception and unfolding of character, and above all the mastery with which character and event is grouped round the figure of Shylock. Master as he is of his art, the poet's temper is still young; the *Merry Wives of Windsor* is a burst of gay laughter; and laughter more tempered, yet full of a sweeter fascination, rings round us in *As You Like It.*

But in the melancholy and meditative Jaques of the last drama we feel the touch of a new and graver mood. Youth, so full and buoyant in the poet till now, seems to have passed almost suddenly away. Though Shakspere had hardly reached forty, in one of his *Sonnets* which cannot have been written at a much later time than this there are indications that he already felt the advance of premature age. And at this moment the outer world suddenly darkened around him. The brilliant circle of young nobles whose friendship he had shared was broken up in 1601 by the political storm which burst in a mad struggle of the Earl of Essex for power. Essex himself fell on the scaffold; his friend and Shakspere's idol, Southampton, passed a prisoner into the Tower; Herbert Lord Pembroke, younger patron of the poet, was banished from the Court. While friends were thus falling and hopes fading without, Shakspere's own mind seems to have been going through a phase of bitter suffering and unrest. In spite of the ingenuity of commentators, it is difficult and even impossible to derive any knowledge of Shakspere's inner history from the *Sonnets;* "the strange imagery of passion which passes over the magic mirror," it has been finely said, "has no tangible evidence before or behind it." [F. T. Palgrave, 1824–97, English poet, critic, and anthologist.]

But its mere passing is itself an evidence of the restlessness and agony within. The change in the character of his dramas gives a surer indication of his change of mood. The fresh joyousness, the keen delight in life and in man, which breathes through Shakspere's early work disappears in comedies such as *Troilus* and *Measure for Measure.* Disappointment, disillusion, a new sense of the evil and foulness that underlies so much of human life, a loss of the old frank trust in its beauty and goodness, threw their gloom over these comedies. Failure seems everywhere. In *Julius Caesar* the virtue of Brutus is foiled by its ignorance of and isolation from mankind; in Hamlet even penetrating intellect proves helpless for want of the capacity of action; the poison of Iago taints the love of Desdemona and the grandeur of Othello; Lear's mighty passion battles helplessly against the wind and the rain; a woman's weakness of frame dashes the cup of her triumph from the hand of Lady Macbeth; lust and self-indulgence blast the heroism of Antony; pride ruins the nobleness of Coriolanus.

But the very struggle and self-introspection that these dramas betray were to give a depth and grandeur to Shakspere's work such as it had never known before. The age was one in which man's temper and powers took a new range and energy. Sidney or [Sir Walter] Raleigh lived not one but a dozen lives at once; the daring of the adventurer, the philosophy of the scholar, the passion of the lover, the fanaticism of the saint, towered into almost superhuman grandeur. Man became conscious of the immense resources that lay within him, conscious of boundless powers that seemed to mock the narrow world in which they moved. All through the age of the Renascence one feels this impress of the gigantic, this giant-like activity, this immense ambition and desire. The very bombast and extravagance of the times reveal cravings and impulses before which common speech broke down. It is this grandeur of humanity that finds its poetic expression in the later work of Shakspere. As the poet penetrated deeper and deeper into the recesses of the soul, he saw how great and wondrous a thing was man. "What a piece of work is a man," cries Hamlet; "how noble in reason; how infinite in faculty; in form and moving how express and admirable; in action how like an angel; in apprehension how like a god; the beauty of the world; the paragon of animals!" It is the wonder of man that spreads before us as the poet pictures the wide speculation of Hamlet, the awful convulsion of a great nature in Othello, the terrible storm in the soul of Lear which blends with the very storm of the heavens themselves, the awful ambition that nerved a woman's hand to dabble itself with the blood of a murdered king, the reckless lust that "flung away a world for love." Amid the terror and awe of these great dramas we learn something of the vast forces of the age from which they sprang. The passion of Mary Stuart, the ruthlessness of Alva, the daring of Drake, the chivalry of Sidney, the range of thought and action in Raleigh or Elizabeth, come better home to us as we follow the mighty series of tragedies which began in *Hamlet* and ended in *Coriolanus*.

—John Richard Green, from "The England of Shakspere," *History of the English People*, volume 2, pp. 472–85

A. C. Bradley "Shakespeare the Man" (1904)

Widely regarded as one of the greatest critics of Shakespeare, especially for his discussions of Shakespeare's tragedies, in this lecture, A. C. Bradley (1851–1935) draws a portrait of Shakespeare, relying less on alleged firsthand testimony than on a probing reading of Shakespearean texts. Concentrating on incident, imagery, and rhetoric, Bradley analyzes the texture of the sentiments and attitudes he finds embedded in the texts, and using an impressionistic method refined by his own critical sensitivity, creates a reading of Shakespeare's disposition, attitudes, and beliefs through his hypotheses regarding the dramatist's feelings about his characters.

Such phrases as 'Shakespeare the man' or 'Shakespeare's personality' are, no doubt, open to objection. They seem to suggest that, if we could subtract from Shakespeare the mind that produced his works, the residue would be the man himself; and that his mind was some pure impersonal essence unaffected by the accidents of physique, temperament, and character. If this were so, one could but echo Tennyson's thanksgiving that we know so little of Shakespeare. But as it is assuredly not so, and as 'Shakespeare the man' really means the one indivisible Shakespeare, regarded for the time from a particular point of view, the natural desire to know whatever can be known of him is not to be repressed merely because there are people so foolish as to be careless about his works and yet curious about his private life. For my own part I confess that, though I should care nothing about the man if he had not written the works, yet, since we possess them, I would rather see and hear him for five minutes in his proper person than discover a new one. And though we may be content to die without knowing his income or even the surname of Mr. W. H., we cannot so easily resign the wish to find the man in his writings, and to form some idea of the disposition, the likes and dislikes, the character and the attitude towards life, of the human being who seems to us to have understood best our common human nature.

The answer of course will be that our biographical knowledge of Shakespeare is so small, and his writings are so completely dramatic, that this wish, however natural, is idle. But I cannot think so. Doubtless, in trying to form an idea of Shakespeare, we soon reach the limits of reasonable certainty; and it is also true that the idea we can form without exceeding them is far from being as individual as we could desire. But it is more distinct than is often supposed, and it is reasonably certain; and although we can add to its distinctness only by more or less probable conjectures, they are not mere guesses, they really have probability in various degrees. On this whole subject there is a tendency at the present time to an extreme skepticism, which appears to me to be justified neither by the circumstances of the particular case nor by our knowledge of human nature in general.

This scepticism is due in part to the interest excited by Mr. (Sidney) Lee's discussion of the Sonnets in his *Life* of Shakespeare [1898], and to the importance rightly attached to that discussion. The Sonnets are lyrical poems of friendship and love. In them the poet ostensibly speaks in his own person and expresses his own feelings. Many critics, no doubt, had denied that he really did so; but they had not Mr. Lee's knowledge, nor had they examined the matter so narrowly as he; and therefore they had not much weakened the general belief that the Sonnets, however conventional or exaggerated their language may sometimes be, do tell us a good deal about their author. Mr. Lee, however, showed far more fully than any previous writer that many of the themes, many even of the ideas, of these poems are commonplaces of Renaissance sonnet-writing; and he came to the conclusion that in the

Sonnets Shakespeare 'unlocked,' not 'his heart,' but a very different kind of armoury, and that the sole biographical inference deducible from them is that 'at one time in his career Shakespeare disdained no weapon of flattery in an endeavour to monopolise the bountiful patronage of a young man of rank.' Now, if that inference is correct, it certainly tells us something about Shakespeare the man; but it also forbids us to take seriously what the Sonnets profess to tell us of his passionate affection, with its hopes and fears, its pain and joy; of his pride and his humility, his self-reproach and self-defense, his weariness of life and his consciousness of immortal genius. And as, according to Mr. Lee's statement, the Sonnets alone of Shakespeare's works 'can be held to throw any illumination on a personal trait,' it seems to follow that, so far as the works are concerned (for Mr. Lee is not specially skeptical as to the external testimony), the only idea we can form of the man is contained in that single inference.

Now, I venture to surmise that Mr. Lee's words go rather beyond his meaning. But that is not our business here, nor could a brief discussion do justice to a theory to which those who disagree with it are still greatly indebted. What I wish to deny is the presupposition which seems to be frequently accepted as an obvious truth. Even if Mr. Lee's view of the Sonnets were indisputably correct, nay, if even, to go much further, the persons and the story in the Sonnets were as purely fictitious as those of *Twelfth Night*, they might and would still tell us something of the personality of their author. For however free a poet may be from the emotions which he simulates, and however little involved in the conditions which he imagines, he cannot (unless he is a mere copyist) write a hundred and fifty lyrics expressive of those simulated emotions without disclosing something of himself, something of the way in which he in particular *would* feel and behave under the imagined conditions. And the same thing holds in principle of the dramas. Is it really conceivable that a man can write some five and thirty dramas, and portray in them an enormous amount and variety of human nature, without betraying anything whatever of his own disposition and preferences? I do not believe that he could do this, even if he deliberately set himself to the task. The only question is how much of himself he would betray. . . .

Of many poets and novelists we know a good deal from external sources. And in these cases we find that the man so known to us appears also in his works, and that these by themselves would have left on us a personal impression which, though imperfect and perhaps in this or that point even false, would have been broadly true. Of course this holds of some writers much more fully than of others; but, except where the work is very scanty in amount, it seems to hold in some degree of all.[1] If so, there is an antecedent probability that it will apply to Shakespeare too. After all, he was human. . . . As a matter of fact, the great majority of Shakespeare's readers—lovers of poetry untroubled by theories and questions—do form from the plays some idea of the man. Knowingly or not, they possess such an idea; and up to a certain point the idea is the same. . . . After I had put together my notes for the present lecture, I re-read Bagehot's essay on Shakespeare the Man, and I read a book by Goldwin Smith and an essay by Leslie Stephen (who, I found, had anticipated a good deal that I meant to say).[2] These three writers, with all their variety, have still substantially the same idea of Shakespeare; and it is the idea of the competent 'general reader' more fully developed. Nor is the value of their agreement in the least diminished by the fact that they make no claim to be Shakespeare scholars. . . .

The remarks I am going to make can have an interest only for those who share the position I have tried to indicate; who believe that the most dramatic of writers must reveal in his writings something of himself, but who recognise that in Shakespeare's case we can expect a reasonable certainty only within narrow limits, which beyond them we have to trust to impressions, the value of which must depend on familiarity with his writings, on freedom from prejudice and the desire to reach any particular result, and on the amount of perception we may happen to possess. I offer my own impressions, insecure and utterly unprovable as I know them to be, simply because those of other readers have an interest for me. . . .

But, before we come to impressions at all, we must look at the scanty store of external evidence: for we may lay down at once the canon that impressions derived from the works must supplement and not contradict this evidence, so far as it appears trustworthy. It is scanty, but it yields a decided outline.

This figure that thou here seest put,
It was for gentle Shakespeare cut:

—so Jonson writes of the portrait in the Folio, and the same adjective 'gentle' is used elsewhere of Shakespeare. It had not in Elizabethan English so confined a meaning as it has now; but it meant something, and I do not remember that their contemporaries called Marlowe or Jonson or Marston 'gentle.' Next, in the earliest extant reference that we have to Shakespeare, the writer [Henry Chettle] says that he himself has seen his 'demeanour' to be 'civil.'[3] It is not saying much; but it is not the first remark an acquaintance would probably have made about Ben Jonson or Samuel Johnson. The same witness adds about Shakespeare that 'divers of worship have reported his uprightness of dealing which argues his honesty.' 'Honesty' and 'honest' in an Elizabethan

passage like this mean more than they would now; they answer rather to our
'honourable' or 'honour'. Lastly we have the witness borne by Jonson in the
words: 'I loved the man, and do honour his memory, on this side idolatry, as
much as any. He was, indeed, honest, and of an open and free nature.' With
this notable phrase, to which I shall have to return, we come to an end of the
testimony of eye-witnesses to Shakespeare the Man (for we have nothing to
do with references to the mere actor or author). It is scanty, and insufficient to
discriminate him from other persons who were gentle, civil, upright in their
dealings, honourable, open, and free: but I submit that there have been not a
few writers to whom all these qualities could not be truly ascribed, and that
the testimony therefore does tell us something definite. To which must be
added that we have absolutely no evidence which conflicts with it. Whatever
Greene in his jealous embitterment might have said would carry little weight,
but in fact, apart from general abuse of actors, he only says that the upstart
had an over-weening opinion of his own capacities.

There remain certain traditions and certain facts; and without discussing
them I will mention what seems to me to have a more or less probable
significance. Stratford stories of drinking bouts may go for nothing, but
not the consensus of tradition to the effect that Shakespeare was a pleasant
and convivial person, 'very good company, and of a very ready and pleasant
smooth wit.'4 That after his retirement to Stratford he spent at the rate of
£1000 a year is incredible, but that he spent freely seems likely enough. The
tradition that as a young man he got into trouble with Sir Thomas Lucy for
deer-stealing (which would probably be an escapade rather than an essay in
serious poaching) is supported by his unsavoury jest about the 'luces' in Sir
Robert Shallow's coat. The more general statement that in youth he was wild
does not sound improbable; and, obscure as the matter is, I cannot regard as
comfortable the little we know of the circumstances of his very early marriage.
A contemporary story of an amorous adventure in London may well be pure
invention, but we have no reason to reject it peremptorily as we should any
similar gossip about Milton. Lastly, certain inferences may safely be drawn
from the facts that, once securely started in London, Shakespeare soon began
to prosper, and acquired, for an actor and playwright, considerable wealth;
that he bought property in his native town, and was consulted sometimes
by fellow-townsmen on matters of business; that he enforced the payment
of certain debts; and that he took the trouble to get a coat of arms. But what
cannot with any logic or any safety be inferred is that he, any more than [Sir
Walter] Scott, was impelled to write simply and solely by the desire to make
money and improve his social position; and the comparative abundance of
business records will mislead only those who are thoughtless enough to forget

that, if they buy a house or sue a debtor, the fact will be handed down, while their kind or generous deeds may be recorded, if at all, only in the statement that they were 'of an open and free nature.'

That Shakespeare was a good and perhaps keen man of business, or that he set store by a coat of arms, we could not have inferred from his writings. But we could have judged from them that he worked hard, and have guessed with some probability that he would rather have been a 'gentleman' than an actor. And most of the other characteristics that appear from the external evidence would, I think, have seemed probable from a study of the works. This should encourage us to hope that we may be right in other impressions which we receive from them. And we may begin with one on which the external evidence has a certain bearing.

Readers of Shakespeare, I believe, imagine him to have been not only sweet-tempered but modest and unassuming. I do not doubt that they are right; and, vague as the Folio portrait and the Stratford bust are, it would be difficult to believe that their subject was an irritable, boastful, or pushing person. But if we confine ourselves to the works, it is not easy to give reasons for the idea that their author was modest and unassuming; and a man is not necessarily so because he is open, free, and very good company. Perhaps we feel that a man who was not so would have allowed much more of himself to appear in his works than Shakespeare does. Perhaps again we think that anything like presumption or self-importance was incompatible with Shakespeare's sense of the ridiculous, his sublime common-sense, and his feeling of man's insignificance. And, lastly, it seems to us clear that the playwright admires and likes people who are modest, unassuming, and plain; while it may perhaps safely be said that those who lack these qualities rarely admire them in others and not seldom despise them. But, however we may justify our impression that Shakespeare possessed them, we certainly receive it; and assuming it to be as correct as the similar impression left by the Waverley Novels indubitably is, I go on to observe that the possession of them does not of necessity imply a want of spirit, or of proper self-assertion or insistence on rights.[5] It did not in Scott, and we have ground for saying that it did not in Shakespeare. If it had, he could not, being of an open and free nature, have prospered as he prospered. He took offence at Greene's attack on him, and showed that he took it. He was 'gentle,' but he liked his debts to be paid. However his attitude as to the enclosure at Welcombe may be construed, it is clear that he had to be reckoned with. It appears probable that he held himself wronged by Sir Thomas Lucy, and, pocketing up the injury because he could not resent it, gave him tit for tat after some fifteen years. The man in the Sonnets forgives his friend easily, but it is not from humility;

and towards the world he is very far from humble. Of the dedication of *The Rape of Lucrece* we cannot judge, for we do not know Shakespeare's relations with Lord Southampton at that date; but, as for the dedication of *Venus and Adonis,* could modesty and dignity be better mingled in a letter from a young poet to a great noble than they are there?

Some of Shakespeare's writings point to a strain of deep reflection and of quasi-metaphysical imagination in his nature; and a few of them seem to reveal a melancholy, at times merely sad, at times embittered or profound, if never hopeless. It is on this side mainly that we feel a decided difference between him and Fielding, and even between him and Scott. Yet nothing in the contemporary allusions or in the traditions would suggest that he was notably thoughtful or serious, and much less that he was melancholy. And although we could lay no stress on this fact if it stood alone, it is probably significant. Shakespeare's writings, on the whole, leave a strong impression that his native disposition was much more gay than grave. They seem always to have made this impression. Fuller tells us that 'though his genius generally was jocular and inclining him to festivity, yet he could, when so disposed, be solemn and serious, as appears by his tragedies.'[6] Johnson agreed with Rymer that his 'natural disposition' led him to comedy; and, although Johnson after his manner distorts a true idea by wilful exaggeration and by perverting distinctions into antitheses, there is truth in his development of Rymer's remark. It would be easy to quote nineteenth century critics to the same effect; and the study of Shakespeare's early works leads to a similar result. It has been truly said that we feel ourselves in much closer contact with his personality in the early comedies and in *Romeo and Juliet* than in *Henry VI* and *Richard III* and *Titus Andronicus*. In the latter, so far as we suppose them to be his own, he seems on the whole to be following, and then improving on, an existing style, and to be dealing with subjects which engage him as a playwright without much appealing to him personally. With *Romeo and Juliet,* on the other hand, and with *Richard II* (which seems clearly to be his first attempt to write historical tragedy in a manner entirely his own), it is different, and we feel the presence of the whole man. The stories are tragic, but it is not precisely the *tragic* aspect of them that attracts him most; and even Johnson's statement, grotesquely false of the later tragedies, that 'in tragedy he is always struggling after some occasion to be comic,' is no more than an exaggeration in respect to *Romeo and Juliet*.[7] From these tragedies, as from *Love's Labour's Lost* and the other early comedies, we should guess that the author was a young man, happy, alert, light-hearted, full of romance and poetry, but full also of fun; blessed with a keen enjoyment of absurdities, but, for all his intellectual subtlety and power, not markedly reflective, and certainly not particularly grave or much inclined to dejection. One might even suspect, I venture to think, that with such a flow of spirits and such exceeding alacrity of mind he might at present be a trifle wanting in feeling and disposed to levity. In any case, if our general impression is correct, we shall not find it hard to believe that the author of these plays and the creator of Falstaff was 'very good company' and a convivial goodfellow; and it might easily happen that he was tempted at times to 'go here and there' in society, and 'make himself a motley to the view' in a fashion that left some qualms behind.[8]

There is a tradition that Shakespeare was 'a handsome well-shaped man.' If the Stratford monument does not lie, he was not in later life a meagre man. And if our notion of his temperament has any truth, he can hardly have been physically feeble, bloodless, or inactive. Most readers probably imagine him the reverse. Even sceptical critics tell us that he was fond of field-sports; and of his familiar knowledge of them there can be no question. Yet—I can but record the impression without trying to justify it—his writings do not at all suggest to me that he was a splendidly powerful creature like [Henry] Fielding, or that he greatly enjoyed bodily exertion, or was not easily tired. He says much of horses, but he does not make one think, as Scott does, that a gallop was a great delight to him. Nor again do I feel after reading him that he had a strong natural love of adventurous deeds, or longed to be an explorer or a soldier. The island of his boyish dreams—if he heard much of voyages as a boy—was, I fancy, the haunt of marmosets and hedgehogs, quaint mooncalves and flitting sprites, lovely colours, sounds and sweet airs that give delight and hurt not, less like Treasure Island than the Coral Island of Ballantyne in the original illustrations, and more full of wonders than of dangers. He would have liked the Arabian Nights better than Dumas. Of course he admired men of action, understood them, and could express their feelings; but we do not feel particularly close to his personality as we read the warrior speeches of Hotspur, Henry, Othello, Coriolanus, as we do when we read of Romeo or Hamlet, or when we feel the attraction of Henry's modesty. In the same way, I suppose nobody feels Shakespeare's personal presence in the ambition of Macbeth or the pride of Coriolanus; many feel it in Macbeth's imaginative terrors, and in the disgust of Coriolanus at the idea of recounting his exploits in order to win votes. When we seem to hear Shakespeare's voice—and we hear it from many mouths besides Romeo's or Hamlet's—it is the voice of a man with a happy, enjoying, but still contemplative and even dreamy nature, not of a man richly endowed with the impulses and feelings either of strenuous action or of self-assertion. If he had drawn a Satan, we should not have felt his personality, as we do Milton's, in Satan's pride and indomitable courage and intolerance of rule.

We know how often Shakespeare uses the antithesis of blood or passion, and judgment or reason; how he praises the due commingling of the two, or the control of the first by the second; how frequently it is the want of such control that exposes his heroes to the attack of Fortune or Fate. What, then, were the passions or the 'affections of the blood' most dangerous to himself? Not, if we have been right, those of pride or ambition; nor yet those of envy, hatred, or revenge; and still less that of avarice. But, in the first place, let us remember Jonson's words, 'he was honest and of an open and free nature,' and let me repeat an observation, made elsewhere in passing, that these words are true also of the great majority of Shakespeare's heroes, and not least of his tragic heroes. Jonson almost quotes Iago:

> The Moor is of a free and open nature,
> That thinks men honest that but seem to be so.

The king says that Hamlet,

> being remiss,
> Most generous, and free from all contrivings,
> Will not peruse the foils.

The words 'open and free' apply no less eminently to Brutus, Lear, and Timon. Antony and Coriolanus are men naturally frank, liberal, and large. Prospero lost his dukedom through his trustfulness. Romeo and Troilus and Orlando, and many slighter characters, are so far of the same type. Now such a free and open nature, obviously, is specially exposed to the risks of deception, perfidy, and ingratitude. If it is also a nature sensitive and intense, but not particularly active or (if the word may be excused) volitional, such experiences will tempt it to melancholy, embitterment, anger, possibly even misanthropy. If it *is* thus active or volitional, it may become the prey of violent and destructive passion, such as that of Othello and of Coriolanus, and such as Lear's would be if he were not so old. These affections, passions, and sufferings of free and open natures are Shakespeare's favourite tragic subject; and his favouritism, surely, goes so far as to constitute a decided peculiarity, not found thus in other tragic poets. Here he painted most, one cannot but think, what his own nature was most inclined to feel. But it would rather be melancholy, embitterment, an inactive rage or misanthropy, than any destructive passion; and it would be a further question whether, and how far, he may at any time have experienced what he depicts. I am speaking here only of his disposition.[9]

That Shakespeare was as much inclined to be a lover as most poets we may perhaps safely assume; but can we conjecture anything further on this subject? I will confine myself to two points. He treats of love romantically, and tragically, and humorously. In the earlier plays especially the humorous aspect of the matter, the aspect so prominent in the *Midsummer-Night's Dream,* the changefulness, brevity, irrationality, of the feeling, is at least as much dwelt on as the romantic, and with at least as much relish:

Lord! what fools these mortals be!

Now, if there is anything peculiar in the pictures here, it is, perhaps, the special interest that Shakespeare seems to take in what we may call the unreality of the feeling of love in an imaginative nature. Romeo as he first appears, and, in a later play, Orsino, are examples of this. They are perfectly sincere, of course, but neither of them is really in love with a woman; each is in love with the state of being in love. This state is able to attach itself to a particular object, but it is not induced by the particular qualities of that object; it is more a dream than a passion, and can melt away without carrying any of the lover's heart with it; and in that sense it is unreal. This weakness, no doubt, is not confined to imaginative natures, but they may well be specially disposed to it (as Shelley was), and Shakespeare may have drawn it from his own experience. The suspicion is strengthened when we think of *Richard II.* In Richard this imaginative weakness is exhibited again, though not in relation to love. He luxuriates in images of his royal majesty, of the angels who guard his divine right, and of his own pathetic and almost sacred sufferings. The images are not insincere, and yet they are like dreams, for they refuse to touch earth and to connect themselves either with his past misdeeds or with the actions he ought now to perform. A strain of a similar weakness appears again in Hamlet, though only as one strain in a much more deep and complex nature. But this is not a common theme in poetry, much less in dramatic poetry.[10] To come to our second question. When Shakespeare painted Cressida or described her through the mouth of Ulysses ('O these encounterers,' etc.), or, again, when he portrayed the love of Antony for Cleopatra, was he using his personal experience? To answer that he *must* have done so would be as ridiculous as to argue that Iago must be a portrait of himself; and the two plays contain nothing which, by itself, would justify us even in thinking that he probably did so. But we have the series of sonnets about the dark lady; and if we accept the sonnets to the friend as to some considerable extent based on fact and expressive of personal feelings, how can we refuse to take the others on the same footing? Even if the stories of the two series were not intertwined, we should have no ground for treating the two in different ways, unless we could say that external evidence, or the general impression we derive from Shakespeare's works, forbids us to believe that he could ever have been entangled in an intrigue like that implied in the second series, or have felt and thought in the manner there portrayed. Being unable to say this, I am compelled, most regretfully, to hold it probable that this series is, in the main, based on personal experience. And I say 'most regretfully,' not merely because one would regret to think that Shakespeare was the victim of a Cressida or even the lover of a Cleopatra, but because the story implied in these sonnets is of quite another kind. They leave, on the whole, a very disagreeable impression. We cannot compare it with the impressions produced, for example, by the 'heathen' spirit of Goethe's Roman *Elegies*, or by the passion of Shakespeare's Antony. In these two cases, widely dissimilar of course, we may speak of 'immorality,' but we are not discomfited, much less disgusted. The feeling and the attitude are poetic, whole-hearted, and in one case passionate in the extreme. But the state of mind expressed in the sonnets about the dark lady is half-hearted, often prosaic, and never worthy of the name of passion. It is uneasy, dissatisfied, distempered, the state of mind of a man who despises his 'passion' and its object and himself, but, standing intellectually far above it, still has not resolution to end it, and only pains us by his gross and joyless jests. In *Troilus and Cressida*—not at all in the portrayal of Troilus's love, but in the atmosphere of the drama—we seem to trace a similar mood of dissatisfaction, and of intellectual but practically impotent contempt.

In this connection it is natural to think of the 'unhappy period' which has so often been surmised in Shakespeare's life. There is not time here to expand the summary remarks made elsewhere on this subject; but I may refer a little more fully to a persistent impression left on my mind by writings which we have reason to assign to the years 1602–6.[11] There is surely something unusual in their tone regarding certain 'vices of the blood,' regarding drunkenness and sexual corruption. It does not lie in Shakespeare's *view* of these vices, but in an undertone of disgust. Read Hamlet's language about the habitual drunkenness of his uncle, or even Cassio's words about his casual excess; then think of the tone of *Henry IV* or *Twelfth Night* or the *Tempest*; and ask if the difference is not striking. And if you are inclined to ascribe it wholly to the fact that *Hamlet* and *Othello* are tragedies, compare the passages in them with the scene on Pompey's galley in *Antony and Cleopatra*. The intent of that scene is terrible enough, but in the tone there is no more trace of disgust than in *Twelfth Night*. As to the other matter, what I refer to is not the transgression of lovers like Claudio and Juliet, nor even light-hearted irregularities like those of Cassio: here Shakespeare's speech has its habitual tone. But, when he is dealing with lechery and corruption, the undercurrent of disgust seems to become audible. Is it not true that in the plays from *Hamlet* to *Timon* that subject, in one shape or another, is continually before us; that the intensity of loathing in Hamlet's language about his mother's lust is unexampled in Shakespeare; that the treatment of the subject in *Measure for Measure*, though occasionally purely humorous, is on the whole quite unlike the treatment in *Henry IV*. or even in the brothel scenes of *Pericles*;[12] that while *Troilus and Cressida* is full of disgust and contempt, there is not a trace of either in *Antony and Cleopatra*, though some of the jesting there is obscene enough; that this same tone is as plainly heard in the unquestioned parts of *Timon*; and that, while it is natural in Timon to inveigh against female lechery when he speaks to Alcibiades and his harlots, there is no apparent reason why Lear in his exalted madness should choose this subject for similar invectives? 'Pah! give me an ounce of civet, good apothecary, to sweeten my imagination'—it is a fainter echo of this exclamation that one seems to hear in the plays of those years. Of course I am not suggesting that it is mainly due, or as regards drunkenness due in the least, to any private experience of Shakespeare's. It may have no connection whatever with that experience. It might well be connected with it only in so far as a man frequently wearied and depressed might be unusually sensitive to the ugly aspects of life. But, if we do not take the second series of sonnets to be purely fanciful, we shall think it probable that to some undefined extent it owed its origin to the experience depicted in them.[13]

There remain the sonnets addressed to the friend. Even if it were possible to discuss the general question about them here, it would be needless; for I accept almost wholly, and in some points am greatly indebted to, the views put forward by Mr. Beeching in his admirable edition, to which I may therefore refer my hearers.[14] I intend only to state the main reason why I believe the sonnets to be, substantially, what they purport to be, and then to touch upon one or two of the points where they seem to throw light on Shakespeare's personality.

The sonnets to the friend are, so far as we know, unique in Renaissance sonnet literature in being a prolonged and varied record of the intense affection of an older friend for a younger, and of other feelings arising from their relations. They have no real parallel in any series imitative of Virgil's second Eclogue, or in occasional sonnets to patrons or patron-friends couched in the high-flown language of the time. The intensity of the feelings expressed, however, ought not, by itself, to convince us that they are personal. The author of the plays could, I make no doubt, have written the most intimate of these poems to a mere creature of his imagination and without ever having felt them except in imagination. Nor is there any but an aesthetic reason why he should not have done so if he had wished. But an aesthetic reason there is; and this is the decisive point. No capable poet, much less a Shakespeare, intending to produce a merely 'dramatic' series of poems, would dream of inventing a story like that of these sonnets, or, even if he did, of treating it as they treat it. The story is very odd and unattractive. Such capacities as it has are but slightly developed. It is left obscure, and some of the poems are unintelligible to us because they contain allusions of which we can make nothing. Now all this is perfectly natural if the story is substantially a real story of Shakespeare himself and of certain other persons; if the sonnets were written from time to time as the relations of the persons changed, and sometimes in reference to particular incidents; and if they were written *for* one or more of these persons (far the greater number for only one), and perhaps in a few cases for other friends,—written, that is to say, for people who knew the details and incidents of which we are ignorant. But it is all unnatural, well-nigh incredibly unnatural, if, with the most sceptical critics, we regard the sonnets as a free product of mere imagination.[15]

Assuming, then, that the persons of the story, with their relations, are real, I would add only two remarks about the friend. In the first place, Mr. Beeching seems to me right in denying that there is sufficient evidence of his standing to Shakespeare and the 'rival' poet or poets in the position of a literary patron; while, even if he did, it appears to me quite impossible to take the language of many of the sonnets as that of interested flattery. And in the second place I should be inclined to push even further Mr. Beeching's view on another point. It is clear that the young man was considerably superior to the actor-dramatist in social position; but any gentleman would be so, and there is nothing to prove that he was more than a gentleman of some note, more than plain 'Mr. W. H.' (for these, on the obvious though not compulsory interpretation of the dedication, seem to have been his initials). It is remarkable besides that, while the earlier sonnets show much deference, the later show very little, so little that, when the writer, finding that he has pained his young friend by neglecting him, begs to be forgiven, he writes almost, if not quite, as an equal. Read, for example, sonnets 109, 110, 120, and ask whether it is probable that Shakespeare is addressing here a great nobleman. It seems therefore most likely (though the question is not of much importance) that the sonnets are, to quote Meres's phrase,[16] his 'sonnets among his private friends.'

If then there is, as it appears, no obstacle of any magnitude to our taking the sonnets as substantially what they purport to be, we may naturally look in them for personal traits (and, indeed, to repeat a remark made earlier, we might still expect to find such traits even if we knew the sonnets to be purely dramatic). But in drawing inferences we have to bear in mind what is implied by the qualification 'substantially.' We have to remember that *some* of these poems may be mere exercises of art; that all of them are poems, and not letters, much less *affidavits;* that they are Elizabethan poems; that the Elizabethan language of deference, and also of affection, is to our minds habitually extravagant and fantastic;[17] and that in Elizabethan plays friends openly express their love for one another as Englishmen now rarely do. Allowance being made, however, on account of these facts, the sonnets will still leave two strong impressions—that the poet was exceedingly sensitive to the charm of beauty, and that his love for his friend was, at least at one time, a feeling amounting almost to adoration, and so intense as to be absorbing. Those who are surprised by the first of these traits must have read Shakespeare's dramas with very inactive minds, and I must add that they seem to be somewhat ignorant of human nature. We do not necessarily love best those of our relatives, friends, and acquaintances who please our eyes most; and we should look askance on anyone who regulated his behaviour chiefly by the standard of beauty; but most of us, I suppose, love any human being of either sex and of any age, the better for being beautiful, and are not the least ashamed of the fact. It is further the case that men who are beginning, like the writer of the sonnets, to feel tired and old, are apt to feel an increased and special pleasure in the beauty of the young.[18] If we remember, in addition, what some critics appear constantly to forget, that Shakespeare was a particularly poetical being, we shall hardly be surprised that the beginning of this friendship seems to have been something like a falling in love; and, if we must needs praise and blame, we should also remember that it became a 'marriage of true minds.'[19] And as to the intensity of the feeling expressed in the sonnets, we can easily believe it to be characteristic of the man who made Valentine and Proteus, Brutus and Cassius, Horatio and Hamlet; who painted that strangely moving portrait of Antonio, middle-aged, sad, and almost indifferent between life and death, but devoted to the young, brilliant spendthrift Bassanio; and who portrayed the sudden compelling enchantment exercised by the young Sebastian over the Antonio of *Twelfth Night.* 'If you will not murder me for your love, let me be your servant.' Antonio is accused of piracy: he may lose his life if he is identified:

I have many enemies in Orsino's court,
But, come what may, I do adore thee so
That danger shall seem sport, and I will go.

The adoration, the 'prostration,' of the writer of the sonnets is of one kind with this.

I do not remember what critic uses the word 'prostration.' It applies to Shakespeare's attitude only in some of the sonnets, but there it does apply, unless it is taken to suggest humiliation. *That* is the term used by [Arthur] Hallam, but chiefly in view of a particular point, namely the failure of the poet to 'resent,' though he 'felt and bewailed,' the injury done him in 'the seduction of his mistress.' Though I think we should substitute 'resent more strongly' for the mere 'resent,' I do not deny that the poet's attitude in this matter strikes us at first as surprising as well as unpleasant to contemplate. But Hallam's explanation of it as perhaps due to the exalted position of the friend, would make it much more than unpleasant; and his language seems to show that he, like many critics, did not fully imagine the situation. It is not easy to speak of it in public with the requisite frankness; but it is necessary to realise that, whatever the friend's rank might be, he and the poet were intimate friends; that, manifestly, it was rather the mistress who seduced the friend than the friend the mistress; and that she was apparently a woman not merely of no reputation, but of such a nature that she might readily be expected to be mistress to two men at one and the same time. Anyone who realises this may call the situation 'humiliating' in one sense, and I cannot quarrel with him; but he will not call it 'humiliating' in respect of Shakespeare's relation to his friend; nor will he wonder much that the poet felt more pain than resentment at his friend's treatment of him. There is something infinitely stranger in a play of Shakespeare's, and it may be symptomatic. Ten Brink called attention to it. Proteus actually offers violence to Sylvia, a spotless lady and the true love of his friend Valentine; and Valentine not only forgives him at once when he professes repentance, but offers to resign Sylvia to him! The incident is to us so utterly preposterous that we find it hard to imagine how the audience stood it; but, even if we conjecture that Shakespeare adopted it from the story he was using, we can hardly suppose that it was so absurd to him as it is to us.[20] And it is not the Sonnets alone which lead us to surmise that forgiveness was particularly attractive to him, and the forgiveness of a friend much easier than resentment. From the Sonnets we gather—and there is nothing in the plays or elsewhere to contradict the impression—that he would not be slow to resent the criticisms, slanders, or injuries of strangers or the world, and that he bore himself towards them with a proud, if silent, self-sufficiency. But, we surmise, for anyone whom he loved

> He carried anger as a flint bears fire;
> Who, much enforced, shows a hasty spark
> And straight is cold again;
>
> [*Julius Caesar*, IV.iii.110–12]

and towards anyone so fondly loved as the friend of the Sonnets he was probably incapable of fierce or prolonged resentment. The Sonnets must not occupy us further; and I will not dwell on the indications they afford that Shakespeare sometimes felt bitterly both the social inferiority of his position as an actor,[21] and its influence on his own character; or that (as we have already conjectured) he may sometimes have played the fool in society, sometimes felt weary of life, and often was overtired by work. It is time to pass on to a few hesitating conjectures about what may be called his tastes.

Some passages of his about music have become household words. It is not downright impossible that, like Bottom, having only a reasonable good ear, he liked best the tongs and the bones; that he wondered, with Benedick, how sheeps-guts should hale souls out of men's bodies; and that he wrote the famous lines in the *Merchant of Venice* and in *Twelfth Night* from mere observation and imagination. But it is futile to deal with skepticism run well-nigh mad, and certainly inaccessible to argument from the cases of poets whose tastes are matter of knowledge. Assuming therefore that Shakespeare was fond of music, I may draw attention to two points. Almost always he speaks of music as having a softening, tranquillising, or pensive influence. It lulls killing care and grief of heart to sleep. It soothes the sick and weary, and even makes them drowsy. Hamlet calls for it in his hysterical excitement after the success of the play scene. When it is hoped that Lear's long sleep will have carried his madness away, music is played as he awakes, apparently to increase the desired 'temperance.' It harmonises with the still and moonlit night, and the dreamy happiness of newly-wedded lovers. Almost all the rare allusions to lively or exciting music, apart from dancing, refer, I believe, to 'the lofty instruments of *war*.' These facts would almost certainly have a personal significance if Shakespeare were a more modern poet. Whether they have any, or have much, in an Elizabethan I do not venture to judge.

The second point is diminutive, but it may be connected with the first. The Duke in *Measure for Measure* observes that music often has

       a charm
To make bad good and good provoke to harm.

If we ask how it should provoke good to harm, we may recall what was said of
the weaknesses of some poetic natures, and that no one speaks more feelingly
of music than Orsino [in *Twelfth Night*]; further, how he refers to music as
'the food of love,' and who it is that almost repeats the phrase.

    Give me some music: music, moody food
    Of us that trade in love:

—the words are Cleopatra's.[22] Did Shakespeare as he wrote them remember, I
wonder, the dark lady to whose music he had listened (Sonnet 128)?

    We should be greatly surprised to find in Shakespeare signs of the
nineteenth century feeling for mountain scenery, but we can no more doubt
that within certain limits he was sensitive to the beauty of nature than
that he was fond of music.[23] The only question is whether we can guess at
any preferences here. It is probably inevitable that the flowers most often
mentioned should be the rose and the lily,[24] but hardly that the violet should
come next and not far behind, and that the fragrance of the violet should be
spoken of more often even than that of the rose, and, it seems, with special
affection. This may be a fancy, and it will be thought a sentimental fancy too;
but poets, like other people, may have favourite flowers; that of Keats, we
happen to know, was the violet.

    Again, if we may draw any conclusion from the frequency and the
character of the allusions, the lark held for Shakespeare the place of honour
among birds; and the lines [II.iii.20 in *Cymbeline*],

    Hark! hark! the lark at heaven's gate sings,
        And Phoebus gins arise,

may suggest one reason for this. The lark, as several other collocations
show, was to him the bird of joy that welcomes the sun; and it can hardly be
doubted that dawn and early morning was the time of day that most appealed
to him. That he felt the beauty of night and of moonlight is obvious; but we
find very little to match the lines in *Richard II.*,

    The setting sun, and music at the close,
    As the last taste of sweets, is sweetest last;

and still less to prove that he felt the magic of evening twilight, the 'heavenliest hour' of a famous passage in [Lord Byron's] *Don Juan*. There is a wonderful line in Sonnet 132,

And that full star that ushers in the even,

but I remember little else of the same kind. Shakespeare, as it happens, uses the word 'twilight' only once, and in an unforgettable passage:

In me thou see'st the twilight of such day
As after sunset fadeth in the west:
Which by and by black night doth take away,
Death's second self that seals up all in rest.
[Sonnet 73]

And this feeling, though not often so solemn, is on the whole the prevailing sentiment in the references to sunset and evening twilight. It corresponds with the analogy between the times of the day and the periods of human life. . . .

Two suggestions may be ventured as to Shakespeare's feelings towards four-footed animals. The first must be very tentative. We do not expect in a writer of that age the sympathy with animals which is so beautiful a trait in much of the poetry of the last hundred and fifty years. And I can remember in Shakespeare scarcely any sign of *fondness* for an animal,—not even for a horse, though he wrote so often of horses. But there are rather frequent, if casual, expressions of pity, in references, for example, to the hunted hare or stag, or to the spurred horse:[25] and it may be questioned whether the passage in *As You Like It* about the wounded deer is quite devoid of personal significance. No doubt Shakespeare thought the tears of Jaques sentimental; but he put a piece of himself into Jaques. And, besides, it is not Jaques alone who dislikes the killing of the deer, but the Duke; and we may surely hear some tone of Shakespeare's voice in the Duke's speech about the life in the forest. Perhaps we may surmise that, while he enjoyed field-sports, he felt them at times to be out of tune with the harmony of nature.

On the second point, I regret to say, I can feel no doubt. Shakespeare did not care for dogs, as Homer did; he even disliked them, as Goethe did. Of course he can write eloquently about the points of hounds and the music of their voices in the chase, and humorously about Launce's love for his cur and even about the cur himself; but this is no more significant on the one side than is his conventional use of 'dog' as a term of abuse on the other. What is significant is the absence of allusion, or (to be perfectly accurate) of sympathetic allusion, to the characteristic virtues of dogs, and the abundance of allusions of an insulting kind. Shakespeare has observed and recorded, in some instances profusely, every vice that I can think of in an ill-conditioned dog. He fawns and cringes and flatters, and then bites the hand that caressed him; he is a coward who attacks you from behind, and barks at you the more the farther off you go; he knows neither charity, humanity, nor gratitude; as he flatters power and wealth, so he takes part against the poor and unfashionable, and if fortune turns against you so does he. The plays swarm with these charges. . . . The things he most loathed in men he found in dogs too. And yet all this might go for nothing if we could set anything of weight against it. But what can we set? Nothing whatever, so far as I remember, except a recognition of courage in bear-baiting, bull-baiting mastiffs. For I cannot quote as favourable to the spaniel the appeal of Helena:

> I am your spaniel; and, Demetrius,
> The more you beat me I will fawn on you:
> Use me but as your spaniel, spurn me, strike me,
> Neglect me, lose me; only give me leave,
> Unworthy as I am, to follow you.
> [*A Midsmmer Night's Dream,* II.i.202–06]

This may show that Shakespeare was alive to the baseness of a spaniel-owner, but not that he appreciated that self-less affection which he describes. It is more probable that it irritated him, as it does many men still; and, as for its implying fidelity, there is no reference, I believe, to the fidelity of the dog in the whole of his works, and he chooses the spaniel himself as a symbol of flattery and ingratitude: his Caesar talks of

> Knee-crooked court'sies and base spaniel-fawning;
> [*Julius Caesar,* III.i.43]

his Antony exclaims:

> the hearts
> That spaniel'd me at heels, to whom I gave
> Their wishes, do discandy, melt their sweets
> On blossoming Caesar.
> [*Antony and Cleopatra,* IV.xii.20–23]

To all that he loved most in men he was blind in dogs. And then we call him universal!

This line of research into Shakespeare's tastes might be pursued a good deal further, but we must return to weightier matters. We saw that he could sympathise with anyone who erred and suffered from impulse, affections of the blood, or even such passions as were probably no danger to himself,— ambition, for instance, and pride. Can we learn anything more about him by observing virtues or types of character with which he appears to feel little sympathy, though he may approve them? He certainly does not show this imperfect sympathy towards self-control; we seem to feel even a special liking for Brutus, and again for Horatio, who has suffered much, is quietly patient, and has mastered both himself and fortune. But, not to speak of coldly selfish natures, he seems averse to bloodless people, those who lack, or those who have deadened, the natural desires for joy and sympathy, and those who tend to be precise.[27] Nor does he appear to be drawn to men who, as we say, try to live or to act on principle; nor to those who aim habitually at self-improvement; nor yet to the saintly type of character. I mean, not that he *could* not sympathise with them, but that they did not attract him. Isabella, in *Measure for Measure,* is drawn, of course, with understanding, but, it seems to me, with little sympathy. Her readiness to abandon her pleading for Claudio, out of horror at his sin and a sense of the justice of Angelo's reasons for refusing his pardon, is doubtless in character; but if Shakespeare had sympathised more with her at this point, so should we; while, as it is, we are tempted to exclaim,

She loves him not, she wants the natural touch; and perhaps if Shakespeare had liked her better and had not regarded her with some irony, he would not have allowed himself, for mere convenience, to degrade her by marrying her to the Duke. Brutus and Cordelia, on the other hand, are drawn with the fullest imaginative sympathy, and they, it may be said, are characters of principle; but then (even if Cordelia could be truly so described) they are also intensely affectionate, and by no means inhumanly self-controlled.

The mention of Brutus may carry us somewhat farther. Shakespeare's Brutus kills Cæsar, not because Caesar aims at absolute power, but because Brutus fears that absolute power may make him cruel. That is not Plutarch's idea, it is Shakespeare's. He could fully sympathise with the gentleness of Brutus, with his entire superiority to private aims and almost entire freedom from personal susceptibilities, and even with his resolution to sacrifice his friend; but he could not so sympathise with mere horror of monarchy or absolute power. And now extend this a little. Can you imagine Shakespeare an enthusiast for an 'idea'; a devotee of divine right, or the rights of Parliament, or any particular form of government in Church or State; a Fifth Monarchy man, or a Quaker, or a thick-and-thin adherent of any compact, exclusive, abstract creed, even if it were as rational and noble as [Giuseppi] Mazzini's? This type of mind, even at its best, is alien from his. . . .

This would be the natural place to discuss Shakespeare's politics if we were to discuss them at all. But even if the question whether he shows any interest in the political differences of his time, or any sympathies or antipathies in regard to them, admits of an answer, it could be answered only by an examination of details; and I must pass it by, and offer only the briefest remarks on a wider question. Shakespeare, as we might expect, shows no sign of believing in what is sometimes called a political 'principle'. The main ideas which, consciously or unconsciously, seem to govern or emerge from his presentation of state affairs, might perhaps be put thus. National welfare is the end of politics, and the criterion by which political actions are to be judged. It implies of necessity 'degree'; that is, differences of position and function in the members of the body politic.[28] And the first requisites of national welfare are the observance of this degree, and the concordant performance of these functions in the general interest. But there appear to be no further absolute principles than these: beyond them all is relative to the particular case and its particular conditions. We find no hint, for example, in *Julius Caesar* that Shakespeare regarded a monarchical form of government as intrinsically better than a republican, or *vice versa*; no trace in *Richard II.* that the author shares the king's belief in his inviolable right, or regards Bolingbroke's usurpation as justifiable. We perceive, again, pretty clearly in several plays a dislike and contempt of demagogues, and an opinion that mobs are foolish, fickle, and ungrateful. But these are sentiments which the most determined of believers in democracy, if he has sense, may share; and if he thinks that the attitude of aristocrats like Volumnia and Coriolanus is inhuman and as inexcusable as that of the mob, and that a mob is as easily led right as wrong and has plenty of good nature in it, he has abundant ground for holding that Shakespeare thought so too. That Shakespeare greatly liked and admired the typical qualities of the best kind of aristocrat seems highly probable; but then this taste has always been compatible with a great variety of political opinions. It is interesting but useless to wonder what his own opinions would have been at various periods of English history: perhaps the only thing we can be pretty sure of in regard to them is that they would never have been extreme, and that he would never have supposed his opponents to be entirely wrong.

We have tried to conjecture the impulses, passions, and errors with which Shakespeare could easily sympathise, and the virtues and types of character which he may have approved without much sympathy. It remains to ask whether we can notice tendencies and vices to which he felt any special antipathy; and it is obvious and safe to point to those most alien to a gentle, open, and free nature, the vices of a cold and hard disposition, self-centred and incapable of fusion with others. Passing over, again, the plainly hideous forms or extremes of such vice, as we see them in characters like Richard III, Iago, Goneril and Regan, or the Queen in *Cymbeline*, we seem to detect a particular aversion to certain vices which have the common mark of baseness; for instance, servility and flattery (especially when deliberate and practised with a view to self-advancement), feigning in friendship, and ingratitude. Shakespeare's *animus* against the dog arises from the attribution of these vices to him, and against them in men are directed the invectives which seem to have a personal ring. There appears to be traceable also a feeling of a special, though less painful, kind against unmercifulness. I do not mean, of course, cruelty, but unforgivingness, and even the tendency to prefer justice to mercy. From no other dramatic author, probably, could there be collected such prolonged and heart-felt praises of mercy as from Shakespeare. He had not at all strongly, I think, that instinct and love of justice and retribution which in many men are so powerful; but Prospero's words [in *The Tempest*],

> they being penitent,
> The sole drift of my purpose doth extend
> Not a jot further,

came from his heart. He perceived with extreme clearness the connection of acts with their consequences; but his belief that in this sense 'the gods are just' was accompanied by the strongest feeling that forgiveness ought to follow repentance, and (if I may so put it) his favourite petition was the one that begins 'Forgive us our trespasses.' To conclude, I have fancied that he shows an unusual degree of disgust at slander and dislike of censoriousness; and where he speaks in the Sonnets of those who censured him he betrays an exceptionally decided feeling that a man's offences are his own affair and not the world's.[29]

Some of the vices which seem to have been particularly odious to Shakespeare have, we may notice, a special connection with prosperity and power. Men feign and creep and flatter to please the powerful and to win their own way to ease or power; and they envy and censure and slander their competitors in the race; and when they succeed, they are ungrateful to their friends and helpers and patrons; and they become hard and unmerciful, and

despise and bully those who are now below them. So, perhaps, Shakespeare
said to himself in those years when, as we imagine, melancholy and
embitterment often overclouded his sky, though they did not obscure his faith
in goodness and much less his intellectual vision. And prosperity and power,
he may have added, come less frequently by merit than by those base arts or
by mere fortune. The divorce of goodness and power was, to Shelley, the 'woe
of the world'; if we substitute for 'goodness' the wider word 'merit,' we may
say that this divorce, with the evil bred by power, is to Shakespeare also the
root of bitterness. This fact, presented in its extreme form of the appalling
cruelty of the prosperous, and the heartrending suffering of the defenceless,
forms the problem of his most tremendous drama. We have no reason to
surmise that his own sufferings were calamitous; and the period which seems
to be marked by melancholy and embitterment was one of outward, or at
least financial, prosperity; but nevertheless we can hardly doubt that he felt
on the small scale of his own life the influence of that divorce of power and
merit. His complaint against Fortune, who had so ill provided for his life,
runs through the Sonnets. Even if we could regard as purely conventional
the declarations that his verses would make his friend immortal, it is totally
impossible that he can have been unaware of the gulf between his own gifts
and those of others, or can have failed to feel the disproportion between his
position and his mind. Hamlet had never experienced

> the spurns
> That patient merit of the unworthy takes,

and that make the patient soul weary of life; the man who had experienced
them was the writer of Sonnet 66, who cried for death because he was tired
with beholding

> desert a beggar born,
> And needy nothing trimmed in jollity,

—a beggarly soul flaunting in brave array. Neither had Hamlet felt in his
own person 'the insolence of office'; but the actor had doubtless felt it
often enough, and we can hardly err in hearing his own voice in dramatic
expressions of wonder and contempt at the stupid pride of mere authority
and at men's slavish respect for it. Two examples will suffice. 'Thou hast seen
a farmer's dog bark at a beggar, and the creature run from the cur? There thou
mightst behold the great image of authority. A dog's obeyed in office': so says
Lear [IV.vi.155–59], when madness has cleared his vision, and indignation

makes the Timon-like verses that follow. The other example is almost too famous for quotation but I have a reason for quoting it:

> man, proud man,
> Drest in a little brief authority,
> Most ignorant of what he's most assured,
>
> His glassy essence, like an angry ape,
> Plays such fantastic tricks before high heaven
> As makes the angels weep; who, with our spleens,
> Would all themselves laugh mortal.
>
> [*Measure for Measure*, II.ii.121–27]

It is Isabella who says that; but it is scarcely in character; Shakespeare himself is speaking.[30]

It is with great hesitation that I hazard a few words on Shakespeare's religion. Any attempt to penetrate his reserve on this subject may appear a crowning impertinence; and, since his dramas are almost exclusively secular, any impressions we may form must here be even more speculative than usual. Yet it is scarcely possible to read him much without such speculations. . . .

Almost all the speeches that can be called pronouncedly religious and Christian in phraseology and spirit are placed in the mouths of persons to whom they are obviously appropriate, either from their position (e.g. bishops, friars, nuns), or from what Shakespeare found in histories (*e.g.* Henry IV., V., and VI.), or for some other plain reason. We cannot build, therefore, on these speeches in the least. On the other hand (except, of course, where they are hypocritical or politic), we perceive in Shakespeare's tone in regard to them not the faintest trace of dislike or contempt; nor can we find a trace anywhere of such feelings, or of irreverence, towards Christian ideas, institutions, or customs (mere humorous irreverence is not relevant here); and in the case of 'sympathetic' characters, living in Christian times but not in any decided sense religious, no disposition is visible to suppress or ignore their belief in, and use of, religious ideas. Some characters, again, Christian or heathen, who appear to be drawn with rather marked sympathy, have strong, if simple, religious convictions (*e.g.* Horatio [in *Hamlet*], Edgar [in *King Lear*], Hermione [in *The Winter's Tale*]); and in others, of whom so much can hardly be said, but who strike many readers, rightly or wrongly, as having a good deal of Shakespeare in them (*e.g.* Romeo and Hamlet), we observe a quiet but deep sense that they and other men are neither their own masters nor responsible only to themselves and other men, but are in the hands of 'Providence' or guiding powers 'above.'[33]

To this I will add two remarks. To every one, I suppose, certain speeches sound peculiarly personal. Perhaps others may share my feeling about Hamlet's words:

> There's a divinity that shapes our ends,
> Rough-hew them how we will;
>
> [V.ii.10–11]

and about those other words of his:

> There are more things in heaven and earth, Horatio,
> Than are dreamt of in your philosophy;
>
> [I.v.167–68]

and about the speech of Prospero ending, 'We are such stuff as dreams are made on'[34] [*The Tempest* IV.i.156]. On the other hand, we observe that Hamlet seems to have arrived at that conviction as to the 'divinity' after reflection, and that, while he usually speaks as one who accepts the received Christian ideas, yet, when meditating profoundly, he appears to ignore them.[35] In the same way the Duke in *Measure for Measure* is for the most part, and necessarily, a Christian; yet nobody would guess it from the great speech, 'Be absolute for death,' addressed by a supposed friar to a youth under sentence to die, yet containing not a syllable about a future life.[36] . . .

Shakespeare, I imagine, was not, in the sense assigned to the word some minutes ago, a religious man. Nor was it natural to him to regard good and evil, better and worse, habitually from a theological point of view. But (this appears certain) he had a lively and serious sense of 'conscience,' of the pain of self-reproach and self-condemnation, and of the torment to which this pain might rise.[37] He was not in the least disposed to regard conscience as somehow illusory or a human invention, but on the contrary thought of it (I use the most non-committal phrase I can find) as connected with the power that rules the world and is not escapable by man. He realised very fully and felt very keenly, after his youth was past and at certain times of stress, the sufferings and wrongs of men, the strength of evil, the hideousness of certain forms of it, and its apparent incurability in certain cases. And he must sometimes have felt all this as a terrible problem. But, however he may have been tempted, and may have yielded, to exasperation and even despair, he never doubted that it is best to be good; felt more and more that one must be patient and must forgive;[38] and probably maintained unbroken a conviction, practical if not formulated, that to be good is to be at peace with that unescapable power. But it is unlikely that he attempted to theorise further on the nature of the power. All was for him, in the end, mystery; and, while we have no reason whatever to attribute to him a belief in the ghosts and oracles he used in his dramas, he had no inclination to play the spy on God or to limit his power by our notions of it. That he had dreams and ponderings about the mystery such as he never put into the mouths of actors I do not doubt; but I imagine they were no more than dreams and ponderings and movings about in worlds unrealised.

Whether to this 'religion' he joined a more or less conventional acceptance of some or all of the usual Christian ideas, it is impossible to tell. There is no great improbability to me in the idea that he did not, but it is more probable to me that he did,—that, in fact, though he was never so tormented as Hamlet, his position in this matter was, at least in middle life (and he never reached old age), much like Hamlet's. If this were so it might naturally happen that, as he grew older and wearier of labour, and perhaps of the tumult of pleasure and thought and pain, his more personal religion, the natural piety which seems to gain in weight and serenity in the latest plays, came to be more closely joined with Christian ideas. But I can find no clear indications that this did happen; and though some have believed that they discovered these ideas displayed in full, though not explicitly, in the *Tempest*, I am not able to hear there more than the stream of Shakespeare's own 'religion' moving with its fullest volume and making its deepest and most harmonious music.[39] . . .

If we were obliged to answer the question which of Shakespeare's plays contains, not indeed the fullest picture of his mind, but the truest expression of his nature and habitual temper, unaffected by special causes of exhilaration or gloom, I should be disposed to choose *As You Like It*. It wants, to go no further, the addition of a touch of Sir Toby or Falstaff, and the ejection of its miraculous conversions of ill-disposed characters. But the misbehaviour of Fortune, and the hardness and ingratitude of men, form the basis of its plot, and are a frequent topic of complaint. And, on the other hand, he who is reading it has a smooth brow and smiling lips, and a heart that murmurs,

> Happy is your grace,
> That can translate the stubbornness of fortune
> Into so quiet and so sweet a style.
>   [II.i.18–20]

And it is full not only of sweetness, but of romance, fun, humour of various kinds, delight in the oddities of human nature, love of modesty and fidelity and high spirit and patience, dislike of scandal and censure, contemplative curiosity, the feeling that in the end we are all merely players, together with a touch of the feeling that

> Then is there mirth in heaven
> When earthly things made even
>   Atone together.
>
> [V.iv.108–10]

And, finally, it breathes the serene holiday mood of escape from the toil, competition, and corruption of city and court into the sun and shadow and peace of the country, where one can be idle and dream and meditate and sing, and pursue or watch the deer as the fancy takes one, and make love or smile at lovers according to one's age.[40]

If, again, the question were put to us, which of Shakespeare's characters reveals most of his personality, the majority of those who consented to give an answer would answer 'Hamlet.' This impression may be fanciful, but it is difficult to think it wholly so, and, speaking for those who share it, I will try to trace some of its sources. There is a good deal of Shakespeare that is not in Hamlet. But Hamlet, we think, is the only character in Shakespeare who could possibly have composed his plays (though it appears unlikely, from his verses to Ophelia, that he could have written the best songs). Into Hamlet's mouth are put what are evidently Shakespeare's own views on drama and acting. Hamlet alone, among the great serious characters, can be called a humorist. When in some trait of another character we seem to touch Shakespeare's personality, we are frequently reminded of Hamlet.[41] When in a profound reflective speech we hear Shakespeare's voice, we usually hear Hamlet's too, and his peculiar humour and turns of phrase appear unexpectedly in persons otherwise unlike him and unlike one another. The most melancholy group of Sonnets (71–74) recalls Hamlet at once, here and there recalls even his words; and he and the writer of Sonnet 66 both recount in a list the ills that make men long for death. And then Hamlet 'was indeed honest and of an open and free nature'; sweet-tempered and modest, yet not slow to resent calumny or injury; of a serious but not a melancholy disposition; and the lover of his friend. And, with these traits, we remember his poet ecstasy at the glory of earth and sky and the marvellous endowments of man; his eager affectionate response to everything noble or sweet in human nature; his tendency to dream and to live in the world of his own mind; his liability to sudden vehement emotion, and his admiration for men whose blood and judgment are better commingled; the overwhelming effect of disillusionment upon him; his sadness, fierceness, bitterness and cynicism. All this, and more: his sensitiveness to the call of duty; his longing to answer to it, and his anguish over his strange delay; the conviction gathering in his tortured soul that man's purposes and failures are divinely shaped to ends beyond his vision; his incessant meditation, and his sense that there are mysteries which no meditation can fathom; nay, even littler traits like his recourse to music to calm his excitement, or his feeling on the one hand that the peasant should not tread on the courtier's heels, and on the other that the mere courtier is spacious in the possession of dirt—all this, I say, corresponds with our impression of Shakespeare, or rather of characteristic traits in Shakespeare, probably here and there a good deal heightened, and mingled with others not characteristic of Shakespeare at all. And if this is more than fancy, it may explain to us why Hamlet is the most fascinating character, and the most inexhaustible, in all imaginative literature. What else should he be, if the world's greatest poet, who was able to give almost the reality of nature to creations totally unlike himself, put his own soul straight into this creation, and when he wrote Hamlet's speeches wrote down his own heart?[42]

Notes

1.   Unquestionably it holds in a considerable degree of Browning, who in *At the Mermaid* and *House* wrote as though he imagined that neither his own work nor Shakespeare's betrayed anything of the inner man. But if we are to criticize those two poems as arguments, we must say that they involve two hopelessly false assumptions, that we have to choose between a self-revelation like Byron's and no self-revelation at all, and that the relation between a poet and his work is like that between the inside and the outside of a house.

2.   Almost all Shakespearean criticism, of course, contains something bearing on our subject; but I have a practical reason for mentioning in particular Mr. Frank Harris's articles in the *Saturday Review* for 1898. A good many of Mr. Harris's views I cannot share, and I had arrived at almost all the ideas expressed in the lecture (except some of the Sonnets questions) before reading his papers. But I found in them also valuable ideas which were quite new to me and would probably be so to many readers. It is a great pity that the articles are not collected and published in a book. [Mr. Harris has published, in *The Man Shakespeare*, the substance of the articles, and also matter which, in my judgment, has much less value.]

3.   He is apologizing for an attack made on Shakespeare in a pamphlet of which he was the publisher and Greene the writer.

4.   It is said of him, indeed, in his lifetime that, had he not played some kingly parts in sport (*i.e.* on the stage), he would have been a companion for a king.

5.   Nor, *vice versa,* does the possession of these latter qualities at all imply, as some writers seem to assume, the absence of the former or of gentleness.

6.   Fuller may be handing down a tradition, but it is not safe to assume this. His comparison, on the other hand, of Shakespeare and Jonson, in their wit-combats, to an English man-of-war and a Spanish great galleon, reads as if his own happy fancy were operating on the reports, direct or indirect, of eye-witnesses.

7.   See, for example, Act IV. Sc. V., to which I know no parallel in the later tragedies.

8.   I allude to Sonnet 110, Mr. Beeching's note on which seems to be unquestionably right: 'There is no reference to the poet's profession of player. The sonnet gives the confession of a favourite of society.' This applies, I think, to the whole group of sonnets (it begins with 107) in which the poet excuses his neglect of his friend, though there are *also* references to his profession and its effect on his nature and his reputation. (By a slip Mr. Beeching makes the neglect last for three years.)

9.   It is perhaps most especially in his rendering of the shock and the effects of *disillusionment* in open natures that we seem to feel Shakespeare's personality. The nature of this shock is expressed in Henry's words to Lord Scroop:

I will weep for thee;
For this revolt of thine, methinks, is like
Another fall of man.

10.   There is nothing of this semi-reality, of course, in the *passion* of love as portrayed, for example, in men so different as Orlando, Othello, Antony, Troilus, whose love for Cressida resembles that of Romeo for Juliet. What I have said of Romeo's 'love' for Rosaline corresponds roughly with Coleridge's view; and, without subscribing to all of Coleridge's remarks, I believe he was right in finding an intentional contrast between this feeling and the passion that displaces it (though it does not follow that the feeling would not have become a genuine passion if Rosaline had been kind). Nor do I understand the notion that Coleridge's view is refuted and even rendered ridiculous by the mere fact that Shakespeare found the Rosaline story in Brooke (Halliwell-Phillipps, *Outlines,* 7th ed., illustrative note 2). Was he compelled then to use whatever he found? Was it his practice to do so? The question is always *why* he used what he found, and *how.* Coleridge's view of this matter, it need hardly be said, is far from indisputable; but it must be judged by our knowledge of Shakespeare's mind and not of his material alone. I may add, as I have referred to Halliwell-Phillipps, that Shakespeare made changes in the story he found; that it is arbitrary to assume (not that it matters) that

Coleridge, who read Steevens, was unaware of Shakespeare's use of Brooke; and that Brooke was by no means a 'wretched poetaster.'

11.   *Hamlet, Measure for Measure, Othello, Troilus and Cressida, King Lear, Timon of Athens.* See *Shakespearean Tragedy,* pp. 79–85, 275–6. I should like to insist on the view there taken that the tragedies subsequent to *Lear* and *Timon* do not show the pressure of painful feelings.

12.   It is not implied that the scenes are certainly Shakespeare's; but I see no sufficient ground for decisively rejecting them.

13.   That experience, certainly in part and probably wholly, belongs to an earlier time, since sonnets 138 and 144 were printed in the *Passionate Pilgrim.* But I see no difficulty in that. What bears little fruit in a normal condition of spirits may bear abundant fruit later, in moods of discouragement and exasperation induced largely by other causes.

14.   *The Sonnets of Shakespeare with an Introduction and Notes,* Ginn & Co., 1904.

15.   I find that Mr. Beeching, in the Stratford Town edition of Shakespeare (1907), has also urged these considerations.

16.   I do not meat to imply that Meres necessarily refers to the sonnets we possess, or that all of these are likely to have been written by 1598.

17.   A fact to be remembered in regard to references to the social position of the friend.

18.   Mr. Beeching's illustration of the friendship of the sonnets from the friendship of Gray and Bonstetten is worth pages of argument.

19.   In 125 the poet repudiates the accusation that his friendship is too much based on beauty.

20.   This does not imply that the Sonnets are as early as the *Two Gentlemen of Verona,* and much less that they are earlier.

21.   This seems to be referred to in lines by John Davies of Hereford, reprinted in Ingleby's *Shakespeare's Centurie of Prayse,* second edition, pp. 58, 84, 94. In the first of these passages, dated 1603 (and perhaps in the second, 1609), there are signs that Davies had read Sonnet 111, a fact to be noted with regard to the question of the chronology of the Sonnets.

22.   'Mistress Tearsheet,' too 'would fain hear some music,' and 'Sneak's noise' had to be sent for (*2 Henry IV.,* II. iv. 12).

23.   It is tempting, though not safe, to infer from the *Tempest* and the great passage in *Pericles* that Shakespeare must have been in a storm at sea; but that he felt the poetry of a sea-storm is beyond all doubt. Few moments in the reading of his works are more overwhelming than that in which, after listening not without difficulty to the writer of the first two Acts of *Pericles,* suddenly, as the third opens, one hears the authentic voice:

Thou god of this great vast, rebuke these surges
That wash both heaven and hell. . . . The seaman's whistle
Is as a whisper in the ears of death,
Unheard.

Knowing that this is coming, I cannot stop to read the Prologue to Act III., though I believe Shakespeare wrote it. How it can be imagined that he did more than touch up Acts I. and II. passes my comprehension.

I may call attention to another point. Unless I mistake, there is nothing in Shakespeare's authorities, as known to us, which corresponds with the feeling of Timon's last speech, beginning,

Come not to me again: but say to Athens,
Timon hath made his everlasting mansion
Upon the beached verge of the salt flood:

a feeling made more explicit in the final speech of Alcibiades.

24.   The lily seems to be in almost all cases the Madonna lily. It is very doubtful whether the lily of the valley is referred to at all.

25.   But there is something disappointing, and even estranging, in Sonnet 50, which, promising to show a real sympathy, cheats us in the end. I may observe, without implying that the fact has any personal significance, that the words about 'the poor beetle that we tread upon' are given to a woman (Isabella), and that it is Marina who says:

I trod upon a worm against my will,
But I wept for it.

26.   Three times in one drama Shakespeare refers to this detestable trait. See *Shakespearean Tragedy*, p. 268, where I should like to qualify still further the sentence containing the qualification 'on the whole.' Good judges, at least, assure me that I have admitted too much against the dog.

27.   Nor can I recall any sign of liking, or even approval, of that 'prudent, *cautious*, self-control' which, according to a passage in Burns, in 'wisdom's root.'

28.   The *locus classicus*, of course, is *Troilus and Cressida*, I, iii, 75 ff.

29.   Of all the evils inflicted by man on man those chosen for mention in the dirge in *Cymbeline*, one of the last plays, are the frown o' the great, the tyrant's stroke, slander, censure rash.

30.   Having written these paragraphs, I should like to disclaim the belief that Shakespeare was habitually deeply discontented with his position in life.

33.   It is only this 'quiet but deep sense' that is significant. No inference can be drawn from the fact that the mere belief in powers above seems to be taken as a matter of course in practially all the characters, good and bad alike. On the other hand there may well be something symptomatic in the

apparent absence of interest in theoretical disbelief in such powers and in
the immortality of the soul. I have observed elsewhere that the atheism of
Aaron does not increase the probablility that the conception of the character
is Shakespeare's.

34.   With the first compare, what to me has, though more faintly, the same
ring, Hermione's

> If powers divine
>
> Behold our human actions, as they do:

with the second, Helena's

> It is not so with Him that all things knows
> As 'tis with us that square our guess by shows;
> But most it is presumption in us when
> The help of heaven we count the act of men:

followed soon after by Lafeu's remark:

> They say miracles are past; and we have our philosophical
> persons to make modern and familiar things supernatural and
> causeless. Hence it is that we make trifles of terrors, ensconcing
> ourselves into seeming knowledge, when we should submit
> ourselves to an unknown fear.

35.   It is worth noting that the reference, which appears in the First Quarto
version of 'To be or not to be,' to 'an everlasting judge,' disappears in the
revised versions.

36.   The suggested inference, of course, is that this speech, thus out of
character, and Hamlet's 'To be or not to be' (though that is in character), show
us Shakespeare's own mind. It has force, I think, but nor compulsory force.
The topics of these speeches are, in the old sense of the word, commonplaces.
Shakespeare may have felt, Here is my chance to show what I can do with
certain feelings and thought of supreme interest to men of all times and place
and modes of belief. It would not follow from this that they are not 'personal,'
but any inference to a non-acceptance of received religious ideas would be
much weakened. ('All the world's a stage' is a patent example of the suggested
elaboration of a commonplace.)

37.   What actions in particular *his* conscience approved and disapproved is
another question and one not relevant here.

38.   This does not at all imply to Shakespeare, so far as we can see, that evil
is never to be forcibly resisted.

39.   I do not mean to reject the idea that in some passages in the *Tempest*
Shakespeare, while he wrote them with a dramatic purpose, also thought of
himself. It seems to me likely. And if so, there *may* have been such a thought
in the words,

And thence retire me to my Milan, where
Every third thought shall be my grave.

and also in those lines about prayer and pardon which close the Epilogue, and
to my ear come with a sudden effect of great seriousness, contrasting most
strangely with their context. If they *had* a grave and personal under-meaning
it cannot have been intended for the audience, which would take the prayer
as addressed to itself.

40.   It may be added that *As You Like It,* though idyllic, is not so falsely
idyllic as some critics would make it. It is based, we may roughly say, on a
contrast between court and country; but those who inhale virtue from the
woodland are courtiers who bring virtue with them, and the country has its
churlish masters and unkind or uncouth maidens.

41.   This has been strongly urged and fully illustrated by Mr. Harris.

42.   It may be suggested that, in the catalogue above, I should have
mentioned that imaginative 'unreality' in love referred to on p. 326. But I do
not see in Hamlet either this, or any sign that he took Ophelia for an Imogen
or even a Juliet, though naturally he was less clearly aware of her deficiencies
than Shakespeare.

I may add, however, another item to the catalogue. We do not feel that
the problems presented to most of the tragic heroes could have been fatal
to Shakespeare himself. The immense breadth and clearness of his intellect
would have saved him from the fate of Othello, Troilus, or Antony. But we do
feel, I think, and he himself may have felt, that he could not have coped with
Hamlet's problem; and there is no improbability in the idea that he may have
experienced in some degree the melancholia of his hero.

GENERAL

Francis Meres (1598)

The existence of a commonplace book, or diary, of the English clergyman Francis Meres (1565–1647) locates Shakespeare in the theatrical landscape of his time. The record offers one opinion of his work that may echo a common opinion about Shakespeare in his era and gives a terminal date for establishing the dates of a few of his plays. The mention of a play called *Love's Labors Won* suggests a play that has not survived. Meres's is not the only allusion to such a play. Stanley Wells and Gary Taylor report in their edition of Shakespeare's work (Oxford, 1988, p. 309) "the discovery in 1953 of a fragment of a bookseller's list that had been used in the binding of a volume published in 1637/8" mentioning "loves labors won."

As the soule *of Euphorbus* was thought to live in *Pythagoras:* so the sweete wittie soule of Ovid lives in mellifluous & hony-tongued *Shakespeare*, witnes his *Venus* and *Adonis*, his *Lucrece*, his sugred Sonnets among his private friends, &c.

As *Plautus* and *Seneca* are accounted the best for Comedy and Tragedy among the Latines ? so *Shakespeare* among ye English is the most excellent in both kinds for the stage; for Comedy, witnes his *Gentlemen of Verona*, his *Errors*, his *Love labors lost*, his *Love labours wonne*, his *Midsummers night dreame*, & his *Merchant of Venice*: for Tragedy his *Richard the 2. Richard the 3. Henry the 4. King Iohn, Titus Andronicus* and his *Romeo and Juliet*.

As *Epius Stolo* said, that the Muses would speake with *Plautus* tongue, if they would speak Latin: so I say that the Muses would speake with *Shakespeares* fine filed phrase, if they would speake English.

—Francis Meres, *Palladis Tamia*, 1598

JOHN WEEVER "AD GULIELMUM SHAKESPEARE" (1599)

Like Meres, John Weever (1576–1632), poet and antiquary, establishes Shakespeare's presence in the London theater world and also names some of his work, concentrating on his poetry but alluding to two of his plays, and, by these mentions helps in establishing their dates.

Honie-tong'd *Shakespeare* when I saw thine issue
I swore *Apollo* got them and none other,
Their rosie-tainted features cloth'd in tissue,
Some heauen born goddesse said to be their mother:
Rose-checkt *Adonis* with his amber tresses,
Faire fire-hot *Venus* charming him to loue her,
Chaste *Lucretia* virgine-like her dresses,
Prowd lust-flung *Tarquine* seeking still to proue her:
Romea Richard; more whose names I know not,
Their sugred tongues, and power attractiue beuty
Say they are Saints althogh that Sts they shew not
For thousands vowes to them subiectiue dutie:
They burn in loue thy children *Shakespear* het them,
Go, wo thy Muse more Nymphish brood beget them.

> —John Weever, "Ad Gulielmum
> Shakespeare," *Epigrammes in the Oldest
> Cut and Newest Fashion*, 1599

LEONARD DIGGES "TO THE MEMORIE OF THE DECEASED AUTHOR MAISTER W. SHAKESPEARE" (1623)

Leonard Digges (1588–1635) was a scholar, poet, and translator. This verse first appeared among the commendatory front matter in the 1623 Folio edition of Shakespeare's work edited by Heminge and Condell. It sounds a common theme that Shakespeare himself broached in his first sonnets, that long after his flesh was decayed and monuments to him became ruins, his spirit would live because it inhabited his works, which are eternal. "As Naso said," refers to Publius Ovidius Naso, the Roman poet Ovid.

Shakespeare, at length thy pious fellowes giue
The world thy Workes: thy Workes, by which, out-liue
Thy Tombe, thy name must; when that stone is rent,
And Time dissolues thy *Stratford* Moniment,
Here we aliue shall view thee still. This Booke,
When Brasse and Marble fade, shall make thee looke
Fresh to all Ages: when Posteritie
Shall loath what's new, thinke all is prodegie
That is not *Shakespeares*; eu'ry Line, each Verse
Here shall reuiue, redeeme thee from thy Herse.
Nor Fire, nor cankring Age, as *Naso* said,
Of his, thy wit-fraught Booke shall once inuade.
Nor shall I e're beleeue, or thinke thee dead
(Though mist) vntill our bankrout Stage be sped
(Impossible) with some new strain t'out-do
Passions of *Iuliet,* and her *Romeo;*
Or till I heare a Scene more nobly take,
Then when thy half-Sword parlying Romans spake.
Till these, till any of thy Volumes rest
Shall with more fire, more feeling be exprest,
Be sure, our *Shakespeare,* thou canst neuer dye,
But crown'd with Lawrell, hue eternally.

—Leonard Digges "To the Memorie
of the Deceased Author Maister W.
Shakespeare," *Mr. William Shakespeares
Comedies, Histories, & Tragedies,* 1623

JOHN HEMINGE AND HENRY CONDELL "TO THE GREAT VARIETY OF READERS" (1623)

John Heminge (1556–1630) and Henry Condell (?–1627) were actors in Shakespeare's company, the King's Men, who gathered his work and printed it, in 1623, in the First Folio. Their short introduction is both an advertisement to the reader to buy the book and an encomium to the author. The importance of the First Folio cannot be stressed enough. Of the 36 plays gathered there, 18 had never been printed before, and some that had already been printed in quarto editions were inaccurate and filled with errors.

From the most able, to him that can but spell: There you are number'd. We had rather you were weighd. Especially, when the fate of all Bookes depends vpon your capacities: and not of your heads alone, but of your purses. Well! It is now publique, & you wil stand for your priuiledges wee know: to read, and censure. Do so, but buy it first. That doth best commend a Booke, the Stationer saies. Then, how odde soeuer your braines be, or your wisedomes, make your licence the same, and spare not. Iudge your sixe-pen'orth, your shillings worth, your fiue shillings worth at a time, or higher, so you rise to the iust rates, and welcome. But, what euer you do, Buy. Censure will not driue a Trade, or make the Iacke go. And though you be a Magistrate of wit, and sit on the Stage at *Black-Friers,* or the *Cock-pit,* to arraigne Playes dailie, know, these Playes haue had their triall alreadie, and stood out all Appeales; and do now come forth quitted rather by a Decree of Court, then any purchas'd Letters of commendation.

It had bene a thing, we confesse, worthie to haue bene wished, that the Author himselfe had liu'd to haue set forth, and ouerseen his owne writings; But since it hath bin ordain'd otherwise, and he by death departed from that right, we pray you do not envie his Friends, the office of their care, and paine, to haue collected & publish'd them; and so to haue publish'd them, as where (before) you were abus'd with diuerse stolne, and surreptitious copies, maimed, and deformed by the frauds and stealthes of iniurious impostors, that expos'd them: euen those, are now offer'd to your view cur'd, and perfect of their limbes; and all the rest, absolute in their numbers, as he conceiued them. Who, as he was a happie imitator of Nature, was a most gentle expresser of it. His mind and hand went together: And what he thought, he vttered with that easinesse, that wee haue scarse receiued from him a blot in his papers. But it is not our prouince, who onely gather his works, and giue them you, to praise him. It is yours that reade him. And there we hope, to your diuers capacities, you will finde enough, both to draw, and hold you: for his wit can no more lie hid, then it could be lost. Reade him, therefore; and againe, and againe: And if then you doe not like him, surely you are in some manifest danger, not to vnderstand him. And so we leaue you to other of his Friends, whom if you need, can bee your guides: if you neede them not, you can leade your selues, and others. And such Readers we wish him.

—John Heminge and Henry Condell,
"To the Great Variety of Readers,"
Mr. William Shakespeares Comedies,
Histories, & Tragedies, 1623

Hugh Holland "Upon the Lines and Life of the Famous Scenicke Poet, Master William Shakespeare" (1623)

Hugh Holland's (1563–1633) commemorative verses appearing in the First Folio are conventional lines lamenting Shakespeare's death and suggesting his immortality. They use the image of his profession as an actor to express Holland's sense of loss and Shakespeare's exit from life and entrance to death and eternal fame.

Those hands, which you so clapt, go now, and wring
You *Britaines* braue; for done are *Shakespeares* dayes:
His dayes are done, that made the dainty Playes,
Which made the Globe of heau'n and earth to ring.
Dry'de is that veine, dryd is the *Thespian* Spring,
Turn'd all to teares, and *Phoebus* clouds his rayes:
That corp's, that coffin now besticke those bayes,
Which crown'd him *Poet* first, then *Poets* King.
If *Tragedies* might any *Prologue* haue,
All those he made, would scarse make one to this:
Where *Fame,* now that he gone is to the graue
(Death publique tyring-house) the *Nuncius* [envoy] is.
For though his line of life went soone about,
The life yet of his lines shall neuer out.

> —Hugh Holland "Upon the Lines and Life of
> the Famous Scenicke Poet, Master William
> Shakespeare," *Mr. William Shakespeares
> Comedies, Histories, & Tragedies,* 1623

Ben Jonson "To the Memory of My Beloued, the Author Mr. William Shakespeare" (1623)

Ben Jonson's tribute to Shakespeare, first printed in the First Folio, reflects Jonson's own sense of himself as a poet as well as his esteem for Shakespeare and his own understanding of human psychology. After assenting that his praise does not come as the result of any suspect motives, he begins to catalog Shakespeare's virtues by showing his superiority even to his contemporaries and his predecessors whether in the art of comedy, represented by socks, or tragedy, represented by the high boots or buskins in which it was performed in classical Greece. Not only does Jonson find Shakespeare still living in his works, but he sees those works illuminating a world darkened by grief at Shakespeare's death. Describing Shakespeare as his own monument, Jonson alludes to William Basse's tributary poem, included in the "Personal" section of this volume, of the preceding year, in which Basse asks Chaucer and other great poets to make room for Shakespeare in their tomb:

> Renowned Spencer lye a thought more nye
> To learned Chaucer, and rare Beaumont lye
> A little neerer Spenser, to make roome
> For Shakespeare in your threefold, fowerfold Tombe.

> —William Basse, 1622

To draw no envy (*Shakespeare*) on thy name,
Am I thus ample to thy Booke, and Fame:
While I confesse thy writings to be such,
As neither *Man*, nor Muse, can praise too much.
'Tis true, and all men's suffrage. But these wayes
Were not the paths I meant vnto thy praise:
For silliest Ignorance on these may light,
Which, when it sounds at best, but eccho's right;
Or blinde Affection, which doth ne're advance
The truth, but gropes, and urgeth all by chance;
Or crafty Malice, might pretend this praise,
And thinke to mine, where it seem'd to raise.
These are, as some infamous Baud, or Whore,
Should praise a Matron. What could hurt her more?
But thou art proofe against them, and indeed
Aboue th'ill fortune of them, or the need.
I, therefore will begin. Soule of the Age!
The applause! delight! the wonder of our Stage!
My *Shakespeare*, rise; I will not lodge thee by
Chaucer, or *Spenser*, or bid *Beaumont* lye
A little further, to make thee a roome:
Thou art a Moniment, without a tombe,
And art aliue still, while thy Booke doth live,
And we haue wits to read, and praise to giue.

That I not mixe thee so, my braine excuses;
I meane with great, but disproportion'd Muses:
For, if I thought my judgement were of yeeres,
I should commit thee surely with thy peeres,
And tell, how farre thou didst our *Lily* out-shine,
Or sporting *Kid,* or *Marlowes* mighty line.
And though thou hadst small *Latine,* and lesse *Greeke,*
From thence to honour thee, I would not seeke
For names; but call forth thund'ring /Æschilus,
Euripides, and *Sophocles* to vs,
Paccuvius, Accius, him of *Cordoua* dead,
To life againe, to heare thy Buskin tread,
And shake a Stage: Or, when thy Sockes were on,
Leaue thee alone, for the comparison
Of all, that insolent *Greece,* or haughtie *Rome*
Sent forth, or since did from their ashes come.
Triumph, my *Britaine,* thou hast one to showe,
To whom all Scenes of *Europe* homage owe.
He was not of an age, but for all time!
And all the Muses still were in their prime,
When like *Apollo* he came forth to warme
Our eares, or like a *Mercury* to charme!
Nature her selfe was proud of his designes,
And ioy'd to weare the dressing of his lines!
Which were so richly spun, and wouen so fit,
As, since, she will vouchsafe no other Wit.
The merry *Greeke,* tart *Aristophanes,*
Neat Terence, witty *Plautus,* now not please;
But antiquated, and deserted lye
As they were not of Natures family.
Yet must I not giue Nature all: Thy Art,
My gentle *Shakespeare,* must enioy a part.
For though the *Poets* matter, Nature be,
His Art doth giue the fashion. And, that he,
Who casts to write a living line, must sweat,
(Such as thine are) and strike the second heat
Upon the *Muses* anvile: turne the same,
(And himselfe with it) that he thinkes to frame;
Or for the lawrell, he may gaine a scorne,

For a good *Poet's* made, as well as borne.
And such wert thou. Looke how the father's face
Lives in his issue, even so, the race
Of *Shakespeare's* minde, and manners brightly shines
In his well toned, and true-filed lines:
In each of which, he seemes to shake a Lance,
As brandish't at the eyes of Ignorance.
Sweet Swan of Auon! what a sight it were
To see thee in our waters yet appeare,
And make those flights upon the bankes of *Thames,*
That so did take *Eliza,* and our *Iames!*
But stay, I see thee in the *Hemisphere*
Aduanc'd, and made a Constellation there!
Shine forth, thou Starre of Poets, and with rage,
Or influence, chide, or cheere the drooping Stage;
Which, since thy flight from hence, hath moum'd like night,
And despaires day, but for thy Volumes light.

—Ben Jonson, "To the Memory of
My Beloued, the Author Mr. William
Shakespeare," *Mr. William Shakespeares
Comedies, Histories, & Tragedies,* 1623

MICHAEL DRAYTON "TO MY MOST DEARELY-LOVED FRIEND HENERY REYNOLDS, ESQUIRE, OF POETS AND POESIE" (1627)

Poet and playwright Michael Drayton's (1563–1631) encomium repeats what had been said in regard to Shakespeare's dramatic range in the First Folio's tributes. It is significant because it demonstrates the wave of admiration that seemed to be rising around Shakespeare's name.

Shakespeare thou hadst as smooth a Comicke vaine,
Fitting the socke, and in thy natural braine,
As strong conception, and as Cleere a rage,
As any one that trafiqu'd with the stage.

—Michael Drayton, "To My Most Dearely-
Loved Friend Henery Reynolds, Esquire,
of Poets and Poesie," *Elegies,* 1627

JOHN MILTON "ON SHAKESPEAR" (1630)

John Milton (1608–74), author of *Paradise Lost*, was an epic poet, a polemical essayist, and a statesman. His tribute to Shakespeare, composed in 1630, was the first of his English poems to appear in print—Milton wrote a significant amount of verse in Latin and was fluent in Greek and Hebrew as well as several modern European languages—and was printed without attribution in the Second Folio edition of Shakespeare's work, in 1632. Here, Milton argues that Shakespeare does not need a monument because the power of his work makes his readers into his monument, turning them into monumental stone by astonishing them with the marvel his works produce.

What needs my *Shakespear* for his honour'd Bones,
The labour of an age in piled Stones,
Or that his hallow'd reliques should be hid
Under a Star-ypointing *Pyramid?*
Dear son of memory, great heir of Fame,
What need'st thou such weak witnes of thy name?
Thou in our wonder and astonishment
Hast built thy self a live-long Monument.
For whilst to th' shame of slow-endeavoring art,
Thy easie numbers flow, and that each heart
Hath from the leaves of thy unvalu'd Book,
Those Delphick lines with deep impressions took,
Then thou our fancy of it self bereaving,
Dost make us Marble with too much conceaving;
And so Sepulcher'd in such pomp dost lie,
That Kings for such a Tomb would wish to die.

—John Milton "On Shakespear," 1630

LEONARD DIGGES "UPON MASTER WILLIAM SHAKESPEARE, THE DECEASED AUTHOUR, AND HIS POEMS" (1640)

Leonard Digges (1588–1635) was a poet and a translator. His stepfather, Thomas Russell, was a friend of Shakespeare's and the executor of his will. Digges's tributary verses appeared posthumously in a 1640 collection of Shakespeare's poems published by John Benson. Digges's assertions that

Shakespeare used no sources and his plays show no influence from other works is inaccurate. Shakespeare freely used the translation of Plutarch's *Lives* by Thomas North, including some of North's language in both *Antony and Cleopatra* and in *Coriolanus*. He borrowed equally from many Continental and British writers for such plays as *Othello*, *Romeo and Juliet*, *The Two Gentlemen of Verona*, and *Hamlet*, to name but a few.

———

Nature onely helpt him, for looke thorow
This whole Booke, thou shalt find he doth not borrow.
One phrase from Greekes, nor Latines imitate,
Nor once from vulgar Languages Translate,
Nor Plagiari-like from others gleane,
Nor begges he from each witty friend a Scene
To peece his Acts with, all that he doth write,
Is pure his owne, plot, language exquisite,
But oh! what praise more powerfull can we give
The dead, then that by him the Kings men live,
His Players, which should they but have shar'd the Fate,
All else expir'd within the short Termes date;
How could the Globe have prospered, since through want
Of change, the Plaies and Poems had growne scant. . . .
So have I seene, when Cesar would appeare,
And on the Stage at halfe-sword parley were,
Brutus and *Cassius:* oh how the Audience
Were ravish'd, with what wonder they went thence,
When some new day they would not brooke a line,
Of tedious (though well laboured) *Catiline;*
Sejanus too was irkesome, they priz'de more
Honest *Iago*, or the jealous Moore.
And though the Fox and subtill Alchimist,
Long intermitted could not quite be mist,
Though these have sham'd all the Ancients, and might raise,
Their Authours merit with a crowne of Bayes.
Yet these sometimes, even at a friends desire
Acted, have scarce defrai'd the Seacoale fire
And doore-keepers: when let but *Falstaffe* come,
Hall, *Poines*, the rest you scarce shall have a roome
All is so pester'd: let but *Beatrice*
And *Benedicke* be seene, loe in a trice

The Cockpit Galleries, Boxes, all are full
To hear *Malvoglio*, that crosse garter'd Gull.
Briefe, there is nothing in his wit fraught Booke,
Whose sound we would not heare, on whose worth looke
Like old coynd gold, whose lines in every page,
Shall passe true currant to succeeding age.

> —Leonard Digges, "Upon Master William
> Shakespeare, the Deceased Authour, and
> His Poems," *Shakespeare's Poems*, 1640

BEN JONSON (1641)

Ben Jonson's recollections of Shakespeare, joined to his critical observations about Shakespeare's strengths and failings, provide posterity with a sense of immediacy that the conversation of a contemporary of Shakespeare's who knew and worked with him can provoke. Shakespeare was one of the actors, in 1598, who appeared in the first performances of Jonson's first important play, *Everyman in His Humour*. Many reminiscences of the time concern the drinking bouts and exchanges of wit the two engaged in. While Shakespeare's art was sprawling and romantic, and showed the savage contradictions that could be yoked uneasily to form a human character, Jonson's was a classically disciplined approach that anatomized the particular character types that defined individuals and fueled their social clashes.

It seems likely that Shakespeare was not guilty of an error, as Jonson judges it, in regard to Caesar, but that Shakespeare is revealing by this speech just the proud self-involvement that would enflame the conspirator's wrath.

I remember, the players have often mentioned it as an honour to Shakspeare, that in his writing (whatsoever he penned) he never blotted out a line. My answer hath been, Would he had blotted a thousand. Which they thought a malevolent speech. I had not told posterity this, but for their ignorance, who chose that circumstance to commend their friend by, wherein he most faulted; and to justify mine own candour: for I loved the man, and do honour his memory, on this side idolatry, as much as any. He was (indeed) honest, and of an open and free nature; had an excellent phantasy, brave notions, and gentle expressions; wherein he flowed with that facility, that sometimes it was necessary he should be stopped: *Sufflaminandus erat*, as Augustus said of Haterius. His wit was in his own power, would the rule of it had been so too. Many times he fell into those things, could not escape laughter: as when he said in the person of Caesar, one speaking to him, "Caesar thou dost me wrong." He replied, "Caesar did never wrong but with just cause," and such like; which were ridiculous. But he redeemed his vices with his virtues. There was ever more in him to be praised than to be pardoned.

—Ben Jonson, *Timber; or Discoveries*, 1641

MARGARET CAVENDISH "LETTER 123" (1664)

Margaret Cavendish, the duchess of Newcastle (1623–73), was a writer, poet, playwright, philosopher, and lady in waiting to King Charles I's wife, Queen Henrietta Maria. Here, responding to criticism that Shakespeare's range was limited in accuracy to portrayals of characters of the lower social class, Cavendish argues that his ability to depict character and types of characters was unlimited as was his ability to discourse, through his characters, on any subject.

Shakespeare did not want Wit, to Express to the Life all Sorts of Persons, of what Quality, Profession, Degree, Breeding, or Birth soever; nor did he want Wit to Express the Divers, and Different Humours, or Natures, or Several Passions in Mankind; and so Well he hath Express'd in his Playes all Sorts of Persons, as one would think he had been Transformed into every one of those Persons he hath Described; and as sometimes one would think he was Really himself the Clown or Jester he Feigns, so one would think, he was also the King, and Privy Counsellor; also as one would think he were Really the Coward he Feigns, so one would think he were the most Valiant, and Experienced Souldier; Who would not think he had been such a man as his Sir *John Falstaff*? and who would not think he had been *Harry* the Fifth? & certainly *Julius Caesar, Augustus Caesar,* and *Antonius,* did never Really Act their parts Better, if so Well, as he hath Described them, and I believe that *Antonius* and *Brutus* did not Speak Better to the People, than he hath Feign'd them; nay, one would think that he had been Metamorphosed from a Man to a Woman, for who could Describe *Cleopatra* Better than he hath done, and many other Females of his own Creating, as *Nan Page,* Mrs. *Page,* Mrs. *Ford,* the Doctors Maid, *Beatrice,* Mrs. *Quickly, Doll Tear-sheet,* and others, too many to Relate? and in his Tragick Vein, he Presents Passions so Naturally, and Misfortunes so Probably, as he Peirces the souls of his Readers with such a True Sense and Feeling thereof, that it Forces Tears through their

Eyes, and almost Perswades them, they are Really Actors, or at least Present at those Tragedies. Who would not Swear he had been a Noble Lover, that could Woo so well? and there is not any person he hath Described in his Book, but his Readers might think they were Well acquainted with them; indeed *Shakespeare* had a Clear Judgment, a Quick Wit, a Spreading Fancy, a Subtil Observation, a Deep Apprehension, and a most Eloquent Elocution; truly, he was a Natural Orator, as well as a Natural Poet, and he was not an Orator to Speak Well only on some Subjects, as Lawyers, who can make Eloquent Orations at the Bar, and Plead Subtilly and Wittily in Law-Cases, or Divines, that can Preach Eloquent Sermons, or Dispute Subtilly and Wittily in Theology, but take them from that, and put them to other Subjects, and they will be to seek; but *Shakespeare's* Wit and Eloquence was General, for, and upon all Subjects, he rather wanted Subjects for his Wit and Eloquence to Work on, for which he was Forced to take some of his Plots out of History, where he only took the Bare Designs, the Wit and Language being all his Own; and so much he had above others, that those, who Writ after him, were Forced to Borrow of him, or rather to Steal from him. . . .

—Margaret Cavendish, "Letter 123,"
CCXI Sociable Letters, 1664

Richard Flecknoe "A Short Discourse of the English Stage" (1664)

Richard Flecknoe (1600–ca. 1678) was a dramatist, poet, and chronicler of his extensive travels. He was the object of the polemical satire *MacFlecknoe* by John Dryden. In this excerpt from his remarks on drama, Flecknoe reformulates the commonplaces of his age: Shakespeare was a poet guided by a natural sensibility; his work has an immediacy and buoyancy; and Jonson's work was accomplished, displaying more art, or labor, than Shakespeare's and was, as a result, ponderous.

For Playes, *Shakespear* was one of the first, who inverted the Dramatick Stile, from dull History to quick Comedy, upon whom *Johnson* [i.e. Ben Jonson] refin'd. . . .

To compare our English Dramatick Poets together (without taxing them) *Shakespear* excelled in a natural Vein, [John] *Fletcher* in Wit, and *Johnson* in Gravity and ponderousness of Style; whose onely fault was, he was too elaborate; and had he mixt less erudition with his Playes, they had been more pleasant and delightful than they are. Comparing him with *Shakespear*, you shall see the difference betwixt Nature and Art; and with *Fletcher,* the difference betwixt Wit and Judgement: Wit being an exuberant thing, like *Nilus* [the Nile], never more commendable then when it overflowes; but Judgement a stayed and reposed thing, always containing it self within its bounds and limits.

—Richard Flecknoe, "A Short Discourse of
the English Stage," *Love's Kingdom,* 1664

JOHN DRYDEN (1668)

John Dryden (1631–1700), in his tribute to Shakespeare, furthers the characterization of him as a natural genius whose talent and sensibility were stronger than his art or power to govern that talent and sensibility. Dryden was a poet, dramatist, essayist, and critic whose own work was governed by his adherence to neoclassical rules of decorum. He adapted several of Shakespeare's plays, including *Antony and Cleopatra,* calling it *All for Love* (1677), conforming them to the taste of his time, of which he was a principal arbiter.

Shakespeare was the man who of all Modern, and perhaps Ancient Poets, had the largest and most comprehensive soul. All the Images of Nature were still present to him, and he drew them not laboriously, but luckily: when he describes any thing, you more than see it, you feel it too. Those who accuse him to have wanted learning, give him the greater commendation: he was naturally learn'd; he needed not the spectacles of Books to read Nature; he look'd inwards, and found her there. I cannot say he is every where alike; were he so, I should do him injury to compare him with the greatest of Mankind. He is many times flat, insipid; his Comick wit degenerating into clenches, his serious swelling into Bombast. But he is alwayes great, when some great occasion is presented to him: no man can say he ever had a fit subject for his wit, and did not then raise himself as high above the rest of Poets,

Quantum lenta solent, inter viburna cupressi. [*How the cypress tree towers above the swaying honeysuckles!*] The consideration of this made Mr. *Hales* of *Eaton* say, That there was no subject of which any Poet ever writ, but he would produce it much better done in *Shakespeare;* and however others are now generally prefer'd before him, yet the Age wherein he liv'd, which had contemporaries with him *Fletcher* and *Johnson,* never equall'd them to him in their esteem: And in the last Kings Court, when Ben's reputation was at highest, Sir *John Suckling*, and with him the greater part of the Courtiers, set our *Shakespeare* far above him.

—John Dryden, *An Essay of*
Dramatick Poesie, 1668

JOHN DRYDEN "DEFENSE OF THE EPILOGUE" (1672)

Dryden's criticisms can seem provincial after nearly three and a half centuries, as does his disdain for certain plays, such as *Measure for Measure, The Winter's Tale* (now highly esteemed) and the history plays, but each age privileges work that conforms to the dictates of its spirit and taste. The Restoration period, in which the English monarchy was reinstated after the regicide, the civil wars, and the Puritan Commonwealth, was concerned with hierarchy, order, formality, rules, manners, and propriety in governance, behavior, and literature.

[A]ll writers have their imperfections and failings. But I may safely conclude in the general, that our [Dryden's and writers who were his contemporaries] improprieties are less frequent, and less gross than theirs [the writers of Shakespeare's era]. One testimony of this is undeniable, that we are the first who have observed them. And certainly, to observe errors is a great step to the correcting of them. But malice and partiality set apart, let any man who understands English read diligently the works of Shakespeare and Fletcher; and I dare undertake that he will find in every page either some solecism of speech, or some notorious flaw in sense; and yet these men are reverenced when we are not forgiven. That their wit is great, and many times their expressions noble, envy itself cannot deny.... But the times were ignorant in which they lived. Poetry was then, if not in its infancy among us, at least not arrived to its vigour and maturity: witness the lameness of their plots; many of which ... were made up of some ridiculous, incoherent story, which in one play many times took up the business of an age. I suppose I need not name *Pericles, Prince of Tyre*, nor the historical plays of Shakespeare. Besides many of the rest, as *The Winter's Tale, Love's Labour Lost, Measure for Measure*, which were either grounded on impossibilities, or at least so meanly written that the comedy neither caused your mirth, nor the serious part your concernment.

—John Dryden, "Defense of the Epilogue,"
The Conquest of Granada, 1672

EDWARD PHILLIPS (1675)

Edward Phillips (1630–96), John Milton's nephew, was the author of *The Mysteries of Love and Eloquence, or The Arts of Wooing and Complimenting,* 1658. His *Theatrum Poetarum Anglicanorum* is a listing of the poets of England with brief commentaries. His picture of Shakespeare follows the accepted attitude of Shakespeare as an untutored and unpolished genius.

―――――――――――

William Shakespeare, the glory of the English Stage; whose nativity at *Stratford-upon-Avon* is the highest honour that town can boast of: from an *Actor* of Tragedies and Comedies he became a *Maker,* and such a *Maker,* that though some others may perhaps pretend to a more exact *decorum* and *economy,* especially in Tragedy; never any expressed a more lofty and tragic height; never any represented Nature more purely to the life: and where the polishments of Art are most wanting, as most probably his learning was not extraordinary, he pleaseth with a certain wild and native elegance: and in all his writings hath an unvulgar style; as well in his *Venus and Adonis,* his *Rape of Lucrece,* and other various poems, as in his dramatics.

—Edward Phillips, *Theatrum Poetarum Anglicanorum,* 1675

JOHN DRYDEN "PREFACE" (1679)

Dryden praises Shakespeare for his skill in the creation of characters. He faults him, however, for instances in which his use of language is bombastic or extravagant rather than sublime. While noting this trait in Shakespeare as a bad influence on the writers of his own age, Dryden blames them rather than Shakespeare for it. He attributes the fault in Shakespeare to the overflow of his genius and gives examples of Shakespeare's verse that display his sublimity and skill in creating complex characters.

―――――――――――

If Shakespeare be allowed, as I think he must, to have made his characters distinct, it will easily be inferred that he understood the nature of the passions: because it has been proved already that confused passions make undistinguishable characters: yet I cannot deny that he has his failings; but they are not so much in the passions themselves as in his manner of expression: he often obscures his meaning by his words, and sometimes makes it unintelligible. I will not say of so great a poet that he distinguished not the

blown puffy style from true sublimity; but I may venture to maintain that
the fury of his fancy often transported him beyond the bounds of judgment,
either in coining of new words and phrases, or racking words which were in
use into the violence of a catachresis. Tis not that I would explode the use of
metaphors from passions, for Longinus thinks 'em necessary to raise it: but to
use 'em at every word, to say nothing without a metaphor, a simile, an image,
or description, is I doubt to smell a little too strongly of the buskin. . . . But
Shakespeare does not often thus; for the passions in his scene between Brutus
and Cassius [in *Julius Caesar*] are extremely natural, the thoughts are such as
arise from the matter, the expression of 'em not viciously figurative. I cannot
leave this subject, before I do justice to that divine poet by giving you one of
his passionate descriptions: 'tis of Richard the Second when he was deposed,
and led in triumph through the streets of London by Henry of Bullingbrook:
the painting of it is so lively, and the words so moving, that I have scarce
read any thing comparable to it in any other language. Suppose you have
seen already the fortunate usurper passing through the crowd, and followed
by the shouts and acclamations of the people; and now behold King Richard
entering upon the scene: consider the wretchedness of his condition, and his
carriage in it; and refrain from pity if you can:

> As in a theatre, the eyes of men,
> After a well-graced actor leaves the stage,
> Are idly bent on him that enters next,
> Thinking his prattle to be tedious:
> Even so, or with much more contempt, men's eyes
> Did scowl on Richard: no man cried, God save him:
> No joyful tongue gave him his welcome home,
> But dust was thrown upon his sacred head,
> Which with such gentle sorrow he shook off,
> His face still combating with tears and smiles
> (The badges of his grief and patience),
> That had not God (for some strong purpose) steel'd
> The hearts of men, they must perforce have melted,
> And barbarism itself have pitied him.
>   [*Richard II*, V.ii.23–31]

To speak justly of this whole matter: 'tis neither height of thought that is
discommended, nor pathetic vehemence, nor any nobleness of expression in
its proper place; but 'tis a false measure of all these, something which is like
'em, and is not them . . . 'tis an extravagant thought, instead of a sublime one;

'tis roaring madness, instead of vehemence; and a sound of words, instead of sense. If Shakespeare were stripped of all the bombast in his passions, and dressed in the most vulgar words, we should find the beauties of his thoughts remaining; if his embroideries were burnt down, there would still be silver at the bottom of the melting-pot: but I fear (at least let me fear it for myself) that we who ape his sounding words have nothing of his thought, but are all outside; there is not so much as a dwarf within our giant's clothes. Therefore, let not Shakespeare suffer for our sakes; 'tis our fault, who succeed him in an age which is more refined, if we imitate him so ill that we copy his failings only, and make a virtue of that in our writings which in his was an imperfection.

For what remains, the excellency of that poet was, as I have said, in the more manly passions; Fletcher's in the softer: Shakespeare writ better betwixt man and man; Fletcher, betwixt man and woman: consequently, the one described friendship better; the other love: yet Shakespeare taught Fletcher to write love: and Juliet, and Desdemona, are originals. 'Tis true, the scholar had the softer soul; but the master had the kinder. Friendship is both a virtue and a passion essentially; love is a passion only in its nature, and is not a virtue but by accident: good nature makes friendship; but effeminacy love. Shakespeare had an universal mind, which comprehended all characters and passions; Fletcher a more confined and limited: for though he treated love in perfection, yet honour, ambition, revenge, and generally all the stronger passions, he either touched not, or not masterly. To conclude all, he was a limb of Shakespeare.

—John Dryden, "Preface" to
Troilus and Cressida (1679)

Nahum Tate "Preface" (1680)

Nahum Tate (1652–1715), appointed laureate of England in 1692, was a poet, librettist—for Henry Purcell's opera *Dido and Aeneas*—and the author of the adaptation of *King Lear* that was more commonly performed than Shakespeare's version for nearly two centuries. Tate, in the following extract, gently challenges what was, still in his time, the accepted notion that Shakespeare was not learned, as evidenced by his portrayal of historical characters. Tate concludes that, whether Shakespeare had closely studied the literature of the past or not, he was a great student of humanity as he observed it himself.

What I have already asserted concerning the necessity of Learning to make a compleat Poet, may seem inconsistent with my reverence for our *Shakespeare*.

Cujus amor semper mihi crescit in Horas.
[Virgil, *Bucolics*, tenth eclogue: For whom my love increases by the hour.]

I confess I cou'd never yet get a true account of his Learning, and am apt to think it more than Common Report allows him. I am sure he never touches on a Roman Story, but the Persons, the Passages, the Manners, the Circumstances, the Ceremonies, all are Roman. And what Relishes yet of a more exact Knowledge, you do not only see a Roman in his Heroe, but the particular Genius of the Man, without the least mistake of his Character, given him by their best Historians. You find his Antony in all the Defects and Excellencies of his Mind, a Souldier, a Reveller, Amorous, sometimes Rash, sometimes Considerate, with all the various Emotions of his Mind. His *Brutus* agen has all the Constancy, Gravity, Morality, Generosity, Imaginable, without the least Mixture of private Interest or Irregular Passion. He is true to him, even in the Imitation of his Oratory, the famous Speech which he makes him deliver, being exactly agreeable to his manner of expressing himself. . . .

But however it far'd with our Author for Book-Learning, 'tis evident that no man was better studied in Men and Things, the most useful Knowledge for a *Dramatic* Writer. He was a most diligent Spie upon Nature, trac'd her through her darkest Recesses, pictur'd her in her just Proportion and Colours; in which Variety 'tis impossible that all shou'd be equally pleasant, 'tis sufficient that all be proper.

Of his absolute Command of the Passions, and Mastery in distinguishing of Characters, you have a perfect Account in (Dryden's) most excellent Criticism before *Troilus and Cressida*: If any Man be a lover of *Shakespeare* and covet his Picture, there you have him drawn to the Life; but for the Eternal Plenty of his Wit on the same Theam, I will only detain you with a few instances of his Reflections on the Person, and Cruel Practices of *Richard* the Third. First of all *Henry* the Sixth bespeaks him in these words:

The owl shriekt at thy birth, an evil sign
Thy Mother felt more than a Mothers Pain,
And yet brought forth less than a Mothers hope;
An indigested Lump, &c.

Richard afterwards makes as bold with himself, where this is part of his Soliloque.

> Cheated of Feature by dissembling Nature,
> Deform'd, unfinish'd, sent before my time
> Into this breathing world, scarce half made up.

Queen *Margaret* cannot hear him mention'd without a new stream of Satyr.

> A Hell-hound that doth Hunt us all to Death,
> That Dog that had his Teeth before his Eyes,
> To worry Lambs and lap their gentle Blood, &c.

And never meets him but she presents him with his Picture;

> Hells black Intelligencer,
> Their Factour to buy *Souls* and send 'em thither.

And again,

> Thou elfish markt abortive Monster,
> Thou that wast seal'd in thy Nativity,
> The Slave of Nature and the son of Hell.
> Thou slander of thy heavy Mothers Womb.

With very many other Taunts to the same purpose.

—Nahum Tate, "Preface" to *The Loyal General*, 1680

NICHOLAS ROWE (1714)

Nicholas Rowe (1674–1718) was the first editor of Shakespeare's plays and his first biographer. It was Rowe who inserted act and scene divisions into the plays. Rowe was a dramatist and a poet. He was appointed England's poet laureate in 1715. Rowe's anecdotal account of Shakespeare's life precedes his edition of Shakespeare's plays.

Inaccurate as it is in many respects, and guided much by hearsay, Rowe's life of Shakespeare became the standard biography of Shakespeare for the eighteenth century, establishing the era's popular sense of Shakespeare as a man and an author. In this excerpt, Rowe surveys Shakespeare's work, pointing to its virtues in the depiction of character, in construction, in expression of thought and sentiment, and in the quality of Shakespeare's poetry. Rowe also explains and excuses those aspects of the plays, the frequent intermingling of comedy with tragedy, for example, that tended to offend the taste and decorum of his own era. Rowe repeats the idea, introduced by Ben Jonson, that Shakespeare was a raw poet of nature whose genius was uninstructed by art and learning. It is an opinion that will serve as an enduring point of contentious debate for Shakespeare's critics through the ages. Reinforcing the idea of Shakespeare's greatness, Rowe compares the action of *Hamlet* to the action in the great Greek tragedian Sophocles' *Electra*.

His Plays are properly to be distinguish'd only into Comedies and Tragedies. Those which are called Histories, and even some of his Comedies, are really Tragedies, with a run or mixture of Comedy amongst 'em. That way of Trage-Comedy was the common Mistake of that Age, and is indeed become so agreeable to the *English* Tast[e], that tho' the severer Critiques among us cannot bear it, yet the generality of our Audiences seem to be better pleas'd with it than with an exact Tragedy. *The Merry Wives of Windsor, The Comedy of Errors,* and *The Taming of the Shrew,* are all pure Comedy; the rest, however they are call'd, have something of both Kinds. 'Tis not very easie to determine which way of Writing he was most Excellent in. There is certainly a great deal of Entertainment in his Comical Humours; and tho' they did not then strike at all Ranks of People, as the Satyr of the present Age has taken the Liberty to do, yet there is a pleasing and a well-distinguish'd Variety in those Characters which he thought fit to meddle with. *Falstaff* is allow'd by every body to be a Master-piece; the Character is always well-sustain'd, tho' drawn out into the length of three Plays; and even the Account of his Death, given by his Old Landlady Mrs. *Quickly,* in the first Act of *Henry* V tho' it be extremely Natural, is yet as diverting as any Part of his Life. If there be any Fault in the Draught he has made of this lewd old Fellow, it is, that tho' he has made him a Thief, Lying, Cowardly, Vain-glorious, and in short every way Vicious, yet he has given him so much Wit as to make him almost too agreeable; and I don't know whether some People have not, in remembrance of the Diversion he had formerly afforded 'em, been sorry to see his Friend *Hal* use him so scurvily, when he comes to the Crown in the End of the Second Part of *Henry* the Fourth. Amongst other Extravagances, in *The Merry Wives of Windsor,* he has made him a Dear-stealer, that he might at the same time remember his *Warwickshire* Prosecutor, under the Name of Justice

Shallow; he has given him very near the same Coat of Arms which *Dugdale,* in his Antiquities of that County, describes for a Family there, and makes the Welsh Parson descant very pleasantly upon 'em. That whole Play is admirable; the Humours are various and well oppos'd; the main Design, which is to cure *Ford* of his unreasonable Jealousie, is extremely well conducted. *Falstaffs Billet-doux,* and Master Slender's

Ah! Sweet Ann *Page!*

are very good Expressions of Love in their Way. In *Twelfth-Night* there is something singularly Ridiculous and Pleasant in the fantastical Steward *Malvolio.* The Parasite and the Vainglorious in *Parolles,* in *All's Well That Ends Well,* is as good as any thing of that Kind in *Plautus* or *Terence. Petruchio,* in *The Taming of the Shrew,* is an uncommon Piece of Humour. The Conversation of *Benedick* and *Beatrice,* in *Much Ado about Nothing,* and of *Rosalind* in *As You Like It,* have much Wit and Sprightliness all along. His Clowns, without which Character there was hardly any Play writ in that Time, are all very entertaining: And, I believe, *Thersites* in *Troilus and Cressida,* and *Apemantus* in *Timon,* will be allow'd to be Master-Pieces of ill Nature, and satyrical Snarling. To these I might add, that incomparable Character of *Shylock* the *Jew,* in *The Merchant of Venice;* but tho' we have seen that Play Receiv'd and Acted as a Comedy, and the Part of the Jew perform'd by an Excellent Comedian, yet I cannot but think it was design'd Tragically by the Author. There appears in it such a deadly Spirit of Revenge, such a savage Fierceness and Fellness, and such a bloody designation of Cruelty and Mischief, as cannot agree either with the Stile or Characters of Comedy. The Play it self, take it all together, seems to me to be one of the most finish'd of any of *Shakespear's.* The Tale indeed, in that Part relating to the Caskets, and the extravagant and unusual kind of Bond given by *Antonio,* is a little too much remov'd from the Rules of Probability: But taking the Fact for granted, we must allow it to be very beautifully written. There is something in the Friendship of *Antonio* to *Bassanio* very Great, Generous and Tender. The whole fourth Act, supposing, as I said, the Fact to be probable, is extremely Fine. But there are two Passages that deserve a particular Notice. The first is, what *Portia* says in praise of Mercy [IV.i.182ff,]; and the other on the Power of Musick [V.i.55ff.]. The Melancholy of *Jaques,* in *As You Like It,* is as singular and odd as it is diverting. And if what *Horace* says

Difficile est proprie communia Dicere,
[It is difficult to say in your own way things that are common to everybody.]

'Twill be a hard Task for any one to go beyond him in the Description of the several Degrees and Ages of Man's Life, tho' the Thought be old, and common enough.

> All the World's a Stage,
> And all the Men and Women meerly Players; [II.vii.139ff.]

... His Images are indeed ev'ry where so lively, that the Thing he would represent stands full before you, and you possess ev'ry Part of it. I will venture to point out one more, which is, I think, as strong and as uncommon as any thing I ever saw; 'tis an Image of Patience. Speaking of a Maid in Love, he says,

> She never told her Love,
> But let Concealment, like a Worm i'th' Bud
> Feed on her Damask Cheek: She pin'd in Thought,
> And ... sate like *Patience* on a Monument,
> Smiling at *Grief.* [*Twelfth Night*, II.iv.114ff.]

What an Image is here given! and what a Task would it have been for the greatest Masters of *Greece* and *Rome* to have express'd the Passions design'd by this Sketch of Statuary? The Stile of his Comedy is, in general, Natural to the Characters, and easie in it self; and the Wit most commonly sprightly and pleasing, except in those places where he runs into Dogrel Rhymes, as in *The Comedy of Errors*, and a Passage or two in some other Plays. As for his Jingling sometimes, and playing upon Words, it was the common Vice of the Age he liv'd in: And if we find it in the Pulpit, made use of as an Ornament to the Sermons of some of the Gravest Divines of those Times; perhaps it may not be thought too light for the Stage.

But certainly the greatness of this Author's Genius does no where so much appear, as where he gives his Imagination an entire Loose, and raises his Fancy to a flight above Mankind and the Limits of the visible World. Such are his Attempts in *The Tempest, Midsummer-Night's Dream, Macbeth* and *Hamlet*. Of these, *The Tempest*, however it comes to be plac'd the first by the former Publishers of his Works, can never have been the first written by him: It seems to me as perfect in its Kind, as almost any thing we have of his. One may observe, that the Unities are kept here with an Exactness uncommon to the Liberties of his Writing: Tho' that was what, I suppose, he valu'd himself least upon, since his Excellencies were all of another Kind. I am very sensible that he does, in this Play, depart too much from that likeness to Truth which ought to be observ'd in these sort of Writings; yet he does it so very finely, that one is easily drawn in to have more Faith for his sake, than Reason does well allow of. His Magick has something in it very Solemn and very Poetical: And that extravagant Character of *Caliban* is mighty well sustain'd, shews a wonderful Invention in the Author, who could strike out such a particular wild Image, and is certainly one of the finest and most uncommon Grotesques that was ever seen. The Observation, which I have been inform'd three very great Men concurr'd in making upon this Part, was extremely just. *That* Shakespear *had not only found out a new Character in his* Caliban, *but had also devisd and adapted a new manner of Language for that Character.* Among the particular Beauties of this Piece, I think one may be allow'd to point out the Tale of *Prospero* in the First Act; his Speech to *Ferdinand* in the Fourth, upon the breaking up the Masque of *Juno* and *Ceres;* and that in the Fifth, where he dissolves his Charms, and resolves to break his Magick Rod.

It is the same Magick that raises the Fairies in *Midsummer Night's Dream,* the Witches in *Macbeth,* and the Ghost in *Hamlet,* with Thoughts and Language so proper to the Parts they sustain, and so peculiar to the Talent of this Writer. But of the two last of these Plays I shall have occasion to take notice, among the Tragedies of Mr. *Shakespear.* If one undertook to examine the greatest part of these by those Rules which are establish'd by *Aristotle,* and taken from the Model of the *Grecian* Stage, it would be no very hard Task to find a great many Faults: But as *Shakespear* liv'd under a kind of mere Light of Nature, and had never been made acquainted with the Regularity of those written Precepts, so it would be hard to judge him by a Law he knew nothing of. We are to consider him as a Man that liv'd in a State of almost universal License and Ignorance: There was no establish'd Judge, but every one took the liberty to Write according to the Dictates of his own Fancy. When one considers, that there is not one Play before him of a Reputation good enough to entitle it to an Appearance on the present Stage, it cannot but be a Matter of great Wonder that he should advance Dramatick Poetry so far as he did. The Fable is what is generally plac'd the first, among those that are reckon'd the constituent Parts of a Tragick or Heroick Poem; not, perhaps, as it is the most Difficult or Beautiful, but as it is the first properly to be thought of in the Contrivance and Course of the whole; and with the Fable ought to be consider'd, the fit Disposition, Order and Conduct of its several Parts. As it is not in this Province of the *Drama* that the Strength and Mastery of *Shakespear* lay, so I shall not undertake the tedious and ill-natur'd Trouble to point out the several Faults he was guilty of in it. His Tales were seldom invented, but rather taken either from true History, or Novels and Romances: And he commonly made use of 'em in that Order, with those Incidents, and that extent of Time in which he found 'em in the Authors from whence he borrow'd them. So *The Winter's Tale,* which is taken from an old Book, call'd, *The Delectable History of* Dorastus *and* Faunia, contains the space of sixteen or seventeen Years, and the Scene is sometimes laid in *Bohemia,* and sometimes in *Sicily,* according to the original Order of the Story. Almost all his Historical Plays comprehend a great length of Time, and very different and distinct Places: And in his *Antony and Cleopatra,* the Scene travels over the greatest Part of the *Roman* Empire. But in Recompence for his Carelessness in this Point, when he comes to another Part of the *Drama, The Manners of his Characters, in Acting or Speaking what is proper for them, and fit to be shown by the Poet,* he may be generally justify'd, and in very many places greatly commended. For those Plays which he has taken from the *English* or *Roman* History, let any Man compare 'em, and he will find the Character as exact in the Poet as the Historian. He seems indeed so far from proposing to himself any one Action for a Subject, that the Title very often tells you, 'tis *The Life of King* John, *King* Richard, &c. What can be more agreeable to the Idea our Historians give *of Henry* the Sixth, than the Picture *Shakespear* has drawn of him! His Manners are every where exactly the same with the Story; one finds him still describ'd with Simplicity, passive Sanctity, want of Courage, weakness of Mind, and easie Submission to the Governance of an imperious Wife, or prevailing Faction: Tho' at the same time the Poet does Justice to his good Qualities, and moves the Pity of his Audience for him, by showing him Pious, Disinterested, a Contemner of the Things of this World, and wholly resign'd to the severest Dispensations of God's Providence. There is a short Scene in the Second Part *of Henry* VI. which I cannot but think admirable in its Kind. Cardinal *Beaufort,* who had murder'd the Duke of *Gloucester,* is shewn in the last Agonies on his Death-Bed, with the good King praying over him. There is so much Terror in one, so much Tenderness and moving Piety in the other, as must touch any one who is capable either of Fear or Pity. In his *Henry* VIII. that Prince is drawn with that Greatness of Mind, and all those good Qualities which are attributed to him in any Account of his Reign. If his Faults are not shewn in an equal degree, and the Shades in this Picture do not bear a just Proportion to the Lights, it is not that the Artist wanted either Colours or Skill in the Disposition of 'em; but the truth, I believe, might be, that he forbore doing it out of regard to Queen *Elizabeth,* since it could have been no very great Respect to the Memory of his Mistress, to have expos'd some certain Parts of her Father's Life upon the Stage. He has dealt much more freely with the Minister of that Great King, and certainly nothing was ever more justly written, than the Character of Cardinal *Wolsey.* He has shewn him Tyrannical, Cruel, and Insolent in his Prosperity; and yet, by a wonderful Address, he makes his Fall and Ruin the Subject of general Compassion. The whole Man, with his Vices and Virtues, is finely and exactly describ'd in the second Scene of the fourth Act. The Distresses likewise of Queen *Katherine*, in this Play, are very movingly touch'd; and tho' the Art of the Poet has skreen'd King *Henry* from any gross Imputation of Injustice, yet one is inclin'd to wish, the Queen had met with a Fortune more worthy of her Birth and Virtue. Nor are the Manners, proper to the Persons represented, less justly observ'd, in those Characters taken from the *Roman* History; and of this, the Fierceness and Impatience of *Coriolanus*, his Courage and Disdain of the common People, the Virtue and Philosophical Temper of *Brutus*, and the irregular Greatness of Mind in M. *Antony*, are beautiful Proofs. For the two last especially, you find 'em exactly as they are describ'd by *Plutarch*, from whom certainly *Shakespear* copy'd 'em. He has indeed follow'd his Original pretty close, and taken in several little Incidents that might have been spar'd in a Play. But, as I hinted before, his Design seems most commonly rather to describe those great Men in the several Fortunes and Accidents of their Lives, than to take any single great Action, and form his Work simply upon that. However, there are some of his Pieces, where the Fable is founded upon one Action only. Such are more especially, *Romeo* and *Juliet, Hamlet*, and *Othello*. The Design in *Romeo* and *Juliet*, is plainly the Punishment of their two Families, for the unreasonable Feuds and Animosities that had been so long kept up between 'em, and occasion'd the Effusion of so much Blood. In the management of this Story, he has shewn something wonderfully Tender and Passionate in the Love-part, and very Pitiful in the Distress. *Hamlet* is founded on much the same Tale with the *Electra* of *Sophocles*. In each of 'em a young Prince is engag'd to Revenge the Death of his Father, their Mothers are equally Guilty, are both concern'd in the Murder of their Husbands, and are afterwards married to the Murderers. There is in the first Part of the *Greek* Tragedy, something very moving in the Grief of *Electra*; but as Mr. [André] D'Acier has observ'd, there is something very unnatural and shocking in the Manners he has given that Princess and *Orestes* in the latter Part. *Orestes* embrues his Hands in the Blood of his own Mother; and that barbarous Action is perform'd, tho' not immediately upon the Stage, yet so near, that the Audience hear *Clytemnestra* crying out to *Æghystus* for Help, and to her Son for Mercy: While *Electra*, her Daughter, and a Princess, both of them Characters that ought to have appear'd with more Decency, stands upon the Stage and encourages her Brother in the Parricide. What Horror does this not raise! *Clytemnestra* was a wicked Woman, and had deserv'd to Die; nay, in the truth of the Story, she was kill'd by her own Son; but to represent an Action of this Kind on the Stage, is certainly an Offence against those Rules of

Manners proper to the Persons that ought to be observ'd there. On the contrary, let us only look a little on the Conduct of *Shakespear*. *Hamlet* is represented with the same Piety towards his Father, and Resolution to Revenge his Death, as *Orestes*; he has the same Abhorrence for his Mother's Guilt, which, to provoke him the more, is heighten'd by Incest: But 'tis with wonderful Art and Justness of Judgment, that the Poet restrains him from doing Violence to his Mother. To prevent any thing of that Kind, he makes his Father's Ghost forbid that part of his Vengeance.

> *But howsoever thou pursu'st this Act,*
> *Taint not thy Mind; nor let thy Soul contrive*
> *Against thy Mother ought; leave her to Heav'n,*
> *And to those Thorns that in her Bosom lodge,*
> *To prick and sting her.* [I.v.84–88]

This is to distinguish rightly between *Horror* and *Terror*. The latter is a proper Passion of Tragedy, but the former ought always to be carefully avoided. And certainly no Dramatick Writer ever succeeded better in raising *Terror* in the Minds of an Audience than *Shakespear* has done. The whole Tragedy of *Macbeth*, but more especially the Scene where the King is murder'd, in the second Act, as well as this Play, is a noble Proof of that manly Spirit with which he writ; and both shew how powerful he was, in giving the strongest Motions to our Souls that they are capable of . . .

—Nicholas Rowe, from "Some Account of the Life, &c. of Mr. William Shakespear," *The Works of Mr. William Shakespear*, Volume 1, pp. xxvi–xxxv

Thomas Purney "Preface" (1717)

Cambridge-educated Thomas Purney (1695–ca. 1730) was the chaplain of Newgate Prison in London. Purney is concerned that the plays of the French playwrights Racine and Corneille are more generally esteemed than those by English playwrights such as Shakespeare and Otway. He attributes the difference to a combative attitude on the part of English critics and more particularly to the French playwrights' adherence to rules that Otway and Shakespeare, particularly, violate.

The rules he is referring to concern, primarily, the unities. According to Aristotle's theories, in a drama there must be a unity of time, place, and action. The play, thus, must consist of one continuous action that occurs in one place and over one period of time and that does not mix,

as Shakespeare often does, tragic and comic elements. A play such as
Shakespeare's *Antony and Cleopatra*, whose action hopscotches around
the globe and jumps over stretches of time, is an example of a play of his
that violates those rules.

What stops, I think, the general and universal Value for our Noblest Authors,
is, Their Faults are Faults against the common known mechanick Rules of
Poetry, as *Shakespear's* Blemishes and [Thomas] *Otway's* are against the Unity
of Place, and mixing Comedy throughout, and the like; which are obvious to
every one: Whereas how few can take the Beauties of *Shakespear,* especially
in the Sentiment, which is often indeed too clouded by the Language. The
French, on the other hand, if they can't come up to our noblest Beauties, they
learn from their *Criticks* to avoid our plainest Faults. And such Writings as
are neither good nor bad, acquire the widest and the easiest Characters for
good. But yet give me a dozen faults, if there's half as many noble Graces
blended with 'em, before a Poem that's as regular as insipid.

'Twere too long to draw a full comparison of *Shakespear,* and *Corneil* or
Racine. But give me leave to appeal a little to the Judgment of the Reader.

Suppose *Shakespear* had given *Corneil* the Character of a fierce Savage
Moor, such as *Othello;* Then told him, that to make his Temper chaufft and
fermented by Jealousie would show such a Character in the finest Light;
how think ye, even then, would *Corneil* have wrote the Play? We may guess
from his own Performances. Would he have given us to the Love between
the Savage and the tender Lady as *Shakespear* has done, Or have drawn a
charming Scene, where the honest old Love-Story would have been finely
talkt over by 'em. How would the subtilness of *Iago* have been shewn in
working up a furious *Warriour?* But worse yet, How would he have drawn
the Strugglings of a great Soul between the fiercest Hatred and the tendrest
Obligations to Love? I fear He must have told us, *Othello* had such Contests
in himself. How would he have described the roughest and most open
Soul in the World biting in his Wrath, and dissembling before the tender
Desdemona? I doubt a few Monologues would have supply'd the place of that.
In short, would not *Corneil* have shewn the Grief of the innocent, surpriz'd,
and gentle *Desdemona,* by a number of fine mournful Sentences between Her
and a Confidant? Ay; and such a Scene would have raised a world of pity in
a *French* Audience.

Such uncommon Characters as *Othello's, Macbeth's, Hamlet's, Jaffeir's,
Monomia's,* &c. are the only difficult one's to draw, the only One's that shine on
the Stage, and the only One's I could never find in the *French* writers of Tragedy.

But there is a Species in Writing which seems natural to our Nation, and inconsistent with the *French* Vivacity; It has never yet been consider'd by any *Critick*, yet constitutes the Soul and Essence of Tragedy. I call this kind, the GLOOMY: And it consists oftner in the general scene or view, than in the Sentiment. For Instance. *Romeo* is wandring among the Trees, and anon espy's a glimering light at *Julia's* Window. And in King LEAR; we see LEAR under a *Hovel* retired in the Night, while Thunder, Rain and Lightning were abroad.

All the Tragedys of *Shakespear* which we call good, abound with the *Gloomy*. And the want of it may be one great reason why *Corneil* and *Racine*, tho' they have so much Spirit in their Expressions, tho' their Thoughts are so rarely vitious, and their Compositions agreeable to the common and easiest Rules, yet want the Life, what shall I call it, the Vis TRAGICA [tragic power], which appears in the good Tragedies of *Shakespear* and *Otway*.

The *English*, as I said, alone have Genius's fitted for the *Gloomy*. But as we never abounded much with *Criticks*, never any has enter'd into the Nature of it. Tho' sure it deserves an entire Discourse. And so sweetly amusing it is to the Soul, That 'twill shine thro' Language even ridiculous; and alone support a Sentiment. As here,

Put out the Light, and then put out the Light.

The Language is a kind of *Pun*, and therefore to Minds that cannot take the Beauty of the Thought divested of it, the line appears absurd.

But the chief use of the GLOOMY (in the Sentiment) is in *Soliloquies;* and would a Tragick-Writer be at pains to be Master of it, he need never write, at least, a bad one. The *Soliloquies* of *Corneil* and *Racine*, are only such because the Person that utters 'em is alone. The Thoughts are exactly of the same kind with those in the *Dialogue* part of the *Play;* without *Solemnity* or *Gloominess*. But what a solemn Awe do *Shakespear's* draw over the Mind. . . .

But Instances were endless; especially out of *Shakespear*. Yet 'twas the finess, I believe, of his Imagination, that fill'd his Tragedys with the GLOOMY; rather then his having 'ere sate down and consider'd the *Pleasures of the Imagination*, and then the fittest Methods to excite those Pleasures. He felt his own Mind most agreeably amused, when'ere the Gloomy overspread it; and most wrote (as was *Ovid* and *Spencer's* way) what most delighted him to write.

The *French* Writers have this to offer for their wanting the Soul and Essence of Tragedy. They generally observe the Mechanick Rules, especially Unity of Place, which *Shakespear* alway break's thro'. Now the GLOOMY, as

I said, is oftnest rais'd by the general Scene or View; by leading the Mind into secret Apartments, and private Places.... But if a Play-Writer would preserve the Unity of Place, it must be by laying his Scene in a Thorough-Fare, in a Palace Yard, before the Door of an House, or in a publick Hall, as *Sophocles, Terence,* and the *French* Writers of Tragedy do. So that by cramping their Genius's by the observation of this Rule (which yet is necessary in the Representation) they cut themselves off from the chief Opportunity of introducing the Gloomy. And even in the Thought, the Gloomy cannot with advantage appear, unless held up and assisted by the Scene. How could this Thought have been supported in *Romeo* and *Juliet*

What light is that, which breaks from yonder Window, &c.

but by *Shakespear's* leading us, with Romeo, into the Secret Retirement of an *Orchat?*
Or what could have furnish'd *Othello's* Soliloquy,

It is the Cause; It is the Cause, my Soul:
Let me not name it to you, ye chast Stars, &c.

had not *Shakespear* lead us in into the Bed-Chamber of *Desdemona* in the Night-time?
In short, if 'tis otherwise introduced, it must be out of the Action; as the Account *of Macbeth's* Lady walking in her Sleep. And *Hotspur's* Wife's relation of his talking in his Sleep with the thoughts and contrivance of a Rebellion.

—Thomas Purney, "Preface" to *Pastorals;*
viz. The Bashful Swain, 1717

William Collins "An Epistle Addrest to Sir Thomas Hanmer on His Edition of Shakespear's Works" (1744)

William Collins (1721–59) was a poet whose verse tended more to resemble the poetry of the coming romanticism of the nineteenth century than the verse defined by the classical discipline of his own. A harbinger of the romantic sensibilities that would inform Shakespeare's work in the nineteenth century, in these lines Collins elevates Shakespeare's freedom over Ben Jonson's discipline and Shakespeare's capacity for rendering both the character of human passion and the nature of historical truth over John Fletcher's skill in representing the tender passions stereotypically attributed to women. Collins fashions the content of his own verse with examples from Shakespeare, focusing on *Richard III*, *Julius Caesar*, and, in a brilliantly succinct piece of character analysis, *Coriolanus*.

Too nicely *Johnson* knew the Critic's Part;
Nature in him was almost lost in Art.
Of softer Mold the gentle *Fletcher* came,
The next in Order, as the next in Name.
With pleas'd Attention 'midst his Scenes we find
Each glowing Thought, that warms the Female Mind;
Each melting Sigh, and ev'ry tender Tear,
The Lover's Wishes and the Virgin's Fear.
His ev'ry strain the *Smiles* and *Graces* own;
But stronger *Shakespear* felt for *Man* alone:
Drawn by his Pen, our ruder Passions stand
Th' unrival'd Picture of his early Hand
Yet He alone to ev'ry Scene could give
Th' Historian's Truth, and bid the Manners live.
Wak'd at his Call I view, with glad Surprize,
Majestic Forms of mighty Monarchs rise.
There *Henry's* Trumpets spread their loud Alarms,
And laurel'd Conquest waits her Hero's Arms.
Here gentler *Edward* claims a pitying Sigh,
Scarce born to Honours, and so soon to die!
Yet shall thy Throne, unhappy Infant, bring
No Beam of Comfort to the guilty King?
The Time shall come, when *Glo'ster's* Heart shall bleed
In Life's last Hours, with Horror of the Deed:
When dreary Visions shall at last present
Thy vengeful Image, in the midnight Tent:
Thy Hand unseen the secret Death shall bear,
Blunt the weak Sword, and break th' oppressive Spear.
Where'er we turn, by Fancy charm'd, we find
Some sweet Illusion of the cheated Mind.
Oft, wild of Wing, she calls the Soul to rove
With humbler Nature, in the rural Grove;

Where Swains contented own the quiet Scene,
And twilight Fairies tread the circled Green:
Drest by her Hand, the Woods and Vallies smile,
And Spring diffusive decks th' *enchanted Isle.*
O more than all in pow'rful Genius blest,
Come, take thine Empire o'er the willing Breast!
Whate'er the Wounds this youthful Heart shall feel,
Thy Songs support me, and thy Morals heal!
There ev'ry Thought the Poet's Warmth may raise,
There native Music dwells in all the Lays.
O might some Verse with happiest Skill persuade
Expressive Picture to adopt thine Aid!
What wond'rous Draughts might rise from ev'ry Page!
What other *Raphaels* Charm a distant Age!
Methinks ev'n now I view some free Design,
Where breathing Nature lives in ev'ry Line:
Chast and subdu'd the modest Lights decay,
Steal into Shade, and mildly melt away.
————And see, where Antony in Tears approv'd,
Guards the pale Relicks of the Chief he lov'd:
O'er the cold Corse the Warrior seems to bend,
Deep sunk in Grief, and mourns his murther'd Friend!
Still as they press, he calls on all around,
Lifts the torn Robe, and points the bleeding Wound.
But who is he, whose Brows exalted bear
A Wrath impatient, and a fiercer Air?
Awake to all that injur'd Worth can feel,
On his own *Rome* he turns th'avenging Steel.
Yet shall not War's insatiate Fury fall,
(So Heav'n ordains it) on the destin'd Wall.
See the fond Mother 'midst the plaintive Train
Hung on his Knees, and prostrate on the Plain!
Touch'd to the Soul, in vain he strives to hide
The Son's Affection, in the Roman's Pride:
O'er all the Man conflicting Passions rise,
Rage grasps the Sword, while *Pity* melts the Eyes.

—William Collins, "An Epistle Addrest
to Sir Thomas Hanmer on His Edition
of Shakespear's Works," 1744

David Hume "Appendix to the Reign of James I" (1754–62)

David Hume (1711–76) was a Scottish philosopher, historian, and economist. In his assessment of Shakespeare's work, he concludes that Shakespeare worked by instinct but was ignorant of art, that he was, consequently, something of a grotesque genius whose work is full of great and picturesque beauty and also great flaws.

If Shakspeare be considered as a MAN, born in a rude age, and educated in the lowest manner, without any instruction, either from the world or from books, he may be regarded as a prodigy; if represented as a poet, capable of furnishing a proper entertainment to a refined or intelligent audience, we must abate much of this eulogy. In his compositions, we regret that many irregularities, and even absurdities, should so frequently disfigure the animated and passionate scenes intermixed with them; and, at the same time, we perhaps admire the more those beauties, on account of their being surrounded with such deformities. A striking peculiarity of sentiment, adapted to a single character, he frequently hits, as it were, by inspiration; but a reasonable propriety of thought he cannot for any time uphold. Nervous and picturesque expressions as well as descriptions abound in him; but it is in vain we look either for purity or simplicity of diction. His total ignorance of all theatrical art and conduct, however material a defect, yet, as it affects the spectator rather than the reader, we can more easily excuse, than that want of taste which often prevails in his productions, and which gives way only by intervals to the irradiations of genius. A great and fertile genius he certainly possessed, and one enriched equally with a tragic and comic vein; but he ought to be cited as a proof, how dangerous it is to rely on these advantages alone for attaining an excellence in the finer arts. And there may even remain a suspicion that we overrate, if possible, the greatness of his genius; in the same manner as bodies often appear more gigantic, on account of their being disproportioned and misshapen.

—David Hume, "Appendix to the Reign of James I," *History of England*, 1754–62

Edward Young (1759)

Like William Collins, poet and clergyman Edward Young (1681–1765) had more of a romantic than a classical sensibility valuing the importance of individual genius over formal compliance with rules of composition and imitation of great literary models. Rather than a liability, he regards Shakespeare's putative lack of learning as an asset, arguing that heavy classical learning diminished Ben Jonson's power and that Shakespeare's innate genius was to know nature and humankind to their very depths.

Shakspeare mingled no water with his wine, lowered his genius by no vapid imitation. Shakspeare gave us a Shakspeare; nor could the first in ancient fame have given us more. Shakspeare is not their son, but brother; their equal, and that in spite of all his faults. Think you this too bold? Consider, in those ancients what is it the world admires? Not the fewness of their faults, but the number and brightness of their beauties; and if Shakspeare is their equal (as he doubtless is) in that which in them is admired, then is Shakspeare as great as they; and not impotence, but some other cause, must be charged with his defects. When we are setting these great men in competition, what but the comparative size of their genius is the subject of our inquiry? And a giant loses nothing of his size, though he should chance to trip in his race. But it is a compliment to those heroes of antiquity to suppose Shakspeare their equal only in dramatic powers; therefore, though his faults had been greater, the scale would still turn in his favour. There is at least as much genius on the British as on the Grecian stage. . . .

Jonson, in the serious drama, is as much an imitator, as Shakspeare is an original. He was very learned, as Samson was very strong, to his own hurt. Blind to the nature of tragedy, he pulled down all antiquity on his head, and buried himself under it. We see nothing of Jonson, nor indeed of his admired (but also murdered) ancients; for what shone in the historian is a cloud on the poet; and *Catiline* might have been a good play, if Sallust had never writ.

Who knows whether Shakspeare might not have thought less, if he had read more? Who knows if he might not have laboured under the load of Jonson's learning. . . . His mighty genius, indeed, through the most mountainous oppression would have breathed out some of his inextinguishable fire; yet, possibly, he might not have risen up into that giant, that much more than common man, at which we now gaze with amazement and delight. Perhaps he was as learned as his dramatic province required; for, whatever other learning he wanted, he was master of two books, unknown to many of the profoundly read, though books which the last conflagration alone can destroy,—the book of nature, and that of man. These he had by heart, and has transcribed many admirable pages of them into his immortal works. These are the fountain-head, whence the Castalian streams of original composition flow; and these are often mudded by other waters,—though waters, in their distinct channel, most wholesome and pure: as two chemical liquors, separately clear as crystal, grow foul by mixture, and offend the sight. So that he had not only as much learning as his dramatic province required, but perhaps, as it could safely bear.

—Edward Young, *Conjectures on Original Composition*, 1759

HENRY HOME, LORD KAMES (1763)

Lord Kames (1696–1782) was a Scottish philosopher and jurist. He argues that Shakespeare's language presents the passions of his characters with fidelity to the nature of the passion expressed. Although he found the way Shakespeare handled dialogue weak in the early plays, in the later ones, his skill in that grew considerably.

Shakspeare is superior to all other writers in delineating passion. It is difficult to say in what part he most excels, whether in moulding every passion to peculiarity of character, in discovering the sentiments that proceed from various tones of passion, or in expressing properly every different sentiment: he disgusts not his reader with general declamation and unmeaning words, too common in other writers: his sentiments are adjusted to the peculiar character and circumstances of the speaker: and the propriety is no less perfect between his sentiments and his diction. That this is no exaggeration, will be evident to every one of taste, upon comparing Shakspeare with other writers in similar passages. If upon any occasion he falls below himself, it is in those scenes where passion enters not: by endeavoring in that case to raise his dialogue above the style of ordinary conversation, he sometimes deviates into intricate thought and obscure expression: sometimes, to throw his language out of the familiar, he employs rhyme. But may it not, in some measure, excuse Shakspeare, I shall not say his works, that he had no pattern, in his own or in any living language, of dialogue fitted for the theatre? At the same time, it ought not to escape observation, that the stream clears in its progress, and that in his later plays he has attained the purity and perfection of dialogue; an observation that, with greater certainty than tradition, will direct us to arrange his plays in the order of time. This ought to be considered by those who rigidly exaggerate every blemish of the finest genius for the drama ever the world enjoyed: they ought also for their own sake to consider, that it is easier to discover his blemishes, which lie generally at the surface, than his beauties, which can be truly relished by those only who dive deep into human nature. One thing must be evident to the meanest capacity, that wherever passion is to be displayed, nature shows itself mighty in him, and is conspicuous by the most delicate propriety of sentiment and expression.

—Henry Home, Lord Kames, *Elements of Criticism*, 1763, chapter 17

SAMUEL JOHNSON (1765)

Samuel Johnson (1709–84) was a critic, moralist, biographer, editor, lexicographer, poet, novelist, and a conversationalist whose life, manner, and wit are preserved in James Boswell's *Life of Johnson* (1791) as well as in his own work. He is often regarded as the pre-eminent man of eighteenth-century London and the foremost literary critic to have written in English. His discussion of Shakespeare in his annotated edition of Shakespeare's plays is informed by his common sense, his contempt of cant, his concern with the influence of history on creativity, his belief in the need for art to be morally instructive, and his copious learning. Johnson's vision of Shakespeare is of a poet more blessed by nature in his powers of observation and expression than by art. Johnson sees Shakespeare as the child of an age in which culture itself was still in its childhood, as a poet less concerned with following accepted rules of composition or of keeping such genres as comedy and tragedy separated in a single work than with probing the depths of human nature and character. Johnson, however, does not only excuse Shakespeare's failure to adhere to such standards as the unities, he challenges the validity of the unities, asserting, for example, that in the playhouse the audience is perfectly capable of negotiating time and space imaginatively should the playwright require it. Johnson is also not blind to what he considers faults in Shakespeare despite his regard for him as a towering figure. Johnson considers Shakespeare stronger in comedy than in tragedy. He is put off by Shakespeare's punning and regards him as lacking in the moral concern to instruct his audience in virtue by choosing rather to please them. Johnson asserts that Shakespeare's diction can be pompous, tangled up, or cold, and that his plots are loose, his endings hasty, and his historical work full of anachronisms.

[B]ecause human judgment, though it be gradually gaining upon certainty, never becomes infallible; and approbation, though long continued, may yet be only the approbation of prejudice or fashion; it is proper to inquire, by what peculiarities of excellence Shakespeare has gained and kept the favour of his countrymen.

Nothing can please many, and please long, but just representations of general nature. Particular manners can be known to few, and therefore few only can judge how nearly they are copied. The irregular combinations of fanciful invention may delight a-while, by that novelty of which the common satiety of life sends us all in quest; but the pleasures of sudden wonder are soon exhausted, and the mind can only repose on the stability of truth.

Shakespeare is above all writers, at least above all modern writers, the poet of nature; the poet that holds up to his readers a faithful mirrour of manners and of life. His characters are not modified by the customs of particular places, unpractised by the rest of the world; by the peculiarities of studies or professions, which can operate but upon small numbers; or by the accidents of transient fashions or temporary opinions: they are the genuine progeny of common humanity, such as the world will always supply, and observation will always find. His persons act and speak by the influence of those general passions and principles by which all minds are agitated, and the whole system of life is continued in motion. In the writings of other poets a character is too often an individual, in those of Shakespeare it is commonly a species.

It is from this wide extension of design that so much instruction is derived. It is this which fills the plays of Shakespeare with practical axioms and domestick wisdom. It was said of Euripides, that every verse was a precept; and it may be said of Shakespeare, that from his works may be collected a system of civil and economical prudence. Yet his real power is not shewn in the splendour of particular passages, but by the progress of his fable, and the tenour of his dialogue; and he that tries to recommend him by select quotations, will succeed like the pedant in Hierocles, who, when he offered his house to sale, carried a brick in his pocket as a specimen.

It will not easily be imagined how much Shakespeare excells in accommodating his sentiments to real life, but by comparing him with other authours. It was observed of the ancient schools of declamation, that the more diligently they were frequented, the more was the student disqualified for the world, because he found nothing there which he should ever meet in any other place. The same remark may be applied to every stage but that of Shakespeare. The theatre, when it is under any other direction, is peopled by such characters as were never seen, conversing in a language which was never heard, upon topicks which will never arise in the commerce of mankind. But the dialogue of this authour is often so evidently determined by the incident which produces it, and is pursued with so much ease and simplicity, that it seems scarcely to claim the merit of fiction, but to have been gleaned by diligent selection out of common conversation, and common occurrences.

Upon every other stage the universal agent is love, by whose power all good and evil is distributed, and every action quickened or retarded. To bring a lover, a lady and a rival into the fable; to entangle them in contradictory obligations, perplex them with oppositions of interest, and harrass them with violence of desires inconsistent with each other; to make them meet in rapture and part in agony; to fill their mouths with hyperbolical joy and outrageous sorrow; to distress them as nothing human ever was distressed; to deliver them as nothing human ever was delivered, is the business of a modern dramatist. For this, probability is violated, life is misrepresented, and language is depraved. But love is only one of many passions, and as it has no great influence upon the sum of life, it has little operation in the dramas of a poet, who caught his ideas from the living world, and exhibited only what he saw before him. He knew, that any other passion, as it was regular or exorbitant, was a cause of happiness or calamity.

Characters thus ample and general were not easily discriminated and preserved, yet perhaps no poet ever kept his personages more distinct from each other. I will not say with Pope, that every speech may be assigned to the proper speaker, because many speeches there are which have nothing characteristical; but perhaps, though some may be equally adapted to every person, it will be difficult to find any that can be properly transferred from the present possessor to another claimant. The choice is right, when there is reason for choice.

Other dramatists can only gain attention by hyperbolical or aggravated characters, by fabulous and unexampled excellence or depravity, as the writers of barbarous romances invigorated the reader by a giant and a dwarf; and he that should form his expectations of human affairs from the play, or from the tale, would be equally deceived. Shakespeare has no heroes; his scenes are occupied only by men, who act and speak as the reader thinks that he should himself have spoken or acted on the same occasion: Even where the agency is supernatural the dialogue is level with life. Other writers disguise the most natural passions and most frequent incidents; so that he who contemplates them in the book will not know them in the world: Shakespeare approximates the remote, and familiarizes the wonderful; the event which he represents will not happen, but if it were possible, its effects would probably be such as he has assigned; and it may be said, that he has not only shewn human nature as it acts in real exigences, but as it would be found in trials, to which it cannot be exposed.

This therefore is the praise of Shakespeare, that his drama is the mirrour of life; that he who has mazed his imagination, in following the phantoms which other writers raise up before him, may here be cured of his delirious extasies, by reading human sentiments in human language; by scenes from which a hermit may estimate the transactions of the world, and a confessor predict the progress of the passions.

His adherence to general nature has exposed him to the censure of criticks, who form their judgments upon narrower principles. [John] Dennis and [Thomas] Rhymer think his Romans not sufficiently Roman; and Voltaire censures his kings as not completely royal. Dennis is offended, that Menenius, a senator of Rome [in *Coriolanus*], should play the buffoon; and Voltaire perhaps thinks decency violated when the Danish usurper [Claudius in *Hamlet*] is represented as a drunkard. But Shakespeare always makes nature predominate over accident; and if he preserves the essential character, is not very careful of distinctions superinduced and adventitious. His story requires Romans or kings, but he thinks only on men. He knew that Rome, like every other city, had men of all dispositions; and wanting a buffoon, he went into the senate-house for that which the senate-house would certainly have afforded him. He was inclined to shew an usurper and a murderer not only odious but despicable; he therefore added drunkenness to his other qualities, knowing that kings love wine like other men, and that wine exerts its natural power upon kings. These are the petty cavils of petty minds; a poet overlooks the casual distinction of country and condition, as a painter, satisfied with the figure, neglects the drapery.

The censure which he has incurred by mixing comick and tragick scenes, as it extends to all his works, deserves more consideration. Let the fact be first stated, and then examined.

Shakespeare's plays are not in the rigorous and critical sense either tragedies or comedies, but compositions of a distinct kind; exhibiting the real state of sublunary nature, which partakes of good and evil, joy and sorrow, mingled with endless variety of proportion and innumerable modes of combination; and expressing the course of the world, in which the loss of one is the gain of another; in which, at the same time, the reveller is hasting to his wine, and the mourner burying his friend; in which the malignity of one is sometimes defeated by the frolick of another; and many mischiefs and many benefits are done and hindered without design.

Out of this chaos of mingled purposes and casualties the ancient poets, according to the laws which custom had prescribed, selected some the crimes of men, and some their absurdities; some the momentous vicissitudes of life, and some the lighter occurrences; some the terrours of distress, and some the gayeties of prosperity. Thus rose the two modes of imitation, known by the names of tragedy and comedy, compositions intended to promote different ends by contrary means, and considered as so little allied, that I do not recollect among the Greeks or Romans a single writer who attempted both.

Shakespeare has united the powers of exciting laughter and sorrow not only in one mind but in one composition. Almost all his plays are divided between serious and ludicrous characters, and, in the successive evolutions of the design, sometimes produce seriousness and sorrow, and sometimes levity and laughter.

That this is a practice contrary to the rules of criticism will be readily allowed; but there is always an appeal open from criticism to nature. The end of writing is to instruct; the end of poetry is to instruct by pleasing. That the mingled drama may convey all the instruction of tragedy or comedy cannot be denied, because it includes both in its alternations of exhibition, and approaches nearer than either to the appearance of life, by shewing how great machinations and slender designs may promote or obviate one another, and the high and the low co-operate in the general system by unavoidable concatenation.

It is objected, that by this change of scenes the passions are interrupted in their progression, and that the principal event, being not advanced by a due graduation of preparatory incidents, wants at last the power to move, which constitutes the perfection of dramatick poetry. This reasoning is so specious, that it is received as true even by those who in daily experience feel it to be false. The interchanges of mingled scenes seldom fail to produce the intended vicissitudes of passion. Fiction cannot move so much, but that the attention may be easily transferred; and though it must be allowed that pleasing melancholy be sometimes interrupted by unwelcome levity, yet let it be considered likewise, that melancholy is often not pleasing, and that the disturbance of one man may be the relief of another; that different auditors have different habitudes; and that, upon the whole, all pleasure consists in variety.

The players, who in their edition divided our authour's works into comedies, histories, and tragedies, seem not to have distinguished the three kinds, by any very exact or definite ideas.

An action which ended happily to the principal persons, however serious or distressful through its intermediate incidents, in their opinion constituted a comedy. This idea of a comedy continued long amongst us, and plays were written, which, by changing the catastrophe, were tragedies to-day and comedies to-morrow.

Tragedy was not in those times a poem of more general dignity or elevation than comedy; it required only a calamitous conclusion, with which the common criticism of that age was satisfied, whatever lighter pleasure it afforded in its progress.

History was a series of actions, with no other than chronological succession, independent on each other, and without any tendency to introduce or regulate the conclusion. It is not always very nicely distinguished from tragedy. There is not much nearer approach to unity of action in the tragedy of *Antony and Cleopatra*, than in the history of *Richard the Second*. But a history might be continued through many plays; as it had no plan, it had no limits.

Through all these denominations of the drama, Shakespeare's mode of composition is the same; an interchange of seriousness and merriment, by which the mind is softened at one time, and exhilarated at another. But whatever be his purpose, whether to gladden or depress, or to conduct the story, without vehemence or emotion, through tracts of easy and familiar dialogue, he never fails to attain his purpose; as he commands us, we laugh or mourn, or sit silent with quiet expectation, in tranquillity without indifference.

When Shakespeare's plan is understood, most of the criticisms of Rhymer and Voltaire vanish away. The play of *Hamlet* is opened, without impropriety, by two sentinels; Iago bellows at Brabantio's window, without injury to the scheme of the play, though in terms which a modern audience would not easily endure; the character of Polonius is seasonable and useful, and the Grave-diggers themselves may be heard with applause.

Shakespeare engaged in dramatick poetry with the world open before him; the rules of the ancients were yet known to few; the publick judgment was unformed; he had no example of such fame as might force him upon imitation, nor criticks of such authority as might restrain his extravagance: He therefore indulged his natural disposition, and his disposition, as Rhymer has remarked, led him to comedy. In tragedy he often writes with great appearance of toil and study, what is written at last with little felicity; but in his comick scenes, he seems to produce without labour, what no labour can improve. In tragedy he is always struggling after some occasion to be comick, but in comedy he seems to repose, or to luxuriate, as in a mode of thinking congenial to his nature. In his tragick scenes there is always something wanting, but his comedy often surpasses expectation or desire. His comedy pleases by the thoughts and the language, and his tragedy for the greater part by incident and action. His tragedy seems to be skill, his comedy to be instinct.

The force of his comick scenes has suffered little diminution from the changes made by a century and a half, in manners or in words. As his personages act upon principles arising from genuine passion, very little modified by particular forms, their pleasures and vexations are communicable to all times and to all places; they are natural, and therefore durable; the adventitious peculiarities of personal habits, are only superficial dies, bright and pleasing for a little while, yet soon fading to a dim tinct, without any remains of former lustre; but the discriminations of true passion are the colours of nature; they pervade the whole mass, and can only perish with the body that exhibits them. The accidental compositions of heterogeneous modes are dissolved by the chance which combined them; but the uniform simplicity of primitive qualities neither admits increase, nor suffers decay. The sand heaped by one flood is scattered by another, but the rock always continues in its place. The stream of time, which is continually washing the dissoluble fabricks of other poets, passes without injury by the adamant of Shakespeare.

If there be, what I believe there is, in every nation, a stile which never becomes obsolete, a certain mode of phraseology so consonant and congenial to the analogy and principles of its respective language as to remain settled and unaltered; this stile is probably to be sought in the common intercourse of life, among those who speak only to be understood, without ambition of elegance. The polite are always catching modish innovations, and the learned depart from established forms of speech, in hope of finding or making better; those who wish for distinction forsake the vulgar, when the vulgar is right; but there is a conversation above grossness and below refinement, where propriety resides, and where this poet seems to have gathered his comick dialogue. He is therefore more agreeable to the ears of the present age than any other authour equally remote, and among his other excellencies deserves to be studied as one of the original masters of our language.

These observations are to be considered not as unexceptionably constant, but as containing general and predominant truth. Shakespeare's familiar dialogue is affirmed to be smooth and clear, yet not wholly without ruggedness or difficulty; as a country may be eminently fruitful, though it has spots unfit for cultivation: His characters are praised as natural, though their sentiments are sometimes forced, and their actions improbable; as the earth upon the whole is spherical, though its surface is varied with protuberances and cavities.

Shakespeare with his excellencies has likewise faults, and faults sufficient to obscure and overwhelm any other merit. I shall shew them in the proportion in which they appear to me, without envious malignity or superstitious veneration. No question can be more innocently discussed than a dead poet's pretensions to renown; and little regard is due to that bigotry which sets candour higher than truth.

His first defect is that to which may be imputed most of the evil in books or in men. He sacrifices virtue to convenience, and is so much more careful to please than to instruct, that he seems to write without any moral purpose. From his writings indeed a system of social duty may be selected, for he that thinks reasonably must think morally; but his precepts and axioms drop casually from him; he makes no just distribution of good or evil, nor is always careful to shew in the virtuous a disapprobation of the wicked; he carries his persons indifferently through right and wrong, and at the close dismisses them without further care, and leaves their examples to operate by chance. This fault the barbarity of his age cannot extenuate; for it is always a writer's duty to make the world better, and justice is a virtue independent on time or place.

The plots are often so loosely formed, that a very slight consideration may improve them, and so carelessly pursued, that he seems not always fully to comprehend his own design.

He omits opportunities of instructing or delighting which the train of his story seems to force upon him, and apparently rejects those exhibitions which would be more affecting, for the sake of those which are more easy.

It may be observed, that in many of his plays the latter part is evidently neglected. When he found himself near the end of his work, and in view of his reward, he shortened the labour, to snatch the profit. He therefore remits his efforts where he should most vigorously exert them, and his catastrophe is improbably produced or imperfectly represented.

He had no regard to distinction of time or place, but gives to one age or nation, without scruple, the customs, institutions, and opinions of another, at the expence not only of likelihood, but of possibility. These faults Pope has endeavoured, with more zeal than judgment, to transfer to his imagined interpolators. We need not wonder to find Hector [in *Troilus and Cressida*] quoting Aristotle, when we see the loves of Theseus and Hippolyta [in *A Midsummer Night's Dream*] combined with the Gothick mythology of fairies. Shakespeare, indeed, was not the only violator of chronology, for in the same age [Sir Philip] Sidney, who wanted not the advantages of learning, has, in his *Arcadia*, confounded the pastoral with the feudal times, the days of innocence, quiet and security, with those of turbulence, violence and adventure.

In his comick scenes he is seldom very successful, when he engages his characters in reciprocations of smartness and contests of sarcasm; their jests are commonly gross, and their pleasantry licentious; neither his gentlemen nor his ladies have much delicacy, nor are sufficiently distinguished from his clowns by any appearance of refined manners. Whether he represented the real conversation of his time is not easy to determine; the reign of Elizabeth is commonly supposed to have been a time of stateliness, formality and reserve, yet perhaps the relaxations of that severity were not very elegant. There must, however, have been always some modes of gayety preferable to others, and a writer ought to chuse the best.

In tragedy his performance seems constantly to be worse, as his labour is more. The effusions of passion which exigence forces out are for the most part striking and energetick; but whenever he solicits his invention, or strains his faculties, the offspring of his throes is tumour, meanness, tediousness, and obscurity.

In narration he affects a disproportionate pomp of diction and a wearisome train of circumlocution, and tells the incident imperfectly in many words, which might have been more plainly delivered in few. Narration in dramatick poetry is naturally tedious, as it is unanimated and inactive, and obstructs the progress of the action; it should therefore always be rapid, and enlivened by frequent interruption. Shakespeare found it an encumbrance, and instead of lightening it by brevity, endeavoured to recommend it by dignity and splendour.

His declamations or set speeches are commonly cold and weak, for his power was the power of nature; when he endeavoured, like other tragick writers, to catch opportunities of amplification, and instead of inquiring what the occasion demanded, to show how much his stores of knowledge could supply, he seldom escapes without the pity or resentment of his reader.

It is incident to him to be now and then entangled with an unwieldy sentiment, which he cannot well express, and will not reject; he struggles with it a while, and if it continues stubborn, comprises it in words such as occur, and leaves it to be disentangled and evolved by those who have more leisure to bestow upon it.

Not that always where the language is intricate the thought is subtle, or the image always great where the line is bulky; the equality of words to things is very often neglected, and trivial sentiments and vulgar ideas disappoint the attention, to which they are recommended by sonorous epithets and swelling figures.

But the admirers of this great poet have most reason to complain when he approaches nearest to his highest excellence, and seems fully resolved to sink them in dejection, and mollify them with tender emotions by the fall of greatness, the danger of innocence, or the crosses of love. What he does best, he soon ceases to do. He is not long soft and pathetick without some idle conceit, or contemptible equivocation. He no sooner begins to move, than he counteracts himself; and terrour and pity, as they are rising in the mind, are checked and blasted by sudden frigidity.

A quibble is to Shakespeare, what luminous vapours are to the traveller; he follows it at all adventures, it is sure to lead him out of his way, and sure to engulf him in the mire. It has some malignant power over his mind, and its fascinations are irresistible. Whatever be the dignity or profundity of his disquisition, whether he be enlarging knowledge or exalting affection, whether he be amusing attention with incidents, or enchaining it in suspense, let but a quibble spring up before him, and he leaves his work unfinished. A quibble is the golden apple for which he will always turn aside from his career, or stoop from his elevation. A quibble, poor and barren as it is, gave him such delight, that he was content to purchase it, by the sacrifice of reason, propriety and truth. A quibble was to him the fatal Cleopatra for which he lost the world, and was content to lose it.

It will be thought strange, that, in enumerating the defects of this writer, I have not yet mentioned his neglect of the unities; his violation of those laws which have been instituted and established by the joint authority of poets and of criticks.

For his other deviations from the art of writing, I resign him to critical justice, without making any other demand in his favour, than that which must be indulged to all human excellence; that his virtues be rated with his failings: But, from the censure which this irregularity may bring upon him, I shall, with due reverence to that learning which I must oppose, adventure to try how I can defend him.

His histories, being neither tragedies nor comedies, are not subject to any of their laws; nothing more is necessary to all the praise which they expect, than that the changes of action be so prepared as to be understood, that the incidents be various and affecting, and the characters consistent, natural and distinct. No other unity is intended, and therefore none is to be sought.

In his other works he has well enough preserved the unity of action. He has not, indeed, an intrigue regularly perplexed and regularly unravelled; he does not endeavour to hide his design only to discover it, for this is seldom the order of real events, and Shakespeare is the poet of nature: But his plan has commonly what Aristotle requires, a beginning, a middle, and an end; one event is concatenated with another, and the conclusion follows by easy consequence. There are perhaps some incidents that might be spared, as in other poets there is much talk that only fills up time upon the stage; but the general system makes gradual advances, and the end of the play is the end of expectation.

To the unities of time and place he has shewn no regard, and perhaps a nearer view of the principles on which they stand will diminish their value, and withdraw from them the veneration which, from the time of Corneille, they have very generally received, by discovering that they have given more trouble to the poet, than pleasure to the auditor.

The necessity of observing the unities of time and place arises from the supposed necessity of making the drama credible. The criticks hold it impossible, that an action of months or years can be possibly believed to pass in three hours; or that the spectator can suppose himself to sit in the theatre, while ambassadors go and return between distant kings, while armies are levied and towns besieged, while an exile wanders and returns, or till he whom they saw courting his mistress, shall lament the untimely fall of his son. The mind revolts from evident falsehood, and fiction loses its force when it departs from the resemblance of reality.

From the narrow limitation of time necessarily arises the contraction of place. The spectator, who knows that he saw the first act at Alexandria, cannot suppose that he sees the next at Rome, at a distance to which not the dragons of Medea could, in so short a time, have transported him; he knows with certainty that he has not changed his place; and he knows that place cannot change itself; that what was a house cannot become a plain; that what was Thebes can never be Persepolis.

Such is the triumphant language with which a critick exults over the misery of an irregular poet, and exults commonly without resistance or reply. It is time therefore to tell him, by the authority of Shakespeare, that he assumes, as an unquestionable principle, a position, which, while his breath is forming it into words, his understanding pronounces to be false. It is false, that any representation is mistaken for reality; that any dramatick fable in its materiality was ever credible, or, for a single moment, was ever credited.

The objection arising from the impossibility of passing the first hour at Alexandria, and the next at Rome, supposes, that when the play opens the spectator really imagines himself at Alexandria, and believes that his walk to the theatre has been a voyage to Egypt, and that he lives in the days of Antony and Cleopatra. Surely he that imagines this may imagine more. He that can take the stage at one time for the palace of the Ptolemies, may take it in half an hour for the promontory of Actium. Delusion, if delusion be admitted, has no certain limitation; if the spectator can be once persuaded, that his old acquaintance are Alexander and Caesar, that a room illuminated with candles is the plain of Pharsalia, or the bank of Granicus, he is in a state of elevation above the reach of reason, or of truth, and from the heights of empyrean poetry, may despise the circumscriptions of terrestrial nature. There is no reason why a mind thus wandering in extasy should count the clock, or why an hour should not be a century in that calenture of the brains that can make the stage a field.

The truth is, that the spectators are always in their senses, and know, from the first act to the last, that the stage is only a stage, and that the players are only players. They come to hear a certain number of lines recited with just gesture and elegant modulation. The lines relate to some action, and an action must be in some place; but the different actions that compleat a story may be in places very remote from each other; and where is the absurdity of allowing that space to represent first Athens, and then Sicily, which was always known to be neither Sicily nor Athens, but a modern theatre.

By supposition, as place is introduced, time may be extended; the time required by the fable elapses for the most part between the acts; for, of so much of the action as is represented, the real and poetical duration is the same. If, in the first act, preparations for war against Mithridates are represented to be made in Rome, the event of the war may, without absurdity, be represented, in the catastrophe, as happening in Pontus; we know that there is neither war, nor preparation for war; we know that we are neither in Rome nor Pontus; that neither Mithridates [132–63 B.C., king of Pontus, now northeastern Turkey] nor Lucullus [Roman general ca. 118 B.C.] are before us. The drama exhibits successive imitations of successive actions, and why may not the second imitation represent an action that happened years after the first; if it be so connected with it, that nothing but time can be supposed to intervene. Time is, of all modes of existence, most obsequious to the imagination, a lapse of years is as easily conceived as a passage of hours. In contemplation we easily contract the time of real actions, and therefore willingly permit it to be contracted when we only see their imitation.

It will be asked, how the drama moves, if it is not credited. It is credited with all the credit due to a drama. It is credited, whenever it moves, as a just picture of a real original; as representing to the auditor what he would himself feel, if he were to do or suffer what is there feigned to be suffered or to be done. The reflection that strikes the heart is not, that the evils before us are real evils, but that they are evils to which we ourselves may be exposed. If there be any fallacy, it is not that we fancy the players, but that we fancy ourselves unhappy for a moment; but we rather lament the possibility than suppose the presence of misery, as a mother weeps over her babe, when she remembers that death may take it from her. The delight of tragedy proceeds from our consciousness of fiction; if we thought murders and treasons real, they would please no more.

Imitations produce pain or pleasure, not because they are mistaken for realities, but because they bring realities to mind. When the imagination is recreated by a painted landscape, the trees are not supposed capable to give us shade, or the fountains coolness; but we consider, how we should be pleased with such fountains playing beside us, and such woods waving over us. We are agitated in reading the history of Henry the Fifth, yet no man takes his book for the field of Agencourt. A dramatick exhibition is a book recited with concomitants that encrease or diminish its effect. Familiar comedy is often more powerful on the theatre, than in the page; imperial tragedy is always less. The humour of Petruchio [in *The Taming of the Shrew*] may be heightened by grimace; but what voice or what gesture can hope to add dignity or force to the soliloquy of *Cato* [Joseph Addison tragedy, 1713].

A play read, affects the mind like a play acted. It is therefore evident, that the action is not supposed to be real, and it follows that between the acts a longer or shorter time may be allowed to pass, and that no more account of space or duration is to be taken by the auditor of a drama, than by the reader of a narrative, before whom may pass in an hour the life of a hero, or the revolutions of an empire.

Whether Shakespeare knew the unities, and rejected them by design, or deviated from them by happy ignorance, it is, I think, impossible to decide, and useless to enquire. We may reasonably suppose, that, when he rose to notice, he did not want the counsels and admonitions of scholars and criticks, and that he at last deliberately persisted in a practice, which he might have begun by chance. As nothing is essential to the fable, but unity of action, and as the unities of time and place arise evidently from false assumptions, and, by circumscribing the extent of the drama, lessen its variety, I cannot think it much to be lamented, that they were not known by him, or not observed: Nor, if such another poet could arise, should I very vehemently reproach him, that his first act passed at Venice, and his next in Cyprus. Such violations of rules merely positive, become the comprehensive genius of Shakespeare, and such censures are suitable to the minute and slender criticism of Voltaire:

Non usque adeo permiscuit imis
Longus summa dies, ut non, si voce Metelli
Serventur leges, malint a Caesare tolli.
["The course of time has not wrought
such confusion but that the laws, if preserved by the voice of Metellus,
would prefer to be annulled by Caesar," Lucan, *Pharsalia*, III.138–40]

Yet when I speak thus slightly of dramatick rules, I cannot but recollect how much wit and learning may be produced against me; before such authorities I am afraid to stand, not that I think the present question one of those that are to be decided by mere authority, but because it is to be suspected, that these precepts have not been so easily received but for better reasons than I have yet been able to find. The result of my enquiries, in which it would be ludicrous to boast of impartiality, is, that the unities of time and place are not essential to a just drama, that though they may sometimes conduce to pleasure, they are always to be sacrificed to the nobler beauties of variety and instruction; and that a play, written with nice observation of critical rules, is to be contemplated as an elaborate curiosity, as the product of superfluous and ostentatious art, by which is shewn, rather what is possible, than what is necessary.

He that, without diminution of any other excellence, shall preserve all the unities unbroken, deserves the like applause with the architect, who shall display all the orders of architecture in a citadel, without any deduction from its strength; but the principal beauty of a citadel is to exclude the enemy; and the greatest graces of a play, are to copy nature and instruct life. . . .

Those whom my arguments cannot persuade to give their approbation to the judgment of Shakespeare, will easily, if they consider the condition of his life, make some allowance for his ignorance.

Every man's performances, to be rightly estimated, must be compared with the state of the age in which he lived, and with his own particular opportunities; and though to the reader a book be not worse or better for the circumstances of the authour, yet as there is always a silent reference of human works to human abilities, and as the enquiry, how far man may extend his designs, or how high he may rate his native force, is of far greater dignity than in what rank we shall place any particular performance, curiosity is always busy to discover the instruments, as well as to survey the workmanship, to know how much is to be ascribed to original powers, and how much to casual and adventitious help. The palaces of Peru or Mexico were certainly mean and incommodious habitations, if compared to the houses of European monarchs; yet who could forbear to view them with astonishment, who remembered that they were built without the use of iron?

The English nation, in the time of Shakespeare, was yet struggling to emerge from barbarity. The philology of Italy had been transplanted hither in the reign of Henry the Eighth; and the learned languages had been successfully cultivated by [John] Lilly, [Thomas] Linacer, and [Sir Thomas] More; by [Reginald, Cardinal] Pole, [John] Cheke, and [Sir Robert] Gardiner; and afterwards by [Sir Thomas] Smith, Clerk, Haddon, and [Roger] Ascham. Greek was now taught to boys in the principal schools; and those who united elegance with learning, read, with great diligence, the Italian and Spanish poets. But literature was yet confined to professed scholars, or to men and women of high rank. The publick was gross and dark; and to be able to read and write, was an accomplishment still valued for its rarity. . . .

Our authour's plots are generally borrowed from novels, and it is reasonable to suppose, that he chose the most popular, such as were read by many, and related by more; for his audience could not have followed him through the intricacies of the drama, had they not held the thread of the story in their hands.

The stories, which we now find only in remoter authours, were in his time accessible and familiar. The fable of *As You Like It,* which is supposed to be copied from Chaucer's *Gamelyn,* was a little pamphlet of those times; and old Mr. [Coley] Cibber remembered the tale of *Hamlet* in plain English prose, which the criticks have now to seek in Saxo Grammaticus.

His English histories he took from English chronicles and English ballads; and as the ancient writers were made known to his countrymen by versions, they supplied him with new subjects; he dilated some of Plutarch's lives into plays, when they had been translated by [Sir Thomas] North.

[Shakespeare's] plots, whether historical or fabulous, are always crowded with incidents, by which the attention of a rude people was more easily caught than by sentiment or argumentation; and such is the power of the marvellous even over those who despise it, that every man finds his mind more strongly seized by the tragedies of Shakespeare than of any other writer; others please us by particular speeches, but he always makes us anxious for the event, and has perhaps excelled all but Homer in securing the first purpose of a writer, by exciting restless and unquenchable curiosity, and compelling him that reads his work to read it through. . . .

Voltaire expresses his wonder, that our authour's extravagances are endured by a nation, which has seen the tragedy of *Cato.* Let him be answered, that Addison speaks the language of poets, and Shakespeare, of men. We find in *Cato* innumerable beauties which enamour us of its authour, but we see nothing that acquaints us with human sentiments or human actions; we place it with the fairest and the noblest progeny which judgment propagates by conjunction with learning, but *Othello* is the vigorous and vivacious offspring of observation impregnated by genius. *Cato* affords a splendid exhibition of artificial and fictitious manners, and delivers just and noble sentiments, in diction easy, elevated and harmonious, but its hopes and fears communicate no vibration to the heart; the composition refers us only to the writer; we pronounce the name of *Cato,* but we think on Addison.

The work of a correct and regular writer is a garden accurately formed and diligently planted, varied with shades, and scented with flowers; the composition of Shakespeare is a forest, in which oaks extend their branches, and pines tower in the air, interspersed sometimes with weeds and brambles, and sometimes giving shelter to myrtles and to roses; filling the eye with awful pomp, and gratifying the mind with endless diversity. Other poets display cabinets of precious rarities, minutely finished, wrought into shape, and polished unto brightness. Shakespeare opens a mine which contains gold and diamonds in unexhaustible plenty, though clouded by incrustations, debased by impurities, and mingled with a mass of meaner minerals.

It has been much disputed, whether Shakespeare owed his excellence to his own native force, or whether he had the common helps of scholastick education, the precepts of critical science, and the examples of ancient authours.

There has always prevailed a tradition, that Shakespeare wanted learning, that he had no regular education, nor much skill in the dead languages. Jonson, his friend, affirms, that *he had small Latin, and less Greek;* who, besides that he had no imaginable temptation to falsehood, wrote at a time when the character and acquisitions of Shakespeare were known to multitudes. His evidence ought therefore to decide the controversy, unless some testimony of equal force could be opposed.

Some have imagined, that they have discovered deep learning in many imitations of old writers; but the examples which I have known urged, were drawn from books translated in his time; or were such easy coincidencies of thought, as will happen to all who consider the same subjects; or such remarks on life or axioms of morality as float in conversation, and are transmitted through the world in proverbial sentences. . . .

The *Comedy of Errors* is confessedly taken from the *Menaechmi* of Plautus; from the only play of Plautus which was then in English. What can be more probable, than that he who copied that, would have copied more; but that those which were not translated were inaccessible?

Whether he knew the modern languages is uncertain. That his plays have some French scenes proves but little; he might easily procure them to be written, and probably, even though he had known the language in the common degree, he could not have written it without assistance. In the story of Romeo and Juliet he is observed to have followed the English translation, where it deviates from the Italian; but this on the other part proves nothing against his knowledge of the original. He was to copy, not what he knew himself, but what was known to his audience.

It is most likely that he had learned Latin sufficiently to make him acquainted with construction, but that he never advanced to an easy perusal of the Roman authours. Concerning his skill in modern languages, I can find no sufficient ground of determination; but as no imitations of French or Italian authours have been discovered, though the Italian poetry was then high in esteem, I am inclined to believe, that he read little more than English, and chose for his fables only such tales as he found translated.

That much knowledge is scattered over his works is very justly observed by [Alexander] Pope, but it is often such knowledge as books did not supply.

He that will understand Shakespeare, must not be content to study him in the closet, he must look for his meaning sometimes among the sports of the field, and sometimes among the manufactures of the shop.

There is however proof enough that he was a very diligent reader, nor was our language then so indigent of books, but that he might very liberally indulge his curiosity without excursion into foreign literature. Many of the Roman authours were translated, and some of the Greek; the Reformation had filled the kingdom with theological learning; most of the topicks of human disquisition had found English writers; and poetry had been cultivated, not only with diligence, but success. This was a stock of knowledge sufficient for a mind so capable of appropriating and improving it.

But the greater part of his excellence was the product of his own genius. He found the English stage in a state of the utmost rudeness; no essays either in tragedy or comedy had appeared, from which it could be discovered to what degree of delight either one or other might be carried. Neither character nor dialogue were yet understood. Shakespeare may be truly said to have introduced them both amongst us, and in some of his happier scenes to have carried them both to the utmost height. . . .

Other writers borrow their characters from preceding writers, and diversify them only by the accidental appendages of present manners; the dress is a little varied, but the body is the same. Our authour had both matter and form to provide; for except the characters of Chaucer, to whom I think he is not much indebted, there were no writers in English, and perhaps not many in other modern languages, which shewed life its native colours. . . .

Nor was his attention confined to the actions of men; he was an exact surveyor of the inanimate world; his descriptions have always some peculiarities, gathered by contemplating things as they really exist. . . . Shakespeare, whether life or nature be his subject, shews plainly, that he has seen with his own eyes; he gives the image which he receives, not weakened or distorted by the intervention of any other mind; the ignorant feel his representations to be just, and the learned see that they are compleat.

—Samuel Johnson, from *Preface
to Shakespeare*, 1765

ELIZABETH MONTAGUE "ON THE PRETERNATURAL BEINGS" (1769)

Arguing that the poets of each era construct their work using the super-stitions, mythologies, and religions of their times, Elizabeth Montague

(1718–1800), writer, literary critic, social reformer, arts patron, society host-ess, and feminist, compares Shakespeare's use of English folk culture with Ben Jonson's use of classical culture—to Shakespeare's advantage. In a fur-ther comparison to the great Greek tragedian Aeschylus, she argues that Shakespeare's conjurations, the ghost of Hamlet's father or the witches in *Macbeth,* are more gripping even than Aeschylus's portrayal of the ghost of the dead king Darius in his play *The Persians.*

Our first theatrical entertainments, after we emerged from gross barbarism, were of the allegorical kind. The Christmas carol, and Carnival shows, the pious pastimes of our holy-days, were turned into pageantries and masques, all symbolical and allegorical. Our stage rose from hymns to the Virgin, and encomiums on the Patriarchs and Saints; as the Grecian tragedies from the hymns to Bacchus. Our early poets added narration and action to this kind of psalmody, as Æschylus had done to the song of the goat. Much more rapid indeed was the progress of the Grecian stage towards perfection. Philosophy, poetry, eloquence, all the fine arts, were in their meridian glory, when the Drama first began to dawn at Athens, and gloriously it shone forth, illumined by every kind of intellectual light.

Shakspeare, in the dark shades of Gothic barbarism, had no resources but in the very phantoms, that walked the night of ignorance and superstition: or in touching the latent passions of civil rage and discord: sure to please best his fierce and barbarous audience, when he raised the bloody ghost, or reared the warlike standard. His choice of these subjects was judicious, if we consider the times in which he lived; his management of them so masterly, that he will be admired in all times.

In the same age, Ben Jonson, more proud of his learning than confident of his genius, was desirous to give a metaphysical air to his works. He composed many pieces of the allegorical kind, established on the Grecian mythology, and rendered his playhouse a perfect pantheon. Shakspeare disdained these quaint devices: an admirable judge of human nature, with a capacity most extensive, and an invention most happy, he contented himself with giving dramatic manners to history, sublimity and its appropriated powers and charms to fiction; and in both these arts he is unequalled. The *Catiline* and *Sejanus* of Jonson are cold, crude, heavy pieces; turgid where they should be great; bombast where they should be sublime; the sentiments extravagant; the manners exaggerated; and the whole undramatically conducted by long senatorial speeches, and flat plagiarisms from Tacitus and Sallust. Such of this author's pieces as he boasts to *be grounded on antiquity and solid learning, and to lay hold on removed mysteries*

[Ben Jonson, prologue to *The Masque of Queens,* Montague's note], have neither the majesty of Shakspeare's serious fables, nor the pleasing sportfulness and poetical imagination of his fairy tales. Indeed if we compare our countryman in this respect, with the most admired writers of antiquity, we shall, perhaps, not find him inferior to them. Æschylus, with greater impetuosity of genius than even Shakspeare, makes bold incursions into the blind chaos of mingled allegory and fable, but he is not so happy in diffusing the solemn shade; in casting the dim, religious light that should reign there. When he introduces his Furies, and other supernatural beings, he exposes them by too glaring a light; causes affright in the spectator, but never rises to the imparting that unlimited terror, which we feel when Macbeth, to his bold address,

How now! ye secret, foul, and midnight hags,
What is't ye do?

is answered,

A deed without a name.

—Elizabeth Montague, from "On the
Preternatural Beings," *An Essay on the
Writings and Genius of Shakspeare,* 1769

EDWARD TAYLOR "ON SHAKESPEAR" (1774)

Edward Taylor (1642–1729) is believed to be the author of the *Cursory Remarks on Tragedy* from which this excerpt is taken. Taylor was born in England. In 1680, he immigrated to the Massachusetts Bay Colony and was a Puritan theologian, a physician, and a poet.

Granting Shakespeare greatness as a writer of comedies and as a poet, Taylor counters the general esteem in which Shakespeare was held, arguing that his works, especially his tragedies, have a savage, undisciplined character that severely tarnishes them, and that Shakespeare's work is, in places, morally reprehensible. The claim that Shakespeare depicted nature truly and freely does not excuse his faults, Taylor argues, asserting that some of what he considers the vulgarities of nature ought not to be depicted but kept hidden. Taylor is loath to forgive Shakespeare his violation of rules like the classical dramatic unities and finds that violation not only to be an artistic blot but a moral one also. He dislikes the intrusion of "low" characters into a scene after the depiction of "noble" characters. In particular, Taylor is repelled by the fact that virtue and virtuous characters suffer in the tragedies and do not triumph. He argues that art is better when it induces in the audience the sense that evil will be punished and the good will be rewarded, thus attempting to direct moral behavior.

It has been the prevailing fashion for some years past to launch out into the most extravagant praises of our countryman Shakespear, and to allot him beyond all competition the first place as a tragic writer. Compared with him, Corneille, Racine, and Voltaire, are fantastic composers, void of historical truth, imitation of character, or representation of manners; mere declaimers, without energy or fire of action, and absurdly introducing, upon all occasions, tedious, insipid, uninteresting love-scenes. But, prejudice apart, is he so transcendentally their superior, and is he the glorious luminary that shines?

> velut inter ignes Luna minores.
> ["like the moon among the lesser fires," Horace]

Shall I venture to proceed further, and ask, if he be in general even a good tragic writer? We have seen what are some of the most material rules for dramatic compositions, as prescribed by Aristotle and other eminent masters in the art of criticism: rules consonant to reason, and calculated to deceive the spectator into a persuasion, that he is interested in a real event, whilst time, place, and action, conspire to strengthen the delusion: rules dictated by the wise, approved by the learned, and adopted by writers of judgment, genius, and taste of all nations. But these were either totally unknown to Shakespear, or wilfully neglected by him. Instead of confining the action to a limited time, he takes in the space of days, months, and even years; instead of adhering to the unity of place, by a preposterous magic he transports the spectator in the shifting of a scene, from Italy to Britain, from Venice to Cyprus, from the court of England to that of France....

His genius therefore is not to be restrained by the shackles of critic laws; his audacious fancy, his enthusiastic fire, are not to submit to the tame institutions of an Aristotle or a [Roman rhetorician] Quintilian. So then he is to be indulged in transgressing the bounds of nature, in neglecting to give to fiction the air of truth, and in imposing the most palpable incongruities and most striking impossibilities on the audience, because he dares. Mr. Pope's partiality seems to have gotten the better of his usual justice and candour, when he observes, that we are not to apply the rules of Aristotle to Shakespear; "for that, says he, would be like trying a man by the laws of one country, who acts under those of another." Yet surely there are laws of general society as well as of particular communities, laws that bind each individual as a citizen of the world; the infringement of which would justly excite the universal indignation and resentment of mankind. In most countries, England excepted, certain positions and rules have been holden sacred and inviolable in the literary as well as in the political word: these did the antient Greek tragedians observe and cultivate, and to these have the most eminent amongst the modern Italians and French scrupulously adhered. But our excentric English tragedian has presumed to quit the beaten track, and has boldly ventured to turn aside into the regions of the most wild, most fantastic imagination. With an unprecedented, with an unpardonable audacity, has he overleaped the pale of credibility, a boundary too confined for his romantic genius. Presented by him with impossibilities instead of the appearance of truth, we remain undeluded spectators. . . .

And although we may be affected by particular passages in any one of his plays, yet the whole of the representation cannot be very interesting on account of its extravagance. Let us not therefore approve, let us not even extenuate those faults in Shakespear, that justice, that common sense, would lead us to condemn in others. But with an impartiality that becomes every man, who dares to think for himself, let us allow him great merit as a comic writer, greater still as a poet, but little, very little, as a tragedian. . . . Perhaps it will be said, that Shakespear wrote, when learning, taste, and manners were pedantic, unrefined, and illiberal; that none but such motley pieces, as his are, could please the greater part of his audience, the illiterate, low-liv'd mechanics; that some of his characters were necessitated to speak their language; and that their bursts of applause were to be purchased even at the expence of decency and common sense. When we consider his situation and circumstances, that in lieu of the

> hospita musis
> Otia, et exemtum curis gravioribus aevum. (Sil. Ital. lib. 12.)
> ["leisurely hospitality of the muses and an age free of grave concerns,"
>   Tiberius Catius Silius Italicus, Roman poet and politician, 25–101]

he was exposed to all the miseries of poverty and want; that to live he was constrained to write, and to adapt himself to the humour of others; it must be acknowledged, that he deserves our pity rather than our censure. But when we come to consider him as a tragic writer, and to weigh his merit as such, a standard must be established, by which our judgments are to be determined: where then are we to look for this nice criterion of merit, but in those works, that have been the delight of past ages, and are the admiration of the present.

Let it not be advanced as a merit, let it not be urged even as an excuse, that Shakespear followed nature in the busy walks of men; that he presented her, as he found her, naked and unadorned: for there are parts of nature that require concealment; there are others too that by the thin transparent veil, by the light, the careless drapery, are greatly heightened and improved. . . .

The scene of the grave-diggers in *Hamlet* is certainly real life, or as it is vulgarly termed, highly natural; yet how misplaced, how unworthy the tragedian. . . .

To the credit of the present times indeed these puerilities are now omitted; let us hope they will not be the only ones, nor let us be afraid to reject what our ancestors, in conformity to the grosser notions then prevalent, beheld with pleasure and applause.

It is not long ago that even a comedy, which had a considerable share of merit, met with an unfavourable reception, on account of a low illiberal dialogue; though it was perfectly adapted to the persons between whom it passed. Nor has there, I believe, been found more than one haughty overgrown critic, who has dared to censure the public for expressing their disapprobation of language, that became a spunging-house indeed, but was highly improper for the stage; which even the comic muse, sportive and mirthful though she be, is not permitted to tread, but with a certain easy politeness, a certain graceful decorum.

It must be acknowledged, that Shakespear abounds in the true sublime; but it must be allowed that he abounds likewise in the low and vulgar. And who is there, that after soaring on eagle wings to unknown regions and empyreal heights, is not most sensibly mortified to be compelled the next moment to grovel in dirt and ordure. In the first case (and if he mounts with Shakespear it will frequently happen) he may chance to be dazzled with the excessive glare, even till his "eye-balls crack. . . ." What a contrast there is between the sublime and the bathos! yet how closely are they united in Shakespear! Fired with the exalted sentiments of his heroes, from whose mouths virtue herself seems to dictate to mankind, we feel our hearts dilate, the current of our blood flow swifter in every vein, and our whole frame wound up to a pitch of dignity unfelt, unknown before. Although we could not expect that our enthusiasm should remain in its full energy and force, yet of itself it would subside by degrees into a benign complacency and universal philanthropy. How cruel is it then to hurry us from heroes and philosophers into a crew of plebeians, grave-diggers, and buffoons; from the bold tropes and figures of nervous and manly eloquence, from the sage lessons of morality, such as a Minerva might have inspired, or a Socrates have taught, to the obscure jest or low quibble, that base counterfeit of wit, which, like the monkey when compared with man, is rendered more disgusting by an unsightly resemblance. . . .

The morals of Shakespear's plays are in general extremely natural and just: yet why must innocence unnecessarily suffer? why must the hoary, the venerable Lear, be brought with sorrow to the grave? Why must Cordelia perish by an untimely fate? the amiable, the dutiful, the innocent Cordelia! She that had already felt the heart-rending anger of a much beloved, but hasty mistaken father! She that could receive, protect, and cherish a poor, infirm, weak, and despised old man, although he had showered down curses on her undeserving head! That such a melancholy catastrophe was by no means necessary, is sufficiently evinced by the manner in which the same play is now performed (in the adaptation of Nahum Tate). Ingratitude now meets with its proper punishment, and the audience now retire, exulting in the mutual happiness of paternal affection, and filial piety. Such, if practicable, should be the winding up of all dramatic representations, that mankind may have the most persuasive allurements to all good actions: for although virtue depressed may be amiable, virtue triumphant must be irresistable.

But it may perhaps be objected by some, that the death of the wicked cannot occasion pity; and if innocence and virtue are not to fall beneath the stroke of oppression and injustice, where is the pathos, where is the tender sympathy? To this it may be answered, in the unmerited misfortunes, in the agonizing distress of the innocent; in seeing the virtuous involuntarily led to the perpetration of some horrid crime, or in the dread apprehension of having already committed it, or tottering on the very brink of perdition. What a critical, what an interesting situation is it to the spectator, when he beholds Merope seemingly reduced to the dreadful alternative of seeing her son perish, or of giving herself to the murderer of her husband? [In Greek mythology, Merope is the wife of the Corinthian king, Polybus, and foster mother of Oedipus. Taylor seems to have confused her with Oedipus's actual mother, Jocasta, wife to Laius, king of Thebes.] Again, what horror do we feel, when we see her with her arm uplifted upon the point of killing that very son, whose death she means to revenge! It is not my design to condemn those tragedies, in which innocence falls a victim to treachery or violence; we see but too many instances of it in real life; consequently it cannot be improper for the stage, which ought to represent living manners. I would be understood therefore not to reject other tragedies, but to give the preference to those, in which death, punishment, or remorse, await the guilty only. And as at all dramatic representations I am to see but an imitation of nature, let the delusion be on the side of virtue, that I may still flatter myself with the pleasing belief, that to be good is to be happy. . . .

In our English bard, what a glow of fancy, what a rapidity of imagination, what a sublimity in diction, what strength, what a distinction of characters, what a knowledge of the human heart! Yet how inattentive to propriety and order, how deficient in grouping, how fond of exposing disgusting as well as beautiful figures! Were we to see a statue, the several component parts of which, when detached and considered separately, would be highly just in themselves, and pleasing to the eye, yet from a want of due correctness, symmetry, and proportion to each other, the whole figure should be not only awkward and disgusting, but even unnatural and monstrous, we should not hesitate to pronounce the sculptor,

> Infelix operis summa quia ponere totum nesciit. (Horat. *de Arte Poet.*)
> ["An unsuccessful craftsman because he is unable to achieve the highest unity," Horace]

Like such a statue are the tragedies of our author; their parts beautiful, their whole inconsistent.

And is then poor Shakespear to be excluded from the number of good tragedians? He is; but let him be banished, like Homer, from the republic of Plato, with marks of distinction and veneration; and may his forehead, like the Grecian bards, be bound with an honourable wreath of ever-blooming flowers.

—Edward Taylor, from "On Shakespear,"
Cursory Remarks on Tragedy, pp. 31–51

HUGH BLAIR (1783)

Hugh Blair (1718–1800) was a Scottish Presbyterian clergyman who published five volumes of his sermons. He was also professor of rhetoric and *belles lettres* at the University of Edinburgh. Blair does not refer directly to the dominant classical critical precepts of the time, but despite the "blemishes" he admits are present in Shakespeare's work, his praise of Shakespeare for virtues such as his "masterly representations of character, ... the liveliness of his descriptions, the force of his sentiments, and his possessing, ... the natural language of passion," signals that the precepts of eighteenth-century classicism are being supplanted by the sensibility that defines nineteenth-century romanticism.

Instances, I admit, there are, of some works that contain gross transgressions of the laws of Criticism, acquiring, nevertheless, a general, and even a lasting admiration. Such are the plays of Shakespeare, which, considered as dramatic poems, are irregular in the highest degree. But then we are to remark, that they have gained the public admiration, not by their being irregular, not by their transgressions of the rules of art, but in spite of such transgressions. They possess other beauties which are comformable to just rules; and the force of these beauties has been so great as to overpower all censure, and to give the Public a degree of satisfaction superior to the disgust arising from their blemishes. Shakespeare pleases, not by his bringing the transactions of many years into one play: not by his grotesque mixtures of Tragedy and Comedy in one piece, nor by the trained thoughts, and affected witticisms, which he sometimes employs. These we consider as blemishes, and impute them to the grossness of the age in which he lived. But he pleases by his animated and masterly representations of characters, by the liveliness of his descriptions, the force of his sentiments, and his possessing, beyond all writers, the natural language of passion: beauties which true Criticism no less teaches us to place in the highest rank, than Nature teaches us to feel.

—Hugh Blair, *Lectures on Rhetoric and Belles-Lettres*, 1783, lecture 3

RICHARD CUMBERLAND (1786)

In this letter, Richard Cumberland (1732–1811), an English dramatist, essayist, and memoirist, suggests there is a fitting comparison to be made between Macbeth and Richard III. He sees in Macbeth moral subtleties that are missing in the forthrightly evil Richard, and he then compares Shakespeare to the great Greek tragedian Aeschylus.

In the second section, labeled with the heading "No. 70," Cumberland continues his discussion of *Macbeth,* focusing on the powerful and baleful influence Lady Macbeth exerts on Macbeth and, as he had compared Shakespeare to Aeschylus in his previous discussion, concludes with a comparison of Lady Macbeth and Queen Clytemnestra from Aeschylus's *Agamemnon.*

There are two very striking characters delineated by our great dramatic poet, which I am desirous of bringing together under one review, and these are *Macbeth* and *Richard the Third.*

The parts which these two persons sustain in their respective dramas, have a remarkable coincidence: both are actuated by the same guilty ambition in the opening of the story: both murder their lawful sovereign in the course of it: and both are defeated and slain in battle at the conclusion of it: yet these two characters, under circumstances so similar, are as strongly distinguished in every passage of their dramatic life by the art of the poet, as any two men ever were by the hand of nature.

Let us contemplate them in the three following periods; viz. The premeditation of their crime; the perpetration of it; and the catastrophe of their death.

Duncan, the reigning king of Scotland, has two sons: Edward the Fourth of England has also two sons; but these kings and their respective heirs do not affect the usurpers Macbeth and Richard in the same degree, for the latter is a prince of the blood royal, brother to the king, and next in consanguinity to the throne after the death of his elder brother the Duke of Clarence: Macbeth, on the contrary, is not in the succession—

> And to be king
> Stands not within the prospect of belief.
> [I.iii.73–74]

His views therefore being farther removed and more out of hope, a greater weight of circumstances should be thrown together to tempt and encourage him to an undertaking so much beyond *the prospect of his belief*. The art of the poet furnishes these circumstances, and the engine which his invention employs, is of a preternatural and prodigious sort. He introduces in the very opening of his scene a troop of sibyls or witches, who salute Macbeth with their divinations, and in three solemn prophetic gratulations hail him Thane of Glamis, Thane of Cawdor, and King hereafter!

> By Sinel's death I know I'm Thane of Glamis;
> But how of Cawdor?
> [I.iii.71–72]

One part of the prophecy therefore is true; the remaining promises become more deserving of belief. This is one step in the ladder of his ambition, and mark how artfully the poet has laid it in his way; no time is lost; the wonderful machinery is not suffered to stand still, for behold a verification of the second prediction, and a courtier thus addresses him from the king—

> And for an earnest of a greater honour,
> He bade me from him call thee Thane of Cawdor.
> [I.iii.104–05]

The magic now works to his heart, and he cannot wait the departure of the royal messenger before his admiration vents itself aside—

> Glamis, and Thane of Cawdor! The greatest is behind.
> [I.iii.115–16]

A second time he turns aside, and unable to repress the emotions, which this second confirmation of the predictions has excited, repeats the same secret observation—

> Two truths are told
> As happy prologues to the swelling act Of the imperial theme.
>   [I.iii.127–29]

A soliloquy then ensues, in which the poet judiciously opens enough of his character to shew the spectator that these preternatural agents are not superfluously set to work upon a disposition prone to evil, but one that will have to combat many compunctious struggles, before it can be brought to yield even to oracular influence. This alone would demonstrate (if we needed demonstration) that Shakspeare, without resorting to the ancients, had the judgment of ages as it were instinctively. From this instant we are apprised that Macbeth meditates an attack upon our pity as well as upon our horror, when he puts the following question to his conscience—

> And make my seated heart knock at my ribs
> Against the use of nature?
>   [I.iii.134–35]

Now let us turn to Richard, in whose cruel heart no such remorse finds place: he needs no tempter: there is here no *dignus vindice nodus* [a knotty issue worth pursuing], nor indeed any *knot* at all, for he is already practised in murder; ambition is his ruling passion, and a crown is in view, and he tells you at his very first entrance on the scene—

> I am determined to be a villain.
>   [I.i.29]

We are now presented with a character full formed and complete for all the savage purposes of the drama.

The barriers of conscience are broken down, and the soul, hardened against shame, avows its own depravity—

> Plots have I laid, inductions dangerous,
> . . . .
> To set my brother Clarence and the king
> In deadly hate the one against the other.
>   [I.i.32–35]

He observes no gradations in guilt, expresses no hesitation, practises no refinements, but plunges into blood with the familiarity of long custom, and gives orders to his assassins to dispatch his brother Clarence with all the unfeeling tranquillity of a Nero or Caligula. Richard, [has] no longer any scruples to manage with his own conscience. . . .

It is manifest therefore that there is an essential difference in the developement of these characters, and that in favour of Macbeth: in his soul cruelty seems to dawn; it breaks out with faint glimmerings, like a winter morning, and gathers strength by slow degrees: in Richard it flames forth at once, mounting like the sun between the tropics, and enters boldly on its career without a herald. As the character of Macbeth has a moral advantage in this distinction, so has the drama of that name a much more interesting and affecting cast: the struggles of a soul, naturally virtuous, whilst it holds the guilty impulse of ambition at bay, affords the noblest theme for the drama, and puts the creative fancy of our poet upon a resource, in which he has been rivalled only by the great father of tragedy Æschylus. . . . Æschylus is justly styled the father of tragedy, but this is not to be interpreted as if he was the inventor of it: Shakspeare with equal justice claims the same title, and his originality is qualified with the same exception: the Greek tragedy was not more rude and undigested when Æschylus brought it into shape, than the English tragedy was when Shakspeare began to write: if therefore it be granted that he had no aids from the Greek theatre (and I think this is not likely to be disputed), so far these great masters are upon equal ground. Æschylus was a warrior of high repute, of a lofty generous spirit, and deep, as it should seem, in the erudition of his times: in all these particulars he has great advantage over our countryman, who was humbly born, of the most menial occupation, and, as it is generally thought, unlearned. Æschylus had the whole epic of Homer in his hands, the *Iliad* [and the] *Odyssey.* . . . [H]e had also a great fabulous creation to resort to amongst his own divinities, characters ready defined, and an audience, whose superstition was prepared for every thing he could offer; he had therefore a firmer and broader stage (if I may be allowed the expression) under his feet, than Shakspeare had: his fables in general are Homeric, and yet it does not follow that we can pronounce for Shakspeare that he is more original in his plots, for I understand that late researches have traced him in all or nearly all: both poets added so much machinery and invention of their own in the conduct of their fables, that whatever might have been the source, still their streams had little or no taste of the spring they flowed from. . . . [I]n his divine personages, Æschylus has the field of heaven, and indeed of hell also, to himself; in his heroic and military characters he has never been excelled; he had too good a model within his own bosom to fail of making those delineations natural: in his imaginary beings also he will be found a respectable, though not an equal rival of our poet; but in the variety of character, in all the nicer touches of nature, in all the extravagances of caprice and humour, from the boldest feature down to the minutest foible, Shakspeare stands alone: such persons as he delineates never came into the contemplation of Æschylus as a poet; his tragedy has no dealing with them; the simplicity of the Greek fable, and the great portion of the drama filled up by the chorus, allow of little variety of character; and the most which can be said of Æschylus in this particular is, that he never offends against nature or propriety, whether his cast is in the terrible or pathetic, the elevated or the simple. His versification, with the intermixture of lyric composition, is more various than that of Shakspeare; both are lofty and sublime in the extreme, abundantly metaphorical, and sometimes extravagant. . . .

Both were subject to be hurried on by an uncontrollable impulse, nor could nature alone suffice for either: Æschylus had an apt creation of imaginary beings at command—

He could call spirits from the vasty deep, And they *would come*—
[cf. *I Henry IV* III.i.52ff.]

Shakspeare, having no such creation in resource, boldly made one of his own; if Æschylus therefore was invincible, he owed it to his armour, and that, like the armour of Æneas, was the work of the gods: but the unassisted invention of Shakspeare seized all and more than superstition supplied to Æschylus.

No. 70

We are now to attend Macbeth to the perpetration of the murder, which puts him in possession of the crown of Scotland; and this introduces a new personage on the scene, his accomplice and wife: she thus developes her own character—

> Come, all you spirits,
> That tend on mortal thoughts, unsex me here,
> And fill me from the crown to the toe topful
> Of direst cruelty; make thick my blood,
> Stop up the access and passage to remorse,
> That no compunctious visitings of nature

Shake my fell purpose, nor keep peace between
Th' effect and it. Come to my woman's breasts,
And take my milk for gall, you murth'ring ministers,
Wherever in your sightless substances
You wait on nature's mischief: come, thick night,
And pall thee in the dunnest smoke of hell!

                    [I.v.41ff.]

Terrible invocation! Tragedy can speak no stronger language, nor could any genius less than Shakspeare's support a character of so lofty a pitch, so sublimely terrible at the very opening. The part which Lady Macbeth fills in the drama has a relative as well as positive importance, and serves to place the repugnance of Macbeth in the strongest point of view; she is in fact the auxiliary of the witches, and the natural influence, which so high and predominant a spirit asserts over the tamer qualities of her husband, makes those witches but secondary agents for bringing about the main action of the drama. This is well worth a remark; for if they, which are only artificial and fantastic instruments, had been made the sole or even principal movers of the great incident of the murder, Nature would have been excluded from her share in the drama, and Macbeth would have become the mere machine of an uncontrollable necessity, and his character, being robbed of its free agency, would have left no moral behind: I must take leave therefore to anticipate a remark, which I shall hereafter repeat, that when Lady Macbeth is urging her Lord to the murder, not a word is dropt by either of the witches or their predictions. It is in these instances of his conduct that Shakspeare is so wonderful a study for the dramatic poet. But I proceed—

Lady Macbeth in her first scene, from which I have already extracted a passage, prepares for an attempt upon the conscience of her husband, whose nature she thus describes—

Yet do I fear thy nature;
It is too full o'th' milk of human kindness
To catch the nearest way.

                    [I.v.17–19]

He arrives before she quits the scene, and she receives him with consummate address—

Great Glamis! worthy Cawdor!
Greater than both by the All-hail hereafter!

                    [I.v.55–56]

These are the very gratulations of the witches; she welcomes him with
confirmed predictions, with the tempting salutations of ambition, not with
the softening caresses of a wife—

> *Macb.*: Duncan comes here to-night.
> *Lady*: And when goes hence?
> *Macb.*: To-morrow, as he purposes.
> *Lady*: Oh never
> Shall sun that morrow see!
> [I.v.59–63]

The rapidity of her passion hurries her into immediate explanation, and he,
consistently with the character she had described, evades her precipitate
solicitations with a short indecisive answer—

> We will speak further—
> [I.v.72]

His reflections upon this interview, and the dreadful subject of it, are soon after
given in soliloquy, in which the poet has mixed the most touching strokes of
compunction with his meditations: he reasons against the villany of the act, and
honour jointly with nature assails him with an argument of double force—

> He's here in double trust;
> First as I am his kinsman and his subject,
> Strong both against the deed; then as his host,
> Who should against the murtherer shut the door,
> Not bear the knife himself.
> [I.vii.12–16]

This appeal to nature, hospitality, and allegiance, was not without its
impression; he again meets his lady, and immediately declares—

> We will proceed no further in this business.
> [I.vii.81]

This draws a retort upon him, in which his tergiversation and cowardice are
satirized with so keen an edge, and interrogatory reproaches are passed so
fast upon him, that, catching hold in his retreat of one small but precious
fragment in the wreck of innocence and honour, he demands a truce from
her attack, and, with the spirit of a combatant who has not yet yielded up his
weapons, cries out—

Pr'thee, peace;

The words are no expletives; they do not fill up a sentence, but they form one: they stand in a most important pass: they defend the breach her ambition has made in his heart; a breach in the very citadel of humanity; they mark the last dignified struggle of virtue, and they have a double reflecting power, which, in the first place, shews that nothing but the voice of authority could stem the torrent of her invective, and in the next place announces that something, worthy of the solemn audience he had demanded, was on the point to follow—and worthy it is to be a standard sentiment of moral truth expressed with proverbial simplicity, sinking into every heart that hears it—

> I dare do all that may become a man,
> Who dares do more is none.
>   [I.vii.46–47]

How must every feeling spectator lament that a man should fall from virtue with such an appeal upon his lips!

"A man is not a coward because he fears to be unjust," is the sentiment of an old dramatic poet [Philonides].

Macbeth's principle is honour; cruelty is natural to his wife; ambition is common to both; one passion favourable to her purpose has taken place in his heart: another still hangs about it, which being adverse to her plot, is first to be expelled, before she can instill her cruelty into his nature. The sentiment above quoted had been firmly delivered, and was ushered in with an apostrophe suitable to its importance; she feels its weight; she perceives it is not to be turned aside with contempt, or laughed down by ridicule, as she had already done where weaker scruples had stood in the way: but, taking sophistry in aid, by a ready turn of argument she gives him credit for his sentiment, erects a more glittering though fallacious logic upon it, and by admitting his objection cunningly confutes it—

> What beast was't then
> That made you break this enterprise to me?
> When you durst do it, then you were a man,
> And to be more than what you were, you wou'd
> Be so much more than man.
>   [I.vii.48–51]

Having thus parried his objection by a sophistry calculated to blind his reason and inflame his ambition, she breaks forth into such a vaunting display of hardened intrepidity, as presents one of the most terrific pictures that was ever imagined—

> I have given suck, and know
> How tender 'tis to love the babe that milks me;
> I wou'd, whilst it was smiling in my face,
> Have pluckt my nipple from its boneless gums,
> And dasht its brains out, had I but so sworn
> As you have done to this.
>
> [I.vii.54–59]

This is a note of horror, screwed to a pitch that bursts the very sinews of nature; she no longer combats with a human weapon, but seizing the flash of the lightning extinguishes her opponent with the stroke: here the controversy must end, for he must either adopt her spirit, or take her life; he sinks under the attack, and offering nothing in delay of execution but a feeble hesitation, founded in fear—"If we should fail"—he concludes with an assumed ferocity, caught from her and not springing from himself—

> I am settled, and bend up
> Each corporal agent to this terrible feat.
>
> [I.vii.79–80]

The strong and sublime strokes of a master impressed upon this scene make it a model of dramatic composition, and I must in this place remind the reader of the observation I have before hinted at, that no reference whatever is had to the auguries of the witches: it would be injustice to suppose that this was other than a purposed omission by the poet; a weaker genius would have resorted back to these instruments: Shakspeare had used and laid them aside for a time; he had a stronger engine at work, and he could proudly exclaim—

> We defy auguries!
>
> [cf. Hamlet V.ii.220]

Nature was sufficient for that work, and to shew the mastery he had over nature, he took his human agent from the weaker sex.

This having passed in the first act, the murder is perpetrated in the succeeding one. The introductory soliloquy of Macbeth, the chimera of the dagger, and the signal on the bell, are awful preludes to the deed. In this dreadful interim, Lady Macbeth, the great superintending spirit, enters to support the dreadful work. It is done: and he returns appalled with sounds; he surveys his bloody hands with horror; he starts from her proposal of going back to besmear the guards of Duncan's chamber, and she snatches the reeking daggers from his trembling hands to finish the imperfect work—

> Infirm of purpose,
> Give me the daggers!
> [II.ii.52–53]

She returns on the scene, the deed which he revolted from is performed, and with the same unshaken ferocity she vauntingly displays her bloody trophies, and exclaims—

> My hands are of your colour, but I shame
> To wear a heart so white.
> [II.ii.63–64]

Fancied noises, the throbbings of his own quailing heart, had shaken the constancy of Macbeth; real sounds, the certain signals of approaching visiters, to whom the situation of Duncan must be revealed, do not intimidate her; she is prepared for all trials, and cooly tells him—

> I hear a knocking
> At the south entry: Retire we to our chamber;
> A little water clears us of this deed.
> How easy is it then!
> [II.ii.64–67]

The several incidents thrown together in this scene of the murder of Duncan, are of so striking a sort as to need no elucidation: they are better felt than described, and my attempts point at passages of more obscurity, where the touches are thrown into shade, and the art of the author lies more out of sight.

Lady Macbeth being now retired from the scene, we may in this interval, as we did in the conclusion of the former paper, permit the genius of Æschylus to introduce a rival murderess on the stage.

Clytemnestra has received her husband Agamemnon, on his return from the capture of Troy, with studied rather than cordial congratulations. He opposes the pompous ceremonies she had devised for the display of his entry, with a magnanimous contempt of such adulation—

Sooth me not with strains
Of adulation, as a girl; nor raise
As to some proud barbaric king, that loves
Loud acclamations echoed from the mouths
Of prostrate worshippers, a clamorous welcome:
Spread not the streets with tapestry; 'tis invidious:
These are the honours we should pay the gods;
For mortal men to tread on ornaments
Of rich embroidery—no; I dare not do it:
Respect me as a man, not as a god.

> (Potter's *Aeschylus*.)

These are heroic sentiments, but in conclusion the persuasions of the wife overcome the modest scruples of the hero, and he enters his palace in the pomp of triumph; when soon his dying groans are echoed from the interior scene, and the adultress comes forth besprinkled with the blood of her husband to avow the murder—

I struck him twice, and twice
He groan'd; then died: a third time as he lay
I gor'd him with a wound; a grateful present
To the stern god, that in the realms below
Reigns o'er the dead: there let him take his seat.
He lay: and spouting from his wounds a stream
Of blood, bedew'd me with these crimson drops.
I glory in them, like the genial earth,
When the warm showers of heav'n descend, and wake
The flowrets to unfold their vermeil leaves.
Come then, ye reverend senators of Argos,
Joy with me, if your hearts be turn'd to joy,
And such I wish them.

> (Potter.)

> —Richard Cumberland, from *The Observer*, number 69, 1786

Charles Dibdin "Shakespear" (1795)

Charles Dibdin (ca. 1745–1815), a singer, actor, dramatist, novelist, and composer of operettas, here argues that Shakespeare's greatness gains him attention, but

the focus of much of that attention has been on inconsequential elements in
his work that are identified as faults by many critics when they are, in fact, not.
These elements, like the insistence on adherence to classical rules of composition and the unities, are themselves faulty, Dibdin asserts. In his homage, Dibdin
celebrates Shakespeare by presenting an anatomy of his qualities, with a focus
on *Romeo and Juliet*, and by repeatedly mocking what he sees as the arrogant
objections of Shakespeare's detractors.

Shakespear whose writings are the offspring of an intuition that mocks
description, that shames the schools, and that ascertains sublimity; whose
knowledge of human nature was profound, penetrating and infallible;
whose morality and philosophy confirm all that was good and wise in the
ancients; whose words are in our mouths, and their irresistable influence
in our hearts; whose eulogium may be felt but cannot be expressed, and
whose own pen alone was equal to the composition of his epitaph: this
Shakespear in the mouths of his fellow creatures is more known for a few
inconsiderable blemishes, sprung from redundant fancy and indispensible
conformity, than for innumerable beauties, delightful as truth, and
commanding as inspiration.

Look at the various authors who by way of compliment to their own
sagacity have deigned so far to honour biography and literature, as to point
out all the blemishes, both as a man and as a writer, of him whose virtue and
whose merit were either above their comprehension, or else their tingling
envy would not allow them to praise. Do we hear from them a word of his
polished manners that made up the delight of the court of Elizabeth; that
laughed Euphuism from the circle, and that endeared him to the friends of
lord Southampton, and various other patrons? Not a syllable. They just allow
that he was a good kind of man, well intentioned, but they never fail, by way
of a drawback, to tell you that he was a bungler at wool combing, that he was
a notorious deer stealer, and that he turned out a very bad actor.

Have we any author who has had the fair disinterestedness, the noble
candour, to indulge himself and gratify the world by any exclusive work that
has instanced the various ways in which Shakespear so greatly commanded
all the passions of the soul; in which, with a portraiture full of imagination
and faithful as nature, he drew ambition, jealousy, tenderness, piety, villainy,
rashness, credulity, licentiousness, and a hundred others with all their shades
and gradations? Not one. We have, however, a little myriad of critics and
hyper-critics who have done his memory the credit to render his works
profitable to themselves, by making holes as fast as tinkers in his reputation

which, they fancy and endeavour to persuade the world they have adroitly mended by patching them up with dross of their own. Well did he say that men's perfections are written in sand their faults in marble.

In my province, I do not consider, if I were ever so inclined, that I have a right to examine the private character of any man, farther than as it may have influenced his public conduct; nor even then, unless it should relate to his connection with the drama. If, by deduction, I can shew that the world has been imposed on by a false character given in favour of any man's works through patronage procured by adulation, meanness, and the fawning arts of a sycophant, it is very fair to place the public and private sentiments of that man by the side of each other, and to appeal to the world, be this or any other the description of his mental blemishes, whether, by that criterion, they have purchased gold or been imposed on by tinsel.

If, on the contrary, I can produce any instances where meekness and modesty have been borne down by rancour and envy, it will be my duty to dwell upon the virtues of him who may have had the public misfortune and the private happiness to possess those qualities; nor can I lay a claim to impartiality, the forwardest requisite of a historian, if I neglect in such cases to deduce, from the heart of the man, the merit of the poet.

Shakespear's genius was so brilliant, his knowledge so wide and universal, his conception so true, and his sentiments so godlike, that to meditate his character is to suppose perfection. Yes, say the cavillers, but his writings are full of faults; and how, as a private man, will he be able to stand or fall upon a comparison with them. Thus quaintness, in complaisance to the time at which he wrote, temporary satire then, perhaps, excellent, now obsolete, and other venial inaccuracies, for it is extremely difficult to call them errors, which we ought not to condemn, or, if we ought, do we easily know how, are quoted to deface his monument of marble, and tortured into as many shapes as envy has snakes, to ornament a sandy heap mistaken by the ignorant for the monument of his commentators.

The writings of Shakespear take in so large and so wonderful an extent of compass, that, while we acknowledge that he wrote better, we are obliged to add that he wrote more than any other dramatic writer. One voluminous author writes tragedies for which he is deservedly celebrated, that after all contain only the representations of a few passions placed in different points of view; another, equally voluminous, writes comedies, with the same just right to celebration, in which a few follies and absurdities are properly ridiculed; Shakespear goes infinitely beyond all this. He takes the whole round of the passions, bends them into every form in which they ought deservedly to be exhibited, exposes them to contempt, holds them up to ridicule, commands for them admiration, conciliates pity, excites terror, and in short displays, in his faithful portraiture of them, every effect that can unlock the anxious mind, or gratify the susceptible fancy; and, when satisfied with exploring and laying open to view the motley group of affections that characterize nature in the beings of this world, he stretches his comprehensive imagination and invents a new world, inhabited with beings the offspring of his own fancy, who in their allegorical character give a refinement to virtue, an aversion to vice, and a ridicule to folly, which no actual representation of them could have had the force or the beauty to convey.

Thus Shakespear, by having left nothing unrepresented either as a positive and naked exhibition of nature, or a deduced and figurative description of her, has gone unequivocally beyond all other writers; and were there nothing else to sanction his astonishing merit and extend his wide fame, he would yet indisputably stand above all dramatic authors ancient and modern.

But, when we consider that there had been no school in which he might study this art, that no dramatic writer since Æschylus, whose soul seems as if it had transmigrated till it was born anew in Shakespear, had been equal to the meritorious task of restoring the glare of Melpomene's [the muse of tragedy's] dagger and perfecting the polish on the mirror of Thalia [the muse of comedy]; when we consider that the theatre in ten years, in the hands of Shakespear, attained all that perfection which it had lost for more than two thousand, and boasted additional perfection never known to it before in the course of the world, it is impossible to contemplate the character of this great man with a degree of wonder equal to its value, which I consider as the highest climax of panegyric; and yet these considerations are never afforded, and all we can learn from writers, whose geniuses would be complimented by the possession of a capacity to comprehend the genius of Shakespear, gives us no more than permission to assert, that he was an extraordinary man, when it was admitted that he had received but an indifferent education, and that, though there were passages in his works of great and wonderful beauty, there were, nevertheless, numerous faults which never ought to be permitted.

As to the faults, I think it will not be very difficult to prove that they are not so numerous not of such magnitude as the world is taught to believe by the critics; I do not care much what they themselves believe on the subject, though I hope for the sake of common sense and their own reputation, they do not believe half they assert; as to the beauties, they are too indelibly impressed on the heart of every one who has heard or read them to need explanation.

But a few words as to the education of Shakespear, for though I am not writing his life I have a great pride in being the historian of his mind. He received the common advantages of learning in what is called a grammar school; that is to say, a place where a boy of any tolerable genius may learn all that the master is capable of teaching him in six months, and where boys in general study for years and at last know nothing.

Whether Shakespear learned little or much at this school makes nothing either for or against my argument. I can very willingly suppose that the scholar was very soon able to teach the master. It was not in this grammar school where he received that education which has wrought his celebrity. It was in the school of nature, who condescended to be his instructress. The lady fell in love with him; was captivated; he was her Adonis, her Endymion, and both her beauty and her chastity yielded to the irresistible impulse; while he, with all the gallantry, yet the delicacy of an honourable lover, and a faithful knight, consecrated his life to the service of his mistress, pleaded her cause, redressed her wrongs, and, with the truest constancy and most ardent gratitude, made her beauty the perpetual theme of his panegyric.

If Æschylus, when, God knows, grammar schools had nothing to do with learning, but when men were called wise because they used first so many words as served simply to express such ideas as nature taught them, and good, because their minds adopted no ideas but what tended to promote general morality: if Æschylus, studying in the school of nature, represented the great actions and glorious achievements of his countrymen, and felt emulously and meritoriously that by that means he should render Greece and human nature a benefit, why should we deny the same merit to Shakespear more than two thousand years afterwards, when grammar schools actually flourished. But it would wrong my cause to waste too much anxiety about it; and nothing but a necessity for strong and incontrovertible argument to cope with the opinions of men, certainly great and reputable, except in their charitable warning to the world of faults in another which are not yet, however, generally discovered, and, after all, not of the magnitude of their own, would have induced me to dwell so minutely on a theme that, with men of fair and candid discrimination, recommends itself and speaks its own eulogium.

The general merit of Shakespear manifests itself in a thousand various ways. Take any one of the passions which he has moulded at will to serve the general purpose of instruction and amusement, and see to what an astonishing pitch he has affected the human heart by a critical and interesting display of it.

Is the passion love? See how he has followed it through all its vicissitudes. The delicate tenderness, the fond impatience, the impetuous ardour, the noble constancy of Romeo and Juliet, perhaps, has not a parallel in language.

To youthful love every thing is possible; and the exquisite nonsense that Shakespear has put into the mouth of the doating, enamoured, yet delicate Juliet, is full of poetic beauty, so boundlessly, so extravagant, and yet so truly natural, that we are equally captivated with her love and her innocence.

The love of Romeo is no less admirably drawn. It is impetuous, thoughtless, and rash, yet manly, noble, and generous; but its characteristic is nature. He leaps the orchard wall and braves the resentment of Juliet's relations, out of love, yet presently, out of this very love, he becomes a coward and puts up with an insult from of those relations; nor is he roused out of this apathy till called upon to revenge the death of his friend.

In the garden scene, surely nothing can be so beautiful as the enchanted, yet respectful, manner in which he listens to the unaffected tenderness, the timid honesty, the techy impatience of Juliet. His love, profound, and awful, recedes from his tongue to his heart; hers, inconsiderate and volatile, flies from her heart to her tongue, till, at length impelled to reply to her fond confession, which disdains all hypocrisy, and derides all subterfuge, they join in interchanging vows, tender and affectionate on her part, manly and honourable on his.

Absence only renders more amiable the noble and exalted minds of those lovers. His despair at hearing the sentence of banishment, his horror at the news of Juliet's death, and his solemn determination to follow her; and her resigned compliance with the friar's stratagem, her awful manner of executing it, and her destroying herself, after every hope has failed her, are masterly pictures of exquisite love.[1]

Were I to go on investigating the various ways in which Shakespear has treated this one passion, I should greatly exceed the limits I am obliged to prescribe for myself. I shall, therefore, for the present pass by the noble and persevering constancy of Imogen [in *Cymbeline*], the patient and endearing tenderness of Desdemona [in *Othello*], the generous and enterprizing affection of Rosalind [in *As You Like It*], the silent and devouring passion of Viola [in *Twelfth Night*], and all those great and unexampled proofs of consummate strength of mind and profound judgment of the human heart in which Shakespear, though he may have been in one instance now and then equalled by a particular author, taking his writings on the passion of love in their full and comprehensive sense, he has clearly excelled every author.

Notes

1.   [French dramatist, critic, and novelist, Louis-Sebastien] Mercier was so charmed with Romeo and Juliet, and so distressed that the lovers should become victims to the unjust and unreasonable enmity of their families, that

he has given the plot a new turn. The play never was performed, but it has all the delicacy, finesse, and truth of that admirable author. Benvolio, having long foreseen the consequence of this family hatred, does his utmost to excite the love of Romeo and Juliet, in order to bring about a reconciliation. He finds both the families averse to his project, and, therefore, connives at a private marriage. Every thing happens as in Shakespear's play. Benvolio, however, in the place of the friar, having from his infancy studied chemistry, administers a potion to Juliet; and, contriving that Romeo should be informed of the death, furnishes him with another. Romeo opens the tomb and finding Juliet apparently dead, drinks the potion and falls down at her side. In the mean, Benvolio having alarmed the two fathers they presently behold their two children in this state. After reading to them a severe lecture, and reproaching them for their conduct and the dreadful consequences of their mutual enmity, he honestly confesses that he has wrought all this; tells them that this seeming death of these lovers is but a sleep; that he alone, however, knows the charm to revive them; and that, if they will discard their unjust anger and vow perpetual amity, their children shall wake and revive the double pleasure of being restored to life and to the arms of their parents; but that, if they hesitate, it will be too late. In that case he knows he shall be considered as their murderer, but that he would rather die than witness a rancour so dishonourable to themselves and such a scandal to human nature. The result is obvious. The lovers revive, and their affection is crowned with the approbation and blessing of their fathers. I shall only add that the Frenchman merely alters the story; he does not attempt to improve upon Shakespear, whose genius he reverences, and to whose productions he had upon all occasions most willingly paid a warm tribute of admiration.

—Charles Dibdin, from "Shakespear," *A Complete
History of the Stage*, volume 3, pp. 14–28, 1795

WILLIAM GODWIN "OF ENGLISH STYLE" (1797)

William Godwin (1756–1836), political philosopher, novelist, husband of author and pioneering feminist Mary Wollstonecraft, father of Mary Shelley (author of *Frankenstein*), and father-in-law of the poet Percy Bysshe Shelley, asserts that Shakespeare's greatness comes in his expression of great passions because, Godwin says, Shakespeare was guided by an impetuous genius that fitted him for the expression of great passions. When Shakespeare must portray events and mental states of less intensity, Godwin finds that he becomes pedantic in his language, remote and needlessly complicated. Godwin gives several examples, but a contemporary reader may find that Godwin is trying to shape Shakespeare to his own specifications as the neoclassical critics did. While they read him with the expectation that he ought to conform to such decorum that the unities of dramatic action demand, Godwin faults him for the lack of a romantic temperament, unable to see the individual characterizations suggested by Shakespeare's idiosyncratic language. Brutus is drawn by Shakespeare as not the sort of man to engage in high-flown oratorical justifications of the sort Godwin desires. Brutus's temperament recoils from stirring passion, and he hopes to justify his part in Caesar's death through quietly convincing reason. In another example Godwin offers, in dialogue with Othello, the duke of Venice is shown to be keeping his distance and being a little officious.

I proceed now to the mention of Shakespear, a writer whom no ingenuous English reader can recollect without the profoundest esteem and the most unbounded admiration. His gigantic mind enabled him in a great degree to overcome the fetters in which the English language was at that period bound. In him we but rarely trace the languid and tedious formality which at that time characterised English composition. His soul was too impetuous, and his sympathy with human passions too entire, not to instruct him in the shortest road to the heart.

But Shakespear for the most part is great only, when great passions are to be expressed. In the calmer and less turbid scenes of life his genius seems in a great degree to forsake him. His wit is generally far fetched, trivial and cold. His tranquil style is perplexed, pedantical, and greatly disfigured with conceits. Of this we will exhibit some examples. They shall be taken from such of his plays as are supposed to have been written in the reign of James the first. It would not have been less easy to have detected similar faults in his earlier plays.

The following is part of the dialogue between the disguised Duke and Isabella in *Measure for Measure,* upon occasion of Angelo's atrocious proposition concerning the pardon of her brother.

Duk.: The hand that hath made you faire, hath made you good: the
    goodnesse that is cheape in beauty, makes beauty briefe in goodnesse;
    but grace being the soule of your complexion, shall keepe the body of
    it ever faire: the assault that *Angelo* hath made to you, Fortune hath
    convaid to my understanding; and, but that frailty hath examples for

his falling, I should wonder at *Angelo:* how will you doe to content
this Substitute, and to save your brother? . . .

Isab.: Let me heare you speake farther; I have spirit to doe anything that
appeares not foule in the truth of my spirit.

Duk.: Vertue is bold, and goodness never fearfull: Have you not heard
speake *of Mariana* the sister of *Fredericke* the great Souldier, who
miscarried at Sea?

Isab.: I have heard of the Lady, and good words went with her name.

Duk.: She should this *Angelo* have married: was affianced to her by oath,
and the nuptial appointed: between which time of the contract, and
limit of the solemnity, her brother *Fredericke* was wrackt at Sea,
having in that perished vessel, the dowry of his sister: but marke how
heavily this befell to the poore Gentlewoman, there she lost a noble
and renouned brother, in his love toward her, ever most kind and
naturall: with him the portion and sinew of her fortune, her marriage
dowry: with both, her combynate-husband, this well seeming *Angelo.*

Isab.: Can this be so? did *Angelo* so leave her?

Duk.: Left her in her teares, and dried not one of them with his comfort:
swallowed his vowes whole, pretending in her, discoveries of dishonor:
in few, bestow'd her on her owne lamentation, which she yet weares
for his sake: and he, a marble of her cares, is washed with them, but
relents not. . . . Goe you to *Angelo,* answer his requiring with a plausible
obedience, agree with his demands to the point: . . . we shall advise
this wronged maid tosteed up your appointment, goe in your place:
if the encounter acknowledge it selfe hereafter, it may compell him to
her recompence; and heere, by this is your brother saved, your honor
untainted, the poore *Mariana* advantaged, and the corrupt Deputy
sealed. (Edit. 1632, commonly called the second folio.) [III.i.182ff.]

Nothing can be of a style more quaint and uncouth, than the letters that
are from time to time introduced in different plays of Shakespear. Take as a
specimen the letter of Posthumus to Imogen in the tragedy of *Cymbeline.*

Ivstice, and your Fathers wrath (should hee take mee in his
Dominion) could not be so cruell to me, as you, (oh the deerest
of Creatures) would even renew me with your eyes. Take notice
that I am in *Cambria* at *Milford-Haven:* what your owne Love, will
out of this advise you, follow. So he wishes you all happinesse, that
remaines loyall to his Vow, and your encreasing in Love.

Leonatus Posthumus.[III.ii.40ff.]

There was probably never a grander occasion of eloquence, than when Brutus ascended the rostrum to vindicate the assassination of Caesar. Nothing but the contagion of the vilest taste in literature, could have led Shakespear to put into his mouth such phrases as the following.

> Be patient till the last. Romans, Countrymen, and Lovers, heare mee for my cause, and be silent, that you may heare. Beleeve me for mine Honor, and have respect to mine Honor, that you may beleeve. Censure me in your Wisedome, and awake your Senses, that you may the better Iudge.————There is Teares, for his Love: Ioy, for his Fortune: Honor, for his Valour: and death for his Ambition.
>
> [*Julius Caesar*, III.ii.13ff.]

I know not how far the great soul of Brutus, if he had condescended to such poor prating as this, could have elevated it by his enunciation: dramatic writers, well acquainted with the stage, often err in this way, thinking rather, how feeble or foolish things may be disguised by an admirable delivery, than what they are in themselves. This I know, that the genuine tendency of such expressions was to procure Brutus to be driven out by the Roman people with hootings, execration and scorn.

We will only add to these examples, the words in which the Duke communicates to Othello his commission for Cyprus. One would think that no function could require greater simplicity of language.

The Turke with a most mighty preparation makes for Cyprus: *Othello*, the Fortitude of the place is best knowne to you. And though we have there a Substitute of most allowed sufficiency; yet opinion, a more Soveraigne Mistris of Effects, throwes a more safe voyce on you: you must therefore be content to slubber the grosse of your new Fortunes, with this more stubborne, and boysterous expedition.

> —William Godwin, "Of English Style,"
> *The Enquirer*, 1797, pp. 388–93

AUGUST WILHELM VON SCHLEGEL
"LECTURE XXIII" (1809)

August Wilhelm von Schlegel (1767–1845) was a German critic, philologist, and translator of Shakespeare's work into German. In this lecture, Schlegel systematically defends Shakespeare against a number of opinions that have, over the course of Shakespearean criticism, gathered around his work: 1) Schlegel attempts to demonstrate that Shakespeare is not devoid of conscious art or great learning, even if his learning was not of the academic sort. 2) He describes two sorts of critical methods that have been used to understand Shakespeare. One examines the parts of a whole work as separate pieces that have been cobbled together. The other method entails studying the whole work and seeing the various parts as emanations from its vital center. 3) Schlegel traces the design of Shakespeare's work. 4) Schlegel discusses Shakespeare's great knowledge of humanity, characters, the passions, the working of the mind, and mental illness. 5) Schlegel defends Shakespeare's word play. 6) Schlegel refutes the argument that Shakespeare's plays are often morally odious and censurable because they "wound our feelings." 7) After discussing Shakespeare's immense accomplishments as a tragedian, Schlegel finds an equal genius in his comedies and focuses on his fools. 8) Schlegel ends his lecture with a discussion and defence of Shakespeare's diction and versification, considering them in the context of Shakespeare's time and as expressive tools that help fashion the quality of thought and feeling his works establish.

Our poet's want of scholarship has been the subject of endless controversy, and yet it is surely a very easy matter to decide. Shakspeare was poor in dead school-cram, but he possessed a rich treasury of living and intuitive knowledge. He knew a little Latin, and even something of Greek, though it may be not enough to read with ease the writers in the original. With modern languages also, the French and Italian, he had, perhaps, but a superficial acquaintance. The general direction of his mind was not to the collection of words but of facts. With English books, whether original or translated, he was extensively acquainted: we may safely affirm that he had read all that his native language and literature then contained that could be of any use to him in his poetical avocations. He was sufficiently intimate with mythology to employ it, in the only manner he could wish, in the way of symbolical ornament. He had formed a correct notion of the spirit of Ancient History, and more particularly of that of the Romans; and the history of his own country was familiar to him even in detail. Fortunately for him it had not as yet been treated in a diplomatic and pragmatic spirit, but merely in the chronicle-style; in other words, it had not yet assumed the appearance of dry investigations respecting the development of political relations, diplomatic negotiations, finances, &c., but exhibited a visible image of the life and movement of an age prolific of great deeds. Shakspeare, moreover, was a nice observer of nature; he knew the technical language of mechanics and artisans; he seems to have been well travelled in the interior of his own country, while of others he inquired diligently of travelled navigators respecting their peculiarity of climate and customs. He thus became accurately acquainted with all the popular usages, opinions, and traditions which could be of use in poetry.

The proofs of his ignorance, on which the greatest stress is laid, are a few geographical blunders and anachronisms. Because in a comedy founded on an earlier tale, he makes ships visit Bohemia, he has been the subject of much laughter. But I conceive that we should be very unjust towards him, were we to conclude that he did not, as well as ourselves, possess the useful but by no means difficult knowledge that Bohemia is nowhere bounded by the sea. He could never, in that case, have looked into a map of Germany, who yet describes elsewhere, with great accuracy, the maps of both Indies, together with the discoveries of the latest navigators.[1] In such matters Shakspeare is only faithful to the details of the domestic stories. In the novels on which he worked, he avoided disturbing the associations of his audience, to whom they were known, by novelties—the correction of errors in secondary and unimportant particulars. The more wonderful the story, the more it ranged in a purely poetical region, which he transfers at will to an indefinite distance. These plays, whatever names they bear, take place in the true land of romance, and in the very century of wonderful love stories. He knew well that in the forest of Ardennes there were neither the lions and serpents of the Torrid Zone, nor the shepherdesses of Arcadia: but he transferred both to it,[2] because the design and import of his picture required them. Here he considered himself entitled to take the greatest liberties. He had not to do with a hair-splitting, hypercritical age like ours, which is always seeking in poetry for something else than poetry; his audience entered the theatre, not to learn true chronology, geography, and natural history, but to witness a vivid exhibition. I will undertake to prove that Shakspeare's anachronisms are, for the most part, committed of set purpose and deliberately. It was frequently of importance to him to move the exhibited subject out of the background of time, and bring it quite near us. Hence in *Hamlet*, though avowedly an old Northern story, there runs a tone of modish society, and in every respect the costume of the most recent period. Without those circumstantialities it would not have been allowable to make a philosophical inquirer of Hamlet, on which trait, however, the meaning of the whole is made to rest. On that account he mentions his education at a university, though, in the age of the true Hamlet of history, universities were not in existence. He makes him study at Wittenberg, and no selection of a place could have been more suitable. The name was very popular: the story of *Dr. Faustus of Wittenberg* had made it well known; it was of particular celebrity in protestant England, as Luther had taught and written there shortly before, and the very name must have immediately suggested the idea of freedom in thinking. I cannot even consider it an anachronism that Richard the Third should speak of Macchiavel. The word is here used altogether proverbially: the contents, at least, of the book entitled *Of the Prince (Del Principe,)* have been in existence ever since the existence of tyrants; Macchiavel was merely the first to commit them to writing. . . .

To me he appears a profound artist, and not a blind and wildly luxuriant genius. I consider, generally speaking, all that has been said on the subject a mere fable, a blind and extravagant error. In other arts the assertion refutes itself; for in them acquired knowledge is an indispensable condition of clever execution. But even in such poets, as are usually given out as careless pupils of nature, devoid of art or school discipline, I have always found, on a nearer consideration of the works of real excellence they may have produced, even a high cultivation of the mental powers, practice in art, and views both worthy in themselves and maturely considered. This applies to Homer as well as to Dante. The activity of genius is, it is true, natural to it, and, in a certain sense, unconscious; and, consequently, the person who possesses it is not always at the moment able to render an account of the course which he may have pursued; but it by no means follows, that the thinking power had not a great share in it. It is from the very rapidity and certainty of the mental process, from the utmost clearness of understanding, that thinking in a poet is not perceived as something abstracted, does not wear the appearance of reflex meditation. That notion of poetical inspiration, which many lyrical poets have brought into circulation, as if they were not in their senses, and like Pythia [the priestess who presided over the oracle of Apollo at Delphos], when possessed by the divinity, delivered oracles unintelligible to themselves—this notion, (a mere lyrical invention,) is least of all applicable to dramatic composition, one of the most thoughtful productions of the human mind. It is admitted that Shakspeare has reflected, and deeply reflected, on character and passion, on the progress of events and human destinies, on the human constitution, on all the things and relations of the world; this is an admission which must be made, for one alone of thousands of his maxims would be a sufficient refutation of whoever should attempt to deny it. So that it was only for the structure of his own pieces that he had no thought to spare? This he left to the dominion of chance, which blew together the atoms of [Greek philosopher] Epicurus. But supposing that, devoid of any higher ambition to approve himself to judicious critics and posterity, and wanting in that love of art which longs for self-satisfaction in the perfection of its works, he had merely laboured to please the unlettered crowd; still this very object alone and the pursuit of theatrical effect, would have led him to bestow attention to the structure and adherence of his pieces. For does not the impression of a drama depend in an especial manner on the relation of the parts to each other? And, however beautiful a scene may be in itself, if yet it be at variance with what the spectators have been led to expect in its particular place, so as to destroy the interest which they had hitherto felt, will it not be at once reprobated by all who possess plain common sense, and give themselves up to nature? The comic intermixtures may be considered merely as a sort of interlude, designed to relieve the straining of the mind after the stretch of the more serious parts, so long as no better purpose can be found in them; but in the progress of the main action, in the concatenation of the events, the poet must, if possible, display even more expenditure of thought than in the composition of individual character and situations, otherwise he would be like the conductor of a puppet-show who has entangled his wires, so that the puppets receive from their mechanism quite different movements from those which he actually intended.

The English critics are unanimous in their praise of the truth and uniform consistency of his characters, of his heartrending pathos, and his comic wit. Moreover, they extol the beauty and sublimity of his separate descriptions, images, and expressions. This last is the most superficial and cheap mode of criticising works of art. Johnson compares him who should endeavour to recommend this poet by passages unconnectedly torn from his works, to the pedant in Hierocles, who exhibited a brick as a sample of his house. And yet how little, and how very unsatisfactorily does he himself speak of the pieces considered as a whole! Let any man, for instance, bring together the short characters which he gives at the close of each play, and see if the aggregate will amount to that sum of admiration which he himself, at his outset, has stated as the correct standard for the appreciation of the poet. It was, generally speaking, the prevailing tendency of the time which preceded our own, (and which has showed itself particularly in physical science,) to consider everything having life as a mere accumulation of dead parts, to separate what exists only in connexion and cannot otherwise be conceived, instead of penetrating to the central point and viewing all the parts as so many irradiations from it. Hence nothing is so rare as a critic who can elevate himself to the comprehensive contemplation of a work of art. Shakspeare's compositions, from the very depth of purpose displayed in them, have been especially liable to the misfortune of being misunderstood. Besides, this prosaic species of criticism requires always that the poetic form should be applied to the details of execution; but when the plan of the piece is concerned, it never looks for more than the logical connexion of causes and effects, or some partial and trite moral by way of application; and all that cannot be reconciled therewith is declared superfluous, or even a pernicious appendage. On these principles we must even strike out from the Greek tragedies most of the choral songs, which also contribute nothing to the development of the action, but are merely an harmonious echo of the impressions the poet aims at conveying. In this they altogether mistake the rights of poetry and the nature of the romantic drama, which, for the very reason that it is and ought to be picturesque, requires richer accompaniments and contrasts for its main groups. In all Art and Poetry, but more especially in the romantic, the Fancy lays claims to be considered as an independent mental power governed according to its own laws.

In an essay on *Romeo and Juliet*,[4] written a number of years ago, I went through the whole of the scenes in their order, and demonstrated the inward necessity of each with reference to the whole; I showed why such a particular circle of characters and relations was placed around the two lovers; I explained the signification of the mirth here and there scattered, and justified the use of the occasional heightening given to the poetical colours. From all this it seemed to follow unquestionably, that with the exception of a few witticisms, now become unintelligible or foreign to the present taste, (imitations of the tone of society of that day,) nothing could be taken away, nothing added, nothing otherwise arranged, without mutilating and disfiguring the perfect work. I would readily undertake to do the same for all the pieces of Shakspeare's maturer years, but to do this would require a separate book. Here I am reduced to confine my observations to the tracing his great designs with a rapid pencil; but still I must previously be allowed to deliver my sentiments in a general manner on the subject of his most eminent peculiarities.

Shakspeare's knowledge of mankind has become proverbial: in this his superiority is so great, that he has justly been called the master of the human heart. A readiness to remark the mind's fainter and involuntary utterances, and the power to express with certainty the meaning of these signs, as determined by experience and reflection, constitutes "the observer of men;" but tacitly to draw from these still further conclusions, and to arrange the separate observations according to grounds of probability, into a just and valid combination, this, it may be said, is to know men. The distinguishing property of the dramatic poet who is great in characterization, is something altogether different here, and which, (take it which way we will,) either includes in it this readiness and this acuteness, or dispenses with both. It is the capability of transporting himself so completely into every situation, even the most unusual, that he is enabled, as plenipotentiary of the whole human race, without particular instructions for each separate case, to act and speak in the name of every individual. It is the power of endowing the creatures of his imagination with such self-existent energy, that they afterwards act in each conjuncture according to general laws of nature: the poet, in his dreams, institutes, as it were, experiments which are received with as much authority as if they had been made on waking objects. The inconceivable element herein, and what moreover can never be learned, is, that the characters appear neither to do nor to say any thing on the spectator's account merely; and yet that the poet simply, by means of the exhibition, and without any subsidiary explanation, communicates to his audience the gift of looking into the inmost recesses of their minds. Hence Goethe has ingeniously compared Shakspeare's characters to watches with crystalline plates and cases, which, while they point out the hours as correctly as other watches, enable us at the same time to perceive the inward springs whereby all this is accomplished.

Nothing, however, is more foreign to Shakspeare than a certain anatomical style of exhibition, which laboriously enumerates all the motives by which a man is determined to act in this or that particular manner. This rage of supplying motives, the mania of so many modern historians, might be carried at length to an extent which would abolish every thing like individuality, and resolve all character into nothing but the effect of foreign or external influences whereas we know that it often announces itself most decidedly in earliest infancy. After all, a man acts so because he is so. And what each man is, that Shakspeare reveals to us most immediately: he demands and obtains our belief, even for what is singular and deviates from the ordinary course of nature. Never perhaps was there so comprehensive a talent for characterization as Shakspeare. It not only grasps every diversity of rank, age, and sex, down to the lispings of infancy; not only do the king and the beggar, the hero and the pickpocket, the sage and the idiot, speak and act with equal truthfulness; not only does he transport himself to distant ages and foreign nations, and portray with the greatest accuracy (a few apparent violations of costume excepted) the spirit of the ancient Romans, of the French in the wars with the English, of the English themselves during a great part of their history, of the Southern Europeans (in the serious part of many comedies), the cultivated society of the day, and the rude barbarism of a Norman foretime; his human characters have not only such depth and individuality that they do not admit of being classed under common names, and are inexhaustible even in conception: no, this Prometheus not merely forms men, he opens the gates of the magical world of spirits, calls up the midnight ghost, exhibits before us the witches with their unhallowed rites, peoples the air with sportive fairies and sylphs; and these beings, though existing only in the imagination, nevertheless possess such truth and consistency, that even with such misshapen abortions as Caliban, he extorts the assenting conviction, that were there such beings they would so conduct themselves. In a word, as he carries a bold and pregnant fancy into the kingdom of nature, on the other hand, he carries nature into the regions of fancy, which lie beyond the confines of reality. We are lost in astonishment at the close intimacy he brings us into with the extraordinary, the wonderful, and the unheard-of.

Pope and Johnson appear strangely to contradict each other, when the first says, "all the characters of Shakspeare are individuals," and the second, "they are species." And yet perhaps these opinions may admit of reconciliation. Pope's expression is unquestionably the more correct. A character which should be merely a personification of a naked general idea could neither exhibit any great depth nor any great variety. The names of genera and species are well known to be merely auxiliaries for the understanding, that we may embrace the infinite variety of nature in a certain order. The characters which Shakspeare has so thoroughly delineated have undoubtedly a number of individual peculiarities, but at the same time they possess a significance which is not applicable to them alone: they generally supply materials for a profound theory of their most prominent and distinguishing property. But even with the above correction, this opinion must still have its limitations. Characterization is merely one ingredient of the dramatic art, and not dramatic poetry itself. It would be improper in the extreme, if the poet were to draw our attention to superfluous traits of character, at a time when it ought to be his endeavour to produce other impressions. Whenever the musical or the fanciful preponderates, the characteristical necessarily falls into the background. Hence many of the figures of Shakspeare exhibit merely external designations, determined by the place which they occupy in the whole: they are like secondary persons in a public procession, to whose physiognomy we seldom pay much attention; their only importance is derived from the solemnity of their dress and the duty in which they are engaged. Shakspeare's messengers, for instance, are for the most part mere messengers, and yet not common, but poetical messengers: the messages which they have to bring is the soul which suggests to them their language. Other voices, too, are merely raised to pour forth these as melodious lamentations or rejoicings, or to dwell in reflection on what has taken place; and in a serious drama without chorus this must always be more or less the case, if we would not have it prosaical.

If Shakspeare deserves our admiration for his characters, he is equally deserving of it for his exhibition of passion, taking this word in its widest signification, as including every mental condition, every tone, from indifference or familiar mirth to the wildest rage and despair. He gives us the history of minds; he lays open to us, in a single word, a whole series of their anterior states. His passions do not stand at the same height, from first to last, as is the case with so many tragic poets, who, in the language of [German critic, philosopher, and dramatist Gotthold Ephraim] Lessing, are thorough masters of the legal style of love. He paints, with inimitable veracity, the gradual advance from the first origin; "he gives," as Lessing says, "a living picture of all the slight and secret artifices by which a feeling steals into our souls, of all the imperceptible advantages which it there gains, of all the stratagems by which it makes every other passion subservient to itself, till it becomes the sole tyrant of our desires and our aversions." Of all the poets, perhaps, he alone has portrayed the mental diseases, melancholy, delirium, lunacy, with such inexpressible and, in every respect, definite truth, that the physician may enrich his observations from them in the same manner as from real cases.

And yet Johnson has objected to Shakspeare that his pathos is not always natural and free from affectation. There are, it is true, passages, though comparatively speaking very few, where his poetry exceeds the bounds of actual dialogue, where a too soaring imagination, a too luxuriant wit, rendered a complete dramatic forgetfulness of himself impossible. With this exception, the censure originated in a fanciless way of thinking, to which everything appears unnatural that does not consort with its own tame insipidity. Hence an idea has been formed of simple and natural pathos, which consists in exclamations destitute of imagery and nowise elevated above every-day life. But energetical passions electrify all the mental powers, and will consequently, in highly-favoured natures, give utterance to themselves in ingenious and figurative expressions. It has been often remarked that indignation makes a man witty; and as despair occasionally breaks out into laughter, it may sometimes also give vent to itself in antithetical comparisons.

Besides, the rights of the poetical form have not been duly weighed. Shakspeare, who was always sure of his power to excite, when he wished, sufficiently powerful emotions, has occasionally, by indulging in a freer play of fancy, purposely tempered the impressions when too painful, and immediately introduced a musical softening of our sympathy.[5] He had not those rude ideas of his art which many moderns seem to have, as if the poet, like the clown in the proverb, must strike twice on the same place. An ancient rhetorician delivered a caution against dwelling too long on the excitation of pity; for nothing, he said, dries so soon as tears; and Shakspeare acted conformably to this ingenious maxim without having learned it. The paradoxical assertion of Johnson that "Shakspeare had a greater talent for comedy than tragedy, and that in the latter he has frequently displayed an affected tone," is scarcely deserving of lengthy notice. For its refutation, it is unnecessary to appeal to the great tragical compositions of the poet, which, for overpowering effect, leave far behind them almost everything that the stage has seen besides; a few of their less celebrated scenes would be quite sufficient. What to many readers might lend an appearance of truth to this assertion are the verbal witticisms, that playing upon words, which Shakspeare not unfrequently introduces into serious and sublime passages, and even into those also of a peculiarly pathetic nature.

I have already stated the point of view in which we ought to consider this sportive play upon words. I shall here, therefore, merely deliver a few observations respecting the playing upon words in general, and its poetical use. A thorough investigation would lead us too far from our subject, and too deeply into considerations on the essence of language, and its relation to poetry, or rhyme, &c.

There is in the human mind a desire that language should exhibit the object which it denotes, sensibly, by its very sound, which may be traced even as far back as in the first origin of poetry. As, in the shape in which language comes down to us, this is seldom perceptibly the case, an imagination which has been powerfully excited is fond of laying hold of any congruity in sound which may accidentally offer itself, that by such means he may, for the nonce, restore the lost resemblance between the word and the thing. For example, how common was it and is it to seek in the name of a person, however arbitrarily bestowed, a reference to his qualities and fortunes,—to convert it purposely into a significant name. Those who cry out against the play upon words as an unnatural and affected invention, only betray their own ignorance of original nature. A great fondness for it is always evinced among children, as well as with nations of simple manners, among whom correct ideas of the derivation and affinity of words have not yet been developed, and do not, consequently, stand in the way of this caprice. In Homer we find several examples of it; the Books of Moses, the oldest written memorial of the primitive world, are, as is well known, full of them. On the other hand, poets of a very cultivated taste, like Petrarch, or orators, like Cicero, have delighted in them. Whoever, in *Richard the Second,* is disgusted with the affecting play of words of the dying John of Gaunt on his own name, should remember that the same thing occurs in the *Ajax* of Sophocles. We do not mean to say that all playing upon words is on all occasions to be justified. This must depend on the disposition of mind, whether it will admit of such a play of fancy, and whether the sallies, comparisons, and allusions, which lie at the bottom of them, possess internal solidity. Yet we must not proceed upon the principle of trying how the thought appears after it is deprived of the resemblance in sound, any more than we are to endeavour to feel the charm of rhymed versification after depriving it of its rhyme. The laws of good taste on this subject must, moreover, vary with the quality of the languages. In those which possess a great number of homonymes, that is, words possessing the same, or nearly the same, sound, though quite different in their derivation and signification, it is almost more difficult to avoid, than to fall on such a verbal play. It has, however, been feared, lest a door might be opened to puerile witticism, if they were not rigorously proscribed. But I cannot, for my part, find that Shakspeare had such an invincible and immoderate passion for this verbal witticism. It is true, he sometimes makes a most lavish use of this figure; at others, he has employed it very sparingly; and at times (for example, in *Macbeth*), I do not believe a vestige of it is to be found. Hence, in respect to the use or the rejection of the play upon words, he must have been guided by the measure of the objects, and the different style in which they required to be treated, and probably have followed here, as in every thing else, principles which, fairly examined, will bear a strict examination.

The objection that Shakspeare wounds our feelings by the open display of the most disgusting moral odiousness, unmercifully harrows up the mind, and tortures even our eyes by the exhibition of the most insupportable and hateful spectacles, is one of greater and graver importance. He has, in fact, never varnished over wild and blood-thirsty passions with a pleasing exterior—never clothed crime and want of principle with a false show of greatness of soul; and in that respect he is every way deserving of praise. Twice he has portrayed downright villains, and the masterly way in which he has contrived to elude impressions of too painful a nature may be seen in Iago and Richard the Third. I allow that the reading, and still more the sight, of some of his pieces, is not advisable to weak nerves, any more than was the *Eumenides* of Eschylus; but is the poet, who can only reach an important object by a bold and hazardous daring, to be checked by considerations for such persons? If the effeminacy of the present day is to serve as a general standard of what tragical composition may properly exhibit to human nature, we shall be forced to set very narrow limits indeed to art, and the hope of anything like powerful effect must at once and for ever be renounced. If we wish to have a grand purpose, we must also wish to have the grand means, and our nerves ought in some measure to accommodate themselves to painful impressions, if, by way of requital, our mind is thereby elevated and strengthened. The constant reference to a petty and puny race must cripple the boldness of the poet. Fortunately for his art, Shakspeare lived in an age extremely susceptible of noble and tender impressions, but which had yet inherited enough of the firmness of a vigorous olden time, not to shrink with dismay from every strong and forcible painting. We have lived to see tragedies of which the catastrophe consists in the swoon of an enamoured princess: if Shakspeare falls occasionally into the opposite extreme, it is a noble error, originating in the fulness of a gigantic strength. And this tragical Titan, who storms the heavens and threatens to tear the world from off its hinges, who, more terrible than Æschylus, makes our hair to stand on end, and congeals our blood with horror, possessed at the same time the insinuating loveliness of the sweetest poesy; he toys with love like a child, and his songs die away on the ear like melting sighs. He unites in his soul the utmost elevation and the utmost depth; and the most opposite and even apparently irreconcilable properties subsist in him peaceably together. The world of spirits and nature have laid all their treasures at his feet: in strength a demi-god, in profundity of view a prophet, in all-seeing wisdom a guardian spirit of a higher order, he lowers himself to mortals as if unconscious of his superiority, and is as open and unassuming as a child.

If the delineation of all his characters, separately considered, is inimitably bold and correct, he surpasses even himself in so combining and contrasting them, that they serve to bring out each other's peculiarities. This is the very perfection of dramatic characterization: for we can never estimate a man's true worth if we consider him altogether abstractedly by himself; we must see him in his relations with others; and it is here that most dramatic poets are deficient. Shakspeare makes each of his principal characters the glass in which the others are reflected, and by like means enables us to discover what could not be immediately revealed to us. What in others is most profound, is with him but surface. Ill-advised should we be were we always to take men's declarations respecting themselves and others for sterling coin. Ambiguity of design with much propriety he makes to overflow with the most praiseworthy principles; and sage maxims are not unfre-quently put in the mouth of stupidity, to show how easily such common-place truisms may be acquired. Nobody ever painted so truthfully as he has done the facility of self-deception, the half self-conscious hypocrisy towards ourselves, with which even noble minds attempt to disguise the almost inevitable influence of selfish motives in human nature. This secret irony of the characterization commands admiration as the profound abyss of acuteness and sagacity; but it is the grave of enthusiasm. We arrive at it only after we have had the misfortune to see human nature through and through; and when no choice remains but to adopt the melancholy truth, that "no virtue or greatness is altogether pure and genuine," or the dangerous error that "the highest perfection is attainable." Here we therefore may perceive in the poet himself, notwithstanding his power to excite the most fervent emotions, a certain cool indifference, but still the indifference of a superior mind, which has run through the whole sphere of human existence and survived feeling.

The irony in Shakspeare has not merely a reference to the separate characters, but frequently to the whole of the action. Most poets who portray human events in a narrative or dramatic form take themselves a part, and exact from their readers a blind approbation or condemnation of whatever side they choose to support or oppose. The more zealous this rhetoric is, the more certainly it fails of its effect. In every case we are conscious that the subject itself is not brought immediately before us, but that we view it through the medium of a different way of thinking. When, however, by a dexterous manoeuvre, the poet allows us an occasional glance at the less brilliant reverse of the medal, then he makes, as it were, a sort of secret understanding with the select circle of the more intelligent of his readers or spectators; he shows them that he had previously seen and admitted the validity of their tacit objections; that he himself is not tied down to the represented subject, but soars freely above it; and that, if he chose, he could unrelentingly annihilate the beautiful and irresistibly attractive scenes which his magic pen has produced. No doubt, wherever the proper tragic enters every thing like irony immediately ceases; but from the avowed raillery of Comedy, to the point where the subjection of mortal beings to an inevitable destiny demands the highest degree of seriousness, there are a multitude of human relations which unquestionably may be considered in an ironical view, without confounding the eternal line of separation between good and evil. This purpose is answered by the comic characters and scenes which are interwoven with the serious parts in most of those pieces of Shakspeare where romantic fables or historical events are made the subject of a noble and elevating exhibition. Frequently an intentional parody of the serious part is not to be mistaken in them; at other times the connexion is more arbitrary and loose, and the more so the more marvellous the invention of the whole, and the more entirely it is become a light revelling of the fancy. The comic intervals everywhere serve to prevent the pastime from being converted into a business, to preserve the mind in the possession of its serenity, and to keep off that gloomy and inert seriousness which so easily steals upon the sentimental, but not tragical, drama. Most assuredly Shakspeare did not intend thereby, in defiance to his own better judgment, to humour the taste of the multitude: for in various pieces, and throughout considerable portions of others, and especially when the catastrophe is approaching, and the mind consequently is more on the stretch and no longer likely to give heed to any amusement which would distract their attention, he has abstained from all such comic intermixtures. It was also an object with him, that the clowns or buffoons should not occupy a more important place than that which he had assigned them: he expressly condemns the extemporizing with which they loved to enlarge their parts.[6] Johnson founds the justification of the species of drama in which seriousness and mirth are mixed, on this, that in real life the vulgar is found close to the sublime, that the merry and the sad usually accompany and succeed one another. But it does not follow that because both are found together, therefore they must not be separable in the compositions of art. The observation is in other respects just, and this circumstance invests the poet with a power to adopt this procedure, because every thing in the drama must be regulated by the conditions of theatrical probability; but the mixture of such dissimilar, and apparently contradictory, ingredients, in the same works, can only be justifiable on principles reconcilable with the views of art, which I have already described. In the dramas of Shakspeare the comic scenes are the antechamber of the poetry, where the servants remain; these prosaic attendants must not raise their voices so high as to deafen the speakers in the presence-chamber; however, in those intervals when the ideal society has retired they deserve to be listened to; their bold raillery, their presumption of mockery, may afford many an insight into the situation and circumstances of their masters.

Shakspeare's comic talent is equally wonderful with that which he has shown in the pathetic and tragic: it stands on an equal elevation, and possesses equal extent and profundity; in all that I have hitherto said, I only wished to guard against admitting that the former preponderated. He is highly inventive in comic situations and motives: it will be hardly possible to show whence he has taken any of them, whereas, in the serious part of his dramas, he has generally laid hold of some well-known story. His comic characterization is equally true, various, and profound, with his serious. So little is he disposed to caricature, that rather, it may be said, many of his traits are almost too nice and delicate for the stage, that they can only be made available by a great actor, and fully understood by an acute audience. Not only has he delineated many kinds of folly, but even of sheer stupidity has he contrived to give a most diverting and entertaining picture. There is also in his pieces a peculiar species of the farcical, which apparently seems to be introduced more arbitrarily, but which, however, is founded on imitation of some actual custom. This is the introduction of the merrymaker, the fool with his cap and bells, and motley dress, called more commonly in England *Clown,* who appears in several comedies, though not in all, but of the tragedies in *Lear* alone, and who generally merely exercises his wit in conversation with the principal persons though he is also sometimes incorporated into the action. In those times it was not only usual for princes to have their court fools, but many distinguished families, among their other retainers, kept such an exhilarating housemate as a good antidote against the insipidity and wearisomeness of ordinary life, and as a welcome interruption of established formalities. Great statesmen, and even ecclesiastics, did not consider it beneath their dignity to recruit and solace themselves after important business with the conversation of their fools; the celebrated Sir Thomas More had his fool painted along with himself by Holbein. Shakspeare appears to have lived immediately before the time when the custom began to be abolished; in the English comic authors who succeeded him the clown is no longer to be found. The dismissal of the fool has been extolled as a proof of refinement; and our honest forefathers have been pitied for taking delight in such a coarse and farcical amusement. For my part, I am rather disposed to believe, that the practice was dropped from the difficulty in finding fools able to do full justice to their parts:[7] on the other hand, reason, with all its conceit of itself, has become too timid to tolerate such bold irony; it is always careful lest the mantle of its gravity should be disturbed in any of its folds; and rather than allow a privileged place to folly beside itself, it has unconsciously assumed the part of the ridiculous; but, alas! a heavy and cheerless ridicule.[8] It would be easy to make a collection of the excellent sallies and biting sarcasms which have been preserved of celebrated court fools. It is well known that they frequently told such truths to princes as are never now told to them.[9] Shakspeare's fools, along with somewhat of an overstraining for wit, which cannot altogether be avoided when wit becomes a separate profession, have for the most part an incomparable humour, and an infinite abundance of intellect, enough indeed to supply a whole host of ordinary wise men.

I have still a few observations to make on the diction and versification of our poet. The language is here and there somewhat obsolete, but on the whole much less so than in most of the contemporary writers, a sufficient proof of the goodness of his choice. Prose had as yet been but little cultivated, as the learned generally wrote in Latin: a favourable circumstance for the dramatic poet; for what has he to do with the scientific language of books? He had not only read, but studied the earlier English poets; but he drew his language immediately from life itself, and he possessed a masterly skill in blending the dialogical element with the highest poetical elevation. I know not what certain critics mean, when they say that Shakspeare is frequently ungrammatical. To make good their assertion, they must prove that similar constructions never occur in his contemporaries, the direct contrary of which can, however, be easily shown. In no language is every thing determined on principle; much is always left to the caprice of custom, and if this has since changed, is the poet to be made answerable for it? The English language had not then attained to that correct insipidity which has been introduced into the more recent literature of the country, to the prejudice, perhaps, of its originality. As a field when first brought under the plough produces, along with the fruitful shoots, many luxuriant weeds, so the poetical diction of the day ran occasionally into extravagance, but an extravagance originating in the exuberance of its vigour. We may still perceive traces of awkwardness, but nowhere of a laboured and spiritless display of art. In general Shakspeare's style yet remains the very best model, both in the vigorous and sublime, and the pleasing and tender. In his sphere he has exhausted all the means and appliances of language. On all he has impressed the stamp of his mighty spirit. His images and figures, in their unsought, nay, uncapricious singularity, have often a sweetness altogether peculiar. He becomes occasionally obscure from too great fondness for compressed brevity; but still, the labour of poring over Shakspeare's lines will invariably meet an ample requital.

The verse in all his plays is generally the rhymeless Iambic of ten or eleven syllables, occasionally only intermixed with rhymes, but more frequently alternating with prose. No one piece is written entirely in prose; for even in those which approach the most to the pure Comedy, there is always something added which gives them a more poetical hue than usually belongs to this species. Many scenes are wholly in prose, in others verse and prose succeed each other alternately. This can only appear an impropriety in the eyes of those who are accustomed to consider the lines of a drama like so many soldiers drawn up rank and file on a parade, with the same uniform, arms, and accoutrements, so that when we see one or two we may represent to ourselves thousands as being every way like them.

In the use of verse and prose Shakspeare observes very nice distinctions according to the ranks of the speakers, but still more according to their characters and disposition of mind. A noble language, elevated above the usual tone, is only suitable to a certain decorum of manners, which is thrown over both vices and virtues, and which does not even wholly disappear amidst the violence of passion. If this is not exclusively possessed by the higher ranks, it still, however, belongs naturally more to them than to the lower; and therefore in Shakspeare dignity and familiarity of language, poetry, and prose, are in this manner distributed among the characters. Hence his tradesmen, peasants, soldiers, sailors, servants, but more especially his fools and clowns, speak almost without exception, in the tone of their actual life. However, inward dignity of sentiment, wherever it is possessed, invariably displays itself with a nobleness of its own, and stands not in need, for that end, of the artificial elegancies of education and custom; it is a universal right of man, of the highest as well as the lowest; and hence also, in Shakspeare, the nobility of nature and morality is ennobled above the artificial nobility of society. Not unfrequently also he makes the very same persons express themselves at times in the sublimest language, and at others in the lowest; and this inequality is in like manner founded in truth. Extraordinary situations, which intensely occupy the head and throw mighty passions into play, give elevation and tension to the soul: it collects together all its powers, and exhibits an unusual energy, both in its operations and in its communications by language. On the other hand, even the greatest men have their moments of remissness, when to a certain degree they forget the dignity of their character in unreserved relaxation. This very tone of mind is necessary before they can receive amusement from the jokes of others, or what surely cannot dishonour even a hero, from passing jokes themselves. Let any person, for example, go carefully through the part of Hamlet. How bold and powerful the language of his poetry when he conjures the ghost of his father, when he spurs himself on to the bloody deed, when he thunders into the soul of his mother! How he lowers his tone down to that of common life, when he has to do with persons whose station demands from him such a line of conduct; when he makes game of Polonius and the courtiers, instructs the player, and even enters into the jokes of the grave-digger. Of all the poet's serious leading characters there is none so rich in wit and humour as Hamlet; hence he it is of all of them that makes the greatest use of the familiar style. Others, again, never do fall into it; either because they are constantly surrounded by the pomp of rank, or because a uniform seriousness is natural to them; or, in short, because through the whole piece they are under the dominion of a passion, calculated to excite, and not, like the sorrow of Hamlet, to depress the mind. The choice of the one form or the other is everywhere so appropriate, and so much founded in the nature of the thing, that I will venture to assert, even where the poet in the very same speech makes the speaker leave prose for poetry, or the converse, this could not be altered without danger of injuring or destroying some beauty or other. The blank verse has this advantage, that its tone may be elevated or lowered; it admits of approximation to the familiar style of conversation, and never forms such an abrupt contrast as that, for example, between plain prose and the rhyming Alexandrines.

Shakspeare's Iambics are sometimes highly harmonious and full sounding; always varied and suitable to the subject, at one time distinguished by ease and rapidity, at another they move along with ponderous energy. They never fall out of the dialogical character, which may always be traced even in the continued discourses of individuals, excepting when the latter run into the lyrical. They are a complete model of the dramatic use of this species of verse, which, in English, since Milton, has been also used in epic poetry; but in the latter it has assumed a quite different turn. Even the irregularities of Shakspeare's versification are expressive; a verse broken off, or a sudden change of rhythmus, coincides with some pause in the progress of the thought, or the entrance of another mental disposition. As a proof that he purposely violated the mechanical rules, from a conviction that too symmetrical a versification does not suit with the drama, and on the stage has in the long run a tendency to lull the spectators asleep, we may observe that his earlier pieces are the most diligently versified, and that in the later works, when through practice he must have acquired a greater facility, we find the strongest deviations from the regular structure of the verse. As it served with him merely to make the poetical elevation perceptible, he therefore claimed the utmost possible freedom in the use of it.

The views or suggestions of feeling by which he was guided in the use of rhyme may likewise be traced with almost equal certainty. Not unfrequently scenes, or even single speeches, close with a few rhyming lines, for the purpose of more strongly marking the division, and of giving it more rounding. This was injudiciously imitated by the English tragic poets of a later date; they suddenly elevated the tone in the rhymed lines, as if the person began all at once to speak in another language. The practice was welcomed by the actors from its serving as a signal for clapping when they made their exit. In Shakspeare, on the other hand, the transitions are more easy: all changes of forms are brought about insensibly, and as if of themselves. Moreover, he is generally fond of heightening a series of ingenious and antithetical sayings by the use of rhyme. We find other passages in continued rhyme, where solemnity and theatrical pomp were suitable, as, for instance, in the mask. . . .

The whole of Shakspeare's productions bear the certain stamp of his original genius, but yet no writer was ever farther removed from every thing like a mannerism derived from habit or personal peculiarities. Rather is he, such is the diversity of tone and colour, which varies according to the quality of his subjects he assumes, a very Proteus [a mythological Greek sea god and shape-shifter]. Each of his compositions is like a world of its own, moving in its own sphere. They are works of art, finished in one pervading style, which revealed the freedom and judicious choice of their author. If the formation of a work throughout, even in its minutest parts, in conformity with a leading idea; if the domination of one animating spirit over all the means of execution, deserves the name of correctness (and this, excepting in matters of grammar, is the only proper sense of the term); we shall then, after allowing to Shakspeare all the higher qualities which demand our admiration, be also compelled, in most cases, to concede to him the title of a correct poet.

Notes

1. *Twelfth Night, or What You Will*—Act iii. Scene ii.

2. *As You Like It.*

4. In the first volume of *Charakteristiken und Kritiken,* published by my brother and myself.

5. A contemporary of the poet, the author of the already-noticed poem, (subscribed I. M. S.,) tenderly felt this while he says—

Yet so to temper passion, that our ears
Take pleasure in their pain, and eyes in tears
Both smile and weep.

6. In Hamlet's directions to the players. Act iii. sc. 2.

7. See Hamlet's praise of Yorick. In *The Twelfth Night,* Viola says:—

This fellow is wise enough to play the fool,
And to do that well craves a kind of wit;
He must observe their mood on whom he jests,
The quality of the persons, and the time;
And like the haggard, check at every feather
That comes before his eye. This is a practice
As full of labour as a wise man's art:
For folly that he wisely shows is fit,
But wise men's folly fall'n quite taints their wit.

8. "Since the little wit that fools have was silenced, the little foolery that wise men have makes a greater show."—*As You Like It.* Act. i., sc. 2.

9. Charles the Bold, of Burgundy, is known to have frequently boasted that he wished to rival Hannibal as the greatest general of all ages. After his defeat of Granson, his fool accompanied him in his hurried flight, and exclaimed, "Ah, your Greece, they have for once Hanniballed us!" If the Duke had given an ear to this warning raillery, he would not so soon afterwards have come to a disgraceful end.

—August Wilhelm von Schlegel, "Lecture
XXIII," *Lectures on Dramatic Art and
Literature,* translated by John Black, 1809

WALTER SCOTT "AN ESSAY ON THE DRAMA" (1814)

Sir Walter Scott (1771–1832), throughout the nineteenth century a highly popular Scottish historical novelist and poet, echoes Edward Young's

belief that Shakespeare's lack of great familiarity with the classics was ben-
eficial, not detrimental, to his art.

The change in the way of approaching and viewing Shakespeare's
work that marks the difference between critics shaped by neoclassicism
and those influenced by the emerging romantic temperament can be seen
in Scott's assessment. He does not challenge his precursors' perceptions
about the nature of Shakespeare's work. He values the work differently
from how they did. Relying on the aesthetics of a heightened sensitivity,
rather than on the precepts of a classical code of composition, he deems
aspects of Shakespeare's writing as genius, whereas previously they had
been seen as undisciplined. Scott argues, additionally, that Shakespeare,
rather than being bound by classical prescriptions, derived his art from the
forms that had already appeared on the English stage and thus expanded
the limits of English drama beyond those set by the classical rules.

The English stage might be considered equally without rule and without
model when Shakspeare arose. The effect of the genius of an individual upon
the taste of a nation is mighty; but that genius, in its turn, is formed according
to the opinions prevalent at the period when it comes into existence. Such was
the case with Shakspeare. Had he received an education more extensive, and
possessed a taste refined by the classical models, it is probable that he also,
in admiration of the ancient Drama, might have mistaken the form for the
essence, and subscribed to those rules which had produced such masterpieces
of art. Fortunately for the full exertion of a genius, as comprehensive and
versatile as intense and powerful, Shakspeare had no access to any models
of which the commanding merit might have controlled and limited his own
exertions. He followed the path which a nameless crowd of obscure writers
had trodden before him; but he moved in it with the grace and majestic step
of a being of a superior order; and vindicated for ever the British theatre from
a pedantic restriction to classical rule. Nothing went before Shakspeare which
in any respect was fit to fix and stamp the character of a national Drama; and
certainly no one will succeed him capable of establishing, by mere authority,
a form more restricted than that which Shakspeare used.

Such is the action of existing circumstances upon genius, and the reaction
of genius upon future circumstances. Shakspeare and Corneille was each the
leading spirit of his age; and the difference between them is well marked by the
editor of the latter:—"*Corneille est inegal comme Shakespeare, et plein de genie
comme lui: mais le genie de Corneille doit a celui de Shakespeare ce qu'un seigneur
est a legard d'un homme de peuple ne avec le même esprit que lui.*" [Corneille

is unequaled like Shakespeare, and full of genius like him: but the genius of Corneille owes to the genius of Shakespeare what a lord does to a man of the people born with the same spirit as his.] This distinction is strictly accurate, and contains a compliment to the English author which, assuredly, the critic did not intend to make. Corneille wrote as a courtier, circumscribed within the imaginary rules and ceremonies of a court, as a chicken is by a circle of chalk drawn round it. Shakspeare, composing for the amusement of the public alone, had within his province, not only the inexhaustible field of actual life, but the whole ideal world of fancy and superstition;—more favourable to the display of poetical genius than even existing realities. Under the circumstances of Corneille, Shakspeare must have been restricted to the same dull, regular, and unvaried system. He must have written, not according to the dictates of his own genius, but in conformity to the mandate of some *Intendant des menus plaisirs* [steward of small pleasures]; or of some minister of state, who, like Cardinal Richelieu, thought he could write a tragedy because he could govern a kingdom. It is not equally clear to what height Corneille might have ascended, had he enjoyed the national immunities of Shakspeare. Each pitched down a landmark in his art. The circle of Shakspeare was so extensive, that it is with advantage liable to many restrictions; that of Corneille included a narrow limit, which his successors have deemed it unlawful to enlarge.

It is not our intention, within the narrow space to which our essay is necessarily limited, to enlarge upon the character and writings of Shakspeare. We can only notice his performances as events in the history of the theatre—of a gigantic character, indeed, so far as its dignity, elevation, and importance are considered; but, in respect of the mere practice of the Drama, rather fixing and sanctioning, than altering or reforming, those rules and forms which he found already established. This we know for certain, that those historical plays or chronicles, in which Shakspeare's muse has thrown a never-fading light upon the history of his country, did, almost every one of them, exist before him in the rude shape of dry dialogue and pitiful buffoonery, stitched into scenes by the elder playwrights of the stage. His romantic Dramas exhibit the same contempt of regularity which was manifested by Marlow, and other writers; for where there was abuse or extreme license upon the stage, the example of Shakespeare may be often quoted as its sanction, never as tending to reform it.

—Walter Scott, "An Essay on the Drama," 1814

Royall Tyler (ca. 1815)

Royall Tyler (1757–1826), American jurist and playwright, argues that Americans, not partial to the English but sharing a common language,

may be seen as the arbiters of Shakespeare's worth. Acknowledging the
validity of the high opinion with which the English regarded Shakespeare,
he states that the playwright's greatness lies predominantly in the human
and behavioral authenticity of his characters.

The English pride themselves on Shakespeare. They enthusiastically admire
his plays and challenge the whole world to produce a dramatic writer of
such universal preeminence. The French wits, with Voltaire as their head,
have been disposed to deny to the Bard of Avon this supreme eminence and
attribute the English opinion of his merits to national prejudice and to an
incorrect if not a barbarous taste. No umpire has yet appeared well qualified
to decide between them.

I conclude on reflection we Americans may be deemed properly qualified.
Familiar with the language in which Shakespeare wrote, free from the
imputation of national prejudice, and if our judgement is in any way bias'd from
the not yet forgotten resentment occasioned by our revolutionary struggle and
the irritation of a more recent war [the War of 1812] and the vulgar aspersions
of her travellers and reviewers, it surely is not inclined to English pretentions.
We, therefore, seem well suited to decide upon the claims of the dramatist and
we think we ought and shall be credited when we say that the English do not
estimate the genius and dramas of the immortal bard too highly.

That their enthusiastic admiration of his plays does not proceed from
national prejudice or incorrect or barbarous taste, but simply from a
familiarity with their vernacular tongue in which he wrote. That Shakespeare's
brilliant imagination by which he repeopled the earth with the offspring of
his own fancy or the splendid and noble passages so often quoted from
his writings and so often vainly attempted to be translated, are but minor
excellences and by far exceeded by that admirable facility and familiarity with
which he penetrates the bosoms of the persons represented by his dramatis
personae, making every one, whether the inmates of the palace or the cottage,
of the ocean, the wilderness or the cavern, whether surrounded by domestic
comforts or cast forth roofless and abandoned to bide the "peltings of the
pitiless storm," whether actuated by passion or bereft of reason, whether grave
or gay, drunk or sober, wise or witty, in love or in debt, pedantic or foolish,
conduct just as a deep knowledge of human nature would make us conclude
persons so situated would naturally act, think and talk, and frequently by
some brief and unobtrusive speech making them develop a whole life of
character. And all this effected in a manner so simple, so natural, and with
such apparent lack of effort that the reader of his dramas is often tempted to

withhold the merit of invention from the bard and to conclude it impossible for people similarly circumstanced to talk and act in any other way than they did. No, the English with all their self complacency do not estimate the genius and dramas of Shakespeare too highly, and the foreigner who can not relish his plays, tho' he may peruse the production of other English poets with pleasure, may rest assured he is still but imperfectly acquainted with the English tongue.

—Royall Tyler, *The Bay Boy,* ca. 1815, chapter 14

SAMUEL TAYLOR COLERIDGE (1818)

Samuel Taylor Coleridge (1772–1834) was a poet who, with William Wordsworth, became one of the leading theoreticians and proponents of English romanticism. He also produced many volumes of philosophical, literary, and social criticism. In these excerpts from his writings on Shakespeare, Coleridge attempts to define what constitutes a poet and to bury the prevalent idea that Shakespeare was an untutored and savage genius of a playwright whose works lacked true and proper form. At the heart of Coleridge's argument is the assertion that form is a quality that arises from the matter at hand rather than an external patterning imposed on it. He argues, additionally, that unity results from "combining many circumstances into one moment of consciousness," not on slavish adherence to mechanical rules. A true poet, moreover, Coleridge asserts, quoting Wordsworth, is able "to make [a reader] almost lose the consciousness of words,—to make him see every thing flashed ['upon his inward eye.']" Shakespeare, Coleridge argues, makes "every thing present to the imagination—both the forms, and the passions which modify those forms, either actually, as in the representations of love, or anger, or other human affections; or imaginatively, by the different manner in which inanimate objects, or objects unimpassioned themselves, are caused to be seen by the mind in moments of strong excitement, and according to the kind of the excitement." As many poets have used Shakespeare as the source for poetry of their own, Coleridge, in his critical encounters with Shakespeare, endeavored to devise a general philosophy of literary criticism arising from his readings of Shakespeare.

Shakspeare, a Poet Generally

Clothed in radiant armour, and authorized by titles sure and manifold, as a poet, Shakspeare came forward to demand the throne of fame, as the dramatic poet of England. His excellencies compelled even his contemporaries to seat him on that throne, although there were giants in those days contending for the same honor.... [H]e had shown himself a poet, previously to his appearance as a dramatic poet; and had no *Lear*, no *Othello*, no *Henry IV*, no *Twelfth Night* ever appeared, we must have admitted that Shakspeare possessed the chief, if not every, requisite of a poet,—deep feeling and exquisite sense of beauty, both as exhibited to the eye in the combinations of form, and to the ear in sweet and appropriate melody; that these feelings were under the command of his own will; that in his very first productions he projected his mind out of his own particular being, and felt, and made others feel, on subjects no way connected with himself, except by force of contemplation and that sublime faculty by which a great mind becomes that, on which it meditates. To this must be added that affectionate love of nature and natural objects, without which no man could have observed so steadily, or painted so truly and passionately, the very minutest beauties of the external world....

Moreover Shakspeare had shown that he possessed fancy, considered as the faculty of bringing together images dissimilar in the main by some one point or more of likeness, as in such a passage as this:—

Full gently now she takes him by the hand,
A lily prisoned in a jail of snow,
Or ivory in an alabaster band;
So white a friend ingirts so white a foe!
                    [*Venus and Adonis*, ll. 361–64]

And still mounting the intellectual ladder, he had as unequivocally proved the indwelling in his mind of imagination, or the power by which one image or feeling is made to modify many others, and by a sort of fusion to force many into one;—that which afterwards showed itself in such might and energy in *Lear*, where the deep anguish of a father spreads the feeling of ingratitude and cruelty over the very elements of heaven;—and which, combining many circumstances into one moment of consciousness, tends to produce that ultimate end of all human thought and human feeling, unity, and thereby the reduction of the spirit to its principle and fountain, who is alone truly one. Various are the workings of this the greatest faculty of the human mind, both passionate and tranquil. In its tranquil and purely pleasurable operation, it acts chiefly by creating out of many things, as they would have appeared in the description of an ordinary mind, detailed in unimpassioned succession, a oneness, even as nature, the greatest of poets, acts upon us, when we open

our eyes upon an extended prospect. Thus the flight of Adonis in the dusk of
the evening:—

> Look! how a bright star shooteth from the sky;
> So glides he in the night from Venus' eye!
>   [ll. 815–16]

How many images and feelings are here brought together without effort
and without discord, in the beauty of Adonis, the rapidity of his flight, the
yearning, yet hopelessness, of the enamored gazer, while a shadowy ideal
character is thrown over the whole! Or this power acts by impressing the
stamp of humanity, and of human feelings, on inanimate or mere natural
objects:—

> Lo! here the gentle lark, weary of rest,
> From his moist cabinet mounts up on high,
> And wakes the morning, from whose silver breast
> The sun ariseth in his majesty,
> Who doth the world so gloriously behold,
> The cedar-tops and hills seem burnish'd gold.
>   [ll. 853–58]

Or again, it acts by so carrying on the eye of the reader as to make him almost
lose the consciousness of words,—to make him see every thing flashed, as
Wordsworth has grandly and appropriately said,—

> *Flashed* upon that inward eye
> Which is the bliss of solitude;—

and this without exciting any painful or laborious attention, without any
anatomy of description, (a fault not uncommon in descriptive poetry)—but
with the sweetness and easy movement of nature. This energy is an absolute
essential of poetry, and of itself would constitute a poet, though not one of the
highest class;—it is, however, a most hopeful symptom, and the *Venus and
Adonis* is one continued specimen of it.

In this beautiful poem there is an endless activity of thought in all the
possible associations of thought with thought, thought with feeling, or with
words, of feelings with feelings, and of words with words.

> Even as the sun, with purple-colour'd face,
> Had ta'en his last leave of the weeping morn,

Rose-cheek'd Adonis hied him to the chase:
Hunting he loved, but love he laughed to scorn.
Sick-thoughted Venus makes amain unto him,
And like a bold-faced suitor 'gins to woo him.
                    [ll. 1–6]

Remark the humanizing imagery and circumstances of the first two lines, and the activity of thought in the play of words in the fourth line. The whole stanza presents at once the time, the appearance of the morning, and the two persons distinctly characterized, and in six simple verses puts the reader in possession of the whole argument of the poem.

Over one arm the lusty courser's rein,
Under the other was the tender boy,
Who blush'd and pouted in a dull disdain,
With leaden appetite, unapt to toy,
She red and hot, as coals of glowing fire,
He red for shame, but frosty to desire:—
                    [ll. 31–36]

This stanza and the two following afford good instances of that poetic power, which I mentioned above, of making every thing present to the imagination—both the forms, and the passions which modify those forms, either actually, as in the representations of love, or anger, or other human affections; or imaginatively, by the different manner in which inanimate objects, or objects unimpassioned themselves, are caused to be seen by the mind in moments of strong excitement, and according to the kind of the excitement,—whether of jealousy, or rage, or love, in the only appropriate sense of the word, or of the lower impulses of our nature, or finally of the poetic feeling itself. It is, perhaps, chiefly in the power of producing and reproducing the latter that the poet stands distinct.

The subject of the *Venus and Adonis* is unpleasing; but the poem itself is for that very reason the more illustrative of Shakspeare. There are men who can write passages of deepest pathos and even sublimity on circumstances personal to themselves and stimulative of their own passions; but they are not, therefore, on this account poets. Read that magnificent burst of woman's patriotism and exultation, Deborah's song of victory; it is glorious, but nature is the poet there. It is quite another matter to become all things and yet remain the same,—to make the changeful god be felt in the river, the lion and the flame;—this it is, that is the true imagination. Shakspeare writes in this poem, as if he were of another planet, charming you to gaze on the movements of Venus and Adonis, as you would on the twinkling dances of two vernal butterflies.

Finally, in this poem and the *Rape of Lucrece*, Shakspeare gave ample proof of his possession of a most profound, energetic, and philosophical mind, without which he might have pleased, but could not have been a great dramatic poet. Chance and the necessity of his genius combined to lead him to the drama his proper province; in his conquest of which we should consider both the difficulties which opposed him, and the advantages by which he was assisted.

Shakspeare's Judgment Equal to His Genius

Thus then Shakspeare appears, from his *Venus and Adonis* and *Rape of Lucrece* alone, apart from all his great works, to have possessed all the conditions of the true poet. Let me now proceed to destroy, as far as may be in my power, the popular notion that he was a great dramatist by mere instinct, that he grew immortal in his own despite, and sank below men of second or third-rate power, when he attempted aught beside the drama—even as bees construct their cells and manufacture their honey to admirable perfection; but would in vain attempt to build a nest. Now this mode of reconciling a compelled sense of inferiority with a feeling of pride, began in a few pedants, who having read that Sophocles was the great model of tragedy, and Aristotle the infallible dictator of its rules, and finding that the *Lear, Hamlet, Othello* and other master-pieces were neither in imitation of Sophocles, nor in obedience to Aristotle,—and not having (with one or two exceptions) the courage to affirm, that the delight which their country received from generation to generation, in defiance of the alterations of circumstances and habits, was wholly groundless,—took upon them, as a happy medium and refuge, to talk of Shakspeare as a sort of beautiful *lusus naturæ*, a delightful monster,—wild, indeed, and without taste or judgment, but like the inspired idiots so much venerated in the East, uttering, amid the strangest follies, the sublimest truths. In nine places out of ten in which I find his awful name mentioned, it is with some epithet of 'wild,' 'irregular,' 'pure child of nature,' &c. If all this be true, we must submit to it; though to a thinking mind it cannot but be painful to find any excellence, merely human, thrown out of all human analogy, and thereby leaving us neither rules for imitation, nor motives to imitate;—but if false, it is a dangerous falsehood;—for it affords a refuge to secret self-conceit,—enables a vain man at once to escape his reader's indignation by general swoln panegyrics, and merely by his *ipse dixit* to treat, as contemptible, what he has not intellect enough to comprehend, or soul to feel, without assigning any reason, or referring his opinion to any demonstrative principle;—thus leaving Shakspeare as a sort of grand Lama, adored indeed, and his very excrements prized as relics, but with no authority or real influence. I grieve that every late voluminous edition of his works would enable me to substantiate the present charge with a variety of facts one tenth of which would of themselves exhaust the time allotted to me. Every critic ... puts on the seven-league boots of self-opinion, and strides at once from an illustrator into a supreme judge, and blind and deaf, fills his three-ounce phial at the waters of Niagara; and determines positively the greatness of the cataract to be neither more nor less than his three-ounce phial has been able to receive. ...

However inferior in ability I may be to some who have followed me, I own I am proud that I was the first in time who publicly demonstrated to the full extent of the position, that the supposed irregularity and extravagancies of Shakspeare were the mere dreams of a pedantry that arraigned the eagle because it had not the dimensions of the swan. ...

Let me, then, once more submit this question to minds emancipated alike from national, or party, or sectarian prejudice:—Are the plays of Shakspeare works of rude uncultivated genius, in which the splendour of the parts compensates, if aught can compensate, for the barbarous shapelessness and irregularity of the whole?—Or is the form equally admirable with the matter, and the judgment of the great poet, not less deserving our wonder than his genius?—Or, again, to repeat the question in other words:—Is Shakspeare a great dramatic poet on account only of those beauties and excellencies which he possesses in common with the ancients, but with diminished claims to our love and honour to the full extent of his differences from them?—Or are these very differences additional proofs of poetic wisdom, at once results and symbols of living power as contrasted with lifeless mechanism—of free and rival originality as contradistinguished from servile imitation, or, more accurately, a blind copying of effects, instead of a true imitation of the essential principles?—Imagine not that I am about to oppose genius to rules. ... The true ground of the mistake lies in the confounding mechanical regularity with organic form. The form is mechanic, when on any given material we impress a pre-determined form, not necessarily arising out of the properties of the material;—as when to a mass of wet clay we give whatever shape we wish it to retain when hardened. The organic form, on the other hand, is innate; it shapes, as it developes, itself from within, and the fulness of its development is one and the same with the perfection of its outward form. Such as the life is, such is the form. Nature, the prime genial artist, inexhaustible in diverse powers, is equally inexhaustible in forms;—each exterior is the physiognomy of the being within,—its true image reflected and thrown out from the concave mirror;—and even such is the appropriate excellence of her chosen poet, of our own Shakspeare,—himself a nature humanized, a genial understanding directing self-consciously a power and an implicit wisdom deeper even than our consciousness. . . .

[D]oes God choose idiots by whom to convey divine truths to man?

Recapitulation, and Summary of the Characteristics of Shakspeare's Drama

. . . It is essential to poetry that it be simple, and appeal to the elements and primary laws of our nature; that it be sensuous, and by its imagery elicit truth at a flash; that it be impassioned, and be able to move our feelings and awaken our affections. . . . [P]oetry, as distinguished from other modes of composition, does not rest in metre, and . . . that it is not poetry, if it make no appeal to our passions or our imagination. One character belongs to all true poets, that they write from a principle within, not originating in any thing without; and that the true poet's work in its form, its shapings, and its modifications, is distinguished from all other works that assume to belong to the class of poetry, as a natural from an artificial flower, or as the mimic garden of a child from an enamelled meadow. In the former the flowers are broken from their stems and stuck into the ground; they are beautiful to the eye and fragrant to the sense, but their colours soon fade, and their odour is transient as the smile of the planter;— while the meadow may be visited again and again with renewed delight, its beauty is innate in the soil, and its bloom is of the freshness of nature. . . .

The stage in Shakspeare's time was a naked room with a blanket for a curtain; but he made it a field for monarchs. That law of unity, which has its foundations, not in the factitious necessity of custom, but in nature itself, the unity of feeling, is every where and at all times observed by Shakspeare in his plays. Read *Romeo and Juliet;*—all is youth and spring;—youth with its follies, its virtues, its precipitancies;—spring with its odours, its flowers, and its transiency; it is one and the same feeling that commences, goes through, and ends the play. The old men, the Capulets and the Montagues, are not common old men; they have an eagerness, a heartiness, a vehemence, the effect of spring; with Romeo, his change of passion, his sudden marriage, and his rash death, are all the effects of youth;—whilst in Juliet love has all that is tender and melancholy in the nightingale, all that is voluptuous in the rose, with whatever is sweet in the freshness of spring; but it ends with a long deep sigh like the last breeze of the Italian evening. This unity of feeling and character pervades every drama of Shakspeare.

—Samuel Taylor Coleridge, from *Shakspeare, with Introductory Remarks on Poetry, the Drama, and the Stage,* 1818, *Literary Remains,* edited by Henry Nelson Coleridge, 1836, volume 2, pp. 53–83

WILLIAM HAZLITT "SHAKESPEARE AND MILTON" (1818)

William Hazlitt (1778–1830) was an English essayist, critic, philosopher, journalist, and painter. The following excerpt presents his anatomy of Shakespeare's genius as a playwright. Hazlitt emphasizes what he sees as Shakespeare's power to become any person and to imagine several persons, fully realized and individualized, reacting to and interacting with one another. He notes, too, the perfection and exactitude of Shakespeare's language. He excuses what others see as Shakespeare's faults, whether regarding the unities or his fondness for word play, punning, and bawdy humor, by noting that they are products of Shakespeare's time and reflections of his role as a theatrical entertainer.

The four greatest names in English poetry, are almost the four first we come to—Chaucer, Spenser, Shakspeare, and Milton. There are no others that can really be put in competition with these. . . .

In comparing these four writers together, it might be said that Chaucer excels as the poet of manners, or of real life; Spenser, as the poet of romance; Shakspeare, as the poet of nature (in the largest use of the term): and Milton, as the poet of morality. . . .

The striking peculiarity of Shakspeare's mind was its generic quality, its power of communication with all other minds—so that it contained a universe of thought and feeling within itself, and had no one peculiar bias, or exclusive excellence more than another. He was just like any other man, but that he was like all other men. He was the least of an egotist that it was possible to be. He was nothing in himself; but he was all that others were, or that they could become. He not only had in himself the germs of every faculty and feeling, but he could follow them by anticipation, intuitively, into all their conceivable ramifications, through every change of fortune or conflict of passion, or turn of thought. He had "a mind reflecting ages past," and present:—all the people that ever lived are there. There was no respect of persons with him. His genius shone equally on the evil and on the good, on the wise and the foolish, the monarch and the beggar. . . . He was like the genius of humanity, changing places with all of us at pleasure, and playing with our purposes as with his own. He turned the globe round for his amusement, and surveyed the generations of men, and the individuals as they passed, with their different concerns, passions, follies, vices, virtues, actions, and motives—as well those that they knew, as those which they did not know, or acknowledge to themselves. The dreams of childhood, the ravings of despair, were the toys of his fancy. Airy beings waited at his call, and came at his bidding. Harmless fairies "nodded to him, and did him curtesies:" and the night-hag bestrode the blast at the command of "his so potent art." The world of spirits lay open to him, like the world of real men and women: and there is the same truth in his delineations of the one as of the other; for if the preternatural characters he describes could be supposed to exist, they would speak, and feel, and act, as he makes them. He had only to think of any thing in order to become that thing, with all the circumstances belonging to it. When he conceived of a character whether real or imaginary, he not only entered into all its thoughts and feelings, but seemed instantly, and as if by touching a secret spring, to be surrounded with all the same objects, "subject to the same skyey influences," the same local, outward, and unforeseen accidents which would occur in reality. Thus the character of Caliban [in *The Tempest*] not only stands before us with a language and manners of its own, but the scenery and situation of the enchanted island he inhabits, the traditions of the place, its strange noises, its hidden recesses, "his frequent haunts and ancient neighbourhood," are given with a miraculous truth of nature, and with all the familiarity of an old recollection. The whole "coheres semblably together" in time, place, and circumstance. In reading this author, you do not merely learn what his characters say,—you see their persons. By something expressed or understood, you are at no loss to decypher their peculiar physiognomy, the meaning of a look, the grouping, the bye-play, as we might see it on the stage. A word, an epithet paints a whole scene, or throws us back whole years in the history of the person represented. So (as it has been ingeniously remarked) when Prospero [in *The Tempest*] describes himself as left alone in the boat with his daughter, the epithet which he applies to her, "Me and thy *crying self*," flings the imagination instantly back from the grown woman to the helpless condition of infancy, and places the first and most trying scene of his misfortunes before us, with all that he must have suffered in the interval. How well the silent anguish of Macduff is conveyed to the reader, by the friendly expostulation of Malcolm [in *Macbeth*]—"What! man, ne'er pull your hat upon your brows!" Again, Hamlet, in the scene with Rosencrantz and Guildenstern, somewhat abruptly concludes his fine soliloquy on life by saying, "Man delights not me, nor woman neither, though by your smiling you seem to say so." Which is explained by their answer—"My lord, we had no such stuff in our thoughts. But we smiled to think, if you delight not in man, what lenten entertainment the players shall receive from you, whom we met on the way:" [II.ii.317ff.]—as if while Hamlet was making this speech, his two old schoolfellows from Wittenberg had been really standing by, and he had seen them smiling by stealth, at the idea of the players crossing their minds. It is not "a combination and a form" of words, a set speech or two, a preconcerted theory of a character, that will do this: but all the persons concerned must have been present in the poet's imagination, as at a kind of rehearsal; and whatever would have passed through their minds on the occasion, and have been observed by others, passed through his, and is made known to the reader.—I may add in passing, that Shakspeare always gives the best directions for the costume and carriage of his heroes. Thus, to take one example, Ophelia['s] . . . account of Hamlet [II.i.77–100]. . . .

How after this airy, fantastic idea of irregular grace and bewildered melancholy any one can play Hamlet, as we have seen it played, with strut, and stare, and antic right-angled sharp-pointed gestures, it is difficult to say, unless it be that Hamlet is not bound, by the prompter's cue, to study the part of Ophelia. The account of Ophelia's death begins thus:

There is a willow hanging o'er a brook,
That shows its hoary leaves in the glassy stream.
                    [IV.vii.166ff]

Now this is an instance of the same unconscious power of mind which is as true to nature as itself. The leaves of the willow are, in fact, white underneath, and it is this part of them which would appear "hoary" in the reflection in the brook. The same sort of intuitive power, the same faculty of bringing every object in nature, whether present or absent, before the mind's eye, is observable in the speech of Cleopatra, when conjecturing what were the employments of Antony in his absence:—"He's speaking now, or murmuring, where's my serpent of old Nile?" [I.v.24–25] How fine to make Cleopatra have this consciousness of her own character, and to make her feel that it is this for which Antony is in love with her! She says, after the battle of Actium, when Antony has resolved to risk another fight, "It is my birthday; I had thought to have held it poor: but since my lord is Antony again, I will be Cleopatra." [III. xiii.185–87] What other poet would have thought of such a casual resource of the imagination, or would have dared to avail himself of it? The thing happens in the play as it might have happened in fact.—That which, perhaps, more than any thing else distinguishes the dramatic productions of Shakspeare from all others, is this wonderful truth and individuality of conception. Each of his characters is as much itself, and as absolutely independent of the rest, as well as of the author, as if they were living persons, not fictions of the mind. The poet may be said, for the time, to identify himself with the character he wishes to represent, and to pass from one to another, like the same soul successively animating different bodies. By an art like that of the ventriloquist, he throws his imagination out of himself, and makes every word appear to proceed from the mouth of the person in whose name it is given. His plays alone are properly expressions of the passions, not descriptions of them. His characters are real beings of flesh and blood; they speak like men, not like authors. One might suppose that he had stood by at the time, and overheard what passed. As in our dreams we hold conversations with ourselves, make remarks, or communicate intelligence, and have no idea of the answer which we shall receive, and which we ourselves make, till we hear it: so the dialogues in Shakspeare are carried on without any consciousness of what is to follow, without any appearance of preparation or premeditation. The gusts of passion come and go like sounds of music borne on the wind. Nothing is made out by formal inference and analogy, by climax and antithesis: all comes, or seems to come, immediately from nature. Each object and circumstance exists in his mind, as it would have existed in reality: each several train of thought and feeling goes on of itself, without confusion or effort. In the world of his imagination, every thing has a life, a place, and being of its own! . . .

The passion in Shakspeare is of the same nature as his delineation of character. It is not some one habitual feeling or sentiment preying upon itself, growing out of itself, and moulding every thing to itself; it is passion modified by passion, by all the other feelings to which the individual is liable, and to which others are liable with him; subject to all the fluctuations of caprice and accident; calling into play all the resources of the understanding and all the energies of the will; irritated by obstacles or yielding to them; rising from small beginnings to its utmost height; now drunk with hope, now stung to madness, now sunk in despair, now blown to air with a breath, now raging like, a torrent. The human soul is made the sport of fortune, the prey of adversity: it is stretched on the wheel of destiny, in restless ecstacy. The passions are in a state of projection. Years are melted down to moments, and every instant teems with fate. We know the results, we see the process. Thus after Iago has been boasting to himself of the effect of his poisonous suggestions on the mind of Othello, "which, with a little act upon the blood, will work like mines of sulphur," he adds—

Look where he comes! not poppy, nor mandragora,
Nor all the drowsy syrups of the East,
Shall ever medicine thee to that sweet sleep
Which thou ow'dst yesterday. [III.iii.327–29]

And he enters at this moment, like the crested serpent, crowned with his wrongs and raging for revenge! The whole depends upon the turn of a thought. A word, a look, blows the spark of jealousy into a flame; and the explosion is immediate and terrible as a volcano. The dialogues in *Lear*, in *Macbeth*, that between Brutus and Cassius [in *Julius Caesar*], and nearly all those in Shakspeare, where the interest is wrought up to its highest pitch, afford examples of this dramatic fluctuation of passion. . . . When Richard II. calls for the looking-glass to contemplate his faded majesty in it, and bursts into that affecting exclamation: "Oh, that I were a mockery-king of snow, to melt away before the sun of Bolingbroke," [*sic*. IV.i.259ff. O that I were a mockery king of snow, / Standing before the sun of Bolingbroke, / To melt myself away in water-drops!] we have here the utmost force of human passion, combined with the ideas of regal splendour and fallen power. . . .

Shakspeare's imagination is of the same plastic kind as his conception of character or passion. "It glances from heaven to earth, from earth to heaven." Its movement is rapid and devious. It unites the most opposite extremes; or, as Puck says, in boasting of his own feats, "puts a girdle round about the earth in forty minutes." [*A Midsummer Night's Dream* II.i.175–76] He seems always hurrying from his subject, even while describing it; but the stroke, like the lightning's, is sure as it is sudden. He takes the widest possible range, but from that very range he has his choice of the greatest variety and aptitude of materials. He brings together images the most alike, but placed at the greatest distance from each other; that is, found in circumstances of the greatest dissimilitude. From the remoteness of his combinations, and the celerity with which they are effected, they coalesce the more indissolubly together. The more the thoughts are strangers to each other, and the longer they have been kept asunder, the more intimate does their union seem to become. Their felicity is equal to their force. Their likeness is made more dazzling by their novelty. They startle, and take the fancy prisoner in the same instant. . . .

Shakspeare's language and versification are like the rest of him. He has a magic power over words: they come winged at his bidding; and seem to know their places. They are struck out at a heat, on the spur of the occasion, and have all the truth and vividness which arise from an actual impression of the objects. His epithets and single phrases are like sparkles, thrown off from an imagination, fired by the whirling rapidity of its own motion. His language is hieroglyphical. It translates thoughts into visible images. It abounds in sudden transitions and elliptical expressions. This is the source of his mixed metaphors, which are only abbreviated forms of speech. These, however, give no pain from long custom. They have, in fact, become idioms in the language. They are the building, and not the scaffolding to thought. We take the meaning and effect of a well-known passage entire, and no more stop to scan and spell out the particular words and phrases, than the syllables of which they are composed. In trying to recollect any other author, one sometimes stumbles, in case of failure, on a word as good. In Shakspeare, any other word but the true one, is sure to be wrong. . . .

It remains to speak of the faults of Shakspeare. They are not so many or so great as they have been represented; what there are, are chiefly owing to the following causes:—The universality of his genius was, perhaps, a disadvantage to his single works; the variety of his resources sometimes diverting him from applying them to the most effectual purposes. He might be said to combine the powers of Aeschylus and Aristophanes, of Dante and Rabelais, in his own mind. If he had been only half what he was, he would perhaps have appeared greater. The natural ease and indifference of his temper made him sometimes less scrupulous than he might have been. He is relaxed and careless in critical places; he is in earnest throughout only in *Timon, Macbeth,* and *Lear.* Again, he had no models of acknowledged excellence constantly in view to stimulate his efforts, and by all that appears, no love of fame. He wrote for the "great vulgar and the small," in his time, not for posterity. If Queen Elizabeth and the maids of honour laughed heartily at his worst jokes, and the catcalls in the gallery were silent at his best passages, he went home satisfied, and slept the next night well. He did not trouble himself about Voltaire's criticisms. He was willing to take advantage of the ignorance of the age in many things; and if his plays pleased others, not to quarrel with them himself. His very facility of production would make him set less value on his own excellences, and not care to distinguish nicely between what he did well or ill. His blunders in chronology and geography do not amount to above half a dozen, and they are offences against chronology and geography, not against poetry. As to the unities, he was right in setting them at defiance. He was fonder of puns than became so great a man. His barbarisms were those of his age. His genius was his own. He had no objection to float down with the stream of common taste and opinion: he rose above it by his own buoyancy, and an impulse which he could not keep under, in spite of himself or others, and "his delights did shew most dolphin-like." [cf. *Antony and Cleopatra* V.ii.88ff]

He had an equal genius for comedy and tragedy; and his tragedies are better than his comedies, because tragedy is better than comedy. His female characters, which have been found fault with as insipid, are the finest in the world. Lastly, Shakspeare was the least of a coxcomb of any one that ever lived, and much of a gentleman.

—William Hazlitt, from "Shakespeare and
Milton," *Lectures on the English Poets,* 1818

THOMAS CAMPBELL (1819)

Thomas Campbell (1777–1844) was a Scottish poet. Considering the problem of the unities, he rejects slavish adherence and admits they can be
observed with flexibility, but he insists that there must be limits to that
flexibility. He does not, however, prevent this scruple from hindering his
appreciation of Shakespeare when Shakespeare wildly violates the unities,
but allows that Shakespeare's genius may lead where it will. The Schlegel
to whom Campbell refers is August Wilhelm von Schlegel, German critic,
philologist, and translator of Shakespeare's work into German.

The bare name of the dramatic unities is apt to excite revolting ideas of
pedantry, arts of poetry, and French criticism. With none of these do I wish
to annoy the reader. I conceive that it may be said of those unities as of fire
and water, that they are good servants but bad masters. In perfect rigour they
were never imposed by the Greeks, and they would be still heavier shackles if
they were closely riveted on our own drama. It would be worse than useless to
confine dramatic action literally and immoveably to one spot, or its imaginary
time to the time in which it is represented. On the other hand, dramatic time
and place cannot surely admit of indefinite expansion. It would be better,
for the sake of illusion and probability, to change the scene from Windsor
to London, than from London to Pekin; it would look more like reality of a
messenger, who went and returned in the course of the play, told us of having
performed a journey often or twenty, rather than of a thousand miles; and if
the spectator had neither that, nor any other circumstance, to make him ask
how so much could be performed in so short a time.

In an abstract view of dramatic art, its principles must appear to lie nearer
to unity than to the opposite extreme of disunion, in our conceptions of
time and place. Giving up the law of unity in its literal rigour, there is still
a latitude of its application which may preserve proportion and harmony in
the drama.

The brilliant and able Schlegel has traced the principles of what he
denominates the romantic, in opposition to the classical drama; and conceives
that Shakspeare's theatre, when tried by those principles, will be found not to
have violated any of the unities, if they are largely and liberally understood.
I have no doubt that Mr. Schlegel's criticism will be found to have proved
this point in a considerable number of the works of our mighty poet. There
are traits, however, in Shakspeare, which, I must own, appear to my humble
judgment incapable of being illustrated by any system or principles of art. I
do not allude to his historical plays, which, expressly from being historical,

may be called a privileged class. But in those of purer fiction, it strikes me that there are licences conceded indeed to imagination's "chartered libertine," but anomalous with regard to anything which can be recognised as principles in dramatic art. When Perdita, [in *The Winter's Tale*] for instance, grows from the cradle to the marriage altar in the course of the play, I can perceive no unity in the design of the piece, and take refuge in the supposition of Shakspeare's genius triumphing and trampling over art. Yet Mr. Schlegel, as far as I have observed, makes no exception to this breach of temporal unity; nor, in proving Shakspeare a regular artist on a mighty scale, does he deign to notice this circumstance, even as the *ultima Thule* of his licence. If a man contends that dramatic laws are all idle restrictions, I can understand him; or if he says that Perdita's growth on the stage is a trespass on art, but that Shakspeare's fascination over and over again redeems it, I can both understand and agree with him. But when I am left to infer that all this is right on romantic principles, I confess that those principles become too romantic for my conception. If Perdita may be born and married on the stage, why may not Webster's Duchess of Malfi, lie-in between the acts, and produce a fine family of tragic children? Her Grace actually does so in Webster's drama, and he is a poet of some genius, though it is not quite so sufficient as Shakspeare's to give a "sweet oblivious antidote" [*Macbeth*, V.iii.44] to such "perilous stuff." [*Macbeth*, V.iii.45] It is not, however, either in favour of Shakspeare's or of Webster's genius that we shall be called on to make allowance, if we justify in the drama the lapse of such a number of years as may change the apparent identity of an individual. . . . On a general view, I conceive it may be said that Shakspeare nobly and legitimately enlarged the boundaries of time and place in the drama; but in extreme cases, I would rather agree with [English dramatist Richard] Cumberland, to waive all mention of his name in speaking of dramatic laws, than accept of those licences for art which are not art, and designate irregularity by the name of order.

—Thomas Campbell, *An Essay
on English Poetry*, 1819

Johann Peter Eckermann (1836)

Johann Peter Eckermann (1792–1854), poet, writer, and tutor, edited Johann Wolfgang von Goethe's forty-volume *Complete Works*, 1839–40. Goethe was a German poet, playwright, novelist, statesman, and scientist whose influence throughout Europe in the humanities, politics, and science was immense.

In this excerpt, Goethe observes that Shakespeare's greatness, while towering, was also a result of the time he lived in, the English Renaissance, a period of exceptional creativity, especially in the drama.

———————— ———————— ————————

We discoursed upon English literature, on the greatness of Shakespeare; and on the unfavourable position held by all English dramatic authors who had appeared after that poetical giant.

"A dramatic talent of any importance," said Goethe, "could not forbear to notice Shakespeare's works; nay, could not forbear to study them. Having studied them, he must be aware that Shakespeare has already exhausted the whole of human nature in all its tendencies, in all its heights and depths, and that in fact there remains for him, the aftercomer, nothing more to do. And how get courage only to put pen to paper, if conscious, in an earnest appreciating spirit, that such unfathomable and unattainable excellences were already in existence!" . . .

I turned the conversation back to Shakespeare. "When he is disengaged from English literature," said I, "and considered as transformed into a German, his greatness seems a miracle. But in the soil of his country, and the atmosphere of his century; studied with his contemporaries and immediate successors—Ben Jonson, [Philip] Massinger [1583–1640], Marlowe, and Beaumont and Fletcher—Shakespeare, though still a being of the most exalted magnitude, appears in some measure accessible. Much is due to the powerfully productive atmosphere of his time."

"You are right," returned Goethe. "It is with Shakespeare as with the mountains of Switzerland. Transplant Mont Blanc at once into the large plain of Luneburg Heath, and we should find no words to express our wonder at its magnitude. Seek it, however, in its gigantic home; go to it over its immense neighbours, the Jungfrau, the Finsteraarhorn, the Eiger, the Wetterhorn, St. Gothard, and Monte Rosa; Mont Blanc will indeed still remain a giant, but it will no longer produce in us such amazement.

"Besides, let him who will not believe," continued Goethe, "that much of Shakespeare's greatness appertains to his great vigorous time, only ask himself the question, whether a phenomenon so astounding would be possible in the present England of 1824, in these evil days of criticizing and hairsplitting journals?"

—Johann Peter Eckermann, *Conversations with
Goethe*, 1836, translated by John Oxenford

Thomas De Quincey "Shakespeare" (1838)

Thomas De Quincey (1785–1859) was an essayist known primarily for his 1822 work, *Confessions of an English Opium Eater*. In this panegyric, comparing

Shakespeare to the foremost classical Greek dramatists, De Quincey praises Shakespeare's originality and superiority in drawing the characters of women, the fluidity and conversational verisimilitude of his dialogue, the verisimilitude with which he creates imaginary characters like fairies, and the quality of the thought and sentiments embedded in his work.

In the gravest sense it may be affirmed of Shakspeare that he is among the modern luxuries of life; that life, in fact, is a new thing, and one more to be coveted, since Shakspeare has extended the domains of human consciousness, and pushed its dark frontiers into regions not so much as dimly descried or even suspected before his time, far less illuminated (as now they are) by beauty and tropical luxuriance of life. For instance, ... the possible beauty of the female character had not been seen as in a dream before Shakspeare called into perfect life the radiant shapes of Desdemona [in *Othello*], of Imogen [in *Cymbeline*], of Hermione [in *The Winter's Tale*], of Perdita [in *The Winter's Tale*], of Ophelia [in *Hamlet*], of Miranda [in *The Tempest*], and many others. The Una of Spenser [in *The Fairie Queen*], earlier by ten or fifteen years than most of these, was an idealised portrait of female innocence and virgin purity, but too shadowy and unreal for a dramatic reality. And, as to the Grecian classics, let not the reader imagine for an instant that any prototype in this field of Shakspearian power can be looked for there. The *Antigone* and the *Electra* of the tragic poets are the two leading female characters that classical antiquity offers to our respect, but assuredly not to our impassioned love. ... They challenge our admiration, severe, and even stern, as impersonations of filial duty, cleaving to the steps of a desolate and afflicted old man, or of sisterly affection, maintaining the rights of a brother under circumstances of peril, of desertion, and consequently of perfect self-reliance. Iphigenia, again, though not dramatically coming before us in her own person, but according to the beautiful report of a spectator, presents us with a fine statuesque model of heroic fortitude. ... These are fine marble groups, but they are not the warm breathing realities of Shakspeare; there is "no speculation" in their cold marble eyes; the breath of life is not in their nostrils; the fine pulses of womanly sensibilities are not throbbing in their bosoms. And, besides this immeasurable difference between the cold moony reflexes of life as exhibited by the power of Grecian art and the true sunny life of Shakspeare, it must be observed that the Antigones, &c., of the antique put forward but one single trait of character ... whereas in Shakspeare all is presented in the *concrete*,—that is to say, not brought forward in relief, as by some effort of an anatomical artist, but embodied and imbedded, so to speak, as by the force of a creative nature, in the complex system of a human life: a life in which all the elements move and play simultaneously, and, with something more than mere simultaneity or coexistence, acting and re-acting each upon the other—nay, even acting by each other and through each other. In Shakspeare's characters is felt for ever a real *organic* life, where each is for the whole and in the whole, and where the whole is for each and in each. They only are real incarnations.

The Greek poets could not exhibit any approximations to *female* character without violating the truth of Grecian life and shocking the feelings of the audience. The drama with the Greeks, as with us, though much less than with us, was a picture of human life; and that which could not occur in life could not wisely be exhibited on the stage. Now, in ancient Greece, women were secluded from the society of men. . . . And hence generally arose for Shakspeare the wider field, and the more astonishing by its perfect novelty, when he first introduced female characters, not as mere varieties or echoes of masculine characters, a Medea or Clytemnestra, or a vindictive Hecuba, the mere tigress of the tragic tiger, but female characters that had the appropriate beauty of female nature; woman no longer grand, terrific, and repulsive, but woman "after her kind"—the other hemisphere of the dramatic world; woman running through the vast gamut of womanly loveliness; woman as emancipated, exalted, ennobled, under a new law of Christian morality; woman the sister and co-equal of man, no longer his slave, his prisoner, and sometimes his rebel. . . .

A second reason which lends an emphasis of novelty and effective power to Shakspeare's female world is a peculiar fact of contrast which exists between that and his corresponding world of men. Let us explain. The purpose and the intention of the Grecian stage was not primarily to develop human *character*, whether in men or in women: human *fates* were its object; great tragic situations under the mighty control of a vast cloudy destiny, dimly descried at intervals, and brooding over human life by mysterious agencies, and for mysterious ends. Man, no longer the representative of an august *will*,—man, the passion-puppet of fate,—could not with any effect display what we call a character, which is a distinction between man and man, emanating originally from the will, and expressing its determinations, moving under the large variety of human impulses. The will is the central pivot of character; and this was obliterated, thwarted, cancelled, by the dark fatalism which brooded over the Grecian stage. That explanation will sufficiently clear up the reason why marked or complex variety of character was slighted by the great principles of the Greek tragedy. And every scholar who has studied that grand drama of Greece with feeling,—that drama, so magnificent, so regal, so stately,—and who has thoughtfully investigated its principles, and its difference from the English drama, will acknowledge that powerful and elaborate character,—character, for instance, that could employ the fiftieth part of that profound analysis which has been applied to Hamlet, to Falstaff, to Lear, to Othello, and applied by Mrs. [Anna Brownell Murphy] Jameson [in *Characteristics of Women,* 1832] so admirably to the full development of Shakspearian heroines,—would have been as much wasted, nay, would have been defeated, and interrupted the blind agencies of fate, just in the same way as it would injure the shadowy grandeur of a ghost to individualize it too much. . . .

In the great world, therefore, of woman, as the interpreter of the shifting phases and the lunar varieties of that mighty changeable planet, that lovely satellite of man [*sic*], Shakspeare stands not the first only, not the original only, but is yet the sole authentic oracle of truth. Woman, therefore, the beauty of the female mind, *this* is one great field of his power. The supernatural world, the world of apparitions, *that* is another: for reasons which it would be easy to give, reasons emanating from the gross mythology of the ancients, no Grecian,[3] no Roman, could have conceived a ghost. That shadowy conception, the protesting apparition, the awful projection of the human conscience, belongs to the Christian mind: and in all Christendom, who, let us ask, who, but Shakspeare, has found the power for effectually working this mysterious mode of being? In summoning back to earth "the majesty of buried Denmark," how like an awful necromancer does Shakspeare appear! All the pomps and grandeurs which religion, which the grave, which the popular superstition had gathered about the subject of apparitions, are here converted to his purpose, and bend to one awful effect. The wormy grave brought into antagonism with the scenting of the early dawn; the trumpet of resurrection suggested, and again as an antagonist idea to the crowing of the cock (a bird ennobled in the Christian mythus by the part he is made to play at the Crucifixion); its starting "as a guilty thing" placed in opposition to its majestic expression of offended dignity when struck at by the partisans of the sentinels; its awful allusions to the secrets of its prison-house; its ubiquity, contrasted with its local presence; its aerial substance, yet clothed in palpable armour; the heart-shaking solemnity of its language, and the appropriate scenery of its haunt, viz. the ramparts of a capital fortress, with no witnesses but a few gentlemen mounting guard at the dead of night,—what a mist, what a *mirage* of vapour, is here accumulated, through which the dreadful being in the centre looms upon us in far larger proportions than could have happened had it been insulated and left naked of this circumstantial pomp! In the *Tempest*, again, what new modes of life, preternatural, yet far as the poles from the spiritualities of religion. Ariel in antithesis to Caliban![4] What is most ethereal to what is most animal! A phantom of air, an abstraction of the dawn and of vesper sunlights, a bodiless sylph on the one hand; on the other a gross carnal monster. . . . In the *Midsummer-Night's Dream*, again, we have the old traditional fairy, a lovely mode of preternatural life, remodified by Shakspeare's eternal talisman. Oberon and Titania remind us at first glance of Ariel; they approach, but how far they recede: they are like—"like, but oh, how different!" And in no other exhibition of this dreamy population of the moonlight forests and forest-lawns are the circumstantial proprieties of fairy life so exquisitely imagined, sustained, or expressed. The dialogue between Oberon and Titania is, of itself, and taken separately from its connexion, one of the most delightful poetic scenes that literature affords. The witches in *Macbeth* are another variety of supernatural life in which Shakspeare's power to enchant and to disenchant are alike portentous. The circumstances of the blasted heath, the army at a distance, the withered attire of the mysterious hags, and the choral litanies of their fiendish Sabbath, are as finely imagined in their kind as those which herald and which surround the ghost in *Hamlet*. There we see the *positive* of Shakspeare's superior power. But now turn and look to the *negative*. At a time when the trials of witches, the royal book on demonology, and popular superstition (all so far useful, as they prepared a basis of undoubting faith for the poet's serious use of such agencies) had degraded and polluted the ideas of these mysterious beings by many mean associations, Shakspeare does not fear to employ them in high tragedy (a tragedy moreover which, though not the very greatest of his efforts as an intellectual whole, nor as a struggle of passion, is *among* the greatest in any view, and positively *the* greatest for scenical grandeur, and in that respect makes the nearest approach of all English tragedies to the Grecian model); he does not fear to introduce, for the same appalling effect as that for which Aeschylus introduced the Eumenides, a triad of old women; . . . yet, relying on his own supreme power to disenchant as well as to enchant, to create and to uncreate, he mixes these women and their dark machineries with the power of armies, with the agencies of kings, and the fortunes of martial kingdoms. Such was the sovereignty of this poet, so mighty its compass!

A third fund of Shakspeare's peculiar power lies in his teeming fertility of fine thoughts and sentiments. From his works alone might be gathered a golden bead-roll of thoughts the deepest, subtlest, most pathetic, and yet most catholic and universally intelligible; the most characteristic, also, and appropriate to the particular person, the situation, and the case, yet, at the same time, applicable to the circumstances of every human being, under all the accidents of life, and all vicissitudes of fortune. But this subject offers so vast a field of observation, it being so eminently the prerogative of Shakspeare to have thought more finely and more extensively than all other poets combined, that we cannot wrong the dignity of such a theme by doing more, in our narrow limits, than simply noticing it as one of the emblazonries upon Shakspeare's shield.

Fourthly, we shall indicate (and, as in the last case, *barely* indicate, without attempting in so vast a field to offer any inadequate illustrations) one mode of Shakspeare's dramatic excellence which hitherto has not attracted any special or separate notice. We allude to the forms of life and natural human passion as apparent in the structure of his dialogue. Among the many defects and infirmities of the French and of the Italian drama, indeed we may say of the Greek, the dialogue proceeds always by independent speeches, replying indeed to each other, but never modified in its several openings by the momentary effect of its several terminal forms immediately preceding. Now, in Shakspeare, who first set an example of that most important innovation, in all his impassioned dialogues, each reply or rejoinder seems the mere rebound of the previous speech. Every form of natural interruption, breaking through the restraints of ceremony under the impulses of tempestuous passion; every form of hasty interrogative, ardent reiteration when a question has been evaded; every form of scornful repetition of the hostile words; every impatient continuation of the hostile statement; in short, all modes and formulae by which anger, hurry, fretfulness, scorn, impatience, or excitement under any movement whatever, can disturb or modify or dislocate the formal bookish style of commencement: these are as rife in Shakspeare's dialogue as in life itself; and how much vivacity, how profound a verisimilitude, they add to the scenic effect as an imitation of human passion and real life, we need not say. A volume might be written illustrating the vast varieties of Shakspeare's art and power in this one field of improvement; another volume might be dedicated to the exposure of the lifeless and unnatural result from the opposite practice in the foreign stages of France and Italy. And we may truly say that, were Shakspeare distinguished from them by this single feature of nature and propriety, he would on that account alone have merited a great immortality.

Notes

3.   It may be thought, however, by some readers, that Aeschylus, in his fine phantom of Darius, has approached the English ghost. As a foreign ghost, we would wish (and we are sure that our excellent readers would wish) to show every courtesy and attention to this apparition of Darius. It has the advantage of being royal, an advantage which it shares with the ghost of the royal Dane. Yet how different, how removed by a total world, from that or any of Shakespeare's ghosts! Take that of Banquo, for instance: how shadowy, how unreal, yet how real! Darius is a mere ghost—a diplomatic ghost. But Banquo—he exists only for Macbeth; the guests do not see him; yet how solemn, how real, how heart-searching he is!

4.   Caliban has not yet been thoroughly fathomed. For all Shakespeare's great creations are like works of nature, subjects of inexhaustible study.

> —Thomas De Quincey, from "Shakespeare,"
> 1838, *Collected Writings*, edited by David
> Masson, 1889, volume 4, pp. 70–79

THOMAS CARLYLE "THE HERO AS POET" (1841)

Thomas Carlyle (1795–1881), the Scottish essayist, historian, satirist, and moralist, proclaims Shakespeare a hero poet, worthy of idolatry, one who speaks the world's voice in his own and who, rather than writing about nature, incarnates the process of nature writing, not through his intellect but through the workings of an oxymoronic "unconscious intellect" working in him.

The picture that Carlyle draws of Shakespeare is of a man so complete in himself that he can seem to be without needs, a man who might have been content to remain in Stratford had not circumstances taken him to London and the theater. Shakespeare's completeness and his intellectual power combined to give him the material and the aptitude, Carlyle asserts, necessary to produce the work he did. Anticipating by more than a decade the central argument of the Baconions—those who claimed Sir Francis Bacon, not Shakespeare, wrote the plays attributed to the latter—that Bacon's work shows the wisdom, learning, all-encompassing enlightenment, and far-seeing understanding that can be discovered in Shakespeare's work. Carlyle argues that, even so, turning the matter of Bacon's prose into those plays is a feat requiring something more than what is contained in Bacon's work. It is a power Carlyle calls "portrait-painting," which he sees in Shakespeare's ability to develop dramatic situations, interactions, and, especially, characters. This power, Carlyle argues, causes Shakespeare's plays to stand as the representations of the practical reality of the European Renaissance world, just as Dante's *Divine Comedy* embodies the spiritual world of medieval Europe.

Shakspeare . . . embodies for us the Outer Life of our Europe as developed [during the Middle Ages], its chivalries, courtesies, humours, ambitions, what practical way of thinking, acting, looking at the world, men then had. As in Homer we may still construe Old Greece; so in Shakspeare and Dante, after thousands of years, what our modern Europe was, in Faith and in Practice, will still be legible. Dante has given us the Faith or soul; Shakspeare, in a not less noble way, has given us the Practice or body. . . . Two fit men: Dante, deep, fierce was the central fire of the world; Shakspeare, wide, placid, far-seeing, as the Sun, the upper light of the world. Italy produced the one world-voice; we English had the honour of producing the other.

Curious enough how, as it were by mere accident, this man came to us. I think always, so great, quiet, complete and self-sufficing is this Shakspeare, had the Warwickshire Squire not prosecuted him for deer-stealing, we had perhaps never heard of him as a Poet! The woods and skies, the rustic Life of Man in Stratford there, had been enough for this man! But indeed that strange outbudding of our whole English Existence, which we call the Elizabethan Era, did not it too come as of its own accord? The 'Tree Igdrasil' [from Norse Mythology, its whose roots and branches hold together the universe] buds and withers by its own laws,—too deep for our scanning. . . . Priceless Shakspeare was the free gift of Nature; given altogether silently;—received altogether silently, as if it had been a thing of little account. . . .

Of this Shakspeare of ours, perhaps the opinion one sometimes hears a little idolatrously expressed is, in fact, the right one; I think the best judgment not of this country only, but of Europe at large, is slowly pointing to the conclusion, That Shakespeare is the chief of all Poets hitherto; the greatest intellect who, in our recorded world, has left record of himself in the way of Literature. On the whole, I know not such a power of vision, such a faculty of thought, if we take all the characters of it, in any other man. Such a calmness of depth; placid joyous strength; all things imaged in that great soul of his so true and clear, as in a tranquil unfathomable sea! It has been said, that in the constructing of Shakspeare's Dramas there is, apart from all other 'faculties' as they are called, an understanding manifested, equal to that in [Sir Francis]

Bacon's *Novum Organum* [1620]. That is true; and it is not a truth that strikes every one. It would become more apparent if we tried, any of us for himself, how, out of Shakspeare's dramatic materials, *we* could fashion such a result! ... [I]t is in what I called Portrait-painting, delineating of men and things, especially of men, that Shakspeare is great. All the greatness of the man comes out decisively here. It is unexampled, I think, that calm creative perspicacity of Shakspeare. The thing he looks at reveals not this or that face of it, but its inmost heart, and generic secret: it dissolves itself as in light before him, so that he discerns the perfect structure of it. Creative, we said: poetic creation, what is this too but *seeing* the thing sufficiently? The *word* that will describe the thing, follows of itself from such clear intense sight of the thing. And is not Shakspeare's *morality,* his valour, candour, tolerance, truthfulness; his whole victorious strength and greatness, which can triumph over such obstructions, visible there too? Great as the world! No *twisted,* poor convex-concave mirror, reflecting all objects with its own convexities and concavities; a perfectly *level* mirror;—that is to say withal, if we will understand it, a man justly related to all things and men, a good man. It is truly a lordly spectacle how this great soul takes-in all kinds of men and objects, a Falstaff, an Othello, a Juliet, a Coriolanus; sets them all forth to us in their round completeness; loving, just, the equal brother of all. *Novum Organum,* and all the intellect you will find in Bacon, is of a quite secondary order; earthy, material, poor in comparison with this. Among modern men, one finds, in strictness, almost nothing of the same rank. Goethe alone, since the days of Shakspeare, reminds me of it. ... If called to define Shakspeare's faculty, I should say superiority of Intellect, and think I had included all under that. What indeed are faculties? We talk of faculties as if they were distinct, things separable; as if a man had intellect, imagination, fancy, &c., as he has hands, feet, and arms. That is a capital error. Then again, we hear of a man's 'intellectual nature,' and of his 'moral nature,' as if these again were divisible, and existed apart. Necessities of language do perhaps prescribe such forms of utterance; we must speak, I am aware, in that way, if we are to speak at all. But words ought not to harden into things for us. It seems to me, our apprehension of this matter is, for most part, radically falsified thereby. We ought to know withal, and to keep forever in mind, that these divisions are at bottom but *names;* that man's spiritual nature, the vital Force which dwells in him, is essentially one and indivisible; that what we call imagination, fancy, understanding, and so forth, are but different figures of the same Power of Insight, all indissolubly connected with each other. ...

If I say, therefore, that Shakspeare is the greatest of Intellects, I have said all concerning him. But there is more in Shakspeare's intellect than we have yet seen. It is what I call an unconscious intellect; there is more virtue in it than he himself is aware of. [German romantic philosopher and writer] Novalis beautifully remarks of him, that those Dramas of his are Products of Nature too, deep as Nature herself. I find a great truth in this saying. Shakspeare's Art is not Artifice; the noblest worth of it is not there by plan or precontrivance. It grows-up from the deeps of Nature, through this noble sincere soul, who is a voice of Nature. The latest generations of men will find new meanings in Shakspeare, new elucidations of their own human being; 'new harmonies with the infinite structure of the Universe; concurrences with later ideas, affinities with the higher powers and senses of man.' ... How much in Shakspeare lies hid; his sorrows, his silent struggles known to himself; much that was not known at all, not speakable at all: like *roots*, like sap and forces working underground! ...

Withal the joyful tranquillity of this man is notable. I will not blame Dante for his misery: it is as battle without victory; but true battle,—the first, indispensable thing. Yet I call Shakspeare greater than Dante, in that he fought truly, and did conquer. Doubt it not, he had his own sorrows: those *Sonnets* of his will even testify expressly in what deep waters he had waded, and swum struggling for his life;—as what man like him ever failed to have to do? It seems to me a heedless notion, our common one, that he sat like a bird on the bough; and sang forth, free and offhand, never knowing the troubles of other men. Not so; with no man is it so. How could a man travel forward from rustic deer-poaching to such tragedy-writing, and not fall-in with sorrows by the way? Or, still better, how could a man delineate a Hamlet, a Coriolanus, a Macbeth, so many suffering heroic hearts, if his own heroic heart had never suffered?—And now, in contrast with all this, observe his mirthfulness, his genuine overflowing love of laughter! You would say, in no point does he *exaggerate* but only in laughter. Fiery objurgations, words that pierce and burn, are to be found in Shakspeare; yet he is always in measure here; never what Johnson would remark as a specially 'good hater.' But his laughter seems to pour from him in floods; he heaps all manner of ridiculous nicknames on the butt he is bantering, tumbles and tosses him in all sorts of horse-play; you would say, with his whole heart laughs. And then, if not always the finest, it is always a genial laughter. Not at mere weakness, at misery or poverty; never. No man who *can* laugh, what we call laughing, will laugh at these things. It is some poor character only *desiring* to laugh, and have the credit of wit, that does so.

Laughter means sympathy; good laughter is not 'the crackling of thorns under the pot.' [*Ecclesiastes* 7:6] Even at stupidity and pretension this Shakspeare does not laugh otherwise than genially. Dogberry and Verges [in *Much Ado about Nothing*] tickle our very hearts; and we dismiss them covered with explosions of laughter: but we like the poor fellows only the better for our laughing; and hope they will get on well there, and continue Presidents of the City-watch. Such laughter, like sunshine on the deep sea, is very beautiful to me.

We have no room to speak of Shakspeare's individual works; though perhaps there is much still waiting to be said on that head. Had we, for instance, all his plays reviewed as *Hamlet*, in [Goethe's novel] *Wilhelm Meister*, is! A thing which might, one day, be done. August Wilhelm Schlegel has a remark on his Historical Plays, *Henry Fifth* and the others, which is worth remembering. He calls them a kind of National Epic. [Soldier, statesman, John Churchill, first Duke of] Marlborough [1650–1722], you recollect, said, he knew no English History but what he had learned from Shakspeare. There are really, if we look to it, few as memorable Histories. The great salient points are admirably seized; all rounds itself off, into a kind of rhythmic coherence; it is, as Schlegel says, *epic*;—as indeed all delineation by a great thinker will be. There are right beautiful things in those Pieces, which indeed together form one beautiful thing. That battle of Agincourt strikes me as one of the most perfect things, in its sort, we anywhere have of Shakspeare's. The description of the two hosts: the worn-out, jaded English; the dread hour, big with destiny, when the battle shall begin; and then that deathless valour: 'Ye good yeomen, whose limbs were made in England!' [*Henry V*, III.i.25–26] There is a noble Patriotism in it,—far other than the 'indifference' you sometimes hear ascribed to Shakspeare. A true English heart breathes, calm and strong, through the whole business; not boisterous, protrusive; all the better for that. There is a sound in it like the ring of steel. This man too had a right stroke in him, had it come to that!

But I will say, of Shakspeare's works generally, that we have no full impress of him there; even as full as we have of many men. His works are so many windows, through which we see a glimpse of the world that was in him. All his works seem, comparatively speaking, cursory, imperfect, written under cramping circumstances; giving only here and there a note of the full utterance of the man. Passages there are that come upon you like splendour out of Heaven; bursts of radiance, illuminating the very heart of the thing: you say, 'That is *true*, spoken once and forever; wheresoever and whensoever there is an open human soul, that will be recognised as true!' Such bursts, however, make us feel that the surrounding matter is not radiant; that it is, in part, temporary, conventional. Alas, Shakspeare had to write for the Globe Playhouse: his great soul had to crush itself, as it could, into that and no other mould. It was with him, then, as it is with us all. No man works save under conditions. . . .

Whoever looks intelligently at this Shakspeare may recognise that he too was a *Prophet*, in his way; of an insight analogous to the Prophetic, though he took it up in another strain. Nature seemed to this man also divine; unspeakable, deep as Tophet [Hell], high as Heaven: 'We are such stuff as Dreams are made of.' [*sic*] . . . But the man sang; did not preach, except musically. We called Dante the melodious Priest of Middle-Age Catholicism. May we not call Shakspeare the still more melodious Priest of a *true* Catholicism, the 'Universal Church' of the Future and of all times? No narrow superstition, harsh asceticism, intolerance, fanatical fierceness or perversion: a Revelation, so far as it goes, that such a thousandfold hidden beauty and divineness dwells in all Nature; which let all men worship as they can! We may say without offence, that there rises a kind of universal Psalm out of this Shakspeare too; not unfit to make itself heard among the still more sacred Psalms. Not in disharmony with these, if we understood them, but in harmony!—I cannot call this Shakspeare a 'Sceptic,' as some do; his indifference to the creeds and theological quarrels of his time misleading them. No: neither unpatriotic, though he says little about his Patriotism; nor sceptic, though he says little about his Faith. Such 'indifference' was the fruit of his greatness withal: his whole heart was in his own grand sphere of worship (we may call it such); these other controversies, vitally important to other men, were not vital to him.

But call it worship, call it what you will, is it not a right glorious thing, and set of things, this that Shakspeare has brought us? For myself, I feel that there is actually a kind of sacredness in the fact of such a man being sent into this Earth. Is he not an eye to us all; a blessed heaven-sent Bringer of Light?—And, at bottom, was it not perhaps far better that this Shakspeare, everyway an unconscious man, was *conscious* of no Heavenly message? . . .

Compared with any speaker or singer one knows, even with Aeschylus or Homer, why should he not, for veracity and universality, last like them? He is *sincere* as they; reaches deep down like them, to the universal and perennial. . . .

Well: this is our poor Warwickshire Peasant, who rose to be Manager of a Playhouse, so that he could live without begging; whom the Earl of Southampton cast some kind glances on; whom Sir Thomas Lucy, many thanks to him, was for sending to the Treadmill! We did not account him a god . . . while he dwelt with us. . . . Which Englishman we ever made, in this land of ours, which million of Englishmen, would we not give-up rather than the Stratford Peasant? There is no regiment of highest Dignitaries that we would sell him for. He is the grandest thing we have yet done. . . . [W]heresoever . . . English men and women are, they will say to one another:

'Yes, this Shakspeare is ours; we produced him, we speak and think by him; we are of one blood and kind with him.'

—Thomas Carlyle, from "The Hero
as Poet," *On Heroes, Hero-Worship
and the Heroic in History,* 1841

THOMAS BABINGTON MACAULAY
"MADAME D'ARBLAY" (1843)

Here, Thomas Babington Macaulay (1800–49), poet, historian, and politician, praises Shakespeare for the depth and complexity of his characters.

Highest among those who have exhibited human nature by means of dialogue, stands Shakspeare. His variety is like the variety of nature, endless diversity, scarcely any monstrosity. The characters of which he has given us an impression, as vivid as that which we receive from the characters of our own associates, are to be reckoned by scores. Yet in all these scores hardly one character is to be found which deviates widely from the common standard, and which we should call very eccentric if we met it in real life. The silly notion that every man has one ruling passion, and that this clue, once known, unravels all the mysteries of his conduct, finds no countenance in the plays of Shakspeare. There man appears as he is, made up of a crowd of passions, which contend for the mastery over him and govern him in turn. What is Hamlet's ruling passion? Or Othello's? Or Harry the Fifth's? Or Wolsey's [in *Henry VIII*]? Or Lear's? Or Shylock's [in *The Merchant of Venice*]? Or Benedick's [in *Much Ado about Nothing*]? Or Macbeth's? Or that of Cassius [in *Julius Caesar*]? Or that of Falconbridge [in *King John*]? But we might go on for ever. Take a single example, Shylock. Is he so eager for money as to be indifferent to revenge? Or so eager for revenge as to be indifferent to money? Or so bent on both together as to be indifferent to the honour of his nation and the law of Moses? All his propensities are mingled with each other, so that, in trying to apportion to each its proper part, we find the same difficulty which constantly meets us in real life. A superficial critic may say, that hatred is Shylock's ruling passion. But how many passions have amalgamated to form that hatred? It is partly the result of wounded pride: Antonio has called him dog. It is partly the result of covetousness: Antonio has hindered him of half a million; and, when Antonio is gone, there will be no limit to the gains of usury. It is partly the result of national and religious feeling: Antonio has spit on the Jewish gaberdine; and the oath of revenge has been sworn by the Jewish Sabbath. We might go through all the characters which we have mentioned, and through fifty more in the same way; for it is the constant manner of Shakspeare to represent the human mind as lying, not under the absolute dominion of one despotic propensity, but under a mixed government, in which a hundred powers balance each other. Admirable as he was in all parts of his art, we most admire him for this, that while he has left us a greater number of striking portraits than all other dramatists put together, he has scarcely left us a single caricature.

—Thomas Babington Macaulay, "Madame D'Arblay," 1843, *Critical, Historical, and Miscellaneous Essays,* 1860, volume 5, pp. 306–07

LEIGH HUNT "SHAKSPEARE" (1845)

Leigh Hunt (1784–1859), English poet, essayist, critic, journalist, and trans-lator, argues that rather than being unlearned, as traditional criticism defined him, Shakespeare shows himself, in fact, often, to be too learned, and his learning caused him, Hunt maintains, to write dialogue that was too allusive and Latinate for his characters.

There is nothing wanting either to the imagination or fancy of Shakspeare. The one is lofty, rich, affecting, palpable, subtle; the other full of grace, playfulness, and variety. He is equal to the greatest poets in grandeur of imagination; to all in diversity of it; to all in fancy; to all in everything else, except in a certain primaeval intensity, such as Dante's and Chaucer's; and in narrative poetry, which (to judge from *Venus and Adonis,* and the *Rape of Lucrece)* he certainly does not appear to have had a call to write. He over-informed it with reflection. It has been supposed that when Milton spoke of Shakspeare as

Fancy's child
Warbling his native wood-notes wild,

the genealogy did him injustice. . . . The propriety of the words, "native wood-notes wild," is not so clear. I take them to have been hastily said by a learned man of an unlearned. But Shakspeare, though he had not a college education, was as learned as any man, in the highest sense of the word, by a scholarly intuition. He had the spirit of learning. He was aware of the education he wanted, and by some means or other supplied it. He could anticipate Milton's own Greek and Latin;

Tortive and errant from his course of growth— [*Troilus and Cressida,*
I.iii.9]
The multitudinous seas incarnardine— [*Macbeth,* II.ii.58]
A pudency so rosy, &c.   [*Cymbeline,* II.v.11]

In fact, if Shakspeare's poetry has any fault, it is that of being too learned;
too over-informed with thought and allusion. . . . He thinks twenty times to
another man's once, and makes all his serious characters talk as well as he
could himself,—with a superabundance of wit and intelligence. He knew,
however, that fairies must have a language of their own; and hence, perhaps,
his poetry never runs in a more purely poetical vein than when he is speaking
in their persons;—I mean it is less mixed up with those heaps of comments
and reflections which, however the wilful or metaphysical critic may think
them suitable on all occasions, or succeed in persuading us not to wish them
absent, by reason of their stimulancy to one's mental activity, are assuredly
neither always proper to dramatic, still less to narrative poetry; nor yet so
opposed to all idiosyncrasy on the writer's part as Mr. Coleridge would have
us believe. It is pretty manifest, on the contrary, that the over-informing
intellect which Shakspeare thus carried into all his writings, must have been
a personal as well as literary peculiarity; and as the events he speaks of are
sometimes more interesting in their nature than even a superabundance
of his comments can make them, readers may be pardoned in sometimes
wishing that he had let them speak a little more briefly for themselves.

—Leigh Hunt, "Shakspeare,"
Imagination and Fancy, 1845

H. N. HUDSON (1848)

The American lecturer and writer on Shakespeare who edited an American
edition of Shakespeare's plays, the Reverend Henry Norman Hudson (1814–
86) begins this homage to Shakespeare with a celebration of what Hudson
sees as his universality and his comprehension of everything human. In
the second part of this excerpt, Hudson condemns the critical opinion
that Shakespeare's plays were immoral, arguing, rather, that Shakespeare,
because of the broad range of his vision and the depth of his understanding, draws evil or immoral characters true to their vices but never gives the
impression, based on the entire play in which they appear, that there is
anything attractive or appealing about those vices. He argues that because
Shakespeare can show vice in both its obscenity and its complexity, his

work actually serves as a truer moral guide than works that are esteemed because of their pious moralizing. Additionally, Hudson argues against critics who resent Shakespeare's failure always to show vice defeated and virtue triumphant, asserting that is, in fact, another indication of the very morality of Shakespeare's work. Hudson warns that virtue ought to be pursued not because of its presumed inevitable success but for itself.

Sensibility

Shakspeare's sensibility is in proportion with his other gifts. His heart is as great and as strong as his head. He feels the beauty and the worth of things as truly and as deeply as he discerns their relations; is alive to the slightest and equal to the strongest impression; nothing stuns and nothing eludes his sensibility. He sympathizes, calmly yet intensely, with all that he finds and all that he makes; he *loves* all things; his soul gushes out in warm virgin-like affection over all the objects of his contemplation, and embraces them in its soft, heavenly radiance. He discerns a soul, a pulse of good even in things that are evil; knows, indeed, that nothing can exist utterly divorced from good of some sort; that it must have some inward harmony to hold it in existence. To this harmony, this innate, indestructible worth, his mind is ever open. He is, therefore, a man of universal benevolence; wishes well of all things; will do his best to benefit them; not, indeed, by injuring others, but by doing them justice; by giving them their due, be they saints, or be they sinners. He is strictly and inexorably impartial, and even shows his love of perfect justice by shedding the sunshine and the rain of his genius alike on the just and on the unjust. For his feelings are the allies, not the rivals, of his other powers; exist in sympathy and reciprocity, not in antagonism with them, and therefore never try to force or tempt him from his loyalty to truth.

With most men, the head and heart will not work together; one of them is always pulling the other under: in thinking, they cease to feel, or in feeling they cease to think; so that, to borrow a figure from Coleridge, they are either like the moon, all light and no heat, or like a stove, all heat and no light. They therefore fail of true wisdom, because they are always using either the head without the heart, or the heart without the head. Shakspeare, on the contrary, everywhere exemplifies "the long pull, and strong pull, and pull altogether," of all the faculties. Thought and feeling with him are always interpenetrating and interworking, and he never fails of wisdom, because he never uses head or heart alone. Notwithstanding, forasmuch as Shakspeare discovers no preference of the good characters to the bad, many think him deficient in moral sensibility; whereas, in fact, he shows the perfection of such sensibility in altogether preferring truth to them both: for there is really nothing more vicious or more vitiating than, what some people seem greatly in love with, the attempting to teach better morality than is taught by nature and Providence. . . .

There are . . . a few men, and perhaps Shakspeare stands at their head, who truly sympathize with something out of themselves; who really feel the true, the beautiful, and the good; nay, whose feeling of these objects comparatively swallows up the feeling of themselves. Shakspeare, it is true, did not talk about his feelings, perhaps was not conscious of them; but that he had them in their truest, deepest form, seems highly probable from the fact, that instead of speaking about *them,* he spoke about the things that inspired them. His love of the true, the beautiful, and the good, was simply too deep and genuine, to be listening to its own voice, or carrying a looking-glass before itself to gaze at its own image; and such is ever the case with souls that are smitten with such objects. For it is the very nature of true feeling to interest us in something out of ourselves. And when we see a man prating about his feelings, we may know at once that he has none. In a word, it is with feeling as with religion; if a man really have any, he will have "none to speak of." Of all men, therefore, Shakspeare was perhaps the least a sentimentalist; strove not at all to reveal the truth and beauty of his feelings, but only to reveal the truth and beauty which he felt. . . .

Nor are Shakspeare's moral sympathies, his sympathy with truth and good, any more just or genuine than his mere human sympathies. He not only knows what we all know, but feels what we all feel, and utters forth the feeling with the same fidelity as he does the knowledge. The hearts of most men are so small, that they cannot fully enter into the feelings of another without ceasing to be themselves; a complete sympathy with the movements of another mind would perhaps swallow up the individuality of their own. But Shakspeare's all-embracing bosom catches and reverberates every note of man's heart. He could reproduce in their utmost depth and intensity the feelings of us all without injury to himself. His sympathies seem to have covered the extremes of human sensibility, so that the feelings of us all might, as it were, be cut out of his, and yet leave his personality entire.

Doubtless it was this omniformity of feeling, as much as any thing, that qualified him, beyond any other man, to be the representative of the whole human family. He was thus in a condition neither to withhold from a character his own, nor to yield him up another's, but simply to give him his due. Hence the strict rigid impartiality of his representations; for among all his characters, we cannot discover from the delineation itself that he had a single favourite, though of course we cannot conceive it possible for any man to regard Edmund and Edgar [in *King Lear*], for example, with the same feelings. It is as if the scenes of his dramas were forced on his observation against his will; himself, meanwhile, being under the most solemn oath to report the truth. . . . Surrounded by the angels and demons which make up the dramatic combination of Lear or Othello, though conscious the while of their inmost thoughts and feelings, such, nevertheless, is the calmness, with which he surveys them, that not the least bias comes in to distort or discolour his representation of them. He thus uniformly leaves the characters to make their own impression upon us; has no opinions or feelings of his own to promulgate through them, but simply to represent them; in a word, he is their mouth-piece, not they his; and he could be the representative of all because he would be the advocate of none. With the honour or shame, the right or wrong of their actions, he has nothing to do; that they are so and act so, is their fault, not his; and his business is, not to reform nor deprave, to censure nor approve them, but simply to tell the truth about them, whithersoever it may lead him. Accordingly, he exhibits neither any utterly worthless, nor any utterly faultless monsters; none too good or too bad to exist; none too high to be loved, or too low to be pitied: even his worst characters (unless we except those two she-tigers, Goneril and Regan [in *King Lear*], and even their blood is red like ours) have some slight fragrance of humanity about them; some indefinable touches which redeem them from utter hatred or utter contempt, and keep them within the pale of human sympathy, or at least of human pity.

Nor does Shakspeare ever bring in any characters as the mere shadows, or instruments, or appendages of others. All the persons, great and small, contain within themselves the reason why they are there and not elsewhere, why they are so and not otherwise. None exist exclusively for others, or exclusively for themselves, but all appear, partly on their own account, with aims, and feelings, and interests of their own. None are forced in merely to supply the place of others, and so merely trifled with till the others can be got ready to resume their place; but each is treated in his turn as if he were the main character in the piece, and speaks and acts, not merely to call up and call out others, but chiefly to utter and impart himself. So true is this, that even when one character comes in as the satellite of another, he does so by a right and an impulse of his own; he is all the while but obeying or rather executing the law of his personality, and has just as much claim on the other for a primary, as the other has on him for a satellite. In a word, Shakspeare, in his mental kingdom, is a prince of absolute power, but at the same time of absolute justice, and always treats those of his subjects as the mightiest who are at the moment beneath his pen: he knows no weighty man, or rather knows no man whatever in his empire, save him who is now speaking, and knows him as such, or even at all, only while he permits him to speak. The consequence of which is, that all the characters are developed, not indeed at equal length, for they have not all the same amount to be developed, but with equal perfectness as far as they go; for to make the dwarf fill the same space as the giant, would be to dilute, not develope the dwarf.

Thus with the fruitfulness of nature Shakspeare also joined the disinterestedness of nature, who concentrates herself alike in the nettle and the oak, the night-shade and the rose, the wasp and the dove. And perhaps his greatest glory, both as a poet and as a man is, that he was no respecter of sects, or parties, or persons, but simply a teller of the truth.

> Born for the universe, he shrunk not his mind,
> Nor to party gave up what was meant for mankind.
> [cf. Oliver Goldsmith's epitaph for Edmund Burke:
> Who, born for the universe, narrowed his mind,
> And to party gave up what was meant for mankind.]

... Hence his works are always humanizing us, fusing our minds, so to speak, out of their selfish isolation, into unanimity and fellowship; in a word, they are a constant discipline of humanity, are filled with those "touches of nature," which "make the whole world kin:" at the voice of his genius the shell of individualism, into which we are so fond of retiring to "suck the paws of our own self-importance," [from Coleridge's *The Improvisatore,* 1827] is perpetually giving way to the ingress and egress of human sympathy. He seems indeed to have lived and worked altogether at the roots of humanity, distilling the very sap and moulding the very elements of the wonderful structure; and knew that all sects and parties were but the transient, differently-shaped leaves which the winds of time would soon blow into oblivion, while the structure itself would remain forever the same.

This universal and impartial humanity is doubtless among the highest qualities of Shakspeare's works; nay, it is among the highest possible qualities of any human productions; for it is the union and interfusion of the deepest reason and the justest feeling. . . . Shakspeare's works, the profoundest of all uninspired [i.e., nonbiblical] writings, are at the same time the most generally intelligible. Striking below the accidents of local and partial nature, he is constantly touching chords that vibrate through the universal mind of man. . . . Shakspeare's characters always affect us as those in real life. Different people, according to their respective feelings and dispositions, take up very different impressions of them. As in the case of actual persons, nothing short of a profound and subtle analysis can arrive at satisfactory conclusions respecting them. To a constant, reflecting student, they seem perpetually developing themselves, and are always undergoing apparent modifications precisely corresponding to the real modifications of the student's own character. Often they are so much addressed to the feelings, so much more is often suggested than is said, that no one can fully expound them, without completely unfolding himself. Always making the persons act and speak from what is implied, as well as from what is disclosed, the poet is perpetually sending us beyond himself to nature, and to the elements of all character. Even when the characters are seen but in part, they are yet capable of being understood and unfolded in the whole; every part being relative and inferring all the others. What is given, be it ever so little, conveys a relish of what is withheld. . . .

From what hath been said, the perceptive, the creative, and the sensitive powers were so exquisitely balanced in Shakspeare's mind, that it is impossible to say which had the lead. That he indefinitely surpassed all other writers in something, is generally allowed; but in what particular faculty or mental activity his great superiority lay, scarce any two are agreed. And this very circumstance is probably decisive of the truth. The real secret of his superiority to all other writers, lies in his having in the highest degree the peculiar faculties of each. It is the absence of any individual preponderance or individual deficiency among his powers, that forms their united perfection; and his towering so far above the rest of mankind is sufficiently explained by the fact, that no one of his faculties towered above the others. . . .

Alleged Immorality

Shakspeare's plays have been frequently charged with immoral tendencies; than which a more unfounded and injurious charge could not well be made. Like various other charges visited upon them, it has generally sprung either from a disposition to fix upon certain detached expressions, or from inability to take in the impression of a vital, organic whole. For morally, as otherwise, a work of art should be regarded in its total impression; and those who can see but one line or one sentence of a poem at once are not competent judges of its moral quality. Undoubtedly there are passages in Shakspeare's works, as indeed there are in the Bible itself, which, taken by themselves, may produce a bad effect; but there cannot be found a whole play, scarcely even a whole scene in them, whose integral impression is not altogether good. . . .

It must be confessed, however, that Shakspeare's own virtue, like that of his purest characters, and like that of the purest men too, was not of that ambitious, pharisaical sort, which is always trying to bolster itself by an outrageous horror of vice, or at least the appearance of vice. Accordingly he never attires sensuality in artificial attractions, nor conceals real impurity under a wrappage of conventional decency, nor throws the drapery of affected delicacy over the movements of guilty passion. If he has occasion for a bad character, he shows him just as he is, and does not attempt to disguise his grossness, or palliate his deformity; and it is surely our own fault if we are captivated by the inward impurity of a character whose outward ugliness ought to offend even our senses. He has sometimes delineated downright villains and sensualists; but he has never volunteered to steal the robes of heaven for them to serve the devil in without offending decency. In all cases, indeed, he has most religiously kept faith with the moral sensibilities which nature has set to guard the purity of the mind, and he seldom violates even the laws of gentility save in obedience to the higher laws of morality. . . .

In Shakspeare, as in nature, virtue shows her finest lessons in contest, or in contrast with vice: if we reject the former and cleave to the latter, the fact proves our impurity, not his; and if we are corrupted by such teachings, it were surely hard to tell what can purify us. He who forsakes Isabella to follow after Angelo [in *Measure for Measure*], or Desdemona to follow after Iago [in *Othello*], may be justly given up as already a spoiled egg. . . .

In heaven's name let decency be preserved, but let it not be piled on in folds and bustles to cover up personal deformity! Obscenity is certainly bad enough, but it is infinitely better than the chaste language of a crafty seducer. It is always well for us to know whom we are with; and our best safeguard against vice, is the very indecency in which it naturally appears. In his uniform observance of these principles Shakspeare has shown a degree of moral purity of which we have few examples in literature. He is indeed sometimes gross, but never false; he may occasionally offend a sense of delicacy, but never deceives and seduces the mind into admiration of unworthy objects; and he carries on no warfare against virtue by endeavoring to entrap our sympathies by the misfortunes of vice. That he should make a Falstaff at once so delightful and so detestable; that he should so charm us with the humour, even while disgusting us with the sensuality of such a being, and so let us into the truth, without drawing us into the love of such a character; really proves the strength of his morality no less than the mastery of his genius. For my part, I dare be known to think Shakspeare's works a far better school of virtuous discipline than half the moral and religious books which are now put into the hands of youth. . . .

Shakspeare, it is true, never lays off the poet to put on the moralist. . . . Morality comes from him as from nature, not in abstract propositions, to set our logic-mills a-going, but in a living form of beauty, to inspire us with love and noble passion. . . .

Another item in the attempted impeachment of Shakspeare's morality is, that he does not always observe, nay, sometimes utterly disregards what are termed the laws of poetical justice; that in his exhibitions moral equity is, to say the least, but very imperfectly administered, often, indeed, not administered at all. He does not encourage virtue by making it always successful, nor discountenance vice by always defeating its aims. In short, a degree of moral confusion reigns in his plays; the innocent often fall under the machinations of the guilty; the guilty often triumph on the ruins of innocence; often both are hurried away in undistinguishable ruin.

Fortunately for Shakspeare's honour, this charge cannot be denied. This rigid dispensation of moral justice, which brings virtue and vice down to a calculation of profit and loss, however favourable it might have been to his popularity, would have been fatal to his morality. And is the not succeeding, the not getting our wages, the worst thing we fear? Most assuredly, then, it is not the worst we shall suffer, and ought to suffer. If we would not rather die as Desdemona than live and thrive as Iago, the more pity for us.

—H. N. Hudson, from *Lectures on Shakspeare*, 1848, volume 1, pp. 64–87

RALPH WALDO EMERSON "SHAKSPEARE; OR, THE POET" (1850)

Ralph Waldo Emerson (1803–82), American essayist, philosopher, and poet, here argues that Shakespeare's greatness does not lie in his originality, that, in fact, Shakespeare was hardly original in his invention but borrowed copiously from numerous sources as was the accepted practice of his time. Shakespeare's greatness, rather, Emerson asserts, is the result of the music of his poetry—Emerson calls it the "tune"—of the design of his works, the philosophy they contain, the complexity of his characters, the immensity of his power to create, and the wisdom he brings to what he creates.

Great genial power . . . consists in not being original at all; in being altogether receptive; in letting the world do all, and suffering the spirit of the hour to pass unobstructed through the mind.

Shakspeare's youth fell in a time when the English people were importunate for dramatic entertainments. The court took offence easily at political allusions and attempted to suppress them. The Puritans, a growing and energetic party, and the religious among the Anglican church, would suppress them. But the people wanted them. Inn-yards, houses without roofs, and extemporaneous enclosures at country fairs were the ready theatres of strolling players. The people had tasted this new joy; and, as we could not hope to suppress newspapers now ... neither then could king, prelate, or puritan, alone or united, suppress an organ which was ballad, epic, newspaper, caucus, lecture, Punch and library, at the same time. Probably king, prelate and puritan, all found their own account in it. It had become, by all causes, a national interest,—by no means conspicuous, so that some great scholar would have thought of treating it in an English history,—but not a whit less considerable because it was cheap and of no account, like a baker's-shop. The best proof of its vitality is the crowd of writers which suddenly broke into this field; Kyd, Marlow, Greene, Jonson, Chapman, Dekker, Webster, Heywood, Middleton, Peele, Ford, Massinger, Beaumont and Fletcher.

The secure possession, by the stage, of the public mind, is of the first importance to the poet who works for it. He loses no time in idle experiments. Here is audience and expectation prepared. In the case of Shakspeare there is much more. At the time when he left Stratford and went up to London, a great body of stage-plays of all dates and writers existed in manuscript and were in turn produced on the boards. Here is the *Tale of Troy,* which the audience will bear hearing some part of, every week; the *Death of Julius Caesar,* and other stories out of Plutarch, which they never tire of; a shelf full of English history, from the chronicles of Brut [legendary founder and first king of Britain] and [King] Arthur, down to the royal Henries, which men hear eagerly; and a string of doleful tragedies, merry Italian tales and Spanish voyages, which all the London 'prentices know. All the mass has been treated, with more or less skill, by every playwright, and the prompter has the soiled and tattered manuscripts. It is now no longer possible to say who wrote them first. They have been the property of the Theatre so long, and so many rising geniuses have enlarged or altered them, inserting a speech or a whole scene, or adding a song, that no man can any longer claim copyright in this work of numbers. Happily, no man wishes to. They are not yet desired in that way. We have few readers, many spectators and hearers. . . .

Shakspeare, in common with his comrades, esteemed the mass of old plays waste stock, in which any experiment could be freely tried. Had the *prestige* which hedges about a modern tragedy existed, nothing could have been done. The rude warm blood of the living England circulated in the play, as in street-ballads, and gave body which he wanted to his airy and majestic fancy. The poet needs a ground in popular tradition on which he may work, and which, again, may restrain his art within the due temperance. It holds him to the people, supplies a foundation for his edifice, and in furnishing so much work done to his hand, leaves him at leisure and in full strength for the audacities of his imagination. In short, the poet owes to his legend what sculpture owed to the temple. Sculpture in Egypt and in Greece grew up in subordination to architecture. It was the ornament of the temple wall. . . .

In point of fact it appears that Shakspeare did owe debts in all directions, and was able to use whatever he found; and the amount of indebtedness may be inferred from [Shakespearean scholar and editor of the plays Edmond] Malone's laborious computations in regard to the first, second and third parts of *Henry* VI., in which, "out of 6,043 lines, 1,771 were written by some author preceding Shakspeare, 2,373 by him, on the foundation laid by his predecessors, and 1,899 were entirely his own." And the proceeding investigation hardly leaves a single drama of his absolute invention. Malone's sentence is an important piece of external history. In *Henry* VIII. I think I see plainly the cropping out of the original rock on which his own finer stratum was laid. The first play was written by a superior, thoughtful man, with a vicious ear. I can mark his lines, and know well their cadence. See Wolsey's soliloquy, and the following scene with Cromwell, where instead of the metre of Shakspeare, whose secret is that the thought constructs the tune, so that reading for the sense will best bring out the rhythm,—here the lines are constructed on a given tune, and the verse has even a trace of pulpit eloquence. But the play contains through all its length unmistakable traits of Shakspeare's hand, and some passages, as the account of the coronation, are like autographs. What is odd, the compliment to Queen Elizabeth is in the bad rhythm.

Shakspeare knew that tradition supplies a better fable than any invention can. If he lost any credit of design, he augmented his resources. . . .

Some able and appreciating critics think no criticism on Shakspeare valuable that does not rest purely on the dramatic merit; that he is falsely judged as poet and philosopher. I think as highly as these critics of his dramatic merit, but still think it secondary. He was a full man, who liked to talk; a brain exhaling thoughts and images, which, seeking vent, found the drama next at hand. Had he been less, we should have had to consider how well he filled his place, how good a dramatist he was,—and he is the best in the world. But it turns out that what he has to say is of that weight as to withdraw some attention from the vehicle. . . . He wrote the airs for all our modern music: he wrote the text of modern life; the text of manners: he drew the man of England and Europe; the father of the man in America; he drew the man, and described the day, and what is done in it: he read the hearts of men and women, their probity, and their second thought and wiles; the wiles of innocence, and the transitions by which virtues and vices slide into their contraries: he could divide the mother's part from the father's part in the face of the child, or draw the fine demarcations of freedom and of fate: he knew the laws of repression which make the police of nature: and all the sweets and all the terrors of human lot lay in his mind as truly but as softly as the landscape lies on the eye. And the importance of this wisdom of life sinks the form, as of Drama or Epic, out of notice. Tis like making a question concerning the paper on which a king's message is written.

Shakspeare is as much out of the category of eminent authors, as he is out of the crowd. He is inconceivably wise; the others, conceivably. A good reader can, in a sort, nestle into Plato's brain and think from thence; but not into Shakspeare's. We are still out of doors. For executive faculty, for creation, Shakspeare is unique. No man can imagine it better. He was the farthest reach of subtlety compatible with an individual self,—the subtlest of authors, and only just within the possibility of authorship. With this wisdom of life is the equal endowment of imaginative and of lyric power. He clothed the creatures of his legend with form and sentiments as if they were people who had lived under his roof; and few real men have left such distinct characters as these fictions. And they spoke in language as sweet as it was fit. Yet his talents never seduced him into an ostentation, nor did he harp on one string. An omnipresent humanity co-ordinates all his faculties. Give a man of talents a story to tell, and his partiality will presently appear. He has certain observations, opinions, topics, which have some accidental prominence, and which he disposes all to exhibit. He crams this part and starves that other part, consulting not the fitness of the thing, but his fitness and strength. But Shakspeare has no peculiarity, no importunate topic; but all is duly given; no veins, no curiosities; no cow-painter, no bird-fancier, no mannerist is he: he has no discoverable egotism: the great he tells greatly; the small subordinately. He is wise without emphasis or assertion; he is strong, as nature is strong, who lifts the land into mountain slopes without effort and by the same rule as she floats a bubble in the air, and likes as well to do the one as the other. This makes that equality of power in farce, tragedy, narrative and love-songs; a merit so incessant that each reader is incredulous of the perception of other readers.

This power of expression, or of transferring the inmost truth of things into music and verse, makes him the type of the poet and has added a new problem to metaphysics. This is that which throws him into natural history, as a main production of the globe, and as announcing new eras, and ameliorations. Things were mirrored in his poetry without loss or blur: he could paint the fine with precision, the great with compass, the tragic and the comic indifferently and without any distortion or favor. He carried his powerful execution into minute details, to a hair point; finishes an eyelash or a dimple as firmly as he draws a mountain; and yet these, like nature's, will bear the scrutiny of the solar microscope.

—Ralph Waldo Emerson, "Shakspeare; or, the Poet," *Representative Men*, 1850

JAMES ANTHONY FROUDE "ENGLAND'S FORGOTTEN WORTHIES" (1852)

James Anthony Froude (1818–94), novelist, historian, editor, and biographer, argues that Shakespeare's characters, far from being creations of an overcharged imagination, are actual representations of the kinds of people who were his contemporaries.

We wonder at the grandeur, the moral majesty of some of Shakespeare's characters, so far beyond what the noblest among ourselves can imitate, and at first thought we attribute it to the genius of the poet, who has outstripped nature in his creations. But we are misunderstanding the power and the meaning of poetry in attributing creativeness to it in any such sense. Shakespeare created, but only as the spirit of nature created around him, working in him as it worked abroad in those among whom he lived. The men whom he draws were such men as he saw and knew; the words they utter were such as he heard in the ordinary conversations in which he joined. At the Mermaid with Raleigh and with Sidney, and at a thousand unnamed English firesides, he found the living originals for his Prince Hals, his Orlandos, his Antonios, his Portias, his Isabellas. The closer personal acquaintance which we can form with the English of the age of Elizabeth, the more we are satisfied that Shakespeare's great poetry is no more than the rhythmic echo of the life which it depicts.

—James Anthony Froude, "England's Forgotten Worthies," 1852, *Short Studies on Great Subjects*, 1890, volume 1, pp. 445–46

JAMES RUSSELL LOWELL "SHAKESPEARE ONCE MORE" (1868)

James Russell Lowell (1819–1891), American poet, critic, social activist, and first editor of *The Atlantic Monthly* magazine, argues that the age in which Shakespeare lived was particularly suited to fostering Shakespeare's genius especially because 1) the English language was not fully formed. It was, Lowell argues, in a stage of development that allowed writers like Shakespeare the freedom to explore and invent the language, to have free reign to develop its depth, breadth, and even its meanings; and 2) the political and social climate of the Elizabethan and Jacobean eras allowed Shakespeare's unfettered aesthetic pursuits because of the order that marked Elizabethan and Jacobean society and that would soon give way to political and social turmoil marked by the regicide in 1649 when Charles I was beheaded, by the Puritan Commonwealth under the Cromwells that followed, and by the neoclassicsm that defined the Restoration of the monarchy in 1661 with the return of Charles II.

It may be doubted whether any language be rich enough to maintain more than one truly great poet,—and whether there be more than one period, and that very short, in the life of a language, when such a phenomenon as a great poet is possible. It may be reckoned one of the rarest pieces of good-luck that ever fell to the share of a race, that (as was true of Shakespeare) its most rhythmic genius, its acutest intellect, its profoundest imagination, and its healthiest understanding should have been combined in one man, and that he should have arrived at the full development of his powers at the moment when the material in which he was to work—that wonderful composite called English, the best result of the confusion of tongues—was in its freshest perfection. . . .

Had Shakespeare been born fifty years earlier, he would have been cramped by a book-language not yet flexible enough for the demands of rhythmic emotion, not yet sufficiently popularized for the natural and familiar expression of supreme thought, not yet so rich in metaphysical phrase as to render possible that ideal representation of the great passions which is the aim and end of Art, not yet subdued by practice and general consent to a definiteness of accentuation essential to ease and congruity of metrical arrangement. Had he been born fifty years later, his ripened manhood would have found itself in an England absorbed and angry with the solution of political and religious problems, from which his whole nature was averse, instead of in that Elizabethan social system, ordered and planetary in functions and degrees . . . where his contemplative eye could crowd itself with various and brilliant picture, and whence his impartial brain . . . could draw its morals of courtly and worldly wisdom, its lessons of prudence and magnanimity. In estimating Shakespeare, it should never be forgotten, that, like Goethe, he was essentially observer and artist, and incapable of partisanship. The passions, actions, sentiments, whose character and results he delighted to watch and to reproduce, are those of man in society as it existed; and it no more occurred to him to question the right of that society to exist than to criticise the divine ordination of the seasons. His business was with men as they were, not with man as he ought to be,—with the human soul as it is shaped or twisted into character by the complex experience of life, not in its abstract essence, as something to be saved or lost. . . . As purely poet, Shakespeare would have come too late, had his lot fallen in that generation. In mind and temperament too exoteric for a mystic, his imagination could not have at once illustrated the influence of his epoch and escaped from it; . . . the equilibrium of his judgment, essential to him as an artist, but equally removed from propagandism, whether as enthusiast or logician, would have unfitted him for the pulpit; and his intellectual being was too sensitive to the wonder and beauty of outward life and Nature to have found satisfaction, as Milton's could, (and perhaps only by reason of his blindness,) in a world peopled by purely imaginary figures. We might fancy him becoming a great statesman, but he lacked the social position which could have opened that career to him. What we mean when we say *Shakespeare,* is something inconceivable either during the reign of Henry the Eighth, or the Commonwealth, and which would have been impossible after the Restoration.

All favorable stars seem to have been in conjunction at his nativity. The Reformation had passed the period of its vinous fermentation, and its clarified results remained as an element of intellectual impulse and exhilaration; there were small signs yet of the acetous and putrefactive stages which were to follow in the victory and decline of Puritanism. Old forms of belief and worship still lingered, all the more touching to Fancy, perhaps, that they were homeless and attainted; the light of sceptic day was baffled by depths of forest where superstitious shapes still cowered, creatures of immemorial wonder, the raw material of Imagination. The invention of printing, without yet vulgarizing letters, had made the thought and history of the entire past contemporaneous; while a crowd of translators put every man who could read in inspiring contact with the select souls of all the centuries. A new world was thus opened to intellectual adventure at the very time when the keel of Columbus had turned the first daring furrow of discovery in that unmeasured ocean which still girt the known earth with a beckoning horizon of hope and conjecture, which was still fed by rivers that flowed down out of primeval silences, and which still washed the shores of Dreamland. Under a wise, cultivated, and firm-handed monarch also, the national feeling of England grew rapidly more homogeneous and intense, the rather as the womanhood of the sovereign stimulated a more chivalric loyalty,—while the new religion, of which she was the defender, helped to make England morally, as it was geographically, insular to the continent of Europe.

If circumstances could ever make a great national poet, here were all the elements mingled at melting-heat in the alembic, and the lucky moment of projection was clearly come. If a great national poet could ever avail himself of circumstances, this was the occasion,—and, fortunately, Shakespeare was equal to it. Above all, we may esteem it lucky that he found words ready to his use, original and untarnished,—types of thought whose sharp edges were unworn by repeated impressions. . . .

It was in London, and chiefly by means of the stage, that a thorough amalgamation of the Saxon, Norman, and scholarly elements of English was brought about. Already, [George] Puttenham, in his *Arte of English Poesy,* declares that the practice of the capital and the country within sixty miles of it was the standard of correct diction, the *jus et norma loquendi* [correct and normal speech]. Already [Edmund] Spenser had almost re-created English poetry,—and it is interesting to observe, that, scholar as he was, the archaic words which he was at first over-fond of introducing are often provincialisms of purely English original. Already [Christopher] Marlowe had brought the English unrhymed pentameter (which had hitherto justified but half its name, by being always blank and never verse) to a perfection of melody, harmony, and variety which has never been surpassed. Shakespeare, then, found a language already to a certain extent *established,* but not yet fetlocked by dictionary and grammar mongers,—a versification harmonized, but which had not yet exhausted all its modulations, nor been set in the stocks by critics who deal judgment on refractory feet, that will dance to Orphean measures of which their judges are insensible. That the language was established is proved by its comparative uniformity as used by the dramatists, who wrote for mixed [i.e., educated and uneducated] audiences, as well as by Ben Jonson's satire upon [John] Marston's neologisms; that it at the same time admitted foreign words to the rights of citizenship on easier terms than now is in good measure equally true. What was of greater import, no arbitrary line had been drawn between high words and low; vulgar then meant simply what was common; poetry had not been aliened from the people by the establishment of an Upper House of vocables, alone entitled to move in the stately ceremonials of verse, and privileged from arrest while they forever keep the promise of meaning to the ear and break it to the sense. The hot conception of the poet had no time to cool while he was debating the comparative respectability of this phrase or that; but he snatched what word his instinct prompted, and saw no indiscretion in making a king speak as his country nurse might have taught him.[2] . . .

We believe that Shakespeare, like all other great poets, instinctively used the dialect which he found current, and that his words are not more wrested from their ordinary meaning than followed necessarily from the unwonted weight of thought or stress of passion they were called on to support. . . .

When I say that Shakespeare used the current language of his day, I mean only that he habitually employed such language as was universally comprehensible,—that he was not run away with by the hobby of any theory as to the fitness of this or that component of English for expressing certain thoughts or feelings. . . .

Shakespeare has been sometimes taxed with the barbarism of profuseness and exaggeration. But this is to measure him by a Sophoclean scale. The simplicity of the antique tragedy is by no means that of expression, but is of form merely. In the utterance of great passions, something must be indulged to the extravagance of Nature; the subdued tones to which pathos and sentiment are limited cannot express a tempest of the soul. The range between the piteous "no more but so," in which Ophelia compresses the heart-break whose compression was to make her mad, and that sublime appeal of Lear to the elements of Nature, only to be matched, if matched at all, in the *Prometheus* [of Aeschylus], is a wide one, and Shakespeare is as truly simple in the one as in the other. The simplicity of poetry is not that of prose, nor its clearness that of ready apprehension merely. To a subtile sense, a sense heightened by sympathy, those sudden fervors of phrase, gone ere one can say it lightens, that show us Macbeth groping among the complexities of thought in his conscience-clouded mind, and reveal the intricacy rather than enlighten it, while they leave the eye darkened to the literal meaning of the words, yet make their logical sequence, the grandeur of the conception, and its truth to Nature clearer than sober daylight could. . . .

Shakespeare's language is no longer the mere vehicle of thought, it has become part of it, its very flesh and blood. The pleasure it gives us is unmixed, direct, like that from the smell of a flower or the flavor of a fruit. . . . In

Shakespeare it is always the higher thing, the thought, the fancy, that is pre-eminent; it is Caesar that draws all eyes, and not the chariot in which he rides, or the throng which is but the reverberation of his supremacy. If not, how explain the charm with which he [Shakespeare] dominates in all tongues, even under the disenchantment of translation? Among the most alien races he is as solidly at home as a mountain seen from different sides by many lands, itself superbly solitary, yet the companion of all thoughts and domesticated in all imaginations.

In description Shakespeare is especially great, and in that instinct which gives the peculiar quality of any object of contemplation in a single happy word that colors the impression on the sense with the mood of the mind. Most descriptive poets seem to think that a hogshead of water caught at the spout will give us a livelier notion of a thunder-shower than the sullen muttering of the first big drops upon the roof. They forget that it is by suggestion, not cumulation, that profound impressions are made upon the imagination. . . . Shakespeare understood perfectly the charm of indirectness, of making his readers seem to discover for themselves what he means to show them. If he wishes to tell that the leaves of the willow are gray on the under side, he does not make it a mere fact of observation by bluntly saying so, but makes it picturesquely reveal itself to us as it might in Nature:—

> There is a willow grows athwart the flood,
> That shows his *hoar* leaves in the glassy stream.
> [*Hamlet,* IV.vii.166–67]

Where he goes to the landscape for a comparison, he does not ransack wood and field for specialties, as if he were gathering simples, but takes one image, obvious, familiar, and makes it new to us either by sympathy or contrast with his own immediate feeling. He always looked upon Nature with the eyes of the mind. Thus he can make the melancholy of autumn or the gladness of spring alike pathetic:—

> That time of year thou mayst in me behold,
> When yellow leaves, or few, or none, do hang
> Upon those boughs that shake against the cold,
> Bare ruined choirs where late the sweet birds sang.
> [Sonnet 28]

Or again:—

From thee have I been absent in the spring,
When proud-pied April, dressed in all his trim,
Hath put a spirit of youth in everything,
That heavy Saturn leaped and laughed with him.
[Sonnet 98]

But as dramatic poet, Shakespeare goes even beyond this, entering so perfectly into the consciousness of the characters he himself has created, that he sees everything through their peculiar mood, and makes every epithet, as if unconsciously, echo and re-echo it. Theseus asks Hermia,—

Can you endure the livery of a nun,
For aye to be in shady cloister mewed,
To live a *barren* sister all your life,
Chanting faint hymns to the *cold fruitless* moon?
[*A Midsummer Night's Dream*, I.i.70–73]

When Romeo must leave Juliet, the private pang of the lovers becomes a property of Nature herself, and

    Envious streaks
Do lace the *severing* clouds in yonder east.
[III.v.7–8]

But even more striking is the following instance from *Macbeth*:—

The raven himself is hoarse
That croaks the fatal enterance of Duncan Under your battlements.
[I.v.39–41]

Here Shakespeare, with his wonted tact, makes use of a vulgar superstition, of a type in which mortal presentiment is already embodied, to make a common ground on which the hearer and Lady Macbeth may meet. After this prelude we are prepared to be possessed by her emotion more fully, to feel in her ears the dull tramp of the blood that seems to make the raven's croak yet hoarser than it is, and to betray the stealthy advance of the mind to its fell purpose. For Lady Macbeth hears not so much the voice of the bodeful bird as of her own premeditated murder, and we are thus made her shuddering accomplices before the fact. Every image receives the color of the mind, every word throbs with the pulse of one controlling passion. The epithet *fatal* makes us feel the implacable resolve of the speaker, and shows us that she is tampering with her conscience by putting off the crime upon the prophecy of the Weird Sisters to which she alludes. In the word *battlements,* too, not only is the fancy led up to the perch of the raven, but a hostile image takes the place of a hospitable; for men commonly speak of receiving a guest under their roof or within their doors. That this is not over-ingenuity, seeing what is not to be seen, nor meant to be seen, is clear to me from what follows. When Duncan and Banquo arrive at the castle, their fancies, free from all suggestion of evil, call up only gracious and amiable images. The raven was but the fantastical creation of Lady Macbeth's over-wrought brain.

> This castle hath a pleasant seat, the air
> Nimbly and sweetly doth commend itself
> Unto our gentle senses.
>   This *guest* of summer,
> The *temple-haunting* martlet, doth approve
> By his *loved mansionry* that the heaven's breath
> Smells *wooingly* here; no jutty, frieze,
> Buttress, or coigne of vantage, but this bird
> Hath made his pendent bed and procreant cradle.
>   [I.vi.1–8]

The contrast here cannot but be as intentional as it is marked. Every image is one of welcome, security, and confidence. The summer, one may well fancy, would be a very different hostess from her whom we have just seen expecting *them.* And why *temple-haunting,* unless because it suggests sanctuary? . . . If all this be accident, it is at least one of those accidents of which only this man was ever capable. . . . Those who criticise his diction as sometimes extravagant should remember that in poetry language is something more than merely the vehicle of thought, that it is meant to convey the sentiment as much as the sense, and that, if there is a beauty of use, there is often a higher use of beauty.

Notes

2.   "Vulgarem locutionem anpellamus eam qua infants adsueflunt ab adsistentibus cum primitus disitnguere voces incipient: vel, quod brevius dici potest, vulgarem locutionem asserimus *quam sine omni regula, nutricem imitantes accepimus.*" Dante, *de Vulg. Eloquio,* Lib I. cap. i.

—James Russell Lowell, from "Shakespeare Once
More," 1868, Works, 1890, volume 3, pp. 151–227

EDWIN P. WHIPPLE "SHAKESPEARE: I" (1869)

Edwin Percy Whipple (1819–86) was an American essayist and critic. In considering the biography of Shakespeare, he separates the life of the external man, about whom little is known, from the life of the inner man he sees distributed throughout the characters and passions manifest in his plays. Whipple argues that Shakespeare's plays indicate that he was able to penetrate and to express the life of every individual.

The biography of Shakespeare, if we merely look at the bulk of the books which assume to record it, is both minute and extensive; but when we subject the octavo or quarto to examination, we find a great deal that is interesting about his times, and some shrewd and some dull guessing about his probable actions and motives, but little about himself except a few dates. He was born in Stratford-on-Avon, in April, 1564, and was the son of John Shakespeare, tradesman, of that place. In 1582, in his nineteenth year, he married Anne Hathaway, aged twenty-six. About the year 1586 he went to London and became a player. In 1589 he was one of the proprietors of the Blackfriars Theatre, and in 1595 was a prominent shareholder in a larger theatre, built by the same company, called the Globe. As a playwright he seems to have served an apprenticeship; for he altered, amended, and added to the dramas of others before he produced any himself. Between the year 1591, or thereabouts, and the year 1613, or thereabouts, he wrote over thirty plays, the precise date of whose composition it is hardly possible to fix. He seems to have made yearly visits to Stratford, where his wife and children resided, and to have invested money there as he increased in wealth. Mr. Emerson has noted, that about the time he was writing *Macbeth*, perhaps the greatest tragedy of ancient or modern times, "he sued Philip Rogers, in the borough-court of Stratford, for thirty-five shillings tenpence, for corn delivered to him at various times." In 1608, Mr. Collier estimates his income at four hundred pounds a year, which, allowing for the decreased value of money, is equal to eight or nine thousand dollars at the present time. About the year 1610, he retired permanently to Stratford, though he continued to write plays for the company with which he was connected. He died on the 23d of April, 1616.

Such is essentially the meagre result of a century of research into the external life of Shakespeare. As there is hardly a page in his writings which does not shed more light upon the biography of his mind, and bring us nearer to the individuality of the man, the antiquaries in despair have been compelled to abandon him to the psychologists; and the moment the transition from external to internal facts is made, the most obscure of men passes into the most notorious. For this personality and soul we call Shakespeare, the recorded incidents of whose outward career were so few and trifling, lived a more various life—a life more crowded with ideas, passions, volitions, and *events*—than any potentate the world has ever seen. Compared with his experience, the experience of Alexander or Hannibal, of Caesar or Napoleon, was narrow and one-sided. He had projected himself into almost all the varieties of human character, and, in imagination, had intensely realized and *lived* the life of each. From the throne of the monarch to the bench of the village alehouse, there were few positions in which he had not placed himself, and which he had not for a time identified with his own. No other man had ever seen nature and human life from so many points of view; for he had looked upon them through the eyes of Master Slender [in *The Merry Wives of Windsor*] and Hamlet, of Caliban [in *The Tempest*] and Othello, of Dogberry [in *Much Ado about Nothing*] and Mark Antony, of Ancient Pistol [in *2Henry IV* and *Henry V*] and Julius Caesar, of Mistress Tearsheet [in *2Henry IV*] and Imogen [in *Cymbeline*], of Dame Quickly [in both parts of *Henry IV*] and Lady Macbeth, of Robin Goodfellow and Titania [in *A Midsummer Night's Dream*], of Hecate [in *Macbeth*] and Ariel [in *The Tempest*]. No king or queen of his time had so completely felt the cares and enjoyed the dignity of the regal state as this playwright, who usurped it by his thought alone; and the freshest and simplest maiden in Europe had no innocent heart-experience which this man could not share,—escaping, in an instant, from the shattered brain of Lear, or the hag-haunted imagination of Macbeth, in order to feel the tender flutter of her soul in his own. And none of these forms, though mightier or more exquisite than the ordinary forms of humanity, could hold or imprison him a moment longer than he chose to abide in it. He was on an excursion through the world of thought and action, to seize the essence of all the excitements of human nature,—terrible, painful, criminal, rapturous, or humorous; and to do this in a short earthly career, he was compelled to condense ages into days, and lives into minutes. He exhausts, in a short time, all the glory and all the agony there is on the throne or on the couch of Henry IV, and then, wearied with royalty, is off to the Boar's Head to have a rouse with Sir John. He feels all the flaming pride and scorn of the aristocrat Corlolanus; his brain widens with the imperial ideas, and his heart beats with the measureless ambition, of the autocrat Caesar; and anon he has donned a greasy apron, plunged into the roaring Roman mob, and is yelling against aristocrat and autocrat with all the gusto of democratic rage. He is now a prattling child, and in a second he is the murderer with the knife at its throat. Capable of *being* all that he actually or imaginatively *sees,* he enters into at will, and abandons at will, the passions that brand or blast other natures. Avarice, malice, envy, jealousy, hatred, revenge, remorse, neither in their separate nor mutual action are strong enough to fasten him; and the same may be said of love and pity and friendship and joy and ecstasy; for behind and within this multiform personality is the person Shakespeare,—serene, self-conscious, vigilant, individualizing the facts of his consciousness, and pouring his own soul into each creation, without ever parting with the personal identity which is at the heart of all, which disposes and co-ordinates all, and which dictates the impression to be left by all.

And this fact conducts us to the question of Shakespeare's individuality. We are prone to place him as a man below other great men, because we make a distinction between the man and his genius. We gather our notion of Shakespeare from the meagre details of his biography, and in his biography he appears little and commonplace,—not by any means so striking a person as Kit Marlowe or Ben Jonson. To this individuality we tack on a universal genius,—which is about as reasonable as it would be to take the controlling power of gravity from the sun and attach it to one of the asteroids. Shakespeare's genius is not something distinct *from* the man; it is the expression *of* the man, just as the sun's attraction is the result of its immense mass. The measure of a man's individuality is his creative power; and all that Shakespeare created he individually included. We must, therefore, if we desire to grasp his greatness, discard from our minds all associations connected with the pet epithets which other authors have condescended to shower upon him, such as "Sweet Will," and "Gentle Shakespeare," and "Fancy's child,"—fond but belittling phrases, as little appropriate as would be the patronizing chatter of the planet Venus about the dear, darling little Sun;—we must discard all these from our conceptions, and consider him primarily as a vast, comprehensive, personal soul and force, that passed from eternity into time, with all the wide aptitudes and affinities for the world he entered bound up in his individual being from the beginning. These aptitudes and affinities, these quick, deep, and varied sympathies, were so many inlets of the world without him; and facts pouring into such a nature were swiftly organized into faculties. Nothing, indeed, amazes us so much, in the biography of Shakespeare's mind, as the preternatural rapidity with which he assimilated knowledge into power, and experience into insight. . . . His soul lay genially open to the world of nature and human life, to receive the objects that went streaming into it, but never parted with the power of reacting upon all it received. This would not be so marvellous had he merely taken in the forms and outside appearances of things. All his perceptions, however, were vital; and the life and force of the objects he drew into his consciousness tugged with his own life and force for the mastery, and ended in simply enriching the spirit they strove to subdue. This indestructible spiritual energy, which becomes mightier with every exercise of might; which plucks out the heart and absorbs the vitality of everything it touches; which daringly commits itself to the fiercest, and joyously to the softest passions, without losing its moral and mental sanity. . . . [A]iming to include everything, [Shakespeare's creative genius] refuses to be included by anything, and in the sweep of its creativeness acts with a confident audacity, as if in it nature were humanized and humanity individualized;—in short, this unexampled energy of blended sensibility, intelligence, and will, is what constitutes the man Shakespeare; and this man is no mere name for an impersonal, unconscious genius, that did its marvels by instinct, no name for a careless playwright who blundered into miracles, but is essentially a person, creating strictly within the limitations of his individuality,—within those limitations appearing to be impersonal only because he is comprehensive enough to cover a wide variety of special natures,—and, above all, a person individually as great, at least, as the sum of his whole works. . . .

Let us, in illustration, glance at his method of creation, as successfully exerted in any one of his great dramas, say *Hamlet,* or *King Lear,* or *Macbeth,* or *Othello.*

He takes a story or a history, with which the people are familiar, the whole interest of which is narrative. He finds it a mere succession of incidents; he leaves it a combination of events. He finds the persons named in it mere commonplace sketches of humanity; he leaves them self-subsisting, individual characters, more real to the mind than the men and women we daily meet.

Now the first fact that strikes us when we compare the original story with Shakespeare's magical transformation of it is, that everything is raised from the actual world into a Shakespearian world. He alters, enlarges, expands, enriches, enlivens, informs, *recreates* everything, lifting sentiment, passion, humor, thought, action, to the level of his own nature. Through incidents and through characters is shot Shakespeare's soul,—a soul that yields itself to every mould of being, from the clown to the monarch, endows every class of character it animates with the Shakespearian felicity and certainty of speech, and, being in *all* as well as in *each,* so connects and relates the society he has called into life, that they unite to form a whole, while existing with perfect distinctness as parts. The characters are not developed by isolation, but by sympathy or collision, and the closer they come together the less they run together. They are independent of each other, and yet necessitate each other. None of them could appear in any other play without exciting disorder; yet in this play their discord conduces to the general harmony. And so tough is the hold on existence of these beings that, though thousands of millions of men and women have been born, have died, and have been forgotten since they were created, and though the actual world has strangely changed, these men and women of Shakespeare's are still alive, and Shakespeare's world still remains untouched by time.

—Edwin P. Whipple, "Shakespeare: I," *The Literature of the Age of Elizabeth,* 1869, pp. 32–56

WILLIAM CULLEN BRYANT "SHAKESPEARE" (1870)

In the following extract, William Cullen Bryant (1794–1878), American poet, journalist, and newspaper editor, argues that Shakespeare is part of the American as well as the British heritage and that English-speaking readers preserve the English language at its apogee by their study of his work and forge a bond with one another, even when they are separated by geography, by holding Shakespeare's language in common.

Shakespeare, though he cannot be called an American poet, as he was not born here and never saw our continent, is yet a poet of the Americans. . . .

It is common to speak of the blood of the ancestor as flowing in the veins of his descendants. . . . The generation which now walks the stage of the world is the reproduction, the re-entrance, in a certain sort, of the generation which has made its exit. The blood that now warms American hearts and gushes through American arteries was once—nearly three hundred years ago, when it ran in the veins of our ancestors in the Old World, and while Shakespeare was yet alive—made to tingle by his potent words. It coursed slowly or swiftly through its purple channels at the will of that great master of the passions. It was quickened and made to glow with indignation at the conduct of Lear's ungrateful daughters; it curdled and was chilled at the sight of the ghost of the royal Dane, and of the sleep-walking murderess in *Macbeth;* it was resolved to tears at the fate of the innocent Desdemona. What American, therefore, who is willing to acknowledge that his ancestors came from the Old World, will fail to claim Shakespeare as his own poet?

It is fortunate that we have in our literature writings of such superlative excellence, so universally read and studied, and, by the exercise of memory, so incorporated into our own minds, as the dramas of Shakespeare. They keep alive the connection between the present and the remote past, and stay the hurrying process of change in certain respects in which change is undesirable. Language is an unstable thing, and, like everything dependent on usage, tends to constant variation; but this tendency has no advantage save as it is demanded by the introduction of new ideas. There are critics who affirm that the English language reached its perfection of expressiveness and copiousness in the time of Queen Elizabeth, and whoever reads the authors of that age will see little cause to wonder at this opinion. Let us congratulate ourselves that we have such an author as Shakespeare, so admired, so loved, to protect our noble language against the capricious innovations of those who read only the authors of yesterday, and that, by dwelling upon what he wrote, the speech of the master minds of his age continues familiar to our ears. There is yet another advantage—that, by tending to preserve the identity of language in regions remote from each other where English is spoken, it keeps alive the remembrance of kindred and brotherhood, and multiplies the pledges of amity and peace between the nations.

—William Cullen Bryant, "Shakespeare," *Prose Writings*, 1884, volume 2, edited by Parke Godwin, pp. 305–06

VICTOR HUGO (1864)

Victor Hugo (1802–85) was a French poet, novelist, dramatist, critic, and statesman. In the following selection, he offers a rhapsodic tribute to Shakespeare, emphasizing the unity of his genius as a dramatist, poet, and philosopher. Hugo counters arguments against Shakespeare's greatness that condemn his lack of sober adherence to the rules of dramatic composition, despite his own respect for them, by praising Shakespeare's opulence, his brio, the power and depth of his imagination, and his ability to penetrate to the heart of his reader's passionate response in the way he elicits the passions of his characters. Considering Shakespeare's skill as a craftsman, Hugo specifically points to and praises Shakespeare's use of double plots in his dramas and shows how his plots and characters mirror one another.

Part II

Book I. Shakespeare—His Genius

II

A poet must at the same time, and necessarily, be a historian and a philosopher. Herodotus and Thales are included in Homer. Shakespeare, likewise, is this triple man. . . . Shakespeare has tragedy, comedy, fairy-land, hymn, farce, grand divine laughter, terror and horror, and, to say all in one word, the drama. He touches the two poles. He belongs to Olympus and to the travelling booth. No possibility fails him.

When he grasps you, you are subdued. Do not expect from him any pity. His cruelty is pathetic. He shows you a mother,—Constance, mother of Arthur [in *King John*]; and when he has brought you to that point of tenderness that your heart is as her heart, he kills her child. He goes farther in horror even than history, which is difficult. He does not content himself with killing Rutland and driving York to despair [in *3 Henry IV*]; he dips in the blood of the son the handkerchief with which he wipes the eyes of the father. He causes elegy to be choked by the drama, Desdemona by Othello. No attenuation in anguish. Genius is inexorable. It has its law and follows it. The mind also has its inclined planes, and these slopes determine its direction. Shakespeare glides toward the terrible. Shakespeare, Aeschylus, Dante, are great streams of human emotion pouring from the depth of their cave the urn of tears. . . .

Shakespeare in philosophy goes at times deeper than Homer. Beyond Priam [in *The Iliad*] there is Lear; to weep at ingratitude is worse than weeping at death. Homer meets envy and strikes it with the sceptre; Shakespeare gives the sceptre to the envious, and out of Thersites [in *Troilus and Cressida*] creates Richard III. Envy is exposed in its nakedness all the better for being clothed in purple; its reason for existing is then visibly altogether in itself. Envy on the throne, what more striking!

Deformity in the person of the tyrant is not enough for this philosopher; he must have it also in the shape of the valet, and he creates Falstaff. The dynasty of commonsense, inaugurated in Panurge [a cowardly libertine in the French writer François Rabelais's *Pantegruel*], continued in Sancho Panza [the squire in *Don Quixote*], goes wrong and miscarries in Falstaff. The rock which this wisdom splits upon is, in reality, lowness. Sancho Panza, in combination with the ass, is embodied with ignorance. Falstaff—glutton, poltroon, savage, obscene, human face and stomach, with the lower parts of the brute—walks on the four feet of turpitude; Falstaff is the centaur man and pig.

Shakespeare is, above all, an imagination. Now,—and this is a truth to which we have already alluded, and which is well known to thinkers,—imagination is depth. No faculty of the mind goes and sinks deeper than imagination. . . .

The poet philosophizes because he imagines. That is why Shakespeare has that sovereign management of reality which enables him to have his way with it; and his very whims are varieties of the true,—varieties which deserve meditation. Does not destiny resemble a constant whim? Nothing more incoherent in appearance, nothing less connected, nothing worse as deduction. Why crown this monster, John? Why kill that child, Arthur [in *King John*]? . . .

What are the *Tempest, Troilus and Cressida, The Two Gentlemen of Verona, The Merry Wives of Windsor*, the *Midsummer Night's Dream, The Winter's Tale*? They are fancy,—arabesque work. The arabesque in art is the same phenomenon as vegetation in nature. The arabesque grows, increases, knots, exfoliates, multiplies, becomes green, blooms, branches, and creeps around every dream. The arabesque is endless; it has a strange power of extension and aggrandizement; it fills horizons, and opens up others; it intercepts the luminous deeds by innumerable intersections; and, if you mix the human figure with these entangled branches, the *ensemble* makes you giddy; it is striking. Behind the arabesque, and through its openings, all philosophy can be seen; vegetation lives; man becomes pantheist; a combination of infinite takes place in the finite; and before such work, in which are found the impossible and the true, the human soul trembles with an emotion obscure and yet supreme. . . .

Man's inner conscience belongs to Shakespeare; he surprises you with it constantly. He extracts from conscience every unforeseen contingence that it contains. Few poets surpass him in this psychical research. Many of the strangest peculiarities of the human mind are indicated by him. He skillfully makes us feel the simplicity of the metaphysical fact under the complication of the dramatic fact. That which the human creature does not acknowledge inwardly, the obscure thing that he begins by fearing and ends by desiring—such is the point of junction and the strange place of meeting for the heart of virgins and the heart of murderers; for the soul of Juliet and the soul of Macbeth. The innocent fears and longs for love, just as the wicked one for ambition. . . .

V

If ever a man was undeserving of the good character of "he is sober," it is most certainly William Shakespeare. Shakespeare is one of the worst rakes that serious aesthetics ever had to lord over.

Shakespeare is fertility, force, exuberance, the overflowing breast, the foaming cup, the brimful tub, the overrunning sap, the overflooding lava, the whirlwind scattering germs, the universal rain of life, everything by thousands, everything by millions, no reticence, no binding, no economy, the inordinate and tranquil prodigality of the creator. To those who feel the bottom of their pocket, the inexhaustible seems insane. Will it stop soon? Never. Shakespeare is the sower of dazzling wonders. At every turn, the image; at every turn, contrast; at every turn, light and darkness.

The poet, we have said, is Nature. Subtle, minute, keen, microscopical like Nature; immense. Not discreet, not reserved, not sparing. Simply magnificent. Let us explain this word, *simple.*

Sobriety in poetry is poverty; simplicity is grandeur. To give to each thing the quantity of space which fits it, neither more nor less, is simplicity. Simplicity is justice. The whole law of taste is in that. Each thing put in its place and spoken with its own word. On the only condition that a certain latent equilibrium is maintained and a certain mysterious proportion preserved, simplicity may be found in the most stupendous complication, either in the style, or in the *ensemble.* These are the arcana of great art. Lofty criticism alone, which takes its starting-point from enthusiasm, penetrates and comprehends these learned laws. Opulence, profusion, dazzling radiancy, may be simplicity. The sun is simple. . . .

For nearly three centuries Shakespeare, this poet all brimming with virility, has been looked upon by sober critics with that discontented air that certain bereaved spectators must have in the seraglio.

Shakespeare has no reserve, no discretion, no limit, no blank. What is wanting in him is that he wants nothing. . . .

Like all lofty minds in full riot of Omnipotence, Shakespeare decants all Nature, drinks it, and makes you drink it. Voltaire reproached him for his drunkenness, and was quite right. Why on earth, we repeat, why has this Shakespeare such a temperament? He does not stop, he does not feel fatigue, he is without pity for the poor weak stomachs that are candidates for the Academy. The gastritis called "good taste," he does not labour under it. He is powerful. What is this vast intemperate song that he sings through ages,—war-song, drinking-song, love-ditty,—which passes from King Lear to Queen Mab [in *Romeo and Juliet*], and from Hamlet to Falstaff, heart-rending at times as a sob, grand as the Iliad? . . .

His poetry has the sharp perfume of honey made by the vagabond bee without a hive. Here prose, there verse; all forms, being but receptacles for the idea, suit him. This poetry weeps and laughs. The English tongue, a language little formed, now assists, now harms him, but everywhere the deep mind gushes forth translucent. Shakespeare's drama proceeds with a kind of distracted rhythm. It is so vast that it staggers; it has and gives the vertigo; but nothing is so solid as this excited grandeur. Shakespeare, shuddering, has in himself the winds, the spirits, the philters, the vibrations, the fluctuations of transient breezes, the obscure penetration of effluvia, the great unknown sap. Thence his agitation, in the depth of which is repose. . . .

Book IV. Criticism

I

Every play of Shakespeare's, two excepted, *Macbeth* and *Romeo and Juliet* (thirty-four plays out of thirty-six), offers to our observation one peculiarity which seems to have escaped, up to this day, the most eniment commentators and critics. . . . It is a double action which traverses the drama, and reflects it on a small scale. By the side of the storm in the Atlantic, the storm in the tea-cup. Thus, Hamlet makes beneath himself a Hamlet: he kills Polonius, father of Laertes,—and there is Laertes opposite him exactly in the same situation he is toward Claudius. There are two fathers to avenge. There might be two ghosts. So, in *King Lear,* side by side and simultaneously, Lear, driven to despair by his daughters Goneril and Regan, and consoled by his daughter Cordelia, is reflected by Gloster, betrayed by his son Edmond, and loved by his son Edgar. The bifurcated idea, the idea echoing itself, a lesser drama copying and elbowing the principal drama, the action trailing its own shadow (a smaller action but its parallel), the unity cut asunder,—surely it is a strange fact. These twin actions have been strongly blamed by the few commentators who have pointed them out. We do not participate in their blame. Do we then approve and accept as good these twin actions? By no means. We recognize them, and this is all. The drama of Shakespeare (we said so with all our might as far back as 1827, in order to discourage all imitation),—the drama of Shakespeare is peculiar to Shakespeare. It is a drama inherent to this poet; it is his own essence; it is himself,—thence his originalities absolutely personal; thence his idiosyncrasies which exist without establishing a law.

These twin actions are purely Shakespearian. Neither Aeschylus nor Molière would admit them; and we certainly would agree with Aeschylus and Molière.

These twin actions are, moreover, the sign of the sixteenth century. . . .

Shakespeare, faithful to the spirit of his time, must needs add Laertes avenging his father to Hamlet avenging his father, and cause Hamlet to be persecuted by Laertes at the same time that Claudius is pursued by Hamlet; he must needs make the filial piety of Edgar a comment on the filial piety of Cordelia, and bring out in contrast, weighed down by the ingratitude of unnatural children, two wretched fathers, each bereaved of a kind light,— Lear mad, and Gloster blind. . . .

V

Imitation is always barren and bad. . . .

[T]he poet starts from his own inner self to come to us. It is that which makes the poet inimitable.

Examine Shakespeare, dive into him, and see how determined he is to be himself. Do not expect any concession from him. It is not egotism, but it is stubbornness. He wills it. He gives to art his orders. . . .

One of the grandeurs of Shakespeare consists in his impossibility to be a model. In order to realize his idiosyncrasy, open one of his plays,—no matter which; it is always foremost and above all Shakespeare.

What more personal than *Troilus and Cressida? A* comic Troy! Here is *Much Ado about Nothing,*—a tragedy which ends with a burst of laughter. Here is the *Winter's Tale,*—a pastoral drama. Shakespeare is at home in his work. Do you wish to see true despotism: look at his fancy. What arbitrary determination to dream! What despotic resolution in his vertiginous flight! What absoluteness in his indecision and wavering! The dream fills some of his plays to that degree that man changes his nature, and is the cloud more than the man. Angelo in *Measure for Measure* is a misty tyrant. He becomes disintegrated, and wears away. Leontes in the *Winter's Tale* is an Othello who is blown away. In *Cymbeline* one thinks that Iachimo will become an Iago, but he melts down. The dream is there,—everywhere. Watch Mamilius [in *The Winter's Tale*], Posthumus [in *Cymbeline*], Hermione, Perdita [in *The Winter's Tale*], passing by. In the *Tempest,* the Duke of Milan has "a brave son," who is like a dream in a dream. Ferdinand alone speaks of him, and no one but Ferdinand seems to have seen him. A brute becomes reasonable: witness the constable Elbow in *Measure for Measure.* An idiot is all at once witty: witness Cloten in *Cymbeline. A* King of Sicily is jealous of a King of Bohemia. Bohemia has a seashore. The shepherds pick up children there [in *The Winter's Tale*]. Theseus, a duke, espouses Hippolyta, the Amazon. Oberon comes in also [in *A Midsummer Night's Dream*]. For here it is Shakespeare's will to dream; elsewhere he thinks.

We say more: where he dreams he still thinks,—with a different but equal depth. Let men of genius remain in peace in their originality.

—Victor Hugo, from *William Shakespeare,*
translated by F. T. Marzials, 1864

Karl Elze "Shakespeare's Character and Conception of Human Nature" (1876)

Karl Elze (1821–89), German Shakespeare scholar and professor of philology, begins by asserting the reasonable proposition that the opinions and beliefs expressed by characters in Shakespeare's plays can be seen only as theirs, not Shakespeare's. He proceeds, however, as in his citation of Belarius's words in *Cymbeline* in regard to reverence or in a conversation about utopia in *The Tempest*, to attribute a character's words to the author. It is probably an inevitability that no critic can fully avoid, and Elze's essay is instructive in the way that it shows how the fundamental beliefs of a critic can find themselves realized in the pronouncements of Shakespeare's characters and how a critic's worldview can influence his understanding and evaluation of what is said in the plays.

Shakespeare's nature was so harmonious that it is difficult to believe that his position towards the State could have been anything else but absolutely in accordance with his position towards the Church and positive religion; in both cases we find him exhibiting the same grand objectivity; which stands as far above the different forms of state as above the different forms of faith. In taking single passages and remarks from Shakespeare's works, we can as little arrive at a general conclusion on this point as with regard to Shakespeare's religious opinions. All Shakespeare's dramatic characters speak of the various forms of government and the different estates, &c, perfectly in accordance with their own individuality, and we have no right, for instance, to assume the political views of Richard II or of Richard III to be the poet's own personal views; for he had no other alternative than to give expression in his histories, to the political opinions peculiar to the day and to the persons represented, and which he found in the works from which he drew his material. It is well known how closely, in this respect, Shakespeare follows Holinshed in his Histories and North's Plutarch in his Roman plays. Shakespeare was, no doubt, anything but a politician himself. . . . He was as far from having thought out a political system for himself as he had planned a religious system, yet he must certainly have been aware that the State is an indispensable and unavoidable means for leading both the human community and the human individual forward on the path to culture and morality, and that the right use of every form of government accomplishes this, although, of course, every form of government is liable to deteriorate. In so far, probably, monarchy and republic—from a theoretical point of view—may have been the same to him;

all he demanded was that the foundations of all human existence—order and law, uprightness and faithfulness, justice and mercy—should be allowed to exert their influence; for, in his opinion, they are the pillars of the State and the Church, inasmuch as they are the basis of every moral community. Beyond these he placed weight only in one other ethical and political factor, that is, in the division and arrangement of the various grades and classes of society, which he thinks ought not to be overstepped either arrogantly or with criminal intention. He does not like to see a peasant tread on the courtier's heel,[1] and terms reverence, which makes distinction of place between high and low, "that angel of the world."[2] [*Cymbeline* IV.ii.248] This can astonish us the less, as the only form of government Shakespeare knew by experience was the monarchical form, which had worked itself out of feudalism, and was controlled more by public opinion than by parliament; hence from childhood he had been accustomed to the distinction of grades in society. In his opinion everyone ought to act in his own sphere as best he can for the good of the whole community, without venturing to grasp at things above or below him; in this way alone, the poet thinks, can the community be prosperous as a whole. This is most fully and completely brought forward in the famous speech of Ulysses in *Troilus and Cressida* (i.3). In connection with this it would seem that the poet considered the things that existed as justified by reason of their very existence. . . . However, the distinction of classes Shakespeare by no means considers an exclusively monarchical institution; he makes the same demand of the republican form of government, as is proved by the opening scene in *Coriolanus.* The fable there related by Menenius Agrippa, of the various members of the body rebelling against the belly, expresses this eloquently enough. And yet here again the reverse of the case has no less its justification in Shakespeare; he attacks and condemns all prejudices respecting class, and considers rank and birth far inferior to virtue and nobility of soul. This is most distinctly taught in *All's Well That Ends Well;* and the admonitory words addressed to the young Count Rousillon (ii. 3), who despises Helena on account of the lowness of her social position, would need to be placed as *pendants* by the side of the speeches of Ulysses and Menenius Agrippa. Such objectivity is all the more confounding, as the admonitory words against class prejudice are not by any means the harangue of a democrat and revolutionist, but are spoken by a royal personage. Any form of government that is not based upon the above-mentioned foundations of all political and social life, the poet denounces and attacks with ridicule as delightful as it is withering. He introduces us to two forms of this description: to the ochlocracy of Jack Cade (in the Second Part of *Henry VI*), and the Utopian state of nature in *The Tempest,* which is an imitation of Montaigne's idea; both forms are so admirably described that they will ever be models of their kind. [Nineteenth-century German philologist] W. König[3] very justly points out that Shakespeare seems to express his own opinion of these two abortions, where "the rabblement" is characterized [in *2 Henry VI,* IV.ii.187ff] by Jack Cade's words, "But then are we in order when we are most out of order," and where the Utopian state is despatched with Alonzo's words, "Thou dost talk nothing to me." [*The Tempest* II.i.175] Shakespeare denounces ochlocracy as well as the socialistic, natural state, because both speak disparagingly of culture. Jack Cade causes the Clerk of Chatham to be executed merely "because he can write, read, and cast accompt," and Lord Say because he erected schools, printing establishments, and paper-mills. The natural state advocated by Gonzalo is altogether wanting in moral foundation: he will have nothing to do with work, or property, or marriage.

Endeavours have not been wanting to represent Shakespeare as having been a good royalist . . . but these endeavours are precisely of the same character as those which maintain the poet to have been a strictly orthodox Christian, no matter whether Protestant or Catholic. It is no doubt true that Shakespeare has given the monarchical form of government an extremely high position, and has repeatedly praised it in enthusiastic terms as the sublime and sanctified climax of all social order; still it must not be overlooked that this praise falls from the lips of kings themselves—or, at all events, from the lips of those in their immediate surroundings—and it is not to be expected that they should have thought or spoken disparagingly of such a subject. It will be sufficient to point to the remarks of Claudius (in *Hamlet,* iv. 5) and to the speeches of Richard II. (iii. 2 and 3). But besides this, the Biblical and very poetical idea that the King rules as the Anointed of the Lord, as the representative of God on earth, corresponds absolutely with the ideas entertained in Shakespeare's day; and "His Sacred Majesty" James I. was so imbued with this idea that he would scarcely allow himself to be regarded as mortal. The . . . idea was part and parcel of the general current of thought of Shakespeare's day, so that even on this account it is difficult to determine how far the idea may have concealed the poet's own personal convictions. . . . [I]n our opinion it would rather seem that Shakespeare entertained no greater respect for regal robes than for the robes of priests, and that the poet might very well have supplemented his remark [in *Measure for Measure*] about the hood not making the monk, by saying that neither do purple robes make a king. The cowl and the ermine are beautiful and venerable symbols, but the appearance must not belie the reality; and here again, as in every other case, the poet lays the main stress upon the man whom the regal mantle envelops. He makes his Henry V state this very clearly (in iv. 1), where he says to John

Bates, "I think the king is but a man, as I am: the violet smells to him as it doth to me; the element shows to him as it doth to me; all his senses have but human conditions; his ceremonies laid by, in his nakedness he appears but a man; and though his affections are higher mounted than ours, yet when they stoop, they stoop with the like wing."[4] These words at the same time remind us of Shylock's famous apostrophe [in the *Merchant of Venice*] ("Hath not a Jew eyes? Hath not a Jew hands?" &c), and show very distinctly, when thus placed side by side, that Shakespeare recognized the rightful claims of the man in the king as well as in the Jew, in the highest as well as the lowest. Shakespeare knows that there are royal criminals, and has depicted them as such in Claudius and Richard III. He knows that royalty has important duties to perform, and he judges kings according to their ability and their endeavour to discharge these duties—and their fate, too, is made dependent upon this. The supreme freedom with which Shakespeare has not only delineated a series of the most different royal personages, but also genuine Roman republicans, makes it impossible to believe that he was an admirer of royalty *quand meme*—in fact, that he can have been attached to any special political system. To what a climax an exaggerated form of royalism and absolutism may be carried is shown by an appalling example in *King Lear*. Lear himself, in his clear moments—but unfortunately too late—recognizes the fact that in a very great measure his absolute power, and the grovelling devotion and flattery of his subjects, are the cause of his misfortunes, as, in fact, they are the cause of his downfall. Without exaggeration, it may be said that Lear is the personification of Absolutism which has lost its reason, Caesarism gone mad, and in him it is shown that absolute power carried to excess, leads to mental aberration as a final consequence. We have here Goethe's warning about "the limitation of the human mind" in the grandest and most overwhelming form. "They flattered me like a dog," says Lear (iv. 6). "They say 'Ay' and 'No' to everything that I said!—'Ay' and 'No,' too, was no good divinity. When the rain came to wet me once, and the wind to make me chatter; when the thunder would not peace at my bidding; there I found 'em, there I smelt 'em out. Go to, they are not men o' their words; they told me I was everything; 'tis a lie, I am not ague-proof." [97–107] If anywhere, the poet seems himself here to speaking through the mouths of his dramatic personages.

But the poet shows his detestation of insolence and arrogance, not only in crowned heads, but also in the king's officials; he chastises them for this at every opportunity, and even Hamlet does not omit to mention "the insolence of office" as one of the greatest plagues of life. The poet, in *Measure for Measure*, says that:—

> Could great men thunder
> As Jove himself does, Jove would neer be quiet,
> For every pelting petty officer
> Would use his heaven for thunder;
> Nothing but thunder!
>
>   [II.ii.110–14]

And when among the lower officials conceit of office and unseemly behaviour are coupled with ignorance and stupidity, the combination is made the target of the poet's most delightful, but, at the same time, of his keenest sarcasm. Shallow, Silence [in *2Henry IV*], Dogberry, Verges [in *Much Ado about Nothing*] and others, are extremely comical characters, but between the lines it is unmistakably evident what the poet's own opinion is of these caricatures of officialism. Absolutism, when carried to excess by rulers or leaders of men, ends in madness, but when carried to excess by subordinates results in absurdity.

Notes

1. *Hamlet*, v. 1.

2. *Cymbeline*, IV. 2, 207.

3. *Shakespeare-Jahrbuch*, vii, 194.

4. See also Henry's monologue in the same scene: *Upon the King! Let us our lives, &c., lay on the King!*

> —Karl Elze, from "Shakespeare's Character
> and Conception of Human Nature,"
> *William Shakespeare: A Literary Biography*,
> translated by L. Dora Schmitz, 1876

HAVELOCK ELLIS "WILLIAM SHAKESPEARE" (1878)

Havelock Ellis (1859–1939), British physician, sexologist, writer, and social reformer, discusses the periods into which Shakespeare's plays are divided and how the plays of the various periods differ from one another particularly with regard to the way his heroines are portrayed.

The transition from the second to the third period of Shakespeare is very gradual. *All's Well That Ends Well* and *Julius Caesar* lie on the borderland. I consider the following to be as near as possible the chronological order of the third period plays; *Hamlet, Measure for Measure, Othello,*

Lear, Macbeth, Antony and Cleopatra, Coriolanus, Troilus and Cressida
(or perhaps after *Measure for Measure*), *Timon*. The women of the first,
second and third periods have much in common. The women of the
fourth period stand quite apart. They [the women of the third period]
are all marked by the absence of what I would call *sweet earthliness*.
Sweetness they may have and too much of it, abundance of earthliness
some of them, but none of them that combination of the two which we
find in Rosalind [*As You Like It*] and Viola [*Twelfth Night*] and Imogen
[*Cymbeline*]. Here they are: Ophelia [*Hamlet*], Isabella [*Measure for
Measure*], Desdemona [*Othello*], Regan, Goneril, Cordelia, [*King Lear*]
Lady Macbeth, Cleopatra, Volumnia, Virgilia [*Coriolanus*], Cressida. It is
as if one were reading Dante.

The transition from the third to the fourth period is of startling
suddenness. *Troilus and Cressida* is as incomprehensible as it is wonderful.
Shakespeare seems to be pouring out all the wealth of his genius in mockery.
The atmosphere of *Timon* is almost unbearable. Then in an interval of little
more than a year, away from the keen irony of the *Troilus,* the fierce satire of
Timon, and we are in the country air of Stratford in *Pericles* and *Cymbeline*
and *Winter's Tale,* breathing the fragrance of flowers, looking at life with the
calm far-away gaze of old age. I can't recall any more wonderful transition in
literature. Shakespeare was long in attaining his maturity. He was about thirty
when he reached the manhood of his genius. But half a lifetime is pressed
together in the brief six years of the third period. When he wrote *The Tempest*
he was old—older at 45 almost than Goethe was at 80. He takes an old man's
joy in the freshness of young boyhood and girlhood; in the beauty of flowers
and sunny air and peace; in the loveliness of repentance and forgiveness and
reconciliation. Not that there is any trace of decay in Shakespeare's later work.
He turned to the sweet Italian tales which had charmed him in youth, and
touched him with a light playful touch, yet full of strength and tenderness
and truth. *Cymbeline* is a lovely play. It was Hazlitt's favourite and he has
criticised it admirably in his *Characters*. I always look upon Imogen as the
noblest, sweetest ideal of womanhood in Shakespeare,—the woman in whom
the elements of character are held in most perfect equilibrium, with indeed
a certain touch of gravity that faintly recalls the third period, and yet with
all the sweet earthliness of Rosalind and Viola. *The Tempest* and *The Winter's
Tale* are scarcely less lovely plays.

—Havelock Ellis, "William Shakespeare,"
1878, *From Marlowe to Shaw,* 1950,
edited by John Gawsworth, pp. 30–31

John Addington Symonds
"Introductory" (1884)

John Addington Symonds (1840–93), English poet, biographer, historian, and literary critic, argues, like Sir Walter Scott before him, that rather than inventing new forms and techniques, Shakespeare, in the composition of his plays, drew from the tradition of the English stage and of English poetry that had directly preceded him and from the theatrical conventions and literary performances that were part of his milieu. While conceding Shakespeare's superiority to his contemporaries, Symonds also acknowledges their eminence, noting how much better they might seem were Shakespeare's work to disappear but how negligible the loss would be were Shakespeare's to remain.

Shakspere forms a focus for all the rays of light which had emerged before his time, and that after him these rays were once more decomposed and scattered over a wide area. Thus at least we may regard the matter from our present point of survey. Yet during Shakspere's lifetime his predominance was by no means so obvious. To explain the defect of intelligence in Shakspere's contemporaries, to understand why they chose epithets like 'mellifluous', 'sweet', and 'gentle', to describe the author of *King Lear, Othello*, and *Troilus and Cressida;* why they praised his 'right happy and copious industry' instead of dwelling on his interchange of tragic force and fanciful inventiveness; why the misconception of his now acknowledged place in literature extended even to Milton and to Dryden, will remain perhaps for ever impossible to every student of those times. But this intellectual obtuseness is itself instructive, when we regard Shakspere as the creature, not as the creator, of a widely diffused movement in the spirit of the nation, of which all his contemporaries were dimly conscious. They felt that behind him, as behind themselves, dwelt a motive force superior to all of them. Instead, then, of comparing him, as some have done, to the central orb of a solar system, from whom the planetary bodies take their light, it would be more correct to say that the fire of the age which burns in him so intensely, burned in them also, more dimly, but independently of him. He represents the English dramatic genius in its fullness. The subordinate playwrights bring into prominence minor qualities and special aspects of that genius. Men like Webster and Heywood, Jonson and Ford, Fletcher and Shirley, have an existence in literature outside Shakspere, and are only in an indirect sense satellites and vassals. Could Shakspere's works be obliterated from man's memory, they would still sustain the honours of the English stage with decent splendour. Still it is only when Shakspere shines among them, highest, purest, brightest of that brotherhood, that the real radiance of his epoch is discernible—that the real value and meaning of their work become apparent.

The more we study Shakspere in relation to his predecessors, the more obliged are we to reverse Dryden's famous dictum that he 'found not, but created first the stage.' The fact is, that he found dramatic form already fixed. When he began to work among the London playwrights, the Romantic Drama in its several species—Comedy, Italian Novella, Roman History, English Chronicle, Masque, Domestic Tragedy, Melodrama—had achieved its triumph over the Classical Drama of the scholars. Rhyme had been discarded, and blank verse adopted as the proper vehicle of dramatic expression. Shakspere's greatness consisted in bringing the type established by his predecessors to artistic ripeness, not in creating a new type. It may even be doubted whether Shakspere was born to be a playwright—whether it was not rather circumstance which led him to assume his place as coryphaeus to the choir of dramatists. The defects of the Romantic form were accepted by him with easy acquiescence, nor did he aim at altering that form in any essential particular. He dealt with English Drama as he dealt with the materials of his plays; following an outline traced already, but glorifying each particular of style and matter; breathing into the clay-figures of a tale his own creator's breath of life, enlarging prescribed incident and vivifying suggested thought with the art of an unrivalled poet-rhetorician, raising the verse invented for him to its highest potency and beauty with inexhaustible resource and tact incomparable in the use of language.

At the same time, the more we study Shakspere in his own works, the more do we perceive that his predecessors, no less than his successors, exist for him; that without him English dramatic art would be but second rate; that he is the keystone of the arch, the justifier and interpreter of his time's striving impulses. The forms he employs are the forms he found in common usage among his fellow-craftsmen. But his method of employing them is so vastly superior, the quality of his work is so incommensurable by any standard we apply to the best of theirs, that we cannot help regarding the plays of Shakspere as not exactly different in kind, but diverse in inspiration. Without those predecessors, Shakspere would certainly not have been what he is. But having him, we might well afford to lose them. Without those successors, we should still miss much that lay implicit in the art of Shakspere. But having him, we could well dispense with them. His predecessors lead up to him, and help us to explain his method. His successors supplement his work, illustrating the breadth and length and depth and versatility of English poetry in that prolific age.

It is this twofold point of view from which Shakspere must be studied in connection with the minor dramatists, which gives them value. It appears that a whole nation laboured in those fifty years' activity to give the world one Shakspere; but it is no less manifest that Shakspere did not stand alone, without support and without lineage. He and his fellow playwrights are interdependent, mutually illustrative; and their aggregated performance is the expression of a nation's spirit.

—John Addington Symonds, "Introductory"
to *Shakspere's Predecessors in the
English Drama*, 1884, pp. 16–19

WALT WHITMAN "A THOUGHT
ON SHAKSPERE" (1886)

Walt Whitman (1819–92), American poet and newspaperman, here considers Shakespeare's work, and even as he concedes its greatness, as a reminder of an antidemocratic aristocratic era, Whitman questions its place in a society devoted to the common people and democratic values.

[F]or all he stands for so much in modern literature, [Shakespeare] stands entirely for the mighty aesthetic sceptres of the past, not for the spiritual and democratic, the sceptres of the future. The inward and outward characteristics of Shakspere are his vast and rich variety of persons and themes, with his wondrous delineation of each and all—not only limitless funds of verbal and pictorial resource, but great excess, superfetation—mannerism, like a fine, aristocratic perfume, holding a touch of musk ... with boundless sumptuousness and adornment, real velvet and gems, not shoddy nor paste— but a good deal of bombast and fustian—(certainly some terrific mouthing in Shakspere!).

Superb and inimitable as all is, it is mostly an objective and physiological kind of power and beauty the soul finds in Shakspere—a style supremely grand of the sort, but in my opinion stopping short of the grandest sort, at any rate for fulfilling and satisfying modern and scientific and democratic American purposes. Think, not of growths as forests primeval, or Yellowstone geysers, or Colorado ravines, but of costly marble palaces, and palace rooms, and the noblest fixings and furniture, and noble owners and occupants to correspond—think of carefully built gardens from the beautiful but sophisticated gardening art at its best, with walks and bowers and artificial lakes, and appropriate statue-groups and the finest cultivated roses and lilies and japonicas in plenty—and you have the tally of Shakspere. The low characters, mechanics, even the loyal henchmen—all in themselves nothing—serve as capital foils to the aristocracy. The comedies (exquisite as they certainly are) bringing in admirably portray'd common characters, have the unmistakable hue of plays, portraits, made for the divertisement only of the elite of the castle, and from its point of view. The comedies are altogether non-acceptable to America and Democracy.

But to the deepest soul, it seems a shame to pick and choose from the riches Shakspere has left us—to criticise his infinitely royal, multiform quality—to gauge, with optic glasses, the dazzle of his sun-like beams.

The best poetic utterance, after all, can merely hint, or remind, often very indirectly, or at distant removes. Aught of real perfection, or the solution of any deep problem, or any completed statement of the moral, the true, the beautiful, eludes the greatest, deftest poet—flies away like an always uncaught bird.

> —Walt Whitman, "A Thought on Shakspere,"
> 1886, *Prose Works*, 1964, volume 2,
> edited by Floyd Stovall, pp. 556–58

W. E. HENLEY "SHAKESPEARE" (1890)

English, poet, critic, and editor William Ernest Henley (1849–1903), in comparing Shakespeare to the Dutch painter Rembrandt van Rijn, acknowledges the greatness and notes the unevenness of both, expresses his amazement at the discrepancies in quality he sees in Shakespeare's work, and scorns those who worship Shakespeare for not being able to accept his faults.

Shakespeare and Rembrandt have in common the faculty of quickening speculation and compelling the minds of men to combat and discussion. About the English poet a literature of contention has been in process of accretion ever since he was discovered to be Shakespeare; and about the Dutch painter and etcher there has gradually accumulated a literature precisely analogous in character and for the most part of equal quality. . . . Both were giants; both were original and individual in the highest sense of the words; both were leagues ahead of their contemporaries, not merely as regards the matter of their message but also in respect of the terms of its delivery; each, moreover—and here one comes upon a capital point of contact and resemblance—each was at times prodigiously inferior to himself. Shakespeare often writes so ill that you hesitate to believe he could ever write supremely well. . . . There are passages in his work in which he reaches such heights of literary art as since his time no mortal has found accessible; and there are passages which few or none of us can read without a touch of that 'burning sense of shame' experienced in the presence of Mr. Poynter's *Diadumene* by the British Matron of *The Times* newspaper. Now, we have got to be so curious in ideals that we cannot away with the thought of imperfection. Our worship must have for its object something flawless, something utterly without spot or blemish. We can be satisfied with nothing less than an entire and perfect chrysolite; and we cannot taste our Shakespeare at his worst without experiencing not merely the burning sense of shame aforesaid but also a frenzy of longing to father his faults upon somebody else—Marlowe for instance, or Green, or Fletcher—and a fury of proving that our divinity was absolutely incapable of them. That Shakespeare varied—that the matchless prose and the not particularly lordly verse of *As You Like It* are by the same hand; that the master to whom we owe our Hamlet is also responsible for Gertrude and King Claudius; that he who gave us the agony of Lear and the ruin of Othello did likewise perpetrate the scene [in *Troilus and Cressida*] of Hector's murder, in manner so poor and in spirit so cynical and vile—is beyond all belief and patience; and we have argued the point to such an extent that we are all of us in Gotham, and a mooncalf like the ascription of whatever is good in Shakespeare to Lord Bacon is no prodigy but a natural birth.

—W. E. Henley, "Shakespeare," *Views and Reviews*, 1890, pp. 101–03

WILLIAM DEAN HOWELLS "SHAKESPEARE" (1891)

After an introduction in which he attacks a slavish and indiscriminate worship of Shakespeare, the American novelist and literary critic William Dean Howells (1837–1920) discusses the joy he gleans from the greatness and vitality evident in *Hamlet* and other of Shakespeare's plays, whether he sees them performed or reads them.

There ought certainly to be some bound beyond which the cult of favorite authors should not be suffered to go. I should keep well within the limit of that early excess now, and should not liken the creation of Shakespeare to the creation of any heavenly body bigger, say, than one of the nameless asteroids that revolve between Mars and Jupiter. Even this I do not feel to be a true means of comparison, and I think that in the case of all great men we like to let our wonder mount and mount, till it leaves the truth behind, and honesty is pretty much cast out as ballast. A wise criticism will no more magnify Shakespeare because he is already great than it will magnify any less man. But we are loaded down with the responsibility of finding him all we have been told he is, and we must do this or suspect ourselves of a want of taste, a want of sensibility. At the same time, we may really be honester than those who have led us to expect this or that of him, and more truly his friends. I wish the time might come when we could read Shakespeare, and Dante, and Homer, as sincerely and as fairly as we read any new book by the least known of our contemporaries. The course of criticism is towards this, but when I began to read Shakespeare I should not have ventured to think that he was not at every moment great. I should no more have thought of questioning the poetry of any passage in him than of questioning the proofs of holy writ. All the same, I knew very well that much which I read was really poor stuff, and the persons and positions were often preposterous. It is a great pity that the ardent youth should not be permitted and even encouraged to say this to himself, instead of falling slavishly before a great author and accepting him at all points as infallible. Shakespeare is fine enough and great enough when all the possible detractions are made, and I have no fear of saying now that he would be finer and greater for the loss of half his work, though if I had heard any one say such a thing then I should have held him as little better than one of the wicked.

Probably no dramatist ever needed the stage less, and none ever brought more to it. There have been few joys for me in life comparable to that of seeing the curtain rise on *Hamlet,* and hearing the guards begin to talk about the ghost; and yet how fully this joy imparts itself without any material embodiment! It is the same in the whole range of his plays: they fill the scene, but if there is no scene they fill the soul. They are neither worse nor better because of the theatre. They are so great that it cannot hamper them; they are so vital that they enlarge it to their own proportions and endue it with something of their own living force. They make it the size of life, and yet they retire it so wholly that you think no more of it than you think of the physiognomy of one who talks importantly to you. I have heard people' say that they would rather not see Shakespeare played than to see him played ill, but I cannot agree with them. He can better afford to be played ill than any other man that ever wrote. Whoever is on the stage, it is always Shakespeare who is speaking to me, and perhaps this is the reason why in the past I can trace no discrepancy between reading his plays and seeing them.

—William Dean Howells, "Shakespeare,"
My Literary Passions, 1891, pp. 58–60

EDMOND SCHERER "SHAKESPEARE" (1891)

Edmond Henri Adolphe Scherer (1815–89), French literary critic, journalist, theologian, and politician, here pays homage to Shakespeare's power to create living characters, to his depth and subtlety of wisdom, and to his lyricism. Scherer faults Shakespeare, however, for sometimes making abrupt transitions in characters' actions.

If there is no drama without action, neither is there any without character. It may be that the creation of character is the highest function of art. There is nothing which more resembles divine power than the exploit by which the poet evokes from the depths of his imagination personages who have never lived, but who thenceforward live forever, and who will take a place in our memories, in our affections, in the realities of our world, exactly as if they had been formed by the hand of the Most High. And if a single creation of this kind suffices to immortalize a writer, what shall we say of a poet who, like Shakespeare, has drawn crowds of characters, all different, all alive, uniting the most distinct physiognomy and the intensest reality to the highest quality of idealism and poetry? The English dramatist is in nothing so marvellous as in this. He is the magician who can give life to anything by his wand; or rather, he is Nature herself, capricious, prodigal, always new, always full of surprises and of profundity. His personages are not what are called heroes; there is no posing in them; there is no abstraction; the idea has become incarnate, and develops itself as a whole, with all the logic of passion, with all the spontaneity of life. The only thing which can be brought against the author is at times a too sharp change—one, so to speak, effected on the stage—in the sentiments of his characters. Aufidius, for example, passes too quickly from hatred to sorrow when he sees Coriolanus fall; and in *Richard III*. Anne accepts with too great ease the ring of the man on whom she has just spit in contempt; while Elizabeth is too quick in giving her daughter to the man who has just massacred her sons. This is certainly turning the corner too sharply, and there is a want of truth in it.

I think that something of the same kind may be said of Shakespeare's style. The language which he puts in the mouths of his characters is not always appropriate—is sometimes far from being appropriate—to the circumstances, even to the characters themselves. The poet delights too much in the expression for itself and its own sake. He dwells on it, he lingers over it, he plays with equivalents and synonyms. Menenius thus complains of the change which has occurred in Coriolanus's humor:—"The tartness of his face sours ripe grapes: when he walks he moves like an engine, and the ground shrinks before his treading: he is able to pierce a corselet with his eye: talks like a knell, and his hum is a battery. He sits in his state as a thing made for Alexander. What he bids be done is finished with his bidding. He wants nothing of a god but eternity and a heaven to throne in" [V.iv.17ff.]—I take this quotation at random to exemplify what I mean. The form in this poet sometimes overruns in this fashion; the expression is redundant and out of proportion to the situation. This remark applies still better to the conceits and the word-plays which Shakespeare, without troubling himself about the occasion, puts in everybody's mouth. The most pathetic speeches are not free from them. It is not that the author is not conscious of the incongruity of these quips.

Do sick men play so nicely with their names? [II.i.84]

asks Richard II of the Duke of Lancaster, and it is certain that his last works have much fewer of these blots than his first. But if there is sometimes ill-placed wit in our poet, what verve is there in this wit, what gayety, what exuberance! With what freedom and caprice does fancy develop itself! How well . . . do excess and license of talent suit this unbounded invention! And we must also say at once that this wit is but one of Shakespeare's qualities. He possesses imagination and feeling in at least equal measure. He has felt everything, has understood everything. No man has lived more, has observed more, has better reproduced the outward world. And yet he is at the same time the most lyrical of poets; he expresses in finished form, in inimitable poetry, all the emotions of the heart. He says things as no one else says them, in a manner at once strange and striking. He has unbelievable depths, subtlenesses of intuition as unbelievable. There rises from his writings a kind of emanation of supreme wisdom; and it seems that their very discords melt into some transcendent harmony. Shakespeare has enlarged the domain of the mind, and, take him all in all, I do not believe that any man has added more than he has to the patrimony of mankind.

—Edmond Scherer, "Shakespeare," *Essays on English Literature,* 1891, translated by George Saintsbury, pp. 47–50

Hallam Tennyson (1897)

Hallam Tennyson (1852–1928) was the son of the English poet Lord
Alfred Tennyson. Henry Hallam, English historian, was the father of
Arthur Hallam, the close friend of Alfred Tennyson, after whose death
Tennyson wrote "In Memoriam" (1849). In the following extracts, Hallam
Tennyson presents observations and insights by his father on several of
Shakespeare's plays.

Of Shakespeare's sonnets he (Tennyson) would say, "Henry Hallam made a
great mistake about them: they are noble. Look how beautiful such lines as
these are:

> The summer flower is to the summer sweet,
> Though to itself it only live and die,
>   [Sonnet 94]

and

> And peace proclaims olives of endless age." [Sonnet 107]

Of Shakespeare's blank verse he said, "Almost any prose can be cut up
into blank verse, but blank verse becomes the finest vehicle of thought in
the language of Shakespeare and Milton. As far as I am aware, no one has
noticed what great Aeschylean lines there are in Shakespeare, particularly in
King John: for instance,

> The burning crest
> Of the old, feeble, and day-wearied sun,
>   [V.iv.34–35]

or again,

> The sepulcher
> Hath oped his ponderous and marble jaws."
>   [*Hamlet*, I.iv.48–50]

He would say, "There are three repartees in Shakespeare which always
bring tears to my eyes from their simplicity.

"One is in *King Lear* when Lear says to Cordelia, 'So young and so
untender,' and Cordelia lovingly answers, 'So young, my lord, and true.' And

in *The Winter's Tale,* when Florizel takes Perdita's hand to lead her to the dance, and says, 'So turtles pair that never mean to part,' and the little Perdita answers, giving her hand to Florizel, I'll swear for 'em.' And in *Cymbeline,* when Imogen in tender rebuke says to her husband,

> Why did you throw your wedded lady from you?
> Think that you are upon a rock; and now
> Throw me again!

and Posthumus does not ask forgiveness, but answers, kissing her,

> Hang there like fruit, my soul, Till the tree die.

After reading *Pericles,* Act V. aloud:
"That is glorious Shakespeare: most of the rest of the play is poor, and not by Shakespeare, but in that act the conception of Marina's character is exquisite."

Of *Henry VI.* he said, "I am certain that *Henry VI.* is in the main not Shakespeare's, though here and there he may have put in a touch, as he undoubtedly did in *The Two Noble Kinsmen.* There is a great deal of fine Shakespeare in that. Spedding insisted that Shakespeare, among the many plays that he edited for the stage, had corrected a play on Sir Thomas More in the British Museum. It is a poor play, but Spedding believed that the corrections were possibly in Shakespeare's actual handwriting.

"I have no doubt that much of *Henry VIII* also is not Shakespeare. It is largely written by Fletcher, with passages unmistakeably by Shakespeare, notably the two first scenes in the first Act, which are sane and compact in thought, expression and simile. I could swear to Shakespeare in the *Field of the Cloth of Gold:*

> To-day the French
> All clinquant, all in gold like heathen gods,
> Shone down the English; and to-morrow they
> *Made Britain India; every man that stood*
> *Show'd like a mine.*
>   [I.i.18–22]

"*Hamlet* is the greatest creation in literature that I know of: though there may be elsewhere finer scenes and passages of poetry. Ugolino and Paolo and Francesca in Dante equal anything anywhere. It is said that Shakespeare was such a poor actor that he never got beyond his ghost in this play, but then the ghost is the most real ghost that ever was. The Queen did not think that Ophelia committed suicide, neither do I.

"Is there a more delightful love-poem than *Romeo and Juliet?* yet it is full of conceits.

"One of the most passionate things in Shakespeare is Romeo's speech:

Amen, amen! but come what sorrow can,
It cannot countervail the exchange of joy
That one short minute gives me in her sight, etc.
[II.vi.3–5]

More passionate than anything in Shelley. No one has drawn the true passion of love like Shakespeare."

For inimitably natural talk between husband and wife he would quote the scene between Hotspur and Lady Percy (*King Henry IV.,* Pt. I.), and would exclaim: "How deliciously playful is that—

In faith, I'll break thy little finger, Harry,
An if thou wilt not tell me all things true!
[II.iii.87f.]

"Macbeth is not, as is too often represented, a noisy swash-buckler; he is a full-furnished, ambitious man. In the scene with Duncan, the excess of courtesy adds a touch to the tragedy. It is like Clytemnestra's profusion to Agamemnon; who, by the way, always strikes me as uncommonly cold and haughty to his wife whom he had not seen for years.

"*King Lear* cannot possibly be acted, it is too titanic. At the beginning of the play Lear, in his old age, has grown half mad, choleric and despotic, and therefore cannot brook Cordelia's silence. This play shows a state of society where men's passions are savage and uncurbed. No play like this anywhere— not even the *Agamemnon*—is so terrifically human.

"Actors do not comprehend that Shakespeare's greatest villains, Iago among them, have always a touch of conscience. You see the conscience working—therein lies one of Shakespeare's pre-eminences. Iago ought to be acted as the 'honest Iago,' not the stage villain; he is the essentially jealous man, not Othello."

—Hallam Tennyson, *Alfred Lord Tennyson:*
A Memoir, 1897, volume 2, pp. 289–92

George Bernard Shaw "Better Than Shakespear?" (1897)

With the curmudgeonly iconoclasm that has become a Shavian trademark, George Bernard Shaw (1856–1950), English dramatist, critic, essayist, socialist reformer, temperance propagandist, and vegetarian, argues in this extract that the allegorical Puritan epic of the soul's journey through earthly hazards to Paradise, *The Pilgrim's Progress* (1678) by John Bunyan, is dramatically and verbally richer, sturdier, more sincere, and more worthwhile than Shakespeare's plays. Note that the line from *Hamlet* that Shaw chooses to dismiss is from a play within the play and, consequently, part of Shakespeare's deliberate pastiche of a high declamatory style rather than an illustration of Shakespearean bombast. Shaw himself rewrote the last act of *Cymbeline* in 1945, thinking to improve it, but admits in the foreword that "my notion that it is a cobbled-up *pasticcio* ... was an unpardonable stupidity," showing that he was able to stand in his own gun sight as well as place others there.

─────·ɤ/ʌ/ɤ·─────   ─────·ɤ/ʌ/ɤ·─────   ─────·ɤ/ʌ/ɤ·─────

When I saw a stage version of *The Pilgrim's Progress* (by G. G. Collingham) announced for production, I shook my head, knowing that Bunyan is far too great a dramatist for our theatre, which has never been resolute enough even in its lewdness and venality to win the respect and interest which positive, powerful wickedness always engages, much less the services of men of heroic conviction. Its greatest catch, Shakespear, wrote for the theatre because, with extraordinary artistic powers, he understood nothing and believed nothing. Thirty-six big plays in five blank verse acts, and (as Mr Ruskin, I think, once pointed out) not a single hero! Only one man in them all who believes in life, enjoys life, thinks life worth living, and has a sincere, unrhetorical tear dropped over his death-bed; and that man—Falstaff! What a crew they are—these Saturday to Monday athletic stockbroker Orlandos, these villains, fools, clowns, drunkards, cowards, intriguers, fighters, lovers, patriots, hypochondriacs who mistake themselves (and are mistaken by the author) for philosophers, princes without any sense of public duty, futile pessimists who imagine they are confronting a barren and unmeaning world when they are only contemplating their own worthlessness, self-seekers of all kinds, keenly observed and masterfully drawn from the romantic-commercial point of view. Once or twice we scent among them an anticipation of the crudest side of Ibsen's polemics on the Woman Question, as in *All's Well That Ends Well*, where the man cuts as meanly selfish a figure beside his enlightened lady doctor wife as Helmer beside Nora; or in *Cymbeline*, where Posthumus, having, as he believes, killed his wife for inconstancy, speculates for a moment on what his life would have been worth if the same standard of continence had been applied to himself. And certainly no modern study of the voluptuous temperament, and the spurious heroism and heroinism which its ecstasies produce, can add much to *Antony and Cleopatra*, unless it were some sense of the spuriousness on the author's part. But search for statesmanship, or even citizenship, or any sense of the commonwealth, material or spiritual, and you will not find the making of a decent vestryman or curate in the whole horde. As to faith, hope, courage, conviction, or any of the true heroic qualities, you find nothing but death made sensational, despair made stage-sublime, sex made romantic, and barrenness covered up by sentimentality and the mechanical lilt of blank verse.

All that you miss in Shakespear you find in Bunyan, to whom the true heroic came quite obviously and naturally. The world was to him a more terrible place than it was to Shakespear; but he saw through it a path at the end of which a man might look not only forward to the Celestial City, but back on his life and say:—'Tho' with great difficulty I am got hither, yet now I do not repent me of all the trouble I have been at to arrive where I am. My sword I give to him that shall succeed me in my pilgrimage, and my courage and skill to him that can get them.' The heart vibrates like a bell to such an utterance as this: to turn from it to 'Out, out, brief candle,' and 'The rest is silence,' and 'We are such stuff as dreams are made on, and our little life is rounded with a sleep' is to turn from life, strength, resolution, morning air and eternal youth, to the terrors of a drunken nightmare.

Let us descend now to the lower ground where Shakespear is not disabled by his inferiority in energy and elevation of spirit. Take one of his big fighting scenes, and compare its blank verse, in point of mere rhetorical strenuousness, with Bunyan's prose. Macbeth's famous cue for the fight with Macduff runs thus:—

Yet I will try the last: before my body
I throw my warlike shield. Lay on, Macduff,
And damned be him that first cries Hold, enough!
                    [V.viii.22–24]

Turn from this jingle, dramatically right in feeling, but silly and resourceless in thought and expression, to Apollyon's cue for the fight in the Valley of Humiliation: 'I am void of fear in this matter. Prepare thyself to die; for I swear by my infernal den that thou shalt go no farther: here will I spill thy soul.' This is the same thing done masterly. Apart from its superior grandeur, force, and appropriateness, it is better claptrap and infinitely better word-music.

Shakespear, fond as he is of describing fights, has hardly ever sufficient energy or reality of imagination to finish without betraying the paper origin of his fancies by dragging in something classical in the style of the Cyclops' hammer falling 'on Mars's armor, forged for proof eterne.' [II.ii.501] Hear how Bunyan does it: 'I fought till my sword did cleave to my hand; and when they were joined together as if the sword grew out of my arm; and when the blood run thorow my fingers, then I fought with most courage.' Nowhere in all Shakespear is there a touch like that of the blood running down through the man's fingers, and his courage rising to passion at it. Even in mere technical adaptation to the art of the actor, Bunyan's dramatic speeches are as good as Shakespear's tirades. Only a trained dramatic speaker can appreciate the terse manageableness and effectiveness of such a speech as this, with its grandiose exordium, followed up by its pointed question and its stern threat: 'By this I perceive thou art one of my subjects; for all that country is mine, and I am the Prince and the God of it. How is it then that thou hast ran away from thy King? Were it not that I hope thou mayst do me more service, I would strike thee now at one blow to the ground.' Here there is no raving and swearing and rhyming and classical allusion. The sentences go straight to their mark; and their concluding phrases soar like the sunrise, or swing and drop like a hammer, just as the actor wants them. I might multiply these instances by the dozen; but I had rather leave dramatic students to compare the two authors at first-hand. In an article on Bunyan lately published in the *Contemporary Review*—the only article worth reading on the subject I ever saw (yes, thank you: I am quite familiar with Macaulay's patronizing prattle about *The Pilgrim's Progress*)—Mr Richard Heath, the historian of the Anabaptists, shews how Bunyan learnt his lesson, not only from his own rough pilgrimage through life, but from the tradition of many an actual journey from real Cities of Destruction (under Alva), with Interpreters' houses and convoy of Greathearts all complete. Against such a man what chance had our poor immortal William, with his 'little Latin' (would it had been less, like his Greek!), his heathen mythology, his Plutarch, his Boccaccio, his Holinshed, his circle of London literary wits, soddening their minds with books and their nerves with alcohol (quite like us), and all the rest of his Strand and Fleet Street surroundings, activities, and interests, social and professional, mentionable and unmentionable? Let us applaud him, in due measure, in that he came out of it no blackguardly Bohemian, but a thoroughly respectable snob; raised the desperation and cynicism of its outlook to something like sublimity in his tragedies; dramatized its morbid, self-centred passions and its feeble and shallow speculations with all the force that was in them; disinfected it by copious doses of romantic poetry, fun, and common sense; and gave to its perpetual sex-obsession the relief of individual character and feminine winsomeness. Also—if you are a sufficiently good Whig—that after incarnating the spirit of the whole epoch which began with the sixteenth century and is ending (I hope) with the nineteenth, he is still the idol of all well-read children. But as he never thought a noble life worth living or a great work worth doing, because the commercial profit-and-loss sheet shewed that the one did not bring happiness nor the other money, he never struck the great vein—the vein in which Bunyan told of that 'man of a very stout countenance' who went up to the keeper of the book of life and said, not 'Out, out, brief candle,' but 'Set down my name, sir,' and immediately fell on the armed men and cut his way into heaven after receiving and giving many wounds.

—George Bernard Shaw, from "Better than Shakespear?," 1897, *Plays and Players,* edited by A. C. Ward, 1952, pp. 152–57

GEORGE SAINTSBURY "SHAKESPEARE" (1898)

George Saintsbury (1845–1933), English writer and literary critic, examining Shakespeare's plays in the presumed order of their composition, discusses the qualities of the early plays as they reflect and improve upon their precursors and suggest the heights that Shakespeare will attain in his latter plays. In his discussion of second-period plays, Saintsbury emphasizes what he calls the completeness of Shakespeare's art, calling attention particularly to the refinements in the development of plot and character. Saintsbury sees Shakespeare reaching an apotheosis of inspiration and expressive power in the great tragedies of passion, character, and fate, of his third period, written in a verse that Saintsbury asserts is unequaled. Saintsbury considers the beauty of the last plays as he sorts out those that are surely by Shakespeare from those that are only partially by him and from those sometimes attributed to him but whose provenance is either highly questionable or impossible.

What really is Shakespeare's earliest dramatic work is, as has been said, in the highest degree uncertain; and of the pieces which are with more or less probability ascribed to his earliest period it is not definitely known how much is his own, how much supplied by or borrowed from others. From the beginning of the play, as distinguished from the interlude, the habit seems to have established itself, in England as in other countries, of constantly reworking old pieces by new hands; and it is probably to some exceptional popularity of Shakespeare as a refashioner in this way that [Robert] Greene's outburst [in 1592 in *A Groatsworth of Wit*] refers. His early pieces, then, may be divided into anticipations, more or less original, of his special masterpiece, the romantic comedy, attempts in the blood-and-thunder melodrama of the time, and probably, in most cases, refashioned chronicle-plays or "histories," a kind, as we have seen, as old as [John] Bale. To the first division belong *Love's Labour's Lost*, the *Two Gentlemen of Verona*, the *Comedy of Errors* (this touching the translated classical play), *Measure for Measure* (?), the series culminating in *A Midsummer Night's Dream*; to the second *Titus Andronicus*; to the last the majority of the great series of the English histories, while *Romeo and Juliet* stands apart as what we may call a romantic tragedy corresponding to the romantic comedy, and promising almost greater things to come.

In all this work, guessing as little as we can, and proceeding as gingerly as possible, we can see the poet's genius growing and settling itself in every possible way. In metre he begins with the lumbering fourteeners, not as yet quite spirited up even by him, the stiff blank verse which even from the first becomes pliant in his hand, the richer but almost stiffer Marlovian hectoring style, the giant fantasies and euphuistic devices of [novelist and playwright John] Lyly, all frequently lapsing into rhymed couplet and even stanza. But almost from the very first there are glimpses, and very soon there are much more than glimpses, of something that we have never seen before. Such a phrase, for instance, to take but the first that occurs, as the

> And shake the yoke of inauspicious stars
> From this world-wearied flesh,

of *Romeo and Juliet* [V.iii.111–12] takes us a long way beyond Marlowe, a longer way beyond [Elizabethan dramatist George] Peek. In both these masters there is a deficiency of vibration in the verse, and a certain poverty, or at least simplicity, of verbal music. "Native wood-notes wild" is rather truer of [playwright George] Peele than of Shakespeare. Even Shakespeare could not often outdo Marlowe in a sort of economy of majesty, the grandeur of a huge blank cliff-face, or of the empty welkin itself. But as his meaning is more complex, farther-ranging, more intricately developed than theirs, so are his versification and his form. The incomparable skill that was to achieve such things as

Peace, peace!
Dost thou not see my baby at my breast
That sucks the nurse asleep?

[*Antony and Cleopatra* V.ii.307–09]

or the famous *Tempest* passage about "such stuff as dreams are made on," confronts us in the making (and a very rapid making) quite early. We find it in the quaint euphuisms of *Love's Labour's Lost*, in the unequal speeches of the *Two Gentlemen* [*of Verona*], even in such a partly farcical medley as the *Comedy of Errors*, and such an ill-mingled mass of farce and tragedy as *Measure for Measure*. The real Shakespeare cannot help snowing himself, if only by a flash of verse here and there; and then we are in presence of something new—of a kind of English poetry that no one has hit upon before, and which, as we cannot but feel, is revolutionising the whole structure and character of English verse. He may rhyme, or he may not rhyme, or he may turn to prose; but always there is the new phrase, the new language, conceited to the despair of pedants, playing on words in a fashion maddening to dullards, not always impeccable from the stricter standpoints of taste, but always instinct with creative genius.

In respect of construction and dramatic conception these early works, as we might expect, are less advanced. The chronicle-play of its nature defies construction of the ordinary kind, though sometimes, as in Marlowe's *Edward II* and Shakespeare's two *Richards*, the actual story may be short and central enough to give something like definite plot. It is, however, remarkable how Shakespeare contrives to infuse into these chronicles, or, as they may be not inaccurately termed, these dramatic romances, something of the unity of the regular play or dramatic epic. He will do it by the most various means— sometimes as in *King John*, by the contrasted attraction of the tragedy of Constance and Arthur and the comedy of the Bastard Falconbridge; sometimes, as in *Henry IV*, by the inclusion of a non-historical character, like Falstaff, of the very first interest and importance, with the subsidiaries necessary to set it off; sometimes, as in *Henry V*, by projecting an idea (in this case the patriotic idea of England) in such a fashion that the whole of the play, humours and all, imposes it on the spectator. But in the miscellaneous plays there is much less unity of construction, and, as yet, the romantic attraction of character is not quite secured. The defeat of the project of seclusion from womankind in *Love's Labour's Lost* might hardly, in any case, have been sufficient by itself, and is certainly not made sufficient; the play, agreeable as it is, loses itself in humours, and episodes, and single combats of wit and love. The central story of the *Two Gentlemen* is not more than enough for an ordinary *nouvelle,* and it may be questioned whether that of *Romeo and Juliet* is in itself much more. But this latter is quintessenced, and exalted to the heavens, by the pure and intense poetic quality of its verse, by the pity of it in the case of the hero and still more the heroine, and by the contrasted flashes of wit and gallantry in Mercutio and Tybalt and the rest. So in the other and lighter masterpiece, *A Midsummer Night's Dream,* which probably belongs to this period, the subtle fidelity to the dream-nature perhaps makes it unnecessary to give, but certainly as a matter of fact excludes, any elaborate character-drawing. Indeed, always and everywhere at this period, Shakespeare's character is far ahead of his plot. Some indeed, to whom critical adhesion can here by no means be given, would maintain that this was always the case, and that to the very last the dazzling and transcendent truth and mastery of the great personages help to blind the reader to the want of that "clockwork" excellence of construction which Jonson could perhaps already give, and was certainly to give before Shakespeare's death. Let it rather be said that Shakespeare at this time had not quite acquired the art of constructing up to his character-level; that later, when he had learnt it, he never cared to give more construction than was necessary for his characters; and that in this he was right. It may be questioned—heresy as the statement will seem to some—whether construction, pitched to the perfection of [Ben Jonson's *Epicoene,* or] The *Silent Woman* [1609] or of [the 1749 novel by Henry Fielding] *Tom Jones,* is not something of a *tour de force,* and whether it does not deserve Bacon's pleasant sneer in another matter, "you may see as good sights in tarts." Life does not consider or contrive so curiously. However this may be, Shakespeare at this time was certainly not "our best plotter"; he was already at times an almost perfect artist in character, as he was a quite perfect poet. Even in such "more rawer" work as the *Two Gentlemen,* "Who is Silvia?" does not more show us the master of lyric than Julia and Lance show us the master of the graver and the lighter, the more passionate and the more frivolous, psychology and ethology. Even in that unequal medley, *Measure for Measure,* the great scene between Isabel and Claudio so far transcends anything that English, anything that European, drama had had to show for nearly two thousand years, that in this special point of view it remains perhaps the most wonderful in Shakespeare. Marlowe has nothing like it; his greatest passages, psychologically speaking, are always monologues; he cannot even attempt the clash and play of soul with soul that is so miraculously given here. Yet, though the play (which some call a comedy!) is not known to have been acted till 1604, its general characteristics put it far earlier. [Most scholars are now in agreement that the play was actually written around 1604.]

The second or middle division of plays may be said to be connected with the first by the link between *Henry IV* and *Henry V*,[1] the latest and most matured of the early batch, and the *Merry Wives of Windsor,* probably the first of the second. The *Merry Wives* itself is a curious study. It has failed to find favour with some, owing to a not ignoble dislike at seeing the degradation or discomfiture of Falstaff, but it must be remembered that Shakespeare, though never cruel with the morbid cruelty of the modern pessimist, is always perfectly awake to the facts of life. . . . It has also been a common saying that the play is little better than a farce. If so, it can only be said that Shakespeare very happily took or made the opportunity of showing how a farce also can pass under the species of eternity. How infinitely do the most farcical of the characters, such as Sir Hugh and Dr. Caius, excel the mere "Vices" of earlier playwrights! Who but Shakespeare had—we may almost say who but Shakespeare has—made an immortal thing of a mere ass, a mere puff-ball of foolish froth like Slender? If Chaucer had had the dramatic as he had the narrative faculty and atmosphere he might have done Mrs. Quickly [in the two parts of *Henry IV* and in *Henry V*], who is a very near relative, in somewhat lower life, of the Wife of Bath, and rapidly ripening for her future experiences in Eastcheap. But Shallow is above even Chaucer, as are also the subtle differentiation between Mrs. Page and Mrs. Ford, and the half-dozen strokes which her creator judged sufficient for sweet Anne Page. As for Falstaff, it is mistaken affection which thinks him degraded, or "translated" Bottom-fashion. He is even as elsewhere, though under an unluckier star.

This completeness exhibits itself, not perhaps in more masterly fashion, but in a somewhat higher and more varied material, in the great trio of Romantic comedies which is supposed to represent the work of the last year or two of the sixteenth century—*Twelfth Night, Much Ado about Nothing,* and *As You Like It.* Whether this order represents the actual composition or not, it certainly represents an intellectual and literary progression of interest and value, though the steps between the three are not wide. *Twelfth Night,* like the *Merry Wives* though not quite to the same extent, is pure comedy with a leaning to farce. The exquisite delicacy of the character of Viola suffuses it with a more romantic tone; but the disasters of Malvolio are even less serious than Falstaff's, and the great appeal of the play lies wholly on the comical side, in the immortal characters of Sir Toby and Sir Andrew, in Feste, the first distinctly and peculiarly Shakespearian clown, in Maria the "youngest wren of nine," in the glorious fooling of the plot against the steward, and the minor *Comedy of Errors* put upon Viola and Sebastian. There is no touch of sadness, though the clown's final song of "The rain it raineth every day" gives a sort of warning note; the whole is sunny, and if less romantically imaginative than *A Midsummer Night's Dream*, it is almost as romantically fanciful.

Much Ado about Nothing changes us from pure comedy to the tragi-comic—indeed, to what threatens at one time to be tragedy undiluted. Perhaps here only, or here and in the *Winter's Tale*, Shakespeare has used tragedy to heighten his comedy, just as he habitually does the opposite; and the effect is good. But it is for the lighter side—for the peerless farce of Dogberry, the almost peerless comedy proper of Benedick and Beatrice—that we love the play. And the attraction of this couple, anticipated very early in Rosaline and Biron [in *Love's Labour's Lost*], is used yet again and with absolutely supreme success in *As You Like It*, one of the topmost things in Shakespeare, the masterpiece of romantic comedy, one of the great type-dramas of the world. Here, as in so many other places, Shakespeare borrowed his theme, and even no small part of his minor situations; but this matters nothing. The *Tale of Gamelyn* [a short narrative poem of the fourteenth century which tells of an older brother's tyranny over a younger brother] is pleasant and vigorous; [Thomas] Lodge's *Rosalynde* is ingenious and fantastically artistic. But *As You Like It* is ... [one] of the few books exhibiting imagination and expression equally married. Rosalind and Touchstone stand, each in his or her own way, alone.

The apparent change in the subject and temper of Shakespeare's work at the beginning of the seventeenth century has been the subject of much idle talk. There is no more reason to believe that he was specially and personally merry when he wrote this group of comedies, than there is to believe that he was sad or embittered during the period which produced *Julius Caesar, Hamlet, Othello, Lear, Macbeth, Antony and Cleopatra*—to which some would add *Troilus and Cressida, Timon*, and even *Measure for Measure*, as well as *Coriolanus*. To the present writer it is pretty certain that *Measure for Measure, Timon*, and *Troilus and Cressida* represent much earlier work, whether or no they had been actually produced. The three Roman plays, *Julius Caesar, Coriolanus*, and *Antony and Cleopatra*, make an interesting section to themselves, which in *Antony and Cleopatra* almost passes into that of romantic tragedy, and so joins the supreme quartette, *Hamlet, Macbeth, Othello*, and *Lear*. In all the Roman plays Shakespeare applied his English-chronicle method pretty exactly to the material that he found in [Thomas] North's [1579 translation of] *Plutarch*, and, since his faculties both of stage-management and of versification were now in complete maturity, with the noblest effect. But in character he does not create much, he only interprets—till we come to the "Serpent of old Nile" and her lover, who are neither the crowned wanton and besotted debauchee of uninspired history, nor the anti-Roman sorceress and victim of Horace's craven-crowing ode, but a real hero and heroine of romance, luckless though not blameless, sympathetic though not ill served.

Much, however, even of *Antony and Cleopatra* is only chronicle, and like the other two, great as they are, falls beneath the magnificent creation of the four great romantic tragedies. In each of these, of course, Shakespeare had again his authorities, and, as his wont, he sometimes followed them closely. But the interest of the four does not depend in the very least upon [Giovanni Battista Giraldi] Cinthio [1504–1573, whose collection of tales, *Hecatommithi*, provided one of the sources for *Othello*] or Saxo [Grammaticus, 1150–1220, whose history of Denmark provided one of Shakespeare's sources for *Hamlet*], upon Geoffrey [of Monmouth, 1100–55, whose *History of the Kings of England* provided Shakespeare with source material for *King Lear* and *Cymbeline*] or [Ralph] Holinshed [whose *Chronicles* provided Shakespeare with material for the history plays as well as *Macbeth, King Lear,* and *Cymbeline*]. Here, as in the great companion comedies, the dramatist breaks quite free; his real themes are human passion and human action at large, caught and embodied for the nonce in individual character and fate. Nowhere else does even Shakespeare lavish his resources as he does in these four plays, and certainly in none does he manifest such power of displaying the irony of life and fate. Viewed from one standpoint, all four are as well entitled to the motto "Vanity of vanities" as Ecclesiastes itself. The love, the heroism, and the great leading qualities of Othello and Macbeth, the filial duty and intellectual subtlety of Hamlet, the generous if reckless and passionate *bonhomie* of Lear, all make shipwreck against the rocks thrown in their way by inauspicious stars, and sought out too often by their own mistakes and crimes. With that supreme genius which distinguishes him from the common playwright, Shakespeare has never made his heroes or heroines types; and this has puzzled many, and driven not a few to despairing efforts to make them out types after all. It is exactly what they are not. Shakespeare was no duped or duping preacher of the ruling passion like his second editor [Alexander Pope, 1725; Nicholas Rowe, 1674–1718, was the first editor of Shakespeare's work in 1709]. *Othello* is indeed the simplest of the four; but even here the character of Iago, which is almost as complex as that of Hamlet, invites a great, from some the greater, part of the interest.

Those who would make Hamlet a mere irresolute, a mere Waverley [the vacillating hero of Walter Scott's 1814 novel of the same name], not only do not supply a full explanation of him even in their terms, but forget that irresolution, at least such as his, is the most complex of qualities. The inability of the will to "let itself go" is partly caused by, much more complicated with, the inability of the intellect to decide. To compare *Lear* with the wretched other play[2] [*i.e., The True Chronicle History of King Leir,* ca. 1590] on the subject, which is beyond all doubt anterior, or with Holinshed, or with Geoffrey's original, is perhaps the very best single means of appreciating the infinite variety and intricacy of Shakespeare's knowledge and expression of humanity. Although the hapless King is always in the Latin sense impotent—incapable of resisting the impulse of the moment—this fault of his is conditioned, coloured, transformed at every instant by circumstances, many of them Shakespeare's own invention, and all rearranged with new effects by him. The gifting, the unexpected fractiousness of Cordelia (and let it be remembered that Cordelia is not a perfect character, that she is as hyper-frank as her sisters are hypocritical), the petty insults at Goneril's, the bolder outrage at Gloster's under the orders of Regan and Cornwall, the terrors of the storm, and the talk (dangerous to already tottering wits) of the sham madman, the rescue even as it is too late, the second fall into the hands of his enemies, and the final blow in the murder of Cordelia—all these engines, all these reagents, the dramatist applies to Lear's headstrong petulance with the most unvarying precision of science, the most unfailing variety of art. We have the ungovernable king and ex-king in twenty different "states," in twenty different relations and presentments, all connected by the central inexorable story. And so in *Macbeth* the hero—ambitious, uxorious, intensely under the influence of nerves and of imagination, as different from the mere "butcher" of Malcolm's insult as his greater but not less complex-souled wife is from a "fiendlike queen" passes before us whole and real, terrible but exact, before, at the crisis of, and in his criminal stage, at once with the fluttering and phantasmagoric variety of a dream, and with an utterly solid and continuous story-interest. The Macbeth who is excited by the prophecy of the witches is exactly the same Macbeth as he who shrinks from the visioned dagger, as he who is struck to a kind of numb philosophising by the cry of women that announces his wife's death.

Of the numberless and magnificent passages of our poetry which these four plays contain it were vain to attempt to speak. It must be sufficient to say that in them the Shakespearian line, which, with its absolute freedom of shifting the pause from the first syllable to the last, its almost absolute freedom of syllabic equivalence, and the infinite variety of cadence which the use of these two means (and no doubt some magic besides) allowed it to attain, is the central fact of English poetry—this line came to its very farthest. We only observe in the plays of the last six or seven years of his life one change, and that not a quite certain one, the inclination to greater indulgence in the redundant syllable which is so exceedingly noticeable in his successors in romantic drama, Beaumont and Fletcher. It is pretty certain that this license, which he had always used to some extent, would never in his hands have reached the excess which we find in them, and which in their followers simply disbands the line into loose ungirt prose, with some reminiscences of verse here and there. But it cannot be considered on the whole an improvement.

The plays of, or probably belonging to, the last period of Shakespeare's life are fewer in proportion than those of either of the preceding periods, but those of them that are certain present interesting characteristics. These are *Cymbeline*, the *Winter's Tale*, and *The Tempest*, the others being *Henry VIII*. and *Pericles*. This last play, which was not included in the first folio of 1623 by Shakespeare's friends and colleagues, Heminge and Condell, presents curious difficulties. Great part of it *must* be Shakespeare's; there is perhaps no part that *might* not be; and the general characteristics of story-management and versification are a very odd mixture of his earliest and his latest manner—a *Love's Labour's Lost* blended with a *Winter's Tale*. Nor do I at least see reason for refusing any part of Henry *VIII.* to Shakespeare, though the prominence of the redundant syllable has made many ascribe it in large part to Fletcher. But about the other three there is no doubt, and certainly there is more excuse than usual for those who read in them a special index of the author's temper in these his last days—of the "calmed and calming *mens adepta*" whereof Fulke Greville [1554–1628, poet, dramatist, biographer] speaks. *Cymbeline* partakes somewhat of the same character as the earlier *Much Ado about Nothing*. It is very nearly a tragedy—indeed, unlike *Much Ado about Nothing*, it contains accomplished tragic incidents in the deaths of the Queen and Cloten. But as far as the interesting personages—Imogen, Iachimo, Posthumus—are concerned, the tragedy is averted, and the whole deserves the name of romantic *drame* in the French sense.

This word, indeed, exactly describes these last three plays, and with ever-increasing appropriateness. Pedants of the bookish theoric of playwright craftsmanship have found fault with the construction of *Cymbeline*, which is admittedly loose, like its fellows—a chronicle or romance rather than an epic, but perfectly sufficient for its own object and purposes. The backbone of A *Winter's Tale* is a little more carefully and distinctly vertebrated, though no doubt the action is rather improbably prolonged, and the statue-scene, in which Hermione is restored to Leontes, does not entirely atone by its extreme beauty for its equally extreme improbability. But here, as always, Shakespeare has done what he meant to do; and here, as always, it is the extremity of critical impertinence to demand from an author not what he meant to do but something that the critic thinks he might, could, should, or ought to have meant. The vivid truth of the Queen's frank courtesy, Leontes' jealous rage (so different from Othello's, yet equally lifelike), the fine lurid presentment of the "coast" of Bohemia, the exquisitely idyllic (a word much abused, yet here applicable) figure of Perdita, the inimitable *brio* of Autolycus, the pendant to Touchstone—to give all these and other things in a pleasing series was what the dramatist intended to do, and he did it.

The splendour of sunset in *The Tempest* can escape no one, and the sternest opponent of guesswork must admit the probable presence of a designed allegory in the figure of Prospero and the burying of the book, the breaking of the staff, at the close. Even if this be thought too fanciful, nowhere has Shakespeare been more prodigal of every species of his enchantment. The exquisite but contrasted grace of Miranda and Ariel, the wonderful creation of Caliban, the varied human criticism in Gonzalo and the bad brothers, the farce-comedy of Stephano and Trinculo, do not more show the illimitable fancy and creative power of the master in scene and character than the passages, not so much scattered as showered over the whole play, show his absolute supremacy in poetry. Both in the blank verse and the lyrics, in the dialogue and the set *tirades,* in long contexts and short phrases alike, he shows himself absolute, with nothing out of reach of his faculty of expression and suggestion, with every resource of verbal music and intellectual demonstration at his command.

The so-called doubtful plays[3] of Shakespeare form an interesting subject, but one which can be dealt with but briefly here. As attributed by older tradition and assertion or by modern guesswork, they amount to "some dozen or sixteen," of which only three, the *Two Noble Kinsmen,* usually printed as Beaumont and Fletcher's, *Edward III,* and *Arden of Feversham,* have any serious claims, though some have seen such in the *Yorkshire Tragedy,* a curious little horror-piece which, however, a dozen other men might have written. Others again, *Fair Em, Locrine, Sir John Oldcastle,* have absolutely nothing but unauthoritative though pretty ancient assertion to recommend them. As for the excepted three, the *Two Noble Kinsmen,* a dramatisation of Chaucer's *Knight's Tale,* has no suggestion of Shakespeare as a whole, but in parts shows extraordinary similarity to his versification. This has tempted some to think that Shakespeare may by chance have found his younger contemporaries (Beaumont, be it remembered, died in the same year with him) working at the play, have looked at it, and have mended or patched here and there for amusement or out of good-nature. *Edward III* has the same similarities of versification, and in part, though a small part, of handling, but it is more suggestive of an extraordinarily clever piece of imitation or inspiration than of actual Shakespearian authorship. *Arden of Feversham,* on the other hand, has no similarities of versification, and does not, in its dealing with the murder of a husband by his wife and her baseborn paramour, suggest Shakespeare's choice of subject, but is closer in some ways than any other play to his handling in character and psychological analysis.

Notes

1.   It is well to say nothing about *Henry VI.*, because, though I have no doubt that this trilogy is, as we have it, in the main Shakespeare's, it is also beyond all doubt, and beyond all others, a refashioning of earlier plays.

2.   To be found, with other similar apparatus, in Hazlitt's *Shakespeare's Library.*

3.   It was not till 1908 that a Shakespearian *Apocrypha*, containing 14 plays, was supplied by the Clarendon Press (Oxford, ed. C. F. Tucker-Brooke). Before this they were scattered in Hazlitt's *Dodsley*, Simpson's *School of Shakespeare*, and elsewhere; though there was a German edition (Halle, 1878–81) and a single vol. Reprint (London, *n.d.*) of the plays added in the later folios.

—George Saintsbury, from "Shakespeare," *A Short History of English Literature*, 1898, pp. 320–29

GEORGE SANTAYANA "THE ABSENCE OF RELIGION IN SHAKESPEARE" (1900)

George Santayana (1863–1952), philosopher, essayist, poet, and novelist, argues that the concerns addressed in Shakespeare's plays are grounded in the world of earthly experience and human society. Although Santayana admits that there are spiritual and metaphysical sensibilities in Shakespeare's work, he finds only a vision of the natural world and nothing of the supernatural in Shakespeare. Unlike the work of Dante or Homer, Santayana asserts, Shakespeare's works do not rise through the agency of a religious imagination to present a cosmic vision, a philosophy of the cosmos, or a map of a beautiful universal order. A reader might respond by asking if that is not the point, that in Shakespeare's cosmology there is no beautiful universal order. There is the order its inhabitants can fashion according to their complex natures or die trying to.

We are accustomed to think of the universality of Shakespeare as not the least of his glories. No other poet has given so many-sided an expression to human nature, or rendered so many passions and moods with such an appropriate variety of style, sentiment, and accent. If, therefore, we were asked to select one monument of human civilization that should survive to some future age, or be transported to another planet to bear witness to the inhabitants there of what we have been upon earth, we should probably choose the works of Shakespeare. In them we recognize the truest portrait and best memorial of man. Yet the archaeologists of that future age, or the cosmographers of that other part of the heavens, after conscientious study of our Shakesperian autobiography, would misconceive our life in one important respect. They would hardly understand that man had had a religion.

There are, indeed, numerous exclamations and invocations in Shakespeare which we, who have other means of information, know to be evidences of current religious ideas. Shakespeare adopts these, as he adopts the rest of his vocabulary, from the society about him. But he seldom or never gives them their original value. When Iago says *"'sblood,"* a commentator might add explanations which should involve the whole philosophy of Christian devotion; but this Christian sentiment is not in Iago's mind, nor in Shakespeare's, any more than the virtues of Heracles and his twelve labours are in the mind of every slave and pander that cries *"hercule"* in the pages of Plautus and Terence. Oaths are the fossils of piety. The geologist recognizes in them the relics of a once active devotion, but they are now only counters and pebbles tossed about in the unconscious play of expression. The lighter and more constant their use, the less their meaning.

Only one degree more inward than this survival of a religious vocabulary in profane speech is the reference we often find in Shakespeare to religious institutions and traditions. There are monks, bishops, and cardinals; there is even mention of saints, although none is ever presented to us in person. The clergy, if they have any wisdom, have an earthly one. Friar Lawrence culls his herbs like a more benevolent Medea; and Cardinal Wolsey flings away ambition with a profoundly Pagan despair; his robe and his integrity to heaven are cold comfort to him. Juliet goes to shrift to arrange her love affairs, and Ophelia should go to a nunnery to forget hers. Even the chastity of Isabella has little in it that would have been out of place in Iphigenia. The metaphysical Hamlet himself sees a "true ghost," but so far reverts to the positivism that underlines Shakespeare's thinking as to speak soon after of that "undiscovered country from whose bourn no traveller returns."

There are only two or three short passages in the plays, and one sonnet, in which true religious feeling seems to break forth. The most beautiful of these passages is that in *Richard II,* which commemorates the death of Mowbray, Duke of Norfolk:—

Many a time hath banished Norfolk fought
For Jesu Christ in glorious Christian field,

Streaming the ensign of the Christian cross
Against black Pagans, Turks, and Saracens;
And, toiled with works of war, retired himself
To Italy; and there, at Venice, gave
His body to that pleasant country's earth,
And his pure soul unto his captain Christ,
Under whose colours he had fought so long.

[IV.i.92–100]

This is tender and noble, and full of an indescribable chivalry and pathos, yet even here we find the spirit of war rather than that of religion, and a deeper sense of Italy than of heaven. More unmixed is the piety of Henry V after the battle of Agincourt:—

O God, thy arm was here;
And not to us, but to thy arm alone,
Ascribe we all!—When, without stratagem,
But in plain shock and even play of battle,
Was ever known so great and little loss,
On one part and on the other?—Take it, God,
For it is none but thine. . . .
Come, go we in procession to the village,
And be it death proclaimed through our host,
To boast of this, or take that praise from God,
Which is his only. . . .
    Do we all holy rites;
Let there be sung Non *nobis* and *Te Deum*.

[IV.viii.108–25]

This passage is certainly a true expression of religious feeling, and just the kind that we might expect from a dramatist. Religion appears here as a manifestation of human nature and as an expression of human passion. The passion, however, is not due to Shakespeare's imagination, but is essentially historical: the poet has simply not rejected, as he usually does, the religious element in the situation he reproduces.[1]

With this dramatic representation of piety we may couple another, of a more intimate kind, from the Sonnets:—

Poor soul, the centre of my sinful earth,
Fooled by these rebels powers that thee array,
Why dost thou pine within and suffer dearth,

Painting thy outward walls so costly gay?
Why so large cost, having so short a lease,
Dost thou upon thy fading mansion spend?
Shall worms, inheritors of this excess,
Eat up thy charge? Is this thy body's end?
Then, soul, live thou upon thy servant's loss,
And let that pine to aggravate thy store;
Buy terms divine by selling hours of dross,
Within be fed, without be rich no more:
Then shalt thou feed on death, that feeds on men,
And death once dead, there's no more dying then.

[Sonnet 146]

This sonnet contains more than a natural religious emotion inspired by a single event. It contains reflection, and expresses a feeling not merely dramatically proper but rationally just. A mind that habitually ran into such thoughts would be philosophically pious; it would be spiritual. The Sonnets, as a whole, are spiritual; their passion is transmuted into discipline. Their love, which, whatever its nominal object, is hardly anything but love of beauty and youth in general, is made to triumph over time by a metaphysical transformation of the object into something eternal. At first this is the beauty of the race renewing itself by generation, then it is the description of beauty in the poet's verse, and finally it is the immortal soul enriched by the contemplation of that beauty. This noble theme is the more impressively rendered by being contrasted with another, with a vulgar love that by its nature refuses to be so transformed and transmuted. "Two loves," cries the poet, in a line that gives us the essence of the whole, "Two loves I have,—of comfort, and despair."

In all this depth of experience, however, there is still wanting any religious image. The Sonnets are spiritual, but, with the doubtful exception of the one quoted above, they are not Christian. And, of course, a poet of Shakespeare's time could not have found any other mould than Christianity for his religion. In our day, with our wide and conscientious historical sympathies, it may be possible for us to find in other rites and doctrines than those of our ancestors an expression of some ultimate truth. But for Shakespeare, in the matter of religion, the choice lay between Christianity and nothing. He chose nothing; he chose to leave his heroes and himself in the presence of life and of death with no other philosophy than that which the profane world can suggest and understand.

This positivism, we need hardly say, was not due to any grossness or sluggishness in his imagination. Shakespeare could be idealistic when he dreamed, as he could be spiritual when he reflected. The spectacle of life did not pass before his eyes as a mere phantasmagoria. He seized upon its principles; he became wise. Nothing can exceed the ripeness of his seasoned judgment, or the occasional breadth, sadness, and terseness of his reflection. The author of *Hamlet* could not be without metaphysical aptitude; *Macbeth* could not have been written without a sort of sibylline inspiration, or the Sonnets without something of the Platonic mind. It is all the more remarkable, therefore, that we should have to search through all the works of Shakespeare to find half a dozen passages that have so much as a religious sound, and that even these passages, upon examination, should prove not to be the expression of any deep religious conception. If Shakespeare had been without metaphysical capacity, or without moral maturity, we could have explained his strange insensibility to religion; but as it is, we must marvel at his indifference and ask ourselves what can be the causes of it. For, even if we should not regard the absence of religion as an imperfection in his own thought, we must admit it to be an incompleteness in his portrayal of the thought of others. Positivism may be a virtue in a philosopher, but it is a vice in a dramatist, who has to render those human passions to which the religious imagination has always given a larger meaning and a richer depth.

Those greatest poets by whose side we are accustomed to put Shakespeare did not forego this advantage. They gave us man with his piety and the world with its gods. Homer is the chief repository of the Greek religion, and Dante the faithful interpreter of the Catholic. Nature would have been inconceivable to them without the supernatural, or man without the influence and companionship of the gods. These poets live in a cosmos. In their minds, as in the mind of their age, the fragments of experience have fallen together into a perfect picture, like the bits of glass in a kaleidoscope. Their universe is a total. Reason and imagination have mastered it completely and peopled it. No chaos remains beyond, or, if it does, it is thought of with an involuntary shudder that soon passes into a healthy indifference. They have a theory of human life; they see man in his relations, surrounded by a kindred universe in which he fills his allotted place. He knows the meaning and issue of his life, and does not voyage without a chart.

Shakespeare's world, on the contrary, is only the world of human society. The cosmos eludes him; he does not seem to feel the need of framing that idea. He depicts human life in all its richness and variety, but leaves that life without a setting, and consequently without a meaning. If we asked him to tell us what is the significance of the passion and beauty he had so vividly displayed, and what is the outcome of it all, he could hardly answer in any other words than those he puts into he mouth of Macbeth:—

To-morrow, and to-morrow, and to-morrow,
Creeps in this petty pace from day to day,
To the last syllable of recorded time;
And all our yesterdays have lighted fools
The way to dusty death. Out, out, brief candle!
Life's but a walking shadow, a poor player
That struts and frets his hour upon the stage
And then is heard no more: it is a tale
Told by an idiot, full of sound and fury, Signifying nothing.

                              [V.vi.19–28]

How differently would Homer or Dante have answered that question! Their tragedy would have been illumined by a sense of the divinity of life and beauty, or by a sense of the sanctity of suffering and death. Their faith had enveloped the world of experience in a world of imagination, in which the ideals of the reason, of the fancy, and of the heart had a natural expression. They had caught in the reality the hint of a lovelier fable,—a fable in which that reality was completed and idealized, and made at once vaster in its extent and more intelligible in its principle. They had, as it were, dramatized the universe, and endowed it with the tragic unities. In contrast with such a luminous philosophy and so well-digested an experience, the silence of Shakespeare and his philosophical incoherence have something in them that is still heathen; something that makes us wonder whether the northern mind, even in him, did not remain morose and barbarous at its inmost core.

But before we allow ourselves such hasty and general inferences, we may well stop to consider whether there is not some simpler answer to our question. An epic poet, we might say, naturally deals with cosmic themes. He needs supernatural machinery because he depicts the movement of human affairs in their generality, as typified in the figures of heroes whose function it is to embody or overcome elemental forces. Such a poet's world is fabulous, because his inspiration is impersonal. But the dramatist renders the concrete reality of life. He has no need of a superhuman setting for his pictures. Such a setting would destroy the vitality of his creations. His plots should involve only human actors and human motives: the *deus ex machina* has always been regarded as an interloper on his stage. The passions of man are his all-sufficient material; he should weave his whole fabric out of them.

To admit the truth of all this would not, however, solve our problem. The dramatist cannot be expected to put cosmogonies on the boards. Miracle-plays become dramatic only when they become human. But the supernatural world, which the playwright does not bring before the footlights, may exist nevertheless in the minds of his characters and of his audience. He may refer to it, appeal to it, and imply it, in the actions and in the sentiments he attributes to his heroes. And if the comparison of Shakespeare with Homer or Dante on the score of religious inspiration is invalidated by the fact that he is a dramatist while they are epic poets, a comparison may yet be instituted between Shakespeare and other dramatists, from which his singular insensibility to religion will as readily appear.

Greek tragedy, as we know, is dominated by the idea of fate. Even when the gods do not appear in person, or where the service or neglect of them is not the moving cause of the whole play,—as it is in the *Bacchae* and the *Hippolytus* of Euripides,—still the deep conviction of the limits and conditions of human happiness underlies the fable. The will of man fulfils the decrees of Heaven. The hero manifests a higher force than his own, both in success and in failure. The fates guide the willing and drag the unwilling. There is no such fragmentary view of life as we have in our romantic drama, where accidents make the meaningless happiness or unhappiness of a supersensitive adventurer. Life is seen whole, although in miniature. Its boundaries and its principles are studied more than its incidents. The human, therefore, everywhere merges with the divine. Our mortality, being sharply defined and much insisted upon, draws the attention all the more to that eternity of Nature and of law in which it is embosomed. Nor is the fact of superhuman control left for our reflection to discover; it is emphatically asserted in those oracles on which so much of the action commonly turns. . . .

We might say . . . that the absence of religion in Shakespeare was a sign of his good sense; that a healthy instinct kept his attention within the sublunary world; and that he was in that respect superior to Homer and to Dante. For, while they allowed their wisdom to clothe itself in fanciful forms, he gave us his in its immediate truth, so that he embodied what they signified. The supernatural machinery of their poems was, we might say, an accidental incumbrance, a traditional means of expression, which they only half understood, and which made their representation of life indirect and partly unreal. Shakespeare, on the other hand, had reached his poetical majority and independence. He rendered human experience no longer through symbols, but by direct imaginative representation. What I have treated as a limitation in him would, then, appear as the maturity of his strength. . . .

Shakespeare . . . is remarkable among the greater poets for being without a philosophy and without a religion. In his drama there is no fixed conception of any forces, natural or moral, dominating and transcending our mortal energies. Whether this characteristic be regarded as a merit or as a defect, its presence cannot be denied.

Note

1.   "And so about foure of the clocke in the afternoone, the Kynge when he saw no apparaunce of enemies, caused the retreite to be blowen, and gathering his army together, gave thankes to almightie god for so happy a victory, causing his prelates and chapleines to sing this psalm, *In exitu Israell de Egipto*, and commandying every man to kneele downe on the grounds at this verse; *Non nobis, domine, non nobis, sed nomini tuo da gloriam*. Which done, he caused *Te Deum*, with certain anthems, to be song, giving laud & praise to god, and not boasting of his owne force or any humaine power." Holinshed.

—George Santayana, "The Absence of
Religion in Shakespeare," *Interpretations of
Poetry and Religion*, 1900, pp. 147–65

William Butler Yeats "At Stratford-on-Avon" (1901)

William Butler Yeats (1865–1939), one of the major poets to write in English, accuses nineteenth-century critics of Shakespeare of misrepresenting and disvaluing his work because of their devotion to a utilitarian philosophy that puts activity, achievement, and concern for practical good ahead of a sweet and contemplative nature, thus, for example, representing the warrior Henry V as a more heroic figure than the lyrical and contemplative Richard II.

III

[F]ierceness is the habit of mind of the Shakespearian critics [of the nineteenth century]. They grew up in a century of utilitarianism, when nothing about a man seemed important except his utility to the State, and nothing so useful to the State as the actions whose effect can be weighed by the reason. The deeds of Coriolanus, Hamlet, Timon, Richard II. had no obvious use, were, indeed, no more than the expression of their personalities, and so it was thought Shakespeare was accusing them, and telling us to be careful lest we deserve the like accusations. It did not occur to the critics that you cannot know a man from his actions, because you cannot watch him in every kind of circumstance, and that men are made useless to the State as often by abundance as by emptiness, and that a man's business may at times be revelation, and not reformation. Fortinbras was, it is likely enough, a better King than Hamlet would have been, Aufidius was a more reasonable man than Coriolanus, Henry V was a better man-at-arms than Richard II, but after all, were not those others who changed nothing for the better and many things for the worse greater in the Divine Hierarchies? Blake has said that 'the roaring of lions, the howling of wolves, the raging of the stormy sea, and the destructive sword are portions of Eternity, too great for the eye of man,' but Blake belonged by right to the ages of Faith, and thought the State of less moment than the Divine Hierarchies. Because reason can only discover completely the use of those obvious actions which everybody admires, and because every character was to be judged by efficiency in action, Shakespearian criticism became a vulgar worshipper of Success. I have turned over many books in the library at Stratford-on-Avon, and I have found in nearly all an antithesis, which grew in clearness and violence as the century grew older, between two types, whose representatives were Richard II, 'sentimental,' 'weak,' 'selfish,' 'insincere,' and Henry V, 'Shakespeare's only hero.' These books took the same delight in abasing Richard II that school-boys do in persecuting some boy of fine temperament, who has weak muscles and a distaste for school games. And they had the admiration for Henry V that school-boys have for the sailor or soldier hero of a romance in some boys' paper. I cannot claim any minute knowledge of these books, but I think that these emotions began among the German critics, who perhaps saw something French and Latin in Richard II, and I know that Professor [Edward] Dowden, whose book I once read carefully, first made these emotions eloquent and plausible. He lived in Ireland, where everything has failed, and he meditated frequently upon the perfection of character which had, he thought, made England successful, for, as we say, 'cows beyond the water have long horns.' He forgot that England, as [Scottish merchant and philanthropist Robert] Gordon has said, was made by her adventurers, by her people of wildness and imagination and eccentricity; and thought that Henry V, who only seemed to be these things because he had some commonplace vices, was not only the typical Anglo-Saxon, but the model Shakespeare held up before England; and he even thought it worth while pointing out that Shakespeare himself was making a large fortune while he was writing about Henry's victories. In Professor Dowden's successors this apotheosis went further; and it reached its height at a moment of imperialistic enthusiasm, of ever-deepening conviction that the commonplace shall inherit the earth, when somebody of reputation, whose name I cannot remember, wrote that Shakespeare admired this one character alone out of all his characters. The Accusation of Sin produced its necessary fruit, hatred of all that was abundant, extravagant, exuberant, of all that sets a sail for shipwreck, and flattery of the commonplace emotions and conventional ideals of the mob, the chief Paymaster of accusation.

IV

I cannot believe that Shakespeare looked on his Richard II with any but sympathetic eyes, understanding indeed how ill-fitted he was to be King, at a certain moment of history, but understanding that he was lovable and full of capricious fancy, 'a wild creature' as [English critic Walter] Pater has called him. The man on whom Shakespeare modelled him had been full of French elegancies, as he knew from Hollingshead, and had given life a new luxury, a new splendour, and been 'too friendly' to his friends, 'too favourable' to his enemies. And certainly Shakespeare had these things in his head when he made his King fail, a little because he lacked some qualities that were doubtless common among his scullions, but more because he had certain qualities that are uncommon in all ages. To suppose that Shakespeare preferred the men who deposed his King is to suppose that Shakespeare judged men with the eyes of a Municipal Councillor weighing the merits of a Town Clerk; and that had he been by when [French poet Paul] Verlaine cried out from his bed, 'Sir, you have been made by the stroke of a pen, but I have been made by the breath of God,' he would have thought the Hospital Superintendent the better man. He saw indeed, as I think, in Richard II the defeat that awaits all, whether they be Artist or Saint, who find themselves where men ask of them a rough energy and have nothing to give but some contemplative virtue, whether lyrical phantasy, or sweetness of temper, or dreamy dignity, or love of God, or love of His creatures. He saw that such a man through sheer bewilderment and impatience can become as unjust or as violent as any common man, any Bolingbroke or Prince John, and yet remain 'that sweet lovely rose.' The courtly and saintly ideals of the Middle Ages were fading, and the practical ideals of the modern age had begun to threaten the unuseful dome of the sky; Merry England was fading, and yet it was not so faded that the Poets could not watch the procession of the world with that untroubled sympathy for men as they are, as apart from all they do and seem, which is the substance of tragic irony.

Shakespeare cared little for the State, the source of all our judgments, apart from its shows and splendours, its turmoils and battles, its flamings out of the uncivilized heart. He did indeed think it wrong to overturn a King, and thereby to swamp peace in civil war, and the historical plays from *Henry IV* to *Richard III*, that monstrous birth and last sign of the wrath of Heaven, are a fulfilment of the prophecy of the Bishop of Carlisle, who was 'raised up by God' to make it; but he had no nice sense of utilities, no ready balance to measure deeds, like that fine instrument, with all the latest improvements, [German literary critic and historian, Georg Gottfried] Gervinus and Professor Dowden handle so skilfully. He meditated as Solomon, not as [utilitarian philosopher Jeremy] Bentham meditated, upon blind ambitions, untoward accidents, and capricious passions, and the world was almost as empty in his eyes as it must be in the eyes of God. . . .

V

. . . I have often had the fancy that there is some one Myth for every man, which, if we but knew it, would make us understand all he did and thought. Shakespeare's Myth, it may be, describes a wise man who was blind from very wisdom, and an empty man who thrust him from his place, and saw all that could be seen from very emptiness. It is in the story of Hamlet, who saw too great issues everywhere to play the trivial game of life, and of Fortinbras, who came from fighting battles about 'a little patch of ground' so poor that one of his Captains would not give 'six ducats' to 'farm it,' and who was yet acclaimed by Hamlet and by all as the only befitting King. And it is in the story of Richard II, that unripened Hamlet, and of Henry V, that ripened Fortinbras. To poise character against character was an element in Shakespeare's art, and scarcely a play is lacking characters that are the complement of one another, and so, having made the vessel of porcelain Richard II, he had to make the vessel of clay Henry V. He makes him the reverse of all that Richard was. He has the gross vices, the coarse nerves, of one who is to rule among violent people, and he is so little 'too friendly' to his friends that he bundles them out of doors when their time is over. He is as remorseless and undistinguished as some natural force, and the finest thing in his play is the way his old companions fall out of it broken-hearted or on their way to the gallows; and instead of that lyricism which rose out of Richard's mind like the jet of a fountain to fall again where it had risen, instead of that phantasy too enfolded in its own sincerity to make any thought the hour had need of, Shakespeare has given him a resounding rhetoric that moves men, as a leading article does to-day. His purposes are so intelligible to everybody that everybody talks of him as if he succeeded, although he fails in the end, as all men great and little fail in Shakespeare, and yet his conquests abroad are made nothing by a woman turned warrior, and that boy he and Katherine were to 'compound,' 'half French, half English,' 'that' was to 'go to Constantinople and take the Turk by the beard,' turns out a Saint, and loses all his father had built up at home and his own life.

Shakespeare watched Henry V. not indeed as he watched the greater souls in the visionary procession, but cheerfully, as one watches some handsome spirited horse, and he spoke his tale, as he spoke all tales, with tragic irony.

—Walter Butler Yeats, from "At Stratford-on-Avon," 1901, *Ideas of Good and Evil*, 1903, pp. 152–64

Ambrose Bierce "The Ravages of Shakspearitis" (1903)

In this extract, American journalist, satirist, and short story writer Ambrose Bierce (1842–1914?) challenges what he sees as a diseased adulation of Shakespeare, arguing that Shakespeare, although he possessed an excess of riches, had little control over his material. Bierce is actually reviving the argument that goes back to Ben Jonson's remarks in *Timber* (1641), when he wished Shakespeare had edited his works more than he did, and to the neoclassical view that Shakespeare was a wild creator who lacked art.

[L]ooking into Mr. Arlo Bates's book, *Talks on Writing English*, . . . I find this passage quoted from [Francis] Jeffrey:

> Everything in him (Shakspeare) is in unmeasured abundance and unequaled perfection—but everything so balanced and kept in subordination as not to jostle or disturb or take the place of another. The most exquisite poetical conceptions, images and descriptions are given with such brevity and introduced with such skill as merely to adorn without loading the sense they accompany. All his excellences, like those of Nature herself, are thrown out together; and, instead of interfering with, support and recommend each other.

This is so fine as to be mostly false. It is true that Shakspeare throws out his excellences in unmeasured abundance and all together; and nothing else in this passage is true. His poetical conceptions, images and descriptions are not "given" at all; they are "turned loose." They came from his brain like a swarm of bees. They race out, as shouting children from a country school. They distract, stun, confuse. So disorderly an imagination has never itself been imagined. Shakspeare had no sense of proportion, no care for the strength of restraint, no art of saying just enough, no art of any kind. He flung about him his enormous and incalculable wealth of jewels with the prodigal profusion of a drunken youth mad with the lust of spending. Only the magnificence and value of the jewels could blind us to the barbarian method of distribution. They dazzle the mind and confound all the criteria of the judgment. Small wonder that the incomparable Voltaire, French, artistic in every fiber and trained in the severe dignities of Grecian art, called this lawless and irresponsible spendthrift a drunken savage.

Of no cultivated Frenchman is the judgment on Shakspeare much milder; the man's "art," his "precision," his "perfection"—these are creations of our Teutonic imaginations . . .

—Ambrose Bierce, "The Ravages of
Shakspearitis," 1903, *Collected Works*,
1911, volume 10, pp. 109–12

LYTTON STRACHEY
"SHAKESPEARE'S FINAL PERIOD" (1904)

Lytton Strachey (1880–1932), British critic and noted biographer of Victorian notables, argues that the perception of Shakespeare's last plays as serene indications of a spirit at peace with mankind and the world is narrow and mistaken.

The whole of the modern criticism of Shakespeare has been fundamentally affected by one important fact. The chronological order of the plays, for so long the object of the vaguest speculation, of random guesses, or at best of isolated 'points,' has been now discovered and reduced to a coherent law. It is no longer possible to suppose that *The Tempest* was written before *Romeo and Juliet*; that *Henry VI* was produced in succession to *Henry V*; or that *Antony and Cleopatra* followed close upon the heels of *Julius Caesar*. Such theories were sent to limbo for ever, when a study of those plays of whose date we have external evidence revealed the fact that, as Shakespeare's life advanced, a corresponding development took place in the metrical structure of his verse. The establishment of metrical tests, by which the approximate position and date of any play can be readily ascertained, at once followed; chaos gave way to order; and, for the first time, critics became able to judge, not only of the individual works, but of the whole succession of the works of Shakespeare.

Upon this firm foundation modern writers have been only too eager to build. It was apparent that the Plays, arranged in chronological order, showed something more than a mere development in the technique of verse—a development, that is to say, in the general treatment of characters and subjects, and in the sort of feelings which those characters and subjects were intended to arouse; and from this it was easy to draw conclusions as to the development of the mind of Shakespeare itself. Such conclusions have, in fact, been constantly drawn. But it must be noted that they all rest upon the tacit assumption, that the character of any given drama is, in feet, a true index to the state of mind of the dramatist composing it. The validity of this assumption has never been proved; it has never been shown, for instance, why we should suppose a writer of farces to be habitually merry; or whether we are really justified in concluding, from the fact that Shakespeare wrote nothing but tragedies for six years, that, during that period, more than at any other, he was deeply absorbed in the awful problems of human existence. It is not, however, the purpose of this essay to consider the question of what are the relations between the artist and his art; for it will assume the truth of the generally accepted view, that the character of the one can be inferred from that of the other. What it will attempt to discuss is whether, upon this hypothesis, the most important part of the ordinary doctrine of Shakespeare's mental development is justifiable.

What then, is the ordinary doctrine? Dr. [Frederick James] Furnivall [1825–1910, a co-founder and editor of the *Oxford English Dictionary* as well as the founder of several literary societies] states it as follows:

> Shakespeare's course is thus shown to have run from the amorousness and fun of youth, through the strong patriotism of early manhood, to the wrestlings with the dark problems that beset the man of middle age, to the gloom which weighed on Shakespeare (as on so many men) in later life, when, though outwardly successful, the world seemed all against him, and his mind dwelt with sympathy on scenes of faithlessness of friends, treachery of relations and subjects, ingratitude of children, scorn of his kind; till at last, in his Stratford home again, peace came to him, Miranda and Perdita in their lovely freshness and charm greeted him, and he was laid by his quiet Avon side.

And the same writer goes on to quote with approval Professor Dowden's

> likening of Shakespeare to a ship, beaten and storm-tossed, but yet entering harbour with sails full-set, to anchor in peace.

Such, in fact, is the general opinion of modern writers upon Shakespeare; after a happy youth and a gloomy middle age he reached at last—it is the universal opinion—a state of quiet serenity in which he died. Professor Dowden's book on *Shakespeare's Mind and Art* gives the most popular expression to this view, a view which is also held by Mr. [Bernhard Aegidius Konrad] ten Brink, by [English Shakespearean scholar] Sir I[srael] Gollancz, and, to a great extent, by [Danish scholar] Dr. [Georg Morris Cohen] Brandes. Professor Dowden, indeed, has gone so far as to label this final period with the appellation of 'On the Heights,' in opposition to the preceding one, which, he says, was passed 'In the Depths.' [Shakespearean biographer and editor of the plays] Sir Sidney Lee, too, seems to find, in the Plays at least, if not in Shakespeare's mind, the orthodox succession of gaiety, of tragedy, and of the serenity of meditative romance.

Now it is clear that the most important part of this version of Shakespeare's mental history is the end of it. That he did eventually attain to a state of calm content, that he did, in fact, die happy—it is this that gives colour and interest to the whole theory. For some reason or another, the end of a man's life seems naturally to afford the light by which the rest of it should be read; last thoughts do appear in some strange way to be really best and truest; and this is particularly the case when they fit in nicely with the rest of the story, and are, perhaps, just what one likes to think oneself. If it be true that Shakespeare, to quote Professor Dowden, 'did at last attain to the serene self-possession which he had sought with such persistent effort'; that, in the words of Dr. Furnivall, 'forgiven and forgiving, full of the highest wisdom and peace, at one with family and friends and foes, in harmony with Avon's flow and Stratford's level meads, Shakespeare closed his life on earth'—we have obtained a piece of knowledge which is both interesting and pleasant. But if it be not true, if, on the contrary, it can be shown that something very different was actually the case, then will it not follow that we must not only reverse our judgment as to this particular point, but also readjust our view of the whole drift and bearing of Shakespeare's 'inner life'?

The group of works which has given rise to this theory of ultimate serenity was probably entirely composed after Shakespeare's final retirement from London, and his establishment at New Place. It consists of three plays— Cymbeline, The Winter's Tale, and The Tempest—and three fragments—the Shakespearean parts of Pericles, Henry VIII, and The Two Noble Kinsmen. All these plays and portions of plays form a distinct group; they resemble each other in a multitude of ways, and they differ in a multitude of ways from nearly all Shakespeare's previous work.

One other complete play, however, and one other fragment, do resemble in some degree these works of the final period; for, immediately preceding them in date, they show clear traces of the beginnings of the new method, and they are themselves curiously different from the plays they immediately succeed—that great series of tragedies which began with Hamlet in 1601 and ended in 1608 with Antony and Cleopatra. In the latter year, indeed,

Shakespeare's entire method underwent an astonishing change. For six years he had been persistently occupied with a kind of writing which he had himself not only invented but brought to the highest point of excellence—the tragedy of character. Every one of his masterpieces has for its theme the action of tragic situation upon character; and, without those stupendous creations in character, his greatest tragedies would obviously have lost the precise thing that has made them what they are. Yet, after *Antony and Cleopatra* Shakespeare deliberately turned his back upon the dramatic methods of all his past career. There seems no reason why he should not have continued, year after year, to produce *Othellos, Hamlets,* and *Macbeths;* instead, he turned over a new leaf, and wrote *Coriolanus.*

Coriolanus is certainly a remarkable, and perhaps an intolerable play: remarkable, because it shows the sudden first appearance of the Shakespeare of the final period; intolerable, because it is impossible to forget how much better it might have been. The subject is thick with situations; the conflicts of patriotism and pride, the effects of sudden disgrace following upon the very height of fortune, the struggles between family affection on the one hand and every interest of revenge and egotism on the other—these would have made a tragic and tremendous setting for some character worthy to rank with Shakespeare's best. But it pleased him to ignore completely all these opportunities; and, in the play he has given us, the situations, mutilated and degraded, serve merely as miserable props for the gorgeous clothing of his rhetoric. For rhetoric, enormously magnificent and extraordinarily elaborate, is the beginning and the middle and the end of *Coriolanus.* The hero is not a human being at all; he is the statue of a demi-god cast in bronze, which roars its perfect periods, to use a phrase of Sir Walter Raleigh's, through a melodious megaphone. The vigour of the presentment is, it is true, amazing; but it is a presentment of decoration, not of life. So far and so quickly had Shakespeare already wandered from the subtleties of *Cleopatra.* The transformation is indeed astonishing; one wonders, as one beholds it, what will happen next.

At about the same time, some of the scenes in *Timon of Athens* were in all probability composed: scenes which resemble *Coriolanus* in their lack of characterisation and abundance of rhetoric, but differ from it in the peculiar grossness of their tone. For sheer virulence of foul-mouthed abuse, some of the speeches in Timon are probably unsurpassed in any literature; an outraged drayman would speak so, if draymen were in the habit of talking poetry. From this whirlwind of furious ejaculation, this splendid storm of nastiness, Shakespeare, we are confidently told, passed in a moment to tranquility and joy, to blue skies, to young ladies, and to general forgiveness.

From 1604 to 1610 [says Professor Dowden] a show of tragic figures, like the kings who pass before Macbeth, filled the vision of Shakespeare; until at last the desperate image of Timon rose before him; when, as though unable to endure or to conceive a more lamentable ruin of man, he turned for relief to the pastoral loves of Prince Florizel and Perdita; and as soon as the tone of his mind was restored, gave expression to its ultimate mood of grave serenity in *The Tempest*, and so ended.

This is a pretty picture, but is it true? It may, indeed, be admitted at once that Prince Florizel and Perdita are charming creatures, that Prospero is 'grave,' and that Hermione is more or less 'serene'; but why is it that, in our consideration of the later plays, the whole of our attention must always be fixed upon these particular characters? Modern critics, in their eagerness to appraise everything that is beautiful and good at its proper value, seem to have entirely forgotten that there is another side to the medal; and they have omitted to point out that these plays contain a series of portraits of peculiar infamy, whose wickedness finds expression in language of extraordinary force. Coming fresh from their pages to the pages of *Cymbeline, The Winter's Tale,* and *The Tempest,* one is astonished and perplexed. How is it possible to fit into their scheme of roses and maidens that 'Italian fiend' the 'yellow Iachimo,' or Cloten, that 'thing too bad for bad report,' or the 'crafty devil,' his mother, [in *Cymbeline*] or Leontes [in *The Winter's Tale*], or Caliban, or Trinculo [in *The Tempest*]? To omit these figures of discord and evil from our consideration, to banish them comfortably to the background of the stage, while Autolycus [in *The Winter's Tale*] and Miranda [in *The Tempest*] dance before the footlights, is surely a fallacy in proportion; for the presentment of the one group of persons is every whit as distinct and vigorous as that of the other. Nowhere, indeed, is Shakespeare's violence of expression more constantly displayed than in the 'gentle utterances' of his last period; it is here that one finds Paulina [in *The Winter's Tale*], in a torrent of indignation as far from 'grave serenity' as it is from 'pastoral love,' exclaiming to Leontes:

What studied torments, tyrant, hast for me?
What wheels? racks? fires? what flaying? boiling
In leads or oils? what old or newer torture
Must I receive, whose every word deserves
To taste of thy most worst? Thy tyranny,
Together working with thy jealousies,

Fancies too weak for boys, too green and idle
For girls of nine, O! think what they have done,
And then run mad indeed, stark mad; for all
Thy by-gone fooleries were but spices of it.
That thou betray'dst Polixenes, 'twas nothing;
That did but show thee, of a fool, inconstant
And damnable ingrateful; nor was't much
Thou would'st have poison'd good Camillo's honour,
To have him kill a king; poor trespasses,
More monstrous standing by; whereof I reckon
The casting forth to crows thy baby daughter
To be or none or little; though a devil
Would have shed water out of fire ere done't.
Nor is't directly laid to thee, the death
Of the young prince, whose honourable thoughts,
Thoughts high for one so tender, cleft the heart
That could conceive a gross and foolish sire
Blemished his gracious dam.
[III.ii.173–96]

Nowhere are the poet's metaphors more nakedly material; nowhere does he verge more often upon a sort of brutality of phrase, a cruel coarseness. Iachimo tells us how:

The cloyed will,
That satiate yet unsatisfied desire, that tub
Both filled and running, ravening first the lamb,
Longs after for the garbage.
[I.vi.46–49]

and talks of:

an eye
Base and unlustrous as the smoky light
That's fed with stinking tallow.
[I.vi.108–10]

'The south fog rot him!' Cloten burst out to Imogen [at II.iii.133], cursing her husband in an access of hideous rage.

What traces do such passages as these show of 'serene self-possession,' of 'the highest wisdom and peace,' or of 'meditative romance'? English critics, overcome by the idea of Shakespeare's ultimate tranquillity, have generally denied to him the authorship of the brothel scenes in *Pericles;* but these scenes are entirely of a piece with the grossness of *The Winter's Tale* and *Cymbeline.*

> Is there no way for men to be, but women
> Must be half-workers?

says Posthumus when he hears of Imogen's guilt.

>   We are all bastards;
> And that most venerable man, which I
> Did call my father, was I know not where
> When I was stamped. Some coiner with his tools
> Made me a counterfeit; yet my mother seemed
> The Dian of that time; so doth my wife
> The nonpareil of this—O vengeance, vengeance!
> Me of my lawful pleasure she restrained
> And prayed me, oft, forbearance; did it with
> A pudency so rosy, the sweet view on't
> Might well have warmed old Saturn, that I thought
>   her
> As chaste as unsunned snow—O, all the devils!—
> This yellow Iachimo, in an hour,—was't not?
> Or less,—at first: perchance he spoke not; but,
> Like a full-acorned boar, a German one,
> Cried, oh! and mounted: found no opposition
> But what he looked for should oppose, and she
> Should from encounter guard.
>   [II.v.1–19]

And Leontes [in *The Winter's Tale*], in a similar situation, expresses himself in images no less to the point. . . .

It is really a little difficult, in the face of such passages, to agree with Professor Dowden's dictum: 'In these latest plays the beautiful pathetic light is always present.'

But how has it happened that the judgment of so many critics has been so completely led astray? Charm and gravity, and even serenity, are to be found in many other plays of Shakespeare. Ophelia is charming, Brutus is grave, Cordelia is serene; are we then to suppose that *Hamlet,* and *Julius Caesar,* and *King Lear* give expression to the same mood of high tranquillity which is betrayed by *Cymbeline, The Tempest,* and *The Winter's Tale?* 'Certainly not,' reply the orthodox writers, 'for you must distinguish. The plays of the last period are not tragedies; they all end happily'—'in scenes,' says Sir. I. Gollancz, 'of forgiveness, reconciliation, and peace.' Virtue, in fact, is not only virtuous, it is triumphant; what would you more?

But to this it may be retorted, that, in the case of one of Shakespeare's plays, even the final vision of virtue and beauty triumphant over ugliness and vice fails to dispel a total effect of horror and of gloom. For, in *Measure for Measure* Isabella is no whit less pure and lovely than any Perdita or Miranda, and her success is as complete; yet who would venture to deny that the atmosphere of *Measure for Measure* was more nearly one of despair than of serenity? What is it, then, that makes the difference? Why should a happy ending seem in one case futile, and in another satisfactory? Why does it sometimes matter to us a great deal, and sometimes not at all, whether virtue is rewarded or not?

The reason, in this case, is not far to seek. *Measure for Measure* is, like nearly every play of Shakespeare's before *Coriolanus,* essentially realistic. The characters are real men and women; and what happens to them upon the stage has all the effect of what happens to real men and women in actual life. Their goodness appears to be real goodness, their wickedness real wickedness; and, if their sufferings are terrible enough, we regret the fact, even though in the end they triumph, just as we regret the real sufferings of our friends. But, in the plays of the final period, all this has changed; we are no longer in the real world, but in a world of enchantment, of mystery, of wonder, a world of shifting visions; a world of hopeless anachronisms, a world in which anything may happen next. The pretences of reality are indeed usually preserved, but only the pretences. Cymbeline is supposed to be the king of a real Britain, and the real Augustus is supposed to demand tribute of him. . . .

[S]trangely remote is the world of Shakespeare's latest period; and it is peopled, this universe of his invention, with beings equally unreal, with creatures either more or less than human, with fortunate princes and wicked step-mothers, with goblins and spirits, with lost princesses and insufferable kings. And of course, in this sort of fairy land, it is an essential condition that everything shall end well; the prince and princess are bound to marry and live happily ever afterwards, or the whole story is unnecessary and absurd; and the villains and the goblins must naturally repent and be forgiven. But it is clear that such happy endings, such conventional closes to fantastic tales, cannot be taken as evidences of serene tranquillity on the part of their maker; they merely show that he knew, as well as anyone else, how such stories ought to end.

Yet there can be no doubt that it is this combination of charming heroines and happy endings which has blinded the eyes of modern critics to everything else. Iachimo, and Leontes, and even Caliban, are to be left out of account, as if, because in the end they repent or are forgiven, words need not be wasted on such reconciled and harmonious fiends. It is true they are grotesque; it is true that such personages never could have lived; but who, one would like to know, has ever met [*The Tempest*'s] Miranda, or become acquainted with [*The Winter's Tale*'s] Prince Florizel of Bohemia? In this land of faery, is it right to neglect the goblins? In this world of dreams, are we justified in ignoring the nightmares? Is it fair to say that Shakespeare was in 'a gentle, lofty spirit, a peaceful, tranquil mood,' when he was creating the Queen in *Cymbeline,* or writing the first two acts of *The Winter's Tale?*

Attention has never been sufficiently drawn to one other characteristic of these plays, though it is touched upon both by Professor Dowden and Dr. Brandes—the singular carelessness with which great parts of them were obviously written. Could anything drag more wretchedly than the *denouement* of *Cymbeline?* And with what perversity is the great pastoral scene in *The Winter's Tale* interspersed with long-winded intrigues, and disguises, and homilies! For these blemishes are unlike the blemishes which enrich rather than lessen the beauty of the earlier plays; they are not, like them, interesting or delightful in themselves; they are usually merely necessary to explain the action, and they are sometimes purely irrelevant. One is, it cannot be denied, often bored, and occasionally irritated, by Polixenes and Camillo [in *The Winter's Tale*] and Sebastian and Gonzalo [in *The Tempest*] and Belarius [in *Cymbeline*]; these personages have not even the life of ghosts; they are hardly more than speaking names, that give patient utterance to involution upon involution. What a contrast to the minor characters of Shakespeare's earlier works!

It is difficult to resist the conclusion that he was getting bored himself. Bored with people, bored with real life, bored with drama, bored, in fact, with everything except poetry and poetical dreams. He is no longer interested, one often feels, in what happens, or who says what, so long as he can find place for a faultless lyric, or a new, unimagined rhythmical effect, or a grand and mystic speech. In this mood he must have written his share in *The Two Noble Kinsmen,* leaving the plot and characters to Fletcher to deal with as he pleased, and reserving to himself only the opportunities for pompous verse. In this mood he must have broken off halfway through the tedious history of *Henry VIII;* and in this mood he must have completed, with all the resources of his rhetoric, the miserable archaic fragment of *Pericles.*

Is it not thus, then, that we should imagine him in the last years of his life? Half enchanted by visions of beauty and loveliness, and half bored to death;

on the one side inspired by a soaring fancy to the singing of ethereal songs, and on the other urged by a general disgust to burst occasionally through his torpor into bitter and violent speech? If we are to learn anything of his mind from his last works, it is surely this.

And such is the conclusion which is particularly forced upon us by a consideration of the play which is in many ways most typical of Shakespeare's later work, and the one which critics most consistently point to as containing the very essence of his final benignity—*The Tempest.* There can be no doubt that the peculiar characteristics which distinguish *Cymbeline* and *The Winter's Tale* from the dramas of Shakespeare's prime, are present here in a still greater degree. In *The Tempest,* unreality has reached its apotheosis. Two of the principal characters are frankly not human beings at all; and the whole action passes, through a series of impossible occurrences, in a place which can only by courtesy be said to exist. The Enchanted Island, indeed, peopled, for a timeless moment, by this strange fantastic medley of persons and of things, has been cut adrift for ever from common sense, and floats buoyed up by a sea, not of waters, but of poetry. Never did Shakespeare's magnificence of diction reach more marvellous heights than in some of the speeches of Prospero, or his lyric art a purer beauty than in the songs of Ariel; nor is it only in these ethereal regions that the triumph of his language asserts itself. It finds as splendid a vent in the curses of Caliban ... The *denouement* itself, brought about by a preposterous piece of machinery, and lost in a whirl of rhetoric, is hardly more than a peg for fine writing. . . .

A comparison naturally suggests itself, between what was perhaps the last of Shakespeare's completed works, and that early drama which first gave undoubted proof that his imagination had taken wings. The points of resemblance between *The Tempest* and *A Midsummer Night's Dream,* their common atmosphere of romance and magic, the beautiful absurdities of their intrigues, their studied contrasts of the grotesque with the delicate, the ethereal with the earthly, the charm of their lyrics, the *verve* of the vulgar comedy—these, of course, are obvious enough; but it is the points of difference which really make the comparison striking. One thing, at any rate, is certain about the wood near Athens—it is full of life. The persons that haunt it—though most of them are hardly more than children, and some of them are fairies, and all of them are too agreeable to be true—are nevertheless substantial creatures, whose loves and jokes and quarrels receive our thorough sympathy; and the air they breathe—the lords and the ladies, no less than the mechanics and the elves—is instinct with an exquisite good-humour, which makes us as happy as the night is long. To turn from Theseus and Titania and Bottom to the Enchanted Island, is to step out of a country lane into a conservatory. The roses and the dandelions have vanished before preposterous cactuses, and fascinating orchids too delicate for the open air; and, in the artificial atmosphere, the gaiety of youth has been replaced by the disillusionment of middle age. Prospero is the central figure of *The Tempest*; and it has often been wildly asserted that he is a portrait of the author—an embodiment of that spirit of wise benevolence which is supposed to have thrown a halo over Shakespeare's later life. But, on closer inspection, the portrait seems to be as imaginary as the original. To an irreverent eye, [Prospero,] the ex-Duke of Milan would perhaps appear as an unpleasantly crusty personage, in whom a twelve years' monopoly of the conversation had developed an inordinate propensity for talking. These may have been the sentiments of Ariel, safe at the Bermoothes; but to state them is to risk at least ten years in the knotty entrails of an oak, and it is sufficient to point out, that if Prospero is wise, he is also self-opinionated and sour, that his gravity is often another name for pedantic severity, and that there is no character in the play to whom, during some part of it, he is not studiously disagreeable. But his Milanese countrymen are not even disagreeable; they are simply dull. 'This is the silliest stuff that e'er I heard,' remarked Hippolyta of Bottom's amateur theatricals [in *A Midsummer Night's Dream*]; and one is tempted to wonder what she would have said to the dreary puns and interminable conspiracies of Alonzo, and Gonzalo, and Sebastian, and Antonio, and Adrian, and Francisco, and other shipwrecked noblemen. At all events, there can be little doubt that they would not have had the entree at Athens.

The depth of the gulf between the two plays is, however, best measured by a comparison of Caliban and his masters with Bottom and his companions. The guileless group of English mechanics, whose sports are interrupted by the mischief of Puck, offers a strange contrast to the hideous trio of the 'jester,' the 'drunken butler,' and the 'savage and deformed slave,' whose designs are thwarted by the magic of Ariel. Bottom was the first of Shakespeare's masterpieces in characterisation, Caliban was the last: and what a world of bitterness and horror lies between them! The charming coxcomb it is easy to know and love; but the 'freckled whelp hag-born' moves us mysteriously to pity and to terror, eluding us for ever in fearful allegories, and strange coils of disgusted laughter and phantasmagorical tears. The physical vigour of the presentment is often so remorseless as to shock us. . . .

You taught me language, and my profit on't
Is, I know how to curse.

[I.ii.363–64]

Is this Caliban addressing Prospero, or Job addressing God? It may be either; but it is not serene, nor benign, nor pastoral, nor 'On the Heights.'

—Lytton Strachey, "Shakespeare's Final Period,"
1904, *Literary Essays*, 1949, pp. 1–15

LEO TOLSTOY (1906)

The great Russian novelist Leo Nikolayevich Tolstoy (1828–1910), whose novels *War and Peace* and *Anna Karenina* place him in the pantheon of the world's enduring writers, in his later years was impelled by a doctrine of utopian anarchism and Christian asceticism to devote himself to social, moral, economic, and spiritual reform. He then renounced his own masterworks and all art and pursuits that did not seem to embody the moral and religious values he held to be essential to mankind's proper calling—earthly virtue—defined by service and renunciation and seen as preparation for death. In this essay, he expresses a profound distaste for Shakespeare's work because of what he considered to be its depravity and its inability to lead men and women to the proper religious attitudes and conduct he thought essential for a world governed by a humanity that expresses divinity. George Orwell, the English essayist and author of *1984* and *Animal Farm*, in his 1947 rebuttal "Lear, Tolstoy, and the Fool," argues that, ironically, Tolstoy's last days were presaged in *King Lear* and observes that Tolstoy's character, his break with his family, his flight from his home, and his death are eerily similar to Lear's.

An artistic, poetic work, particularly a drama, must first of all excite in the reader or spectator the illusion that whatever the person represented is living through, or experiencing, is lived through or experienced by himself. For this purpose it is as important for the dramatist to know precisely what he should make his characters both do and say as what he should not make them say and do, so as not to destroy the illusion of the reader or spectator. Speeches, however eloquent and profound they may be, when put into the mouth of dramatic characters, if they be superfluous, or unnatural to the position and character, destroy the chief condition of dramatic art—the illusion, owing to which the reader or spectator lives in the feelings of the persons represented. Without putting an end to the illusion, one may leave much unsaid—the reader or spectator will himself fill this up, and sometimes, owing to this, his illusion is even increased, but to say what is superfluous is the same as to overthrow a statue composed of separate pieces and thereby scatter them, or to take away the lamp from a magic lantern: the attention of the reader or spectator is distracted, the reader sees the author, the spectator sees the actor, the illusion disappears, and to restore it is sometimes impossible; therefore without the feeling of measure there can not be an artist, and especially a dramatist.

Shakespeare is devoid of this feeling. His characters continually do and say what is not only unnatural to them, but utterly unnecessary. I do not cite examples of this, because I believe that he who does not himself see this striking deficiency in all Shakespeare's dramas will not be persuaded by any examples and proofs. It is sufficient to read *King Lear,* alone, with its insanity, murders, plucking out of eyes, Gloucester's jump, its poisonings, and wranglings—not to mention *Pericles, Cymbeline, The Winter's Tale, The Tempest*—to be convinced of this. Only a man devoid of the sense of measure and taste could produce such types as *Titus Andronicus* or *Troilus and Cressida,* or so mercilessly mutilate the old drama *King Leir.*

Gervinus endeavors to prove that Shakespeare possessed the feeling of beauty, "Schonheit's sinn," but all Gervinus's proofs prove only that he himself, Gervinus, is completely destitute of it. In Shakespeare everything is exaggerated: the actions are exaggerated, so are their consequences, the speeches of the characters are exaggerated, and therefore at every step the possibility of artistic impression is interfered with. Whatever people may say, however they may be enraptured by Shakespeare's works, whatever merits they may attribute to them, it is perfectly certain that he was not an artist and that his works are not artistic productions. Without the sense of measure, there never was nor can be an artist, as without the feeling of rhythm there can not be a musician. Shakespeare might have been whatever you like, but he was not an artist.

"But one should not forget the time at which Shakespeare wrote," say his admirers. "It was a time of cruel and coarse habits, a time of the then fashionable euphemism, *i.e.,* artificial way of expressing oneself—a time of forms of life strange to us, and therefore, to judge about Shakespeare, one should have in view the time when he wrote. In Homer, as in Shakespeare, there is much which is strange to us, but this does not prevent us from appreciating the beauties of Homer," say these admirers. But in comparing Shakespeare with Homer, as does Gervinus, that infinite distance which separates true poetry from its semblance manifests itself with especial force. However distant Homer is from us, we can, without the slightest effort, transport ourselves into the life he describes, and we can thus transport ourselves because, however alien to us may be the events Homer describes, he believes in what he says and speaks seriously, and therefore he never exaggerates, and the sense of measure never abandons him. This is the reason why, not to speak of the wonderfully distinct, lifelike, and beautiful characters of Achilles, Hector, Priam, Odysseus, and the eternally touching scenes of Hector's leave-taking, of Priam's embassy, of Odysseus's return, and others—the whole of the *Iliad* and still more the *Odyssey* are so humanly near to us that we feel as if we ourselves had lived, and are living, among its gods and heroes. Not so with Shakespeare. From his first words, exaggeration is seen: the exaggeration of events, the exaggeration of emotion, and the exaggeration of effects. One sees at once that he does not believe in what he says, that it is of no necessity to him, that he invents the events he describes, and is indifferent to his characters—that he has conceived them only for the stage and therefore makes them do and say only what may strike his public; and therefore we do not believe either in the events, or in the actions, or in the sufferings of the characters. Nothing demonstrates so clearly the complete absence of esthetic feeling in Shakespeare as comparison between him and Homer. The works which we call the works of Homer are artistic, poetic, original works, lived through by the author or authors; whereas the works of Shakespeare—borrowed as they are, and, externally, like mosaics, artificially fitted together piecemeal from bits invented for the occasion—have nothing whatever in common with art and poetry.

VIII

At the beginning of the last century, when Goethe was dictator of philosophic thought and esthetic laws, a series of casual circumstances made him praise Shakespeare. The esthetic critics caught up this praise and took to writing their lengthy, misty, learned articles, and the great European public began to be enchanted with Shakespeare. The critics, answering to the popular interest, and endeavoring to compete with one another, wrote new and ever new essays about Shakespeare; the readers and spectators on their side were increasingly confirmed in their admiration, and Shakespeare's fame, like a lump of snow, kept growing and growing, until in our time it has attained that insane worship which obviously has no other foundation than "suggestion."

Shakespeare finds no rival, not even approximately, either among the old or the new writers. Here are some of the tributes paid to him.

"Poetic truth is the brightest flower in the crown of Shakespeare's merits;" "Shakespeare is the greatest moralist of all times;" "Shakespeare exhibits such many-sidedness and such objectivism that they carry him beyond the limits of time and nationality;" "Shakespeare is the greatest genius that has hitherto existed;" "For the creation of tragedy, comedy, history, idyll, idyllistic comedy, esthetic idyll, for the profoundest presentation, or for any casually thrown off, passing piece of verse, he is the only man. He not only wields an unlimited power over our mirth and our tears, over all the workings of passion, humor, thought, and observation, but he possesses also an infinite region full of the phantasy of fiction, of a horrifying and an amusing character. He possesses penetration both in the world of fiction and of reality, and above this reigns one and the same truthfulness to character and to nature, and the same spirit of humanity;" "To Shakespeare the epithet of Great comes of itself; and if one adds that independently of his greatness he has, further, become the reformer of all literature, and, moreover, has in his works not only expressed the phenomenon of life as it was in his day, but also, by the genius of thought which floated in the air has prophetically forestalled the direction that the social spirit was going to take in the future (of which we see a striking example in Hamlet),—one may, without hesitation, say that Shakespeare was not only a great poet, but the greatest of all poets who ever existed, and that in the sphere of poetic creation his only worthy rival was that same life which in his works he expressed to such perfection."

The obvious exaggeration of this estimate proves more conclusively than anything that it is the consequence, not of common sense, but of suggestion. The more trivial, the lower, the emptier a phenomenon is, if only it has become the subject of suggestion, the more supernatural and exaggerated is the significance attributed to it. The Pope is not merely saintly, but most saintly, and so forth. So Shakespeare is not merely a good writer, but the greatest genius, the eternal teacher of mankind.

Suggestion is always a deceit, and every deceit is an evil. In truth, the suggestion that Shakespeare's works are great works of genius, presenting the height of both esthetic and ethical perfection, has caused, and is causing, great injury to men.

This injury is twofold: first, the fall of the drama, and the replacement of this important weapon of progress by an empty and immoral amusement; and secondly, the direct depravation of men by presenting to them false models for imitation.

Human life is perfected only through the development of the religious consciousness, the only element which permanently unites men. The development of the religious consciousness of men is accomplished through all the sides of man's spiritual activity. One direction of this activity is in art. One section of art, perhaps the most influential, is the drama.

Therefore the drama, in order to deserve the importance attributed to it, should serve the development of religious consciousness. Such has the drama always been, and such it was in the Christian world. But upon the appearance of Protestantism in its broader sense, i.e., the appearance of a new understanding of Christianity as of a teaching of life, the dramatic art did not find a form corresponding to the new understanding of Christianity, and the men of the Renaissance were carried away by the imitation of classical art. This was most natural, but the tendency was bound to pass, and art had to discover, as indeed it is now beginning to do, its new form corresponding to the change in the understanding of Christianity.

But the discovery of this new form was arrested by the teaching arising among German writers at the end of the eighteenth and beginning of the nineteenth centuries—as to so-called objective art, *i.e.,* art indifferent to good or evil—and therein the exaggerated praise of Shakespeare's dramas, which partly corresponded to the esthetic teaching of the Germans, and partly served as material for it. If there had not been exaggerated praise of Shakespeare's dramas, presenting them as the most perfect models, the men of the eighteenth and nineteenth centuries would have had to understand that the drama, to have a right to exist and to be a serious thing, must serve, as it always has served and can not but do otherwise, the development of the religious consciousness. And having understood this, they would have searched for a new form of drama corresponding to their religious understanding.

But when it was decided that the height of perfection was Shakespeare's drama, and that we ought to write as he did, not only without any religious, but even without any moral, significance, then all writers of dramas in imitation of him began to compose such empty pieces as are those of Goethe, Schiller, Hugo, and, in Russia, of Pushkin, or the chronicles of Ostrovski, Alexis Tolstoy, and an innumerable number of other more or less celebrated dramatic productions which fill all the theaters, and can be prepared wholesale by any one who happens to have the idea or desire to write a play. It is only thanks to such a low, trivial understanding of the significance of the drama that there appears among us that infinite quality of dramatic works describing men's actions, positions, characters, and frames of mind, not only void of any spiritual substance, but often of any human sense.

Let not the reader think that I exclude from this estimate of contemporary drama the theatrical pieces I have myself incidentally written. I recognize them, as well as all the rest, as not having that religious character which must form the foundation of the drama of the future.

The drama, then, the most important branch of art, has, in our time, become the trivial and immoral amusement of a trivial and immoral crowd. The worst of it is, moreover, that to dramatic art, fallen as low as it is possible to fall, is still attributed an elevated significance no longer appropriate to it. Dramatists, actors, theatrical managers, and the press—this last publishing in the most serious tone reports of theaters and operas—and the rest, are all perfectly certain that they are doing something very worthy and important.

The drama in our time is a great man fallen, who has reached the last degree of his degradation, and at the same time continues to pride himself on his past of which nothing now remains. The public of our time is like those who mercilessly amuse themselves over this man once so great and now in the lowest stage of his fall.

Such is one of the mischievous effects of the epidemic suggestion about the greatness of Shakespeare. Another deplorable result of this worship is the presentation to men of a false model for imitation. If people wrote of Shakespeare that for his time he was a good writer, that he had a fairly good turn for verse, was an intelligent actor and good stage manager—even were this appreciation incorrect and somewhat exaggerated—if only it were moderately true, people of the rising generation might remain free from Shakespeare's influence. But when every young man entering into life in our time has presented to him, as the model of moral perfection, not the religious and moral teachers of mankind, but first of all Shakespeare, concerning whom it has been decided and is handed down by learned men from generation to generation, as an incontestable truth, that he was the greatest poet, the greatest teacher of life, the young man can not remain free from this pernicious influence. When he is reading or listening to Shakespeare the question for him is no longer whether Shakespeare be good or bad, but only: In what consists that extraordinary beauty, both esthetic and ethical, of which he has been assured by learned men whom he respects, and which he himself neither sees nor feels? And constraining himself, and distorting his esthetic and ethical feeling, he tries to conform to the ruling opinion. He no longer believes in himself, but in what is said by the learned people whom he respects. I have experienced all this. Then reading critical examinations of the dramas and extracts from books with explanatory comments, he begins to imagine that he feels something of the nature of an artistic impression. The longer this continues, the more does his esthetical and ethical feeling become distorted. He ceases to distinguish directly and clearly what is artistic from an artificial imitation of art. But, above all, having assimilated the immoral view of life which penetrates all Shakespeare's writings, he loses the capacity of distinguishing good from evil. And the error of extolling an insignificant, inartistic writer—not only not moral, but directly immoral—executes its destructive work.

This is why I think that the sooner people free themselves from the false glorification of Shakespeare, the better it will be.

First, having freed themselves from this deceit, men will come to understand that the drama which has no religious element at its foundation is not only not an important and good thing, as it is now supposed to be, but the most trivial and despicable of things. Having understood this, they will have to search for, and work out, a new form of modern drama, a drama which will serve as the development and confirmation of the highest stage of religious consciousness in men.

Secondly, having freed themselves from this hypnotic state, men will understand that the trivial and immoral works of Shakespeare and his imitators, aiming merely at the recreation and amusement of the spectators, can not possibly represent the teaching of life, and that, while there is no true religious drama, the teaching of life should be sought for in other sources.

—Leo Tolstoy, from *On Shakespeare,*
translated by V. Tchertkoff and I. F.
M., 1906, pp. 78–82, 115–124

GEORGE EDWARD WOODBERRY
"SHAKSPERE" (1907)

George Edward Woodberry (1855–1930), American literary critic, editor, and poet, traces the development of Shakespeare's style, seeing a movement from lyricism to action to the activity of mind as figured in the play of wit and intellect. He sees in Shakespeare's work the "victory of dramatic over purely poetic diction," and considers that to be a "victory of action over illusion." Turning from action to character, Woodberry argues that the model personality that pervades Shakespeare's work is the aristocratic personality, whose roots are in the Italian Renaissance, and that such a personality is defined by the play of individual power in the human encounter with the world and experience.

Action is the core of the drama; it is what gives attractive and arresting power to the word "dramatic," focuses the attention, makes the eye look and the spirit expect at the fall of those syllables. To Shakspere, in his youth, immersed and absorbed in the dramatic movement that made a captive servant of him, mind, moods, energy, ambition, hope—that overmastered him with what was to be his fate therein, life was the object of his thoughts, but life primarily as a story. The story of life was there before him in the old plays on the stage, in the books he read, in the tales he thumbed over; at first a story of English Kings and Italian lovers, of the convulsions of state, heart-break and the words of clowns, comic confusions, tragic discords, enchanted woodlands.

He found the chronicle plays in vogue, fragments of history; and here and there, beginning his art, he re-established a scene, heightened a dialogue, concentrated a passion of anger or pity; it was piecemeal work by which he came to the power at last of defining a plot, a play of his own, an interpretation and representation of the story in a way of his own. The material he used was external, given to him, persons and incidents; he did not invent them, he found them; and his manipulation of them at first was, naturally, mainly in the language, the verbal investiture of person, act, scene, that part of the work which was most flexible, most plastic, readiest for a youthful hand and most tempting for lips that had suddenly unlocked a flood of such poesy, eloquence and passion in speech, colours of nature and the heart, as had never before poured from an English fount. It is this flow of language, vehement or smooth or impassioned, reflecting natural beauty of personal graces, prone to pathos and sentiment, rhetorical, dragging along with it all the affectations of the hour, experimenting with its own powers, intoxicated with its own poetry, exuberant with its own life—it is this marvellously musical, facile, intellectual power of language, this mastery that is not merely verbal, but is of the essence of expression, poetic not purely dramatic—it is this that in the earlier works plays over the story, atmospheres it, inhabits it, and in its surplus of light, feeling and imagery, in its lyrical effusion, overflows without submerging the dramatic interest, threatens the eminence of the action. From *Love's Labour's Lost* to *A Midsummer Night's Dream*, this lyrical obsession mounts prevailing; thereafter it recedes—the tints of the morning, the bloom of spring, the hour of the bloom of life had passed. Shakspere, loosing the passion of language to the full as never English poet did, had not lost his foothold on the reality of life, on the story, the drama, the action; and, deepening in his dramatic faculty he came, in the end, to that subtile mastery of language which belongs only to the greatest genius, lords of the brief and broken phrase. Four words created light; and something of that same miracle lingers in the power of the poet who is truly divine. The gradual victory of dramatic over purely poetic diction in Shakspere reflects the victory of life itself, of the action over the illusion of life, in him.

There was a second rivalry with the dramatic instinct in Shakspere besides this of the lyrical impulse. It lay in the intellectual temptation, the power of the naked thought. What is technically called the sentiment, that is, the wise saying, the axiomatic verse in which the reflecting mind is condensed with a purely intellectual value, was an inheritance of the drama from old time; and Shakspere, particularly in his middle life, was apt at linking such counsels together or in developing them from the dialogue. It is an analogous faculty that he employs in those wit-combats of the characters that are pre-eminently intellectual in tone. The wit of Rosalind and Beatrice is more closely united to the dialogue; but in the passages of advice, from Biron's gentle sermon on love to the sage wisdom of Polonius and Ulysses, and even on to Prospero's great farewell there is a recurring interruption of the action in play after play, due to the emergence of thought in control of the scene; and as Shakspere's lyricism give to the plays that atmosphere which isolates them among the works of dramatic genius and sets them apart in an unapproached realm of creative art, so his wisdom gives to them that intellectual dilatation by which they excel all others in majesty of mind. Other dramatists have represented life with equal impressiveness in its being, but none have represented life so conscious of its own significance. Here again, as in his lyrical moment, Shakspere in his intellectual moment seems to depart from the story, the drama, the action, but he does not really depart, or if he does so it is only to bring back to the drama the offerings of all the Muses. And in a third tributary element of the drama, in the spectacle, while he uses the embellishment of the scene to the full measure of what his times allowed, he introduces the masque as an adjunct, like a song or a dance, harmonious with the scene but not an essential of the action. These three things, then, diction, sentiment and spectacle, which were the open temptation to woo him from the essential dramatic point of view, the action, he either overcame or successfully subdued them to the enrichment and enlargement of the action; the main drift of his art, the main purpose of his mind were the same, with whatever slackening or bending of the current, toward the story of life pre-eminently, toward character and event, toward reality in its most human form. Beginning with the more intractable material of history, he came to use preferably romantic story in which his imagination was more free in creative power; and in the end, to such a height did this power reach that he seemed to create not only character and event, but also the world in which they had their being; to such a complete victory did his dramatic instinct, prevailing over all other impulses, carry him who always remained at heart a dramatist.

Shakspere was so completely a dramatist, interested in the action of life, that when he took the autobiographical mask in the Sonnets he seems transformed into his opposite, into the lyrical poet unlocking his own heart; here, it has been believed, he told his dearest secrets, his intimacies, the most sweet and bitter disgraces of his days and nights, his springs and autumns; and so inspired is the dramatic action of his mind in this play in the forms of the sonnet, if it be such, that it is only by an effort of detachment, by reflection and judgment, that one sees there only the working of that supreme faculty under the appearances of personality. The secret of the Sonnets has been so many times discovered, and escaped in the discovery, that this view, now best supported, may justly have its lease of life in turn, and the physical basis of fact on which the poet's imagination worked—such strands and suggestions of actuality as he used in the romances—may be found in Southampton's personality; but the black lady, the dear, disloyal friend, the rival poet will still wear in their faces, have in their form and moving, an insoluble mystery, because, whatever the drama, they move in a cloud of lyricism, intense with tenderness, sorrow, unavailing cries, that here all seems the form and substance of the soul itself. A dramatist who makes his own soul the scene of the drama, using the forms of personality, must necessarily leave a mysterious work; but in the Sonnets what is plain is the drama, what is obscure is only the basis of the drama, whether it be fact or convention, or mingled of both; whatever be the personal element, it is conceived, handled, developed dramatically, its truth is at bottom dramatic truth.

And if it be difficult to trace Shakspere's personality with any assured steps in the Sonnets, how much less is it to be probed in the plays proper! Those attempts that have been made to correlate the bare facts of his history with the sequence of his works, to synchronize his life-moods with the comedies and the tragedies, to make the plays render up the spiritual states of the man in his personal being, are ingenious; but the conditions of production, when Elizabeth might ask any day for a *Merry Wives of Windsor*, or some noble family desire a hymeneal spectacle like *A Midsummer Night's Dream*, or James be pleased with a Scotch theme, or the public itself, little indulgent to the moods of those who provide entertainment, might have to be recaptured to the play—such conditions are little favourable to "periods" of the private soul. . . . Shakspere was a dramatist by nature as well as by profession, or he became subdued to what he worked in; he was the servant of the public; and, much more, he was fascinated by life in its externality, life as it was in other men, other times, other places; he was insatiate in informing himself of its story in history, in novels and romances, in ancient and modern authors, wherever it was to be found. He was not that egotist who writes himself large and calls that the world; art in him was not self-revealing, it was the revelation of a world that had been from the foundation of being and would continue when his works were buried deeper than any plummet could sound. This objectivity, this self-effacement in art, this interest in the story of life, this absorption in life's movement, in action, is Shakspere's gift of greatness. It explains his limitations. Spirituality, properly speaking, the celestial immortality of man's nature, is not found in Shakspere either in character, thought or aspiration. The religious life sleeps in his works; and many a generation will marvel at it. He was interested in life, the action of life; and that is a thing confined to this world. He is mundane, secular, in a way scientific; he saw the spectacle as it is in time.

The second main consideration bearing on Shakspere's genius is the fact that the world he saw, dealt with and knew was an aristocratic world. It was given to him first historically, in those chronicles in which his hand learned to mould the human stuff, a kingly world of the Henrys, the Richards and John, with feudal challenge, battle incidents, the life of the council, murders in prisons or on the block, treasons, dethronements, the sorrows of queens, Norfolk, Hotspur and Falconbridge; a life focussed on aristocratic fortunes and pivoted on aristocratic power. To Shakspere the people was always the mob, and negligible. The sphere of humour, too, in which the vulgar enters, is dependent on the aristocratic sphere from the comedy of the camp-fire and the tavern to Bottom's craftsmen and the court clowns, up to Lear's Fool. Later, the Roman plays gave him the same aristocratic state in an antique form, dictatorial, imperial, with the mob of citizens though more in evidence, more contemptible. The ordered world for him was the world of courtly life; all else, though contiguous or entering in for entertainment or service or in the mass of battle, was essentially subordinated, exteriorized, as environment. The romances, which, after the chronicles, had given him the raw material, reinforced his conception of life as an aristocratic structure by expanding it socially into a community of gentlefolk, Venetian, Veronan, Paduan, in Arden, Attica, Illyria, or on French or English meadows; a life where everything breathed civility, the sentiment of high breeding in chivalry and courtesy, the cult of phrase, the dress and behaviour, the interests, ambitions, intrigues, recreations, language, manners and customs of an aristocratic ideal. Even in those regions of the imagination, where he reared his own state in its lordliest form, with the effect of an incantation of genius, in the English realm of Lear, the Scotch court of Macbeth, the throne of Denmark, the Venetian principality of Cyprus, the Egypt of Antony, or in the woods of Cymbeline, the country-side of Perdita, the island-kingdom of Prospero, he impressed upon it aristocracy in its most majestic, noble and gentle forms as the seal of its being. Shakspere's genius is, in fact, the finest flower of the aristocratic ideal of life. . . .

Personality, the essential fruit of aristocracy, the crowning victory of nature in working out her will, came forth from the Italian Renaissance in one of its highest forms, the form of superb personal power. . . . [S]tripped to its essentials it is no more than the individual will to live, the dominance of that will, the ideal of conquering the world to oneself, of subduing life, of having one's way, one's will, one's desire, of the assertion of the power to live that is the thirst of great souls. The aristocratic ideal of life in the Italian

Renaissance developed in the central line of its advance in history this idea of
the dominance of the personal will in life, the prepotency of individuality; and
in so doing it freed human faculty, energy and desire in a way and to a degree
which gave to Italy its brilliant period of many-sided genius and impelled the
human spirit in every civilized country and recaptured the lost provinces of
Rome to the dominion of a spiritual civilization the seat of whose power is in
the ideals of men. . . . Though not a material conquest, it was vaster in control
than that of Alexander or of the elder antique Rome. Shakspere took its full
impact, lived in it, fed on it, absorbed its passions, its principles, its being,
became its spirit in the North, was its transcendent and overwhelming genius
in literature, its greatest monument in time. This is Shakspere's position; he
was the flower of the aristocratic ideal of life. . . .

The dawn of the Renaissance spirit, incarnating itself in English dramatic
poetry, was in Marlowe, who was perhaps in his own passion of life more
at one with the heart of the Renaissance than was Shakspere, but he was
less nobly, less perfectly, less splendidly, at one with it in its manifold
fulness of expression. Marlowe first put on the stage the career of great
passions, characters of immeasurable ambition and unquenchable thirst;
but in *Tamerlane, The Jew of Malta* and *Faustus,* the theme is not sufficiently
correlated with the real play of fact and force in human affairs, it is seized
with too much intellectual abstraction and presented too spectacularly and
fragmentarily in the scenes. . . . Shakspere followed Marlowe in turning to
English history for the material of his art. The idea of tragedy was, indeed,
already defined for him in the European tradition as a thing of the fall of
princes, of royal misfortune and the vicissitude of splendid fates; and in this
way Shakspere's tragic course was charted out for him beforehand; but in
working out dramatically the lots of the English kings he also kept a close
hold on the idea of a life-force in personality determining temperament,
character and the issues of the action. What in Marlowe was extravagantly
set forth as the fixed idea in his characters, bearing almost the impress of
madness, remains in Shakspere, but subdued to the requirements of the
environment and of human nature, to probability. *Richard II* is a pathetic
instance of the fall of a prince, but the story is linked with that infatuation of
the idea of divine right which is the dominant idea of Richard, absorbs the
eloquence, grace and chivalry of his nature and contains his fate. In *Richard
III,* the prepotency of the selfish force develops its bloody way with a power
to take possession of the king's soul that recalls the self-maddening tyranny
of the Roman emperors, till he becomes the fiend, the enemy of society and
of the state itself, whose fall clears the air like a departing thunderstorm.
Romeo exhibits the mastering of passion in the youthful soul; love in him

is ecstasy. The dominance of the personal will, possessed by an idea inciting it, asserting itself with unbridled desire, naturally leads to madness, and in Shakspere's great characters of this sort mania is never far off; in Macbeth there is the capital instance of the blending of the borders between reason and unreason, and, as is Shakspere's way, this elemental trait in the play permeates it, objectified in the witches, reduplicated in Lady Macbeth, but concentrated in the vivid mental action, the bodily starts and stares, the repeated challenge of fate, in Macbeth's shaking but never quite dethroned "state of man." *Timon* is a lesser illustration. *Hamlet* and *Lear* thrust this part of life into the foreground; and in *Othello,* the near neighborhood of the excess of life to madness, of the noble nature to ruin through its own power to live, to be possessed by a passion, an idea, a sorrow, is the ground of its tragic scene. The personal will is necessarily anti-social, and hence opens in its career the whole field of tragic conflict in endless ways; the drama is its natural scope in art, and there it is the most potent power to conjure with; it is, by far, the most interesting thing in the whole of that action of life which Shakspere contemplated so absorbingly. The Renaissance spirit concentrated and intensified the sense of it, carried it to the extreme, made an ideal of it, in history; Shakspere took it over into the sphere of imagination and then gave such examples of it in the transcendent forms of art that his characters became, each in its kind, the supreme models of what is possible to human nature and faculty in personal force, the types of man.

—George Edward Woodberry, "Shakspere,"
Great Writers, 1907, pp. 183–216

J. J. JUSSERAND "WHAT TO EXPECT OF SHAKESPEARE" (1911)

In this excerpt, Jean Jules Jusserand (1855–1932), French author and dip-lomat, confronts and refutes the criticisms of several eminent critics that Shakespeare's work is without a moral purpose or use. While they may not be written with didactic purpose and designed to instruct, by their very nature as works that please, Shakespeare's plays evoke a sensory response, enlarging the sympathies of the heart and teaching readers and audiences pity for one another and for one another's failings.

I

... In the course of ages, while praise and admiration were becoming boundless, an anxious note has been sounded from time to time, the more striking that it came from admirers. Two examples will be enough to make the point clear. While stating that "the stream of time, which is continually washing the dissoluble fabrics of other poets, passes without injury by the adamant of Shakespeare," Dr. Johnson, who wanted his very dictionary to be morally useful through the examples selected by him for each word,[3] stated that Shakespeare, in spite of his beginning "to assume the dignity of an ancient, and claim the privilege of established fame," had for his "first defect that to which may be imputed most of the evils in books or in men. He sacrifices virtue to convenience, and is so much more careful to please than to instruct that he seems to write without any moral purpose. . . . It is always a writer's duty to make the world better."[4]

Nearer our time, another, no enemy like Tolstoi, who considers that Shakespeare "has the basest and most vulgar conception of the world,"[5] but a passionate admirer, Emerson, for whom Shakespeare was not *a* poet, but *the* poet, the "representative" poet wrote: "And now, how stands the account of man with this bard and benefactor, when, in solitude, shutting our ears to the reverberations of his fame, we seek to strike the balance? Solitude has austere lessons. He converted the elements, which waited on his command, into entertainments. He was master of the revels to mankind. As long as the question is of talent and mental power, the world of men has not his equal to show. But when the question is as to life, and its materials, and its auxiliaries, how does it profit me? What does it signify? It is but a *Twelfth Night,* or *Midsummer-Night's Dream,* or a *Winter Evening's Tale:* what signifies another picture more or less?"[6]

So spoke Emerson in one of those Essays which [Victorian critic and poet] Matthew Arnold went so far as to describe as "the most important work done in English prose" in the nineteenth century.

What is it then that we possess? What can we expect of Shakespeare? Is the treasure in this bewitching garden of Hesperides mere glitter, or is it real gold? Do we listen to the seer that can help solve our problems, answer our doubts, instruct our ignorance, soften the hardness of our hearts, brace our courage? Or does the great book whose fame fills the world offer us mere revels, vain dreams and tales, no moral purpose of value, virtue sacrificed to convenience, such evanescent food as was served on Prospero's table for the unworthy?

III

. . . The part of . . . [his audience, composed mostly of common people seeking to be moved and entertained] as a contributor to Shakespeare's plays, can scarcely be over-estimated—a real contributor to whom it seemed at times as if Shakespeare had passed on the pen to scribble as it pleased, or the chalk to draw sketches on the wall. What such people would like, and what they would tolerate, is what gave those plays, which he never thought of after the performance, the unique, the marvellous, the portentous shape in which we find them. Great is the *de facto* responsibility of such a public; great that of Shakespeare too for having never denied it anything; great rather would that have been if he had not purposely intended to please only those living men, assembled in his theatre, on whom his own fortune depended; "For we," even Dr. Johnson had to acknowledge, "For we that live to please, must please to live."

From the writing of his plays, however, Shakespeare expected not one thing but two; first, immediate success with his public, and all that depended on it; second, the pleasant, happy, delightful satisfaction of a function of his brain duly exercised. This for us is the chief thing, what saved him in spite of himself: to the coarse food his groundlings wanted he added the ethereal food which has been for ages the relish of the greatest in mankind, while it had proved quite acceptable to his groundlings too. He added this as a supererogatory element because it was in him to do so, because it gave him no more trouble than to put in quibbles, jokes, or massacres, and because experience had shown him that, while it was not at all necessary to success, it did not hurt, and was received with a good grace. It was for him the exercise of a natural function, as it is for a good tree to produce good fruit.

Hence the strange nature of that work, touching all extremes, the model of all that should be aimed at, and of much that should be avoided; of actual use both ways. Prompt writing, as he had no choice (he had to live), the courting of a public whose acceptance of his work was indispensable, explain, with his prodigious, heaven-bestowed genius, how the best and the worst go together, hand in hand, in his plays, those flashes of a light that will never fade, and those concessions to the popular taste (indecencies, brutalities, mystifications, tortures, coarse jokes, over-well-explained complications), or the advantage so often taken by him of the fact that the public will not know, will not remember, will not mind. "He omits," says Dr. Johnson, "opportunities of instructing or delighting which the train of his story seems to force upon him"; the reason being that, in some cases, such opportunities did not occur to him at once and that he had little time for reconsidering; given his public, that would do. Hence also his anachronisms, his faulty geography, his indifference to real facts, so complete that he would not have stretched out his hand to take a book and verify the place of a city or the date of an event, nor would he have asked his future son-in-law, the physician, whether a human being that has been smothered can still speak. He offers to his groundlings, and not to this learned age of which he never thought and which has no right to complain, a reign of King John without *Magna Charta*, but with plenty of gunpowder . . .

IV

... More than one of the gravest questions that, from the beginning, have troubled mankind would be put in vain to [Shakespeare] the poet, for to them he has no answer. What he does is to place the problem before us with such force that he obliges us to think seriously of those serious questions; hence of use, though of a different use than is sometimes said.

Concerning religions he does not take sides, as is evidenced by the fact that discussions are still renewed now and then (though there is little room for doubt) as to what faith he belonged to. The lesson he gives us is, however, a great one; it was a rare one in his day, and it is summed up in the word "toleration."

No problem is put oftener and more vividly before his audience than that of death and of the hereafter. To this he has no answer. In their calmest moods his personages hope for sleep: "Our little life is rounded with a sleep." Oftener he and they (he in the sonnets, they in the plays) pore over the prospect of physical dissolution, when the time shall come to leave "this vile world, with vilest worms to dwell." [Sonnet 71, l. 4] We still "go we know not where," and no Isabella, be she almost a nun, and bound by her part in the play to act as a consoler, has any word to clear Claudio's doubts or ours. "If I must die," says Claudio, sadly,

I will encounter darkness as a bride,
and hug it in mine arms.
[*Measure for Measure,* III.i.83–85]

... As a patriot his teachings are of the common sort. Patriotism has two sides: it concerns our own country considered in itself, then our country considered in relation to others. The first kind of duty, the most natural and easiest, is admirably fulfilled by the warm-hearted, the sound, and thorough Englishman that the poet was, justly proud of the great deeds of glorious ancestors: most men feel that way without any teaching....

As to the other side of patriotism, Shakespeare writes not only as a man of his day, but as a man who had to echo his public's feelings: an echo can make no change. To understand that to picture the vanquished as a huge crew of cowards, traitors, and scoundrels, afraid of their own shadow, was *not* to increase the glory of a victory, proved beyond the reasoning capacity of the crowd at the Globe. The poet allows them to have their own way, to hold his pen, and write in his plays their own views of what an enemy must have been. They were his only care; unborn posterity and ratiocinating critics that would come to life long after the plays were dead, as he believed, could have on him no influence.

On those great social problems which, in this modern world of ours, fill so much space in the thoughts of all, Shakespeare again expresses himself with the force and pregnancy of a man of incomparable genius; but he speaks as a man of his time and of his *milieu*, not as a man above them. The foibles of the uneducated masses, their credulity, their fickleness, their alternate fits of enthusiasm and depression, their aptitude to cruelty, their inability to understand, are depicted with the stern accuracy of a clear-eyed, unfriendly observer. The counterpart of such vices, or the extenuating circumstances resulting from involuntary ignorance, hardship, and misery, are scarcely visible anywhere. The people, throughout the plays, are the same people, with the same faults, be they the Romans of *Coriolanus* or of *Caesar,* or the English of Jack Cade [in *2Henry VI*], or even the Danes of *Hamlet* (with their selection of Laertes for a king); they are the people. Shakespeare no more hesitates to hold them up to the laughter and scorn of their brethren in the pit, than Molière hesitated to make the real court marquesses laugh at the marquesses in his comedies, or than to-day's playwrights hesitate to ask a middle-class audience to laugh at the faults and folly of middle-class characters. Shakespeare's lesson may be of use to statesmen, scarcely to the people themselves, since for a useful castigation of the many, the most efficacious factor is love.

On one more question of keen, though less general, interest, we would appeal in vain to Shakespeare the playwright; that is for information about himself. Few men . . . have allowed less of their personality to appear in works dealing so directly with the human passions.

V

Far above any . . . single questions rises the one of general import, propounded by Dr. Johnson, Emerson, and others: that of the permanent impression left by the plays on listeners or readers.

During the whole period to which Shakespeare belongs, and before his day too and long after, in his country and out of it, most men agreed that plays must moralize and improve mankind: they have other *raisons d'être,* but this is the chief one. Tragedy and comedy, said [French poet, Pierre de] Ronsard are, above all, "didascaliques et enseignantes." [didactic, like a stage direction, and instructive]. . . .

The only shackles Shakespeare was loaded with were the needs and tastes of his public. They were heavy enough, but they were the only ones. The absence of others is so complete and so unique that this characteristic is among the most singular offered to our wonder by his works. Barring this single exception, no poet cast on the wide world a freer and clearer gaze. He wrote unhampered by traditions, rules, religious systems. He gave himself the pleasure of showing once that he knew dramatic rules existed, but he left them alone because they were "caviare to the general," [*Hamlet*, II.ii.446f.] and he depended on "the general." They were probably, besides, not so very sweet to him either. The final result is that, strange as it may seem, he stands much nearer Aristotle than many of Aristotle's learned followers. The great philosopher did nothing but sum up the teachings of good sense and adapt them to Greek manners. The great poet did nothing but follow the teachings of good sense, as given him by his own sound nature, and adapt them to English wants. . . .

On the question of morality, Aristotle makes it quite evident that his own ideal is a drama in which vice is punished or even has no place; but he clearly states also that the rational end of dramatic poetry is not to moralize but to give pleasure. . . .

On this question, as on that of "rules"—mere suggestions, not "rules" in Aristotle's intentions—Shakespeare's attitude was the same. He would not go out of his way either to secure or to avoid an ethical conclusion or conformity to rules. His plays were truly written "without any moral purpose," that is, instruction was not their object. But to conclude that they do not therefore instruct at all is to wander from truth. First, in some plays the events represented are, as in real life, so full of meaning that the moral is no less obvious than in any classical tragedy with a confidant or a chorus to tell us what to think; and even, at times, the hero tells us that. No one can escape the lesson to be drawn from the fate of Macbeth, of Coriolanus, of Antony, of poor Falstaff and his wild companions. . . .

In many cases, however, it seems as if the evil power so often at play in Greek tragedies, and in real life too, were leading the innocent to their destruction: Othello, Desdemona, Hamlet, as worthy of pity as Oedipus; fatality imposing on them tasks for which nature has not armed them, or offering them temptations to which they would not have yielded had they been less generous. Are those plays of no moral use, or is their use limited to those maxims and pregnant sayings which Corneille considered one of the chief causes of a tragedy's usefulness, and which abound in Shakespeare—. . .

The fate of a Hamlet, an Ophelia, a Desdemona, an Othello, carries, to be sure, no concrete moral with it; the noblest, the purest, the most generous, sink into the dark abyss after agonizing tortures, and one can scarcely imagine what, being human, with human foibles, they could have avoided to escape their misery. Their story was undoubtedly written "without any moral purpose," but not without any moral effect. It obliges human hearts to melt, it teaches them pity.

Notes

3.   "When I first collected these authorities, I was desirous that every quotation should be useful to some other end than the illustration of a word. I therefore extracted from philosophers principles of science, from historians remarkable facts, from chymists complete processes, from divines striking exhortations, from poets beautiful descriptions." Preface to his *Dictionary of the English Language,* 1755.

4.   *Preface to Shakespeare,* 1765. John Dennis, a passionate admirer of the poet, gave in Nov., 1719, under the title *The Invader of His Country,* a remodeled version of *Coriolanus,* with a new ending, so as to add a moral sadly lacking, he thought, in Shakespeare's play.

5.   And according to whom his glory can be explained only as being one of those contagious mental diseases which now and then afflict mankind, like the crusades, the belief in sorcerers and the "passion for tulips which, at a certain time, invaded the whole of Holland." Tolstoi's *Shakespeare,* translated into French by Bienstock.

6.   *Representative Men: Seven Lectures,* Boston, 1850, pp. 213, 214.

—J. J. Jusserand, from "What to Expect of
Shakespeare," 1911, *The School for Ambassadors
and Other Essays,* 1925, pp. 293–322

TEXTUAL HISTORY

ALEXANDER POPE "THE PREFACE OF THE EDITOR" (1725)

Alexander Pope (1688–1744), poet, critic, satirist, and translator of Homer, was, along with Samuel Johnson, the predominant literary force of the eighteenth century. His verse was a well-disciplined construction of rhymed couplets; his subject, the foibles, manners, and morals of his society. Pope was the second editor of Shakespeare's work. (Nicholas Rowe was the first, in 1709. The First Folio of 1623 was a collection of Shakespeare's plays, not an edition. Its inestimable value lies in its existence. Without it, we would not have many of Shakespeare's plays at all. But the problems it bequeathed, textual problems that result from mangled, garbled, erroneous typesettings, are thorny and numerous and have been the source of enormous editorial work and sometimes bitter disputation among editors ever since.)

In the following introduction to his edition, Pope describes the textual confusion, sloppiness, and corruptions an editor encounters who tries to sort through quartos (texts pre-existing the First Folio that are often unreliable, having been pirated, carelessly prepared, or printed from the imperfect memory of players; quartos are not always inferior texts, but they often offer texts greatly at variance with the First Folio), later folios, variants, and emendations in the effort to put together and annotate a reliable text.

I shall now lay before the reader some of those almost innumerable Errors, which have risen from one source, the ignorance of the Players, both as his actors, and as his editors. . . .

It is not certain that any one of his Plays was published by himself. During the time of his employment in the Theatre, several of his pieces were printed separately in Quarto. What makes me think that most of these were not publish'd by him, is the excessive carelessness of the press: every page is so scandalously false spelled, and almost all the learned or unusual words so intolerably mangled, that it's plain there either was no Corrector to the press at all, or one totally illiterate. If any were supervised by himself, I should fancy the two parts of *Henry the 4th,* and *Midsummer-Night's Dream* might have been so: because I find no other printed with any exactness; and (contrary to the rest) there is very little variation in all the subsequent editions of them. There are extant two Prefaces, to the first quarto edition of *Troilus and Cressida* in 1609, and to that of *Othello;* by which it appears, that the first was publish'd without his knowledge or consent, and even before it was acted, so late as seven or eight years before he died: and that the latter was not printed till after his death. The whole number of genuine plays which we have been able to find printed in his life-time, amounts but to eleven. And of some of these, we meet with two or more editions by different printers, each of which was whole heaps of trash different from the other: which I should fancy was occasion'd, by their being taken from different copies, belonging to different Playhouses.

The folio edition (in which all the plays we now receive as his, were first collected) was published by two Players, *Heming* and *Condell,* in 1623, seven years after his decease. They declare, that all the other editions were stolen and surreptitious, and affirm theirs to be purged from the errors of the former. This is true as to the literal errors, and no other; for in all respects else it is far worse than the Quartos:

First, because the additions of trifling and bombast passages are in this edition far more numerous. For whatever had been added, since those Quartos, by the actors, or had stolen from their mouths into the written parts, were from thence conveyed into the printed text, and all stand charged upon the Author. He himself complained of this usage in *Hamlet,* where he wishes that *those who play the Clowns wou'd speak no more than is set down for them.* (Act. 3. Sc. 4.) But as a proof that he could not escape it, in the old editions of *Romeo and Juliet* there is no hint of a great number of the mean conceits and ribaldries now to be found there. In others, the low scenes of Mobs, Plebeians and Clowns, are vastly shorter than at present: And I have seen one in particular (which seems to have belonged to the playhouse, by having the parts divided with lines, and the Actors names in the margin) where several of those very passages were added in a written hand, which are since to be found in the folio.

In the next place, a number of beautiful passages which are extant in the first single editions, are omitted in this: as it seems, without any other reason, than their willingness to shorten some scenes: These men (as it was said of *Procrustes*) either lopping, or stretching an Author, to make him just fit for their Stage.

This edition is said to be printed from the *Original Copies*; I believe they meant those which had lain ever since the Author's days in the playhouse, and had from time to time been cut, or added to, arbitrarily. It appears that this edition, as well as the Quartos, was printed (at least partly) from no better copies than the *Prompter's Book,* or *Piece-meal Parts* written out for the use of the actors: For in some places their very[1] names are thro' carelessness set down instead of the *Persona Dramatis:* And in others the notes of direction to the *Property-men* for their *Moveables,* and to the *Players* for their *Entries,*[2] are inserted into the Text, thro' the ignorance of the Transcribers.

The Plays not having been before so much as distinguish'd by Acts and Scenes, they are in this edition divided according as they play'd them; often where there is no pause in the action, or where they thought fit to make a breach in it, for the sake of Musick, Masques, or Monsters.

Sometimes the scenes are transposed and shuffled backward and forward; a thing which could no otherwise happen, but by their being taken from separate and piece-meal-written parts.

Many verses are omitted intirely, and others transposed; from whence invincible obscurities have arisen, past the guess of any Commentator to clear up, but just where the accidental glympse of an old edition enlightens us.

Some Characters were confounded and mix'd, or two put into one, for want of a competent number of actors. Thus in the Quarto edition of *Midsummer-Night's Dream,* Act. 5. *Shakespear* introduces a kind of Master of the Revels called *Philostratus:* all whose part is given to another character (that of *Egeus*) in the subsequent editions: So also in *Hamlet* and *King Lear.* This too makes it probable that the Prompter's Books were what they call'd the Original Copies.

From liberties of this kind, many speeches also were put into the mouths of wrong persons, where the Author now seems chargeable with making them speak out of character: Or sometimes perhaps for no better reason, than that a governing Player, to have the mouthing of some favourite speech himself, would snatch it from the unworthy lips of an Underling.

Prose from verse they did not know, and they accordingly printed one for the other throughout the volume. . . .

From what has been said, there can be no question but had *Shakespear* published his works himself (especially in his latter time, and after his retreat from the stage) we should not only be certain which are genuine; but should find in those that are, the errors lessened by some thousands. If I may judge from all the distinguishing marks of his style, and his manner of thinking and writing, I make no doubt to declare that those wretched plays, *Pericles, Locrine, Sir John Oldcastle, Yorkshire Tragedy, Lord Cromwell, The Puritan,* and *London Prodigal,* cannot be admitted as his. And I should conjecture of some of the others, (particularly *Love's Labour Lost, The Winter's Tale,* and *Titus Andronicus)* that only some characters, single scenes, or perhaps a few particular passages, were of his hand. It is very probable what occasion'd some Plays to be supposed *Shakespear's* was only this; that they were pieces produced by unknown authors, or fitted up for the Theatre while it was under his administration: and no owner claiming them, they were adjudged to him. . . . Yet the Players themselves, *Hemings* and *Condell,* afterwards did *Shakespear* the justice to reject those eight plays in their edition; tho' they were then printed in his name, in every body's hands, and acted with some applause; (as we learn from what *Ben Johnson* says of *Pericles* in his *Ode on the New Inn.)* That *Titus Andronicus* is one of this class I am the rather induced to believe, by finding the same Author openly express his contempt of it in the *Induction* to *Bartholomew-Fair,* in the year 1614, when *Shakespear* was yet living. And there is no better authority for these latter sort, than for the former, which were equally published in his life-time.

If we give into this opinion, how many low and vicious parts and passages might no longer reflect upon this great Genius, but appear unworthily charged upon him? And even in those which are really his, how many faults may have been unjustly laid to his account from arbitrary Additions, Expunctions, Transpositions of scenes and lines, confusion of Characters and Persons, wrong application of Speeches, corruptions of innumerable Passages by the Ignorance, and wrong Corrections of 'em again by the Impertinence, of his first Editors? From one or other of these considerations, I am verily perswaded, that the greatest and the grossest part of what are thought his errors would vanish, and leave his character in a light very different from that disadvantageous one, in which it now appears to us.

This is the state in which *Shakespear's* writings lye at present; for since the above-mentioned Folio Edition, all the rest have implicitly followed it, without having recourse to any of the former, or ever making the comparison between them. It is impossible to repair the Injuries already done him; too much time has elaps'd, and the materials are too few. In what I have done I have rather given a proof of my willingness and desire, than of my ability, to do him justice. I have discharg'd the dull duty of an Editor, to my best judgment, with more labour than I expect thanks, with a religious abhorrence of all innovation, and without any indulgence to my private sense or conjecture. The method taken in this Edition will show it self. The various Readings are fairly put in the margin, so that every one may compare 'em; and those I have prefer'd into the Text are constantly *ex fide Codicum* [critically re-evaluated], upon authority. The Alterations or Additions which *Shakespear* himself made, are taken notice of as they occur. Some suspected passages which are excessively bad, (and which seem Interpolations by being so inserted that one can intirely omit them without any chasm, or deficience in the context) are degraded to the bottom of the page; with an Asterisk referring to the places of their insertion. The Scenes are mark'd so distinctly that every removal of place is specify'd; which is more necessary in this Author than any other, since he shifts them more frequently: and sometimes without attending to this particular, the reader would have met with obscurities. The more obsolete or unusual words are explained. Some of the most shining passages are distinguish'd by comma's in the margin; and where the beauty lay not in particulars but in the whole, a star is prefix'd to the scene. This seems to me a shorter and less ostentatious method of performing the better half of Criticism (namely the pointing out an Author's excellencies) than to fill a whole paper with citations of fine passages, with *general Applauses,* or *empty Exclamations* at the tail of them. There is also subjoin'd a Catalogue of those first Editions by which the greater part of the various readings and of the corrected passages are authorised, (most of which are such as carry their own evidence along with them.) These Editions now hold the place of Originals, and are the only materials left to repair the deficiences or restore the corrupted sense of the Author: I can only wish that a greater number of them (if a greater were ever published) may yet be found, by a search more successful than mine, for the better accomplishment of this end.

I will conclude by saying of *Shakespear,* that with all his faults, and with all the irregularity of his *Drama,* one may look upon his works, in comparison of those that are more finish'd and regular, as upon an ancient majestick piece of *Gothick* Architecture, compar'd with a neat Modern building: The latter is more elegant and glaring, but the former is more strong and more solemn. It must be allow'd, that in one of these there are materials enough to make many of the other. It has much the greater variety, and much the nobler apartments; tho' we are often conducted to them by dark, odd, and uncouth passages. Nor does the Whole fail to strike us with greater reverence, tho' many of the Parts are childish, ill-plac'd, and unequal to its grandeur.

Notes

1.   *Much Ado about Nothing.* Act 2. *Enter Prince* Leonato, Claudio, *and* Jack Wilson, *instead of* Balthasar. *And in Act 4.* Cowley, *and* Kemp, *constantly thro' a whole scene.* (Edit. Fol. of 1623, and 1632.)

Such as

——My Queen is murder'd! *Ring the little Bell*

——His nose grew as sharp as a pen, and *a table of Greenfield's, &c.*

> —Alexander Pope, from "The Preface
> of the Editor," *The Works of Mr. William
> Shakespear,* 1725, volume 1, pp. xiv–xxiv

LEWIS THEOBALD "INTRODUCTION" (1726)

Lewis Theobald (1688–1744), in 1733, published his own edition of Shakespeare in seven volumes. It was a significant advance in Shakespearean scholarship, producing, up until then, the most reliable texts of the plays, derived from collation, emendation, and annotation of extant texts. It was superior to Pope's edition, which Theobald criticizes in the following excerpt. For his pains, Pope conferred on Theobald the crown of dunces in his satire of 1728, *The Dunciad.* Pope also incorporated many of Theobald's corrections of Pope's edition in his own second edition of the same year.

I have very often declar'd, and that in a number of Companies, that what thro' the *Indolence,* what thro' the *Ignorance* of his EDITORS, we have scarce any Book in the *English* Tongue more fertile of Errors, than the Plays of SHAKESPEARE. And, I believe, whenever I have fall'n on this subject, I have not fail'd to express my Wish, that some fine *Genius,* equal to the task, would befriend the Memory of this immortal Poet, and contribute to the Pleasure of the present and of future Times, in retrieving, as far as possible, the *original Purity* of his *Text,* and rooting out that vast Crop of *Errors,* which has almost choak'd up his *Beauties.*

It was no small Satisfaction therefore to me, when I first heard Mr. POPE had taken upon him the Publication of SHAKESPEARE. I very reasonably expected, from his known Talents and Abilities, from his uncommon Sagacity and Discernment, and from his unwearied Diligence and Care of informing himself by an happy and extensive Conversation, we should have had our Author come out as perfect, as the want of *Manuscripts* and *original Copies* could give us a Possibility of hoping. I may dare to say, a great Number of SHAKESPEARE's Admirers, and of Mr. POPE's too, (both which I sincerely declare myself,) concurred in this Expectation: ... and that he would not have sate down contented with performing, as he calls it himself, the *dull Duty* of an EDITOR only. SHAKESPEARE's Works have always appear'd to me like what he makes his HAMLET compare the World to, an *unweeded Garden grown to Seed*: And I am sorry there is still reason to complain, the *Weeds* in him are so very sparingly thin'd, that, not to speak out of compass, a thousand *rank* and *unsightly* ones are left to stare us in the Face, and clog the Delight of the expected Prospect.

It must necessarily happen, that where the Assistance of *Manuscripts* is wanting to set an Author's Meaning right, and rescue him from those Errors which have been transmitted down thro' a Series of incorrect Editions, and a long Intervention of Time, many Passages must be desperate, and past a Cure, and their true Sense irretrievable, either to Care, or the Sagacity of Conjecture. . . .

I HAVE so great an Esteem for Mr. POPE, and so high an Opinion of his Genius and Excellencies, that I beg to be excused from the least Intention of derogating from his Merits, in this Attempt to restore the true Reading of SHAKESPEARE . . . for I am assuming a Task here, which this learned *Editor* [Pope] seems purposely (I was going to say, with too nice a Scruple) to have declined.

To explain myself, I must be obliged to make a short Quotation from Mr. POPE, in his Preface to SHAKESPEARE: "In what I have done," says he, "I have rather given a Proof of my Willingness and Desire, than of my Ability to do him Justice. I have discharg'd the dull Duty of an *Editor*, to my best Judgment, with more Labour than I expect Thanks, with a *religious Abhorrence* of all *Innovation*, and without any Indulgence to my private Sense or Conjecture." I cannot help thinking this Gentleman's *Modesty* in this Point too *nice* and *blameable*; and that what he is pleased to call a *religious Abhorrence* of *Innovation*, is downright *Superstition*: Neither can I be of Opinion, that the Writings of SHAKESPEARE are so *venerable*, as that we should be excommunicated from good Sense, for daring to *innovate properly*; or that we ought to be as cautious of altering *their* Text, as we would That of the *sacred Writings*. . . .

We should shew very little Honesty, or Wisdom, to play the Tyrants with any Author's Text; to raze, alter, innovate, and overturn, at all Adventures, and to the utter Detriment of his Sense and Meaning: But to be so very reserv'd and cautious, as to interpose no Relief or Conjecture, where it manifestly labours and cries out for Assistance, seems . . . absurd. . . .

I don't know whether I am mistaken in Judgment, but I have always thought, that whenever a *Gentleman* and a *Scholar* turns Editor of any Book, he at the same Time commences *Critick* upon his *Author*; and that wherever he finds the Reading suspected, manifestly corrupted, deficient in Sense, and unintelligible, he ought to exert every Power and Faculty of the Mind to supply such a Defect, to give Light and restore Sense to the Passage, and, by a reasonable Emendation, to make that satisfactory and consistent with the Context, which before was so absurd, unintelligible, and intricate.

THIS is a *Task,* which, as I above intimated, Mr. POPE has *purposely disclaim'd,* and which I . . . have taken upon my self to prosecute. I am not insensible under what Disadvantages I must set out upon such a Work, and against such an Antagonist. . . . But as I have laid it down as a Rule to myself not to be arbitrary, fantastical, or wanton, in my Conjectures upon our Author, I shall venture to aim at some little Share of Reputation, in endeavouring to restore Sense to Passages in which no Sense has hitherto been found; or, failing in that Hope, must submit to incur, which I should be very unwilling to do, the Censure of a rash and vain Pretender.

As SHAKESPEARE stands, or at least ought to stand, in the Nature of a Classic Writer, and, indeed, he is corrupt enough to pass for one of the oldest Stamp, every one, who has a Talent and Ability this Way, is at liberty to make his Comments and Emendations upon him. . . .

No Vein of Pedantry, or Ostentation of useless Criticism, incited me to this Work: It is a Sacrifice to the Pleasure of SHAKESPEARE's Admirers in general; and should it fail of all the Success which I wish, it may chance to work this good Effect, That many will be tempted to read this Poet with a more diligent Eye than hitherto: The Consequence of which will be, that better Criticks will make their own Observations, with more Strength than I can pretend; and this Specimen prove only an Invitation to lead them into nobler Corrections. If, however, till that happens, where SHAKESPEARE has yet, thro' all his Editions, labour'd under flat Nonsense, and invincible Darkness, I can, by the Addition or Alteration of a single letter, or two, give him both Sense and Sentiment, who will be so unkind to say, this is a trifling or unwarrantable Attempt? . . .

I am sorry that the Use and Intention of this Undertaking ties me down to the Necessity of one unpleasant Office, That of setting right the Faults in Pointing, and those meerly literal, committed by the Printer, and continued by too negligent a Revisal. This is the Drudgery of Correction, in which I could wish to have been spar'd, there being no Pleasure in the Execution of it, nor any Merit, but that of dull Diligence, when executed. But, *unpleasant* as it is, even this Part must be dispens'd with; and all that I can do, to ease myself or Readers in it, is to mark these minute Corrections with all possible Brevity, and proceed to more important Matter.

I CAN scarce suspect it will be thought, if I begin my Animadversions upon the Tragedy of HAMLET, that I have been partial to myself in picking out this Play, as one more fertile in Errors than any of the rest: On the contrary, I chose it for Reasons quite opposite. It is, perhaps, the best known, and one of the most favourite Plays of our Author: For these thirty Years last past, I believe, not a Season has elaps'd, in which it has not been perform'd on the Stage more than once; and, consequently, we might presume it the most purg'd and free from Faults and Obscurity. Yet give me Leave to say, what I am ready to prove, it is not without very gross Corruptions. Nor does it stand by itself for Faults in Mr. *POPE's* Edition: No, it is a Specimen only of the epidemical Corruption, if I may be allowed to use that Phrase, which runs thro' all the Work. . . .

IF *HAMLET* has its Faults, so has every other of the Plays; and I therefore only offer it as a Precedent of the same Errors, which, every body will be convinced before I have done, possess every Volume and every Play in this Impression.

BUT to proceed from Assertion to Experiment: In order to which I shall constantly be obliged, that the Emendations may stand in a fairer Light, to quote the Passages as they are read, with some part of their Context, in Mr. *POPE's* Edition; and likewise to prefix a short Account of the Business and Circumstances of the Scenes from which the faulty Passages are drawn; that the Readers may be inform'd at a single View, and judge of the Strength and Reason of the Emendation, without a Reference to the Plays themselves for that purpose. But this will be in no kind necessary, where Faults of the Press are only to be corrected: Where the Pointing is wrong, perhaps, That may not be alone the Fault of the Printer; and therefore I may sometimes think myself obliged to assign a Reason for my altering it.

As every Author is best expounded and explain'd in *One* Place, by his own Usage and Manner of Expression in *Others;* wherever our Poet receives an Alteration in his Text from any of my *Corrections* or *Conjectures,* I have throughout en-deavour'd to support what I offer by *parallel Passages,* and *Authorities* from himself: Which, as it will be my best Justification, where my Attempts are seconded with the Concurrence of my Readers; so, it will be my best Excuse for those Innovations, in which I am not so happy to have them think with me.

I HAVE likewise all along, for the greater Ease and Pleasure of the Readers, distinguish'd the Nature of my Corrections by a short marginal Note to each of them, viz. *False Pointing, False Print, Various Reading, Passage omitted, Conjectural Emendation, Emendation,* and the like; so that every body will at once be appriz'd what Subject-matter to expect from every respective Division.

—Lewis Theobald, "Introduction,"
Shakespeare Restored, 1726, pp. i–viii

Henry Fielding (1752)

Henry Fielding (1707–54), magistrate, playwright, and author of *Tom Jones*, in the midst of a century of often turgid and fussy disputes among sometimes self-aggrandizing editors of Shakespeare regarding textual readings, emendations, conjectures, and alterations, offers this fanciful, conclusive critical restoration of the "To be or not to be" soliloquy from *Hamlet*.

SIR,

You are sensible, I believe, that there is nothing in this Age more fashionable, than to criticise on Shakespeare; I am indeed told, that there are not less than 200 Editions of that Author, with Commentaries, Notes, Observations, &c. now preparing for the Press; as nothing therefore is more natural than to direct one's Studies by the Humour of the Times, I have myself employed some leisure Hours on that great Poet. I here send you a short Specimen of my Labours, being some Emendations of that most celebrated Soliloquy in Hamlet, which, as I have no Intention to publish Shakespeare myself, are very much at the Service of any of the 200 Critics abovementioned.

I am, &c.

Hamlet, Act III. Scene 2.
To be, or not to be, that is the question.

This is certainly very intelligible; but if a slight Alteration were made in the former Part of the Line, and an easy Change was admitted in the last Word, the Sense would be greatly improved. I would propose then to read thus;

To be, or not. To be! That is the BASTION.

That is the strong Hold. The Fortress. So Addison in *Cato.*

Here will I hold—

The military Terms which follow, abundantly point out this Reading.

Whether 'tis nobler in the *Mind* to *suffer*
The *Slings* and Arrows of outragious Fortune,
Or *to take Arms against a Sea* of Troubles,
And by opposing end them.

Suffering is, I allow, a Christian Virtue; but I question whether it hath ever been ranked among the heroic Qualities. Shakespeare certainly wrote BUFFET; and this leads us to supply Man for Mind; Mind being alike applicable to both Sexes, whereas Hamlet is here displaying the most masculine Fortitude. *Slings* and *Arrows* in the succeeding Line, is an Impropriety which could not have come from our Author; the former being the Engine which discharges, and the latter the Weapon discharged. To the Sling, he would have opposed the Bow; or to Arrows, Stones. Read therefore WINGED ARROWS; that is, feathered Arrows; a Figure very usual among Poets: So in the classical Ballad of *Chevy Chase*;

> The Grey-Goose Wing that was thereon
> In his Heart's Blood was wet.

The next Line is undoubtedly corrupt—to take Arms against a Sea, can give no Man, I think, an Idea; whereas by a slight Alteration and Transposition all will be set right, and the undoubted Meaning of Shakespeare restored.

> Or *tack* against an *Arm 'oth' Sea* of Troubles,
> And by composing end them.

By composing himself to Sleep, as he presently explains himself. What shall I do? says Hamlet. Shall I *buffet* the Storm, or shall I tack about and go to Rest?

> —To *die,* to sleep;
> No more; and by a Sleep to say we end
> The Heartach, and the thousand natural Shocks
> The Flesh is Heir to; 'tis a *Consummation*
> Devoutly to be wished. *To die,* to sleep;
> To sleep, perchance to dream;—

What to die first, and to go to sleep afterwards; and not only so, but to dream too?—But tho' his Commentators were dreaming of Nonsense when they read this Passage, Shakespeare was awake when he writ it. Correct it thus;

> —To lie to sleep.

i.e. To go to sleep, a common Expression; Hamlet himself expressly says he means *no more;* which he would hardly have said, if he had talked of

Death, a Matter of the greatest and highest Nature: And is not the Context a Description of the Power of Sleep, which every one knows puts an End to the Heart-ach, the Tooth-ach, and indeed every Ach? So our Author in his *Macbeth*, speaking of this very Sleep, calls it

> Balm of hurt Minds, great Nature's *second Course.*

Where, by the bye, instead of second Course, I read SICKEN'D DOSE; this being, indeed, the Dose which Nature chuses to apply to all her Shocks, and may be therefore well said *devoutly to be wished for;* which surely cannot be so generally said of Death.—But how can Sleep be called a *Consummation?*—The true Reading is certainly *Consultation;* the Cause for the Effect, a common Metonymy, *i.e.* When we are in any violent Pain, and a Set of Physicians are met in a *Consultation,* it is to be hoped the Consequence will be a sleeping Dose. Death, I own, is very devoutly to be apprehended, but seldom wished, I believe, at least by the Patient himself, at all such Seasons.

For natural *Shocks,* I would read *Shakes;* indeed I know only one Argument which can be brought in Justification) of the old Reading; and this is, that *Shock* hath the same Signification, and is rather the better Word. In such Cases, the Reader must be left to his Choice.

> For in that Sleep of Death what Dreams may come,
> When we have *shuffled* off this mortal Coil,
> Must give us Pause—

Read and print thus:

> For in that Sleep, of Death what Dreams may come?
> When we have *scuffled* off, this mortal *Call,*
> Must give us Pause—

i.e. Must make us stop. *Shuffle* is a paultry Metaphor, taken from playing at Cards; whereas *scuffle* is a noble and military Word.

> The Whips and Scorns of Time.

Undoubtedly *Whips* and *Spurs.*

> When he himself might his *Quietus* make
> With a bare *Bodkin.*

With a bare *Pipkin*. The Reader will be pleased to observe, that Hamlet, as we have above proved, is here debating whether it were better to go to sleep, or to keep awake; as an Argument for the affirmative, he urges that no Man in his Senses would bear *The Whips and Scorns of Time, the Oppressor's Wrong,* &c. when he himself, without being at the Expence of an Apothecary, might make his *Quietus, or sleeping Dose,* with a bare PIPKIN, the cheapest of all Vessels, and consequently within every Man's Reach.

   —Who would Fardles bear,
   To groan and sweat under a weary Life?

Who indeed would bear any thing for such a Reward? The true Reading is

   —Who would for th' Ales bear
   To groan, &c.

Who would bear the Miseries of Life, for the Sake of the Ales. In the Days of Shakespeare, when Diversions were not arrived at that Degree of Elegance to which they have been since brought, the Assemblies of the People for Mirth were called by the Name of an ALE. This was the Drum or Rout of that Age, and was the Entertainment of the better Sort, as it is at this Day of the Vulgar. Such are the *Easter-Ales* and the *Whitsun-Ales,* at present celebrated all over the West of England. The Sentiment therefore of the Poet, is this; *Who would bear the Miseries of Life, to enjoy the Pleasures of it;* which latter Word is by no forced Metaphor called THE ALES OF LIFE.

   And makes us rather bear the Ills we have,
   Than fly to others that we know not of.

This, I own, is Sense as it stands; but the Spirit of the Passage will be improved, if we read

   Than try *some others,* &c.
   —Thus the native Hue of Resolution,
   Is sicklied o'er with the pale Cast of Thought.

Read,

   —Thus the native Blue of Resolution,
   Is pickled o'er in a stale Cask of Salt.

This restores a most elegant Sentiment; I shall leave the Relish of it therefore with the Reader, and conclude by wishing that its Taste may never be obliterated by any future Alteration of this glorious Poet.

—Henry Fielding, from *The Covent-Garden Journal*, number 31, April 18, 1752

SAMUEL JOHNSON (1756)

In his justification for undertaking a new edition of Shakespeare's plays, Dr. Johnson reviews the faults of previous editions, focusing on the ineptitudes of scholarship that mar them because of previous editors' ignorance of the language and usage of Shakespeare's time and because of their lack of familiarity with Shakespeare's sources. Johnson, with his reputation as a lexicographer established—his dictionary had appeared the previous year—advertises that he will not only collate texts to establish the best reading, and undertake textual comparisons using parallel passages from Shakespeare and relevant passages from other authors, but that he will also offer annotations and paraphrases in order to untangle thorny passages, include relevant material from previous editors, and, consequently, establish a sequence of relevant Shakespeare commentary and criticism for the future. The edition appeared in eight volumes in 1765 and is famous for both Johnson's preface and for his notes, which are frequently printed independently of the texts of the plays.

When the works of Shakespeare are, after so many editions, again offered to the publick, it will doubtless be enquired, why Shakespeare stands in more need of critical assistance than any other of the English writers, and what are the deficiencies of the late attempts, which another editor may hope to supply.

The business of him that republishes an ancient book is, to correct what is corrupt, and to explain what is obscure. To have a text corrupt in many places, and in many doubtful, is, among the authours that have written since the use of types, almost peculiar to Shakespeare. Most writers, by publishing their own works, prevent all various readings, and preclude all conjectural criticism. Books indeed are sometimes published after the death of him who produced them, but they are better secured from corruptions than these unfortunate compositions. They subsist in a single copy, written or revised by the authour; and the faults of the printed volume can be only faults of one descent.

But of the works of Shakespeare the condition has been far different: he sold them, not to be printed, but to be played. They were immediately copied for the actors, and multiplied by transcript after transcript, vitiated by the blunders of the penman, or changed by the affectation of the player; perhaps enlarged to introduce a jest, or mutilated to shorten the representation; and printed at last without the concurrence of the authour, without the consent of the proprietor, from compilations made by chance or by stealth out of the separate parts written for the theatre: and thus thrust into the world surreptitiously and hastily, they suffered another depravation from the ignorance and negligence of the printers, as every man who knows the state of the press in that age will readily conceive.

It is not easy for invention to bring together so many causes concurring to vitiate a text. No other authour ever gave up his works to fortune and time with so little care: no books could be left in hands so likely to injure them, as plays frequently acted, yet continued in manuscript: no other transcribers were likely to be so little qualified for their task as those who copied for the stage, at a time when the lower ranks of the people were universally illiterate: no other editions were made from fragments so minutely broken, and so fortuitously reunited; and in no other age was the art of printing in such unskilful hands.

With the causes of corruption that make the revisal of Shakespeare's dramatick pieces necessary, may be enumerated the causes of obscurity, which may be partly imputed to his age, and partly to himself.

When a writer outlives his contemporaries, and remains almost the only unforgotten name of a distant time, he is necessarily obscure. Every age has its modes of speech, and its cast of thought; which, though easily explained when there are many books to be compared with each other, become sometimes unintelligible, and always difficult, when there are no parallel passages that may conduce to their illustration. Shakespeare is the first considerable authour of sublime or familiar dialogue in our language. Of the books which he read, and from which he formed his stile, some perhaps have perished, and the rest are neglected. His imitations are therefore unnoted, his allusions are undiscovered, and many beauties, both of pleasantry and greatness, are lost with the objects to which they were united, as the figures vanish when the canvas has decayed.

It is the great excellence of Shakespeare, that he drew his scenes from nature, and from life. He copied the manners of the world then passing before him, and has more allusions than other poets to the traditions and superstition of the vulgar; which must therefore be traced before he can be understood.

He wrote at a time when our poetical language was yet unformed, when the meaning of our phrases was yet in fluctuation, when words were adopted at pleasure from the neighbouring languages, and while the Saxon was still visibly mingled in our diction. The reader is therefore embarrassed at once with dead and with foreign languages, with obsoleteness and innovation. In that age, as in all others, fashion produced phraseology, which succeeding fashion swept away before its meaning was generally known, or sufficiently authorised: and in that age, above all others, experiments were made upon our language, which distorted its combinations, and disturbed its uniformity.

If Shakespeare has difficulties above other writers, it is to be imputed to the nature of his work, which required the use of the common colloquial language, and consequently admitted many phrases allusive, elliptical, and proverbial, such as we speak and hear every hour without observing them; and of which, being now familiar, we do not suspect that they can ever grow uncouth, or that, being now obvious, they can ever seem remote.

These are the principal causes of the obscurity of Shakespeare; to which may be added that fulness of idea, which might sometimes load his words with more sentiment than they could conveniently convey, and that rapidity of imagination which might hurry him to a second thought before he had fully explained the first. But my opinion is, that very few of his lines were difficult to his audience, and that he used such expressions as were then common, though the paucity of contemporary writers makes them now seem peculiar. . . .

Another impediment, not the least vexatious to the commentator, is the exactness with which Shakespeare followed his authours. Instead of dilating his thoughts into generalities, and expressing incidents with poetical latitude, he often combines circumstances unnecessary to his main design, only because he happened to find them together. Such passages can be illustrated only by him who has read the same story in the very book which Shakespeare consulted.

He that undertakes an edition of Shakespeare, has all these difficulties to encounter, and all these obstructions to remove.

The corruptions of the text will be corrected by a careful collation of the oldest copies, by which it is hoped that many restorations may yet be made: at least it will be necessary to collect and note the variations as materials for future criticks, for it very often happens that a wrong reading has affinity to the right.

In this part all the present editions are apparently and intentionally defective. The criticks did not so much as wish to facilitate the labour of those that followed them. The same books are still to be compared; the work that has been done, is to be done again, and no single edition will supply the reader with a text on which he can rely as the best copy of the works of Shakespeare.

The edition now proposed will at least have this advantage over others. It will exhibit all the observable varieties of all the copies that can be found, that, if the reader is not satisfied with the editor's determination, he may have the means of chusing better for himself.

Where all the books are evidently vitiated, and collation can give no assistance, then begins the task of critical sagacity; and some changes may well be admitted in a text never settled by the authour, and so long exposed to caprice and ignorance. But nothing shall be imposed, as in the Oxford edition, without notice of the alteration; nor shall conjecture be wantonly or unnecessarily indulged.

It has been long found, that very specious emendations do not equally strike all minds with conviction, nor even the same mind at different times; and therefore, though perhaps many alterations may be proposed as eligible, very few will be obtruded as certain. In a language so ungrammatical as the English, and so licentious as that of Shakespeare, emendatory criticism is always hazardous; nor can it be allowed to any man who is not particularly versed in the writings of that age, and particularly studious of his authour's diction. There is danger lest peculiarities should be mistaken for corruptions, and passages rejected as unintelligible, which a narrow mind happens not to understand.

All the former criticks have been so much employed on the correction of the text, that they have not sufficiently attended to the elucidation of passages obscured by accident or time. The editor will endeavour to read the books which the authour read, to trace his knowledge to its source, and compare his copies with their originals. If in this part of his design he hopes to attain any degree of superiority to his predecessors, it must be considered, that he has the advantage of their labours; that part of the work being already done, more care is naturally bestowed on the other part; and that, to declare the truth, Mr. Rowe and Mr. Pope were very ignorant of the ancient English literature; Dr. Warburton was detained by more important studies; and Mr. Theobald, if fame be just to his memory, considered learning only as an instrument of gain, and made no further enquiry after his authour's meaning, when once he had notes sufficient to embellish his page with the expected decorations.

With regard to obsolete or peculiar diction, the editor may perhaps claim some degree of confidence, having had more motives to consider the whole extent of our language than any other man from its first formation. He hopes, that, by comparing the works of Shakespeare with those of writers who lived at the same time, immediately preceded, or immediately followed him, he shall be able to ascertain his ambiguities, disentangle his intricacies, and recover the meaning of words now lost in the darkness of antiquity.

When therefore any obscurity arises from an allusion to some other book, the passage will be quoted. When the diction is entangled, it will be cleared by a paraphrase or interpretation. When the sense is broken by the suppression of part of the sentiment in pleasantry or passion, the connection will be supplied. When any forgotten custom is hinted, care will be taken to retrieve and explain it. The meaning assigned to doubtful words will be supported by the authorities of other writers, or by parallel passages of Shakespeare himself.

The observation of faults and beauties is one of the duties of an annotator, which some of Shakespeare's editors have attempted, and some have neglected. For this part of his task, and for this only, was Mr. Pope eminently and indisputably qualified: nor has Dr. Warburton followed him with less diligence or less success. But I have never observed that mankind was much delighted or improved by their asterisks, commas, or double commas; of which the only effect is, that they preclude the pleasure of judging for ourselves, teach the young and ignorant to decide without principles; defeat curiosity and discernment, by leaving them less to discover; and at last shew the opinion of the critick, without the reasons on which it was founded, and without affording any light by which it may be examined.

The editor, though he may less delight his own vanity, will probably please his reader more, by supposing him equally able with himself to judge of beauties and faults, which require no previous acquisition of remote knowledge. A description of the obvious scenes of nature, a representation of general life, a sentiment of reflection or experience, a deduction of conclusive argument, a forcible eruption of effervescent passion, are to be considered as proportionate to common apprehension, unassisted by critical officiousness; since, to conceive them, nothing more is requisite than acquaintance with the general state of the world, and those faculties which he must always bring with him who would read Shakespeare.

But when the beauty arises from some adaptation of the sentiment to customs worn out of use, to opinions not universally prevalent, or to any accidental or minute particularity, which cannot be supplied by common understanding, or common observation, it is the duty of a commentator to lend his assistance.

The notice of beauties and faults thus limited will make no distinct part of the design, being reducible to the explanation of obscure passages.

The editor does not however intend to preclude himself from the comparison of Shakespeare's sentiments or expression with those of ancient or modern authours, or from the display of any beauty not obvious to the students of poetry; for as he hopes to leave his authour better understood, he wishes likewise to procure him more rational approbation.

The former editors have affected to slight their predecessors: but in this edition all that is valuable will be adopted from every commentator, that posterity may consider it as including all the rest, and exhibiting whatever is hitherto known of the great father of the English drama.

—Samuel Johnson, *Proposals for Printing,*
by Subscription, the Dramatick Works
of William Shakespeare, 1756

James Russell Lowell
"Shakespeare Once More" (1868)

James Russell Lowell (1819–91) considers the history of the editions of Shakespeare's plays. He emphasizes the debt we owe to John Heminge and Henry Condell for having gathered Shakespeare's plays and thus preserved them in the First Folio of 1623, which Lowell celebrates despite its many textual faults. He then posits the characteristics necessary for an ideal editor of Shakespeare's works.

The hold which Shakespeare has acquired and maintained upon minds so many and so various, in so many vital respects utterly unsympathetic and even incapable of sympathy with his own, is one of the most noteworthy phenomena in the history of literature. That he has had the most inadequate of editors, that, as his own Falstaff was the cause of the wit, so he has been the cause of the foolishness that was in other men, (as where Malone ventured to discourse upon his metres, and Dr. Johnson on his imagination,) must be apparent to every one,—and also that his genius and its manifestations are so various, that there is no commentator but has been able to illustrate him from his own peculiar point of view or from the results of his own favorite studies. But to show that he was a good common lawyer, that he understood the theory of colors, that he was an accurate botanist, a master of the science of medicine, especially in its relation to mental disease, a profound metaphysician, and of great experience and insight in politics,—all these, while they may very well form the staple of separate treatises, and prove, that, whatever the extent of his learning, the range and accuracy of his knowledge were beyond precedent or later parallel, are really outside the province of an editor.

We doubt if posterity owe a greater debt to any two men living in 1623 than to the two obscure actors who in that year published the first folio edition of Shakespeare's plays. But for them, it is more than likely that such of his works as had remained to that time unprinted would have been irrecoverably lost, and among them were *Julius Caesar, The Tempest,* and *Macbeth.* But are we to believe them when they assert that they present to us the plays which they reprinted from stolen and surreptitious copies "cured and perfect of their limbs," and those which are original in their edition "absolute in their numbers as he [Shakespeare] conceived them"? Alas, we have read too many theatrical announcements, have been taught too often that the value of the promise was in an inverse ratio to the generosity of the exclamation-marks, too easily to believe that! . . .

What, then, is the value of the first folio as an authority? For eighteen of the plays it is the only authority we have, and the only one also for four others in their complete form. It is admitted that in several instances Heminge and Condell reprinted the earlier quarto impressions with a few changes, sometimes for the better and sometimes for the worse; and it is most probable that copies of those editions (whether surreptitious or not) had taken the place of the original prompter's books, as being more convenient and legible. Even in these cases it is not safe to conclude that all or even any of the variations were made by the hand of Shakespeare himself. And where the players printed from manuscript, is it likely to have been that of the author? The probability is small that a writer so busy as Shakespeare must have been during his productive period should have copied out their parts for the actors himself, or that one so indifferent as he seems to have been to the immediate literary fortunes of his works should have given much care to the correction of copies, if made by others. The copies exclusively in the hands of Heminge and Condell were, it is manifest, in some cases, very imperfect, whether we account for the fact by the burning of the Globe Theatre or by the necessary wear and tear of years, and (what is worthy of notice) they are plainly more defective in some parts than in others. *Measure for Measure* is an example of this, and we are not satisfied with being told that its ruggedness of verse is intentional, or that its obscurity is due to the fact that Shakespeare grew more elliptical in his style as he grew older. Profounder in thought he doubtless became; though in a mind like his, we believe that this would imply only a more absolute supremacy in expression. But, from whatever original we suppose either the quartos or the first folio to have been printed, it is more than questionable whether the proof-sheets had the advantage of any revision other than that of the printing-office. [Shakespeare editor George] Steevens was of opinion that authors in the time of Shakespeare never read their own proof-sheets; and Mr. [James] Spedding, in his recent edition of Bacon, comes independently to the same conclusion. We may be very sure that Heminge and Condell did not, as vicars, take upon themselves a disagreeable task which the author would have been too careless to assume.

Nevertheless, however strong a case may be made out against the Folio of 1623, whatever sins of omission we may lay to the charge of Heminge and Condell, or of commission to that of the printers, it remains the only text we have with any claims whatever to authenticity. It should be deferred to as authority in all cases where it does not make Shakespeare write bad sense, uncouth metre, or false grammar, of all which we believe him to have been more supremely incapable than any other man who ever wrote English. Yet we would not speak unkindly even of the blunders of the Folio. They have put bread into the mouth of many an honest editor, publisher, and printer for the last century and a half. . . . [W]ith Shakespeare . . . the more we have familiarized ourselves with the operations of our own consciousness, the more do we find, in reading him, that he has been beforehand with us, and that, while we have been vainly endeavouring to find the door of his being, he has searched every nook and cranny of our own. While other poets and dramatists embody isolated phases of character and work inward from the phenomenon to the special law which it illustrates, he seems in some strange way unitary with human nature itself, and his own soul to have been the law and life-giving power of which his creations are only the phenomena. . . .

That Shakespeare did not edit his own works must be attributed, we suspect, to his premature death. That he should not have intended it is inconceivable. Is there not something of self-consciousness in the breaking of Prospero's wand and burying his book,—a sort of sad prophecy, based on self-knowledge of the nature of that man who, after such thaumaturgy, could go down to Stratford and live there for years, only collecting his dividends from the Globe Theatre, lending money on mortgage, and leaning over his gate to chat and bandy quips with neighbors? His mind had entered into every phase of human life and thought, had embodied all of them in living creations;—had he found all empty, and come at last to the belief that genius and its works were as phantasmagoric as the rest, and that fame was as idle as the rumor of the pit? However this may be, his works have come down to us in a condition of manifest and admitted corruption in some portions, while in others there is an obscurity which may be attributed either to an idiosyncratic use of words and condensation of phrase, to a depth of intuition for a proper coalescence with which ordinary language is inadequate, to a concentration of passion in a focus that consumes the lighter links which bind together the clauses of a sentence or of a process of reasoning in common parlance, or to a sense of music which mingles music and meaning without essentially confounding them. We should demand for a perfect editor, then, first, a thorough glossological knowledge of the English contemporary with Shakespeare; second, enough logical acuteness of mind and metaphysical training to enable him to follow recondite processes of thought; third, such a conviction of the supremacy of his author as always to prefer his thought to any theory of his own; fourth, a feeling for music, and so much knowledge of the practice of other poets as to understand that Shakespeare's versification differs from theirs as often in kind as in degree; fifth, an acquaintance with the world as well as with books; and last, what is, perhaps, of more importance than all, so great a familiarity with the working of the imaginative faculty in general, and of its peculiar operation in the mind of Shakespeare, as will prevent his thinking a passage dark with excess of light, and enable him to understand fully that the Gothic Shakespeare often superimposed upon the slender column of a single word, that seems to twist under it, but does not,—like the quaint shafts in cloisters,—a weight of meaning which the modern architects of sentences would consider wholly unjustifiable by correct principle.

—James Russell Lowell, from "Shakespeare Once More," 1868, *Works*, 1890, volume 3, pp. 166–73

Thomas Spencer Baynes
"New Shakespearian Interpretations" (1872)

Before offering scholarly additions, founded on his study of Elizabethan and Jacobean texts, to the critical and explanatory notes that have been accumulated by Shakespearean scholars and editors, Thomas Spencer Baynes (1823–87), English philosopher, essayist, journalist, professor of logic and literature, editor of the ninth edition of the *Encyclopedia Britannica*, and a Shakespearean scholar, traces and evaluates the history of editorial philosophies and practices with which the succession of editors have approached Shakespearean texts. His own contributions regarding the metaphorical basis for various terms Shakespeare used come from Elizabethan texts relating to hunting and hawking.

The oldest and most authoritative editions of Shakespeare are, it is well known, crowded with verbal errors, textual corruptions, and metrical obscurities. They include, indeed, almost every species of literary and typographical confusion which haste, ignorance, and carelessness in the multiplication and fortuitous printing of manuscript copies could produce. After a century and a half of critical labour embracing three great schools of editors and commentators, the text of these dramas is only now partially purged from the obvious blots and stains that disfigure the earliest editions. And it is only within the last ten years that the results of this prolonged critical labour have been condensed, and exhibited in a thoroughly scientific shape, by the acute and learned editors of the Cambridge *Shakespeare*.

By means of this most useful and scholarlike edition, any cultivated and intelligent reader may form some estimate of the net result and general value of Shakespearian criticism. A comparison of the best modern readings with those of the Quartos and Folios will show in what numberless instances the text has been corrected, amended, and even restored. Those who have never made such a comparison would be surprised to find how many familiar phrases and passages, some too regarded as peculiarly Shakespearian, are due to the happy conjectures of successive textual scholars. Rowe and Pope, the first critical editors, being themselves poets, are peculiarly felicitous in their suggested emendations. But even the more prosaic Theobald's single-minded and persistent devotion was surprisingly successful in the same direction. His labours were, however, still more fruitful in restoring neglected readings from the First Folio which neither of his predecessors had consulted with any care. The first school of critics, indeed, brought native sagacity rather than minute or accurate learning to the task of clearing up the difficulties of Shakespeare's text. They satisfied themselves with correcting the more obvious misprints of the Folios, and endeavouring to relieve, by conjectural emendations, some of their corruptest passages.

The second school of editors, represented by [Edward] Capell, [George] Steevens, and [Edmund] Malone, were diligent students of the Elizabethan literature, and found no difficulty therefore in explaining many words and phrases that had perplexed and baffled their predecessors. For elucidating the obscurities of the text, they relied more on illustration than on conjectured emendation. Many passages which the early editors, through ignorance of Elizabethan manners, usages, and allusions, had regarded as corrupt, were amply vindicated from the charge by the more exact and minute knowledge of the later. The third, and more recent schools of editors and critics, represented by [biographer of Shakespeare and editor of a pictorial edition of his plays Charles] Knight, and [scholar, editor, and alleged forger of Shakespeare-related documents John Payne] Collier, [Scottish clergyman, literary historian, editor, and Elizabethan scholar Alexander] Dyce, and [Shakespearean scholar and chessmaster Howard] Staunton while combining the distinctive excellences of the previous schools, have specially developed what may be regarded as the most fruitful branch of Shakespearian criticism—that of apt and illuminating illustrations from contemporary literature. The researches of Knight, Dyce, and Staunton in particular have satisfactorily explained many phrases and allusions regarded by previous editors as hopelessly ambiguous and obscure, if not altogether unintelligible. While thus working in the right direction, the modern school has, however, exemplified afresh the conflict between authority and criticism which must always prevail with regard to an original text, at once so important and so defective as that of Shakespeare's dramas. Mr. Knight, in his admiration of the First Folio, yielded a somewhat exclusive deference to authority. Mr. Collier, again, partly no doubt from the accident of possessing the Perkin's Folio, went to the other extreme, becoming the champion of conjectural emendation in its most licentious forms. Mr. Dyce and Mr. Staunton hold the balance comparatively even, but in the hands of the Cambridge editors it again inclines more decisively towards the side of authority. On the whole, the result of recent criticism and research has been to strengthen the position of the First Folio, and check the recurrent tendency to get rid of textual difficulties by ingenious, but often rash and ignorant, conjecture.

This result is in all respects a satisfactory one. Conjectural emendation is at best a double-edged instrument, to be wielded in safety only on rare occasions and by the most skillful hands. The eager Shakespearian student is, however, continually tempted to cut the Gordian knot of a difficulty by its summary use. The temptation should be steadfastly resisted, on pain, for the most part, of reading into the poet's lines a foreign and prosaic sense, instead of bringing fully out their real but latent meaning. In the majority of cases the practice of substituting his own language for the poet's simply depraves the text, and injures the finer sensibilities of the critic. Those who indulge in it too freely, however naturally gifted, soon lose that respect for the poet's words, and scrupulous care for his meaning, which is the foundation of all sound and illuminating criticism.

There is little danger of any excess in the other main department of critical labour, that of illustrating from appropriate sources the obscurer terms and allusions of Shakespeare's text. In this direction there is still ample scope, "room and verge enough," [Thomas Gray, from Ode VI, The Bard] for the labours of Shakespearian students. The fact is in itself one of the most striking proofs of Shakespeare's marvellous universality. That anything should remain to be elucidated after the life-long devotion of so many learned and acute commentators is surprising enough. But Shakespeare's vision of life is so wide, his moral insight so profound, his knowledge and sympathies so vitalised and universal, and his command of language so absolute, that every part in the wide circle of contemporary learning and experience may throw some light on his pages. In particular, his birthright of pregnant speech is so imperial that he seems to appropriate by a kind of royal prerogative the more expressive elements of diction in every department of human attainment and activity. No section of life or thought is too humble for his regard; none too lofty for his sympathetic appreciation. The day-spring of his serene and glorious intellect illuminates and vivifies the whole. The more prominent features of that great world are familiar to all cultivated English readers. The order and organisation of the several parts have been diligently studied and eloquently expounded by the critics. But there are still hidden nooks and obscure recesses which even the most curious and painstaking observers have failed to explore. On these, special investigation and persistent research may yet throw some light. Such researches are, moreover, within the reach of students who could hardly be considered Shakespearian scholars in the higher and technical sense of the term. The complete Shakespearian scholar ought to have a minute and exhaustive, but at the same time vital acquaintance with the whole Elizabethan period, its entire universe of knowledge and experience. This can only be gained by the thorough and prolonged study of its history and literature, including the most fugitive and evanescent productions, such as songs, ballads, and chap-books, squibs and letters, pamphlets and broadsides. Few even of the more devoted Shakespearian critics have reached this ideal standard. Many hands, however, make light work, and much may be done in the way of Shakespearian interpretation by the separate contributions of students who have been able to cultivate only a small portion of the wide field. The humblest labourer may add his mite to the constantly-accumulating stores of sterling commentary and illustration.

Many of the sources whence elucidations of Shakespeare's obscure passages may be drawn lie on the surface, and are well known. His writings abound, for example, with terms and phrases, similes, metaphors, and allusions derived from field sports, such as hunting and hawking; from games of chance and skill, such as cards and dice, bowls and tennis; from the military and self-defensive arts, such as archery and fencing; from fashionable pastimes, such as music and dancing; and from popular natural history—the whole folk-flora and folk-fauna of the time. The more obvious, and many of the more obscure allusions connected with these branches of popular knowledge and practice, have been amply explained by successive editors. Some, however, have been overlooked, and in the present paper we purpose giving a few illustrations of these neglected allusions. We shall offer an explanation of some passages in Shakespeare, either given up by critics and commentators as hopelessly unintelligible, or only very imperfectly and erroneously explained. So far at least as we are acquainted with

Shakespearian criticism, most of the explanations now proposed of obscure terms, phrases, and allusions are new,—have not been in any way anticipated by previous writers on the subject. Even a very partial acquaintance with the wide field of Shakespearian criticism suggests, however, the propriety of some hesitation and reserve in announcing novelties of interpretation. Every persistent student of Shakespeare must have found, again and again, that what he at first imagined to be discoveries had been anticipated by previous writers, illustrious or obscure. In general, however, the best modern editions represent in a condensed form, either in notes or glossary, the main results of previous criticism. If they leave a difficulty unnoticed, or give only a vague and conjectural explanation, it may be assumed with tolerable certainty that no better solution has yet been offered. In the same way the Variorum edition gives the main results of Shakespearian criticism up to the date of its publication. In offering the following elucidations as novelties, it is meant therefore that they solve difficulties left unexplained by the Variorum edition, by modern editors, by the ablest independent critics, such as [Francis] Douce, [Robert E.] Hunter, [William Sidney] Walker, and [Richard Grant] White, and, so far as the writer is aware, by all previous commentators on Shakespeare.

We may begin with a few illustrations from popular field sports, which in Shakespeare's day meant very much hawking and hunting. These furnish the poet with almost inexhaustible materials of imagery and allusion. In particular, the sportive warfare in the fields and woods with the nobler kinds of chase and game afforded the aptest phrases, similes, and metaphors for picturing vividly the sterner realities of martial conflict, "the pride, pomp, and circumstance of glorious war" [*Othello*, III.iii.351] Such references occur again and again, and many of them are even now only partially explained. In *Coriolanus,* for example, in the wonderful scene between the servants in the house of Aufidius, such an allusion occurs. While the servants who had resisted the intruder are talking together in the hall about the sudden arrival and ceremonious entertainment of their master's great enemy, a third hastily approached from the banqueting-room with the news that it has been just determined, at the suggestion of Coriolanus, to march against Rome.

> *Sec. Serv.:* Why, then we shall have a stirring world again. This peace is
>   nothing, but to rust iron, increase tailors, and breed ballad-makers.
> *First Serv.:* Let me have war, say I; it exceeds peace as far as day does
>   night; it's spritely, waking, audible, and *full of vent.* Peace is a very
>   apoplexy, lethargy, mulled, deaf, sleepy, insensible; a getter of more
>   bastard children than war's a destroyer of men.
>   [IV.v.230–38]

Here the phrase "full of vent," the reading of the Folio's, has so perplexed the critics that more than one has proposed to substitute for it "full of vaunt." The Folio text is, however, perfectly accurate, and peculiarly expressive, although it has never yet been correctly explained. The only explanation attempted is that of Johnson, repeated by subsequent editors, that "full of vent" means "full of rumour, full of materials of discourse." This, however, is a mere conjecture, and not a happy one, as it altogether misses the distinctive meaning of the phrase. Vent is a technical term in hunting to express the scenting of the game by the hounds employed in the chase. Both noun and verb are habitually used in this sense. Their exact meaning and use will be made clear by an extract or two from Turbervile's translation of *Du Fouilloux,* the popular manual of hunting in Shakespeare's day. The first extract refers to the wiles and subtleties of the hart when keenly pressed in the chase: "When a hart feeles that the hounds hold in after him, he fleeth and seeketh to beguile them with change in sundry sortes, for he will seeke other harts and deare at lare, and rowseth them before the houndes to make them hunt change; therewithall he will lie flat down upon his belly in some of their layres, and so let the houndes overshoot him, and because they should have no sent of him, nor *vent* him, he will trusse all his four feet under his belly, and will blow and breath upon the ground in some moist place, in such sort that I have seen the houndes passe by such an hart within a yard of him and never *vent* him." Further on, the author, speaking of the hart, says again expressly: "When he smelleth or *venteth* anything, we say he hath this or that in the wind." In the same way, when the hound vents anything, he pauses to verify the scent, and then, full of eager excitement, strains in the leash to be after the game that is thus perceived to be a-foot. The following extract from the rhyming report of a huntsman upon sight of a hart in pride of grease illustrates this:—

My Liege, I went this morning on my quest;
My hound did sticke, and seemed to *vent* some beast.

... The use of the noun is exemplified in another hunting rhyme, or huntsman's soliloquy, entitled "The Blazon of the Hart," which is of special interest from the vividness of the picture it brings before us:—

... Then take my hound, in lyam me behind,
The stately hart in fryth or fell to find.
And while I seeke his slott where he hath fedde,
The sweet byrdes sing, to cheare my drowsie head.

And when my hound doth straine upon good *vent*
I must confesse, the same doth me content....

The technical meaning and use of the word in these passages is sufficiently clear, and it will be seen how happily Shakespeare employs it. To strain at the lyam or leash "upon good vent" is in Shakespeare's phrase to be "full of vent," or in other words keenly excited, full of pluck and courage, of throbbing energy and impetuous desire, in a word, full of all the kindling stir and commotion of anticipated conflict. This is not only in harmony with the meaning of the passage, but gives point and force to the whole description. War is naturally personified as a trained hound roused to animated motion by the scent of game, giving tongue, and straining in the slips at the near prospect of the exciting chase. This explanation justifies the reading of the Folios, *"sprightly walking,* audible, full of vent," or at least affords a better explanation of it than has yet been offered. With a single exception the early reading has been rejected by all modern editors, including, strangely enough, Mr. Knight and the Cambridge editors. The exception is Mr. Staunton, who, however, while retaining the older reading, fails to understand it, and misinterprets the passage. He explains "sprightly walking" as "quick moving or marching," with evident reference to military movements, and with regard to the special phrase under review, he says boldly "vent is voice, utterance." But the previous epithet, audible, gives this feature of the description, *vent* referring not to sound at all, but to the quick perception of the game, and the signs of eagerness, such as kindled eye, dilated nostril, and muscular impatience, which keen relish for the sport produces. In such a connection "sprightly walking" would refer to the more lively and definite advance arising from the discovery of good vent as compared with the dissatisfied snuffings and uncertain progress when nothing is in view. The description thus includes quickened motion, eager tongue, and intense physical excitement. The passage finds an exact parallel in Henry V.'s spirited address to his soldiers before Harfleur:—

And you, good yeomen,
Whose limbs were made in England, show us here
The mettle of your pasture. . . .
                    [III.i.25–32]

The . . . reference to "the mettle of your pasture" is also derived from the *Noble Art of Venerie.* The colour of the stag, the size and texture of his antlers, his strength of wind and limb, and powers of endurance, depended very much upon the country in which he was reared, and especially upon the kind of pasture on which he browsed. . . . Before leaving the subject, we may notice that the word "vent" in its technical sense is used by Shakespeare's contemporaries, especially the poets, such as [Edmund] Spenser and [Michael] Drayton. The following extract from the graphic account of stag-hunting in the fourteenth song of [Drayton's] *Polyolbion* illustrates this:—

> Now when the hart doth heare
> The oft-bellowing hounds to *vent* his secret leyre,
> He rouzing rusheth out, and through the brakes doth
>   drive. . . .

It need hardly be added that *vent* in this sense is, like so many of the terms of venery, taken directly from the French, to vent the game being simply to wind, or have wind of the game. Shakespeare's very expression, indeed, exists as a French phrase, and is given to illustrate the special meaning of the noun as a hunting term.

Again, Shakespeare uses the word *train* more than once in its technical hunting sense, the most striking instance of this special use being found in *Macbeth*. When Malcolm, in order to test the sincerity of Macduff's devotion, heaps vices on himself, until Macduff, in a burst of noble sorrow and indignation, renounces his enterprise in despair, Malcolm, satisfied with the result, explains the motive of his conduct as follows:—

> *Mal:* . . . Devilish Macbeth By many of these *trains* hath sought to win
>   me Into his power. . . .
>   [IV.iii.117–19]

It has not been noticed that *trains* in this extract is a technical term both in hawking and hunting; in hawking for the lure, thrown out to reclaim a falcon given to ramble, or "rake out" as it is called, and thus in danger of escaping from the fowler; and in hunting for the bait trailed along the ground, and left exposed to tempt the animal from his lair or covert, and bring him fairly within the power of the lurking huntsman. . . .

The play of *Hamlet* supplies another illustration of hunting terms only partially explained.

In the conversation about the players between Hamlet, Rosencrantz and Guildenstern a technical term occurs, which, though sometimes rightly understood, is often erroneously interpreted, and has never been traced or elucidated in its primary meaning and use:—

Ham.: Why did you laugh, then, when I said, man delights not me?
Ros.: To think, my lord, if you delight not in man, what lenten
 entertainment the players shall receive from you: we *coted* them on
 the way, and hither are they coming to offer you service.
[II.ii.322ff.]

Here *cote,* in the older spelling *coat,* is usually explained, even by modern editors, according to its etymology rather than according to its actual use, while none seem to be aware of its special technical meaning. Thus Mr. Collier interprets the phrase "we coted them" to mean "we overtook them," or, strictly, "came side by side with them," and Mr. Staunton boldly gives the latter part of this explanation as the full meaning of the term—"coted them"—"came alongside of them." [Robert] Nares, again, while stating that the term is employed in coursing, gives the same erroneous interpretation, "coted," *i.e.,* "went side by side," and seems to have no real knowledge of its technical use. Mr. Dyce quotes from [Thomas] Caldecott a pertinent example of its use in contemporary literature, but he appears undecided as to the exact signification of the word, and unacquainted with its special secondary meaning. Both verb and noun are, however, sporting terms used in coursing of every kind, whether of the stag, the fox, or the hare. *Cote* in this technical sense is applied to a brace of greyhounds slipped together at the stag or hare, and means that one of the dogs outstrips the other and reaches the game first. . . . To cote is thus not simply to overtake, but to overpass, to outstrip, this being the distinctive meaning of the term. If one dog were originally behind the other, the cote would of course involve overtaking as its condition, but overtaking simply is not coting. Going beyond is the essential point, the term being usually applied under circumstances where overtaking is impossible—to dogs who start together and run abreast until the cote takes place. So Rosencrantz and Guildenstern, having coted the players in their way, reach the palace first, and have been for some time in conversation with Hamlet before the strolling company arrive. In its secondary or metaphorical use, the word uniformly retains the same distinctive meaning. In the literature of the time, to cote others in wealth, beauty, or worth, is to excel them in these respects. . . .

In connection with coursing, we may note the discussion that has arisen among the commentators on the meaning of *lym* or *lyam,* and *leash,* as applied to hounds. In the well-known rhyming list of dogs given by Edgar in his assumed character of Poor Tom in *King Lear,* one of the kinds specified is *lym,* or, in other words, lym-hound; and in the first part of *Henry* IV., *leash* is used for three, in the phrase "a leash of drawers," [II.iv.7] immediately afterwards enumerated as Tom, Dick, and Francis. There has been some hesitation amongst the editors as to the exact technical meaning and use of these terms. But a single extract from the old *Art of Venerie* settles the question:—

> We finde some difference of termes between hounds and greyhounds. As of greyhounds two make a brase, and of hounds a couple. Of greyhounds three make a *lease*, and of hounds a couple and a halfe. We let slippe a greyhound, and we cast off a hound. The string wherewith we leade a greyhound is called a *lease*, and for a hound a *lyame*.

It has been conjectured with much probability that another word, *uncape*, used in the *Merry Wives of Windsor*, must have been a technical term in fox-hunting. It occurs in the humorous scene where the jealous Ford, accompanied by a posse of his friends and neighbours, arrives at his own house, resolved to hunt for the disturber of his peace, whom he declares to be harboured there by the guilty connivance of his wife. On entering the house, he meets the servants going out with the buck-basket in which Falstaff is almost smothered beneath the soiled linen:—

> *Ford*: . . . Here, here, here, be my keys: ascend my chambers; search, seek, find out: I'll warrant we'll unkennel the fox. Let me stop this way first. *[Locks the door.]* So now *uncape*.
> [III.iii.160ff.]

Here it seems clear from the context that *uncape* must be a term connected with fox-hunting, but no instance of its technical use has been discovered, and hardly any two editors agree as to its exact meaning. [William] Warburton asserts, with his usual confidence, that it means "to dig out the fox when earthed"; while [George] Stevens maintains that the term refers to a bag-fox. "The allusion is," he says, "to the stopping every hole at which a fox could enter before they uncape or turn him out of the bag in which he was brought." [Thomas] Hanmer substituted the reading *uncouple* [in his 1744 edition]; and Nares, in support of this interpretation, and with a special eye to Stevens' note, says that "Falstaff is the fox, and he is supposed to be hidden, or kenneled, somewhere in the house; no expression therefore relative to a bag-fox can be applicable, because such a fox would be already in the hands of the hunters. The *uncaping* is decidedly to begin the hunt after him; when the holes for escape had been stopped." This seems from the context to be the real meaning of the word.

It must indicate the commencement of the hunt, or, in other words, the uncoupling of the hounds. But the text need not be altered to bring out this signification. Though no example of its technical use has yet been found, there can be little doubt that uncape was a sporting term locally or colloquially employed instead of uncouple. Nor, after all, is it very difficult to explain its origin and use in this sense. Turbervile, after stating that amongst other differences "the greyhound hath his collar and the hound his couples," intimates the existence of many more technical terms, of which those he gives are simply the most usual. Cape might very well have been one of the terms for collar or couple, as it undoubtedly had this meaning in Shakespeare's day. In the sixteenth and seventeenth centuries, while cape meant, as it still does, the top or upper part of a garment, it was usually restricted to a much smaller portion than the word designates now—a part encircling the neck rather than covering the shoulders. It meant, in fact, a neckband, most commonly of the kind termed a falling-band; in other words, a collar. . . . Shakespeare himself uses it . . . as another word for neckband or collar. In the *Taming of the Shrew*, amongst the directions given to the tailor by Grumio for the making of Katharina's robe or dress, are specified, "a loose-bodied gown with a *small compassed cape*." Here the epithet compassed means circular, so that the item is equivalent to a small circular collar, or falling band around the throat. Whether cape is a technical term in fox-hunting or not, Shakespeare was therefore perfectly entitled to use it, as he evidently does, in the *Merry Wives of Windsor*, as a synonym for couple or collar. As given in the old pictures, the broad, loose, indented leather bands or collars to which the lyam or leash was attached, completely realise the contemporary notion of a cape, and no mistake could possibly arise from the use of the term in this sense. The words *uncape, uncollar,* or *uncouple* would each mean the same thing, while all would be easily, if not equally intelligible.

We may conclude the allusions to hunting by an illustration or two of the beautiful passage in the *Midsummer Night's Dream*, where Theseus celebrates the music of his hounds in full cry . . . [cites IV.i.106-29] . . . Shakespeare might probably enough, as the commentators suggest, have derived his knowledge of Cretan and Spartan hounds from [Arthur] Golding's translation of Ovid, where they are commemorated in the description of Actaeon's tragical chase and death. But in enumerating the points of the slow, sure, deep-mouthed hound, it can hardly be doubted he had in view the celebrated Talbot breed nearer home. A contemporary writer celebrates the virtues of these hounds in terms that recall Shakespeare's own description:—

Next to hunting, hawking was perhaps the most popular field sport in Shakespeare's day. In many parts of the country, indeed, it was more in vogue, or, at least, more habitually pursued, than hunting itself. . . .

—Thomas Spencer Baynes, "New Shakespearian Interpretations," 1872, *Shakespeare Studies*, 1894, pp. 300–57

C. M. Ingleby "The Still Lion Discovered" (1875)

Shakespearean scholar Clement Mansfield Ingleby (1823–86) objects to what he sees as the wholesale damage inflicted on Shakespearean texts by critic-editors he finds impertinent in their assumption that their conjectures about possibly obscure passages are superior to the doubtful and possibly corrupt originals.

We may say of Shakespeare's text what Thomas De Quincey said of Milton's:

ON ANY ATTEMPT TO TAKE LIBERTIES WITH A PASSAGE OF *HIS*, YOU FEEL AS WHEN COMING, IN A FOREST, UPON WHAT SEEMS A DEAD LLON; PERHAPS HE MAY NOT BE DEAD, BUT ONLY SLEEPING, NAY PERHAPS HE MAY NOT BE SLEEPING, BUT ONLY SHAMMING. YOU MAY BE PUT DOWN WITH SHAME BY SOME MAN READING THE LINE OTHERWISE,

or, we add, reading it in the light of more extended or more accurate knowledge.

Here lies the covert danger of emendation. It is true that the text of Shakespeare, as it comes down to us—"the latest seed of time" [from "Godiva," 1842, by Alfred, Lord Tennyson]—in the folio 1623, as well as in the early quartos, is very corrupt. It is corrupt on two accounts. As to the text of the quartos, there was no proper editorial supervision, since the editions were intended merely for the accommodation of playgoers; the text was therefore imperfect not only in form but in substance as well. As to the text of the folio, the supervision of Messrs. Heminge and Condell seems to have been confined to the selection of copies for the printers, Messrs. Jaggard and Blount; and some of those were playhouse copies, which had been curtailed for representation, and certain other were copies of quarto editions; while the correction of the press was probably left to the 'reader' of the printing-house,[1] who certainly could not have exercised any extraordinary vigilance in his vocation. Accordingly we have imperfect copies at first, and a misprinted text at last.

The corrupt and mutilated condition in which the Greek and Roman Classics, especially the Greek, have been handed down to modern times is the sufficient reason for that latitude of conjectural criticism which has been brought to bear on their ancient texts. If we had to deal with an English text which bore like evidences of dilapidation, we should naturally have recourse to the same means for its correction. But such is not the case with the works of any English author who has assumed the proportions of a classic: not Chaucer, nor Shakespeare, nor Milton, is a venerable ruin demanding restoration; though Shakespeare, far more than Milton, has suffered corruption, and that by the very nature of the vehicle to which he committed his thoughts; exactly as the 'Last Supper' of Leonardo da Vinci has incurred an amount of destruction which it might have escaped had it been painted on wood or on canvass. Such corruption, however, as infects the works of Shakespeare touches but comparatively small, and often isolated, portions of the text, offering no very serious obstacle to the general reader, who is not exacting or scrupulous in the interpretation of his author's phraseology. Patches of indictable nonsense, which have hitherto defied all attempts at elucidation, there are, as we shall soon see, in some of the plays; yet it is no very violent proceeding to regard them as parts of the inferior work of a joint-author, or as interpolations by the players, or as matter adopted by Shakespeare from the older play on which his own was founded. But the critical student is naturally intolerant of every unexplored obscurity and every unresolved difficulty; and an editor who works for students as well as for general readers feels himself bound to apply to the text all the available resources of criticism. The example of the ancient Classics, and the capital success which rewarded the vigilance and invention of scholars in that field, could not fail to determine the method on which the recension of Shakespeare was to be attempted by the verbal critics.

As the natural result, the text has been subjected to a conjectural criticism which owns no restraint and systematically violates every principle of probability and of propriety. Obsolete phraseology and archaic allusion are treated as cases of corruption: the language, where corrupt, instead of being restored or amended, is modernized and *improved:* and the idiom, instead of being expounded and illustrated, is accommodated to the prevailing grammatical standard. By this means more fatuous and incapable nonsense has been manufactured for Shakespeare than can be found in any of the ancient copies of his plays. . . .

Shakespeare died without, so far as we know, having made the attempt to collect and print his works. Of this fact an unnecessary difficulty has been made. A much more self-conscious genius than Shakespeare has himself given us the clue to its solution, a clue of which all writers, save Thomas Carlyle,[5] have failed to perceive the significance. Goethe confessed to Eckermann that he never reperused any of his poems when once it was completed and printed, unless impelled to the task by the demand for a new edition; and that he then read it with no self-complacency, but rather dissatisfaction. Why was this? Simply because he felt a *Widerwille*, or distaste, towards the offspring of his less matured self, by reason of its inadequacy to express his great ideal—the 'unbodied figure of the thought that gave 't surmised shape.' He had outgrown his own powers, in the grander sense of that phrase: never, like poor Swift, living to look back with wonder and horror on the glory of a genius that he owned no more, but prejudicially contrasting his past self with the greater present. . . .

[I]t is a fact that the first collection of [Shakespeare's] plays was published six or seven years after his death; and it is a matter of certainty that the folio of 1623 was printed from inaccurate quarto editions and mutilated stagecopies. This is the 'case' of those who advocate the rights of unlimited conjecture; and we frankly make the concession, that our text needs emendation. But, before they can be permitted to conjecture, we require of them to find out where the corruptions lie. If a man's body be diseased, the seat of the disease can generally be determined, between the patient and the doctor: in some cases, however, the malady baffles alike research and experiment.

In the case of Shakespeare's text, the diagnosis is infinitely perplexed: (1) from the multitude of obscurities and difficulties that beset it: (2) from the close resemblance that often subsists between those obscurities which spring from the obsolete language or the archaic allusions, and those which are wholly due to the misreading or misprinting of the text. Our healthy parts are so like our diseased parts, that the doctor sets about the medicinal treatment of that which needs no cure; and the patient's body is so full of those seeming anomalies, that his life is endangered by the multiplicity of agencies brought to bear on his time-worn frame.

What, if there are cases in which those *kyrioi synomotai* [gentlemen conspirators] archaic phraseology and textual corruption, unite their powers against us? Why, in such cases, it is most likely that the critic would be utterly baffled: that he would be unable to restore the lost integrity even by the combined forces of exposition and conjecture. Now it so happens that after all that contemporary literature and conjectural criticism could do for Shakespeare's immortal works, there is a residue of about thirty-five to forty passages which have defied all attempts to cure their immortal nonsense. Does it not seem likely that the perplexity in such cases is due to the joint action of those two sources of obscurity, and our inability to *persever* or discriminate the one from the other? We shall see. The *vintage* afforded by these remarks may be thus expressed. Conjectural criticism is legitimate; for it is needful to the perfection of the text: but no critic can be licensed to exercise it whose knowledge and culture do not guarantee these three great pre-requisites: (1) a competent knowledge of the orthography, phraseology, prosody, as well as the language of arts and customs, prevalent in the time of Shakespeare: (2) a delicate ear for the rhythm of verse and prose:[6] (3) a reverential faith in the resources of Shakespeare's genius.

The present time seems most fitting for the treatment of the question: To what extent, and in what manner, may conjectural criticism be safely exercised? For the last twenty years the text of Shakespeare has been subjected to a process, which for its wholesale destructiveness and the arrogance of its pretensions is wholly without parallel. The English press has teemed with works, from Mr. J. P. Collier's pseudo-antique Corrector down to the late Mr. Staunton's papers 'On Unsuspected Corruptions in the Text of Shakespeare,' most of which, in our judgment, have achieved no other result than that of corrupting and betraying the ancient text. We allow that some of the conjectures thus put forth are invaluable, and certain other may be entertained for careful consideration; but the mass we repudiate as impertinent and barbarous. We deny the need for any wholesale change, and impute great ignorance to the assailants:—not to insist on matters of taste, which it is proverbially difficult to make matters of controversy. We are fully able to prove the strength of our position, by showing that the passages attacked are proof against innovations by the power of their own sense. To do this at full length and in complete detail would require the dimensions of a large volume: to teach the general truth by the force of particular examples is all that we now propose to accomplish. This is our aim: to exemplify the growth of the written English language in relation to the text of Shakespeare: to point out the dangers incident to all tampering with special words and phrases in it: to examine and defend certain of its words and phrases which have suffered the wrongs of so-called emendation; and finally to discuss the general subject of the emendation of the text, and to adduce some examples of passages reclaimed or restored through this means. Having accomplished this, we shall gladly leave the old text, with its legion of archaisms and corruptions, to the tender mercies of those critics whose object is to conserve what is sound and to restore what is corrupt, and not at all to improve what, to their imperfect judgment and limited knowledge, seems unsatisfactory. To the arbitration of such critics we submit the question, whether in any particular case a word or phrase which is intelligible to the well-informed reader, however strange or uncouth, does or does not fulfil the utmost requirements of the cultivated mind, regard being had to the context, the situation, and the speaker.

Notes

1. Not improbably Edward Blount, Isaac Jaggard's partner. See *Notes and Queries*, 2nd S. iii. 7.

5. Consult his *Shooting Niagara, and after?*

6. The late Mr. Staunton was deficient in this. Such a symptosis as would be introduced into the text by reading, in *Macbeth*, 'Making the *green zone* red' and '*cleanse* the *clogg'd* bosom,' &c., would (to borrow De Quincey's happy phrase) 'splinter the teeth of a crocodile,' and make the adder shake her ears.

—C. M. Ingleby, "The Still Lion Discovered,"
Shakespeare Hermeneutics, 1875, pp. 1–12

EDMUND GOSSE "THE AGE OF ELIZABETH" (1897)

Edmund Gosse (1849–1928), a late Victorian poet and critic, scoffs at the degree of critical and scholarly attention bestowed on establishing the exact pedigree of Shakespearean texts and at the search for an exact knowledge of what in the plays is by Shakespeare and what may be additions by other hands. Gosse argues, implicitly, that the great plays are recognizable without such aid and stand out from what he considers the lesser ones for our appreciation, and that is all that matters.

From 1593 to 1610 . . . the volcanic forces of Elizabethan literature were preeminently at work. During these seventeen years Spenser was finishing the *Faerie Queen*, [Francis] Bacon and [Anglican theologian Richard] Hooker were creating modern prose, Jonson was active, and Beaumont and Fletcher beginning to be prominent. These, to preserve our mountain simile, were majestic masses in the landscape, but the central cone, the truncation of which would reduce the structure to meanness, and would dwarf the entire scheme of English literature, was Shakespeare. Very briefly, we may remind ourselves of what his work for the press in those years consisted. He published no dramatic work until 1597. The plays to which his name is, with more or less propriety, attached, are thirty-eight in number; of these, sixteen appeared in small quarto form during the poet's lifetime, and the title-pages of nine or ten of these "stolen and surreptitious" editions, originally sold at sixpence each, bear his name. We have the phenomenon, therefore, of a bibliographical indifference to posterity rare even in that comparatively unlettered age. It is curious to think that, if all Shakespeare's MSS. had been destroyed when he died, we should now possess no *Macbeth* and no *Othello,* no *Twelfth Night* and no *As You Like It.* In 1623 the piety of two humble friends, Heminge and Condell—whose names deserve to be carved on the forefront of the Temple of Fame—preserved for us the famous folio text. But the conditions under which that text was prepared from what are vaguely called Shakespeare's "papers" must have been, and obviously were, highly uncritical. The folio contained neither *Pericles* nor the *Two Noble Kinsmen,* yet participation in these is plausibly claimed for Shakespeare. What other omissions were there, what intrusion of lines not genuinely his?

This question has occupied an army of investigators, whose elaborate and conflicting conjectures have not always been illuminated with common sense. More than a hundred years ago, one of the wittiest of our poets represented the indignant spirit of Shakespeare as assuring his emendators that it would be

Better to bottom tarts and cheesecakes nice
Than thus be patched and cobbled in one's grave,
   ["William Shakespeare to Mrs Anne, Regular Servant
    to the Revd Mr Precentor of York," Thomas Gray]

and since that date whole libraries have been built over the complaining ghost. Within the last quarter of a century, systems by which to test the authenticity and the chronology of the plays have been produced with great confidence, metrical formulas which are to act as reagents and to identify the component parts of a given passage with scientific exactitude. Of these "verse-tests" and "pause-tests" no account can here be given. That the results of their employment have been curious and valuable shall not be denied; but there is already manifest in the gravest criticism a reaction against excess of confidence in them. At one time it was supposed that the "end-stopt" criterium, for instance, might be dropped, like a chemical substance, on the page of Shakespeare, and would there immediately and finally determine minute quantities of Peele or Kyd, that a fragment of Fletcher would turn purple under it, or a greenish tinge betray a layer of [William] Rowley [ca. 1585–1626]. It is not thus that poetry is composed; and this ultra-scientific theory showed a grotesque ignorance of the human pliability of art.

Yet, although the mechanical artifice of this class of criticism carries with it its own refutation, it cannot but have been useful for the reader of

Shakespeare that this species of alchemy should be applied to his text. It has dispersed the old superstition that every word printed within the covers of the folio must certainly be Shakespeare's in the sense in which the entire text of Tennyson or of Victor Hugo belongs to those poets. We are now content to realise that much which is printed there was adapted, edited, or accepted by Shakespeare; that he worked in his youth in the studios of others, and that in middle life younger men painted on his unfinished canvases. But there must be drawn a distinction between Shakespeare's share in the general Elizabethan dramatisation of history, where anybody might lend a hand, and the creation of his own sharply individualised imaginative work. If the verse-tester comes probing in *Macbeth* for bits of [John] Webster, we send him packing about his business; if he likes to analyse *Henry VI.* he can do no harm, and may make some curious discoveries. With the revelation of dramatic talent in England there had sprung up a desire to celebrate the dynastic glories of the country in a series of chronicle-plays. It is probable that every playwright of the period had a finger in this gallery of historical entablatures, and Shakespeare, too, a modest artisan, stood to serve his apprenticeship here[,] before[,] in *Richard III*[,] he proved that his independent brush could excel the brilliant master-worker Marlowe in Marlowe's own approved style. He proceeded to have a chronicle in hand to the close of his career, but he preserved for this class of work the laxity of evolution and lack of dramatic design which he had learned in his youth; and thus, side by side with plays the prodigious harmony of which Shakespeare alone could have conceived or executed, we have an epical fragment, like *Henry V*, which is less a drama by one particular poet, than a fold of the vast dramatic tapestry woven to the glory of England by the combined poetic patriotism of the Elizabethans. Is the whole of what we read here implicit Shakespeare, or did another hand combine with his to decorate this portion of the gallery? It is impossible to tell, and the reply, could it be given, would have no great critical value. *Henry V* is not *Othello*.

—Edmund Gosse, from "The Age of
Elizabeth," *Modern English Literature:
A Short History*, 1897, pp. 104–07

SOURCES

JOHN DENNIS (1712)

The English playwright and critic John Dennis (1657–1734) defines Shakespeare as a natural genius whose work, great as he believes it is, was diminished and marred by Shakespeare's lack of education and by his ignorance of classical authors and of the rules of poetic and dramatic art. Shakespeare's work, Dennis complains, fails to conform to accepted precepts of composition, like adherence to rules of poetic justice or to the unities. Moreover, Dennis faults Shakespeare for factual historical inaccuracies and anachronisms and for deviations from Dennis's own view of history and his own understanding of historical characters. He faults Shakespeare for writing plays that differed from the plays he thinks they ought to be.

When Dennis is not hamstrung by his and his age's prejudices regarding artistic proprieties and conventions and the accepted way to present events, characters, and social classes, however, and when he examines particular aspects of Shakespeare's plays, as he does with *Coriolanus*, he shows an acute understanding of the characters and the action, even as he would endeavor to correct what he sees as faults in their construction or representation.

Students of the history of critical attitudes toward Shakespeare's learning or want of it, and of how his independence from classical or neo-classical models and conventions was judged, might contrast Dennis's essay with Edward Young's 1759 *Conjectures on Original Composition*, in which Young regards Shakespeare's putative lack of learning as an asset, arguing that classical learning and adherence to models would likely have hobbled his art rather than improved it. Later writers like Jusserand and Lowell return to the problem of learning and "errors" in Shakespeare and

dismiss them, as Lowell writes, in 1868, "As if Shakespeare's world were one
which [Flemish mapmaker Gerardus] Mercator could have projected."

Letter I

Shakespear was one of the greatest Genius's that the World e'er saw for the
Tragick Stage. Tho' he lay under greater Disadvantages than any of his
Successors, yet had he greater and more genuine Beauties than the best and
greatest of them. And what makes the brightest Glory of his Character, those
Beauties were entirely his own, and owing to the Force of his own Nature;
whereas his Faults were owing to his Education, and to the Age that he liv'd
in. One may say of him as they did of *Homer*, that he had none to imitate,
and is himself inimitable. His Imaginations were often as just, as they were
bold and strong. He had a natural discretion which never cou'd have been
taught him, and his Judgment was strong and penetrating. He seems to have
wanted nothing but Time and Leisure for Thought, to have found out those
Rules of which he appears so ignorant. His Characters are always drawn
justly, exactly, graphically, except where he fail'd by not knowing History or
the Poetical Art. He has for the most part more fairly distinguish'd them than
any of his Successors have done, who have falsified them, or confounded
them, by making Love the predominant Quality in all. He had so fine a
Talent for touching the Passions, and they are so lively in him, and so truly in
Nature, that they often touch us more without their due Preparations, than
those of other Tragick Poets, who have all the Beauty of Design and all the
Advantage of Incidents. His Master-Passion was Terror, which he has often
mov'd so powerfully and so wonderfully, that we may justly conclude, that if
he had had the Advantage of Art and Learning, he wou'd have surpass'd the
very best and strongest of the Ancients. His Paintings are often so beautiful
and so lively, so graceful and so powerful, especially where he uses them in
order to move Terror; that there is nothing perhaps more accomplish'd in our
English Poetry. His Sentiments for the most part in his best Tragedies, are
noble, generous, easie and natural, and adapted to the Persons who use them.
His Expression is in many Places good and pure after a hundred Years; simple
tho' elevated, graceful tho' bold, and easie tho' strong. He seems to have been
the very Original of our *English* Tragical Harmony; that is the Harmony of
Blank Verse, diversified often by Dissyllable and Trissyllable Terminations.
For that Diversity distinguishes it from Heroick Harmony, and bringing it
nearer to common Use, makes it more porper to gain Attention, and more fit
for Action and Dialogue. Such Verse we make when we are writing Prose; we
make such Verse in common Conversation.

If *Shakespear* had these great Qualities by Nature, what would he not have been, if he had join'd to so happy a Genius Learning and the Poetical Art. For want of the latter, our Author has sometimes made gross Mistakes in the Characters which he has drawn from History, against the Equality and Conveniency of Manners of his Dramatical Persons. Witness *Menenius* in the following Tragedy, whom he has made an errant Buffoon, which is a great Absurdity. For he might as well have imagin'd a grave majestick *jack-Pudding*, as a Buffoon in a *Roman* Senator. *Aufidius* the General of the *Volscians* is shewn a base and a profligate Villain. He has offended against the Equality of the Manners even in his Hero himself. For *Coriolanus* who in the first part of the Tragedy is shewn so open, so frank, so violent, and so magnanimous, is represented in the latter part by *Aufidius,* which is contradicted by no one, a flattering, fawning, cringing, insinuating Traytor.

For want of this Poetical Art, *Shakespear* has introduced things into his Tragedies, which are against the Dignity of that noble Poem, as the Rabble in *Julius Caesar,* and that in *Coriolanus; tho'* that in *Coriolanus* offends not only against the Dignity of Tragedy, but against the Truth of History likewise, and the Customs of Ancient *Rome,* and the Majesty of the *Roman* People, as we shall have occasion to shew anon.

For want of this Art, he has Incidents less moving, less surprizing, and less wonderful. He has been so far from seeking those fine Occasions to move with which an Action furnish'd according to Art would have furnish'd him; that he seems rather to have industriously avoided them. He makes *Coriolanus,* upon his Sentence of Banishment, take his leave of his Wife and his Mother out of sight of the Audience, and so has purposely as it were avoided a great occasion to move.

If we are willing to allow, that *Shakespear* by sticking to the bare Events of History, has mov'd more than any of his Successors, yet his just Admirers must confess, that if he had had the Poetical Art, he would have mov'd ten times more. For 'tis impossible that by a bare Historical Play he could move so much as he would have done by a Fable.

We find that a Romance entertains the generality of Mankind with more Satisfaction than History, if they read only to be entertain'd; but if they read History thro' Pride or Ambition, they bring their Passions along with them, and that alters the case. Nothing is more plain than that even in an Historical Relation some Parts of it, and some Events, please more than others. And therefore a Man of Judgment, who sees why they do so, may in forming a Fable, and disposing an Action, please more than an Historian can do. For the just Fiction of a Fable moves us more than an

Historical Relation can do, for the two following Reasons: First, by reason
of the Communication and mutual Dependence of its Parts. For if Passion
springs from Motion, then the Obstruction of that Motion or a counter
Motion must obstruct and check the Passion: And therefore an Historian
and a Writer of Historical Plays passing from Events of one nature to Events
of another nature without a due Preparation, must of necessity stifle and
confound one Passion by another. The second Reason why the Fiction of
a Fable pleases us more, than an Historical Relation can do, is, because in
an Historical Relation we seldom are acquainted with the true Causes of
Events, whereas in a feign'd Action which is duly constituted, that is, which
has a just beginning, those Causes always appear. For 'tis observable, that
both in a Poetical Fiction and an Historical Relation, those Events are the
most entertaining, the most surprizing, and the most wonderful, in which
Providence most plainly appears. And 'tis for this Reason that the Author
of a just Fable, must please more than the Writer of an Historical Relation.
The Good must never fail to prosper, and the Bad must be always punish'd:
Otherwise the Incidents, and particularly the Catastrophe which is the
grand Incident, are liable to be imputed rather to Chance, than to Almighty
Conduct and to Sovereign Justice. The want of this impartial Distribution
of Justice makes the *Coriolanus of Shakespear* to be without Moral. 'Tis
true indeed *Coriolanus* is kill'd by those Foreign Enemies with whom he
had openly sided against his Country, which seems to be an Event worthy
of Providence, and would look as if it were contriv'd by infinite Wisdom,
and executed by supreme Justice, to make *Coriolanus* a dreadful Example
to all who lead on Foreign Enemies to the Invasion of their native Country;
if there were not something in the Fate of the other Characters, which
gives occasion to doubt of it, and which suggests to the Sceptical Reader
that this might happen by accident. For *Aufidius* the principal Murderer of
Coriolanus, who in cold Blood gets him assassinated by Ruffians, instead
of leaving him to the Law of the Country, and the Justice of the *Volscian*
Senate, and who commits so black a Crime,. not by any erroneous Zeal, or
a mistaken publick Spirit, but thro' Jealousy, Envy, and inveterate Malice;
this Assassinator not only survives, and survives unpunish'd, but seems to
be rewarded for so detestable an Action; by engrossing all those Honours
to himself which *Coriolanus* before had shar'd with him. But not only
Aufidius, but the Roman Tribunes, *Sicinius* and *Brutus*, appear to me to
cry aloud for Poetick Vengeance. For they are guilty of two Faults, neither
of which ought to go unpunish'd: The first is in procuring the Banishment
of *Coriolanus*. If they were really jealous, that *Coriolanus* had a Design on
their Liberties, when he stood for the Consulship, it was but just that they

should give him a Repulse; but to get the Champion and Defender of their Country banish'd upon a pretended Jealousy was a great deal too much, and could proceed from nothing but that Hatred and Malice which they had conceiv'd against him, for opposing their Institution. Their second Fault lay in procuring this Sentence by indirect Methods, by exasperating and inflaming the People by Artifices and Insinuations, by taking a base Advantage of the Open-heartedness and Violence of *Coriolanus,* and by oppressing him with a Sophistical Argument, that he aim'd at Sovereignty, because he had not delivered into the Publick Treasury the Spoils which he had taken from the *Antiates.* As if a Design of Sovereignty could be reasonably concluded from any one Act; or any one could think of bringing to pass such a Design, by eternally favouring the Patricians, and disobliging the Populace. For we need make no doubt, but that it was among the young Patricians that *Coriolanus* distributed the Spoils which were taken from the *Antiates;* whereas nothing but caressing the Populace could enslave the *Roman* People, as Caesar afterwards very well saw and experienc'd. So that this Injustice of the Tribunes was the original Cause of the Calamity which afterwards befel their Country, by the Invasion of the *Volscians,* under the Conduct of *Coriolanus.* And yet these Tribunes at the end of the Play, like *Aufidius,* remain unpunish'd. But indeed *Shakespear* has been wanting in the exact Distribution of Poetical Justice not only in his *Coriolanus,* but in most of his best Tragedies, in which the Guilty and the Innocent perish promiscuously; as *Duncan* and *Banquo* in *Mackbeth,* as likewise Lady *Macduffe* and her Children; *Desdemona* in *Othello; Cordelia, Kent,* and *King Lear,* in the Tragedy that bears his Name; *Brutus* and *Porcia* in *Julius Caesar,* and young *Hamlet* in the Tragedy of *Hamlet.* For tho' it may be said in Defence of the last, that *Hamlet* had a Design to kill his Uncle who then reign'd; yet this is justify'd by no less than a Call from Heaven, and raising up one from the Dead to urge him to it. The Good and the Bad then perishing promiscuously in the best of *Shakespear's* Tragedies, there can be either none or very weak Instruction in them: For such promiscuous Events call the Government of Providence into Question, and by Scepticks and Libertines are resolv'd into Chance. I humbly conceive therefore that this want of Dramatical Justice in the Tragedy *of Coriolanus,* gave occasion for a just Alteration, and that I was oblig'd to sacrifice to that Justice *Aufidius* and the Tribunes, as well as *Coriolanus.* Thus have we endeavour'd to shew, that for want of the Poetical Art, *Shakespeare* lay under very great Disadvantages. At the same time we must own to his Honour, that he has often perform'd Wonders without it. . . . [W]e may justly conclude, that *Shakespear* would have wonderfully surpass'd himself, if Art had been join'd to Nature. . . .

Letter II

... I shall proceed to shew under what Disadvantages *Shakespear* lay for
want of being conversant with the Ancients. But because I have lately been in
some Conversation, where they would not allow, but that he was acquainted
with the Ancients, I shall endeavour to make it appear that he was not; and
the shewing that in the Method in which I pretend to convince the Reader
of it, will sufficiently prove, what Inconveniencies he lay under, and what
Errors he committed for want of being conversant with them. But here we
must distinguish between the several kinds of Acquaintance: A Man may be
said to be acquainted with another who never was but twice in his Company;
but that is at the best a superficial Acquaintance, from which neither very
great Pleasure nor Profit can be deriv'd. Our Business is here to shew, that
Shakespear had no familiar Acquaintance with the *Grecian* and *Roman*
Authors. For if he was familiarly conversant with them, how comes it to pass
that he wants Art? Is it that he studied to know them in other things; and
neglected that only in them, which chiefly tends to the Advancement of the
Art of the Stage? Or is it that he wanted Discernment to see the Justness, and
the Greatness, and the Harmony of their Designs, and the Reasonableness
of those Rules upon which those Designs are founded? Or how come his
Successors to have that Discernment which he wanted, when they fall so
much below him in other things? How comes he to have been guilty of the
grossest Faults in Chronology, and how come we to find out those Faults?
In his Tragedy of *Troylus* and *Cressida,* he introduces *Hector* speaking of
Aristotle, who was born a thousand Years after the Death of *Hector.* In the
same Play mention is made of *Milo,* which is another very great Fault in
Chronology. *Alexander* is mention'd in *Coriolanus,* tho' that Conqueror of
the Orient liv'd above two hundred Years after him. In this last Tragedy he
has mistaken the very Names of his Dramatick Persons, if we give Credit to
Livy. For the Mother of *Coriolanus* in the Roman Historian is *Vetturia,* and
the Wife is *Volumnia.* Whereas in *Shakespear* the Wife is *Virgilia,* and the
Mother *Volumnia.* And the *Volscian* General in *Shakespear* is *Tullus Aufidius,*
and *Tullus Attius* in *Livy.* How comes it that he takes *Plutarch's* Word, who
was by Birth a *Grecian,* for the Affairs of Rome, rather than that of the
Roman Historian, if so be that he had read the latter? Or what Reason can be
given for his not reading him, when he wrote upon a *Roman* Story, but that
in *Shakespear's* time there was a Translation of *Plutarch,* and there was none
of Livy? If *Shakespear* was familiarly conversant with the *Roman* Authors,
how came he to introduce a Rabble into *Coriolanus,* in which he offended not
only against the Dignity of Tragedy, but the Truth of Fact, the Authority of
all the *Roman* Writers, the Customs of Ancient *Rome,* and the Majesty of the

Roman People? By introducing a Rabble into *Julius Caesar,* he only offended against the Dignity of Tragedy. For that part of the People who ran about the Streets upon great Festivals, or publick Calamities, or publick Rejoicings, or Revolutions in Government, are certainly the Scum of the Populace. But the Persons who in the Time of *Coriolanus,* rose in Vindication of their just Rights, and extorted from the Patricians the Institution of the Tribunes of the People, and the Persons by whom afterwards *Coriolanus* was tried, were the whole Body of the Roman People to the Reserve of the Patricians, which Body included the *Roman* Knights, and the wealthy substantial Citizens, who were as different from the Rabble as the Patricians themselves, as qualify'd as the latter to form a right Judgment of Things, and to contemn the vain Opinions of the Rabble. So at least *Horace* esteems them, who very well knew his Countrymen. . . .

If *Shakespear* was so conversant with the Ancients, how comes he to have introdue'd some Characters into his Plays, so unlike what they are to be found in History? In the Character of *Menenius* in the following Tragedy, he has doubly offended against that Historical Resemblance. For first whereas *Menenius* was an eloquent Person, *Shakespear* has made him a downright Buffoon. And how is it possible for any Man to conceive a *Ciceronian Jack-Pudding?* Never was any Buffoon eloquent, or wise, or witty, or virtuous. All the good and ill Qualities of a Buffoon are summ'd up in one Word, and that is a Buffoon. And secondly, whereas *Shakespear* has made him a Hater and Contemner and Villifier of the People, we are assur'd by the *Roman* Historian that *Menenius* was extremely popular. He was so very far from opposing the Institution of the Tribunes, as he is represented in *Shakespear,* that he was chiefly instrumental in it. After the People had deserted the City, and sat down upon the sacred Mountain, he was the chief of the Delegates whom the Senate deputed to them, as being look'd upon to be the Person who would be most agreeable to them. In short, this very *Menenius* both liv'd and dy'd so very much their Favourite, that dying poor he had pompous Funerals at the Expence of the *Roman* People.

Had *Shakespear* read either *Sallust* or *Cicero,* how could he have made so very little of the first and greatest of Men, as that *Caesar* should be but a Fourth-rate Actor in his own Tragedy? How could it have been that seeing *Caesar,* we should ask for *Caesar?* That we should ask, where is his unequall'd Greatness of Mind, his unbounded Thirst of Glory, and that victorious Eloquence, with which he triumph'd over the Souls of both Friends, and Enemies, and with which he rivall'd *Cicero* in Genius as he did *Pompey* in Power? How fair an Occasion was there to open the Character of *Caesar* in the first Scene between *Brutus* and *Cassius?* For when *Cassius* tells *Brutus* that *Caesar* was but a Man like them, and had the same natural Imperfections which they had, how natural had it been for *Brutus* to reply, that *Caesar* indeed had their Imperfections of Nature, but neither he nor *Cassius* had by any means the great Qualities of *Caesar*: neither his Military Virtue, nor Science, nor his matchless Renown, nor his unparallell'd Victories, his unwearied Bounty to his Friends, nor his Godlike Clemency to his Foes, his Beneficence, his Munificence, his Easiness of Access to the meanest *Roman*, his indefatigable Labours, his incredible Celerity, the Plausibleness if not Justness of his Ambition, that knowing himself to be the greatest of Men, he only sought occasion to make the World confess him such. In short, if *Brutus,* after enumerating all the wonderful Qualities of *Caesar,* had resolv'd in spight of them all to sacrifice him to publick Liberty, how had such a Proceeding heighten'd the Virtue and the Character of *Brutus?* But then indeed it would have been requisite that *Caesar* upon his Appearance should have made all this good. And as we know no Principle of human Action but human, Sentiment only, *Caesar* who did greater Things, and had greater Designs than the rest of the *Romans,* ought certainly to have outshin'd by many Degrees all the other Characters of his Tragedy. *Caesar* ought particularly to have justified his Actions, and to have heighten'd his Character, by shewing that what he had done, he had done by Necessity; that the *Romans* had lost their *Agrarian,* lost their Rotation of Magistracy, and that consequently nothing but an empty Shadow of publick Liberty remain'd. . . . .

I am apt to believe that if *Shakespear* had been acquainted with [Roman history as Dennis undertood and has just recounted it], we had had from him quite another Character of *Caesar* than that which we now find in him. He might then have given us a Scene something like that which *Corneille* has so happily us'd in his *Cinna;* something like that which really happen'd between *Augustus, Meccenas* and *Agrippa.* He might then have introduced *Caesar,* consulting *Cicero* on the one side, and on the other *Anthony,* whether he should retain that absolute Sovereignty, which he had acquir'd by his Victory, or whether he should re-establish and immortalize Liberty. That would have been a Scene, which might have employ'd the finest Art and the utmost force of a Writer. That had been a Scene in which all the great Qualities of *Caesar* might have been display'd. . . .

I come now to the main Argument, which some People urge to prove that *Shakespear* was conversant with the Ancients. For there is, say they, among *Shakespear's* Plays, one call'd *The Comedy of Errors,* which is undeniably an Imitation of the *Menechmi* of *Plautus.* Now *Shakespear,* say they, being conversant with *Plautus,* it undeniably follows that he was acquainted with the Ancients; because no Roman Author could be hard to him who had conquer'd *Plautus*. To which I answer, that the Errors which we have mention'd above are to be accounted for no other way, but by the want of knowing the Ancients, or by downright want of Capacity. But nothing can be more absurd or more unjust than to impute it to want of Capacity. For the very Sentiments of *Shakespear* alone are sufficient to shew, that he had a great Understanding: And therefore we must account some other way for his Imitation of the *Menechmi*. . . .

I believe [that Shakespeare] was able to do what Pedants call construe, but that he was able to read *Plautus* without Pain and Difficulty I can never believe. Now I appeal to you, Sir, what time he had between his Writing and his Acting, to read any thing that could not be read with Ease and Pleasure. We see that our Adversaries themselves acknowledge, that if *Shakespear* was able to read *Plautus* with Ease, nothing in Latinity could be hard to him. How comes it to pass then, that he has given us no Proofs of his familiar Acquaintance with the Ancients, but this Imitation of the *Menechmi*, and a Version of two Epistles of Ovid? How come it that he had never read *Horace*? . . . [H]ow comes it that in his *Troylus and Cressida* . . . he runs counter to the Instructions which *Horace* has given for the forming the Character of *Achilles?*

[He] is nothing but a drolling, lazy, conceited, overlooking Coxcomb; so far from being the honour'd *Achilles*, the Epithet that *Homer*, and *Horace* after him give him, that he is deservedly the Scorn and the Jest of the rest of the Characters, even to that Buffoon *Thersites*.

Tho' *Shakespear* succeeded very well in Comedy, yet his principal Talent and his chief Delight was Tragedy. If then *Shakespear* was qualify'd to read *Plautus* with Ease, he could read with a great deal more Ease the Translations of *Sophocles* and *Euripides*. And tho' by these Translations he would not have been able to have seen the charming colouring of those great Masters, yet would he have seen all the Harmony and the Beauty of their great and their just Designs. He would have seen enough to have stirr'd up a noble Emulation in so exalted a Soul as his. How comes it then that we hear nothing from him, of the *Oedipus*, the *Electra*, the *Antigone* of *Sophocles*, of the *Iphigenia's*, the *Orestes*, the *Medea*, the *Hecuba* of *Euripides?* How comes it that we see nothing in the Conduct of his Pieces, that shews us that he had the least Acquaintance with any of these great Master-pieces? Did *Shakespear* appear to be so nearly touch'd with the Affliction of *Hecuba* for the Death of *Priam*, which was but daub'd and bungled by one of his Countrymen, that he could not forebear introducing it as it were by Violence into his own *Hamlet*, and would he make no Imitation, no Commendation, not the least Mention of the unparallell'd and inimitable Grief of the *Hecuba of Euripides?* How comes it, that we find no Imitation of any ancient Play in Him but the *Menechmi* of *Plautus?* How came he to chuse a Comick preferably to the Tragick Poets? Or how comes he to chuse *Plautus* preferably to *Terence,* who is so much more just, more graceful, more regular, and more natural? Or how comes he to chuse the *Menechmi* of *Plautus,* which is by no means his Master-piece, before all his other Comedies? I vehemently suspect that this Imitation of the *Menechmi,* was either from a printed Translation of that Comedy which is lost, or some Version in Manuscript brought him by a Friend, or sent him perhaps by a Stranger, or from the original Play it self recommended to him, and read to him by some learned Friend.

—John Dennis, from *Essay on the Genius and Writings of Shakespear,* 1712

LEWIS THEOBALD "PREFACE" (1734)

In 1733, Theobald published his own edition of Shakespeare in seven volumes. It was a significant advance in Shakespearean scholarship, producing, up until then, the most reliable texts of the plays, derived from collation, emendation, and annotation of extant texts. In this excerpt from his preface, he considers the extent of Shakespeare's learning and his flexible use of ancient material.

It has been allow'd on all hands, how far our Author was indebted to *Nature;* it is not so well agreed, how much he ow'd to *Languages* and acquir'd *Learning.* The Decisions on this Subject were certainly set on Foot by the Hint from *Ben Jonson,* that he had small *Latin* and less *Greek:* And from this Tradition, as it were, Mr. *Rowe* has thought fit peremptorily to declare, that, "It is without Controversy, he had no Knowledge of the Writings of the ancient Poets, for that in his Works we find no Traces of any thing which looks like an Imitation of the Ancients. For the Delicacy of his Taste (continues he,) and the natural Bent of his own great Genius (equal, if not superior, to some of the Best of theirs;) would certainly have led him to read and study them with so much Pleasure, that some of their fine Images would naturally have insinuated themselves into, and been mix'd with, his own Writings; so that his not copying, at least, something from them, may be an Argument of his never having read them." I shall leave it to the Determination of my Learned Readers, from the numerous Passages, which I have occasionally quoted in my Notes, in which our Poet seems closely to have imitated the Classics, whether Mr. Rowe's Assertion be so absolutely to be depended on. The Result of the Controversy must certainly, either way, terminate to our Author's Honour: how happily he could imitate them, if that Point be allow'd; or how gloriously he could think like them, without owing any thing to Imitation.

Tho' I should be very unwilling to allow *Shakespeare* so poor a Scholar, as Many have labour'd to represent him, yet I shall be very cautious of declaring too positively on the other side of the Question: that is, with regard to my Opinion of his Knowledge in the dead Languages. And therefore the Passages, that I occasionally quote from the *Classics,* shall not be urged as Proofs that he knowingly imitated those Originals; but brought to shew how happily he has express'd himself upon the same Topicks. A very learned Critick of our own nation has declar'd, that a Sameness of Thought and Sameness of Expression too, in Two Writers of a different Age, can hardly happen, without a violent Suspicion of the Latter copying from his Predecessor. I shall not therefore run any great Risque of a Censure, tho' I should venture to hint, that the Resemblance, in Thought and Expression, of our Author and an Antient (which we should allow to be Imitation in One, whose Learning was not question'd) may sometimes take its Rise from Strength of Memory, and those Impressions which he ow'd to the School. And if we may allow a Possibility of This, considering that, when he quitted the School, he gave into his Father's Profession and way of Living, and had, 'tis likely, but a slender Library of Classical Learning; and considering what a Number of Translations, Romances, and Legends, started about his Time, and a little before; (most of which, 'tis very evident, he read;) I think, it may easily be reconcil'd, why he rather schemed his *Plots* and *Characters* from these more latter Informations, than went back to those Fountains, for which he might entertain a sincere Veneration, but to which he could not have so ready a Recourse.

In touching on another Part of his Learning, as it related to the Knowledge of *History* and *Books,* I shall advance something, that, at first sight, will very much wear the Appearance of a Paradox. For I shall find it no hard Matter to prove, that from the grossest Blunders in History, we are not to infer his real Ignorance of it: Nor from a greater Use of *Latin* Words, than ever any other *English* Author used, must we infer his Knowledge of that Language.

A Reader of Taste may easily observe, that tho' *Shakespeare,* almost in every Scene of his historical Plays, commits the grossest Offences against Chronology, History, and Antient Politicks; yet This was not thro' Ignorance, as is generally supposed, but thro' the two powerful Blaze of his Imagination; which, when once raised, made all acquired Knowledge vanish and disappear before it. For Instance, in his *Timon,* he turns *Athens,* which was a perfect Democrasy, into an Aristocrasy; while he ridiculously gives a Senator the Power of banishing *Alcibiades.* On the contrary, in *Coriolanus,* he makes

Rome, which at that time was a perfect Aristocrasy, a Democrasy full as ridiculously, by making the People choose *Coriolanus* Consul: Whereas, in Fact, it was not till the Time of *Manlius Torquatus,* that the People had a Right of choosing one Consul. But this Licence in him, as I have said, must not be imputed to Ignorance: since as often we may find him, when Occasion serves, reasoning up to the Truth of History; and throwing out Sentiments as justly adapted to the Circumstances of his Subject, as to the Dignity of his Characters, or Dictates of Nature in general.

Then, to come to his Knowledge of the *Latin* Tongue, 'tis certain, there is a surprising Effusion of *Latin* Words made *English,* far more than in any one *English* Author I have seen; but we must be cautious to imagine, this was of his own doing. For the *English* Tongue, in his Age, began extremely to suffer by an Inundation of Latin; and to be overlaid, as it were, by its Nurse, when it had just began to speak by her before-prudent Care and Assistance. And this, to be sure, was occasion'd by the Pedantry of those two Monarchs, *Elizabeth* and *James,* Both great *Latinists.* For it is not to be wonder'd at, if both the Court and Schools, equal Flatterers of Power, should adapt themselves to the Royal Taste. This, then, was the Condition of the *English* Tongue when *Shakespeare* took it up: like a Beggar in a rich Wardrobe. He found the pure native *English* too cold and poor to second the Heat and Abundance of his Imagination: and therefore was forc'd to dress it up in the Robes, he saw provided for it: rich in themselves, but ill-shaped; cut out to an air of Magnificence, but disproportion'd and cumbersome. To the Costliness of Ornament, he added all the Graces and Decorum of it. It may be said, this did not require, or discover a Knowledge of the *Latin.* To the first, I think, it did not; to the second, it is so far from discovering it, that, I think, it discovers the contrary . . . abounds in the Words of it, but has few or none of its Phrases. . . . This I take to be the truest *Criterion* to determine this long agitated Question.

It may be mention'd, tho' no certain Conclusion can be drawn from it, as a probable Argument of his having read the Antients; that He perpetually expresses the Genius of *Homer,* and other great Poets of the Old World, in animating all the Parts of his Descriptions; and, by bold and breathing Metaphors and Images, giving the Properties of Life and Action to inanimate Things. He is a Copy too of those *Greek* Masters in the infinite use of *compound* and *de-compound Epithets.* I will not, indeed, aver, but that One with *Shakespeare's* exquisite Genius and Observation might have traced these glaring Characteristics of Antiquity by reading *Homer* in [George] *Chapman's* Version.

—Lewis Theobald, from "Preface," *The Works of Shakespeare,* volume 1, pp. xxvii–xxxiii

Peter Whalley (1748)

In the form of a dialogue, scholar and clergyman Peter Whalley (1722–91), citing examples from ancient authors, considers the kinds of natural learning and the instances and suggestions of classical learning in Shakespeare's plays. In addition, he discusses the positive effect of Shakespeare's natural genius, which he sees to be unconstrained by strict rules of art, upon his composition.

The common Accusation hath been, as you say, that [Shakespeare] wanted Learning: Confining, I presume, the Meaning of that Word to an Acquaintance and Intimacy with the dead Languages; yet this is in Effect but a greater Commendation. *Johnson,* however, it must be owned, did not think so; not being so naturally learned, he was willing to derive the greatest Honour from his acquired Riches, and the Spoils which he had obtained from the *Greek* and *Latin* Authors: And this was good Policy in him, who, if he wanted not Imagination, was never yet reckoned to have much to spare. He placed his chief Perfection in this Article, the Fashion of the Times concurring to approve it; and what by this Means he detracted from the Sum *of Shakespeare's* Merit, was added to increase his own: For by industriously supporting this Opinion, he intended to secure the Palm to himself.

I am rather, interposed *Neander,* inclined to believe, that considering the honourable Testimony which *Johnson* hath left of his *beloved Shakespeare,* and the Favours he had received from him, I can hardly believe he would be guilty of that Ingratitude to diminish the Reputation of his Benefactor. However the Competition began, it certainly divided the Critics of that Age; and I think that *Johnson* himself hints at it in this Passage from one of his own Plays; "She may censure Poets, and Authors, and Stiles, and compare 'em, [Samuel] *Daniel* with *Spenser, Johnson* with the other Youth, and so forth. . . .'"

Shakespeare has been deservedly esteemed the *Homer,* the Father of our Dramatic Poetry, as being the most irresistible Master of the Passions; possessed of the same creative Power of Imagination; abounding with a vast Assemblage of Ideas, and a rich Redundancy of Genius and Invention. And I think, added *Neander,* that he may be considered to deserve that Title in another Light, as having, like him, furnished many Poets and Tragedians of succeeding Times with the noblest Images and Thoughts. . . .

However, with all these Superiorities, and with a Dignity equal to the divinest of the Ancients, he had the Fortune to resemble them in the least desirable. Part of their Circumstances; as he met with the Fatality, peculiar almost to distinguished Writers, of being transmitted to Posterity full of

Errors and Corruptions. It would appear almost incredible, that the Writings of an Author of so late a Date, should be thus extremely faulty and incorrect; and that his Works, like the Province *of Africa* to the ancient *Romans,* should yield his Commentators such a continual harvest of Victory and Triumphs; but it happens at the same time, to prevent all Surprize, that we are not only assured of the Fact, but in some measure likewise both of the Cause and Manner of it.

This then being the Case, returned *Eugenius,* can it be any longer a Wonder why certain Adventurers in Criticism have so ardent an Esteem for *Shakespeare,* when he gives them the most delightful Opportunity of trying their Skill upon his Plays, and of indulging a Disposition for Guesses and Conjecture, the darling Passion of our modern Critics. Besides the Correctness of the Text, which is equally necessary to the right understanding him in common with all other Authors; it may not be improper to consider a few Particulars, which may possibly explain the Singularity of some Places, and give us a little Insight into the Learning of *Shakespeare.*

To begin with his Plots, the Ground-work and Basis of the whole: These are usually taken from some History or Novel; he follows the Thread of the Story as it lies before him, and seldom makes any Addition or Improvement to the Incidents arising from it: He copies the old Chronicles almost *verbatim,* and gives a faithful Relation of the several Characters they have left us of our Kings and Princes. It is needless to remark, how erroneous this must render the Plan of his Drama, and what Violation it must necessarily offer to the Unities, as prescribed by *Aristotle.* Yet it does not in the least abate my Veneration for our Poet, that the *French Connoisseurs* have fixed on him the Imputation of Ignorance and Barbarism. It would agree, I believe, as little with their Tempers to be freed from a sovereign Authority in the Empire of Wit and Letters, as in their civil Government. [For the French, a]n absolute Monarch must preside over [all] Affairs. . . . But notwithstanding the Imperfection, and even the Absurdity of the Plots of *Shakespeare,* he continues unrivaled for his masterly Expression of the Characters and Manners; and the proper Execution of these is undoubtedly more useful, and perhaps more conducive to the Ends of Tragedy, than the Design and Conduct of the Plot. A great Part of this unjustifiable Wildness of the Fable, must be placed to the Taste and Humour of the Times; the People had been used to the Marvellous and Surprizing in all their Shews and Sports; they had seen different Kingdoms, in different Quarters of the World, engaged in the same Scene of Business, and could not be hastily confined from so unlimited a Latitude to a narrower Compass. I allow their Appetites to have been much depraved; yet probably some kind of *Regimen,* not very different from what they were before accustomed to, was the properest Method to bring them to a better. Nevertheless, were we to make a Dissection of [Shakespeare's] Plays, we should discover more Art and Judgment than we are commonly aware of, both in the Contrast and Consistency of his principal Characters, and in the different Under-parts, which are all made subservient towards carrying on the main Design; and we should observe, that still there was a Simplicity of Manner, which Nature only can give, and as wonderful a Diversity. *Homer* is admired for that Perfection of Beauty which represents Men as they are affected in Life, and shews us in the Persons of others, the Oppositions of Inclination, and the Struggles between the Passions of Self-love, and those of Honour and Virtue, which we often feel in our own Breasts. This is that Excellence for which he is deservedly admired, as much as for the Variety of his Characters. May we not apply this Remark with an equal Propriety to *Shakespeare,* in whom we find as surprizing a Difference, and as natural and distinct a Preservation of his Characters?

And is not this agreeable Display of Genius, interposed *Neander,* infinitely preferable to that studied Regularity and lifeless Drawing practised by our latter Poets? in whom we meet with either a constant Resemblance, or Antithesis both of Scenes and Persons; the natural Result of a confined and scanty Imagination! I am tempted to compare such Performances to that perpetual Sameness or Repetition which prevails in our modern Taste of Gardens. . . . Yet I believe, however earnestly we contend for Nature, that we are neither of us inclined to exclude the Direction of Art from interposing in the Drama: It gives a heightning and *Relief* to Nature, and at the same time curbs the extravagance of Fancy, and circumscribes it within proper Bounds. All I would establish by this Remark, is the Opinion of *Longinus,* preferring a Composition with some Faults of this kind, which is wrote with Genius and Sublimity, to one of greater Regularity and Correctness, that is not animated with equal Life and Spirit. . . . Rules may probably assist and set off a Genius, tho' they can never give Perfection where that is wanting.

If all the Instances, (said) *Eugenius,* which I shall hereafter mention, do not come fully up to the Point which we propose to settle, yet they will convince us at least that *Shakespeare* could not think like the Ancients, and express himself with an equal Simplicity. . . . I have placed here the Volumes all before me, with some Strictures which I have made from Antiquity, and shall begin with pointing out a Passage in the *Tempest,* where the Sentiment is full in the Spirit of *Homer.* It is *Prospero's* Answer to his Daughter.

Be collected:
No more Amazement; tell your piteous Heart,

There's no Harm done.

(Act I. Sc. 2)

Would not you think that the Poet was imitating those Places in the other, where his Heroes are rouzing up their Courage to take Heart of Grace? ...

We may observe also in the same Play a remarkable Example of his Knowledge in the ancient Poetic Story; when Ceres in the Masque speaks thus to *Iris* upon the Approach of *Juno:*

> High Queen of State,
> Great *Juno* comes; I know her by her Gait.
> [IV.I.101–02]

Here methinks now is no small Mark of the Judgment of our Author, in selecting this peculiar Circumstance for the Discovery of *Juno.* ... And his *Decorum* of the Character is perfectly consistent, and her Attendance upon the Wedding intirely agreeable to her Office.

Let us turn now to the next Play, where a Passage stops us at the very beginning. *Theseus* complains thus of the Tardiness of Time;

> Oh, methinks, how slow
> This old Moon wanes! she lingers my desires
> Like to a Stepdame, or a Dowager
> Long withering out a young Man's Revenue.
> (*Midsummer-Nights Dream,* Act I. Sc. 1. [3–6])

Suppose we were to put this into a *Latin* Dress, could any Words express it more exactly, than these of *Horace,*

> Ut piger Annus
> Pupillis, quos dura premit custodia matrum,
> Sic mihi tarda fluunt, ingrataque tempora.
> [Long as the slow year for pupils who would be free of harsh parental
>   custody
> So for me is this slow and unpleasant time of waiting, *Epistles,* book I. v. 21]

Pass we on from these to *Measure for Measure,* where in the second Scene of the third Act, *Claudio* gives us such an Image of the intermediate State after Death, as bears a great Resemblance to the *Platonic* Purgations described by *Virgil.*

Ay, but to die, and go we know not where;
the delighted Spirit
To bathe in fiery Floods, or to reside
In thrilling Regions of thick-ribbed Ice,
To be imprison'd in the viewless Winds,
And blown with restless Violence round about The pendant World, &c.

(Aeneid, L. IV. 739, *&* seq.*)*

The next Instance which I have observed to demand our Notice, occurs in *Much Ado about Nothing;* where the Thought is very natural and obvious, founded on a Failing common to Human Nature. What we have we prize not to its worth Whilst we enjoy it; but being lack'd and lost, Why, then we rack the Value; then we find

The Virtue that Possession would not shew us Whilst it was ours.

(Act IV. Sc. 1. [217–21])

You may have seen, perhaps, the same Sentiment in many Classic Authors; but the most analogous, and which would almost tempt one to believe the Poet had it directly before him. *Shakespeare's* Translation of these Verses, if I may take the Liberty to call it so, tho' something diffused and paraphrastical, exceeds, in my humble Opinion, the Original; for the Proposition being diversified so agreeably, makes a deeper Impression on the Mind and Memory.

If we compare the Description of the wounded Stag, in *As You Like It,* with *Virgil's* Relation of the Death of the same Creature, we shall find that *Shakespeare's* is as highly finished and as masterly as the other:

The wretched Animal heav'd forth such Groans, That their Discharge did
   stretch his Leathern Coat Almost to bursting; and the big round Tears
   Cours'd one another down his innocent Cheeks
In piteous Chase.

(Act II. Sc. 1. [36–40])

What an exquisite Image this of dumb Distress, and of a wounded Animal languishing in the Agonies of Pain! . . .

I now turn to the Tragedy of *King Lear,* where his passionate Exclamations against his Daughters, appear to have been copied from the *Thyestes* of *Seneca* . . .

I will have such Revenges on you both
That all the World shall—

I will do such things,
What they are yet I know not; but they shall be
The Terrors of the Earth.

(Act II. Sc. 2.)

Fac quod nulla posteritas probet,
Sed nulla taceat: aliquod audendum est nefas Atrox, cruentum:
(Act II. v. 192, & seq.) Haud, quid sit, scio. Sed grande quiddam est.

(Ibid. 270.)

And in the fourth Act we meet with a Passage which deserves our Attention upon a double Account. *Gloster* lamenting the Abuses which had been put both on himself and his Son *Edgar,* wishes that he might find him; and expresseth himself thus,

O dear Son, *Edgar,*
The Food of thy abused Father's Wrath;
Might I but live to *see* thee in my *Touch* I'd say,
I had Eyes again.

(Act IV. Sc. 1. [21–24])

To say nothing of the *Oculate Manus* [the hand's eye] of the Comic Poet [Plautus, in his comedy *Asinaria*], you may remark in these Lines a Contrariety of Metaphor equally bold and elegant; of which you may find many Examples in the ancient—Tragedians, and particularly in *Aeschylus,* the *Athenian Shakespeare.* The whole of it has a remarkable Affinity to the Lamentation of *Oedipus* in his Blindness, desiring that his Daughters might be brought him . . .

Oh, might I once but have them in my Touch,
Weep o'er their Sorrows, and lament our Fate.
With either Hand to touch their tender Forms,
Would make me think that I had Eyes again.

There is another Passage in *King Lear,* which though not taken expressly from any particular Author, is directly the Language of the Ancients upon such Occasions. They were frequently induced by Misfortunes to deny the Justice and Equity of Heaven; and when they poured forth their Complaints, we heard of nothing but *Superum Crimina, & Deorum Iniquitas* [the crimes of heaven and the iniquity of the gods]. *Claudian* [Roman poet of the fourth century A.D.], who was sceptically inclined, and questioned the Knowledge and Wisdom of Providence, at length acquitted the Gods, and was convinced by the Punishment of *Rufinus* [fourth-century A.D. Roman governor in Constantinople indicted for treason]. . . .

The Close of the Period in *Shakespeare* is exactly of the same kind:

> Take Physic, *Pomp*,
> Expose thy self to feel what Wretches feel,
> That thou mayest shake the Superflux to them,
> *And shew the Heavens more just.*
> (Act III. Sc. 4. [33–36])

The Thought in both Poets is evidently false, not being founded upon Truth and Reason, and is parallel to many of the stoical Extravagancies of [Roman poet] *Lucan.*

By continuing our Progress, we come to the first Part of *Henry* the IVth, where we have an humorous Application of a *Greek* Proverb: "How long is't ago, *Jack,* says *Hal* to *Falstaff,* since thou saw'st thy own Knee? *Fal.* My own Knee? When I was about thy Years, *Hal,* I could have crept into any *Alderman's Thumb Ring.*" Creeping through a Ring was a Phrase usually applied to such as were extremely thin; for this Reason the old Woman in *Aristophanes* makes use of it in that Sense. . . .

"You may draw me," says she, "very easily through a Ring." "Ay," replies *Chremylus,* "if that Ring was about the Size of a Hoop." From this we may proceed to the second Part of *Henry* the IVth, where we meet with a political Observation of *Warwick's,* who accounts for the Disloyalty *of Northumberland,* by observing that he had proved faithless to King *Richard:*

> There is a History in all Men's Lives,
> Figuring the Nature of the Times deceased:
> The which observ'd, a Man may prophesy
> With a near Aim of the Main Chance of things
> As yet not come to Life; which in their Seeds,
> And weak Beginnings lie intreasured,
> (Act III. Sc. 1. [80–85])

A Section of Antoninus will confirm and illustrate the Remark of *Shakespeare:* I will read it to you, as I find it translated by Mr. [theater critic and theologian Jeremy] *Collier.* "By looking back into History, and considering the Fate and Revolutions of Government, you will be able to form a Guess, and almost prophesy upon the future; for things past, present, and to come are strangely uniform and of a Colour, and are commonly cast in the same Mould. So that upon the Matter, forty Years of Human Life may serve for a Sample of ten thousand." *Lib.* VII. *Sect* 49.

The next Place remarkable which offers itself, is the Parting between *Suffolk* and Queen *Mary,* in the 2d Part of *Henry* VI. Act III. Sc. 2 [360–64].

> A Wilderness is populous enough,
> So *Suffolk* had thy heavenly Company;
> For where thou art, there is the World itself,
> With every several Pleasure in the World;
> And where thou art not, Desolation.

This is the antient Language of Love and Friendship, and employed by [Roman poet] *Tibullus* to his own Mistress.

—Peter Whalley, from *An Enquiry into the*
Learning of Shakespeare, 1748, pp. 12–84

J. Payne Collier "On the Six Old Plays to Which Shakespeare Was, or Is Supposed to Have Been, Indebted" (1831)

John Payne Collier (1789–1883) was a Shakespearean scholar and editor whose reputation has been marred by the evidence that he presented material he had forged as authentic Elizabethan documents, particularly an edition of the Second Folio of 1632, called the Perkins Folio because that surname appeared on the title page. In it, there are notations in the handwriting of what Collier represented to be an old "corrector." In this excerpt, he carefully describes the debt six of Shakespeare's plays owe to their precursors.

The six old plays on which, it is asserted by [George] Steevens, Shakespeare 'founded' his *Measure for Measure, Comedy of Errors, Taming of the Shrew, King John, Henry the Fifth* and *King Lear* are the following:—

The History of Promos and Cassandra, printed in 1578.
The Troublesome Reign of King John, printed in 1591.
The Famous Victories of Henry the Fifth, acted prior to 1588, probably published in 1594, and certainly printed in 1598.

The Taming of a Shrew, printed in 1594.
The Chronicle History of Leir, King of England, probably published in
    1594, and certainly printed in 1605.
Menaechmi, taken out of Plautus, printed in 1595.

When Steevens reprinted these pieces in 1779, he ventured upon no
argument nor explanation to prove how, and to what extent Shakespeare was
under obligation to their authors: with respect to the last, of which I shall speak
first, it may now be taken for granted that he did not make the slightest use of it.
Menaechmi taken out of Plautus, by W. W. (perhaps W[illiam]. Warner) did not
appear, in all probability, until several years after *The Comedy of Errors* (which
has been supposed to be founded upon it) had been brought upon the stage.
[Edmond] Malone assigns *The Comedy of Errors* to 1592, and we may conclude
with tolerable safety that it had its origin in that or in the following year. Although
there is no trace of any similarity between it and the translation of the *Menachmi*
by W. W., yet there is little doubt that *The Comedy of Errors* was founded upon
an older English play, which was an adaptation of the *Menachmi* much anterior
to 1595. On new-year's night 1576–7, the children of Paul's acted *The History
of Error* at Hampton Court. This fact is recorded by Malone,[1] but he has not
remarked also, that it was repeated on Twelfth-night, 1582–3; for although by
mistake, in the account of the Revels at that date, it is called 'A History of *Ferrar,*'
the person who made out the list of plays, writing from the sound only, meant
probably the same piece as the *History of Error.* This play may have been the
foundation of Shakespeare's *Comedy of Errors,* and the circumstance, that he
borrowed certain parts from the old *History of Error,* will explain all that the
commentators have said regarding doggrel verses, and the apparent authorship of
two different persons in the same play. The doggrel fourteen-syllable verses given
to the Dromios are precisely such as were used in dramatic performances not long
before the period when Shakespeare began to write for the stage; and, as Malone
himself has observed, he most likely obtained the designations of Antipholus
erraticus [wandering] and Antipholus *surreptus* [hidden], which are found in the
old copy of the *Comedy of Errors,*[2] from this source. We may, therefore, very safely
dismiss from our consideration the translation of *Mencechmi* by W. W., on the
grounds, that Shakespeare did not use it, and that it was not printed until some
time after he had commenced his theatrical career.

It is, I think, equally certain that the other five old plays, above enumerated,
were written anterior to the date of any of Shakespeare's productions: four
of them were published anonymously, and there is by no means sufficient
ground for the supposition entertained by some of the German critics, that
they were the juvenile works of our great dramatist, who subsequently altered

and improved them. They bear no resemblance to his style, as exhibited in
his undoubted performances; and nothing is more clear than that at the time
when he commenced his career, and afterwards, it was the constant custom
for dramatic poets to revive, amend, and make additions to, productions
which had once been popular, but which required novelty and adaptation to
the improvements of the age. Judging from internal and external evidence,
I should be inclined to place the five old plays in the following order, with
reference to the dates at which they were produced, and according to that
arrangement I shall speak of each:—1. *Promos and Cassandra*. 2. *Henry the
Fifth*. 3. *King John*. 4. *King Leir*. 5. *Taming of a Shrew*.

    Promos and Cassandra was written by a poet of considerable celebrity in his
day, George Whetstone, and it came from the press of Richard Jones in 1578:
it is divided into a first and second part; and, perhaps, the most remarkable
circumstance connected with the performance is one that has not hitherto been
noticed; viz.; that the first part is entirely in rhyme, while in the second are
inserted considerable portions of blank-verse, put only into the mouth of the
King, as if it better suited the royal dignity. This fact might appear to militate
against the position, elsewhere maintained in this work, that blank-verse was
not employed upon the common, popular stage until 1586 or 1587, did we not
know that *Promos and Cassandra* never was performed, either in public or
private. Whetstone himself gives us this information, in his *Heptameron of Civil
Discourses,* 1582: he there inserts a translation of the original novel on which
he constructed his play,[3] and in a marginal note he observes: 'this Historie,
for rarenes therof, is lively set out in a Comedie by the Reporter of the whole
worke, but yet never presented upon stage.' It is likely that there was some
interval between the penning of the first and of the second parts of *Promos
and Cassandra,* and that in that interval the author had acquired a taste for
blank-verse, and therefore employed it, never designing the piece for popular
representation, for which on this account, among others, he might think it
unfit. The year 1578 is an early date for the use of blank-verse for dramatic
purposes, and a short extract will show sufficiently that Whetstone had not
much improved upon the few examples already set. The King first addresses
Cassandra, (who answers to Shakespeare's Isabella,) who has appealed to him,
and he afterwards turns to Promos, the wicked deputy.

Thy forced fault was free from evill intent,
So long, no shame can blot thee any way;
And though at full I hardly may content thee,
Yet, as I may assure thyselfe I wyl.
Thou wycked man, might it not thee suffice,

By worse then force to spoyle her chastitie,
But, heaping sinne on sinne, against thy oth
Hast cruelly her brother done to death?
This over proofe ne can but make me thinke
That many waies thou hast my subjectes wrongd;
For how canst thou with justice use thy swaie,
When thou thy selfe dost make thy will a lawe?
Thy tyranny made mee this progresse make,
How so for sport tyl nowe I colloured it,
Unto this ende, that I might learne at large
What other wronges by power thou hast wrought.

This quotation shows also one principal variation in the conduct of the story as related by Shakespeare. In *Promos and Cassandra,* the King sends the hero as his Viceroy into Hungary; but hearing of his tyranny and misrule, he makes a 'progress' thither, as if 'for sport,' to ascertain the truth: he does not, like the Duke in *Measure for Measure,* withdraw from his court, and in disguise watch over the administration of justice by his substitute.[4]

It has been observed that Shakespeare in no instance adopted the names of the *dramatis persona* of Whetstone, but this will not at all establish that he did not use *Promos and Cassandra;* for Whetstone has in like manner varied from Cinthio, whose novel he professed to follow, and where the hero is called Juriste, and the heroine Epitia. It is, however, not improbable that there was another version of the Italian tale current at the time, and possibly in a dramatic form, in which Shakespeare might find the name of Vincentio inserted in his *dramatis personae,* although throughout the play he is only called the Duke. He may have caught Isabella from Whetstone's *Heptameron,* 1582, because there a lady of that name is made the narrator of the novel in question from Cinthio.

Although the first part of *Promos and Cassandra* is in rhyme, the author has introduced variety into his measure, and he changes at will from ten-syllable to fourteen-syllable lines, making them rhyme sometimes in couplets, and sometimes alternately, two of the lines having no corresponding termination: thus, when Andrugio, the brother, recommends his sister, Cassandra, to comply with the guilty wishes of Promos, as the least of two evils, she replies, with some spirit,

And of these evils, the least, I hold, is death,
To shun whose dart we can no mean devyse:
Yet honor lives when death hath done his worst.
Thus fame then lyfe is of farre more comprise.

This, however, is a comparatively rare instance, the regularity of rhyme, either in couplets or alternate, being usually observed. Besides those engaged in the serious part of the representation, Whetstone introduced many characters, parasites, cheats, pandars, bawds, prostitutes, bullies, and rustics, in order to give variety to the performance, the story of which drags heavily through the two parts to which it is extended. . . .

On the whole, although it seems clear that Shakespeare kept Whetstone's *Promos and Cassandra* in his eye, it is probable that he also made use of some other dramatic composition or novel, in which the same story was treated.

In *Measure for Measure* we have seen that Shakespeare compressed Whetstone's two plays into one, but he expanded the single play *of The famous Victories of Henry the Fifth*[5] over three performances, inserting hints from it in his two parts of *Henry IV.* and in his *Henry V.* He, however, also resorted to the chroniclers, and especially to Holinshed, for other circumstances of an historical kind, while he seems to have trusted to his own resources for most of the comic characters, scenes, and incidents. *The famous Victories of Henry the Fifth* opens with a robbery committed by Prince Henry (throughout called Henry V) and some of his wild companions, among whom is Sir John Oldcastle, a fat knight, who also goes by the familiar name of Jockey. The question whether Shakespeare did or did not take the hint of his Falstaff from this corpulent personage, and whether in fact Falstaff was not, in the first instance, called Sir John Oldcastle, is argued at length in Malone's Shakespeare by [James] Boswell, xvi. 410,[6] &c. This point is only important, as it relates to the obligation of Shakespeare for the bare hint of such a delightful creation as Falstaff. If Shakespeare were indebted thus far, he owes little else to the old *Henry the Fifth* that can now be traced, and it certainly has not come down to us in a shape to make it probable that he would avail himself of much that he found in it. Here and there lines more or less remotely resemble, and the strongest likeness that has yet been discovered is where, in Shakespeare, (Act v. Sc. 2,) Katherine asks, 'Is it possible dat I should love the enemy of France? which runs thus in the older play, 'How should I love thee, which is my father's enemy?'

The play of *The famous Victories of Henry the Fifth* was entered on the Stationers' books in 1594, and although no copy of that date has been found, it was probably, as I have already remarked, then printed:[7] the date of its authorship was, however, more remote, and it is unquestionable that it was acted prior to 1588, because [Elizabethan comic actor Richard] Tarleton, who is recorded to have played in it the two parts of the Judge, who was struck by Prince Henry, and Derrick, the clown, died in that year. I should be inclined to fix it not long after 1580, and it was perhaps played by the

Queen's players who were selected from the companies of several noblemen in 1583, and of whom Tarleton was one. The circumstance that the whole of it is in prose deserves observation: it might be thought in 1583, or soon afterwards, that the jingle of rhyme did not well suit an historical subject on the stage, and we have learnt from [English satirist] Stephen Gosson, that, prior to 1579, prose plays had been acted at the Belsavage: the experiment, therefore, by the author of the old *Henry the Fifth*, was not a new one, although the present may be the earliest extant instance of an heroic story so treated.[8] Nevertheless, by the time it was printed, blank-verse had completely superseded both rhyme and prose: the publisher seems, on this account, to have chopped up much of the original prose into lines of various lengths in order to look like some kind of measure, and now and then he has contrived to find lines of ten syllables each, that run with tolerable smoothness, and as if they had been written for blank-verse. The following is a short example, the passage commencing with a regular verse terminated by a trochee: it is Prince Henry's speech [in *The Famous Victories*] in excuse for taking away the crown while his father slept—

Most soveraigne lord, and welbeloved father,
I came into your chamber to comfort the melancholy
Soule of your body, and finding you at that time
Past all recovery and dead, to my thinking,
God is my witnesse, and what should I doo
But with weeping tears lament the death of you, my
        father;
And after that, seeing the crown, I took it.
And tell me, father, who might better take it then I,
After your death? but seeing you live,
I most humbly render it into your majesties hands,
And the happiest man alive that my father live:
And live, my lord and father, for ever.
        [*The Famous Victories of Henry the Fifth*, ll.897–918]

The excuse is the same in Shakespeare *(Henry IV.* Pt. ii., A. iv., Sc. 4.), but it is not necessary to show here how differently it is urged and enforced. Among minor resemblances, which prove that Shakespeare had the old *Henry the Fifth* before him, when he wrote his play upon the events of that reign, may be noticed the refusal of the French King to allow his son, the Dauphin, to endanger his person with the English.[9] Little as Shakespeare, in the serious part of his composition, has derived from the older historical play, his obligations are still lighter with reference to the comic portions. After Prince Henry has struck the Chief Justice and has been liberated from prison, in the old *Henry the Fifth* he has a conversation with Sir John Oldcastle, Ned and Tom, his companions in his robberies at Gads-hill. Sir John Oldcastle, speaking of Henry IV, says, 'He is a good old man: God take him to his mercy;' and the Prince, addressing Ned, observes, 'So soon as I am King, the first thing I will do shall be to put my Lord Chief Justice out of office, and thou shalt be my Lord Chief Justice of England.' The reply of Ned resembles, even verbally, that of Falstaff when the Prince of Wales tells him *(Henry IV.* Pt. i., A. i., Sc. 2.) that when he is King he shall have the hanging of the thieves. Ned says, in the older play—

Shall I be Lord Chief Justice?
By Gog's wounds, I'll be the bravest Lord Chief Justice
That ever was in England.

The character of Derrick, the clown, runs through the whole piece, and that Tarleton was able to make anything out of such unpromising materials affords strong evidence of the original resources of that extraordinary performer.

The Troublesome Reign of John, King of England, is in two parts, and bears the marks of more than one hand in its composition: the first part, and especially the earlier portion of it, is full of rhymes, while in the second part they comparatively seldom occur, which may be said to establish that the one was written nearer the date when rhyme was first discarded. The blank-verse of the second part is also a decided improvement upon that of the first part: it is less cumbrous and more varied, though still monotonous in its cadences. Malone, upon conjecture only, attributed the old *King John* to [Robert] Greene or [George] Peele,[10] and some passages in the second part would do credit to either. In the opening of it is a beautiful simile, which Shakespeare might have used had he not been furnished, on the same occasion, with another from the abundant store of his own fancy: that which he employs has, perhaps, more novelty, but assuredly less grace, and both are equally appropriate. Arthur has thrown himself from the tower, and is found dead: Shakespeare calls his body

An empty casket, where the jewel of life
By some damn'd hand was robb'd and ta'en away.
                              [V.i.40–41]

The author of the second part of the old *King John* describes the dead body as a

withered flower,
Who in his life shin'd like the morning's blush,
Cast out of door.

Shakespeare may be said to have borrowed nothing from this piece beyond an unimportant historical blunder, pointed out by Steevens: as to his having 'preserved the greatest part of the conduct' of the elder production, both writers very much followed the chroniclers of the time. Our great dramatist has however displayed, as usual, his superior skill in framing the plot, and, with a single omission, he has brought into the compass of his one play the incidents that are tediously extended through the two parts of the old *King John*. That omission is the plunder of the abbey of Swinstead by Falconbridge, when he finds a nun concealed in the apartment of the Abbot, and a friar hidden in that of the Abbess.

The characters in both performances are nearly the same; but while, in the old play, they are comparatively only instruments of utterance, Shakespeare breathes a spirit of life into his historical personages, and they live again in his lines. Shakespeare may be criticised for a century, but after all we shall only arrive at this point—that we admire him above all others, because he is, more than all others, the poet of actual existence.

The story of Lear and his Daughters is full of moral impossibilities, and Shakespeare's play, founded upon it, is the triumph of sympathy over improbability. Our feelings are deeply interested from the first scene to the last; yet the events, out of which those scenes arise, could scarcely have occurred in any state of society. The old *Chronicle History of King Leir*, as it is called on the title-page, was most likely published in 1594, when it was entered for that purpose on the Stationers' books;[11] while it is probable that Shakespeare's tragedy, on the same subject, was not produced until 1605. He seems to have introduced more variance than usual in his conduct of the plot, and especially to have changed the conclusion, which, in the old play, is managed with great simplicity, and with the observance of that poetical justice which Shakespeare has been blamed by some for disregarding. In the *Chronicle History*, Lear is restored to his throne, after the defeat and exile of his two wicked daughters, while Cordelia (so she is there named) and her husband, the King of France, after reposing awhile with the old King, return to their own dominions. Shakespeare has given a new interest to his performance, by the episode of Glocester and his two sons, which contributes to enforce the same moral lesson. The faithful Fool is likewise new to him; and it need not be stated how much that character adds to the effect of the awful scenes in which he is introduced. The madness of Lear is not to be traced in the old play; and I am satisfied, from the language of the ballad,[12] that it was founded upon Shakespeare's tragedy, and not, as some have supposed, Shakespeare's tragedy upon it. The hint of the part of Kent is undoubtedly taken from the Perillus of the *Chronicle History;* but the latter is a poor, spiritless lamenter over the injuries of Cordelia, in the earlier scenes, and in the progress of the play, instead of contrasting with Lear, he not only partakes the sufferings, but shares the imbecilities of the old abdicated monarch. In the *Chronicle History,* one of the daughters sends a messenger, to murder her father and Perillus in a wood; and the most affecting scene in the piece is that in which the two old men so plead for their lives, that the assassin is unable to perform the duty he had undertaken. In the *Chronicle History,* the two wicked daughters are not married, until their husbands have been bribed by the offer of the division of the kingdom, and the union of Cordelia with the King of France is most absurdly conducted. The King of France, with one of his nobles, visits England as a pilgrim, and meeting Cordelia, driven from her father's court, they fall in love with each other on the spot, he not knowing that she is a Princess, nor she that he is a King. Old Lear puts on the dress of a shipman, when he flies to France from Ragan and Gonorill, and there is accidentally met by Cordelia and her royal spouse, who are making a journey to the sea-side in disguise.

Nothing can be more tame and mechanical than the whole of the dialogue of the *Chronicle History,* which Malone, with great injustice, conjectures to have been written by Thomas Kyd.

The last of the six old plays is that to which Shakespeare was most indebted: all the principal situations, and part of the language of his *Taming of the Shrew* are to be found in the 'pleasant conceited History called the Taming of a Shrew,' a work of very considerable talent, as evinced by the conduct of the plot, the nature of the characters, and the versification of the dialogue. It was printed in 1594; and I shall give the title of this edition at length, because it was unknown to Malone, Steevens, and the rest of the modern commentators:[13]—'A pleasant conceited Historie called The taming of a Shrew. As it was sundry times acted by the Right honourable the Earle of Pembrooke his servants. Printed at London by Peter Short, and are to be sold by Cuthbert Burbie, at his shop at the Royall Exchange. 1594.' Although it is not enumerated by Meres, in 1598, among the plays Shakespeare had then written, and although in Act iv. Scene 1, it contains an allusion to [Thomas] Heywood's *Woman Killed with Kindness,* which was not produced until after 1600, Malone finally fixed upon 1596 as the date when the *Taming of the Shrew* was produced. His earlier conjecture of 1606 seems much more probable, and his only reason for changing his mind was that the versification resembled 'the old comedies antecedent to the time' of Shakespeare, and in this notion he was certainly well-founded. I am however satisfied, that more than one hand (perhaps at distant dates) was concerned in it, and that Shakespeare had little to do with any of the scenes in which Katherine and Petruchio are not engaged. The underplot much resembles the dramatic style of William Haughton, author of an extant comedy, called *Englishmen for my Money*, which was produced prior to 1598.

[Bishop Richard] Hurd gives Shakespeare great praise for 'the excellence of the moral design' of the Induction to his *Taming of the Shrew*, not being aware that the credit due on this account belongs to the author of the original comedy of 1594.[14] Shakespeare has, indeed, made very material changes, both of persons and dialogue; but the lesson enforced by the one and by the other is the same. As the copy of the old *Taming of a Shrew* of 1594 is a great curiosity,[15] and as very little attention has been hitherto paid to the Induction, as it stands in the original of Shakespeare's comedy, I shall quote from it *literatim* at greater length than usual, in order to show the nature and degree of our great dramatist's obligation.

Enter a Tapster, beating out of his doores Slie droonken.
Tapster: You whorson droonken slave, you had best
 be gone,
And empty your droonken panch somewhere else,
For in this house thou shalt not rest to night.
 [Exit Tapster.
Slie: Tilly vally, by crisee Tapster Ile fese you anon,
Fil's the tother pot, and alls paid for, looke you.
I doo drinke it of mine owne Instigation: *Omne bene.*
Heere lie a while. Why, Tapster, I say,
Fil's a fresh cushen heere,
Heigh ho, heer's good warme lying.
 [He fals asleepe.
 Enter a Nobleman and his men from hunting.
Lord: Now that the gloomie shaddow of the night,
Longing to view Orion's drisling lookes,
Leapes from th' antarticke world unto the skie
And dims the welkin with her pitchie breath,
And darkesome night oreshades the christall heavens,
Heere breake we off our hunting for to night.
Cupple uppe the hounds, let us hie us home,
And bid the huntsman see them meated well,

For they have all deserv'd it well to daie.

But soft, what sleepie fellow is this lies heere?

Or is he dead, see one what he dooth lacke?-

Servingman: My Lord, tis nothing but a drunken sleepe.

His head is too heavie for his bodie,

And he hath drunke so much that he can go no
     furder.

Lord: Fie, how the slavish villaine stinkes of drinke.

Ho, sirha, arise! What! so sound asleepe?

Go take him uppe, and beare him to my house,

And beare him easilie for feare he wake,

And in my fairest chamber make a fire,

And set a sumptuous banquet on the boord,

And put my richest garmentes on his backe,

Then set him at the table in a chaire.

When that is doone, against he shall awake,

Let heavenlie musicke play about him still.

Go two of you awaie, and beare him hence,

And then Ile tell you what I have devised,

But see in any case you wake him not.

                       [Exeunt two with Slie

Now take my cloake, and give me one of yours.

Al fellowes now, and see you take me so,

For we will waite upon this droonken man,

To see his countnance when he dooth awake,

And finde himselfe clothed in such attire.

With heavenly musicke sounding in his eares,

And such a banquet set before his eies,

The fellow sure will thinke he is in heaven:

But we will [be] about him when he wakes;

And see you call him Lord at everie word,

And offer thou him his horse to ride abroad,

And thou his hawkes, and houndes to hunt the
     deere,

And I will aske what sutes he meanes to weare,

And what so ere he saith, see you doo not laugh,

But still perswade him that he is a Lord.

     Enter one.

Mess.: And it please your honour, your plaiers be
     com,

And doo attend your honour's pleasure here.
Lord: The fittest time they could have chosen out.
Bid one or two of them come hither straight;
Now will I fit my selfe accordinglie,
For they shall play to him when he awakes.
   Enter two of the players with packs at their backs, and a boy.
Now, sirs, what store of plaies have you?
San.[der]: Marrie, my lord, you maie have a
  Tragicall,
Or a commoditie, or what you will.
The other: A Comedie thou shouldst say: souns,
thout shame us all.
Lord: And what's the name of your Comedie?
San.: Marrie, my lord, 'tis calde The taming of a
  shrew.
'Tis a good lesson for us, my lord, for us y' are
married men.
Lord: The taming of a shrew, that's excellent sure.
Go see that you make you readie straight,
For you must play before a lord to-night.
Say you are his men and I your fellow,
Hee's something foolish, but what so ere he saies,
See that you be not dasht out of countenance.

The reprint made by Steevens, in 1779, from the edition of the old *Taming of a Shrew,* (mentioned by Sir J. Harington in 1596,[16]) will enable the reader to judge how far Shakespeare, and, as I suppose, his coadjutor, were aided by the previous drama; and as the resemblance runs through the whole performance, it is not necessary to point out particular instances. Shakespeare's *Taming of the Shrew* is deficient in the conclusion, for we there hear nothing of Sly after the play is ended. In the old piece of 1594, he is again borne to the door of the ale-house, and there left asleep: it is related in the following manner.

Then enter two bearing of Slie in his owne apparell, and leaves him where
  they found him, and then goes out: then enter the Tapster.
Tapster: Now that the darkesome night is overpast,
And dawning day appeares in cristall skie,
Now must I haste abroad: but soft, who's this?
What, Slie, O wondrous! hath he laine heere all
night?

Tie wake him: I thinke hee's starved by this,
But that his belly was so stufft with ale.
What now, Slie, awake for shame!
Slie: Sim, gives some more wine: what all the
Players gone: am not I a Lord?
Tapster: A Lord, with a murrin: come, art thou drunken still?
Slie: Who's this? Tapster, O Lord sirha, I have had
the bravest dreame to-night, that ever thou
heardest in all thy life.
Tapster: I, mary, but you had best get you home,
For your wife will course you for dreaming heere
to-night.
Slie: Wil she? I know now how to tame a shrew;
I dreamt upon it all this night till now,
And thou hast wakt me out of the best dreame
That ever I had in all my life: but Ile to my
Wife presently, and tame her too, and if she anger
me.
Tapster: Nay, tarry, Slie, for He go home with thee,
And heare the rest that thou hast dreamt to-night.

[Exeunt omnes.

The variations between the copies of 1594 and 1607 are not material, the latter being a reprint from the former; unless, as [editor of an 1875 ten-volume Shakespeare edition Isaac] Reed asserts, there was an intermediate edition in 1596.[17] One circumstance has not been remarked by the commentators, viz., that the scene of the old *Taming of a Shrew* is laid in Athens, and that the names of the characters are a mixture of Greek, Latin, Italian, English, and Scotch. Shakespeare transferred it to Padua, and altered the *dramatis persona,* observing in this particular, and some others, more dramatic propriety.

Notes

1.   *Shakespeare* by Boswell, iv. 151.

2.   It was not printed until it appeared in the folio of 1623. Meres mentions it in 1598.

3.   From *La Seconda Parte de gli Hecatommithi di M. Giovanbatista Giraldi Cinthio.* Deca 8, Nov. 5, p. 415. Edit. 1565.

4.   Shakespeare may have taken his title, *Measure for Measure,* from a short moral observation in Act v., Scene 4, of the first part of *Promos and Cassandra:*

who others doth deceyve,
Deserves himself *like measure* to receive.

5.   Malone (*Shakespeare* by Boswell, iii. 307) inserts, from Henslowe's Diary, a notice, under the date of the 26th of May, 1597, of a play called 'Harey the *fifte* Life and Death,' and in a note he adds, 'This could not have been the play already mentioned, because in that Henry does not die; nor could it have been Shakespeare's play.' His difficulty upon this point arose simply from his not being able to read the MS. of Henslowe, where it stands, as all must acknowledge who know anything of the handwriting of the time, not 'Harey the *fifte*,' but 'Harey the *firste*,' showing that there was an old historical play upon the life and death of Henry I. The play of 'Harey the V.' is entered in Henslowe's Diary as performed on the 28th of November, 1595, being then, no doubt, a revival, with improvements, of the piece now under consideration—*The famous Victories of Henry the Fifth.*

6.   Dr. Farmer (founding himself on a passage in Nathaniel Field's *Amends for Ladies,* 1618) was the first to broach this notion, and the balance of evidence seems to be decidedly in his favour; supposing the fact to be so, another question has arisen out of it, why Shakespeare subsequently made the change? It has been suggested that he did so to avoid confounding the two characters, the Sir John Oldcastle of the old *Henry the Fifth* being 'a mere pampered glutton.' The point, when he made the change, does not seem to have been examined, and at all events it is quite evident from Field's comedy that, even after the change was made, Falstaff was still known to the multitude by the name of Oldcastle. *Amends for Ladies* could not have been written before 1611, yet there Falstaff's description of honour is mentioned by a citizen of London as if it had been delivered by Sir John Oldcastle.

7.   The play had, perhaps, been revived about 1592 or 1593, as Nash mentions it in his *Pierce Pennilesse.* That revival may have led Shakespeare to take up and improve the same subject; and the success of Shakespeare's play might occasion the printing of the old *Henry the Fifth* in opposition to it, or to take advantage of temporary popularity.

8.   Gascoigne's *Supposes,* translated by Ariosto, we have seen was in prose; but that was only a comedy, and it was acted, not at a public theatre, but before the Society of Gray's Inn.

9.   *Henry V.* Act iii. Sc. 6, and *Six Old Plays,* ii. 357.

10.   In a note on Act v. Sc. 7 of *King John,* Malone cites a corresponding passage from *Lust's Dominion,* and if his reasoning were founded on fact, we might infer that Marlow, as well as Greene and Peele, was concerned in the production of the old King John. The truth, however, is that Marlow had

nothing to do with the authorship of *Lust's Dominion,* although it has been invariably assigned to him, until in the last edition of Dodsley's *Old Plays* it was irrefragably proved, that Marlow had been dead five years before some of the historical events in *Lust's Dominion* occurred. *Vide* Dodsley's *Old Plays,* ii. 311. 1825.

11.   It was played by Henslowe's company, as we find by his Diary, on the 6th April, 1593.

12.   Malone's *Shakespeare* by Boswell, x. 297.

13.   Pope seems to have had a copy of the edition of 1594, but afterwards it was lost sight of for about a century, and has only very recently been recovered. It was entered on the Stationers' books on 2d May, 1594, and, no doubt, appeared soon afterwards. Steevens reprinted from a copy dated 1607, having seen no earlier edition.

14.   Unless Warston be correct in his statement (*Hist. Engl. Poet.,* iv. 118,) that it was derived from a collection of Tales by Richard Edwards (author of *Damon and Pythias,* &c.) printed in 1570, which was among the books of Collins at Chichester. No such collection is now known to be in existence.

15.   It was bought by that very intelligent bookseller, Mr T. Rodd, of Newport-street, out of the Catalogue of Longman and Co. for the year 1817; and it was subsequently sold by auction for 20*l.* It occupies forty-six quarto pages besides the title.

16.   In his *Metamorphosis of Ajax* printed in that year.

17.   Malone's *Shakespeare* by Boswell, ii. 341.

> —J. Payne Collier "On the Six Old Plays to Which Shakespeare Was, or Is Supposed to Have Been, Indebted," *The History of English Dramatic Poetry,* 1831, volume 3, pp. 61–83

PAUL STAPFER "SHAKESPEARE'S CLASSICAL KNOWLEDGE" (1880)

Paul Stapfer (1840–1917) was a French literary scholar and teacher. Among his works are essays on Molière, Jean Racine, Victor Hugo, Michel de Montaigne, and Johann Wolfgang von Goethe. After arguing that inquiries about the extent and sources of Shakespeare's classical learning are of little real significance, undertaken to satisfy the vanity of scholars rather than to illuminate the work of the poet, and that assumptions about the range of his knowledge may be mistaken, he reviews and criticizes the work of a number of commentators and discusses some classical allusions and sources in Shakespeare's plays and where and how Shakespeare may have come upon them.

The question as to whether Molière was able to read Aristophanes, Terence and Plautus, in the original, would hardly be likely to excite a very lively interest in the mind of any Frenchman. Molière is held to be a great comic poet by his countrymen, and it may be doubted whether, if they were shown that over and above that he was also a good Greek and Latin scholar, it would greatly add to their estimation of him, or if it were proved that classical authors were only known to him through translations whether their admiration for the author of the "Misanthrope" would suffer any diminution. But in England people think and feel otherwise, and the question regarding Shakespeare's knowledge of Greek and Latin, would appear to be of vast importance in their eyes, to judge from the extraordinary eagerness with which it has generally been discussed. The combatants in this strange dispute are even more curious than the debated point itself, for—admitting for an instant the truth of the most unfavourable conclusions with regard to Shakespeare's classical learning—it is difficult to understand how such an avowal could be harmful to his glory, and that, on the contrary, it should not rather redound to his credit, and redouble our wonder and admiration for the wealth and penetrative power of a genius able, by itself alone, to furnish so many marvellous beauties that have hitherto been, to a certain extent, attributed to study and to the imitation of others. But though the controverted point has no intrinsic importance, the controversy itself is both amusing and instructive.

Great value is attached by the English, who are at heart an aristocratic people, to the distinctions inherited by noble birth and to those gained at the universities; the greatest recommendation a man can have is a title of nobility, the next is a university degree. While a democratic Frenchman, in spite of the small amount of personal merit or renown he may possess, affects as a matter of good taste to conceal his title or degree, an Englishman always proclaims and displays them; dukes and earls, those even whose talents and real worth have made-them justly famous, are as exacting on this point as the obscurest of country squires; the Bachelor of Arts with his honours fresh upon him is not more careful to write after his name the initials of the degree he has just taken than are Oxford and Cambridge professors of long standing. Influenced by this national prejudice in favour of birth or, in default of that, of the certificate in due official form of a university education as a passport to a position in society, it would almost seem as if Englishmen had been a little ashamed of this poor William Shakespeare, who not only was no lord or earl, like Lord Buckhurst, but was not even a graduate of either of the universities, as Marlowe, Greene, Peele, Lyly, Lodge, Gascoigne, and, in short, as nearly all the other dramatic authors of his time were; and also as if they held it necessary for the honour of England to show that he might have been at any rate a Bachelor of Arts.

Another reason for the passionate interest with which English critics have fought over this point may be found in their evident predilection, when dealing with poets, for adding a few more units, whether great or small, to the sum of clearly ascertained biographical facts: it matters not that the discovery should be insignificant to the last degree—that it is a fact is all-sufficient. And an excellent opportunity for research of a precise and not too abstract nature, and for questions of small facts, is afforded in the measurement of the exact amount of Shakespeare's classical learning. The subject opens a fine field for erudition. Aesthetics, taste, feeling, philosophy and thought are quite unnecessary here, and all that is wanted is to ferret out and scrape together and pile up higher and higher, mountains of notes, proceeding after the manner of rats. . . .

It is in this philosophical spirit that I wish to approach the task of making out the inventory of Shakespeare's intellectual furniture in the way of learning, endeavouring to extract from the mass of dry details some ideas of general interest, and taking especial care to avoid falling into the weakness of imagining that the *genius loci* [spirit of a place] can suffer either increase or diminution of glory from the riches or poverty of the house he dwells in. It is necessary first of all to get rid of a most senseless but common confusion which has too often prevailed in the discussion touching the amount of Shakespeare's knowledge, by which the knowledge of languages has been and still is continually confounded with learning strictly so called. Yet they are assuredly two very different things. A knowledge of languages is a key wherewith to unlock the treasures of learning, but it is not learning itself. There are persons who think the key so curious that they pass their whole life in examining it, without once using it to open anything whatever,—of such are grammarians. But it is better to get into literature by a false key or by any other means, no matter what, than to rest contented with studying the ingenious mechanism of the right key; it is better to read translations of Homer and the Greek tragedians than to be satisfied with being well up in our Greek conjugations and syntax. Few men have been as learned as Goethe; few men have imbibed the Hellenic spirit and have understood it as he did, yet Goethe did not know Greek. Did Shakespeare know Greek, and did he know Latin? The whole question has been reduced to these pedantic limits, and no higher idea has been conceived of the education of a poet. While some have denied him all knowledge of classical languages, others have exaggerated his acquaintance with them,—both assertions, in spite of their contradictory nature, affording equal satisfaction to the vanity of critics; for a pedant can make as much capital by exposing the ignorance of a man of genius, as he can by the opportunity afforded him by the learning possessed by the author under review, to display his own erudition.

The origin of the debate is to be found in a line written by Ben Jonson, in an enthusiastic epistle "to the memory of his beloved William Shakespeare," in which he exclaims that the great poet England had just lost outweighed all antiquity, though he knew "small Latin and less Greek." This line has occasioned as much wrangling and hairsplitting as any text in Perseus [last king of Macedonia] or Lycophron [Greek poet of the third century B.C.]; for what, it has been asked, does Ben Jonson mean by "small Latin"? In the estimation of a mighty classical scholar like himself, a very respectable knowledge of Latin might rank as a small matter. And then, it was further remarked, he does not say "no Greek" although his metre would have perfectly allowed of his doing so, but "less Greek." Therefore—oh joy!—Shakespeare did know a little Greek. . . .

And finally, in spite of the sincerely affectionate tone of Ben Jonson's epistle, it has been hinted that the "small Latin and less Greek" might have been dictated by secret jealousy; and since then it has dropped out of account.

In the eighteenth century Warburton and divers other learned commentators, finding curious points of resemblance between Shakespeare and Sophocles, Euripides, Lucian, etc., had no hesitation in concluding that he had both read and copied the Greek writers. It was in 1767 that [Shakespearean scholar and master of Emmanuel College, Cambridge] Dr. [Richard] Farmer's famous essay on the learning of Shakespeare appeared.

In comparing the text of Shakespeare's Roman tragedies with Sir Thomas North's English translation of Plutarch's Lives from the French of Amyot, Farmer showed that Shakespeare had borrowed entirely from that translation,—that he had copied many phrases and even whole pages from it without taking any pains to verify its accuracy by the slightest examination of the original text, as he everywhere follows the English version blindfold, even to its errors and mistranslations. For example, in the third act of *Antony and Cleopatra*, Octavius, speaking of the illustrious lovers, says—

> Unto her
> He gave the 'stablishment of Egypt; made her
> Of lower Syria, Cyprus, *Lydia,* Absolute Queen.

Lydia is a mistake for Lybia, of which Plutarch speaks, but the mistake is made both by Amyot and by North. Again, in the fourth act, Octavius, when challenged by Antony whom he had just defeated, answers—

> My messenger
> He hath whipt with rods; dares me to personal
>   combat,
> Caesar to Antony. Let th' old ruffian know
> I have many other ways to die; meantime,
> Laugh at his challenge.

"I have many other ways to die" is a mistranslation; Plutarch says not "I have" but "he has," that is, that Antony has many other ways to die. His sentence, translated word for word, runs thus: "After this, Antony sent to defy Caesar to single combat, and received for answer that he might find other means of ending his life." Amyot cannot be said to be in fault here, he translates it: "And another time Antony sent to challenge Caesar to single combat. Caesar sent him word that he had many other ways of dying than that;" but Shakespeare was misled by the ambiguous use of the word *he*, which is also found in the English version by North, "Caesar answered that he had many other ways to die than so."

Shakespeare's Timon composes the following epitaph for his tomb:—

> Here lies a wretched corse, of wretched soul bereft:
> Seek not my name; a plague consume you wicked
>   caitiffs left!
> Here lie I Timon; who, alive, all living men did hate:
> Pass by, and curse thy fill; but pass and stay not here
>   thy gait.

This epitaph is taken word for word (one word only being changed) from Sir Thomas North, who here thinks it well to follow Amyot's example of turning the lines into verse. Shakespeare's version, or that which is attributed to him, for *Timon of Athens* is full of incoherencies and doubtful passages,—presents the strange anomaly of uniting in one, two perfectly distinct epitaphs, distinguished as such by North and by Amyot, as well as by Plutarch: one is by Timon himself, the other by the poet Callimachus. It is absurd to say, "Seek not my name," and two lines further on, "Here lie I Timon." In North the passage is, "On the tomb was written this epitaph:—

Here lies a wretched corse of wretched soul bereft,
Seek not my name; a plague consume you wicked
　　　wretches left.

It is reported that Timon himself when he lived made this epitaph; for
that which is commonly rehearsed was not his, but made by the poet
Callimachus:—

Here lie I Timon, who alive all living men did hate:
Pass by and curse thy fill, but pass and stay not here
　　　thy gait.

Turning to *Julius Caesar,* we find Antony (Act III. Sc. 2) saying, when reading
Caesar's will to the people:—

Moreover, he hath left you all his walks,
His private arbours, and new-planted orchards,
On *this* side Tiber.

"On this side Tiber," writes Shakespeare. Plutarch wrote *peran tou potamou,*
"*across* the Tiber," but Shakespeare was misled by North, who had been
misled by Amyot.

He bequeathed unto every citizen of Rome twenty-
five drachmas a man, and he left his gardens and
arbours unto the people, which he had on *this* side of
the river of Tyber.

But the most striking instances of Shakespeare borrowing from North
occur in *Coriolanus,* where, in the hero's speech to Aufidius, demanding his
hospitality and alliance, and in that of Volumnia to her son, in which she
beseeches him not to war upon Rome,[1] Shakespeare has done little more,
says Dr. Farmer, than throw the very words of North into blank verse. The
best and most conclusive part of Dr. Farmer's essay is his demonstration of
the third-handedness of Shakespeare's knowledge of Plutarch, but it contains
also several other curious little revelations; as, for example, that concerning
the plagiarism from [Greek lyric poet] Anacreon that commentators have
been pleased to detect in the following passages from *Timon of Athens* (Act
IV., Sc. 3):—

The sun's a thief, and with his great attraction
Robs the vast sea. The moon's an arrant thief,
And her pale fire she snatches from the sun.
The sea's a thief, whose liquid surge resolves
The moon into salt tears. The earth's a thief,
That feeds and breeds by a composture stolen
From general excrement: each thing's a thief.

Dr. Farmer shows that, even supposing it impossible for Shakespeare, "who was generally able to think for himself," to have originated it, it cannot be quoted as a proof of his knowledge of Greek, seeing that Anacreon's ode had been translated several times into Latin, French, and English, before the end of the sixteenth century, notably by Ronsard in his drinking song:—

La terre les eaux va buvant;
L'arbre la boit par la racine;
La mer salie boit le vent,
Et le soleil boit la marine.
Le soliel est bu de la lune;
Tout boit, soit en haut ou en bas;
Suivant cette regie commune,
Pourquoi done ne boirions nous pas?

It was not only in the case of Greek authors that Shakespeare gladly availed himself of translations, for as Farmer shows, in many instances where it would have been easy for him to consult the Latin originals he preferred having recourse to English translations, as is the case, for example, with Prospero's address to his attendant spirits in the *Tempest*.

Ye elves of hills, of standing lakes, and groves,

which Warburton took to be copied from Ovid, but which a comparison of texts clearly proves to be borrowed not from the Latin poet but from the English translation by Arthur Golding in 1567.

Farmer makes some very sensible remarks on the subject of Shakespeare's frequent allusions to classical fables and memories. To infer from these allusions that Shakespeare had read Ovid, Virgil, and Homer, at any rate in English, and had himself drunk at the fountainhead of Greek and Latin antiquity, is a quite uncalled-for conclusion. The literature of the Middle

Ages and of the Renaissance had popularized all the legends of antiquity, and turned them into current coin long before translations of Greek authors were in people's hands. To quote an example, Shakespeare, in the *Midsummer Night's Dream,* happens to mention Dido, and thereupon commentators carefully point out that there was no translation of Virgil's *Aeneid* in Shakespeare's time. But what does that matter? "The fate of Dido had been sung very early by [English poet John] Gower [Shakespere uses him as a choral figure in *Pericles*], [English poet Geoffrey] Chaucer and [English monk and poet John] Lydgate; [English dramatist Christopher] Marlowe had even already introduced her to the stage."

Another passage in the *Midsummer Night's Dream* shows that Shakespeare knew of the distinction made by Ovid between Cupid's two sets of arrows, some of them being pointed with lead, and others with gold; and again the question arises whether he derived this directly from Ovid, in either Latin or English. He may possibly have done so, but still such a conclusion is perfectly unnecessary, as "Cupid's arrows appear with their characteristic differences in [English Renaissance courtier, soldier, poet, Henry Howard, Earl of] Surrey, in [Sir Philip] Sidney, in [Edmund] Spenser, and in every sonneteer of the Elizabethan period." . . .

The conclusions that Dr. Farmer draws are, however, exaggerated, and overstep his premises; he is of opinion that he has proved that Shakespeare knew neither Greek nor Latin, but in reality he has only shown that the poet made use of translations from both languages as much as possible, and besides this, that independently of any translations, much of his classical knowledge may have been culled from the literature of the Middle Ages and of the Renaissance.

In criticising Shakespeare's attainments, Dr. Farmer fell into the egregious folly of speaking in a strain of impertinent conceit; it is as if the little man—for little he must assuredly have been—was eaten up with vanity, and was bursting to show that he knew more of Greek and Latin than Shakespeare did.

Of the same order of research and of the same spirit was another equally famous work that appeared in the eighteenth century—*Illustrations of Shakespeare,* containing an essay "On the Anachronisms and Some Other Incongruities of Shakspere," by Francis Douce. In this big book, bristling with erudition but devoid of talent, and very foolish and irreverent towards Shakespeare, the poet's historical and geographical blunders are pointed out with pedantic and ponderous care, and without the least understanding of the subject; but an inquiry into Shakespeare's anachronisms, and the further criticism of Douce's book, must be reserved for another chapter.

When Shakespeare was looked upon as an "intoxicated savage," his literary learning was, naturally enough, held in small esteem, and rated lower than it really deserved; but when a complete revolution in opinion was introduced by Schlegel and Coleridge, who proclaimed that he must no longer be regarded as a mere child of nature, but as a wise and enlightened artist knowing perfectly what he was about, people fell into the opposite extreme, and entertained the most extravagant notions as to the extent and depth of his acquirements. Our own century has discovered that Shakespeare knew everything, like Dr. Pancrace, in Molière's comedy of the *Mariage Forcé* [*The Forced Marriage,* 1664], "fables, mythology, and history, grammar, poetry, rhetoric, dialectics and sophistry; mathematics, arithmetic, optics, oneiro-criticism and physics." A legal system, a treatise on mental maladies, a complete guide-book to country life, lessons on ornithology, entomology, and botany have all been extracted from his works; while from the propriety with which he uses technical terms appertaining to military matters, to hunting and to jurisprudence, it has been concluded that he must have been a soldier, a poacher, and a lawyer. Several of his titles to the professorship of universal knowledge have escaped my memory, but those already mentioned make up a tolerably long list, in which Shakespeare figures as a doctor, a lawyer, an agriculturist, a zoologist, a botanist, a hunter and a soldier.

A complete ethnological system has also been discovered in his works by Mr. O'Connell, the author of a New Exegesis *of Shakespeare,* published in 1859, according to whom "that which constitutes the novel and peculiar greatness of Shakespeare, is that being the first to rise to a wider and, at the same time, deeper contemplation of human nature, he has depicted, not only individuals and families, but has also sketched the character of the principal European races. While Aeschylus and the ancient drama limited the sphere of action to the family, the founder of the modern drama carried it further, and included larger groups in conformity with the general progress made in the knowledge of men and of nature. What Asia Minor and Hellas were to the Athenians, Europe, in its vast extent, was to the English people in the days of the Renaissance. The subjects of the Aeschylean drama were the house of Pelopides and that of Labdacides; those of Shakespeare were the Germanic, Italian, and Celtic races: in this system, Iago represents the character of the Italian, Hamlet the Teutonic, and Macbeth the Celtic race."[2] It was this exaggerated notion of Shakespeare's learning and philosophy which also gave rise to the famous paradox, brought forward from time to time by some lunatic, that Shakespeare never existed, and that his name was only a fictitious one, adopted by the most learned and philosophical thinker of the time, Francis Bacon!

To rehabilitate Shakespeare as a Latin scholar was a task that lay very close to the hearts of his commentators, and they entered upon it with such eagerness and simplicity, that the disinterested observer feels quite bewildered, and tries in vain to decide which of the two sides is the more ridiculous—the one which Shakespeare's presumed ignorance rendered vainglorious of its own learning, or the other which thought the poet's glory would be enhanced by showing that he might have carried off a prize for Latin verse. As a sample of the extremely acrimonious language in which those of Coleridge's school speak of "the detractors of Shakespeare's learning," may be quoted the passage in which [Charles] Knight, the well-known editor and critic of Shakespeare, expresses his appreciation of Dr. Farmer's essay:—

> He wrote an essay on the learning of Shakespeare which has not one passage of solid criticism from the first page to the last, and if the name and the works of Shakespeare were to perish, and one copy could be miraculously preserved, the only inference from the book would be, that William Shakespeare was a very obscure and ignorant man whom some misjudging admirers had been desirous to exalt into an ephemeral reputation, and that Richard Farmer was a very distinguished and learned man who had stripped the mask off the pretender.

That such a passage should ever have been written is almost inconceivable, not on account of the hard measure dealt out to Dr. Farmer, but because of the singular notion implied in it, that if Dr. Farmer were right in alleging Shakespeare's ignorance of languages, the poet would be a mere pretender to the crown of fame. For my part, I am most willing to grant Shakespeare's acquaintance with Greek and Latin, not so much for the honour of the poet, as to gratify Mr. Knight, since he takes the matter so much to heart; I believe, and will give my reasons for believing further on, that Shakespeare at all events knew Latin,—only, in truth, the strange arguments with which this view has sometimes been upheld makes one doubt whether it can possibly be the truer one.

In the second part of *Hamlet*, Polonius, in introducing the players to the Prince, praises their skill, and says, that for them, "Seneca cannot be too heavy, nor Plautus too light;" that simply is, as the German critic [Nikolaus] Delius justly remarks, "They can act with facility both the comic Plautus and the tragic Seneca." There is no hidden subtlety of meaning in the two adjectives, *heavy* and *light*. But Knight discovers in them an admirably profound and concise definition of the talent of Seneca and of Plautus.

In *Hamlet*, Shakespeare gives in a word the characteristics of two ancient dramatists; his criticism is decisive as to his familiarity with the originals, "Seneca cannot be too heavy, nor Plautus too light."

In the *Comedy of Errors* (Act V., Sc. 1), a servant rushes in, crying—

O mistress, mistress, shift and save yourself!
My master and his man are both broke loose,
Beaten the maids a-row, and bound the doctor,
Whose beard they have singed off with brands of fire;
And ever as it blazed they threw on him
Great pails of puddled mire to quench the hair.

This, it appears, is an imitation of Virgil, for in the twelfth book of the *Aeneid* (lines 298, and following), we read:—

Corinaeus took a lighted brand from the altar, and at the moment when Ebusus was about to strike him he threw it in his face, the flames surrounded him, and his huge beard caught fire and burnt with a great smell of burning.

Thus, whenever the incident of a beard maliciously set on fire occurs in literature, we must go back to Virgil as its source; as, for instance, in *Tristram Shandy*, where Sterne shows us Susannah setting fire with her candle to Dr. Slop's wig (Vol. VI., Ch. III.), who, in a passion, flings in her face the cataplasm that had been prepared for little Tristram. Again, the passage in which Shakespeare, in *As You Like It*, has described the death of a stag, and "the big, round tears coursing one another down his innocent nose" (Act II., Sc. 1), must presumably be derived from the seventh book of the *Aeneid*;— and yet, is it not possible that so great a poacher might have seen such a sight for himself?

But when we find Knight placing a passage in which Shakespeare puts the eulogy of blows into Dromio's mouth, side by side with one in which Cicero celebrates the praise of learning, we begin to think that we are dreaming, and rub our eyes and read the paragraph over again:—

"When I am cold he heats me with beating; when I am warm he cools me with beating; I am waked with it when I sleep; raised with it when I sit; driven out of doors with it when I go from home; welcomed home with it when I return" (*Comedy of Errors*, Act IV., Sc. 4.): "Literature," says Cicero, "is the exercise of youth and the charm of old age; adorning fortune, it also offers in adversity a refuge and a consolation; the delight of the domestic hearth, easily enjoyed everywhere, it bears us company at night, travelling, and in the country."[3]

As to Greek authors, Knight hardly ventures to affirm positively that Shakespeare read them in the original, but he evidently wishes to intimate as much to his readers. When comparing Shakespeare's misanthrope with that of Lucian, he complacently passes in review the numberless points of resemblance between them, and significantly observes that no translation of Lucian had appeared in Shakespeare's time; as, however, the subject of Timon the Misanthrope was popular before then, and had even appeared on the stage, Knight is obliged to admit that Shakespeare may have known it in its principal details without having had recourse to the original in Greek.

In the historical drama of *Henry V.* (Act I., Sc. 2) we read:—

> While that the armed hand doth fight abroad, The advised head defends
>   itself at home;
> For argument, through high, and low, and lower, Put into parts, doth
>   keep in one concent; Congreeing in a full and natural close,
> Like music. [178–83]

Then, after a very poetical comparison of the "work of honeybees" to a well-governed state, there follows a series of similes, all tending to set forth the truth that—

> So may a thousand actions, once afoot,
> End in one purpose, and be all well borne
> Without defeat.

The same idea is met with in Plato's *Republic,* as well as in a fragment, preserved by Augustine, of Cicero's long-lost treatise, *De Republica.*[4] Knight, in his edition of Shakespeare, gives the following note on this subject:—

> The words of Cicero, to which the lines of Shakespeare have so close a resemblance, form part of a fragment of that portion of his lost treatise *De Republica* which is presented to us only in the writings of St. Augustin. The first question therefore is, Had Shakespeare read the fragment in St. Augustin? But Cicero's *De Republica* was, as far as we know, an adaptation of Plato's *Republic,* the sentence we have quoted is almost literally to be found in Plato; and what is still more curious, the lines of Shakespeare are more deeply imbued with

the Platonic philosophy than the passage of Cicero. They develope unquestionably the great Platonic doctrine of the Triunity of the three principles in man, with the idea of a state. The particular passage in Plato's *Republic* to which we refer is in Book IV, and may be thus rendered: "It is not alone wisdom and strength which make a state simply wise and strong, but it (order), like that harmony called the diapason, is diffused throughout the whole state, making both the weakest and the strongest, and the middling people concent the same melody." Again, "the harmonic power of political justice is the same as that musical concent which connects the three chords, the octave, the bass and the fifth." There was no translation of Plato in Shakespeare's time except a single dialogue by Spenser.

In a question of this kind, in which, to whatever side we may incline, it is impossible to lay claim to absolute certainty, it is well to keep within the bounds of a prudent and modest reserve; but one rule that always holds good is from among the various explanations of a fact to choose out the simplest.

What has here to be accounted for is the presence in Shakespeare's works of a passage which is imbued with the spirit of platonism, and is so beautifully expressed, and so full of an antique wisdom and philosophy that it might have been written by Plato himself. It must, in the first place, be remembered that the comparison of a well-ordered government to a concert in which every instrument plays its part, or to a bee-hive, has long since become a commonplace in literature. Ever since it was set in circulation by Plato and Cicero in their respective treatises on the *Republic,* there has probably been no ancient philosopher or poet from whose writings some analogous simile could not be quoted. In the time of the Renaissance Plato was held in the highest favour by English poets; as Coleridge tells us, "the star of serenest brilliance in the glorious constellation of Elizabeth's court, our England's Sir Philip Sidney, held high converse with Spenser on the idea of supersensual beauty." Lyly, the author of *Euphues,* borrowed the name of his hero from Plato's *Republic,* and his romance teems with comparisons between human governments and those presented to us in nature, especially in the case of bees. The tedious length of his exemplification places it far below the poetry of Shakespeare's passage, and makes it infinitely less worthy to be compared to the antique model, but it is precisely in such cases as this that we catch a glimpse of genius at work in one of its most marvellous operations, by virtue of which, diving through all the prolixity and exaggeration that a whole host of imitators have lost themselves in, it re-discovers an ancient conception, and makes it live again in all its first freshness and truth: for there is a brotherhood among all great minds, and Shakespeare happening to meet with the enfeebled expression of what had once been a thought of Plato's, was able to re-think it, almost back to its original form. A most striking example of this power or resurrection, which is the birthright of genius, is afforded in the character of Cressida, as will be seen further on. In all probability Shakespeare knew nothing of the poem of the obscure Norman trouvère who first conceived the idea of the brilliant coquette, but amidst all the more or less clumsy alterations made by numberless imitators of [the French author of a 40,000-line-poem *The Romance of Troy*] Benoit de Sainte-More, he has grasped the essential features of her character with sure and unerring hand.

Amongst the many minor points of resemblance in details to the texts of classical antiquity, so abundantly offered by Shakespeare's plays, those which touch upon philosophy possess the greatest chance of being interesting, as in them we may hope to meet not only with words, but with at least a few reflected rays of thought. Professor Nebler, of the University of Berne, has dedicated one chapter of his book on Shakespeare (*Aufsätz über Shakespeare* [*An Essay on Shakespeare*]) to pointing out all the passages in which Shakespeare alludes to the name or ideas of an ancient philosopher, and from his pages I have culled the following sentences, adding those I have gathered from my own reading of Shakespeare.

Nothing could well be more poetical than the opening of the fifth act of the *Merchant of Venice*. Jessica and Lorenzo are sitting one summer's night in Portia's garden, singing the eternal hymn of love, while the exquisite grace and charm of the duet is enhanced by the classical reminiscences more or less vague and inaccurate, which mingle with their strains:—

Lor: The moon shines bright:—in such a night as this,
When the sweet wind did gently kiss the trees,
And they did make no noise,—in such a night,
Troilus, methinks, mounted the Trojan walls,
And sighed his soul toward the Grecian tents,
Where Cressid lay that night.[5]
Jes.: In such a night
Did Thisbe fearfully o'ertrip the dew;
And saw the lion's shadow ere himself,
And ran dismayed away.
Lor.: In such a night
Stood Dido with a willow in her hand[6]
Upon the wild sea-banks, and waft her love
To come again to Carthage.

Jes.: In such a night
Medea gather'd the enchanted herbs
That did renew old Aeson.
Lor: . . . Look how the floor of heaven
Is thick inlaid with patines of bright gold,
There's not the smallest orb which thou behold'st
But in his motion like an angel sings;
Still quiring to the young-eyed cherubins:
Such harmony is in immortal souls.
But whilst this muddy vesture of decay
Doth grossly close it in, we cannot hear it.

The idea of the music of the spheres belongs primarily to the philosophy or rather to the poetry of Plato; and the same thought is finely expressed by Cicero in the fragment known under the title of *The Dream of Scipio*. In *Antony and Cleopatra*, Cleopatra, bewailing Antony's death, compares his voice to the "tuned spheres" (Act V., Sc. 2); and in *Twelfth Night* Olivia pays the same compliment to the page in disguise, with whom she is in love. Pericles, prince of Tyre, in his ecstasy at finding his daughter Marina, suddenly hears sounds of music unheard by the others, which he calls the music of the spheres.

The name of Aristotle occurs in the first scene of the *Taming of the Shrew*, but there is a more curious mention of him in *Troilus and Cressida*, Act II., Sc. 2. In the council held by Priam, Troilus and Paris with the unreflective impetuosity of youth vote for the continuation of the war; but Hector, no less calm and prudent than brave, maintains that it would be right as well as politic to restore the wife of Menelaus to her lawful husband, and reproves his two scatter-brained brothers, saying—

Paris and Troilus, you have both said well;
And on the cause and question now in hand
Have glozed,—but superficially; not much
Unlike young men, whom Aristotle thought
Unfit to hear moral philosophy.

For Hector to speak of Aristotle is an amusing anachronism, but it is difficult to decide whether Shakespeare fell into it intentionally or through inadvertence, the humorous licence which runs through the whole play lending probability to the former suggestion; just as Goethe, it may be remembered, has been pleased to put the name of Luther into the mouth of

Faust. It would be as idle to conclude, as [Georg Gottfried] Gervinus does, on the strength of Hector's speech, that Shakespeare had read Aristotle's *Ethics,* as it would be to imagine that every poet of the present day who alludes to a tenet of the Cartesian philosophy or of eclecticism or of positivism has necessarily read the works of [French philosopher, René] Des Cartes, of [French philosopherm Victor] Cousin, or of [French philosopher] Auguste Comte. In his *De Augmentis,* [Francis] Bacon quotes Aristotle's same opinion of young men, and strangely enough makes precisely the same mistake that Shakespeare does; it being politics, not moral philosophy, for which the Greek philosopher deemed young men unfit. [The Greek mathematician and mystic] Pythagoras is several times mentioned in Shakespeare, and always with some ironical allusion to his doctrine of the transmigration of souls. The lively Gratiano, in the *Merchant of Venice,* tells Shylock that he must have been a wolf in a former existence (Act IV., Sc. 1); Rosalind, in *As You Like It,* has a confused recollection of having once been an Irish rat (Act III., Sc. 2); and in *Twelfth Night,* the clown, when mocking and jeering at Malvolio, advises him not to kill a woodcock lest he should thereby dislodge the soul of his grandmother (Act IV., Sc. 2.). The authority of Pythagoras is invoked by name in each of these three passages.

Shakespeare alludes to [pre-Socratic Greek philosopher] Heraclitus, though without mentioning his name, in Act I., Sc. 2, of the *Merchant of Venice,* in which Portia says of one of her suitors, the melancholy and morose County Palatine, that when he grows old he will become like the weeping philosopher.

[Greek philosopher] Epicurus is only treated as the voluptuous materialist of common tradition, and is thus presented in *Antony and Cleopatra* (Act II., Sc. 1); in *King Lear* (Act I., Sc. 4); in *Macbeth* (Act V., Sc. 3) and in the *Merry Wives of Windsor* (Act II., Sc. 2).

The only mention of Socrates occurs in the *Taming of the Shrew,* where, as may readily be guessed, it is not as the philosopher but as the husband that he is alluded to: Petruchio replies to his friend's report of Katharine's shrewish disposition, "Be she as curst and shrewd as Socrates' Xantippe she moves me not." (Act I., Sc. 2.)

Shakespeare, it may be noted, is fond of laughing at philosophers, which indeed is not only allowable but is in fact a highly philosophical proceeding; for if, as [French mathematician, physicist, and religious philosopher Blaise] Pascal says, "to laugh at philosophy is really to philosophize," to laugh at philosophers is still more so. In *Much Ado about Nothing* (Act V., Sc. 1), Leonato observes that—

There was never yet philosopher
That could endure the toothache patiently;
However they have writ the style of gods,
And made a push at chance and sufferance.

In *King John*, Constance, after the loss of her son Arthur, says to Cardinal Pandulph (Act III., Sc. 4.)—

I am not mad;—I would to heaven I were!
For then 'tis like I should forget myself;
O, if I could, what grief should I forget!—
Preach some philosophy to make me mad.

And King Lear calls Edgar, who is counterfeiting madness, his *philosopher*.

But Shakespeare especially makes fun of the truisms philosophers are wont to deal in—commonplace truths which noodles admire as profound thoughts and to which the seven wise men of Greece are so greatly indebted for their fame. Touchstone, in *As You Like It*, deals continually in sentences in imitation of the seven sages; as, for instance, when he gravely says to William the simple countryman, who opens his eyes wide at hearing such fine words (Act V., Sc. 1)—

I do now remember a saying: "The fool doth think he is wise, but the wise man knows himself to be a fool." The heathen philosopher, when he had a desire to eat a grape, would open his lips when he put it into his mouth, meaning thereby, that grapes were meant to eat and lips to open.

Sir Hugh Evans, in the *Merry Wives of Windsor*, thinks with equal truth that lips are a part of the mouth, an opinion which he says he shares with many philosophers. Falstaff displays no less wisdom when, in acting the part of King Henry, he thus addresses his royal son:—

There is a thing Harry which thou hast often heard of, and it is known to many in our land by the name of pitch; this pitch, as *ancient writers do report*, doth defile; so doth the company thou keepest. (*King Henry IV.*, Pt. I., Act. II., Sc. 4.)

Any learned scholar who took a delight in what I confess seems to me the barren and ungrateful task of pointing out all the passages in Shakespeare capable of serving as a text, or pretext, for classical quotations would have to distinguish three separate classes: first, the passages borrowed directly from ancient authors; second, those borrowed indirectly; third, mere coincidences. The distinction is not always easy to make; as, for instance, when Ophelia is buried, Laertes takes last leave of her in the touching and poetic words:—

> Lay her i' the earth;
> And from her fair and unpolluted flesh
> May violets spring!
>   (Act V., Sc. 1.)

And in [Roman poet, satirist, and Stoic philosopher] Persius we find—

> Non nunc e manibus istis,
> Non nunc e tumulo fortunataque favilla Nascentur viola?
> [Now from these hands,
> From this rich and glowing mound will not violets be born?]

Did Shakespeare borrow this, or is it a mere coincidence? Polonius says of Hamlet's madness, that "Though this be madness, yet there is method in it:" upon which a commentator remarks that this is precisely Horace's line—"Insanire paret certa ratione modoque." [Madness can surely appear to be rational and measured.] Yet I think that without Horace's line, Polonius's speech would be just as it is. Again, when Hamlet speaks of "the undiscovered country from whose bourn no traveller returns," it is natural to recall the fine lines of Catullus:—

> Qui nunc it per iter tenebricosum,
> Illuc, unde negant redire quemquam.
> [Who now goes along that dusky way to the place from which they say
>   nobody returns.]

But there is not the slightest necessity to thrust in a remark that no English translation of Catullus had yet appeared; surely the imagination of both poets may have met here.

Sleep, as an image of death, is a well-known idea, and appears under various forms—in *Macbeth*, "this downy sleep, death's counterfeit;" in *Cymbeline*, "Sleep, the ape of death," and in the *Midsummer Night's Dream*, "Death counterfeiting sleep;" but a critic must have but a poor opinion of Shakespeare's imagination to suppose the comparison was suggested to him by a passage translated by Marlowe from Ovid.

Coriolanus says, "I shall be loved when I am lacked" (Act IV., Sc. 1), and the same thought occurs in *Antony and Cleopatra:*—

The ebb'd man, ne'er loved till ne'er worth love,
Comes dear'd by being lacked;

in connection with which is quoted Horace's line—

Extinctus amabitur idem;
[Dead, the same man (who is hated now) will be loved]

and to this there is no objection, but we ought also to note the old proverb: "When people are missed then they are mourned."

In the *Two Gentlemen of Verona,* when Proteus tells Silvia that Valentine is dead, she answers:—

In his grave
Assure thyself my love is buried.
(Act IV., Sc. 2.)

As Dido [in the *Aeneid*] affirms, in like manner, that [her husband] Sicheus has borne her love with him into the tomb:—

Ille habeat secum servetque sepulchro,
[he has it and keeps it with him in the tomb]

we are left to decide whether Shakespeare obtained Silvia's answer from Virgil, or from the natural feeling of the heart. In the *Tempest,* Miranda says to Ferdinand (Act III., Sc. 1)—

I am your wife, if you will marry me;
If not I'll die your maid; to be your fellow
You may deny me; but I'll be your servant,
Whether you will or no.

This is so completely the natural language of passion, while at the same time the five exquisite lines of Catullus[7] rush so irresistibly into the mind, that it is very embarrassing to decide whether we have here a coincidence or a case of borrowing.

The same thing occurs in the passage in the *Comedy of Errors,* in which Adriana says to Antipholus:—

> Come, I will fasten on this sleeve of thine: Thou art an elm, my husband, I, a vine; Whose weakness, married to thy stronger state, Makes me with thy strength to communicate.
>
> (Act II., Sc. 2.)

Shakespeare may very well have imitated Catullus:—

> Lenta, qui, velut assitas
> Vitis implicat arbores,
> Implicabitur in tuum
> Complexum;
> [Just as a supple vine entwines with trees planted nearby, he will become entangled in your embrace.]

but in Beaumont's and Fletcher's *Elder Brother,* the scholar, Charles, says to his servant, "Marry thyself to understanding, Andrew" (Act II., Sc. 4); and in [Molière's, Les] *Femmes Savantes* [1672, *The Learned Ladies*] Armande says to Henriette, in exactly the same spirit and in almost the same terms, "Marry yourself to philosophy, my sister," without Molière having imitated Beaumont and Fletcher.

But the quotation of classical authors would only form the easier portion of the task of drawing up a list of all the passages in Shakespeare in which some reminiscence of antiquity is evoked, for it would be requisite to show by what means the poet came to know them, whether it was from contemporaneous literature, or through translations, or from the originals. For instance, in *Troilus and Cressida,* we read—

> For to be wise and love
> Exceeds man's might; that dwells with gods above.

This thought is first met with in Publius Syrus, a Latin author of the first century before Christ, and accordingly, commentators began by saying, that Shakespeare had translated a passage direct from Publius Syrus. But later on, the discovery was made by some learned bookworm, of an English translation of Publius Syrus, by Taverner, published in 1553, at the end of a little duodecimo volume called the *Distichs of Cato;* and it then seemed more natural to suppose that it was through this translation that Shakespeare had acquired his knowledge of Publius Syrus. This is not all, however, for another learned bookworm found the same thought in [John] Marston's play of *The Dutch Courtezan* (1605), and in Spenser's *Shepheardes Calender;* from this time the third explanation was adopted, more likely to be true than either of the two others, that Shakespeare had simply borrowed the passage of Publius Syrus [first century B.C. Latin writer of maxims] from the current literature of the day. Examples of this sort are innumerable, *ab uno disce omnes* [everything is learned from one thing]. However great a reader of ancient authors Shakespeare may have been, it will be readily admitted on all hands that the writers of his own time and country were those he knew best; and not the faintest shadow of disparagement is thrown over his fame by our agreeing with Dr. Farmer, that he was more familiar with translations than with the originals. In the *Taming of the Shrew,* for instance, we read—

Young budding virgin, fair and fresh and sweet,
Whither away; or where is thy abode?
Happy the parents of so fair a child;
Happier the man, whom favourable stars
Allot thee for his lovely bedfellow!
[IV.v.37–41]

The first thought of this salutation belongs to Homer; from whom it was borrowed by Ovid; [Arthur] Golding translated Ovid, and Shakespeare knew and imitated Golding, as is admitted, not only by Steevens, but even by Delius. It matters little whether a translation intervened or not,—the perfume of antiquity clings none the less to Shakespeare's passage, and it could not be more Homeric if he had transcribed it straight from the *Odyssey.*

There are, however, lines which, to all appearances, were translated, or imitated, from the classics by Shakespeare himself. In the *Comedy of Errors,* Aegeon begins the account of his tragic history with these words:—

A heavier task could not have been imposed
Than I to speak my griefs unspeakable.
[I.i.31ff.]

This beginning resembles too closely the even then familiar and well-known "Infandum regina jubes renovare dolorem," [O, Queen, you command me to revive inexpressible sorrows, *Aeneid,* book II, line 3] to leave room for any doubt as to its having been directly borrowed. Further on, when speaking of the storm in which his ship perished Aegeon describes the obscured light of heaven, and how everything—

> Did but convey into our fearful minds
> A doubtful warrant of immediate death.

Virgil's line:—

> Praesentemque viris intentant omnia mortem,
> [And everything promises instant death to men, *Aeneid*, I, 91,]

is here very closely followed.
   In the *Tempest* (Act IV., Sc. 1), we read—

> Highest queen of state,
> Great Juno comes; I know her by her gait,

which is evidently a recollection of the "Incedo Regina." In the *Taming of the Shrew*, Petruchio, after having said of Katharine, "Be she as curst and shrewd as Socrates' Xantippe," adds, "Were she as rough as are the swelling Adriatic seas," which is a close translation of the "Improbo iracundior Adria," in Horace's well-known ode to Lydia, "Donec gratus eram." [While I was loved.]
   Shakespeare frequently introduces Latin words and phrases into his text; as, for instance, in the last-named comedy, he quotes two lines from Ovid,[8] and a line from Terence,[9] which last line does not indeed exactly tally with the text of the Latin author, and which it has been proved Shakespeare took from Lilly's Latin Grammar; but he could have taken it with equal ease from Terence. He heads his poem of *Venus and Adonis* with a Latin epigraph, and we may rest assured that, to a nature as free from every kind of pedantry and pretence as his was, it would have been utterly repugnant to affect a knowledge he did not really possess. Shakespeare, we need not doubt, knew Latin as well as any man of his time; and in his time the educated portion of the public knew it better than they do now.
   At Stratford-on-Avon, where Shakespeare was born, there was a free grammar school, which could be entered under the three conditions of residing in the town; being seven years old; and knowing how to read. Little William Shakespeare was sent by his father to the school, probably in 1571, when he had attained the age of seven, and knew how to read. The school hours were decidedly long—from daybreak to dark in winter, from

six in the morning to six at night in the summer, excepting intervals for meals and recreation. Here Latin was certainly taught, and perhaps—but this is not equally certain—Greek, French, and Italian. Terence, Virgil, Cicero, Sallust and Caesar were the principal authors read by the boys, while they learned the rules of grammar from [John] Lilly, [fourth century A.D. Roman grammarian and rhetorician Aelius] Donatus, or [Italian humanist, educator, and rhetorician Lorenzo] Valla. Various traditions, all agreeing on one point, relate that about 1578, that is, after about seven years of schooling, Shakespeare was removed from the school before having finished his regular course of study. His father seems at this time to have been undergoing a crisis in his pecuniary affairs, and as the family was both numerous and poor, it is hardly likely that young Shakespeare found time after leaving school to continue his studies. Added to which, he married at the age of eighteen, and by the time he was twenty-one found himself the father of a son and two daughters, and under such circumstances his hours of studious leisure must necessarily have been few. He became an actor, although as his sonnets show, not without some suffering to his pride from the humiliations attaching to the position; he touched up old plays and was ready to turn his hand to anything for which he could get paid, and thus earn a livelihood. In short, the beginning of his dramatic career was rude enough, and left him no time for any occupation of which the aim was other than present and practical utility, none consequently for the patient and thorough study which alone deserves the name. He absorbed knowledge from a thousand channels with ravenous activity, not to keep it and meditate upon it, but in order to give out again immediately whatever he had learned. As money came in, immunity from want came with it; yet even when no longer under the burden of necessity, Shakespeare's reading preserved to the end of his life the hasty character that it had at the beginning; his materials were never slowly accumulated, and carefully stored up in the memory for some grand monumental edifice in the future, but were eagerly seized upon with a view to immediate use. It was on this account that he fastened upon North's translation of Plutarch, a translation at secondhand, taken from the French of Amyot, and consequently doubly liable to inaccuracies, without troubling himself in the least as to what they would think of it at Chaeronea [a town in Greece near Thebes]. Capable of building up a palace out of such stones as it furnished him with, he cared little as to the intrinsic value of the raw material;—the work of transformation was no secret to him. And in the same way, it was not on account of an insufficient knowledge of Latin that he preferred to use the

English translation of Ovid's *Metamorphoses* rather than the original, but because he read English more quickly, and less time was lost.

Seven years at school are enough to enable a lad to read easy passages in Latin fluently and to puzzle out the harder bits. In the sixteenth century Latin was still almost a living language; the world was only just emerging from the Middle Ages when it had been constantly spoken, and many men of letters and of learning continued to write it. It was in fact an ordinary element in the education of both men and women, and there is no shadow of reason for refusing it to Shakespeare. In all probability the *Menaechmi* of Plautus was read by him in the original, no English translation having appeared till some years after the *Comedy of Errors*. The various conjectures as to the means by which Shakespeare could have known the old comedian all proceed upon the unfounded assumption of Shakespeare's incapacity, in case of need, to get through a Latin play by himself.

[German literary historian Georg Gottfried] Gervinus, on the other hand, affirms that Shakespeare was deeply versed in Seneca and Plautus, which is saying a good deal. It is extremely probable that he should have read, either in Latin or more likely still in English, all Seneca's plays, so well known and greatly admired as they then were, and also several of Plautus's, but Gervinus speaks of an intimate familiarity, which is not an assertion that should have been advanced without proof I know of no instance in which Shakespeare has copied Plautus except in the *Comedy of Errors,* and not even that has been completely demonstrated to be directly borrowed. In Act V., Sc. 4, of *Cymbeline,* Jupiter, seated on an eagle, descends amidst thunder and lightning and pronounces his decrees in the same antique metre that [Jacobean dramatist Thomas] Heywood and [translator John] Studley had employed in their translation[s] of Seneca: such is the only proof given by Gervinus of Shakespeare's thorough acquaintance with the Latin tragedian. Warburton took the line in *Antony and Cleopatra* (Act IV., Sc. 10)—

Let me lodge Lichas on the horns o' the moon,

to be imitated from Seneca's *Hercules,* but Steevens deems it more likely to have been borrowed from Book IX of the *Metamorphoses.* Gervinus adds:—

If Shakespeare had had occasion at any time to name
his ideal, and to denote the highest examples of
dramatic art which lay before him, he would have
named none but Plautus and Seneca.

In spite of this purely gratuitous assertion, the conclusion arrived at in our preceding chapter must be repeated and maintained: that Shakespeare's feelings towards classical antiquity were those of complete indifference, that he considered it only as a rich mine of wealth, in which light it stood on exactly the same footing in his regard as the legends of the Middle Ages, and the traditions of English history.

[English historian Henry] Hallam, who advances no opinion lightly, notices the occurrence of numerous Latinisms in Shakespeare's works, "phrases, unintelligible and improper, except in the sense of their primitive roots," such as, "Things base and vile, holding no *quantity*," for value; rivers that have "overborn their continents," the continente ripa" of Horace; "*compact* of imagination;" "something of great *constancy*," for consistency; "sweet Pyramis *translated* there," "the law of Athens, which by no means we may extenuate:" "expressions which it is not very likely that one, who did not understand their proper meaning, would have introduced into poetry." Hallam's remark is repeated by Gervinus; and Mr. S. Neil, the author of a very careful critical biography of Shakespeare, has no hesitation in saying that the poet's language is strongly tinged with Latinisms.

With regard to Greek, we may boldly affirm that he did not know it. Even admitting that he may have learned the declensions and verbs at school, such knowledge would have been quite insufficient to enable him to read a Greek author in the original. Every one knows that Greek is not learned at school, and Hallam declares that if in the sixteenth century men were better versed in Latin than they are now, the case was different with Greek. The extent of Shakespeare's knowledge of it may therefore fairly be measured by that of a school-boy of the present time, whose studies have been broken off unfinished, the result being the most absolute ignorance. But there was no occasion for Knight to make apologies for the great poet on this account—he is not singular in his ignorance, and even Schiller and Goethe, as their correspondence attests, read Homer, Aristotle, and the tragedians in translations.

In discussing the question of Shakespeare's learning, it must never be left out of sight, that poets are possessed of an instrument which is not in the hand of every student—the instrument of genius.

> Great artists [M. (French critic and historian Hypolyte) Taine has well said] have no need to learn,—they guess. I have seen such an one, by means of a suit of armour, a costume, or a collection of old furniture, penetrate more deeply into the spirit of the Middle Ages than three savants put together. They rebuild, naturally and surely,

in the same way that they build up, by virtue of an inspiration that lends wings to reasoning.

If we take the word "learning" in its large and liberal sense, and no longer reduce the question to a miserable pedantic wrangling over his more or less of Greek and Latin, then, of all men that ever lived, Shakespeare is one of the most learned.

> Armed with indefatigable curiosity, he was an incessant reader [writes Philarete Chasles] and made himself acquainted with all the current literature of the day: [John] Harrington's [1591] translation of [*Orlando Furioso*, 1516, by Italian poet Ludovico] Ariosto, [Jacques] Amyot's and [Thomas] North's translations of Plutarch, [Edward] Fairfax's [1600 translation of Torquato] Tasso['s *Gerusaleme liberate*, Jerusalem Delivered, 1576, 1593] and [John] Florio's translation of [French essayist Michel de] Montaigne were in his hands as soon as published. He read the travels of Sir Walter Raleigh, and a translation of those of [Richard] Hakluyt, and of the *Week* [or *The Creation of the World*, 1578], by [Guillaume de Salluste] Du Bartas. Stories, histories, plays, chronicles, theological works, amorous sonnets, everything printed in the sixteenth century, everything that fell into his hands, all was devoured by him, and his plays form a complete encyclopedia of his times.

[François] Rabelais, too, he knew, a recollection of whom is found in two of his comedies.[10] And what an open door into classical antiquity he possessed in Montaigne's essays! Besides these, Pliny's *Natural History* was another book in his library; in *Antony and Cleopatra* (Act III. Sc. 7), there is a learned dissertation on the Nile, and in *Troilus and Cressida* (Act V., Sc.3), Troilus reproaches Hector for his clemency towards the vanquished, which he says, "better fits a lion than a man,"—a notion belonging to Pliny the Elder, who observes that "the lion alone of all wild beasts is gentle to those that humble themselves before him, and will not touch any such upon their submission, but spareth what creature soever lieth prostrate before him."

Like all men of real learning, Shakespeare was fully conscious of his ignorance. The greatest stores of knowledge that any man has ever possessed are as nothing in comparison with the infinite number of things of which he is ignorant. A dark night lies all around us, and the more brightly our little torch burns, the better are we able to gauge the depth of blackness. In one of his sonnets (LXXVIII.), the image chosen by Shakespeare to describe an immense abyss is the distance that separates learning from his "rude ignorance," and elsewhere he says that ignorance is the malediction of God, and that learning is the very wing that bears us up to heaven.

Pope's reflection on this subject is very acute, in which he suggests that Shakespeare's ignorance was exaggerated for the sake of opposition and of symmetry, to form a sharper contrast with the vast learning of Ben Jonson. There is, perhaps, no more pernicious source of error in criticism than this mania for contrasting celebrated contemporaries in hard and fast lines;—because Shakespeare is full of fancy, Ben Jonson is set down as having none. . . . [A]fter all, it is childish to discuss the amount of learning possessed by an author who has taught the whole world, and from whom statesmen declare they have drawn their first notions of politics and history.

Notes

1.   "Should we be silent and not speak, etc"—Act V., Sc. 3.

2.   Littré, *Littérature et histoire.*

3.   Haec studia adolescentiam agunt, senectutem, oblectant secundas res ornant, adversis perfugium ac solatium praebent, delctant domi, non impediunt foris, pernoctant nobiscum, peregrinantur, rusticantur.

4.   Theobald was the first of Shakespeare's commentators to whom it occurred to quote this passage, which runs as follows: "Ut un fidibus ac tibias atque cantu ipso ac vocibus, concentus est quidam tenendus ex distinctis sonis, quen immutatum ac discrepantem aures eruditae ferre non possunt, isque concentus ex dissimillimarum vocum moderatione concors tamen efficitur et congruens: sic ex summis et infirmis et mediis interjectis ordinibus, ut sonis, moderata ratione civitas consensus disimillimarum concinit, et quae harmonia a musicis dicitur in cantu, ea est in civitate concordia, arctissimum atque optimum omni in republica vinculum incolumitatis:quae sine justitia nullo pacto esse potest."

5.   A recollection of Chaucer.

6.   Steevens notes this passage as a proof out of many that Shakespeare was no reader of the classics.

7.   Si tibi non cordi fuerant connubial nostra
     Attamen in vestras potuisti ducere sedes
     Quae tibi jucundo famularer serva labore,
     Candida permulcens liquidis vestigial lymphis
     Purpureave tuum consternens veste cubile.

8.   Hac ibat Simois, his est Sigeia tellus,
     Hic steterat Priami regia celsa senis
     (Act. III., Sc. 1.)

9.   Redime te captum, quam queas, minimo.
      (Act. I., Sc. 1.)

10.   In *As You Like It* (Act III., Sc. 2), Rosalind says to Celia, "Answer me ione word;" to which Celia answers, "You must borrow me Gargantua's mouth first, 'tis a word great for any mouth of this age's size." In *Love's Labour's Lost,* the schoolmaster's name is Holofernes.

—Paul Stapfer, "Shakespeare's Classical
Knowledge," *Shakespeare and Classical Antiquity,*
translated by Emily J. Carey, pp. 73–106

AUTHORSHIP CONTROVERSY

Delia Bacon "William Shakespeare and His Plays: An Inquiry Concerning Them" (1856)

Delia Bacon (1811–59) was born in Tallmadge, Ohio, a city founded by her father, David Bacon. He had been a missionary and proselytized among the indigenous people in Michigan. Delia was a schoolteacher and held classes in history and literature that were designed especially for women. She was also an abolitionist. Around 1852, she began a fervent campaign, with the missionary zeal she had perhaps inherited from her father, to show that Shakespeare, the actor, whom she vilified, was not Shakespeare the author of the plays attributed to a particular actor named Shakespeare. She further asserted that those plays contained a secret, ancient, and subversive divine wisdom that needed to be spread. She conceived of her work as a literary duty, devotedly striving against the errors of received opinion, which she excoriated as if it were a deliberate conspiracy against the truth. Her prose tends to rush, colored by sarcasm and propelled by an inspired manic energy and an anger directed against the player, Shakespeare, whom she regards as incapable of writing the plays attributed to him. Her work took her to England. There, she met with Thomas Carlyle, who had written, in 1841, of Shakespeare as a hero to be worshiped, and Nathaniel Hawthorne, who later wrote about his meeting with her in the introduction to the book he helped her get published, despite his not being in the same camp with Bacon in regard to the authorship of Shakespeare's plays. Many subsequent writers were caught up in the current of her passion. Her work became the wellspring for much prose echoing her beliefs and for many critical refutations of it.

How can we undertake to account for the literary miracles of antiquity, while this great myth of the modern ages still lies at our own door, unquestioned?

This vast, magical, unexplained phenomenon which our own times have produced under our own eyes, appears to be, indeed, the only thing which our modern rationalism is not to be permitted to meddle with. For, here the critics themselves still veil their faces, filling the air with mystic utterances which seem to say, that to this shrine at least, for the footstep of the common reason and the common sense, there is yet no admittance. But how can they instruct us to take off here the sandals which they themselves have taught us to wear into the inmost *sekos* of the most ancient sanctities?

THE SHAKESPEARE DRAMA—its import, its limitations, its object and sources, its beginning and end—for the modern critic, that is surely now the question.

What, indeed, should we know of the origin of the Homeric poems? Twenty-five hundred years ago, when those mystic characters, which the learned Phenician and Egyptian had brought in vain to the singing Greek of the Heroic Ages, began, in the new modifications of national life which the later admixtures of foreign elements created, at length to be put to their true uses, that song of the nation, even in its latest form, was already old on the lips of the learned, and its origin a tradition. All the history of that wonderful individuality, wherein the inspirations of so many ages were at last united— the circumstance, the vicissitude, the poetic life that had framed that dazzling mirror of old time, and wrought in it those depths of clearness—all had gone before the art of writing and memories had found its way into Greece, or even the faculty of perceiving the actual had begun to be developed there.

And yet are the scholars of our time content to leave this matter here, where they find it! With these poetic remains in their hands, the monuments of a genius whose date is ante-historical, are they content to know of their origin only what Alexander and Plato could know, what Solon and Pisistratus were fain to content themselves with, what the Homerids themselves received of him as their ancestral patron!

No: with these works in their hands to-day, reasoning from them alone, with no collateral aids, with scarce an extant monument of the age from which they come to us, they are not afraid to fly in the face of all antiquity with their conclusions. . . .

Two hundred and fifty years ago, *our* poet—our Homer—was alive in the world. Two centuries and a half ago, when the art of letters was already millenniums old in Europe, when the art of printing had already been in use a century and a half, in the midst of a cotemporary historical illumination which has its equal nowhere in history, those works were issued that have given our English life and language their imperishable claim in the earth, that have made the name in which they come to us a word by itself, in the human speech; and, to this hour, we know of their origin hardly so much as we knew of the origin of the Homeric epics, when the present discussions in regard to them commenced, *not* so much,—not a hundredth part so much, as we now know of Pharaoh's, who reigned in the valley of the Nile, ages before the invasion of the Hyksos.

But with these products of the national life in our hands, with all the cotemporary light on their implied conditions which such an age as that of Elizabeth can furnish, are we going to be able to sit still much longer, in a period of historical inquiry and criticism like this, under the gross impossibilities which the still accepted theory on this subject involves?

The age which has put back old Homer's eyes, safe, in his head again, after he had gone without them well nigh three thousand years; the age which has found, and labeled, and sent to the museum, the skull in which the pyramid of Cheops was designed, and the lions which "the mighty hunter before the Lord" ordered for his new palace on the Tigris some millenniums earlier; the age in which we have abjured our faith in Romulus and Remus, is surely one in which we may be permitted to ask this question.

Shall this crowning literary product of that great epoch, wherein these new ages have their beginning, vividly arrayed in its choicest refinements, flashing everywhere on the surface with its costliest wit, crowded everywhere with its subtlest scholasticisms, betraying, on every page, its broadest, freshest range of experience, its most varied culture, its profoundest insight, its boldest grasp of comprehension—shall this crowning result of so many preceding ages of growth and culture, with its essential, and now palpable connection with the new scientific movement of the time from which it issues, be able to conceal from us, much longer, its history?—Shall we be able to accept in explanation of it, much longer, the story of the Stratford poacher?

The popular and traditional theory of the origin of these works was received and transmitted after the extraordinary circumstances which led to its first imposition had ceased to exist, because, in fact, no one had any motive for taking the trouble to call it in question. The common disposition to receive, in good faith, a statement of this kind, however extraordinary—the natural intellectual preference of the affirmative proposition at hand, as the explanation of a given phenomenon, when the negative or the doubt compels one to launch out for himself, in search of new positions—this, alone, might serve to account for this result, at a time when criticism, as yet, was not; when the predominant mental habit, on all ordinary questions, was still that of passive acceptance, and the most extraordinary excitements, on questions of the most momentous interest, could only rouse the public mind to assume, temporarily, any other attitude.

And the impression which these works produced, even in their first imperfect mode of exhibition, was already so profound and extraordinary, as to give to all the circumstances of their attributed origin a blaze of notoriety, tending to enhance this positive force in the tradition. Propounded as a fact, not as a theory, its very boldness—its startling improbability—was made at once to contribute to its strength; covering, beforehand, the whole ground of attack. The wonderful origin of these works was, from the first, the predominant point in the impression they made—the prominent marvel in those marvels, around which all the new wonders, that the later criticism evolved, still continued to arrange themselves.

For the discoveries of this criticism had yet no tendency to suggest any new belief on this point. In the face of all that new appreciation of the works themselves, which was involved in them, the story of that wondrous origin could still maintain its footing;—through all the ramifications of this criticism, it still grew and inwound itself, not without vital limitation, however, to the criticism thus entangled. But these new discoveries involved, for a time, conclusions altogether in keeping with the tradition.

This new force in literature, for which books contained no precedent—this new manifestation of creative energy, with its self-sustained vitalities; with its inexhaustible prodigality, mocking nature herself; with its new grasp of the whole circuit of human aims and activities;—this force, so unlike anything that scholasticism or art had ever before produced, though it came, in fact, with the sweep of all the ages—moved with all their slow accumulation—could not account for itself to those critics, as anything but a new and mystic manifestation of nature—a new upwelling of the occult vital forces, underlying our phenomenal existence—invading the historic order with one capricious leap, laughing at history, telling the laboring ages that their sweat and blood had been in vain.

And the tradition at hand was entirely in harmony with this conception. For, to this superhuman genius, bringing with it its own laws and intuitions from some outlying region of life, not subject to our natural conditions, and not to be included in our "philosophy," the differences between man and man, natural or acquired, would, of course, seem trivial. What could any culture, or any merely natural endowment accomplish, that would furnish the required explanation of this result? And, by way of defining itself as an agency wholly supernal, was it not, in fact, necessary that it should select, as its organ, one in whom the natural conditions of the highest intellectual manifestations were obviously, even grossly, wanting?

With this theory of it, no one need find it strange that it should pass in its selection those grand old cities, where learning sat enthroned with all her time-honored array of means and appliances for the development of mental resource—where the genius of England had hitherto been accomplished for all its triumphs—and that it should pass the lofty centres of church and state, and the crowded haunts of professional life, where the mental activities of the time were gathered to its conflicts; where, in hourly collision, each strong individuality was printing itself upon a thousand others, and taking in turn from all their impress; where, in the thick coming change of that "time-bettering age," in its crowding multiplicities, and varieties, and oppositions, life grew warm and in the old the new was stirring, and in the many, the one; where wit, and philosophy, and fancy, and humor, in the thickest onsets of the hour, were learning to veil, in courtly phrase, in double and triple meanings, in crowding complexities of conceits and unimagined subtleties of form, the freedoms that the time had nurtured; where genius flashed up from all her hidden sources, and the soul of the age—"the mind reflecting ages past"—was collecting itself, and ready, even then, to leap forth, "not-for an age, but for all time."

And, indeed, was it not fitting that this new inspiration, which was to reveal the latent forces of nature, and her scorn of conditions—fastening her contempt for all time upon the pride of human culture at its height—was it not fitting, that it should select this moment of all others, and this locality, that it might pass by that very centre of historical influences, which the court of Elizabeth then made,—that it might involve in its perpetual eclipse that immortal group of heroes, and statesmen, and scholars, and wits, and poets, with its enthroned king of thought, taking all the past for his inheritance, and claiming the minds of men in all futurity, as the scene and limit of his dominion? Yes, even he—he, whose thought would grasp the whole, and keep his grasp on it perpetual—speaks to us still out of that cloud of mockery that fell upon him, when "Great Nature" passed him by—even him—with his immortal longings, with his world-wide aims, with his new mastery of her secrets, too, and his new sovereignty over her, to drop her crown of immortality—lit with the finest essence of that which makes his own page immortal—on the brow of the pet horseboy at Blackfriars—the wit and good fellow of the London link-holders, the menial *attache* and *eleve* of the play-house—the future actor, and joint proprietor, of the New Theatre on the Bankside.

Who quarrels with this movement? Who does not find it fitting and pleasant enough? Let the "thrice three muses" go into mourning as deep as they will for this desertion—as desertion it was—for we all know that to the last hour of his life, this fellow cared never a farthing for them, but only for his gains at their hands;—let learning hide as she best may, her baffled head in this disgrace—who cares?—who does not rather laugh with great creating nature in her triumph?

At least, who would be willing to admit, for a moment, that there was one in all that cotemporary circle of accomplished scholars, and men of vast and varied genius, capable of writing these plays; and who feels the least difficulty in supposing that "this player here," as Hamlet terms him—the whole force of that outburst of scorn ineffable bearing on the word, and on that which it represented to him—who doubts that this player is most abundantly and superabundantly competent to it?

Now that the deer-stealing fire has gone out of him, now that this youthful impulse has been taught its conventional social limits, sobered into the mild, sagacious, witty "Mr. Shakespeare of the Globe," distinguished for the successful management of his own fortunes, for his upright dealings with his neighbors, too, and "his facetious grace in writing," patronized by men of rank, who include his theatre among their instrumentalities for affecting the popular mind, and whose relations to him are, in fact, identical with those which Hamlet sustains to the players of *his* piece, what is to hinder this Mr. Shakespeare—the man who keeps the theatre on the Bankside—from working himself into a frenzy when he likes, and scribbling out unconsciously Lears, and Macbeths, and Hamlets, merely as the necessary dialogue to the spectacles he professionally exhibits; ay, and what is to hinder his boiling his kettle with the manuscripts, too, when he has done with them, if he chooses?

What it would be madness to suppose the most magnificently endowed men of that wondrous age could accomplish—its real men, those who have left their lives in it, woven in its web throughout—what it would be madness to suppose these men, who are but men, and known as such, could accomplish, this Mr. Shakespeare, actor and manager, of whom no one knows anything else, shall be able to do for you in "the twinkling of an eye," without so much as knowing it, and there shall be no words about it.

And are not the obscurities that involve his life, so impenetrably in fact, the true Shakespearean element? In the boundless sea of negations which surrounds that play-house, surely he can unroll himself to any length, or gamer himself into any shape or attitude, which the criticism in hand may call for. There is nothing to bring up against him, with one's theories. For, here in this daylight of our modern criticism, in its noontide glare, has he not contrived to hide himself in the profoundest depths of that stuff that myths are made of? Who shall come in competition with him here? Who shall dive into the bottom of that sea to pluck his drowned honors from him?

Take, one by one, the splendid men of this Elizabethan age, and set them down with a *Hamlet* to write, and you will say beforehand, such an one can not do it, nor such an one,—nor *he,* with that profoundest insight and determination of his which taught him to put physical nature to the question that he might wring from her her secrets; but humanity, human nature, of course, has none worth noting for him;—oh no; he, with his infinite wit and invention, with his worlds of covert humor, with his driest prose, pressed, bursting with Shakspearean beauty, he could not do it; nor *he,* with his Shakespearean acquaintance with life, with his Shakespearean knowledge of men under all the differing social conditions, at home and abroad, by land and by sea, with his world-wide experiences of nature and fortune, with the rush and outbreak of his fiery mind kindling and darting through all his time; he, with his Shakespearean grace and freedom, with his versatile and profound acquirements, with his large, genial, generous, prodigal, Shakespearean soul that would comprehend all, and ally itself with all, he could not do it; neither of these men, nor both of them together, nor all the wits of the age together:— but this Mr. Shakespeare of the Globe, this mild, respectable, obliging man, this "Johannes Factotum" (as a cotemporary calls him, laughing at the idea of *his* undertaking "a blank verse," [The "contemporary" is Robert Greene, writing, in 1592, in *A Groatsworth of Wit.*]) *is there any difficulty here? Oh no! None in the world: for,* in the impenetrable obscurity of that illimitable greenroom of his, "by the mass, he is anything, and he can do anything and that roundly too."

Is it wonderful? And is not that what we like in it? Would you make a man of him? With this miraculous inspiration of his, would you ask anything else of him? Do you not see that you touch the Shakespearean essence, with a question as to motives, and possibilities? Would he be Shakespeare still, if he should permit you to hamper him with conditions? What is the meaning of that word, then? And will you not leave him to us? Shall we have no Shakespeare? Have not we scholars enough, and wits enough, and men, of every other kind of genius, enough,—but have we many Shakespeares?—that you should wish to run this one through with your questions, this one, great, glorious, infinite impossibility, that has had us in its arms, all our lives from the beginning. If you dissolve him do you not dissolve us with him? If you take him to pieces, do you not undo us, also?

Ah, surely we did not need this master spirit of our race to tell us that there is that in the foundation of this human soul, "that loves to apprehend more than cool reason ever comprehends," nay, that there is an infinity in it, that finds her ordinances too straight, that will leap from them when it can, and shake the head at her. And have we not all lived once in regions full of people that were never compelled to give an account of themselves in any of these matters? And when, precisely, did we pass that charmed line, beyond which these phantoms cannot come? When was the word definitively spoken which told us that the childhood of the race was done, or that its grown-up children were to have henceforth no conjurors? Who yet has heard the crowing of that cock, "at whose warning, whether in earth or air, the extravagant and erring spirit hies to his confine?" The nuts, indeed, are all cracked long ago, whence of old the fairy princess, in her coach and six, drove out so freely with all her regal retinue, to crown the hero's fortunes; and the rusty lamp, that once filled the dim hut of poverty with eastern splendors, has lost its capabilities. But, when our youth robbed us of these, had it not marvels and impossibilities of its own to replace them with, yet more magical; and surely, manhood itself, the soberest maturity, can not yet be without these substitutes; and it is nature's own voice and outcry that we hear whenever one of them is taken from us.

Let him alone! We have lecturers enough and professors enough already. Let him alone! We will keep this one mighty conjuror, still, even in the place where men most do congregate, and nobody shall stir a hair on his impossible old head, or trouble him with a question. He shall stand there still, pulling interminable splendors out of places they never could have been in; that is the charm of it; he shall stand there rubbing those few sickly play-house manuscripts of his, or a few old, musty play-house novels, and wringing from them the very wine of all our life, showering from their greasy folds the gems and gold of all the ages! He shall stand there spreading, in the twinkling of an eye, for a single night in a dirty theatre, "to complete a purchase that he has a mind to," the feasts of the immortal gods; and before our lips can, by any chance, have reached even the edge of those cups, that open down into infinity, when the show has served his purpose, he shall whisk it all away again, and leave no wreck behind, except by accident; and none shall remonstrate, or say to him, "wherefore?" He shall stand there, still, for us all—the magician; nature's one, complete, incontestible, gorgeous triumph over the impossibilities of reason.

For the primary Shakespearean condition involves at present, not merely the accidental absence of those external means of intellectual enlargement and perfection, whereby the long arts of the ages are made to bring to the individual mind their last results, multiplying its single forces with the life of all;—but it requires also, the absence of all personal intellectual tastes, aims, and pursuits; it requires that this man shall be below all other men, in his sordid incapacity for appreciating intellectual values; it requires that he shall be able, not merely to witness the performance of these plays, not merely to hear them and read them for himself, but to compose them; it requires him to be able to compose the *Tempest,* and *Othello,* and *Macbeth,* without suspecting that there is anything of permanent interest in them—anything that will outlast the spectacle of the hour.

The art of writing had been already in use, twenty-five centuries in Europe, and a Shakespeare, one would think, might have been able to form some conception of its value and applications; the art of printing had been in use on the continent a century and a half, and it was already darting through every civilized corner of it, and through England, too, no uncertain intimations of its historic purport—intimations significant enough "to make bold power look pale" already—and one would think a Shakespeare might have understood its message. But no! This very spokesman of the new era it ushers in, trusted with this legacy of the new-born times; this man, whom we all so look up to, and reverence, with that inalienable treasure of ours in his hands, which even Ben Jonson knew was not for him, "nor for an age—but for all time," why this Jack Cade [a character in *II Henry VI* who foments rebellion among the people against the nobility] that he is must needs take us back three thousand years with it, and land us at the gates of Ilium! The arts of humanity and history, as they stood when Troy was burned, must save this treasure for us, and be our means of access to it! He will leave this work of his, into which the ends of the world have come to be inwrought for all the future, he will leave it where Homer left his, on the lips of the mouthing "rhapsodists!"

Apparently, indeed, he will be careful to teach these "robustious, periwig-pated fellows" their proper relations to him. He will industriously instruct them how to pronounce his dialogue, so as to give the immediate effect intended; controlling even the gesticulations, insisting on the stops, ruling out utterly the town-crier's emphasis; and, above all, protesting, with a true author's jealousy, against interpolation or any meddling with his text. Indeed, the directions to the players, which he puts into the mouth of Hamlet—involving, as they do, not merely the nice sensibility of the artist, and his nervous, instinctive, esthetic, acquaintance with his art, but a thorough scientific knowledge of its principles—these directions would have led us to infer that he would, at least, know enough of the value of his own works to avail himself of the printing press, for their preservation, and not only that, they would have led us to expect from him a most exquisitely careful revision of his proofs. But how is it? He destroys, we are given to understand, the manuscripts of his unpublished plays, and we owe to accident, and to no care of him whatever, his works as they have come to us. Did ever the human mind debase itself to the possibility of receiving such nonsense as this, on any subject, before?

He had those manuscripts! He had those originals which publishers and scholars would give millions now to purchase a glimpse of; he had the original *Hamlet,* with its last finish; he had the original *Lear,* with his own final readings; he had them all—all, pointed, emphasized, directed, as they came from the gods; he had them all, all finished as the critic of *Hamlet* and *Midsummer Night's Dream* must have finished them; and he left us to wear out our youth, and squander our lifetime, in poring over and setting right the old, garbled copies of the playhouse! He had those manuscripts, and the printing-press had been at its work a hundred years when he was born, but he was not ashamed to leave the best wits and scholars of all succeeding ages, with Pope and Johnson at their head, to exhaust their ingenuity, and sour their dispositions, and to waste their golden hours, year after year, in groping after and guessing out his hidden meanings!

He had those manuscripts! In the name of that sovereign reason, whose name he dares to take upon his lips so often, what did he do with them? Did he wantonly destroy them? No! Ah, no! he did not care enough for them to take that trouble. No, he did not do that! That would not have been in keeping with the character of this most respectable impersonation of the Genius of the British Isle, as it stands set up for us at present to worship. Some worthy, domestic, private, economic use, doubtless, they were put to. For, is not he a private, economical, practical man—this Shakespeare of ours—with no stuff and nonsense about him—a plain, true-blooded Englishman, who minds his own business, and leaves other people to take care of theirs? Is not this our Shakespeare? Is it not the boast of England, that he is just that, and nothing else? "What did he do with them?" He gave them to his cook, or Dr. Hale put up potions for his patients in them, or Judith, poor Judith—who signified her relationship to the author of *Lear,* and the *Tempest,* and her right to the glory of the name he left her, by the very extraordinary kind of "mark" which she affixes to legal instruments—poor Judith may have curled her hair to the day of her death with them, without dreaming of any harm. "What did he do with them?" And whose business is it? Weren't they his own? If he chose to burn them up, or put them to some private use, had not he a perfect *right* to do it?

No! Traitor and miscreant! No! What did you do with them? You have skulked this question long enough. You will have to account for them. You will have to tell us what you did with them. The awakening ages will put you on the stand, and you will not leave it until you answer the question, "What did you do with them?"

And yet, do not the critics dare to boast to us, that he did compose these works for his own private, particular ends only? Do they not tell us, as if it were a thing to be proud of, and "a thing to thank God on," with uplifted eyes, and speechless admiration points, that he did "die, and leave the world no copy?" But who is it that insists so much, so strangely, so repetitiously, upon the wrong to humanity, the fraud done to nature, when the individual fails to render in his account to time of all that nature gives him? Who is it that writes, obscurely, indeed, so many sonnets, only to ring the changes on this very subject, singing out, point by point, not the Platonic theory, but his own fresh and beautiful study of great nature's law, and his own new and scientific doctrine of conservation and advancement? And who is it that writes, unconsciously, no doubt, and without its ever occurring to him that it was going to be printed, or to be read by any one?

> *Thyself* and *thy belongings*
> *Are not thine own* so proper, as to waste
> *Thyself upon thy virtues,* them on thee.
> [*Measure for Measure,* I.i.29–31]

For here is the preacher of another doctrine, which puts the good that is private and particular where the sovereignty that is in nature puts it:

> Heaven doth with us, as *we with torches do;*
> Not light them for themselves. For if our virtues
> Did not go forth of us, 'twere all alike
> As if we had them not. Spirits are not finely touched
> But to fine issues, and nature never lends
> The smallest scruple of her excellence,
> But, like a thrifty goddess, she determines
> Herself the glory of a creditor,
> Both thanks and use.
> [*Measure for Measure,* I.i.32–40]

Truly the man who writes in this style, with such poetic iteration, might put in Hamlet's plea, when his critics accuse him of unconsciousness:

> Bring me to the test
> And I the matter will reword; which madness
> Would gambol from.
> [III.iv.143–45]

What infirmity of blindness is it, then, that we charge upon this "god of our idolatry!" And what new race of Calibans are we, that we should be called upon to worship this monstrous incongruity—this Trinculo—this impersonated moral worthlessness? Oh, stupidity, past finding out! "The myriad-minded one," the light of far-off futurities was in him, and he knew it not! While the word was on his lips, and he reasoned of it, he heeded it not! He, at whose feet all men else are proud to sit, came to him, and found no reverence. The treasure for us all was put into his hands, and—he did not waste it—he did not keep it laid up in a napkin, he did not dig in the earth, and hide his lord's money; no, he used it! he used it for his own despicable and sordid ends, "to complete purchases that he had a mind to," and he left us to gather up "the arts and fragments" as best we may. And they *dare* to tell us this of him, and men believe it, and to this hour his bones are canonized, to this hour his tomb is a shrine, where the genius of the cool, sagacious, clear-thoughted Northern Isle is worshiped, under the form of a mad, unconscious, intellectual possession—a dotard inspiration, incapable of its own designs, wanting in the essential attribute of all mental power—self-cognition.

And yet, who would be willing to spare, now, one point in that time-honored, incongruous whole? Who would be willing to dispense with the least of those contradictions, which have become, in the progressive development of our appreciation of these works, so inextricably knit together, and thereby inwrought, as it were, into our inmost life? Who can, in fact, fairly convince himself, now, that deer-stealing and link-holding, and the name of an obscure family in Stratford—common enough there, though it means what it does to us—and bad, or indifferent performances, at a Surrey theatre, are not really, after all, essential preliminaries and concomitants to the compositon of a *Romeo and Juliet*, or a *Midsummer Night's Dream*, or a *Twelfth Night*? And what Shakespeare critic, at least, could persuade himself, now, that any other motive than the purchase of the Globe theatre, and that capital messuage or tenement in Stratford, called the New Place, with the appurtenances thereof, and the lands adjoining, and the house in Henley street, could by any possibility have originated such works as these?

And what fool would undertake to prove, now, that the fact of the deer-stealing, or any other point in the traditionary statement, may admit of question? Certainly, if we are to have an historical or traditionary Shakespeare of any kind, out of our present materials, it becomes us to protest, with the utmost severity, against the least meddling therewith. If they are not sufficiently meagre already—if the two or three historical points we have, or seem to have, and the miserable scraps and fragments of gossip, which the painful explorations of two centuries have, at length, succeeded in rescuing from the oblivion to which this man's time consigned him—if these points are to be encroached upon, and impaired by criticism, we may as well throw up the question altogether. In the name of all that is tangible, leave us what there is of affirmation here. Surely we have negations enough already. If he did not steal the deer, will you tell us what one mortal thing he did do? He wrote the plays. But, did the man who wrote the plays do nothing else? Are there not some foregone conclusions in them?—some intimations, and round ones, too, that he who wrote them, be he who he may, has had experiences of some sort? Do such things as these, that the plays are full of, begin in the fingers' end? Can you find them in an ink-horn? Can you sharpen them out of a goose-quill? Has your Shakespeare wit and invention enough for that?

But the man was a player, and the manager of a playhouse, and these are plays that he writes. And what kind of play is it that you find in them—and what is the theatre—and who are the actors? Has this man's life been all *play*? Has there been no earnest in it?—no acting in his own name? Had *he* no part of his own in time, then? Has he dealt evermore with secondhand reports, unreal shadows, and mockeries of things? ... [W]hat honest man would want a Shakespeare at this hour of the day, that was not written by that same irregular, lawless, wild, reckless, facetious, law-despising, art-despising genuis of a "Will" that did steal the deer? Is not this the Shakespeare we have had on our shelves with our bibles and prayer-books, since our great grandsires' times? The next step will be to call in question Moses in the bulrushes, and Pharaoh's daughter.

And what is to become, too, under this supposition, of that exquisite specimen of the player's merciless wit, and "facetious grace in writing," which attracted the attention of his cotemporaries, and left such keen impressions on the minds of his fellow-townsmen? What is to become, in this case, of the famous lampoon on Sir Thomas Lucy, nailed up on the park gate, rivaling in Shakespearean grace and sharpness another Attic morceau from the same source—the impromptu on "John-a-Combe?" These remains of the poet, which we find accredited to him in his native village, "with likelihood of truth enough," among those who best knew him, have certainly cost the commentators too much trouble to be lightly relinquished; and, unquestionably, they do bear on the face of them most unmistakable symptoms of the player's wit and the Stratford origin.

No! no! We cannot spare the deer-stealing. As the case now stands, this one, rich, sparkling point in the tradition, can by no means be dispensed with. Take this away, and what becomes of our traditional Shakespeare? He goes! The whole fabric tumbles to pieces, or settles at once into a hopeless stolidity. But for the mercurial lightning, which this youthful reminiscence imparts to him—this single indication of a suppressed tendencey to an heroic life—how could that heavy, retired country gentleman, late manager of the Globe and the Blackfriars theatres, be made to float at any convenient distance above the earth, in the laboring conceptions of the artists whose business it is to present his apotheosis to us? Enlarge the vacant platitudes of that forehead as you will—pile up the artificial brains in the frontispiece to any height which the credulity of an awe-struck public will hesitate to pronounce idiotic—huddle the allegorical shapes about him as thickly as you will, and yet, but for the twinkle which this single reminiscence leaves, this one solitary "proof of liberty," "the flash and outbreak of a fiery mind of general assault," how could the old player and showman be made to sit the bird of Jove so comfortably as he does, on his way to the waiting Olympus?

But, after all, it is not this old actor of Elizabeth's time, who exhibited these plays at his theatre in the way of his trade, and cared for them precisely as a tradesman would—cared for them as he would have cared for tin kettles, or earthern pans and pots, if they had been in his line, instead; it is not this old tradesman; it is not this old showman and hawker of plays; it is not this old lackey, whose hand is on all our heart-strings, whose name is, of mortal names, the most awe-inspiring.

The Shakespeare of Elizabeth and James, who exhibited at his theatre as plays, among many others surpassing them in immediate theatrical success, the wonderful works which bore his name—works which were only half printed, and that surreptitiously, and in detached portions during his life-time, which, seven years after his death, were first collected and published by authority in his name, accompanied, according to the custom of the day, with eulogistic verses from surviving brother poets—this yet living theatrical Shakespeare, is a very different one from the Shakespeare of our modern criticism;—the Shakespeare, brought out, at length, by more than two centuries of readings and the best scholarly investigation of modern times, from between the two lids of that wondrous folio.

The faintly limned outlines of the nucleus which that name once included, are all gone long ago, dissolved in the splendors, dilated into the infinities which this modern Shakespeare dwells in. It is Shakespeare the author, that we now know only, the author of these worlds of profoundest art—these thought-crowded worlds, which modern reading discovers in these printed plays of his. It is the posthumous Shakespeare of the posthumous volume, that we now know only. No, not even that; it is only the work itself that we now know by that name—the phenomenon and not its beginning. For, with each new study of the printed page, further and further behind it, deeper and deeper into regions where no man so much as undertakes to follow it, retreats the power, which is for us all already, as truly as if we had confessed it to ourselves, the unknown, the unnamed.

What does this old player's name, in fact, stand for with us now? Inwrought not into all our literature merely, but into all the life of our modern time, his unlearned utterances our deepest lore, which "we are toiling all our lives to find," his mystic page, the page where each one sees his own life inscribed, point by point, deepening and deepening with each new experience from the cradle to the grave; what is he to us now? Is he the teacher of our players only? What theatres hold now his school? What actors' names stand now enrolled in its illustrious lists? Do not all our modern works incorporate his lore into their essence, are they not glittering on their surface everywhere, with ever new, unmissed jewels from his mines? Which of our statesmen, our heroes, our divines, our poets, our philosophers, has not learned of him; and in which of all their divergent and multiplying pursuits and experiences do they fail to find him still with them, still before them?

The name which has stood to us from the beginning, for all this—which has been inwrought into it, which concentrates it in its unity—cannot now be touched. It has lost its original significance. It means this, and this only to us. It has drunk in the essence of all this power, and light, and beauty, and identified itself with it. Never, perhaps, can it well mean anything else to us.

You cannot christen a world anew, though the name that was given to it at the font prove an usurper's. With all that we now know of that heroic scholar, from whose scientific dream the New World was made to emerge at last, in the face of the mockeries of his time, with all that appreciation of his work which the Old World and the New alike bestow upon it, we cannot yet separate the name of his rival from his hard-earned triumph. What name is it that has drunk into its melody, forever, all the music of that hope and promise, which the young continent of Columbus still whispers—in spite of old European evils planted there—still whispers in the troubled earth? Whose name is it that stretches its golden letters, now, from ocean to ocean, from Arctic to Antarctic, whose name now enrings the millions that are born, and live, and die, knowing no world but the world of that patient scholar's dream—no reality, but the reality of his chimera?

What matters it? Who cares? "What's in a name?" Is there any voice from that hero's own tomb, to rebuke this wrong? No. He did not toil, and struggle, and suffer, and keep his manly heart from breaking, to the end, that those millions might be called by *his* name. Ah, little know they, who thus judge of works like his, what roots such growths must spread, what broad, sweet currents they must reach and drink from. If the millions are blessed there, if, through the heat and burden of his weary day, man shall at length attain, though only after many an erring experience and fierce rebuke, in that new world, to some height of learning, to some scientific place of peace and rest, where worlds are in harmony, and men are as one, he will say, in God's name, Amen! For, on the heights of endurance and self renunciation, where the divine is possible with men, we have one name.

What have we to do with this poor peasant's name, then, so hallowed in all our hearts, now, with household memories, that we should seek to tear it from the countless fastenings which time has given it? This name, chosen at least of fortune, if not of nature, for the place it occupies, dignified with all that she can lend it—illustrious with her most lavish favoritism—has she not chosen to encircle it with honors which make poor those that she saves for her kings and heroes? Let it stand, then, and not by grace of fortune only, but by consent of one who could afford to leave it such a legacy. For he was one whom giving did not impoverish—he had wealth enough of his own and to spare, and honors that he could not part with. . . .

Condemned to refer the origin of these works to the vulgar, illiterate man who kept the theatre where they were first exhibited, a person of the most ordinary character and aims, compelled to regard them as the result merely of an extraordinary talent for pecuniary speculation in this man, how could we, how could any one dare to see what is really in them? With this theory overhanging them, though we threw our most artistic lights upon it, and kept it out of sight when we could, what painful contradictory mental states, what unacknowledged internal misgivings were yet involved in our best judgments of them. How many passages were we compelled to read "trippingly," with the "mind's eye," as the players were first taught to pronounce them on the tongue; and if, in spite of all our slurring, the inner depths would open to us, if anything, which this theory could not account for, would, notwithstanding, obtrude itself upon us, we endeavored to believe that it must be the reflection of our own better learning, and so, half lying to ourselves, making a wretched compromise with our own mental integrity, we still hurried on.

Condemned to look for the author of Hamlet himself—the subtle Hamlet of the university, the courtly Hamlet, "the glass of fashion and the mould of form"—in that dirty, doggish group of players, who come into the scene summoned like a pack of hounds to his service, the very tone of his courtesy to them, with its princely condescension, with its arduous familiarity, only serving to make the great, impassable social gulf between them the more evident—compelled to look in that ignominious group, with its faithful portraiture of the players of that time (taken from the life by one who had had dealings with them), for the princely scholar himself in his author, how could we understand him—the enigmatical Hamlet, with the thought of ages in his foregone conclusions?

With such an origin, how could we see the subtlest skill of the university, not in Hamlet and Horatio only, but in the work itself, incorporated in its essence, pervading its execution? With such an origin as this, how was it possible to note, not in this play only, but in all the Shakespeare drama, what, otherwise, we could not have failed to observe, the tone of the highest Elizabethan breeding, the very loftiest tone of that peculiar courtly culture, which was then, and but *just* then, attaining its height, in the competitions among men of the highest social rank, and among the most brilliant wits and men of genius of the age, for the favor of the learned, accomplished, sagacious, wit-loving maiden queen;—a culture which required not the best acquisitions of the university merely, but acquaintance with life, practical knowledge of affairs, foreign travel and accomplishments, and, above all, the last refinements of the highest Parisian breeding. For "your courtier" must be, in fact, "your picked man of countries." He must, indeed, "get his behavior everywhere." He must be, in fact and literally, the man of "the world."

But for this prepossession, in that daring treatment of court-life which this single play of *Hamlet* involves, in the entire freedom with which its conventionalities are handled, how could we have failed to recognize the touch of one habitually practiced in its refinements? how could we have failed to recognize, not in this play only, but in all these plays, the poet whose habits and perceptions have been moulded in the atmosphere of these subtle social influences. He cannot shake off this influence when he will. He carries the court perfume with him, unconsciously, wherever he goes, among mobs of artisans that will not "keep their teeth clean;" into the ranks of "greasy citizens" and "rude mechanicals;" into country feasts and merry-makings; among "pretty low-born lasses," "the queens of curds and cheese," and into the heart of that forest, "where there is no clock." He looks into the Arden and into Eastcheap from the court stand-point, not from these into the court, and he is as much a prince with Poins and Bardolph as he is when he enters and throws open to us, without awe, without consciousness, the most delicate mysteries of the royal presence.

Compelled to refer the origin of these works to the sordid play-house, who could teach us to distinguish between the ranting, unnatural stuff and bombast which its genuine competitions elicited, in their mercenary appeals to the passions of their audience, ministering to the most vicious tastes, depraving the public conscience, and lowering the common standard of decency, getting up "scenes to tear a cat in,"—"out-Heroding Herod," and going regularly into professional fits about Hecuba and Priam and other Trojans,—who could teach us to distinguish between the tone of this original, genuine, play-house fustian, and that of the "dozen of sixteen lines" which Hamlet will at first, for some earnest purpose of his own, with the consent and privity of *one* of the players, cause to be inserted in it? Nay, thus blinded, we shall not, perhaps, be able to distinguish from this foundation that magnificent whole, with which, from such beginnings, this author will, perhaps, ultimately replace his worthless originals, altogether; that whole in which we shall see, one day, not the burning Ilium, not the old Danish court of the tenth century, but the yet living, illustrious Elizabethan age, with all its momentous interests still at stake, with its yet palpitating hopes and fears, with its new-born energies, bound but unconquerable, already heaving, and muttering through all their undertone; that magnificent whole, where we shall see, one day, "the very abstract and brief chronicle of the time," the "very body of the age, its form and pressure," under any costume of time and country, or under the drapery of any fiction, however absurd or monstrous, which this author shall find already popularized to his hands, and available for his purposes. Hard, indeed, was the time, ill bestead was the spirit of the immemorial English freedom, when the genius of works such as these, was compelled to stoop to such a scene, to find its instruments.

How could we understand from such a source, while that wretched player was still crying it for his own worthless ends, this majestic exhibition of our common human life from the highest intellectual and social stand-point of that wondrous age, letting in, on all the fripperies and affectations, the arrogance and pretension of that illustrious centre of social life, the new philosophic beam, and sealing up in it, for all time, "all the uses and customs" of the world that then was? Arrested with that transparent petrefaction, in all the rushing life of the moment, and set, henceforth, on the table of philosophic halls for scientific illustration; its gaudy butterflies impaled upon the wing, in their perpetual gold; its microscopic insects, "spacious in the possession of land and dirt," transfixed in all the swell and flutter of the moment; its fantastic apes, unrobed for inextinguishable mortal laughter and celestial tears, still playing, all unconsciously, their solemn pageants through; how could the showman explain all this to us—how could the player tell us what it meant?

How could the player's mercenary motive and the player's range of learning and experiment give us the key to this new application of the human reason to the human life, from the new vantage ground of thought, but just then rescued from the past, and built up painfully from all its wreck? How could we understand, from such a source, this new, and strange, and persevering application of thought to life, not merely to society and to her laws, but to nature, too; pursuing her to her last retreats, and holding everywhere its mirror up to her, reflecting the whole boundary of her limitations; laying bare, in its cold, clear, pure depths, in all their unpolite, undraped scientific reality, the actualities which society, as it is, can only veil, and the evils which society, as it is, can only hide and palliate?

In vain the shrieking queen remonstrates, for, it is the impersonated reason whose clutch is on her, and it says, you go not hence till you have seen the inmost part of you. But does all this tell on the thousand pounds? Is the ghost's word good for that?

No wonder that Hamlet refused to speak, or to be commanded to any utterance of harmony, let the critics listen, and entreat as they would, while this illiterate performer, who knew no touch of all that divine music of his, from its lowest note to the top of his key, was still sounding him and fretting him. We shall take another key and another interpreter with us when we begin to understand a work which comprehends, in its design, all our human aims and activities, and tracks them to their beginnings and ends; which demands the ultimate, scientific perpetual reason in all our life—a work which dares to defer the punishment of the crime that society visits with her most dreaded penalties, till all the principles of the human activity have been collected; till all the human conditions have been explored; till the only universal rational human principle is found—a work which dares to defer the punishment of the crime that society condemns, till its principle has been tracked through the crime which she tolerates; through the crime which she sanctions; through the crime which she crowns with all her honors.

We are, indeed, by no means insensible to the difference between this Shakespeare drama, and that on which it is based, and that which surrounds it. We do, indeed, already pronounce that difference, and not faintly, in our word *Shakespeare*; for that is what the word now means with us, though we received it with no such significance. Its historical development is but the next step in our progress.

Yes, there were men in England then, who had heard somewhat of those masters of the olden time, high Eschylus and Sophocles—men who had heard of Euripides, too, and next, Aristophanes—men who had heard of Terence, and not of Terence only, but of his patrons—men who had heard of Plato, too, and of his master. There were men in England, in those days, who knew well enough what kind of an instrumentality the drama had been in its original institution, and with what voices it had then spoken; who knew, also, its permanent relations to the popular mind, and its capability for adaptation to new social exigencies; men, quick enough to perceive, and ready enough to appreciate to the utmost, the facilities which this great organ of the wisdom of antiquity offered for effectual communication between the loftiest mind, at the height of its culture, and that mind of the world in which this, impelled by no law of its own ordaining, seeks ever its own self-completion and perpetuity.

And where had this mighty instrument of popular sway, this mechanism for moving and moulding the multitude, its first origin, but among men initiated in the profoundest religious and philosophic mysteries of their time, among men exercised in the control and administration of public affairs; men clothed even with imperial sway, the joint administrators of the government of Athens, when Athens sat on the summit of her power, the crowned mistress of the seas, the imperial ruler of "a thousand cities." . . .

And there were men in England, in the age of Elizabeth, who had mastered the Greek and Roman history, and not only that, but history of their own institutions—men who knew precisely what kind of crisis in human history that was which they were born to occupy. And they had seen the indigenous English drama struggling up, through the earnest, but childish, exhibitions of the cathedral—through "Miracles," and "Mysteries," and "Moralities," [early forms of pre-Shakespearean drama dedicated to instilling spectators with religious, moral, and social virtues] to be arrested, in its yet undeveloped vigor, with the unfit and unyielding forms of the finished Grecian art; and when, too, by the combined effect of institutions otherwise at variance, all that had, till then, made its life, was suddenly abstracted from it. The royal ordinances which excluded it, henceforth, from all that vital range of topics which the censorship of a capricious and timorous despotism might include among the interdicted questions of church and state, found it already expelled from the religious sanctuaries—in which not the drama only, but all that which we call art, *par excellence,* has its birth and nurture. And that was the crisis in which the pulpit began to open its new drain upon it, having only a vicious play-house, where once the indefinite priestly authority had summoned all the soul to its spectacles, and the long-drawn aisle, and fretted vault, had lent to them their sheltering sanctities; where once, as of old, the Athenian temple had pressed its scene into the heart of the Athenian hill—the holy hill—and opened its subterranean communication with Eleusis, while its centre was the altar on which the gods themselves threw incense. [Eleusis was the site, in ancient Greece, of religious observances, known as the Eleusinian Mysteries, which began around 1600 B.C. The Eleusinian Mysteries celebrated the goddess Demeter, or Ceres, the goddess of vegetation and nurture and her daughter Persephone, or Proserpine, who had been stolen from her by the god Hades, or Pluto, and taken to the Underworld to be his bride. The Eleusinian Mysteries effected the union of the worshippers with the divinities and conferred on the worshippers elevated, even divine powers and immortality.]

And yet, there was a moment in the history of the national genius, when, roused to its utmost—stimulated to its best capability of ingenuity and invention—it found itself constrained to stoop at its height, even to the threshold of this same degraded play-house. There were men in England, who knew what latent capacities that debased instrument of genius yet contained within it—who knew that in the master's hand it might yet be made to yield, even then, and under those conditions, better music than any which those old Greek sons of song had known how to wake in it.

These men knew well enough the proper relation between the essence of the drama and its form. "Considering poetry in respect to the verse, and not to the argument," says one, "though men in learned languages may tie themselves to ancient measures; yet, in modern languages, it seems to me as free to make new measures as to make new dances; and, in these things, the sense is a better judge than the art." Surely, a Schlegel himself could not give us a truer Shakespearean rule than that. Indeed, if we can but catch them when the wind is south-south-west—these grave and oracular Elizabethan wits—we shall find them putting two and two together, now and then, and drawing inferences, and making distinctions which would have much surprised their "uncle-fathers" and "aunt-mothers" at the time, if they had but noted them. But, as they themselves tell us, "in regard to the rawness and unskillfulness of the hands through which they pass, the greatest matters are sometimes carried in the weakest ciphers." Even over their own names, and in those learned tongues of theirs, if we can but once find their stops, and the skill to command them to any utterance of harmony, they will discourse to us, in spite of the disjointed times, the most eloquent music.

For, although they had, indeed, the happiness to pursue their studies under the direct personal supervision of those two matchless scholars, "Eliza and one James," whose influence in the world of letters was then so signally felt, they, nevertheless, evidently ventured to dip into antiquity a little on their own account, and that, apparently, without feeling called upon to render in a perfectly unambiguous report in full of all that they found there, for the benefit of their illustrious patrons, to whom, of course, their literary labors are dedicated. There seemed, indeed, to be no occasion for unpegging the basket on the house's top, and trying conclusions in any so summary manner.

These men distinctly postpone, not their personal reputation only, but the interpretation of their avowed works, to freer ages. There were sparrows abroad then. The tempest was already "singing in the wind," for an ear fine enough to catch it; but only invisible Ariels could dare "to play" then *on pipe and tabor,* [stage direction]. "Thought is free," but only base Trinculos and low-born Stephanos could dare to whisper to it. "That is the tune of our catch, played by the picture of—Nobody."

Yes, there was one moment in that nation's history, wherein the costume, the fable, the scenic effect, and all the attractive and diverting appliances and concomitants of the stage, even the degradation into which it had fallen, its known subserviency to the passions of the audience, its habit of creating a spectacle merely, all combined to furnish to men, in whom the genius of the nation had attained its highest form, freer instrumentalities than the book, the pamphlet, the public document, the parliament, or the pulpit, when all alike were subject to an oppressive and despotic censorship, when all alike were forbidden to meddle with their own proper questions, when cruel maimings and tortures old and new, life-long imprisonment, and death itself, awaited, not a violation of these restrictions merely, but a suspicion of an intention, or even wish, to violate them—penalties which England's noblest men suffered, on suspicion only.

There was one moment in that history, in which the ancient drama had, in new forms, its old power; when, stamped and blazoned on its surface everywhere, with the badges of servitude it had yet leaping within the indomitable heart of its ancient freedom, the spirit of the immemorial European liberties, which Magna Charta had only recognized, and more than that, the freedom of the new ages that were then beginning, "the freedom of the chainless mind." There was one moment in which all the elements of the national genius, that are now separated and incorporated in institutions as wide apart, at least, as earth and heaven, were held together, and that in their first vigor, pressed from without into ther old Greek conjunction. That moment there was; it is chronicled; we have one word for it; we call it—Shakespeare!

Has the time come at last, or has it not yet come, in which this message of the new time can be laid open to us? This message from the lips of one endowed so wondrously, with skill to utter it; endowed, not with the speaker's melodious tones and subduing harmonies only, but with the teacher's divinely glowing heart, with the ambition that seeks its own in all, with the love that is sweeter than the tongues of men and angels. Are we, or are we not, his legatees? Surely this new summing up of all the real questions of our common life, from such an elevation in it, this new philosophy of all men's business and desires, cannot be without its perpetual vital uses. For, in all the points on which the demonstration rests, these diagrams from the dissolving views of the past are still included in the problems of the present.

And if, in this new and more earnest research into the true ends and meanings of this greatest of our teachers, the poor player who was willing enough to assume the responsibility of these works, while they were still plays—theatrical exhibitions only, and quite in his line for the time; who might, indeed, be glad enough to do it for the sake of the princely patronage that henceforth encompassed his fortunes, even to the granting of a thousand pounds at a time, if that were needed to complete his purchase—if this good man, sufficiently perplexed already with the developments which the modern criticism has by degrees already laid at his door, does here positively refuse to go any further with us on this road, why e'en let us shake hands with him and part, he as his business and desire shall point him, "for every man hath business and desire, such as it is," and not without a grateful recollection of the good service he has rendered us.

The publisher of these plays let his name go down still and to all posterity on the cover of it. They *were* his plays. He brought them out,—he and his firm. They took the scholar's text, that dull black and white, that mere ink and paper, and made of it a living, speaking, many-colored, glittering reality, which even the groundlings of that time could appreciate, in some sort. What was Hamlet to them, without his "inky cloak" and his "forest of feathers" and his "razed shoes" and "the roses" on them? And they came out of this man's bag—he was the owner of the "wardrobe" and of the other "stage properties." He was the owner of the manuscripts; and if he came honestly by them, whose business was it to inquire any further, then? If there was no one who chose, just then, to claim the authorship of them, whose else should they be? Was not the actor himself a poet, and a very facetious one, too? Witness the remains of him, the incontestible poetical remains of him, which *have* come down to us. What if his ill-natured cotemporaries, whose poetic glories he was eclipsing forever with those new plays of his, did assail him on his weak points, and call him, in the face of his time, "a *Johannes Factotum*," and held up to public ridicule his particular style of acting, plainly intimating that it was chargeable with that very fault which the prince of Denmark directs his tragedians to omit—did not the blundering editor of that piece of offensive criticism get a decisive hint from some quarter, that he might better have withheld it; and was it not humbly retracted and hushed up directly? Some of the earlier anonymous plays, which were included in the collection published, after this player's decease, as the plays of William Shakespeare, are, indeed, known to have been produced anonymously at other theatres, and by companies with which this actor had never any connection; but the poet's company and the player's were, as it seems, two different things; and that is a fact which the criticism and history of these plays, as it stands at present, already exhibits. Several of the plays which form the nucleus of the Shakespeare drama had already been brought out, before the Stratford actor was yet in a position to assume that relation to it which proved so advantageous to his fortunes. Such as nucleus of the Shakespeare drama there was already, when the name which this actor bore, with such orthographical variations as the purpose required, began to be assumed as the name and device of that new sovereignty of genius which was then first rising and kindling behind its cloud, and dimming and overflowing with its greater glory all the less, and gilding all it shone on. The machinery of these theatrical establishments offered, indeed, the most natural and effective, as well as, at that time, on other accounts, the most convenient mode of exhibition for that particular class of subjects which the genius of this particular poet naturally inclined him to meddle with. He had the most profoundly philosophical reasons for preferring that mode of exhibiting his poems, as will be seen hereafter.

And, when we have once learned to recognize the actor's true relations to the works which have given to his name its anomalous significance, we shall be prepared, perhaps, to accept, at last, this great offer of aid in our readings of these works, which has been lying here now two hundred and thirty years, unnoticed; then, and not till then, we shall be able to avail ourselves, at last, of the aid of those "friends of his," to whom, two hundred and thirty years ago, "knowing that his wit could no more lie hid than it could be lost," the editors of the first printed collection of these works venture to refer us; "those other friends of his, whom, IF WE NEED, can be our *guides*; and, IF WE NEED THEM NOT, we are able to lead ourselves and others, and such readers they wish him."

If we had accepted either of these two conditions—if we had found ourselves with those who need this offered guidance, or with those who need it not—if we had but gone far enough in our readings of these works to feel the want of that aid, from exterior sources, which is here proffered us—there would not have been presented to the world, at this hour, the spectacle—the stupendous spectacle—of a nation referring the origin of its drama—a drama more noble, and learned, and subtle than the Greek—to the invention—the accidental, unconscious invention—of a stupid, ignorant, illiterate, third-rate play-actor.

If we had, indeed, but applied to these works the commonest rules of historical investigation and criticism, we might, ere this, have been led to inquire, on our own account, whether "this player here," who brought them out, might not possibly, in an age like that, like the player in *Hamlet*, have had some friend, or "friends," who, could, "an' if they would," or "an' if they might," explain his miracles to us, and the secret of his "poor cell."

If we had accepted this suggestion, the true Shakespeare would not have been now to seek. In the circle of that patronage with which this player's fortunes brought him in contact, in that illustrious company of wits and poets, we need not have been at a loss to find the philosopher who writes, in his prose as well, and over his own name also,

In Nature's INFINITE BOOK OF SECRESY,
A little I can read;—
[*Antony and Cleopatra,* I.ii.8–9]

we should have found one, at least, furnished for that last and ripest proof of learning which the drama, in the unmiraculous order of the human development, must constitute; that proof of it in which philosophy returns from history, from its noblest fields, and from her last analysis, with the secret and material of the creative synthesis—with the secret and material of art. With this direction, we should have been able to identifiy, ere this, the Philosopher who is only the Poet in disguise—the Philosopher who calls himself the New Magician—the Poet who was toiling and plotting to fill the globe with his Arts, and to make our common, everyday human life poetical—who would have *all* our life, and not a part of it, learned, artistic, beautiful, religious.

We should have found, ere this, ONE, with learning broad enough, and deep enough, and subtle enough, and comprehensive enough, one with nobility of aim and philosophic and poetic genius enough, to be able to claim his own, his own immortal progeny—undwarfed, unblinded, undeprived of one ray or dimple of that all-pervading reason that informs them; one who is able to re-claim them, even now, "cured and perfect in their limbs, and absolute in their numbers, as he conceived them." . . .

—Delia Bacon, "William Shakespeare and His Plays: An Inquiry Concerning Them," *Putnam's Monthly,* January 1856, pp. 1–19

NATHANIEL HAWTHORNE "RECOLLECTIONS OF A GIFTED WOMAN" (1863)

One of the great American writers of the nineteenth century and the author of *The Scarlet Letter,* Nathaniel Hawthorne (1804–64) describes a meeting with Delia Bacon. While not crediting her theories about the authorship of Shakespeare's plays and, in fact, judging her to have become quite extreme in her obsessions, Hawthorne treats her with a gracious generosity of spirit, even providing the introduction to her book and suggesting, in addition, the idea that the depth of Shakespeare's work tends to invite readers to find in it matter that they may, if they choose, use to reflect their own lives back to them. Readers familiar with Hawthorne's stories will find in the character of Delia Bacon and in the incidents he describes a person and a subject that seem made for just his hand, with the gothic combination of obsession, overwrought intellect, dangerous curiosity, spooky settings, forbidden knowledge, and overwrought emotional sensitivity.

She (Delia Bacon) was very communicative about her theory, and would have been much more so had I desired it; but, being conscious within myself of a sturdy unbelief, I deemed it fair and honest rather to repress than draw her out upon the subject. Unquestionably, she was a monomaniac; these overmastering ideas about the authorship of Shakespeare's Plays, and the deep political philosophy concealed beneath the surface of them, had completely thrown her off her balance; but at the same time they had wonderfully developed her intellect, and made her what she could not otherwise have become. It was a very singular phenomenon: a system of philosophy growing up in this woman's mind without her volition,—contrary, in fact, to the determined resistance of her volition,—and substituting itself in the place of everything that originally grew there. To have based such a system on fancy, and unconsciously elaborated it for herself, was almost as wonderful as really to have found it in the plays. But, in a certain sense, she did actually find it there. Shakespeare has surface beneath surface, to an immeasurable depth, adapted to the plummet-line of every reader; his works present many phases of truth, each with scope large enough to fill a contemplative mind. Whatever you seek in him you will surely discover, provided you seek truth. There is no exhausting the various interpretation of his symbols; and a thousand years hence a world of new readers will possess a whole library of new books, as we ourselves do, in these volumes old already. I had half a mind to suggest to Miss Bacon this explanation of her theory, but forbore, because (as I could readily perceive) she had as princely a spirit as Queen Elizabeth herself, and would at once have motioned me from the room.

I had heard, long ago, that she believed that the material evidences of her dogma as to the authorship, together with the key of the new philosophy, would be found buried in Shakespeare's grave. Recently, as I understood her, this notion had been somewhat modified, and was now accurately defined and fully developed in her mind, with a result of perfect certainty. In Lord [Francis] Bacon's Letters, on which she laid her finger as she spoke, she had discovered the key and clew to the whole mystery. There were definite and minute instructions how to find a will and other documents relating to the conclave of Elizabethan philosophers, which were concealed (when and by whom she did not inform me) in a hollow space in the under surface of Shakespeare's gravestone. Thus the terrible prohibition to remove the stone was accounted for. The directions, she intimated, went completely and precisely to the point, obviating all difficulties in the way of coming at the treasure, and even, if I remember right, were so contrived as to ward off any troublesome consequences likely to ensue from the interference of the parish-officers. All that Miss Bacon now remained in England for—indeed, the object for which she had come hither, and which had kept her here for three years past—was to obtain possession of these material and unquestionable proofs of the authenticity of her theory.

She communicated all this strange matter in a low, quiet tone; while, on my part, I listened as quietly, and without any expression of dissent. Controversy against a faith so settled would have shut her up at once, and that, too, without in the least weakening her belief in the existence of those treasures of the tomb; and had it been possible to convince her of their intangible nature, I apprehend that there would have been nothing left for the poor enthusiast save to collapse and die. She frankly confessed that she could no longer bear the society of those who did not at least lend a certain sympathy to her views, if not fully share in them; and meeting little sympathy or none, she had now entirely secluded herself from the world. In all these years, she had seen Mrs. [feminist educational reformer Eliza Ware Rotch] Farrar a few times, but had long ago given her up; Carlyle once or twice, but not of late, although he had received her kindly; Mr. [fifteenth president of the United States James] Buchanan, while Minister in England, had once called on her; and General Campbell, our Consul in London, had met her two or three times on business. With these exceptions, which she marked so scrupulously that it was perceptible what epochs they were in the monotonous passage of her days, she had lived in the profoundest solitude. She never walked out; she suffered much from ill-health; and yet, she assured me, she was perfectly happy.

I could well conceive it; for Miss Bacon imagined herself to have received (what is certainly the greatest boon ever assigned to mortals) a high mission in the world, with adequate powers for its accomplishment; and lest even these should prove insufficient, she had faith that special interpositions of Providence were forwarding her human efforts. This idea was continually coming to the surface, during our interview. She believed, for example, that she had been providentially led to her lodging-house, and put in relations with the good-natured grocer and his family; and, to say the truth, considering what a savage and stealthy tribe the London lodging-house keepers usually are, the honest kindness of this man and his household appeared to have been little less than miraculous. Evidently, too, she thought that Providence had brought me forward—a man somewhat connected with literature—at the critical juncture when she needed a negotiator with the booksellers; and, on my part, though little accustomed to regard myself as a divine minister, and though I might even have preferred that Providence should select some other instrument, I had no scruple in undertaking to do what I could for her. Her book, as I could see by turning it over, was a very remarkable one, and worthy of being offered to the public, which, if wise enough to appreciate it, would be thankful for what was good in it and merciful to its faults. It was founded on a prodigious error, but was built up from that foundation with a good many prodigious truths. And, at all events, whether I could aid her literary views or no, it would have been both rash and impertinent in me to attempt drawing poor Miss Bacon out of her delusions, which were the condition on which she lived in comfort and joy, and in the exercise of great intellectual power. So I left her to dream as she pleased about the treasures of Shakespeare's tombstone, and to form whatever designs might seem good to herself for obtaining possession of them. I was sensible of a lady-like feeling of propriety in Miss Bacon, and a New England orderliness in her character, and, in spite of her bewilderment, a sturdy common-sense, which I trusted would begin to operate at the right time, and keep her from any actual extravagance. And as regarded this matter of the tombstone, so it proved.

The interview lasted about an hour, during which she flowed out freely, as to the sole auditor, capable of any degree of intelligent sympathy, whom she had met with in a very long while. Her conversation was remarkably suggestive, alluring forth one's own ideas and fantasies from the shy places where they usually haunt. She was indeed an admirable talker, considering how long she had held her tongue for lack of a listener,—pleasant, sunny, and shadowy, often piquant, and giving glimpses of all a woman's various and readily changeable moods and humors; and beneath them all there ran a deep and powerful undercurrent of earnestness, which did not fail to produce in the listener's mind something like a temporary faith in what she herself believed so fervently. But the streets of London are not favorable to enthusiasms of this kind, nor, in fact, are they likely to flourish anywhere in the English atmosphere; so that, long before reaching Paternoster Row [a small street in London that had been the home to booksellers and publishers], I felt that it would be a difficult and doubtful matter to advocate the publication of Miss Bacon's book. Nevertheless, it did finally get published.

Months before that happened, however, Miss Bacon had taken up her residence at Stratford-on-Avon, drawn thither by the magnetism of those rich secrets which she supposed to have been hidden by Raleigh, or Bacon, or I know not whom, in Shakespeare's grave, and protected there by a curse, as pirates used to bury their gold in the guardianship of a fiend. She took a humble lodging and began to haunt the church like a ghost. But she did not condescend to any stratagem or underhand attempt to violate the grave, which, had she been capable of admitting such an idea, might possibly have been accomplished by the aid of a resurrection-man [one whose specialty was digging up corpses, often for medical research]. As her first step, she made acquaintance with the clerk, and began to sound him as to the feasibility of her enterprise and his own willingness to engage in it. The clerk apparently listened with not unfavorable ears; but as his situation (which the fees of pilgrims, more numerous than at any Catholic shrine, render lucrative) would have been forfeited by any malfeasance in office, he stipulated for liberty to consult the vicar. Miss Bacon requested to tell her own story to the reverend gentleman, and seems to have been received by him with the utmost kindness, and even to have succeeded in making a certain impression on his mind as to the desirability of the search. As their interview had been under the seal of secrecy, he asked permission to consult a friend, who, as Miss Bacon either found out or surmised, was a practitioner of the law. What the legal friend advised she did not learn; but the negotiation continued, and certainly was never broken off by an absolute refusal on the vicar's part. He, perhaps, was kindly temporizing with our poor countrywoman, whom an Englishman of ordinary mould would have sent to a lunatic asylum at once. I cannot help fancying, however, that her familiarity with the events of Shakespeare's life, and of his death and burial (of which she would speak as if she had been present at the edge of the grave), and all the history, literature, and personalities of the Elizabethan age, together with the prevailing power of her own belief, and the eloquence with which she knew how to enforce it, had really gone some little way toward making a convert of the good clergyman. If so, I honor him above all the hierarchy of England.

The affair certainly looked very hopeful. However erroneously, Miss Bacon had understood from the vicar that no obstacles would be interposed to the investigation, and that he himself would sanction it with his presence. It was to take place after nightfall; and all preliminary arrangements being made, the vicar and clerk professed to wait only her word in order to set about lifting the awful stone from the sepulchre. So, at least, Miss Bacon believed; and as her bewilderment was entirely in her own thoughts, and never disturbed her perception or accurate remembrance of external things, I see no reason to doubt it, except it be the tinge of absurdity in the fact. But, in this apparently prosperous state of things, her own convictions began to falter. A doubt stole into her mind whether she might not have mistaken the depository and mode of concealment of those historic treasures; and, after once admitting the doubt, she was afraid to hazard the shock of uplifting the stone and finding nothing. She examined the surface of the gravestone, and endeavored, without stirring it, to estimate whether it were of such thickness as to be capable of containing the archives of the Elizabethan club. She went over anew the proofs, the clews, the enigmas, the pregnant sentences, which she had discovered in Bacon's Letters and elsewhere, and now was frightened to perceive that they did not point so definitely to Shakespeare's tomb as she had heretofore supposed. There was an unmistakably distinct reference to a tomb, but it might be Bacon's, or Raleigh's, or Spenser's; and instead of the "Old Player," as she profanely called him, it might be either of those three illustrious dead, poet, warrior, or statesman, whose ashes, in Westminster Abbey, or the Tower burial-ground, or wherever they sleep, it was her mission to disturb. It is very possible, moreover, that her acute mind may always have had a lurking and deeply latent distrust of its own fantasies, and that this now became strong enough to restrain her from a decisive step.

But she continued to hover around the church, and seems to have had full freedom of entrance in the daytime, and special license, on one occasion at least, at a late hour of the night. She went thither with a dark-lantern, which could but twinkle like a glow-worm through the volume of obscurity that filled the great dusky edifice. Groping her way up the aisle and towards the chancel, she sat down on the elevated part of the pavement above Shakespeare's grave. If the divine poet really wrote the inscription there, and cared as much about the quiet of his bones as its deprecatory earnestness would imply, it was time for those crumbling relics to bestir themselves under her sacrilegious feet. But they were safe. She made no attempt to disturb them; though, I believe, she looked narrowly into the crevices between Shakespeare's and the two adjacent stones, and in some way satisfied herself that her single strength would suffice to lift the former, in case of need. She threw the feeble ray of her lantern up towards the bust, but could not make it visible beneath the darkness of the vaulted roof. Had she been subject to superstitious terrors, it is impossible to conceive of a situation that could better entitle her to feel them, for, if Shakespeare's ghost would rise at any provocation, it must have shown itself then; but it is my sincere belief, that, if his figure had appeared within the scope of her dark-lantern, in his slashed doublet and gown, and with his eyes bent on her beneath the high, bald forehead, just as we see him in the bust, she would have met him fearlessly, and controverted his claims to the authorship of the plays, to his very face. She had taught herself to contemn "Lord Leicester's groom" (it was one of her disdainful epithets for the world's incomparable poet) so thoroughly, that even his disembodied spirit would hardly have found civil treatment at Miss Bacon's hands.

Her vigil, though it appears to have had no definite object, continued far into the night. Several times she heard a low movement in the aisles: a stealthy, dubious footfall prowling about in the darkness, now here, now there, among the pillars and ancient tombs, as if some restless inhabitant of the latter had crept forth to peep at the intruder. By and by the clerk made his appearance, and confessed that he had been watching her ever since she entered the church.

About this time it was that a strange sort of weariness seems to have fallen upon her: her toil was all but done, her great purpose, as she believed, on the very point of accomplishment, when she began to regret that so stupendous a mission had been imposed on the fragility of a woman. Her faith in the new philosophy was as mighty as ever, and so was her confidence in her own adequate development of it, now about to be given to the world; yet she wished, or fancied so, that it might never have been her duty to achieve this unparalleled task, and to stagger feebly forward under her immense burden of responsibility and renown. So far as her personal concern in the matter went, she would gladly have forfeited the reward of her patient study and labor for so many years, her exile from her country and estrangement from her family and friends, her sacrifice of health and all other interests to this one pursuit, if she could only find herself free to dwell in Stratford and be forgotten. She liked the old slumberous town, and awarded the only praise that ever I knew her to bestow on Shakespeare, the individual man, by acknowledging that his taste in a residence was good, and that he knew how to choose a suitable retirement for a person of shy, but genial temperament. And at this point, I cease to possess the means of tracing her vicissitudes of feeling any further. In consequence of some advice which I fancied it my duty to tender, as being the only confidant whom she now had in the world, I fell under Miss Bacon's most severe and passionate displeasure, and was cast off by her in the twinkling of an eye. It was a misfortune to which her friends were always particularly liable; but I think that none of them ever loved, or even respected, her most ingenuous and noble, but likewise most sensitive and tumultuous character, the less for it.

At that time her book was passing through the press. Without prejudice to her literary ability, it must be allowed that Miss Bacon was wholly unfit to prepare her own work for publication, because, among many other reasons, she was too thoroughly in earnest to know what to leave out. Every leaf and line was sacred, for all had been written under so deep a conviction of truth as to assume, in her eyes, the aspect of inspiration. A practised book-maker, with entire control of her materials, would have shaped out a duodecimo volume full of eloquent and ingenious dissertation,—criticisms which quite take the color and pungency out of other people's critical remarks on Shakespeare,— philosophic truths which she imagined herself to have found at the roots of his conceptions, and which certainly come from no inconsiderable depth somewhere. There was a great amount of rubbish, which any competent editor would have shovelled out of the way. But Miss Bacon thrust the whole bulk of inspiration and nonsense into the press in a lump, and there tumbled out a ponderous octavo volume, which fell with a dead thump at the feet of the public, and has never been picked up. A few persons turned over one or two of the leaves, as it lay there, and essayed to kick the volume deeper into the mud; for they were the hack critics of the minor periodical press in London, than whom, I suppose, though excellent fellows in their way, there are no gentlemen in the world less sensible of any sanctity in a book, or less likely to recognize an author's heart in it, or more utterly careless about bruising, if they do recognize it. It is their trade. They could not do otherwise. I never thought of blaming them. It was not for such an Englishman as one of these to get beyond the idea that an assault was meditated on England's greatest poet. From the scholars and critics of her own country, indeed, Miss Bacon might have looked for a worthier appreciation, because many of the best of them have higher cultivation, and finer and deeper literary sensibilities than all but the very profoundest and brightest of Englishmen. But they are not a courageous body of men; they dare not think a truth that has an odor of absurdity, lest they should feel themselves bound to speak it out. If any American ever wrote a word in her behalf, Miss Bacon never knew it, nor did I. Our journalists at once republished some of the most brutal vituperations of the English press, thus pelting their poor countrywoman with stolen mud, without even waiting to know whether the ignominy was deserved. And they never have known it, to this day, nor ever will.

The next intelligence that I had of Miss Bacon was by a letter from the mayor of Stratford-on-Avon. He was a medical man, and wrote both in his official and professional character, telling me that an American lady, who had recently published what the mayor called a "Shakespeare book," was afflicted with insanity. In a lucid interval she had referred to me, as a person who had some knowledge of her family and affairs. What she may have suffered before her intellect gave way, we had better not try to imagine. No author had ever hoped so confidently as she; none ever failed more utterly. A superstitious fancy might suggest that the anathema on Shakespeare's tombstone had fallen heavily on her head, in requital of even the unaccomplished purpose of disturbing the dust beneath, and that the "Old Player" had kept so quietly in his grave, on the night of her vigil, because he foresaw how soon and terribly he would be avenged. But if that benign spirit takes any care or cognizance of such things now, he has surely requited the injustice that she sought to do him—the high justice that she really did—by a tenderness of love and pity of which only he could be capable. What matters it though she called him by some other name? He had wrought a greater miracle on her than on all the world besides. This bewildered enthusiast had recognized a depth in the man whom she decried, which scholars, critics, and learned societies, devoted to the elucidation of his unrivalled scenes, had never imagined to exist there. She had paid him the loftiest honor that all these ages of renown have been able to accumulate upon his memory. And when, not many months after the outward failure of her lifelong object, she passed into the better world, I know not why we should hesitate to believe that the immortal poet may have met her on the threshold and led her in, reassuring her with friendly and comfortable words, and thanking her (yet with a smile of gentle humor in his eyes at the thought of certain mistaken speculations) for having interpreted him to mankind so well.

I believe that it has been the fate of this remarkable book never to have had more than a single reader. I myself am acquainted with it only in insulated chapters and scattered pages and paragraphs. But, since my return to America, a young man of genius and enthusiasm has assured me that he has positively read the book from beginning to end, and is completely a convert to its doctrines. It belongs to him, therefore, and not to me,—whom, in almost the last letter that I received from her, she declared unworthy to meddle with her work,—it belongs surely to this one individual, who has done her so much justice as to know what she wrote, to place Miss Bacon in her due position before the public and posterity.

—Nathaniel Hawthorne, "Recollections of
a Gifted Woman," *Our Old Home,* 1863

NATHANIEL HOLMES
"PHILOSOPHER AND POET" (1866)

A professor of law at Harvard University, Nathaniel Holmes (1837–1902) cites the wealth of philosophical intelligence and poetic eloquence in the plays attributed to Shakespeare, as well as what he regards to be the paucity of opportunity for preparation, in schooling and learning, for the development of that sort of knowledge and talent in the person regarded to be Shakespeare. Seeing exactly that kind of scholarship, knowledge, eloquence, and mental acuity in the work and accomplishment of English essayist, scientist, philosopher, and jurist Francis Bacon, Holmes argues that it was Bacon who wrote what are called Shakespeare's plays. He sees Bacon as the harbinger of the new and the bringer of wisdom into a world lacking a true metaphysical philosophy, a world in need of a philosophy that can provide a sense of universal order to supplant the Judeo-Christian worldview that Holmes respects but finds worn out and no longer adequate.

Shakespeare has long been considered by all that speak the English tongue, and by the learned of other nations likewise, as the greatest of dramatic poets. The ancients had but one Homer: the moderns have but one Shakespeare. And these two have been fitly styled "the Twin Stars of Poesy" in all the world. These plays have kept the stage better than any other for nearly three centuries. They have been translated into several foreign languages; a vast amount of critical erudition has been expended upon them; and numerous editions have been printed, and countless numbers of copies have been distributed, generation after generation, increasing in a kind of geometrical progression, through all ranks and classes of society from the metropolitan palace to the frontier cabin, until it may almost be said, that if there be anywhere a family possessing but two only books, the one may be the Bible, but the other is sure to be Shakespeare.

Nevertheless, the plays have been understood and appreciated rather according to existing standards of judgment than according to all that was really in them. In general, our English minds seem to have been aware that their poet was more or less philosophical, or rather that he was a kind of universal genius; but that he was a Platonic thinker, a transcendental metaphysician and philosopher, an idealist and a realist all in one, not many seem to have discovered. Coleridge certainly had some inkling of this fact, and to Carlyle, it stood perfectly clear, that Shakespeare "does not look at a thing, but into it, through it; so that he constructively comprehends it, can take it asunder, and put it together again; the thing melts, as it were, into light under his eye, and anew *creates* itself before him." That is to say, he is a Thinker in the highest of all senses: he is a Poet. For Goethe, as for Shakespeare, the world lies all translucent, all *fusible* we might call it, encircled with WONDER; the Natural in reality the Supernatural, for to the seer's eyes both become one."[1] And so also Gervinus concludes upon the question of "the realistic or ideal treatment," that "he is sometimes the one, sometimes the other, but in reality

neither, because he is both at once."[2] Deep searching criticism, on this side of
the sea, has been able to sound the depths and scale the heights of the Higher
Philosophy of Bacon, and it is almost equally clear that it has discovered in it
the world-streaming providence of Shakespeare. "The English shrink from a
generalization," says Emerson. "They do not look abroad into universality, or
they draw only a bucket-full at the fountain of the First Philosophy for their
occasion, and do not go to the springhead. Bacon, who said this, is almost
unique among his countrymen in that faculty, at least among the prose-
writers. Milton, who was the stair or high table-land to let down the English
genius from the summits of Shakespeare, used this privilege sometimes in
poetry, more rarely in prose. For a long interval afterwards, it is not found."[3]
We know how Bacon attained to these heights; but it is not explained how
the unlearned William Shakespeare reached these same "summits" of all
philosophy, otherwise than by a suggestion of "the specific gravity" of inborn
genius. Have we any evidence outside of these plays, that this "dry light"
of nature was greater in William Shakespeare than in Francis Bacon? In
Bacon, as in the plays, we have not only the inborn genius, but a life of study,
knowledge, science, philosophy, art, and the wealth of all learning. Are these
things to be counted as nothing? Then we may as well abolish the universities,
burn the libraries; and shut up the schools, as of no use:—

> Hang up philosophy:
> Unless philosophy can make a Juliet,
> Displant a town, reverse a Prince's doom,
> It helps not, it prevails not: talk no more.
> *(Romeo and Juliet,* Act III. Sc. 3 [57–60])

For the most part, all that has been seen in Shakespeare has been
considered as the product of some kind of natural genius or spontaneous
inspiration. The reason has been nearly this, that since Bacon, if [Irish
philosopher George] Berkeley be excepted, England, or the English language,
has never had a philosophy at all: we have had nothing but a few sciences and
a theology. Bacon's Summary Philosophy, or Philosophy itself, seems to have
fallen still-born from his delivery, a dead letter to our English mind. It was
not grasped, and the existence of it in his works seems to have been forgotten.
No English, or American, philosopher has yet appeared to review, expound,
and complete it, in any systematic manner: this work has been left to those
who are said to hold dominion of the air. Some there have been, doubtless,
as capable as any of undertaking to give a complete systematic statement of
all philosophy; but they probably knew too well what kind of an undertaking

that would be, when a perfect work might require not only a divine man, but a book as large as the Book of God's Works. The men that are called philosophers among us are occupied with physical science only. What Bacon endeavored to re-organize, and constitute anew, as methods and instruments for obtaining a broader and surer "foundation" for a higher metaphysical philosophy, they appear to have mistaken for the whole of science and the sum total of all certain knowledge, excepting only a fantastical kind of traditional supernatural knowledge, for the most part, completely ignoring metaphysics; and, as a matter of course, they have given us as little conception of a philosophy of the universe, and, with all their physical science, have had as little to give, as a Humboldt's Cosmos, or that prodigious Frenchman, M. Auguste Comte.

Besides a physical science we have had *only* a theology, taking old Hebrew and some later Greek literature for all divine revelation; the Mosaic cosmogony for the constitution of the universe; [Archbishop James] Usher's chronology [of the history of the world from the creation] for an account of all time on this earth; Adamic genealogy for an ethnology of the human race; Jesus of Nazareth for the creator of the whole world and sole saviour of mankind; and some five or six fantastic miracles for all the boundless and eternal wonders of the creation. These old ones are nearly worn out, and are fast becoming obsolete: indeed, they are already well-nigh extinct. It is high time they were laid up on a shelf, and labelled to be studied hereafter as fossils of the theological kingdom; and preachers, opening their eyes, should cast about for a new set, at least, out of all the universe of miracles that surround them, and henceforth found their preaching on them. There would then be much less trouble about faith, and infidelity to myths and superstitions might become fidelity to God and his truth.

And so, having no philosophy, and no conception of the possibility of any, and nothing to give the name to, our English mind has appropriated the word as a superfluous synonym for physical science, and scarcely allowed free scope to that. . . .

German scholars of [a] modern school [of philosophy], (which has done something toward a critical exegesis of the fundamental and eternal laws of thought, the true nature of substance or matter, a true knowledge of cause and "the mode of that thing which is uncaused," a sound and rational psychology, and some more scientific, intelligible, and satisfactory account of the constitution of this universe, and of the order of divine providence and the destiny of man in it:—in fine, a Universal Philosophy), whether special students of this philosophy, or debtors to its results for their ideas and methods, have been filled with admiration of the super-eminent genius of

Shakespeare. "The poetry of Shakespeare," says Frederick Schlegel, "has much accord with the German mind." Goethe, despairing to excel him, ranks him first among modern poets, and honors. Hamlet with a place in the *Wilhelm Meister;* and [German romantic writer Jean Paul] Richter no less, discovering at once the amazing depth of his philosophy, makes him rule sovereign in the heart of his Albano [the hero of Richter's 1801 novel *Titan*],—"not through the breathing of living characters, but by lifting him up out of the loud kingdom of earth into the silent realm of infinity."[5] How wonderful, indeed, is all this! Is it, then, that we have here a born genius, to whose all-seeing vision schools and libraries, sciences and philosophies, were unnecessary,—were an idle waste of time, forsooth?—whose marvellous intuition grasped all the past and saw through all the present? whose prophetic insight spans the future ages as they roll up, measures the highest wave of the modern learning and philosophy, and follows backward the tide of civilization, arts, and letters, to the very borders of the barbaric lands?—before whose almost superhuman power, time and place seem to vanish and disappear, as if it had become with him "an everlasting Now and Here"? or, as if it had pleased the Divine Majesty to send another Messiah upon our earth, knowing all past, all present, and all future, to be leader, guide, and second Saviour of mankind? What greater miracle need be!

Being translated into German, Shakespeare became "the father of German literature," says Emerson. But it so happens, that the parts of him, which have been more especially quoted as the basis of this German appreciation, are precisely those, which have been least noticed at home, or if seen, appreciated on quite other grounds. Those transparent characters, which, said Goethe, are "like watches with crystalline plates and cases," where the whole frame and order of discovery are placed, as it were *sub oculos,* under the very eye, and those most pregnant passages, which are written, like the *Faust,* or the [Wilhelm] Meister [a play and a novel by Goethe], with a double aspect, whether because it was then dangerous to write otherwise, or because the highest art made such writing necessary and proper, being the highest wisdom as well as that true poetry which requires the science of sciences and "the purest of all study for knowing it," making these plays magic mirrors like "the universal world" itself, in which any looker may see as much as he is able to see and no more, have passed in the general mind for little more than ingenious poetical conceptions, powerful strokes of stage eloquence, or merely fanciful turns of expression; or if, sometimes, anything deeper may have been half discovered in them, some suspected smack of infidelity may have thrown the trammelled reader, all of a sudden, into a grim silence—a sort of moody astonishment,—very much as if he had

accidentally laid his hand upon an electric eel;—as if a true man should fear
to be infidel to anything but God and the eternal truth of things, or as if more
credence were due to a traditional mythology of the Egyptianized, or the
Grecianized, Hebrews than to the best teachings of the wisest living men and
the most enlightened philosophy. It has been said, that the *Hamlet* was not
discovered to be anything wonderful till within the Nineteenth Century. In
truth, these new wonders of Shakespeare are precisely the parts, qualities, and
characteristics of him, wherein the higher philosophy of Bacon is displayed,
and which are to be understood and comprehended in their full meaning and
drift by those only, who stand upon the same high cliff and platform whereon
he stood alone of all his contemporaries, that topmost height and narrow
strait, "where one but goes abreast," in an age, and almost without an English
rival down to our time. German scholars, as well as some later English, by
the help of this same higher philosophy, in the new Kantian instauration of it,
have been enabled to ascend to this elevated platform; and being there, they
discover the transcendent genius of Shakespeare in the philosophy, culture,
science, and true art, which belonged only to Bacon. And therein and thereby
is it further proven, that this "our Shakespeare" was no other than Francis
Bacon himself; and William Shakespeare ceases to be that "unparelleled
mortal" he has been taken for, that title being justly transferred to the man
to whom it more properly pertains. So, for the most part, in all times, has
the philosopher been robbed of his glory. We worship in Jesus what belongs
to Plato; in Shakespeare, what belongs to Bacon; and in many others, what
belongs to the real philosopher, the actual teacher, the true saviour, and to
Philosophy Herself.

All that gives peculiarity and preeminence to these plays is to be found
in Bacon; vast comprehension, the profoundest philosophic depth, the subtle
discrimination of differences and resemblances, matured wisdom, vigor and
splendor of imagination, accurate observation of nature, extensive knowledge
of men and manners, the mighty genius and the boundless wit, the brevity
of expression and pregnant weight of matter, a fine aesthetic appreciation
of the beautiful, the classical scholarship, familiarity with law, courts, and
legal proceedings, with the metaphysic of jurisprudence, with statesmen and
princes, ladies and courtiers, and that proper sense (which belonged to the
age) of the dignity, sovereign duties, power and honor of the throne and king,
the sovereign power in the State;—all this, and more than can be named,
belongs to both writings, and therefore to one author. Here was a man that
could be a Shakespeare. Coleridge, Schlegel, Goethe, Jean Paul Richter,
Carlyle, Emerson, Delia Bacon, Gervinus, and, doubtless, many more, clearly
saw that the real Shakespeare must have been such a man, in spite of all the

biographies. "Ask your own hearts," says Coleridge, "ask your own common sense, to conceive the possibility of this man being ... the anomalous, the wild, the irregular genius of our daily criticism! What! are we to have miracles in sport? Or, I speak reverently, does God choose idiots by whom to convey divine truths to man?"[6] And yet, even Coleridge failed to discover, that "the morning star, the guide, the pioneer of true philosophy," was not William Shakespeare, but Francis Bacon.

The last and most conclusive proof of all is that general, inwrought, and all-pervading identity, which is to be found in these writings, when carefully studied, and which, when it is looked for and seen, is appreciated and convinces, like the character of a handwriting, by an indescribable genuineness and an irresistible force of evidence. In the words of A. W. Schlegel, speaking of Shakespeare, "On all the stamp of his mighty spirit is impressed."[7] The distinguishing qualities of Bacon's prose style are precisely those which belong to the poet, namely, breadth of thought, depth of insight, weight of matter, brevity, force, and beauty of expression, brilliant metaphor, using all nature as a symbol of thought, and that supreme power of imagination that is necessary to make him an artistic creator, adding man to the universe; qualities, which mark that mind only which God hath framed "as a mirrour or glass, capable of the image of the universal world." His speeches display these qualities. The oratorical style of that day seems to have been more close and weighty than in our times: it was full of strength and earnestness. Lord [English jurist, member of Parliament, and author of works on English common law Edward] Coke spoke in thunderbolts, huge, Cyclopean, tremendous: he went to the very pith and heart of the matter, at once, and his speech was always *"multum in parvo."* [much in little] But in him [Coke], it was vigor without grace, power without splendor, or beauty, and ability unillumined by the divine light of genius. When we know that Bacon had been such a poet, it ceases to be a wonder that he was such an orator as he was. The mind that had been conceiving dramatic speeches, at this rate, during a period of thirty years or more, could never address a court, a parliament, or a king, otherwise than in the language, style, and imagery of poetry. In short, Bacon's prose is Shakespearean poetry, and Shakespeare's poetry is Baconian prose. Nor did these qualities altogether escape the recognition of one, who had an eye to see, an ear to hear, and a soul to comprehend: says Ben Jonson, "There happened in my time one noble speaker, who was full of gravity in his speaking. His language, where he could spare, or pass by a jest, was nobly censorious. No man ever spoke more neatly, more pressly, more weightily, or suffered less emptiness, less idleness, in what he uttered. No member of his speech but consisted of his own graces. His hearers could not cough or look aside from him without loss. He commanded where he spoke and had his judges angry and pleased at his devotion. No man had their affections more in his power. The fear of every man who heard him was lest he should make an end." And again he says, "My conceit of his person was never increased toward him by his place or honors; but I have and do reverence him for the greatness that was only proper to himself, in that he seemed to me ever by his works one of the greatest men, and most worthy of admiration that had been in many ages." [Historian and writer James] Howell, another contemporary, says of him, likewise, that "he was the eloquentest that was born in this isle."

What manner of man, then, have we here for our Shakespeare? A child well born, a highly educated youth, a precocious manhood, and an all-comprehending intelligence; a retired and most diligent student, who felt that he was "fitter by nature to hold a book than play a part," and whose studies, like Plato's, or Cicero's, ended only with life; an original thinker always; a curious explorer into every branch, and a master in nearly all parts, of human learning and knowledge; a brilliant essayist, an ingenious critic, a scientific inventor, a subtle, bold, and all-grasping philosopher; an accurate and profound legal writer; a leading orator and statesman, a counsellor of sovereigns and princes, a director in the affairs of nations, and, in spite of all faults, whether his own, or of his time, or of servants whose rise was his fall, "the justest Chancellor that had been in the five changes since Sir Nicholas Bacon's [courtier and politician, Francis Bacon's father] time," and though frail, not having "the fountain of a corrupt heart," but being one to whose known virtue "no accident could do harm, but rather help to make it manifest"; a prodigious wit, a poetic imaginator, an artistic creator, an institutor of the art of arts and the science of sciences; a seer into the Immortal Providence, and the veritable author of the Shakespeare Drama: in truth, not (as Howell supposed) a rare exception to the fortune of an orator, a lawyer, and a philosopher, as he was, but true still to "the fortune of all poets commonly to die beggars," dying as a philosopher and a poet, "poor out of a contempt of the pelf of fortune as also out of an excess of generosity";—his life, on the whole, and to the last, a sacrifice for the benefit of all science, all future ages, and all mankind. Surely, we may exclaim with Coleridge, not without amazement still: "Merciful, wonder-making Heaven! What a man was this Shakespeare! Myriad-minded, indeed, he was."

Notes

1. Essays, III. 209.
2. *Shakespeare Comm.* (London, 1863), II. 569.

3. *English Traits*, 244.
5. *Titan*, by Brooks, I. 154.
6. *Notes on Shakespeare, Works*, IV. 56.
7. *Lectures on Dram. Lit.*, 302.

—Nathaniel Holmes, "Philosopher and Poet," *The
Authorship of Shakespeare*, 1866, pp. 589–601

James Spedding "On the Authorship of the Plays Attributed to Shakespeare" (1867)

Drawing on his own twenty-five years as a scholar and editor of the works of Francis Bacon, James Spedding (1808–81) advances a number of arguments in order to refute Nathaniel Holmes's claim that Bacon was the author of Shakespeare's plays. Spedding's principal refutation of Holmes's argument that Bacon's accomplishments testify to his authorship lies in the proposition that "It is not the famous man that becomes a great inventor; the great inventor becomes a famous man." The argument that Bacon was a writer of prodigious accomplishment does not provide grounds for attributing Shakespeare's plays to him. Rather, Spedding argues that genius and creativity emerge from unlikely sources. In defense of this proposition, Spedding draws on the life and accomplishment of a series of great figures in the arts and sciences, among them nineteenth-century English novelist Charles Dickens and pioneering physicist and chemist Michael Faraday, whose boyhoods and employments offer no particular indication of their later genius and accomplishments.

From a letter to Professor Nathaniel Holmes, 15th February, 1867.
I have read your book on the authorship of Shakespeare faithfully to the end, and if my report of the result is to be equally faithful, I must declare myself not only unconvinced, but undisturbed. To ask me to believe that the man who was accepted by all the people of his own time, to many of whom he was personally known, as the undoubted author of the best plays then going, was not the author of them—is like asking me to believe that Charles Dickens was not the author of Pickwick. To ask me to believe that a man who was famous for a variety of other accomplishments, whose life was divided between public business, the practice of a laborious profession, and private study of the art of investigating the material laws of nature,—a man of large acquaintance, of note from early manhood, and one of the busiest men of his time—but who

was never suspected of wasting time in writing poetry, and is not known to have written a single blank verse in all his life,—that this man was the author of fourteen comedies, ten historical plays, and eleven tragedies, exhibiting the greatest and the greatest variety of excellence that has been attained in that kind of composition,—is like asking me to believe that Lord Brougham was the author not only of Dickens' novels, but of Thackeray's also, and of Tennyson's poems besides. That the author of Pickwick was a man called Charles Dickens I know upon no better authority than that upon which I know that the author of Hamlet was a man called William Shakespeare. And in what respect is the one more difficult to believe than the other? A boy born and bred like Charles Dickens was unlikely a priori to become famous over Europe and America for a never-ending series of original stories, as a boy born and bred like William Shakespeare to become the author of the most wonderful series of dramas in the world. It is true that Shakespeare's gifts were higher and rarer; but the wonder is that any man should have possessed them, not that the man to whose lot they fell was the son of a poor man called John Shakespeare, and that he was christened William. That he was not a man otherwise known to the world is not strange at all. Nature's great lottery being open to everybody, the chances that the supreme prize will be drawn by an unknown man are as the numbers of the unknown to the known—millions to hundreds. It is not the famous man that becomes a great inventor; the great inventor becomes a famous man. Faraday was a bookbinder's apprentice, who in binding a copy of Mrs. [Jane] Marcet's Conversations on Chemistry [1825], was attracted to the study, got employed as an assistant to [chemist] Sir Humphrey Davy—an assistant in so humble a capacity that wishing to make the acquaintance of some of the scientific men on the continent, he actually went with him to Geneva as his servant—and by his own genius, virtue, and industry, made himself the most famous man (probably) now living in England. [Scottish poet Robert] Burns was a ploughman. Keats was a surgeon's apprentice. George Stephenson [inventor of a safety lamp for miners, builder of the first steam locomotives, and pioneer developer of railway lines] a lad employed in a colliery. Newton did not become Newton because he was sent to Cambridge; he was sent to Cambridge because he was Newton—because he had been endowed by nature with the singular gifts which made him Newton. But for the genius which nature gave them without any consideration of position or advantages, what would have been known of any one of these?

If Shakespeare was not trained as a scholar or a man of science, neither do the works attributed to him show traces of trained scholarship or scientific education. Given the faculties (which nature bestows as freely on the poor as on the rich), you will find that all the acquired knowledge, art, and dexterity which the Shakespearian plays imply, were easily attainable by a man who was labouring in his vocation and had nothing else to do. Or if you find this difficult to believe of such a man as you assume Shakespeare to have been, try Bacon. Suppose Francis Bacon, instead of being trained as a scholar, a statesman, and a lawyer, and seeking his fortune from the patronage of the great, had been turned loose into the world without means or friends, and joined a company of players as the readiest resource for a livelihood. Do you doubt that he would soon have tried his hand at writing a play? that he would have found out how to write better plays than were then the fashion? that he would have cultivated an art which he found profitable and prosperous, and sought about for such knowledge as would help him in it,—reading his Plutarch, and his Seneca, and his Hollinshead, and all the novels and play-books that came in his way; studying life and conversation by all the opportunities which his position permitted; and generally seeking to enrich his thought with observation? Do not you think that Francis Bacon would have been capable of learning in that way everything which there is any reason to think the writer of the Shakespearian plays knew? And if Francis Bacon could, why could not William Shakespeare?

If therefore your theory involved no difficulties of its own—if you merely proposed the substitution of one man for another—I should still have asked why I should doubt the tradition;—where was the difficulty which made the old story hard to believe. I see none. That which is extraordinary in the case, and against which therefore there lies prima facie [at first glance] some presumption, is that any man should possess such a combination of faculties as must have met in the author of these plays. But that is a difficulty which cannot be avoided. There must have been somebody in whom the requisite combination of faculties did meet: for there the plays are: and by supposing that this somebody was a man who at the same time possessed a combination of other faculties, themselves sufficient to make him an extraordinary man too, you do not diminish the wonder but increase it. Aristotle was an extraordinary man. Plato was an extraordinary man. That two men each severally so extraordinary should have been living at the same time in the same country, was a very extraordinary thing. But would it diminish the wonder to suppose the two to be one? So I say of Bacon and Shakespeare. That a human being possessed of the faculties necessary to make a Shakespeare should exist, is extraordinary. That a human being possessed of the faculties necessary to make a Bacon should exist, is extraordinary. That two such human beings should have been living in London at the same time was more extraordinary still. But that one man should have existed possessing the faculties and opportunities necessary to make both, would have been the most extraordinary thing of all.

You will not deny that tradition goes for *something:* that in the absence of any reason for doubting it, the concurrent and undisputed testimony to a fact of all who had the best means of knowing it, is a reason for believing it: or at least for thinking it more probable than any other given fact, not compatible with it, which is not so supported. On this ground alone, without inquiring further, I believe that the author of the plays published in 1623 was a man called William Shakespeare. It was believed by those who had the best means of knowing: and I know no reason for doubting it. The reasons for doubting which you suggest seem all to rest upon a latent assumption that William Shakespeare could not have possessed any remarkable faculties: a fact which would no doubt settle the question if it were established. But what should make me think so? It was not the opinion of anybody who was acquainted with him, so far as we know; and why was a man of that name less likely than another to possess remarkable faculties?

With one to whom the simple story as it comes presents no difficulty, you will not expect that the other considerations which you urge should have much weight. Resemblances both in thought and language are inevitable between writers nourished upon a common literature, addressing popular audiences in a common language, and surrounded by a common atmosphere of knowledge and opinion. But to me, I confess, the resemblances between Shakespeare and Bacon are not so striking as the differences. Strange as it seems that two such minds, both so vocal, should have existed within each other's hearing without mutually affecting each other, I find so few traces of any influence exercised by Shakespeare upon Bacon, that I have great doubt whether Bacon knew any more about him than [four-time prime minister of England William] Gladstone (probably) knows about [playwright and editor of the English humor magazine *Punch*] Tom Taylor (in his dramatic capacity). Shakespeare may have derived a good deal from Bacon. He had no doubt read the *Advancement of Learning* and the first edition of the *Essays,* and most likely had frequently heard him speak in the Courts and the Star Chamber. But among all the parallelisms which you have collected with such industry to illustrate the identity of the writer, I have not observed one in which I should not have inferred from the difference of style a difference of hand. Great writers, especially being contemporary, have many features in common; but if they are really great writers they write naturally, and nature is always individual. I doubt whether there are five lines together to be found in Bacon which could be mistaken for Shakespeare, or five lines in Shakespeare which could be mistaken for Bacon, by one who was familiar with their several styles and practised in such observations. I was myself well read in Shakespeare before I began with Bacon; and I have been forced to cultivate what skill I have in distinguishing Bacon's style to a high degree; because in sifting the genuine from the spurious I had commonly nothing but the style to guide me. And to me, if it were proved that any one of the plays attributed to Shakespeare was really written by Bacon, not the least extraordinary thing about it would be the power which it would show in him of laying aside his individual peculiarities and assuming those of a different man.

If you ask me what I say to Bacon's own confession in the case of *Richard II*, I say that your inference is founded entirely upon a misconstruction of a relative pronoun. "About the same time I [Bacon is being quoted in regard to a reply he made to a question put by Queen Elizabeth] remember an answer of mine in a matter which had some affinity with my lord's cause, *which* though it grew from me went after about in others' names." I [Spedding] say that "which" means not the *matter* but the *answer*.[1] You [Holmes] make it appear to refer to the "matter" only by inserting "and" (p. 251, 1. 8), which is not in the original: and if so there is an end of your whole superstructure. When the queen asked him [Bacon] whether there was not treason in Dr. [John] Hayward's history of the first year of Henry IV, he [Bacon] parried the question by an evasive answer; [i.e., "surely I find none, but for felony very many," alluding to the number of sentences in the work that seemed to resemble similar sentences to be found in the work of the Roman historian Tacitus] which was quoted afterwards and ascribed in conversation to other people, but was really his own. Even if it were possible to believe that the "matter" in question was the play of *Richard II*, the only inference that could be drawn as to the authorship is that the ostensible author was a doctor. But for my part I can see nothing in it but a reference to Dr. Hayward's historical tract.

These are my reasons for rejecting your theory. If you had fixed upon anybody else rather than Bacon as the true author—anybody of whom I knew nothing—I should have been scarcely less incredulous; because I deny that a *prima facie* case is made out for questioning Shakespeare's title. But if there were any reason for supposing that somebody else was the real author, I think I am in a condition to say that, whoever it was, it was not Bacon. The difficulties which such a supposition would involve would be almost innumerable and altogether insurmountable. But if what I have said does not excuse me from saying more, what I might say more would be equally ineffectual.

I ought perhaps to apologize for speaking with such confidence on the question of style in a matter where my judgment is opposed to yours. But you must remember that style is like hand-writing—not easy to recognize at first, but unmistakable when you are familiar enough with it. When some twenty-five years ago I began the work of collating the manuscripts with the printed copies, and plunged into a volume of miscellaneous letters written in the beginning of the seventeenth century, I could scarcely distinguish one hand from another, and it was some time before I discovered which was Bacon's own. But after a little of the close and continuous attention which collating and copying involves, I began to feel as if I could know it through all its varieties, from the stateliest Italian to the most sprawling black-letter, and almost swear to a semi-colon. And I am convinced that I could produce many cases in which the most expert palaeographers and facsimilists would at the first view pronounce two hands different, yet find on examination that they were the same. Now it is the same with a man's manner of expressing himself. The unconscious gestures of the style, scarcely discernible at first, are scarcely mistakable after. The time may have been—I do not know—when I could have believed the style of *Hamlet* and of the *Advancement of Learning* to be the style of the same man: and the time may yet come when you will yourself wonder that you did not perceive the difference.

Notes

1.   Professor Holmes had assumed the "story of the first year of King Henry IV." (which was the matter in question) to be the Shakespearian play of Richard II.: and argued that, in saying that "it [namely the play] grew from him," Bacon confessed himself the real author. Mr. H. allows that he had misconstrued "which," and that this point of the confession must be given up, but remains otherwise satisfied that Bacon *was* the author and that the queen knew it.

—James Spedding, "On the Authorship of
the Plays Attributed to Shakespeare," 1867,
Reviews and Discussions, 1879, pp. 369–75

James Freeman Clarke "Did Shakespeare Write Bacon's Works?" (1881)

In order to show the absurdity of Nathaniel Holmes's claim that Francis Bacon wrote the plays attributed to Shakespeare, James Freeman Clarke (1810–88), an American Unitarian minister, writer, and abolitionist, marshals evidence and devises arguments to show that it is far more likely that Shakespeare wrote Bacon's work. In the course of asserting this position, Clarke illuminates the conditions that existed for gathering knowledge and describes the intellectual climate during the last decades of the sixteenth century in England.

The greatest of English poets is Shakespeare. The greatest prose writer in English literature is probably Lord Bacon. Each of these writers, alone, is a marvel of intellectual grandeur. It is hard to understand how one man, in a few years, could have written all the masterpieces of Shakespeare,—thirty-six dramas, each a work of genius such as the world will never let die. It is a marvel that from one mind could proceed the tender charm of such poems as *Romeo and Juliet, As You Like It,* or *The Winter's Tale;* the wild romance of *The Tempest,* or of *The Midsummer Night's Dream;* the awful tragedies of *Lear, Macbeth,* and *Othello;* the profound philosophy of *Hamlet;* the perfect fun of *Twelfth Night,* and *The Merry Wives of Windsor,* and the reproductions of Roman and English history. It is another marvel that a man like Lord Bacon, immersed nearly all his life in business, a successful lawyer, an ambitious statesman, a courtier cultivating the society of the sovereign and the favorites of the sovereign, should also be the founder of a new system of philosophy, which has been the source of many inventions and new sciences down to the present day; should have critically surveyed the whole domain of knowledge, and become a master of English literary style. Each of these phenomena is a marvel; but put them together, and assume that one man did it all, and you have, not a marvel, but a miracle. Yet, this is the result which the monistic tendency of modern thought has reached. Several critics of our time have attempted to show that Lord Bacon, besides writing all the works usually attributed to him, was also the author of all of Shakespeare's plays and poems.

This theory was first publicly maintained by Miss Delia Bacon in 1857. It had been, before, in 1856, asserted by an Englishman, William Henry Smith, but only in a thin volume printed for private circulation. This book made a distinguished convert in the person of Lord Palmerston, who openly declared his conviction that Bacon was the author of Shakespeare's plays. Two papers by [lawyer and founder of the Shakespeare Society of New York James] Appleton Morgan, written in the same sense, appeared last year in *Appleton's Journal.* But far the most elaborate and masterly work in support of this attempt to dethrone Shakespeare, and to give his seat on the summit of Parnassus to Lord Bacon, is the book by Judge [Nathaniel] Holmes, published in 1866. He has shown much ability, and brought forward every argument which has any plausibility connected with it.

Judge Holmes was, of course, obliged to admit the extreme antecedent improbability of his position. Certainly it is very difficult to believe that the author of such immortal works should have been willing, for any reason, permanently to conceal his authorship; or, if he could hide that fact, been willing to give the authorship to another; or, if willing, should have been able so effectually to conceal the substitution as to blind the eyes of all mankind down to the days of Miss Delia Bacon and Judge Holmes.

What, then, are the arguments used by Judge Holmes? The proofs he adduces are mainly these: (1st) That there are many coincidences and parallelisms of thought and expression between the works of Bacon and Shakespeare; (2d) that there is an amount of knowledge and learning in the plays, which Lord Bacon possessed, but which Shakespeare could hardly have had. Besides these principal proofs, there are many other reasons given which are of inferior weight—a phrase in a letter of [English courtier and eventual Roman Catholic priest] Sir Tobie Matthew; another sentence of Bacon himself, which might be possibly taken as an admission that he was the author of *Richard II.*; the fact that some plays which Shakespeare certainly did not write were first published with his name or his initials. But his chief argument is that Shakespeare had neither the learning nor the time to write the plays, both of which Lord Bacon possessed; and that there are curious coincidences between the plays and the prose works.

These arguments have all been answered, and the world still believes in Shakespeare as before. But I have thought it might be interesting to show how easily another argument could be made of an exactly opposite kind—how easily all these proofs might be reversed. I am inclined to think that if we are to believe that one man was the author of the plays and the philosophy, it is much more probable that Shakespeare wrote the works of Bacon than that Bacon wrote the works of Shakespeare. For there is no evidence that Bacon was a poet as well as a philosopher; but there is ample evidence that Shakespeare was a philosopher as well as a poet. This, no doubt, assumes that Shakespeare actually wrote the plays; but this we have a right to assume, in the outset of the discussion, in order to stand on an equal ground with our opponents.

The Bacon vs. Shakespeare argument runs thus: "Assuming that Lord Bacon wrote the works commonly attributed to him, there is reason to believe that he also wrote the plays and poems commonly attributed to Shakespeare."

The counter argument would then be: "Assuming that Shakespeare wrote the plays and poems commonly attributed to him, there is reason to believe that he also wrote the works commonly attributed to Bacon."

This is clearly the fair basis of the discussion. What is assumed on the one side on behalf of Bacon we have a right to assume on the other on behalf of Shakespeare. But before proceeding on this basis, I must reply to the only argument of Judge Holmes which has much apparent weight. He contends that it was impossible for Shakespeare, with the opportunities he possessed, to acquire the knowledge which we find in the plays. Genius, however great, cannot give the knowledge of medical and legal terms, nor of the ancient languages. Now, it has been shown that the plays afford evidence of a great knowledge of law and medicine; and of works in Latin and Greek, French and Italian. How could such information have been obtained by a boy who had no advantages of study except at a country grammar-school, which he left at the age of fourteen, who went to London at twenty-three and became an actor, and who spent most of his life as actor, theatrical proprietor, and man of business?

This objection presents difficulties to us, and for our time, when boys sometimes spend years in the study of Latin grammar. We cannot understand the rapidity with which all sorts of knowledge were imbibed in the period of the Renaissance. Then every one studied everything. Then Greek and Latin books were read by prince and peasant, by queens and generals. Then all sciences and arts were learned by men and women, by young and old. Thus speaks [author of *The Anatomy of Melancholy*, 1621] Robert Burton—who was forty years old when Shakespeare died: "What a world of books offers itself, in all subjects, arts and sciences, to the sweet content and capacity of the reader! In arithmetic, geometry, perspective, opticks, astronomy, architecture, *sculptura, pictura,* of which so many and elaborate treatises have lately been written; in mechanics and their mysteries, military matters, navigation, riding of horses, fencing, swimming, gardening, planting, great tomes of husbandry, cookery, faulconry, hunting, fishing, fowling; with exquisite pictures of all sports and games. What vast tomes are extant in law, physic, and divinity, for profit, pleasure, practice. Some take an infinite delight to study the very languages in which these books were written: Hebrew, Greek, Syriac, Chaldee, Arabick, and the like." This was the fashion of that day, to study all languages, all subjects, all authors. A mind like that of Shakespeare could not have failed to share this universal desire for knowledge. After leaving the grammar-school, he had nine years for such studies before he went to London. As soon as he began to write plays, he had new motives for study; for the subjects of the drama in vogue were often taken from classic story.

But Shakespeare enjoyed another source of gaining knowledge besides the study of books. When he reached London, five or six play-houses were in full activity, and new plays were produced every year in vast numbers. New plays were then in constant demand, just as the new novel and new daily or weekly paper are called for now. The drama was the periodical literature of the time. Dramatic authors wrote with wonderful rapidity, borrowing their subjects from plays already on the stage, and from classic or recent history.

[Christopher] Marlowe, [Robert] Greene, [John] Lyly, [George] Peele, [Thomas] Kyd, [author of *Rosalynde,* a source of *As You Like It,* Thomas] Lodge, [Thomas] Nash, [Henry] Chettle, [Anthony] Munday, [Robert] Wilson, were all dramatic writers before Shakespeare. Philip Henslowe, a manager or proprietor of the theaters, bought two hundred and seventy plays in about ten years. Thomas Heywood wrote a part or the whole of two hundred and twenty plays during his dramatic career. Each acted play furnished material for some other. They were the property of the playhouses, not of the writers. One writer after another had accused Shakespeare of indifference to his reputation, because he did not publish a complete and revised edition of his works during his life. How could he do this, since they did not belong to him, but to the theater? Yet every writer was at full liberty to make use of all he could remember of other plays, as he saw them acted; and Shakespeare was not slow to use this opportunity. No doubt he gained knowledge in this way, which he afterward employed much better than the authors from whom he took it.

The first plays printed under Shakespeare's name did not appear till he had been connected with the stage eleven years. This gives time enough for him to have acquired all the knowledge to be found in his books. That he had read Latin and Greek books we are told by Ben Jonson; though that great scholar undervalued, as was natural, Shakespeare's attainments in those languages.

But Ben Jonson himself furnishes the best reply to those who think that Shakespeare could not have gained knowledge of science or literature because he did not go to Oxford or Cambridge. What opportunities had Ben Jonson? A brick-layer by trade, called back immediately from his studies to use the trowel; then running away and enlisting as a common soldier; fighting in the Low Countries; coming home at nineteen, and going on the stage; sent to prison for fighting a duel—what opportunities for study had he? He was of a strong animal nature, combative, in perpetual quarrels, fond of drink, in pecuniary troubles, married at twenty, with a wife and children to support. Yet Jonson was celebrated for his learning. He was master of Greek and Latin literature. He took his characters from [late second-, early third-century rhetorician and grammarian] Athenaeus, [Greek-speaking rhetorician and orator] Libanius, Philostratus. Somehow he had found time for all this study. "Greek and Latin thought," says [Hippolyte] Taine, "were incorporated with his own, and made a part of it. He knew alchemy, and was as familiar with alembics, retorts, crucibles, etc., as if he had passed his life in seeking the philosopher's stone. He seems to have had a specialty in every branch of knowledge. He had all the methods of Latin art—possessed the brilliant conciseness of Seneca and [Roman poet] Lucan." If Ben Jonson—a brick-layer, a soldier, a fighter, a drinker—could yet get time to acquire this vast knowledge, is there any reason why Shakespeare, with much more leisure, might not have done the like? He did not possess as much Greek and Latin lore as Ben Jonson, who, probably, had Shakespeare in his mind when he wrote the following passage in his *Poetaster.*

> His learning savors not the school-like gloss
> That most consists in echoing words and terms,
> And soonest wins a man an empty name;
> Nor any long or far-fetched circumstance
> Wrapt in the curious generalties of art—
> But a direct and analytic sum
> Of all the worth and first effects of art.
> And for his poesy, 'tis so rammed with life,
> That it shall gather strength of life with being,
> And live hereafter more admired than now.

The only other serious proof offered in support of the proposition that Lord Bacon wrote the immortal Shakespearean drama is that certain coincidences of thought and language are found in the works of the two writers. When we examine them, however, they seem very insignificant. Take, as an example, two or three, on which Judge Holmes relies, and which he thinks very striking.

Holmes says (page 48) that Bacon quotes Aristotle, who said that "young men were no fit hearers of moral philosophy," and Shakespeare says *(Troilus and Cressida):*

> Unlike young men whom Aristotle thought
> Unfit to hear moral philosophy.

But since Bacon's remark was published in 1605, and *Troilus and Cressida* did not appear until 1609, Shakespeare might have seen it there, and introduced it into his play from his recollection of the passage in the *Advancement of Learning.*

Another coincidence mentioned by Holmes is that both writers use the word "thrust": Bacon saying that a ship "thrust into Weymouth"; and Shakespeare, that "Milan was thrust from Milan." He also thinks it cannot be an accident that both frequently use the word "wilderness," though in very different ways. Both also compare Queen Elizabeth to a "star." Bacon makes Atlantis an island in mid ocean; and the island of Prospero is also in mid ocean. Both have a good deal to say about "mirrors," and "props," and like phrases.

Such reasoning as this has very little weight. You cannot prove two contemporaneous writings to have proceeded from one author by the same words and phrases being found in both; for these are in the vocabulary of the time, and are the common property of all who read and write.

My position is that if either of these writers wrote the works attributed to the other, it is much more likely that Shakespeare wrote the philosophical works of Bacon, than that Bacon wrote the poetical works of Shakespeare. Assuming then, as we have a right to do in this argument, that Shakespeare wrote the plays, what reasons are there for believing that he also wrote the philosophy?

First. This assumption will explain at once that hitherto insoluble problem of the utter contradiction between Bacon's character and conduct, and his works. How could he have been, at the same time, what Pope calls him—

The wisest, brightest, meanest of mankind?
[*An Essay on Man,* line 282]

He was, in his philosophy, the leader of his age, the reformer of old abuses, the friend of progress. In his conduct, he was, as Macaulay has shown, "far behind his age—far behind Sir Edward Coke; clinging to exploded abuses, withstanding the progress of improvement, struggling to push back the human mind." In his writings, he was calm, dignified, noble. In his life, he was an office-seeker through long years, seeking place by cringing subservience to men in power, made wretched to the last degree when office was denied him, addressing servile supplications to noblemen and to the sovereign. To gain and keep office he would desert his friends, attack his benefactors, and make abject apologies for any manly word he might have incautiously uttered. His philosophy rose far above earth and time, and sailed supreme in the air of universal reason. But "his desires were set on things below. Wealth, precedence, titles, patronage, the mace, the seals, the coronet, large houses, fair gardens, rich manors, massy services of plate, gay hangings," were "objects for which he stooped to everything, and endured everything." These words of Macaulay have been thought too severe. But we defy any admirer of Bacon to read his life, by Spedding, without admitting their essential truth. How was it possible for a man to spend half of his life in the meanest of pursuits, and the other half in the noblest?

This great difficulty is removed if we suppose that Bacon, the courtier and lawyer, with his other ambitions, was desirous of the fame of a great philosopher; and that he induced Shakespeare, then in the prime of his powers, to help him write the prose essays and treatises which are his chief works. He has himself admitted that he did actually ask the aid of the dramatists of his time in writing his books. This remarkable fact is stated by Bacon in a letter to Tobie Matthew, written in June, 1623, in which he says that he is devoting himself to making his writings more perfect—instancing the *Essays* and the *Advancement of Learning*—"by the help of some good pens, which forsake me not." One of these pens was that of Ben Jonson, the other might easily have been that of Shakespeare. Certainly there was no better pen in England at that time than his.

When Shakespeare's plays were being produced, Lord Bacon was fully occupied in his law practice, his parliamentary duties, and his office-seeking. The largest part of the Shakespeare drama was put on the stage, as modern research renders probable, in the ten or twelve years beginning with 1590. In 1597, Shakespeare was rich enough to buy the new place at Stratford-on-Avon, and was also lending money. In 1604, he was part owner of the Globe Theater, so that the majority of the plays which gained for him this fortune must have been produced before that time. Now these were just the busiest years of Bacon's life. In 1584, he was elected to Parliament. About the same time, he wrote his famous letter to Queen Elizabeth. In 1585, he was already seeking office from [Queen Elizabeth's chief of spying and intelligence operations and father-in-law of Sir Philip Sidney, Francis] Walsingham and [Scottish peer Michael Balfour, Lord] Burleigh. In 1586, he sat in Parliament for Taunton, and was active in debate and on committees. He became a bencher in the same year, and began to plead in the courts of Westminster. In 1589, he became Queen's counsel, and member of Parliament for Liverpool. After this, he continued active, both in Parliament and at the bar. He sought, by the help of [Robert Devereux, Second Earl of] Essex, to become Attorney-General. From that period, as crown lawyer, his whole time and thought were required to trace and frustrate the conspiracies with which the kingdom was full. It was evident that during these years he had no time to compose fifteen or twenty of the greatest works in any literature.

But how was Shakespeare occupied when Bacon's philosophy appeared? The *Advancement of Learning* was published in 1605, after most of the plays had been written, as we learn from the fact of Shakespeare's purchase of houses and lands. The *Novum Organum* was published in 1620, after Shakespeare's death. But it had been written years before; revised, altered, and copied again and again—it is said twelve times. Bacon had been engaged upon it during thirty years, and it was at last published incomplete and in fragments. If Shakespeare assisted in the composition of this work, his death in 1616 would account, at once, for its being left unfinished. And Shakespeare would have had ample time to furnish the ideas of the *Organum* in the last years of his life, when he had left the theater. In 1613, he bought a house in Black Friars, where Ben Jonson also lived. Might not this have been that they might more conveniently cooperate in assisting Bacon to write the *Novum Organum?*

When we ask whether it would have been easier for the author of the philosophy to have composed the drama, or the dramatic poet to have written the philosophy, the answer will depend on which is the greater work of the two. The greater includes the less, but the less cannot include the greater. Now the universal testimony of modern criticism in England, Germany, and France declares that no larger, deeper, or ampler intellect has ever appeared than that which produced the Shakespeare drama. This "myriad-minded" poet was also philosopher, man of the world, acquainted with practical affairs, one of those who saw the present and foresaw the future. All the ideas of the Baconian philosophy might easily have had their home in this vast intelligence. Great as are the thoughts of the *Novum Organum* they are far inferior to that world of thought which is in the drama. We can easily conceive that Shakespeare, having produced in his prime the wonders and glories of the plays, should in his after leisure have developed the leading ideas of the Baconian philosophy. But it is difficult to imagine that Bacon, while devoting his main strength to politics, to law, and to philosophy, should have, as a mere pastime for his leisure, produced in his idle moments the greatest intellectual work ever done on earth.

If the greater includes the less, then the mind of Shakespeare includes that of Bacon, and not the reverse. This will appear more plainly if we consider the quality of intellect displayed respectively in the drama and the philosophy. The one is synthetic, creative; the other analytic, critical. The one puts together, the other takes apart and examines. Now, the genius which can put together can also take apart; but it by no means follows that the power of taking apart implies that of putting together. A watch-maker, who can put a watch together, can easily take it to pieces; but many a child who has taken his watch to pieces has found it impossible to put it together again.

When we compare the Shakespeare plays and the Baconian philosophy, it is curious to see how the one is throughout a display of the synthetic intellect, and the other of the analytic. The plays are pure creation, the production of living wholes. They people our thought with a race of beings who are living persons, and not pale abstractions. These airy nothings take flesh and form, and have a name and local habitation forever on the earth. Hamlet, Desdemona, Othello, Miranda, are as real people as Queen Elizabeth or Mary of Scotland. But when we turn to the Baconian philosophy, this faculty is wholly absent. We have entered the laboratory of a great chemist, and are surrounded by retorts and crucibles, tests and re-agents, where the work done is a careful analysis of all existing things, to find what are their constituents and their qualities. Poetry creates, philosophy takes to pieces and examines.

It is, I think, an historic fact, that while those authors whose primary quality is poetic genius have often been also, on a lower plane, eminent as philosophers, there is, perhaps, not a single instance of one whose primary distinction was philosophic analysis, who has also been, on a lower plane, eminent as a poet. Milton, [Italian poet who established the sonnet as a poetic form] Petrarch, [Johann Wolfgang von] Goethe, [Roman poet and author of *On the Nature of* Things Titus] Lucretius, [French writer, philosopher, and author of *Candide,* 1759, François-Marie Arouet] Voltaire, [Samuel Taylor] Coleridge, were primarily and eminently poets; but all excelled, too, in a less degree, as logicians, metaphysicians, men of science, and philosophers. But what instance have we of any man like Bacon, chiefly eminent as lawyer, statesman, and philosopher, who was also distinguished, though in a less degree, as a poet? Among great lawyers, is there one eminent also as a dramatic or lyric author? Cicero tried it, but his verses are only doggerel. In [John] Lord Campbell's list of the lord chancellors and chief-justices of England, no such instance appears. If Bacon wrote the Shakespeare drama, he is the one exception to an otherwise universal rule. But if Shakespeare cooperated in the production of the Baconian philosophy, he belongs to a class of poets who have done the same. Coleridge was one of the most imaginative of poets. His *Christabel* and *Ancient Mariner* are pure creations. But in later life he originated a new system of philosophy in England, the influence of which has not ceased to be felt to our day. The case would be exactly similar if we suppose that Shakespeare, having ranged the realm of imaginative poetry in his youth, had in his later days of leisure cooperated with Bacon and Ben Jonson in producing the *Advancement of Learning* and the *Novum Organum.* We can easily think of them as meeting, sometimes at the house of Ben Jonson, sometimes at that of Shakespeare in Black Friars, and sometimes guests at that private house built by Lord Bacon for purposes of study, near his splendid palace of Gorhambury. "A most ingeniously contrived house," says Basil Montagu, "where, in the society of his philosophical friends, he devoted himself to study and meditation." [John] Aubrey tells us that he had the aid of [political philosopher and author of *Leviathan* Thomas] Hobbes in writing down his thoughts. Lord Bacon appears to have possessed the happy gift of using other men's faculties in his service. Ben Jonson, who had been a thorough student of chemistry, alchemy, and science in all the forms then known, aided Bacon in his observations of nature. Hobbes aided him in giving clearness to his thoughts and his language. And from Shakespeare he may have derived the radical and central ideas of his philosophy. He used the help of Dr. Playfer to translate his philosophy into Latin. Tobie Matthew gives him the last argument of Galileo for the Copernican system. He sends his works to others, begging them to correct the thoughts and the style. It is evident, then, that he would have been glad of the concurrence of Shakespeare, and that could easily be had, through their common friend, Ben Jonson.

If Bacon wrote the plays of Shakespeare, it is exceedingly difficult to give any satisfactory reason for his concealment of that authorship. He had much pride, not to say vanity, in being known as an author. He had his name attached to all his other works, and sent them as presents to the universities, and to individuals, with letters calling their attention to these books. Would he have been willing permanently to conceal the fact of his being the author of the best poetry of his time? The reasons assigned by Judge Holmes for this are not satisfactory. They are: his desire to rise in the profession of the law, the low reputation of a play-writer, his wish to write more freely under an *incognito,* and his wish to rest his reputation on his philosophical works. But if he were reluctant to be regarded as the author of *Lear* and *Hamlet,* he was willing to be known as the writer of "Masques," and a play about [King] Arthur, exhibited by the students of Gray's Inn. It is an error to say that the reputation of a play-writer was low. Judge Holmes, himself, tells us that there was nothing remarkable in a barrister of the inns of court writing for the stage. Ford and Beaumont were both lawyers as well as eminent play-writers. Lord Buckhurst, Lord Brooke, Sir Henry Wotton, all wrote plays. And we find nothing in the Shakespeare dramas which Bacon need have feared to say under his own name. It would have been ruin to [English politician] Sir Philip Francis to have avowed himself the author of *Junius* [a political pamphlet accusing Warren Hastings, governor general of Bengal, of corruption]. But the Shakespeare plays satirized no one, and made no enemies. If there were any reasons for concealment, they certainly do not apply to the year 1623, when the first folio appeared, which was after the death of Shakespeare and the fall of Bacon. The acknowledgment of their authorship at that time could no longer interfere with Bacon's rise. And it would be very little to the credit of his intelligence to assume that he was not then aware of the value of such works, or that he did not desire the reputation of being their author. It would have been contrary to his very nature not to have wished for the credit of that authorship.

On the other hand, there would be nothing surprising in the fact of Shakespeare's laying no claim to credit for having assisted in the composition of the *Advancement of Learning*. Shakespeare was by nature as reticent and modest as Bacon was egotistical and ostentatious. What a veil is drawn over the poet's personality in his sonnets! We read in them his inmost sentiments, but they tell us absolutely nothing of the events of his life, or the facts of his position. And if, as we assume, he was one among several who helped Lord Bacon, though he might have done the most, there was no special reason why he should proclaim that fact.

Gervinus has shown, in three striking pages, the fundamental harmony between the ideas and mental tendencies of Shakespeare and Bacon. Their philosophy of man and of life was the same. If, then, Bacon needed to be helped in thinking out his system, there was no one alive who would have given him such stimulus and encouragement as Shakespeare. This also may explain his not mentioning the name of Shakespeare in his works; for that might have called too much attention to the source from which he received this important aid.

Nevertheless, I regard the monistic theory as in the last degree improbable. We have two great authors, and not one only. But if we are compelled to accept the view which ascribes a common source to the Shakespeare drama and the Baconian philosophy, I think there are good reasons for preferring Shakespeare to Bacon as the author of both. When the plays appeared, Bacon was absorbed in pursuits and ambitions foreign to such work; his accepted writings show no sign of such creative power; he was the last man in the world not to take the credit of such a success, and had no motive to conceal his authorship. On the other hand, there was a period in Shakespeare's life when he had abundant leisure to cooperate in the literary plans of Bacon; his ample intellect was full of the ideas which took form in those works; and he was just the person neither to claim any credit for lending such assistance nor to desire it.

There is, certainly, every reason to believe that among his other ambitions, Bacon desired that of striking out a new path of discovery, and initiating a better method in the study of nature. But we know that, in doing this, he sought aid in all quarters, and especially among Shakespeare's friends and companions. It is highly probable, therefore, that he became acquainted with the great dramatist, and that Shakespeare knew of Bacon's designs and became interested in them. And if so, who could offer better suggestions than he; and who would more willingly accept them than the overworked statesman and lawyer, who wished to be also a philosopher?

Finally, we may refer those who believe that the shape of the brow and head indicates the quality of mental power, to the portraits of the two men. The head of Shakespeare, according to all the busts and pictures which remain to us, belongs to the type which antiquity has transmitted to us in the portraits of Homer and Plato. In this vast dome of thought there was room for everything. The head of Bacon is also a grand one, but less ample, less complete—less

Teres, totus atque rotundus.

[Finished and completely rounded off.]

[Horace, *Satires*, II.vii.78]

These portraits therefore agree with all we know of the writings, in showing us which, and which only, of the two minds was capable of containing the other.

> —James Freeman Clarke, "Did Shakespeare Write Bacon's Works?" *The North American Review*, February 1881, pp. 163–75

IGNATIUS DONNELLY "A WORD PERSONAL" (1888)

Ignatius Loyola Donnelly (1831–1901) was a lawyer, politician, member of the U.S. Congress from Minnesota, candidate for vice president of the United States for the People's Party in 1900, and supporter of women's suffrage and of utopian agrarian communities. He argued that there was an elaborate code system inside the plays attributed to Shakespeare that indicates the plays were written by Bacon. The code apparently also conveys other secret information, but Donnelly was not explicit about what that is. Donnelly's writing often is of questionable coherence and is more prone to announcing that there is some mystery to be revealed than it is inclined to lay out anything specific. It is often self-reflexive, apologetic, and defensive. Donnelly's labors were more often subject to ridicule than viewed with respect. As Hawthorne suggested, with a generous understanding of the psychology of human need, in his remarks on Delia Bacon, interpretations of Shakespeare's work can sometimes hint at something deep within the psyche of the interpreter as opposed to revealing something about the works themselves.

Report me and my causes right
To the unsatisfied.

(Hamlet, v.5.)

I began this book with an apology; I end it with another. No one can be more conscious of its defects than I am. So great a subject demanded the utmost care, deliberation and perfection; while my work has, on the other hand, been performed with the utmost haste and under many adverse circumstances.

It was my misfortune to have announced, in 1884, that I believed I had found a Cipher in the Plays. From the time I put forth that claim until the copy was placed in the hands of the publishers, I made no effort to advertise my book. But the assertion was so startling, and concerned writings of such universal interest, that it could not be suffered to fall unnoticed. I felt, at the same time, that I owed some duties to the nineteenth century, as well as to the sixteenth, and hence my work was greatly broken in upon by public affairs. After a time the reading world became clamorous for the proofs of my surprising assertion; and many were not slow to say that I was either an impostor or a lunatic. Goaded by these taunts, I made arrangements to publish before I was really ready to do so; and then set to work, under the greatest strain and the highest possible pressure, to try to keep my engagements with my publishers. But the reader can readily conceive how slowly such a Cipher work as this must have advanced, when every word was a sum in arithmetic, and had to be counted and verified again and again. In the meantime upon my poor devoted head was let loose a perfect flood-tide of denunciation, ridicule and misrepresentation from three-fourths of the newspapers of America and England. I could not pause in my work to defend myself, but had to sit, in the midst of an arctic winter, and patiently endure it all, while working from ten to twelve hours every day, at a kind of mental toil the most exhausting the human mind is capable of.

These facts will, I trust, be my excuse for all the crudeness, roughness, repetitions and errors apparent in these pages.

In the Patent Office they require the inventor to state clearly what he claims. I will follow that precedent.

> I admit, as I have said before, that my workmanship in the elaboration of the Cipher is not perfect. There are one or two essential points of the Cipher rule that I have not fully worked out. I think that I see the complete rule, but I need more leisure to elaborate and verify it abundantly, and reduce my workmanship to mathematical exactness.

But I claim that, beyond a doubt, *there is a Cipher in the so-called Shakespeare Plays.*

The proofs are *cumulative.* I have shown a thousand of them. No honest man can, I think, read this book through and say that there is nothing extraordinary, unusual and artificial in the construction of the text of *1st* and *2nd Henry IV.* No honest man will, I think, deny the multitudinous evidences I present that the text, words, brackets and hyphens have been adjusted arithmetically to the necessity of matching the ends of scenes and fragments of scenes with certain root-numbers of a Cipher. . . .

[R]emember how *heart* is spelled *hart* where it refers to Shakspere's sister; remember how *and it* is spelled *ant,* and not *and't,* where allusion is had to Bacon's *aunt;* remember how *dear* is spelt *deere* when it refers to *deer;* remember how *sperato* is separated by a hair space into *sperato,* so as to give the terminal syllable to *Shake-sper;* remember how the rare word *rabbit* is found in the text precisely cohering, arithmetically, with *hunting.* Then turn to the Cipher story on page 79 of the Folio, where not only scattered words come out, but where whole long series of words are so adjusted, with the aid of the brackets and hyphens, as to follow precisely the order of the words in the play! Then remember how every part of this Cipher story fits precisely into what we know historically to be true; and, although much of it is new, that part is, in itself, probable and reasonable.

The world will either have to admit that there is a Cipher in the Plays, or that in the construction of this narrative I have manifested an ingenuity as boundless as that which I have attributed to Bacon. But I make no such claim. No ingenuity could *create the words* necessary to tell this extraordinary story, unless they were in the text. Take Bulwer's *Richelieu,* or Byron's *Manfred,* or Goldsmith's *She Stoops to Conquer,* or any other dramatic composition of the last hundred years, and you will seek in vain for even one-tenth of the significant words found herein; and as to making any of these modern plays tell a coherent, historical tale, by counting *with the same number* from the ends of scenes and fragments of scenes, it would be altogether and absolutely impossible.

I do not blame any man for having declared *a priori* against the possibility of there being a Cipher in the Plays. On the face of it such a claim is improbable, and, viewed from our nineteenth century standpoint, and in the light of our free age, almost absurd. I could not, in the first instance, have believed it myself. I advanced to the conception slowly and reluctantly. I expected to find only a brief assertion of authorship, a word or two to a column. If any man had told me five years ago that these two plays were such an exquisite and intricate piece of microscopic mosaic-work as the facts show them to be, I should have turned from him with contempt. I could not have believed that any man would involve himself in such incalculable labor as is implied in the construction of such a Cipher. We may say the brain was abnormal that created it. But how, after all, can we judge such an intellect by the ordinary standard of mankind? If he sought immortality he certainly has achieved it, for, once the human family grasps the entirety of this inconceivable work, it will be drowned in an ocean of wonder. The Plays may lose their charm; the English language may perish; but tens of thousands of years from now, if the world and civilization endure, mankind will be talking about this extraordinary welding together of fact and fiction; this tale within a tale; this sublime and supreme triumph of the human intellect. Beside it the *Iliad* will be but as the rude song of wandering barbarians, and *Paradise Lost* a temporary offshoot of Judaism.

I trust no honest man will feel constrained, for consistency's sake, because he has judged my book unheard, to condemn it heard. It will avail nothing to assail me. I am not at issue. And you cannot pound the life out of a fact with your fists. A truth has the indestructibility of matter. It is part of God: the threads of continuity tie it to the throne of the Everlasting.

Edmund Burke said in a debate in Parliament about the population of the American colonies: "While we are disputing they grow to it." And so, even while the critics are writing their essays, to demonstrate that all I have revealed is a fortuitous combination of coincidence, keen and able minds will be taking up my imperfect clues and reducing the Cipher rule to such perfection that it will be as useless to deny the presence of the sun in the heavens as to deny the existence of the inner story in the Plays.

And what a volume of historical truths will roll out of the text of this great volume! The inner life of kings and queens, the highest, perhaps the basest, of their kind; the struggles of factions in the courts; the interior view of the birth of religions; the first colonization of the American continent, in which Bacon took an active part, and something of which is hidden in *The Tempest*; the death of Mary Queen of Scots; the Spanish Armada, told in *Love's Labor Lost*; the religious wars on the continent; the story of Henry of Navarre; the real biography of Essex; the real story of Bacon's career; his defense of his life, hidden in *Henry VIII.*, his own downfall, in cipher, being told in the external story of the downfall of Wolsey. What historical facts may we not expect, of which that account of the introduction of "the dreaded and incurable malady" into England is a specimen; what philosophical reflections; what disquisitions on religion; what profound and unrestrained meditations! It will be, in short, the inner story of the most important era in human history, told by the keenest observer and most powerful writer that has ever lived. And then think of the light that will be thrown upon the Plays themselves; their purposes, their history, their meaning! A great light bursting from a tomb, and covering with its royal effulgence the very cradle of English Literature.

And so I trust my long-promised book to the tender mercies of my fellow-men, saying to them in the language of the old rhyme:

Be to its faults a little blind, And to its virtues very kind.

—Ignatius Donnelly, "A Word Personal,"
*The Great Cryptogram: Francis Bacon's
Cipher in the So-Called Shakespeare
Plays,* 1888, volume 2, pp. 889–94

G. K. CHESTERTON
"SENSATIONALISM AND A CIPHER" (1902)

Gilbert Keith Chesterton (1874–1936), English writer of poetry, essays, literary criticism, journalism, biography, detective stories, and Christian apologetics, was known for his wit; his sense of paradox; his scorn for capitalism, fascism, and socialism; and for his Zionism. In the following essay, he confutes the Baconian hypothesis with scorn, arguing that its practitioners are literal-minded people absorbed by a "delirium of detail." Great and difficult works of literature have historically been regarded, he writes, by small-minded people, as containing secret, coded meanings within them. Chesterton implicitly contrasts the Baconian's cynical need, motivated, he thinks, by a skeptical disposition to "dethrone" Shakespeare with what he conceives as the truer and more noble impulse to deify him, as Thomas Carlyle does, including him among the heroes to be worshiped, as his extraordinary, even incomprehensible greatness deserves. Chesterton attempts to show the absurdity of the Baconian position by postulating other theories of one writer's work being another's, finding spurious clues in the poetry of William Butler Yeats, for example, that prove his work was really written by a contemporaneous British prime minister. Chesterton notes that, for all the talk of a cipher, of a hidden narrative in the plays, none of the advocates of the theory that one exists ever says exactly what it is. Chesterton concludes his defense of Shakespeare by a strong indictment of Bacon's character, arguing that the sublime work of Shakespeare could hardly come from so tarnished a man as Bacon.

I

The revival of the whole astonishing Bacon-Shakespeare business is chiefly interesting to the philosophical mind as an example of the power of the letter which killeth and of how finally and murderously it kills. Baconianism is, indeed, the last wild monstrosity of literalism; it is a sort of delirium of detail. A handful of printers' types, a few alphabetical comparisons are sufficient to convince the Baconians of a proposition which is fully as fantastic historically as the proposition that the Battle of Waterloo was won by [English poet] Leigh Hunt disguised as [Arthur Wellesley, the duke of] Wellington, or that the place of Queen Victoria for the last forty years of her reign was taken by [Irish writer, feminist, and anti-vivisectionist] Miss Frances Power Cobbe. Both these hypotheses are logically quite possible. The dates agree; the physical similarity is practically sufficient. Briefly, in fact, there is nothing to be said against the propositions except that every sane man is convinced that they are untrue.

Let us consider for a moment the Baconian conception from the outside. A sensational theory about the position of Shakespeare was certain in the nature of things to arise. Men of small imagination have sought in every age to find a cipher in the indecipherable masterpieces of the great. Throughout the Middle Ages the whole of the *Aeneid,* full of the sad and splendid eloquence of Virgil, was used as a conjuring book. Men opened it at random, and from a few disconnected Latin words took a motto and an omen for their daily work. In the same way men in more modern times have turned to the Book of Revelation full of the terrible judgment, and yet more terrible consolation of a final moral arbitration, and found in it nothing but predictions about Napoleon Bonaparte and attacks on the English Ritualists. Everywhere, in short, we find the same general truth—the truth that facts can prove anything and that there is nothing so misleading as that which is printed in black and white. Almost everywhere and almost invariably the man who has sought a cryptogram in a great masterpiece has been highly exhilarated, logically justified, morally excited, and entirely wrong.

If, therefore, we continue to study Baconianism from the outside—a process which cannot do it or any other thesis any injustice—we shall come more and more to the conclusion that it is in itself an inevitable outcome of the circumstances of the case and the tendencies of human nature. Shakespeare was by the consent of all human beings a portent. If he had lived some thousand years earlier, people would have turned him into a god. As it is, people can apparently do nothing but attempt to turn him into a Lord Chancellor. But their great need must be served. Shakespeare must have his legend, his whisper of something more than common origin. They must at least make of him a mystery, which is as near as our century can come to a miracle. Something sensational about Shakespeare was bound ultimately to be said, for we are still the children of the ancient earth, and have myth and idolatry in our blood. But in this age of a convention of scepticism we cannot rise to an apotheosis. The nearest we can come to it is a dethronement.

So much for the *a priori* probability of a Baconian theory coming into existence. What is to be said of the *a priori* probability of the theory itself; or, rather, to take the matter in its most lucid order, what is the theory? In the time roughly covered by the latter part of the reign of Queen Elizabeth and the earlier part of the reign of James I, there arose a school of dramatists who covered their country with glory and filled libraries with their wild and wonderful plays. They differed in type and station to a certain extent: some were scholars, a few were gentlemen, most were actors and many were vagabonds. But they had a common society, common meeting-places, a common social tone. They differed in literary aim and spirit: to a certain extent some were great philosophic dramatists, some were quaint humorists, some mere scribblers of a sort of halfwitted and half-inspired melodrama. But they all had a common style, a common form and vehicle, a common splendour, and a common error in their methods. Now, the Baconian theory is that one of these well-known historical figures—a man who lived their life and shared their spirit, and who happened to be the most brilliant in the cultivation of their particular form of art—was, as a matter of fact, an impostor, and that the works which his colleagues thought he had written in the same spirit and the same circumstances in which they had written theirs, were not written by him, but by a very celebrated judge and politician of that time, whom they may sometimes have seen when his coach-wheels splashed them as he went by.

Now, what is to be said about the *a priori* probability of this view, which I stated, quite plainly and impartially above? The first thing to be said, I think, is that a man's answer to the question would be a very good test of whether he had the rudiments of a historical instinct, which is simply an instinct which is capable of realizing the way in which things happen. To many this will appear a vague and unscientific way of approaching the question. But the method I now adopt is the method which every reasonable being adopts in distinguishing between fact and fiction in real life. What would any man say if he were informed that in the private writings of Lord Rosebery that statesman claimed to have written the poems of Mr. W. B. Yeats? Certainly, he could not deny that there were very singular coincidences in detail. How remarkable, for instance, is the name Primrose [Yeats and his family lived at 21 Fitzroy Road in Primrose Hill from 1867 to 1874], which is obviously akin to modest rose, and thus to "Secret Rose." On the top of this comes the crushing endorsement of the same idea indicated in the two words, "rose" and "bury." The remarks of the ploughman in the *Countess Kathleen* [1892] (note the rank in the peerage selected) would be anxiously scanned for some not improbable allusion to a furrow; and everything else, the statesman's abandonment of Home Rule, the poet's aversion to Imperialism, would be all parts of Lord Rosebery's cunning. But what, I repeat, would a man say if he were asked if the theory were probable? He would reply, "The theory is as near to being impossible as a natural phenomenon can be. I know Mr. W. B. Yeats, I know how he talks, I know what sort of a man he is, what sort of people he lives among, and know that he is the man to have written those poems. I know Lord Rosebery too, and what sort of a life his is, and I know that he is not."

Now, we know, almost as thoroughly as we should know the facts of this hypothetical case, the facts about Bacon and Shakespeare. We know that Shakespeare was a particular kind of man who lived with a particular kind of men, all of whom thought much as he thought and wrote much as he wrote. We know that Bacon was a man who lived in another world, who thought other thoughts, who talked with other men, who wrote another style, one might almost say another language. . . . For the moment it is sufficient to point out that the Baconian hypothesis has against it the whole weight of historical circumstance and the whole of that supra-logical realization which some of us call transcendentalism, and most of us common sense.

II

In a previous article I drew attention to the general spirit in which the Baconian question must be approached. That spirit involves the instinct of culture which does not consist merely in knowing the fact, but in being able to imagine the truth. The Baconians imagine a vain thing, because they believe in facts. Their historical faculty is a great deal more like an ear for music. One of the matters, for example, which is most powerfully concerned in the Bacon-Shakespeare question is the question of literary style, a thing as illogical as the bouquet of a bottle of wine. It is the thing, in short, which makes us quite certain that the sentence quoted in *The Tragedy of Sir Francis Bacon* ["An Appeal for further investigation and research" by Harold Bayley, published in 1902, arguing that Bacon was the author of the plays attributed to Shakespeare] from his secret narrative, "The Queen looked pale from want of rest, but was calm and compos'd," was never written by an Elizabethan. Having explained the essentials of the method as they appear to me, I now come to the study of the mass of the Baconian details. They are set forth in a kind of resumé of various Baconian theories in *The Tragedy of Sir Francis Bacon* by Harold Bayley (Grant Richards). The work is an astonishing example of this faculty of putting out the fire of truth with the fuel of information. Mr. Bayley has collected with creditable industry an enormous number of fragmentary facts and rumours. He has looked at the water-marks in the paper used by the Rosicrucians and Jacobean dramatists. He has examined the tail-pieces and ornamental borders of German and Belgian printers. He has gone through the works of Bacon and Shakespeare and a hundred others, picking out parallel words and allusions, but all the time he is completely incapable of realizing the great and glaring truism which lies at the back of the whole question, the simple truism that a million times nought is nought. He does not see, that is, that though a million coincidences, each of which by itself has a slight value, may make up a probability, yet a million coincidences, each of which has no value in itself, make up nothing at all.

What are the sort of coincidences upon which Mr. Bayley relies? The water-mark used in some book is the design of a bunch of grapes. Bacon says, in the *Novum Organum:* "I pledge mankind in liquor pressed from countless grapes." Another water-mark represents a seal. Somebody said about Bacon that he became Lord Keeper of the Great Seal of England and of the great seal of nature. The rose and the lily were symbols used by the Rosicrucians; there are a great many allusions to roses and lilies in Shakespeare. A common printer's border consists of acorns. Bacon somewhere alludes to his fame growing like an oak tree. Does not Mr. Bayley see that no conceivable number of coincidences of this kind would make an account more probable or even more possible? Anyone in any age might talk about clusters of grapes or design clusters of grapes; anyone might make an ornament out of acorns; anyone might talk about growing like a tree. I look down at my own floor and see the Greek key pattern round the oilcloth, but it does not convince me that I am destined to open the doors of Hellenic mystery. Mr. Bayley undoubtedly produces a vast number of these parallels, but they all amount to nothing. In my previous article I took for the sake of argument the imaginary case of Lord Rosebery and Mr. W. B. Yeats. Does not Mr. Bayley see that to point out one genuine coincidence, as that Lord Rosebery paid secret cheques to Mr. Yeats, might indicate something, but to say that they both walked down Piccadilly, that they both admired Burne-Jones, that they both alluded more than once to the Irish question, in short that they both did a million things that are done by a million other people, does not approach even to having the faintest value or significance. This then, is the first thing to be said to the Baconian spirit, that it does not know how to add up a column of noughts.

The second thing to be said is rather more curious. If there is a cipher in the Shakespearian plays, it ought presumably to be a definite and unmistakable thing. It may be difficult to find, but when you have found it you have got it. But the extraordinary thing is that Mr. Bayley and most other Baconians talk about the Baconian cipher as they might talk about "a touch of pathos" in [Thomas] Hood's poetry, or "a flavour of cynicism" in [William Makepeace] Thackeray's novels, as if it were a thing one became faintly conscious of and suspected, without being able to point it out. If anyone thinks this unfair, let him notice the strange way in which Mr. Bayley talks about previous Baconian works. "In 1888 Mr. Ignatius Donnelly claimed to have discovered a cipher story in the first folio of Shakespeare's plays. In his much abused but little read and less refuted book, *The Great Cryptogram,* he endeavoured to convince the world of the truth of his theory. Partly by reason of the complexity of his system, the full details of which he did not reveal, and partly owing to the fact that he did not produce any definite assertion of authorship, but appeared to have stumbled into the midst of a lengthy narrative, the world was not convinced, and Mr. Donnelly was greeted with Rabelaisian laughter. He has since gone to the grave unwept, unhonoured, and unsung, and his secret has presumably died with him. The work of this writer was marred by many extravagant inferences, but *The Great Cryptogram* is nevertheless a damning indictment which has not yet been answered." Again, on the second Baconian demonstration, "Dr. [Detroit physician who in the early 1900s argued for Bacon's authorship of Shakespeare's plays Orville W.] Owen gave scarcely more than a hint of how his alleged cipher worked." The brain reels at all this. Why do none of the cipherists seem to be sure what the cipher is or where it is? A man publishes a huge book to prove that there is a cryptogram, and his secret dies with him. Another man devotes another huge book to giving "scarcely more than a hint of it." Are these works really so impenetrable that no one knows whether they all revealed the same cipher or different ciphers? If they pointed to the same cipher it seems odd that Mr. Bayley does not mention it. If their ciphers were different we can only conclude that the great heart of America is passionately bent on finding a cipher in Shakespeare—anyhow, anywhere, and of any kind.

Finally, there is one thing to be said about a more serious matter. In the chapter called "Mr. William Shakespeare" the author has an extraordinary theory that Shakespeare could not have been the author of the works under discussion because those works rise to the heights of mental purity, and the little we know of Shakespeare's life would seem to indicate that it was a coarse and possibly a riotous one. "Public opinion," he says solemnly, "asks us to believe that this divine stream of song, history, and philosophy sprang from so nasty and beastly a source." There is not much to be said about an argument exhibiting so strange an ignorance of human nature. The argument could equally be used to prove that Leonardo da Vinci could not paint, that [French writer, popular orator, and statesman known for his scandalous love affairs Honoré Gabriel Riqueti, Comte de] Mirabeau, could not speak, and that [Robert] Burns's poems were written by the parson of his parish. But surely there is no need to say this to the Baconians. They should be the last people in the world to doubt the possibility of the conjunction of genius with depravity. They trace their sublime stream of song to a corrupt judge, a treacherous friend, a vulgar sycophant, a man of tawdry aims, of cowardly temper, of public and disgraceful end. He killed his benefactor for hire, and the Baconians would improve this and say that he killed his brother. We know little of Shakespeare's vices, but he might have been a scarecrow of profligacy and remained a man worthier to create Portia than the Lord Verulam [Bacon] whom all history knows. The matter is a matter of evidence, and sentiment has little concern with it. But if we did cherish an emotion in the matter it would certainly be a hope that "the divine stream of song" might not be traced to "so nasty and beastly a source" as Francis Bacon.

> —G. K. Chesterton, "Sensationalism and a
> Cipher," *Chesterton on Shakespeare*, edited
> by Dorothy Collins, 1971, pp. 179–86

MARK TWAIN "IS SHAKESPEARE DEAD?" (1909)

Born Samuel Langhorne Clemens (1835–1910), Mark Twain was a figure of his times, a great American humorist, satirist, iconoclast, social critic, practical joker, adventurer, entrepreneur, and the author of *Adventures of Tom Sawyer* and *Adventures of Huckleberry Finn*. In the following essay, he tosses himself into the "Shakespeare or Bacon" controversy, apparently as a Baconist, but the wary reader may be encouraged to wonder if Twain is not assuming a literary persona and satirizing the entire enterprise by the number of his digressions, the bombast of his bluster, the capriciousness of his arguments, his preliminary confession of how he first came to take the side he seems so completely to advocate, and the world-weary introductory remarks about "claimants," among whom this essay, ironically, without including him in that induction, must place Bacon. Whether or not he is bluffing, Twain's argument essentially recycles the Baconians' argument that Francis Bacon had the kind of education, training, and social position apparently requisite for writing the plays attributed to Shakespeare that Shakespeare himself lacked. Twain also asserts that Bacon's acknowledged writings show that he had the kind of wit, style, and wisdom that his advocate here claims might have enabled him to write the plays of Shakespeare. These qualities are missing, Twain and the Baconians argue, from anything we have by Shakespeare—except, it might be argued in return, from his plays.

Twain's claim that Shakespeare went unregarded in his own day is undercut by such testimonies as Francis Meres's, in 1598. After naming several of Shakespeare's plays that, he has seen, Meres says, "the Muses would speak with *Shakespeares* fine filed phrase, if they would speake English." The following year, John Weever stated that Shakespeare's poetry could be written by Apollo, the god of poetry and music. John Davies, in a 1611 encomium, calls Shakespeare "our English Terrence," referring to the great Roman comic playwright. In 1622, William Basse ranks Shakespeare with Chaucer and Spenser. Ben Jonson, in 1623, praises Shakespeare's "wit." Then, in his posthumously published *Timber* (1640), Jonson famously describes the condition of Shakespeare's manuscripts as mostly free from strikethroughs. In his 1841 essay, Thomas Carlyle argues that all the similarities to or prerequisites for the content of Shakespeare's plays that one can find in Bacon's admirable works, nevertheless, do not by themselves contain the ineffable quality that might transform them into the art that distinguishes Shakespeare's plays.

I

Scattered here and there through the stacks of unpublished manuscript which constitute this formidable Autobiography and Diary of mine, certain chapters will in some distant future be found which deal with "Claimants"—claimants historically notorious: Satan, Claimant; the Golden Calf, Claimant; the Veiled Prophet of Khorassan [a tale in the poem *Lalla Rookh* by Irish poet Thomas Moore, about an eighth-century Arabian prophet who claims to be God], Claimant; Louis XVII., Claimant; William Shakespeare, Claimant; Arthur Orton [who claimed with some success until he was tried and imprisoned as a fraud, to be the heir to an English baronetcy], Claimant; Mary Baker G[lover] Eddy [founder of Christian Science], Claimant—and the rest of them. Eminent Claimants, successful Claimants, defeated Claimants, royal Claimants, pleb Claimants, showy Claimants, shabby Claimants, revered Claimants, despised Claimants, twinkle star-like here and there and yonder through the mists of history and legend and tradition—and, oh, all the darling tribe are clothed in mystery and romance, and we read about them with deep interest and discuss them with loving sympathy or with rancorous resentment, according to which side we hitch ourselves to. It has always been so with the human race. There was never a Claimant that couldn't get a hearing, nor one that couldn't accumulate a rapturous following, no matter how flimsy and apparently unauthentic his claim might be. Arthur Orton's claim that he was the lost Tichborne baronet come to life again was as flimsy as Mrs. Eddy's that she wrote *Science and Health* from the direct dictation of the Deity; yet in England near forty years ago Orton had a huge army of devotees and incorrigible adherents, many of whom remained stubbornly unconvinced after their fat god had been proven an impostor and jailed as a perjurer, and to-day Mrs. Eddy's following is not only immense, but is daily augmenting in numbers and enthusiasm. Orton had many fine and educated minds among his adherents, Mrs. Eddy has had the like among hers from the beginning. Her Church is as well equipped in those particulars as is any other Church. Claimants can always count upon a following, it doesn't matter who they are, nor what they claim, nor whether they come with documents or without. It was always so. Down out of the long-vanished past, across the abyss of the ages, if you listen, you can still hear the believing multitudes shouting for Perkin Warbeck [claimant to the throne of England] and Lambert Simnel [also a claimant to the English throne].

A friend has sent me a new book, from England—*The Shakespeare Problem Restated*—well restated and closely reasoned; and my fifty years' interest in that matter—asleep for the last three years—is excited once more. It is an interest which was born of Delia Bacon's book—away back in that ancient day—1857, or maybe 1856. About a year later my pilot-master, Bixby, transferred me from his own steamboat to the *Pennsylvania,* and placed me under the orders and instructions of George Ealer—dead now, these many, many years. I steered for him a good many months—as was the humble duty of the pilot-apprentice: stood a daylight watch and spun the wheel under the severe superintendence and correction of the master. He was a prime chess-player and an idolater of Shakespeare. He would play chess with anybody; even with me, and it cost his official dignity something to do that. Also—quite uninvited—he would read Shakespeare to me; not just casually, but by the hour, when it was his watch and I was steering. He read well, but not profitably for me, because he constantly injected commands into the text. That broke it all up, mixed it all up, tangled it all up—to that degree, in fact, that if we were in a risky and difficult piece of river an ignorant person couldn't have told, sometimes, which observations were Shakespeare's and which were Ealer's. For instance:

What man dare, I dare!
Approach thou *what are* you laying in the leads for? what a hell of an
　　idea! like the rugged ease her off a little, ease her off! rugged Russian
　　bear, the armed rhinoceros or the *there* she goes! meet her, meet
　　her! didn't you *know* she'd smell the reef if you crowded it like that?
　　Hyrcan tiger; take any shape but that and my firm nerves she'll be

in the woods the first you know! stop the starboard! come ahead
strong on the larboard! back the starboard! . . . *Now* then, you're all
right; come ahead on the starboard; straighten up and go 'long, never
tremble: or be alive again, and dare me to the desert *damnation* can't
you keep away from that greasy water? pull her down! snatch her!
snatch her baldheaded! with thy sword; if trembling I inhabit then,
lay in the leads!—no, only the starboard one, leave the other alone,
protest me the baby of a girl. Hence horrible shadow! eight bells—that
watchman's asleep again, I reckon, go down and call Brown yourself,
unreal mockery, hence!

He certainly was a good reader, and splendidly thrilling and stormy and
tragic, but it was a damage to me, because I have never since been able to
read Shakespeare in a calm and sane way. I cannot rid it of his explosive
interlardings, they break in everywhere with their irrelevant, "What in hell
are you up to *now!* pull her down! more! *more!*—there now, steady as you
go," and the other disorganizing interruptions that were always leaping from
his mouth. When I read Shakespeare now I can hear them as plainly as I
did in that long-departed time—fifty-one years ago. I never regarded Ealer's
readings as educational. Indeed, they were a detriment to me.

His contributions to the text seldom improved it, but barring that detail
he was a good reader; I can say that much for him. He did not use the book,
and did not need to; he knew his Shakespeare as well as Euclid ever knew his
multiplication table.

Did he have something to say—this Shakespeare-adoring Mississippi
pilot—anent Delia Bacon's book?

Yes. And he said it; said it all the time, for months—in the morning watch,
the middle watch, and dog watch; and probably kept it going in his sleep. He
bought the literature of the dispute as fast as it appeared, and we discussed
it all through thirteen hundred miles of river four times traversed in every
thirty-five days—the time required by that swift boat to achieve two round
trips. We discussed, and discussed, and discussed, and disputed and disputed;
at any rate, *he* did, and I got in a word now and then when he slipped a cog
and there was a vacancy. He did his arguing with heat, with energy, with
violence; and I did mine with the reserve and moderation of a subordinate
who does not like to be flung out of a pilot-house that is perched forty feet
above the water. He was fiercely loyal to Shakespeare and cordially scornful
of Bacon and of all the pretensions of the Baconians. So was I—at first. And
at first he was glad that that was my attitude. There were even indications
that he admired it; indications dimmed, it is true, by the distance that lay

between the lofty boss-pilotical altitude and my lowly one, yet perceptible to me; perceptible, and translatable into a compliment—compliment coming down from above the snow-line and not well thawed in the transit, and not likely to set anything afire, not even a cub-pilot's self-conceit; still a detectable compliment, and precious.

Naturally it flattered me into being more loyal to Shakespeare—if possible—than I was before, and more prejudiced against Bacon—if possible—than I was before. And so we discussed and discussed, both on the same side, and were happy. For a while. Only for a while. Only for a very little while, a very, very, very little while. Then the atmosphere began to change; began to cool off.

A brighter person would have seen what the trouble was, earlier than I did, perhaps, but I saw it early enough for all practical purposes. You see, he was of an argumentative disposition. Therefore it took him but a little time to get tired of arguing with a person who agreed with everything he said and consequently never furnished him a provocative to flare up and show what he could do when it came to clear, cold, hard, rose-cut, hundred-faceted, diamond-flashing *reasoning*. That was his name for it. It has been applied since, with complacency, as many as several times, in the Bacon-Shakespeare scuffle. On the Shakespeare side.

Then the thing happened which has happened to more persons than to me when principle and personal interest found themselves in opposition to each other and a choice had to be made: I let principle go, and went over to the other side. Not the entire way, but far enough to answer the requirements of the case. That is to say, I took this attitude—to wit, I only *believed* Bacon wrote Shakespeare, whereas I *knew* Shakespeare didn't. Ealer was satisfied with that, and the war broke loose. Study, practice, experience in handling my end of the matter presently enabled me to take any new position almost seriously; a little bit later, utterly seriously; a little later still, lovingly, gratefully, devotedly; finally: fiercely, rabidly, uncompromisingly. After that I was welded to my faith, I was theoretically ready to die for it, and I looked down with compassion not unmixed with scorn upon everybody else's faith that didn't tally with mine. That faith, imposed upon me by self-interest in that ancient day, remains my faith to-day, and in it I find comfort, solace, peace, and never-failing joy. You see how curiously theological it is. The "rice Christian" of the Orient goes through the very same steps, when he is after rice and the missionary is after *him*; he goes for rice, and remains to worship.

Ealer did a lot of our "reasoning"—not to say substantially all of it. The slaves of his cult have a passion for calling it by that large name. We others do not call our inductions and deductions and reductions by any name at all.

They show for themselves what they are, and we can with tranquil confidence leave the world to ennoble them with a title of its own choosing.

Now and then when Ealer had to stop to cough, I pulled my induction-talents together and hove the controversial lead myself: always getting eight feet, eight and a half, often nine, sometimes even quarter-less-twain—as *I* believed; but always "no bottom," as *he* said. [Twain is using a nautical metaphor. Boatmen dropped a rope into the water to measure its depth. Ealer is telling him his argument has some depth but that he has not gotten to the bottom of the issue.]

I got the best of him only once. I prepared myself. I wrote out a passage from Shakespeare—it may have been the very one I quoted awhile ago, I don't remember—and riddled it with his wild steamboatful interlardings. When an unrisky opportunity offered, one lovely summer day, when we had sounded and buoyed a tangled patch of crossings known as Hell's Half Acre, and were aboard again and he had sneaked the *Pennsylvania* triumphantly through it without once scraping sand, and the A. T. *Lacey* had followed in our wake and got stuck and he was feeling good, I showed it to him. It amused him. I asked him to fire it off—*read* it; read it, I diplomatically added, as only *he* could read dramatic poetry. The compliment touched him where he lived. He did read it; read it with surpassing fire and spirit; read it as it will never be read again; for *he* knew how to put the right music into those thunderous interlardings and make them seem a part of the text, make them sound as if they were bursting from Shakespeare's own soul, each one of them a golden inspiration and not to be left out without damage to the massed and magnificent whole.

I waited a week, to let the incident fade; waited longer; waited until he brought up for reasonings and vituperation my pet position, my pet argument, the one which I was fondest of, the one which I prized far above all others in my ammunition-wagon—to wit, that Shakespeare couldn't have written Shakespeare's works, for the reason that the man who wrote them was limitlessly familiar with the laws, and the law-courts, and law-proceedings, and lawyer-talk, and lawyer-ways—and if Shakespeare was possessed of the infinitely divided Stardust that constituted this vast wealth, *how* did he get it, and *where* and *when?*

"From books."

From books! That was always the idea. I answered as my readings of the champions of my side of the great controversy had taught me to answer: that a man can't handle glibly and easily and comfortably and successfully the argot of a trade at which he has not personally served. He will make mistakes; he will not, and cannot, get the trade-phrasings precisely and exactly right; and the moment he departs, by even a shade, from a common trade-form, the reader who has served that trade will know the writer *hasn't*. Ealer would not be convinced; he said a man could learn how to correctly handle the subtleties and mysteries and free-masonries of *any* trade by careful reading and studying. But when I got him to read again the passage from Shakespeare with the interlardings, he perceived, himself, that books couldn't teach a student a bewildering multitude of pilot-phrases so thoroughly and perfectly that he could talk them oft" in book and play or conversation and make no mistake that a pilot would not immediately discover. It was a triumph for me. He was silent awhile, and I knew what was happening—he was losing his temper. And I knew he would presently close the session with the same old argument that was always his stay and his support in time of need; the same old argument, the one I couldn't answer, because I dasn't—the argument that I was an ass, and better shut up. He delivered it, and I obeyed.

Oh dear, how long ago it was—how pathetically long ago! And here am I, old, forsaken, forlorn, and alone, arranging to get that argument out of somebody again.

When a man has a passion for Shakespeare, it goes without saying that he keeps company with other standard authors. Ealer always had several high-class books in the pilothouse, and he read the same ones over and over again, and did not care to change to newer and fresher ones. He played well on the flute, and greatly enjoyed hearing himself play. So did I. He had a notion that a flute would keep its health better if you took it apart when it was not standing a watch; and so, when it was not on duty it took its rest, disjointed, on the compass-shelf under the breastboard. When the *Pennsylvania* blew up and became a drifting rack-heap freighted with wounded and dying poor souls (my young brother Henry among them), pilot Brown had the watch below, and was probably asleep and never knew what killed him; but Ealer escaped unhurt. He and his pilot-house were shot up into the air; then they fell, and Ealer sank through the ragged cavern where the hurricane-deck and the boiler-deck had been, and landed in a nest of ruins on the main deck, on top of one of the unexploded boilers, where he lay prone in a fog of scald and deadly steam. But not for long. He did not lose his head—long familiarity with danger had taught him to keep it, in any and all emergencies. He held his coat-lapels to his nose with one hand, to keep out the steam, and scrabbled around with the other till he found the joints of his flute, then he took measures to save himself alive, and was successful. I was not on board. I had been put ashore in New Orleans by Captain Klinefelter. The reason—however, I have told all about it in the book called *Old Times on the Mississippi*, and it isn't important, anyway, it is so long ago.

III

How curious and interesting is the parallel—as far as poverty of biographical details is concerned—between Satan and Shakespeare. It is wonderful, it is unique, it stands quite alone, there is nothing resembling it in history, nothing resembling it in romance, nothing approaching it even in tradition. How sublime is their position, and how overtopping, how sky-reaching, how supreme—the two Great Unknowns, the two Illustrious Conjecturabilities! They are the best-known unknown persons that have ever drawn breath upon the planet.

For the instruction of the ignorant I will make a list, now, of those details of Shakespeare's history with are *facts*—verified facts, established facts, undisputed facts.

Facts

He was born on the 23rd of April, 1564.

Of good farmer-class parents who could not read, could not write, could not sign their names.

At Stratford, a small back settlement which in that day was shabby and unclean, and densely illiterate. Of the nineteen most important men charged with the government of the town, thirteen had to "make their mark" in attesting important documents, because they could not write their names.

Of the first eighteen years of his life *nothing* is known. They are a blank.

On the 27th of November (1582) William Shakespeare took out a license to marry Anne Whateley.

Next day William Shakespeare took out a license to marry Anne Hathaway. She was eight years his senior.

William Shakespeare married Anne Hathaway. In a hurry. By grace of a reluctantly granted dispensation there was but one publication of the banns.

Within six months the first child was born.

About two (blank) years followed, during which period *nothing at all happened to Shakespeare,* so far as anybody knows.

Then came twins—1585. February.

Two blank years follow.

Then—1587—he makes a ten-year visit to London, leaving the family behind.

Five blank years follow. During this period *nothing happened to him,* as far as anybody actually knows.

Then—1592—there is mention of him as an actor.

Next year—1593—his name appears in the official list of players.

Next year—1594—he played before the queen. A detail of no consequence: other obscurities did it every year of the forty-five of her reign. And remained obscure.

Three pretty full years follow. Full of play-acting. Then

In 1597 he bought New Place, Stratford.

Thirteen or fourteen busy years follow; years in which he accumulated money, and also reputation as actor and manager.

Meantime his name, liberally and variously spelt, had become associated with a number of great plays and poems, as (ostensibly) author of the same.

Some of these, in these years and later, were pirated, but he made no protest.

Then—1610–11—he returned to Stratford and settled down for good and all, and busied himself in lending money, trading in tithes, trading in land and houses; shirking a debt of forty-one shillings, borrowed by his wife during his long desertion of his family; suing debtors for shillings and coppers; being sued himself for shillings and coppers; and acting as confederate to a neighbor who tried to rob the town of its rights in a certain common, and did not succeed.

He lived five or six years—till 1616—in the joy of these elevated pursuits. Then he made a will, and signed each of its three pages with his name.

A thoroughgoing business man's will. It named in minute detail every item of property he owned in the world—houses, lands, sword, silver-gilt bowl, and so on—all the way down to his "second-best bed" and its furniture.

It carefully and calculatingly distributed his riches among the members of his family, overlooking no individual of it. Not even his wife: the wife he had been enabled to marry in a hurry by urgent grace of a special dispensation before he was nineteen; the wife whom he had left husbandless so many years; the wife who had had to borrow forty-one shillings in her need, and which the lender was never able to collect of the prosperous husband, but died at last with the money still lacking. No, even this wife was remembered in Shakespeare's will.

He left her that "second-best bed."

And *not another thing;* not even a penny to bless her lucky widowhood with.

It was eminently and conspicuously a business man's will, not a poet's.

It mentioned *not a single book.*

Books were much more precious than swords and silver-gilt bowls and second-best beds in those days, and when a departing person owned one he gave it a high place in his will.

The will mentioned *not a play, not a poem, not an unfinished literary work, not a scrap of manuscript of any kind.*

Many poets have died poor, but this is the only one in history that has died *this* poor; the others all left literary remains behind. Also a book. Maybe two.

If Shakespeare had owned a dog—but we need not go into that: we know he would have mentioned it in his will. If a good dog, Susanna would have got it; if an inferior one his wife would have got a dower interest in it. I wish he had had a dog, just so we could see how painstakingly he would have divided that dog among the family, in his careful business way.

He signed the will in three places.

In earlier years he signed two other official documents.

These five signatures still exist.

There are *no other specimens of his penmanship in existence.* Not a line.

Was he prejudiced against the art? His granddaughter, whom he loved, was eight years old when he died, yet she had had no teaching, he left no provision for her education, although he was rich, and in her mature womanhood she couldn't write and couldn't tell her husband's manuscript from anybody else's—she thought it was Shakespeare's.

When Shakespeare died in Stratford *it was not an event.* It made no more stir in England than the death of any other forgotten theater-actor would have made. Nobody came down from London; there were no lamenting poems, no eulogies, no national tears—there was merely silence, and nothing more. A striking contrast with what happened when Ben Jonson, and Francis Bacon, and Spenser, and Raleigh, and the other distinguished literary folk of Shakespeare's time passed from life! No praiseful voice was lifted for the lost Bard of Avon; even Ben Jonson waited seven years before he lifted his.

So far as anybody actually knows and can prove, Shakespeare of Stratford-on-Avon never wrote a play in his life.

So far as anybody knows and can prove, he never wrote a letter to anybody in his life.

So far as any one knows, he received only one letter during his life.

So far as any one knows and can prove, Shakespeare of Stratford wrote only one poem during his life. This one is authentic. He did write that one—a fact which stands undisputed; he wrote the whole of it; he wrote the whole of it out of his own head. He commanded that this work of art be engraved upon his tomb, and he was obeyed. There it abides to this day. This is it:

Good friend for Iesus sake forbeare
To digg the dust encloased heare:
Blest be ye man yt spares thes stones
And curst be he yt moves my bones.

In the list as above set down will be found *every positively known* fact of Shakespeare's life, lean and meager as the invoice is. Beyond these details we know not *a thing* about him. All the rest of his vast history, as furnished by the biographers, is built up, course upon course, of guesses, inferences, theories, conjectures—an Eiffel Tower of artificialities rising sky-high from a very flat and very thin foundation of inconsequential facts.

IV. Conjectures

The historians "suppose" that Shakespeare attended the Free School in Stratford from the time he was seven years old till he was thirteen. There is no *evidence* in existence that he ever went to school at all.

The historians "infer" that he got his Latin in that school—the school which they "suppose" he attended.

They "suppose" his father's declining fortunes made it necessary for him to leave the school they supposed he attended, and get to work and help support his parents and their ten children. But there is no evidence that he ever entered or returned from the school they suppose he attended.

They "suppose" he assisted his father in the butchering business; and that, being only a boy, he didn't have to do full-grown butchering, but only slaughtered calves. Also, that whenever he killed a calf he made a high-flown speech over it. This supposition rests upon the testimony of a man who wasn't there at the time; a man who got it from a man who could have been there, but did not say whether he was or not; and neither of them thought to mention it for decades, and decades, and decades, and two more decades after Shakespeare's death (until old age and mental decay had refreshed and vivified their memories). They hadn't two facts in stock about the long-dead distinguished citizen, but only just the one: he slaughtered calves and broke into oratory while he was at it. Curious. They had only one fact, yet the distinguished citizen had spent twenty-six years in that little town—just half his lifetime. However, rightly viewed, it was the most important fact, indeed almost the only important fact, of Shakespeare's life in Stratford. Rightly viewed. For experience is an author's most valuable asset; experience is the thing that puts the muscle and the breath and the warm blood into the book he writes. Rightly viewed, calf-butchering accounts for *Titus Andronicus*, the only play—ain't it?—that the Stratford Shakespeare ever wrote; and yet it is the only one everybody tries to chouse him out of, the Baconians included.

The historians find themselves "justified in believing" that the young Shakespeare poached upon Sir Thomas Lucy's deer preserves and got haled before that magistrate for it. But there is no shred of respectworthy evidence that anything of the kind happened.

The historians, having argued the thing that *might* have happened into the thing that *did* happen, found no trouble in turning Sir Thomas Lucy into Mr. Justice Shallow. They have long ago convinced the world—on surmise and without trustworthy evidence—that Shallow is Sir Thomas.

The next addition to the young Shakespeare's Stratford history comes easy. The historian builds it out of the surmised deer-stealing, and the surmised trial before the magistrate, and the surmised vengeance-prompted satire upon the magistrate in the play: result, the young Shakespeare was a wild, wild, wild, oh, *such* a wild young scamp, and that gratuitous slander is established for all time! It is the very way Professor Osborn and I built the colossal skeleton brontosaur that stands fifty-seven feet long and sixteen feet high in the Natural History Museum, the awe and admiration of all the world, the stateliest skeleton that exists on the planet. We had nine bones, and we built the rest of him out of plaster of Paris. We ran short of plaster of Paris, or we'd have built a brontosaur that could sit down beside the Stratford Shakespeare and none but an expert could tell which was biggest or contained the most plaster.

Shakespeare pronounced *Venus and Adonis* "the first heir of his invention," apparently implying that it was his first effort at literary composition. He should not have said it. It has been an embarrassment to his historians these many, many years. They have to make him write that graceful and polished and flawless and beautiful poem before he escaped from Stratford and his family—1586 or '87—age, twenty-two, or along there; because within the next five years he wrote five great plays, and could not have found time to write another line.

It is sorely embarrassing. If he began to slaughter calves, and poach deer, and rollick around, and learn English, at the earliest likely moment—say at thirteen, when he was supposably wrenched from that school where he was supposably storing up Latin for future literary use—he had his youthful hands full, and much more than full. He must have had to put aside his Warwickshire dialect, which wouldn't be understood in London, and study English very hard. Very hard indeed; incredibly hard, almost, if the result of that labor was to be the smooth and rounded and flexible and letter-perfect English of the *Venus and Adonis* in the space often years; and at the same time learn great and fine and unsurpassable literary *form*.

However, it is "conjectured" that he accomplished all this and more, much more: learned law and its intricacies; and the complex procedure of the law-courts; and all about soldiering, and sailoring, and the manners and customs and ways of royal courts and aristocratic society; and likewise accumulated in his one head every kind of knowledge the learned then possessed, and every kind of humble knowledge possessed by the lowly and the ignorant; and added thereto a wider and more intimate knowledge of the world's great literatures, ancient and modern, than was possessed by any other man of his time—for he was going to make brilliant and easy and admiration-compelling use of these splendid treasures the moment he got to London. And according to the surmisers, that is what he did. Yes, although there was no one in Stratford able to teach him these things, and no library in the little village to dig them out of. His father could not read, and even the surmisers surmise that he did not keep a library.

It is surmised by the biographers that the young Shakespeare got his vast knowledge of the law and his familiar and accurate acquaintance with the manners and customs and shop-talk of lawyers through being for a time the *clerk of a Stratford court;* just as a bright lad like me, reared in a village on the banks of the Mississippi, might become perfect in knowledge of the Bering Strait whale-fishery and the shop-talk of the veteran exercises of that adventure-bristling trade through catching catfish with a "trot-line" Sundays. But the surmise is damaged by the fact that there is no evidence—and not even tradition—that the young Shakespeare was ever clerk of a law-court.

It is further surmised that the young Shakespeare accumulated his law-treasures in the first years of his sojourn in London, through "amusing himself" by learning book-law in his garret and by picking up lawyer-talk and the rest of it through loitering about the law-courts and listening. But it is only surmise; there is no *evidence* that he ever did either of those things. They are merely a couple of chunks of plaster of Paris.

There is a legend that he got his bread and butter by holding horses in front of the London theaters, mornings and afternoons. Maybe he did. If he did, it seriously shortened his law-study hours and his recreation-time in the courts. In those very days he was writing great plays, and needed all the time he could get. The horse-holding legend ought to be strangled; it too formidably increases the historian's difficulty in accounting for the young Shakespeare's erudition—an erudition which he was acquiring, hunk by hunk and chunk by chunk, every day in those strenuous times, and emptying each day's catch into next day's imperishable drama.

He had to acquire a knowledge of war at the same time; and a knowledge of soldier-people and sailor-people and their ways and talk; also a knowledge of some foreign lands and their languages: for he was daily emptying fluent streams of these various knowledges, too, into his dramas. How did he acquire these rich assets?

In the usual way: by surmise. It is *surmised* that he traveled in Italy and Germany and around, and qualified himself to put their scenic and social aspects upon paper; that he perfected himself in French, Italian, and Spanish on the road; that he went in Leicester's expedition to the Low Countries, as soldier or sutler or something, for several months or years—or whatever length of time a surmiser needs in his business—and thus became familiar with soldiership and soldier-ways and soldier-talk and generalship and general-ways and general-talk, and seamanship and sailor-ways and sailor-talk.

Maybe he did all these things, but I would like to know who held the horses in the mean time; and who studied the books in the garret; and who frollicked in the law-courts for recreation. Also, who did the call-boying and the play-acting.

For he became a call-boy; and as early as '93 he became a "vagabond"—the law's ungentle term for an unlisted actor; and in '94 a "regular" and properly and officially listed member of that (in those days) lightly valued and not much respected profession.

Right soon thereafter he became a stockholder in two theaters, and manager of them. Thenceforward he was a busy and flourishing business man, and was raking in money with both hands for twenty years. Then in a noble frenzy of poetic inspiration he wrote his one poem—his only poem, his darling—and laid him down and died:

Good friend for Iesus sake forbeare
To digg the dust enclosed heare:
Blest be ye man yt spares thes stones
And curst be he yt moves my bones.

He was probably dead when he wrote it. Still, this is only conjecture. We have only circumstantial evidence. Internal evidence.

Shall I set down the rest of the Conjectures which constitute the giant Biography of William Shakespeare? It would strain the Unabridged Dictionary to hold them. He is a brontosaur: nine bones and six hundred barrels of plaster of Paris.

V. "We May Assume"

In the Assuming trade three separate and independent cults are transacting business. Two of these cults are known as the Shakespearites and the Baconians, and I am the other one—the Brontosaurian.

The Shakespearite knows that Shakespeare wrote Shakespeare's Works; the Baconian knows that Francis Bacon wrote them; the Brontosaurian doesn't really know which of them did it, but is quite composedly and contentedly sure that Shakespeare *didn't,* and strongly suspects that Bacon *did.* We all have to do a good deal of assuming, but I am fairly certain that in every case I can call to mind the Baconian assumers have come out ahead of the Shakespearites. Both parties handle the same materials, but the Baconians seem to me to get much more reasonable and rational and persuasive results out of them than is the case with the Shakespearites. The Shakespearite conducts his assuming upon a definite principle, an unchanging and immutable law: which is: 2 and 8 and 7 and 14, added together, make 165. I believe this to be an error. No matter, you cannot get a habit-sodden Shakespearite to cipher-up his materials upon any other basis. With the Baconian it is different. If you place before him the above figures and set him to adding them up, he will never in any case get more than 45 out of them, and in nine cases out of ten he will get just the proper 31.

Let me try to illustrate the two systems in a simple and homely way calculated to bring the idea within the grasp of the ignorant and unintelligent. We will suppose a case: take a lap-bred, house-fed, uneducated, inexperienced kitten; take a rugged old Tom that's scarred from stem to rudder-post with the memorials of strenuous experience, and is so cultured, so educated, so limitlessly erudite that one may say of him "all cat-knowledge is his province"; also, take a mouse. Lock the three up in a holeless, crackless, exitless prison-cell. Wait half an hour, then open the cell, introduce a Shakespearite and a Baconian, and let them cipher and assume. The mouse is missing: the question to be decided is, where it is? You can guess both verdicts beforehand. One verdict will say the kitten contains the mouse; the other will as certainly say the mouse is in the tom-cat.

The Shakespearite will Reason like this—(that is not my word, it is his). He will say the kitten *may have been* attending school when nobody was noticing; therefore *we are warranted in assuming* that it did so; also, it *could have been* training in a court-clerk's office when no one was noticing; since that could have happened, *we are justified in assuming* that it did happen; it *could have studied catology in a garret* when no one was noticing—therefore it *did;* it *could have* attended cat-assizes on the shed-roof nights, for recreation, when no one was noticing, and have harvested a knowledge of cat court-forms and cat lawyer-talk in that way: it *could* have done it, therefore without a doubt it *did;* it *could have* gone soldiering with a war-tribe when no one was noticing, and learned soldier-wiles and soldier-ways, and what to do with a mouse when opportunity offers; the plain inference, therefore, is that that is what it *did.* Since all these manifold things *could* have occurred, we have *every right to believe* they did occur. These patiently and painstakingly accumulated vast acquirements and competences needed but one thing more—opportunity—

to convert themselves into triumphant action. The opportunity came, we have the result; *beyond shadow of question* the mouse is in the kitten.

It is proper to remark that when we of the three cults plant a "We *think we may assume*," we expect it, under careful watering and fertilizing and tending, to grow up into a strong and hardy and weather-defying *"there isn't a shadow of a doubt"* at last—and it usually happens.

We know what the Baconian's verdict would be: *"There is not a rag of evidence that the kitten has had any training, any education, any experience qualifying it for the present occasion, or is indeed equipped for any achievement above lifting such unclaimed milk as comes its way; but there is abundant evidence—unassailable proof, in fact—that the other animal is equipped, to the last detail, with every qualification necessary for the event. Without shadow of doubt the tom-cat contains the mouse.*

VI

When Shakespeare died, in 1616, great literary productions attributed to him as author had been before the London world and in high favor for twenty-four years. Yet his death was not an event. It made no stir, it attracted no attention. Apparently his eminent literary contemporaries did not realize that a celebrated poet had passed from their midst. Perhaps they knew a play-actor of minor rank had disappeared, but did not regard him as the author of his Works. "We are justified in assuming" this.

His death was not even an event in the little town of Stratford. Does this mean that in Stratford he was not regarded as a celebrity of *any* kind?

"We are privileged to assume"—no, we are indeed *obliged* to assume—that such was the case. He had spent the first twenty-two or twenty-three years of his life there, and of course knew everybody and was known by everybody of that day in the town, including the dogs and the cats and the horses. He had spent the last five or six years of his life there, diligently trading in every big and little thing that had money in it; so we are compelled to assume that many of the folk there in those said latter days knew him personally, and the rest by sight and hearsay. But not as a *celebrity*? Apparently not. For everybody soon forgot to remember any contact with him or any incident connected with him. The dozens of townspeople, still alive, who had known of him or known about him in the first twenty-three years of his life were in the same unremembering condition: if they knew of any incident connected with that period of his life they didn't tell about it. Would they if they had been asked? It is most likely. Were they asked? It is pretty apparent that they were not. Why weren't they? It is a very plausible guess that nobody there or elsewhere was interested to know.

For seven years after Shakespeare's death nobody seems to have been interested in him. Then the quarto was published, and Ben Jonson awoke out of his long indifference and sang a song of praise and put it in the front of the book. Then silence fell *again.*

For sixty years. Then inquiries into Shakespeare's Stratford life began to be made, of Stratfordians. Of Stratfordians who had known Shakespeare or had seen him? No. Then of Stratfordians who had seen people who had known or seen people who had seen Shakespeare? No. Apparently the inquiries were only made of Stratfordians who were not Stratfordians of Shakespeare's day, but later comers; and what they had learned had come to them from persons who had not seen Shakespeare; and what they had learned was not claimed as *fact,* but only as legend—dim and fading and indefinite legend; legend of the calf-slaughtering rank, and not worth remembering either as history or fiction.

Has it ever happened before—or since—that a celebrated person who had spent exactly half of a fairly long life in the village where he was born and reared, was able to slip out of this world and leave that village voiceless and gossipless behind him—utterly voiceless, utterly gossipless? And permanently so? I don't believe it has happened in any case except Shakespeare's. And couldn't and wouldn't have happened in his case if he had been regarded as a celebrity at the time of his death.

When I examine my own case—but let us do that, and see if it will not be recognizable as exhibiting a condition of things quite likely to result, most likely to result, indeed substantially *sure* to result in the case of a celebrated person, a benefactor of the human race. Like me.

My parents brought me to the village of Hannibal, Missouri, on the banks of the Mississippi, when I was two and a half years old. I entered school at five years of age, and drifted from one school to another in the village during nine and a half years. Then my father died, leaving his family in exceedingly straitened circumstances; wherefore my book-education came to a standstill forever, and I became a printer's apprentice, on board and clothes, and when the clothes failed I got a hymn-book in place of them. This for summer wear, probably. I lived in Hannibal fifteen and a half years, altogether, then ran away, according to the custom of persons who are intending to become celebrated. I never lived there afterward. Four years later I became a "cub" on a Mississippi steamboat in the St. Louis and New Orleans trade, and after a year and a half of hard study and hard work the U.S. inspectors rigorously examined me through a couple of long sittings and decided that I knew every inch of the Mississippi—thirteen hundred miles—in the dark and in the day—as well as a baby knows the way to its mother's paps day or night. So they licensed me as a pilot—knighted me, so to speak—and I rose up clothed with authority, a responsible servant of the United States Government.

Now then. Shakespeare died young—he was only fifty-two. He had lived in his native village twenty-six years, or about that. He died celebrated (if you believe everything you read in the books). Yet when he died nobody there or elsewhere took any notice of it; and for sixty years afterward no townsman remembered to say anything about him or about his life in Stratford. When the inquirer came at last he got but one fact—no, *legend*—and got that one at second hand, from a person who had only heard it as a rumor and didn't claim copyright in it as a production of his own. He couldn't, very well, for its date antedated his own birth-date. But necessarily a number of persons were still alive in Stratford who, in the days of their youth, had seen Shakespeare nearly every day in the last five years of his life, and they would have been able to tell that inquirer some first-hand things about him if he had in those last days been a celebrity and therefore a person of interest to the villagers. Why did not the inquirer hunt them up and interview them? Wasn't it worth while? Wasn't the matter of sufficient consequence? Had the inquirer an engagement to see a dog-fight and couldn't spare the time?

It all seems to mean that he never had any literary celebrity, there or elsewhere, and no considerable repute as actor and manager.

Now then, I am away along in life—my seventy-third year being already well behind me—yet *sixteen* of my Hannibal schoolmates are still alive to-day, and can tell—and do tell—inquirers dozens and dozens of incidents of their young lives and mine together; things that happened to us in the morning of life, in the blossom of our youth, in the good days, the dear days, "the days when we went gipsying, a long time ago." Most of them creditable to me, too. One child to whom I paid court when she was five years old and I eight still lives in Hannibal, and she visited me last summer, traversing the necessary ten or twelve hundred miles of railroad without damage to her patience or to her old-young vigor. Another little lassie to whom I paid attention in Hannibal when she was nine years old and I the same, is still alive—in London—and hale and hearty, just as I am. And on the few surviving steamboats—those lingering ghosts and remembrancers of great fleets that plied the big river in the beginning of my water-career—which is exactly as long ago as the whole invoice of the life-years of Shakespeare numbers—there are still findable two or three river-pilots who saw me do creditable things in those ancient days; and several white-headed engineers; and several roustabouts and mates; and several deck-hands who used to heave the lead for me and send up on the still night air the "Six—feet—*scant!*" that made me shudder, and the "M-a-r-k—*twain!*" that took the shudder away, and presently the darling "By the d-e-e-p—*four!*" that lifted me to heaven for joy.[1] They know about me, and can tell. And so do printers, from St. Louis to New York; and so do newspaper reporters, from Nevada to San Francisco. And so do the police. If Shakespeare had really been celebrated, like me, Stratford could have told things about him; and if my experience goes for anything, they'd have done it.

VII

If I had under my superintendence a controversy appointed to decide whether Shakespeare wrote Shakespeare or not, I believe I would place before the debaters only the one question, *Was Shakespeare ever a practising lawyer?* and leave everything else out.

It is maintained that the man who wrote the plays was not merely myriad-minded, but also myriad-accomplished: that he not only knew some thousands of things about human life in all its shades and grades, and about the hundred arts and trades and crafts and professions which men busy themselves in, but that he could *talk* about the men and their grades and trades accurately, making no mistakes. Maybe it is so, but have the experts spoken, or is it only Tom, Dick, and Harry? Does the exhibit stand upon wide, and loose, and eloquent generalizing—which is not evidence, and not proof—or upon details, particulars, statistics, illustrations, demonstrations?

Experts of unchallengeable authority have testified definitely as to only one of Shakespeare's multifarious craft-equipments, so far as my recollections of Shakespeare-Bacon talk abide with me—his law-equipment. I do not remember that Wellington or Napoleon ever examined Shakespeare's battles and sieges and strategies, and then decided and established for good and all that they were militarily flawless; I do not remember that any Nelson, or Drake, or Cook ever examined his seamanship and said it showed profound and accurate familiarity with that art; I don't remember that any king or prince or duke has ever testified that Shakespeare was letter-perfect in his handling of royal court-manners and the talk and manners of aristocracies; I don't remember that any illustrious Latinist or Grecian or Frenchman or Spaniard or Italian has proclaimed him a past-master in those languages; I don't remember—well, I don't remember that there is *testimony*—great testimony—imposing testimony—unanswerable and unattackable testimony as to any of Shakespeare's hundred specialties, except one—the law.

Other things change, with time, and the student cannot trace back with certainty the changes that various trades and their processes and technicalities have undergone in the long stretch of a century or two and find out what their processes and technicalities were in those early days, but with the law it is different: it is mile-stoned and documented all the way back, and the master of that wonderful trade, that complex and intricate trade, that awe-compelling trade, has competent ways of knowing whether Shakespeare-law is good law or not; and whether his law-court procedure is correct or not, and whether his legal shop-talk is the shop-talk of a veteran practitioner or only a machine-made counterfeit of it gathered from books and from occasional loiterings in Westminster.

Richard H. Dana served two years before the mast, and had every experience that falls to the lot of the sailor before the mast of our day. His sailor-talk flows from his pen with the sure touch and the ease and confidence of a person who has *lived* what he is talking about, not gathered it from books and random listenings. Hear him:

> Having hove short, cast off the gaskets, and made the bunt of each sail fast by the jigger, with a man on each yard, at the word the whole canvas of the ship was loosed, and with the greatest rapidity possible everything was sheeted home and hoisted up, the anchor tripped and cat-headed, and the ship under headway.

Again:

> The royal yards were all crossed at once, and royals and skysails set, and, as we had the wind free, the booms were run out, and all were aloft, active as cats, laying out on the yards and booms, reeving the studding-sail gear; and sail after sail the captain piled upon her, until she was covered with canvas, her sails looking like a great white cloud resting upon a black speck.

Once more. A race in the Pacific:

> Our antagonist was in her best trim. Being clear of the point, the breeze became stiff, and the royal-masts bent under our sails, but we would not take them in until we saw three boys spring into the rigging of the *California;* then they were all furled at once, but with orders to our boys to stay aloft at the top-gallant mast-heads and loose them again at the word. It was my duty to furl the fore-royal; and while standing by to loose it again, I had a fine view of the scene. From where I stood, the two vessels seemed nothing but spars and sails, while their narrow decks, far below, slanting over by the force of the wind aloft, appeared hardly capable of supporting the great fabrics raised upon them. The *California* was to windward of us, and had every advantage; yet, while the breeze was stiff we held our own. As soon as it began to slacken

she ranged a little ahead, and the order was given to loose the royals. In an instant the gaskets were off and the bunt dropped. "Sheet home the fore-royal!"—"Weather sheet's home!"—"Lee sheet's home!"—"Hoist away, sir!" is bawled from aloft. "Overhaul your clewlines!" shouts the mate. "Aye-aye, sir, all clear!"—"Taut leech! belay! Well the lee brace; haul taut to windward!" and the royals are set.

What would the captain of any sailing-vessel of our time say to that? He would say, "The man that wrote that didn't learn his trade out of a book, he has *been* there!" But would this same captain be competent to sit in judgment upon Shakespeare's seamanship—considering the changes in ships and ship-talk that have necessarily taken place, unrecorded, unremembered, and lost to history in the last three hundred years?

It is my conviction that Shakespeare's sailor-talk would be Choctaw to him. For instance—from *The Tempest:*

Master: Boatswain!

Boatswain: Here, master; what cheer?

Master: Good, speak to the mariners: fall to 't, yarely, or we run ourselves to ground; bestir, bestir!

(Enter *mariners.*)

Boatswain: Heigh, my hearts! cheerly, cheerly, my hearts! yare, yare! Take in the topsail. Tend to the master's whistle. Down with the topmast! yare! lower, lower! Bring her to try wi' the main course. Lay her a-hold, a-hold! Set her two courses. Off to sea again; lay her off.

That will do, for the present; let us yare a little, now, for a change.

If a man should write a book and in it make one of his characters say, "Here, devil, empty the quoins into the standing galley and the imposing-stone into the hell-box; assemble the comps around the frisket and let them jeff for takes and be quick about it," I should recognize a mistake or two in the phrasing, and would know that the writer was only a printer theoretically, not practically.

I have been a quartz miner in the silver regions—a pretty hard life; I know all the palaver of that business: I know all about discovery claims and the subordinate claims; I know all about lodes, ledges, outcroppings, dips, spurs, angles, shafts, drifts, inclines, levels, tunnels, air-shafts, "horses," clay casings, granite casings; quartz mills and their batteries; arastras, and how to charge them with quicksilver and sulphate of copper; and how to clean them up, and how to reduce the resulting amalgam in the retorts, and how to cast the bullion into pigs; and finally I know how to screen tailings, and also how to hunt for something less robust to do, and find it. I know the argot of the quartz-mining and milling industry familiarly; and so whenever Bret Harte introduces that industry into a story, the first time one of his miners opens his mouth I recognize from his phrasing that Harte got the phrasing by listening—like Shakespeare—I mean the Stratford one—not by experience. No one can talk the quartz dialect correctly without learning it with pick and shovel and drill and fuse.

I have been a surface miner—gold—and I know all its mysteries, and the dialect that belongs with them; and whenever Harte introduces that industry into a story I know by the phrasing of his characters that neither he nor they have ever served that trade.

I have been a "pocket" miner—a sort of gold mining not findable in any but one little spot in the world, so far as I know. I know how, with horn and water, to find the trail of a pocket and trace it step by step and stage by stage up the mountain to its source, and find the compact little nest of yellow metal reposing in its secret home under the ground. I know the language of that trade, that capricious trade, that fascinating buried-treasure trade, and can catch any writer who tries to use it without having learned it by the sweat of his brow and the labor of his hands.

I know several other trades and the argot that goes with them; and whenever a person tries to talk the talk peculiar to any of them without having learned it at its source I can trap him always before he gets far on his road.

And so, as I have already remarked, if I were required to superintend a Bacon-Shakespeare controversy, I would narrow the matter down to a single question—the only one, so far as the previous controversies have informed me, concerning which illustrious experts of unimpeachable competency have testified: *Was the author of Shakespeare's Works a lawyer?*—a lawyer deeply read and of limitless experience? I would put aside the guesses and surmises, and perhapses, and might-have-beens, and could-have-beens, and must-have-beens, and we-are-justified-in-presumings, and the rest of those vague specters and shadows and indefinitenesses, and stand or fall, win or lose, by the verdict rendered by the jury upon that single question. If the verdict was Yes, I should feel quite convinced that the Stratford Shakespeare, the actor, manager, and trader who died so obscure, so forgotten, so destitute of even village consequence, that sixty years afterward no fellow-citizen and friend of his later days remembered to tell anything about him, did not write the Works.

IX

Did Francis Bacon write Shakespeare's Works?

Nobody knows.

We cannot say we *know* a thing when that thing has not been proved. Know is too strong a word to use when the evidence is not final and absolutely conclusive. We can infer, if we want to, like those slaves. No, I will not write that word, it is not kind, it is not courteous. The upholders of the Stratford-Shakespeare superstition call us the hardest names they can think of, and they keep doing it all the time; very well, if they like to descend to that level, let them do it, but I will not so undignify myself as to follow them. I cannot call them harsh names; the most I can do is to indicate them by terms reflecting my disapproval; and this without malice, without venom.

To resume. What I was about to say was, those thugs have built their entire superstition upon *inferences,* not upon known and established facts. It is a weak method, and poor, and I am glad to be able to say our side never resorts to it while there is anything else to resort to.

But when we must, we must; and we have now arrived at a place of that sort. Since the Stratford Shakespeare couldn't have written the Works, we infer that somebody did. Who was it, then? This requires some more inferring.

Ordinarily when an unsigned poem sweeps across the continent like a tidal wave whose roar and boom and thunder are made up of admiration, delight, and applause, a dozen obscure people rise up and claim the authorship. Why a dozen, instead of only one or two? One reason is, because there are a dozen that are recognizably competent to do that poem. Do you remember "Beautiful Snow"? Do you remember "Rock Me to Sleep, Mother, Rock Me to Sleep"? Do you remember "Backward, turn backward, O Time, in thy flight! Make me a child again just for to-night"? I remember them very well. Their authorship was claimed by most of the grownup people who were alive at the time, and every claimant had one plausible argument in his favor, at least—to wit, he could have done the authoring; he was competent.

Have the Works been claimed by a dozen? They haven't. There was good reason. The world knows there was but one man on the planet at the time who was competent—not a dozen, and not two. A long time ago the dwellers in a far country used now and then to find a procession of prodigious footprints stretching across the plain—footprints that were three miles apart, each footprint a third of a mile long and a furlong deep, and with forests and villages mashed to mush in it. Was there any doubt as to who made that mighty trail? Were there a dozen claimants? Were there two? No—the people knew who it was that had been along there: there was only one Hercules.

There has been only one Shakespeare. There couldn't be two; certainly there couldn't be two at the same time. It takes ages to bring forth a Shakespeare, and some more ages to match him. This one was not matched before his time; nor during his time; and hasn't been matched since. The prospect of matching him in our time is not bright.

The Baconians claim that the Stratford Shakespeare was not qualified to write the Works, and that Francis Bacon was. They claim that Bacon possessed the stupendous equipment—both natural and acquired—for the miracle; and that no other Englishman of his day possessed the like; or, indeed, anything closely approaching it.

Macaulay, in his Essay, has much to say about the splendor and horizonless magnitude of that equipment. Also, he has synopsized Bacon's history—a thing which cannot be done for the Stratford Shakespeare, for he hasn't any history to synopsize. Bacon's history is open to the world, from his boyhood to his death in old age—a history consisting of known facts, displayed in minute and multitudinous detail; *facts,* not guesses and conjectures and might-have-beens.

Whereby it appears that he was born of a race of statesmen, and had a Lord Chancellor for his father, and a mother who was "distinguished both as a linguist and a theologian: she corresponded in Greek with Bishop [John] Jewell, and translated his *Apologia* from the Latin so correctly that neither he nor Archbishop [of Canterbury Matthew] Parker could suggest a single alteration." It is the atmosphere we are reared in that determines how our inclinations and aspirations shall tend. The atmosphere furnished by the parents to the son in this present case was an atmosphere saturated with learning; with thinkings and ponder-ings upon deep subjects; and with polite culture. It had its natural effect. Shakespeare of Stratford was reared in a house which had no use for books, since its owners, his parents, were without education. This may have had an effect upon the son, but we do not know, because we have no history of him of an informing sort. There were but few books anywhere, in that day, and only the well-to-do and highly educated possessed them, they being almost confined to the dead languages. "All the valuable books then extant in all the vernacular dialects of Europe would hardly have filled a single shelf"—imagine it! The few existing books were in the Latin tongue mainly. "A person who was ignorant of it was shut out from all acquaintance—not merely with Cicero and Virgil, but with the most interesting memoirs, state papers, and pamphlets of his own time"—a literature necessary to the Stratford lad, for his fictitious reputation's sake, since the writer of his Works would begin to use it wholesale and in a most masterly way before the lad was hardly more than out of his teens and into his twenties.

At fifteen Bacon was sent to the university, and he spent three years there. Thence he went to Paris in the train of the English Ambassador, and there he mingled daily with the wise, the cultured, the great, and the aristocracy of fashion, during another three years. A total of six years spent at the sources of knowledge; knowledge both of books and of men. The three spent at the university were coeval with the second and last three spent by the little Stratford lad at Stratford school supposedly, and perhapsedly, and maybe, and by inference—with nothing to infer from. The second three of the Baconian six were "presumably" spent by the Stratford lad as apprentice to a butcher. That is, the thugs presume it—on no evidence of any kind. Which is their way, when they want a historical fact. Fact and presumption are, for business purposes, all the same to them. They know the difference, but they also know how to blink it. They know, too, that while in history-building a fact is better than a presumption, it doesn't take a presumption long to bloom into a fact when *they* have the handling of it. They know by old experience that when they get hold of a presumption-tadpole he is not going to *stay* tadpole in their history-tank; no, they know how to develop him into the giant four-legged bullfrog *olfact,* and make him sit up on his hams, and puff out of his chin, and look important and insolent and come-to-stay; and assert his genuine simon-pure authenticity with a thundering bellow that will convince everybody because it is so loud. The thug is aware that loudness convinces sixty persons where reasoning convinces but one. I wouldn't be a thug, not even if—but never mind about that, it has nothing to do with the argument, and it is not noble in spirit besides. If I am better than a thug, is the merit mine? No, it is His. Then to Him be the praise. That is the right spirit.

They "presume" the lad severed his "presumed" connection with the Stratford school to become apprentice to a butcher. They also "presume" that the butcher was his father. They don't know. There is no written record of it, nor any other actual evidence. If it would have helped their case any, they would have apprenticed him to thirty butchers, to fifty butchers, to a wilderness of butchers—all by their patented method "presumption." If it will help their case they will do it yet; and if it will further help it, they will "presume" that all those butchers were his father. And the week after, they will *say* it. Why, it is just like being the past tense of the compound reflexive adverbial incandescent hypodermic irregular accusative Noun of Multitude; which is father to the expression which the grammarians call Verb. It is like a whole ancestry, with only one posterity.

To resume. Next, the young Bacon took up the study of law, and mastered that abstruse science. From that day to the end of his life he was daily in close contact with lawyers and judges; not as a casual onlooker in intervals between holding horses in front of a theater, but as a practising lawyer—a great and successful one, a renowned one, a Launcelot of the bar, the most formidable lance in the high brotherhood of the legal Table Round; he lived in the law's atmosphere thenceforth, all his years, and by sheer ability forced his way up its difficult steeps to its supremest summit, the Lord-Chancellorship, leaving behind him no fellow-craftsman qualified to challenge his divine right to that majestic place.

When we read the praises bestowed by [adamant Baconian, James Plaisted Wilde] Lord Penzance, and the other illustrious experts upon the legal condition and legal aptnesses, brilliances, profundities, and felicities so prodigally displayed in the Plays, and try to fit them to the historyless Stratford stage-manager, they sound wild, strange, incredible, ludicrous; but when we put them in the mouth of Bacon they do not sound strange, they seem in their natural and rightful place, they seem at home there. Please turn back and read them again. Attributed to Shakespeare of Stratford they are meaningless, they are inebriate extravagancies—intemperate admirations of the dark side of the moon, so to speak; attributed to Bacon, they are admirations of the golden glories of the moon's front side, the moon at the full—and not intemperate, not overwrought, but sane and right, and justified. "At every turn and point at which the author required a metaphor, simile, or illustration, his mind ever turned *first* to the law; he seems almost to have *thought* in legal phrases; the commonest legal phrases, the commonest of legal expressions, were ever at the end of his pen." That could happen to no one but a person whose *trade* was the law; it could not happen to a dabbler in it. Veteran mariners fill their conversation with sailor-phrases and draw all their similes from the ship and the sea and the storm, but no mere *passenger* ever does it, be he of Stratford or elsewhere; or could do it with anything resembling accuracy, if he were hardy enough to try. Please read again what Lord [John] Campbell and the other great authorities have said about Bacon when they thought they were saying it about Shakespeare of Stratford.

X. The Rest of the Equipment

The author of the Plays was equipped, beyond every other man of his time, with wisdom, erudition, imagination, capaciousness of mind, grace, and majesty of expression. Every one has said it, no one doubts it. Also, he had humor, humor in rich abundance, and always wanting to break out. We have no evidence of any kind that Shakespeare of Stratford possessed any of these gifts or any of these acquirements. The only lines he ever wrote, so far as we know, are substantially barren of them—barren of all of them.

> Good friend for Iesus sake forbeare
> To digg the dust encloased heare:
> Blest be ye man yt spares thes stones
> And curst be he yt moves my bones.

Ben Jonson says of Bacon, as orator:

> His language, *where he could spare and pass by a jest,* was nobly censorious. No man ever spoke more neatly, more pressly, more weightily, or suffered less emptiness, less idleness, in what he uttered. No member of his speech but consisted of his (its) own graces. The fear of every man that heard him was lest he should make an end.

From [Thomas Babington] Macaulay:

> He continued to distinguish himself in Parliament, particularly by his exertions in favor of one excellent measure on which the King's heart was set—the union of England and Scotland. It was not difficult for such an intellect to discover many irresistible arguments in favor of such a scheme. He conducted the great case of the *Post Nati* in the Exchequer Chamber; and the decision of the judges—a decision the legality of which may be questioned, but the beneficial effect of which must be acknowledged—was in a great measure attributed to his dexterous management.

Again:

> While actively engaged in the House of Commons and in the courts of law, he still found leisure for letters and philosophy. The noble treatise on the *Advancement of Learning,* which at a later period was expanded into the *De Augmentis,* appeared in 1605.
>
> The *Wisdom of the Ancients,* a work which, if it had proceeded from any other writer, would have been considered as a masterpiece of wit and learning, was printed in 1609.
>
> In the mean time the *Novum Organum* was slowly proceeding. Several distinguished men of learning had been permitted to see portions of that extraordinary book, and they spoke with the greatest admiration of his genius.

Even [diplomat and founder of the Bodlian Library at Oxford] Sir Thomas Bodley, after perusing the *Cogitate et Visa* [*Thoughts and Appearances*], one of the most precious of those scattered leaves out of which the great oracular volume was afterward made up, acknowledged that "in all proposals and plots in that book, Bacon showed himself a master workman"; and that "it could not be gainsaid but all the treatise over did abound with choice conceits of the present state of learning, and with worthy comtemplations of the means to procure it."

In 1612 a new edition of the *Essays* appeared, with additions surpassing the original collection both in bulk and quality.

Nor did these pursuits distract Bacon's attention from a work the most arduous, the most glorious, and the most useful that even his mighty powers could have achieved, "the reducing and recompiling," to use his own phrase, "of the laws of England."

To serve the exacting and laborious offices of Attorney-General and Solicitor-General would have satisfied the appetite of any other man for hard work, but Bacon had to add the vast literary industries just described, to satisfy his. He was a born worker.

The service which he rendered to letters during the last five years of his life, amid ten thousand distractions and vexations, increase the regret with which we think on the many years which he had wasted, to use the words of Sir Thomas Bodley, "on such study as was not worthy such a student."

He commenced a digest of the laws of England, a History of England under the Princes of the House of Tudor, a body of National History, a Philosophical Romance. He made extensive and valuable additions to his Essays. He published the inestimable *Treatise De Augmentis Scientiarum* [*On Increasing Knowledge*].

Did these labors of Hercules fill up his time to his contentment and quiet his appetite for work? Not entirely:

The trifles with which he amused himself in hours of pain and languor bore the mark of his mind. *The best jest-book in the world* is that which he dictated from memory, without referring to any book, on a day on which illness had rendered him incapable of serious study.

Here are some scattered remarks (from Macaulay) which throw light upon Bacon, and seem to indicate—and maybe demonstrate—that he was competent to write the Plays and Poems:

> With great minuteness of observation he had an amplitude of comprehension such as has never yet been vouchsafed to any other human being. The *Essays* contain abundant proofs that no nice feature of character, no peculiarity in the ordering of a house, a garden, or a court-masque, could escape the notice of one whose mind was capable of taking in the whole world of knowledge.... His understanding resembled the tent which the fairy Paribanou gave to Prince Ahmed: fold it, and it seemed a toy for the hand of a lady; spread it, and the armies of powerful Sultans might repose beneath its shade.
>
> The knowledge in which Bacon excelled all men was a knowledge of the mutual relations of all departments of knowledge.
>
> In a letter written when he was only thirty-one, to his uncle, Lord Burleigh, he said, "I have taken all knowledge to be my province."
>
> Though Bacon did not arm his philosophy with the weapons of logic, he adorned her profusely with all the richest decorations of rhetoric.
>
> The practical faculty was powerful in Bacon; but not, like his wit, so powerful as occasionally to usurp the place of his reason and to tyrannize over the whole man.

There are too many places in the Plays where this happens. Poor old dying John of Gaunt volleying second-rate puns at his own name, is a pathetic instance of it. "We may assume" that it is Bacon's fault, but the Stratford Shakespeare has to bear the blame.

> No imagination was ever at once so strong and so thoroughly subjugated. It stopped at the first check from good sense.
>
> In truth, much of Bacon's life was passed in a visionary world— amid things as strange as any that are described in the *Arabian Tales*.... Yet in his magnificent daydreams there was nothing wild—nothing but what sober reason sanctioned.
>
> Bacon's greatest performance is the first book of the *Novum Organum* ... Every part of it blazes with wit, but with wit which is employed only to illustrate and decorate truth. No book ever made

so great a revolution in the mode of thinking, overthrew so many prejudices, introduced so many new opinions.

But what we most admire is the vast capacity of that intellect which, without effort, takes in at once all the domains of science— all the past, the present and the future, all the errors of two thousand years, all the encouraging signs of the passing times, all the bright hopes of the coming age.

He had a wonderful talent for packing thought close and rendering it portable.

His eloquence would alone have entitled him to a high rank in literature.

It is evident that he had each and every one of the mental gifts and each and every one of the acquirements that are so prodigally displayed in the Plays and Poems, and in much higher and richer degree than any other man of his time or of any previous time. He was a genius without a mate, a prodigy not matable. There was only one of him; the planet could not produce two of him at one birth, nor in one age. He could have written anything that is in the Plays and Poems. He could have written this:

The cloud-cap'd towers, the gorgeous palaces,
The solemn temples, the great globe itself,
Yea, all which it inherit, shall dissolve,
And, like an insubstantial pageant faded, Leave not a rack behind.
We are such stuff As dreams are made on,
and our little life Is rounded with a sleep.

Also, he could have written this, but he refrained:

Good friend for Iesus sake forbeare
To digg the dust encloased heare:
Blest be ye man yt spares thes stones
And curst be he yt moves my bones.

When a person reads the noble verses about the cloud-cap'd towers, he ought not to follow it immediately with Good friend for Iesus sake forbeare, because he will find the transition from great poetry to poor prose too violent for comfort. It will give him a shock. You never notice how commonplace and unpoetic gravel is until you bite into a layer of it in a pie.

XI

Am I trying to convince anybody that Shakespeare did not write Shakespeare's Works? Ah, now, what do you take me for? Would I be so soft as that, after having known the human race familiarly for nearly seventy-four years? It would grieve me to know that any one could think so injuriously of me, so uncomplimentarily, so unadmiringly of me. No, no, I am aware that when even the brightest mind in our world has been trained up from childhood in a superstition of any kind, it will never be possible for that mind, in its maturity, to examine sincerely, dispassionately, and conscientiously any evidence or any circumstance which shall seem to cast a doubt upon the validity of that superstition. I doubt if I could do it myself. We always get at second hand our notions about systems of government; and high tariff and low tariff; and prohibition and anti-prohibition; and the holiness of peace and the glories of war; and codes of honor and codes of morals; and approval of the duel and disapproval of it; and our beliefs concerning the nature of cats; and our ideas as to whether the murder of helpless wild animals is base or is heroic; and our preferences in the matter of religious and political parties; and our acceptance or rejection of the Shakespeares and the Arthur Ortons and the Mrs. Eddys. We get them all at second hand, we reason none of them out for ourselves. It is the way we are made. It is the way we are all made, and we can't help it, we can't change it. And whenever we have been furnished a fetish, and have been taught to believe in it, and love it and worship it, and refrain from examining it, there is no evidence, howsoever clear and strong, that can persuade us to withdraw from it our loyalty and our devotion. In morals, conduct, and beliefs we take the color of our environment and associations, and it is a color that can safely be warranted to wash. Whenever we have been furnished with a tar baby ostensibly stuffed with jewels, and warned that it will be dishonorable and irreverent to disembowel it and test the jewels, we keep our sacrilegious hands off it. We submit, not reluctantly, but rather gladly, for we are privately afraid we should find, upon examination, that the jewels are of the sort that are manufactured at North Adams, Mass.

I haven't any idea that Shakespeare will have to vacate his pedestal this side of the year 2209. Disbelief in him cannot come swiftly, disbelief in a healthy and deeply-loved tar baby has never been known to disintegrate swiftly; it is a very slow process. It took several thousand years to convince our fine race—including every splendid intellect in it—that there is no such thing as a witch; it has taken several thousand years to convince that same fine race—including every splendid intellect in it—that there is no such person as Satan; it has taken several centuries to remove perdition from the Protestant

Church's program of post-mortem entertainments; it has taken a weary long time to persuade American Presbyterians to give up infant damnation and try to bear it the best they can; and it looks as if their Scotch brethren will still be burning babies in the everlasting fires when Shakespeare comes down from his perch.

We are The Reasoning Race. We can't prove it by the above examples, and we can't prove it by the miraculous "histories" built by those Stratfordolaters out of a hatful of rags and a barrel of sawdust, but there is a plenty of other things we can prove it by, if I could think of them. We are The Reasoning Race, and when we find a vague file of chipmunk-tracks stringing through the dust of Stratford village, we know by our reasoning powers that Hercules has been along there. I feel that our fetish is safe for three centuries yet. The bust, too—there in the Stratford Church. The precious bust, the priceless bust, the calm bust, the serene bust, the emotionless bust, with the dandy mustache, and the putty face, unseamed of care—that face which has looked passionlessly down upon the awed pilgrim for a hundred and fifty years and will still look down upon the awed pilgrim three hundred more, with the deep, deep, deep, subtle, subtle, subtle, expression of a bladder.

Notes

1.   Four fathoms—twenty-four feet.

—Mark Twain, from "Is Shakespeare Dead?"
1909, *The Complete Essays of Mark Twain,*
edited by Charles Neider, 1963, pp. 407–49

Chronology

1564   William Shakespeare christened at Stratford-on-Avon April 26.

1582   Marries Anne Hathaway in November.

1583   Daughter Susanna born, baptized on May 26.

1585   Twins Hamnet and Judith born, baptized on February 2.

1587   Shakespeare goes to London, without family.

1589–90   *Henry VI, Part 1* written.

1590–91   *Henry VI, Part 2* and *Henry VI, Part 3* written.

1592–93   *Richard III* and *The Two Gentlemen of Verona* written.

1593   Publication of *Venus and Adonis*, dedicated to the Earl of Southampton; the *Sonnets* probably begun.

1593   *The Comedy of Errors* written.

1593–94   Publication of *The Rape of Lucrece*, also dedicated to the Earl of Southampton. *Titus Andronicus* and *The Taming of the Shrew* written.

1594–95   *Love's Labour's Lost, King John*, and *Richard II* written.

1595–96   *Romeo and Juliet* and *A Midsummer Night's Dream* written.

1596   Son Hamnet dies.

1596–97   *The Merchant of Venice* and *Henry IV, Part 1* written; purchases New Place in Stratford.

1597–98   *The Merry Wives of Windsor* and *Henry IV, Part 2* written.

1598–99   *Much Ado about Nothing* written.

1599   *Henry V, Julius Caesar*, and *As You Like It* written.

1600–01   *Hamlet* written.

1601   *The Phoenix and the Turtle* written; father dies.

1601–02   *Twelfth Night* and *Troilus and Cressida* written.

1602–03   *All's Well That Ends Well* written.

1603   Shakespeare's company becomes the King's Men.

1604   *Measure for Measure* and *Othello* written.

1605	*King Lear* written.
1606	*Macbeth* and *Antony and Cleopatra* written.
1607	Marriage of daughter Susanna on June 5.
1607–08	*Coriolanus, Timon of Athens,* and *Pericles* written.
1608	Mother dies.
1609	Publication, probably unauthorized, of the quarto edition of the *Sonnets.*
1609–10	*Cymbeline* written.
1610–11	*The Winter's Tale* written.
1611	*The Tempest* written. Shakespeare returns to Stratford, where he will live until his death.
1612	*A Funeral Elegy* written.
1612–13	*Henry VIII* written; The Globe Theatre destroyed by fire.
1613	*The Two Noble Kinsmen* written (with John Fletcher).
1616	Daughter Judith marries on February 10; Shakespeare dies April 23.
1623	Publication of the First Folio edition of Shakespeare's plays.

Index